American River Road Beyond 2017

American River Road Beyond 2017

Journey Love, Murder, Decay, and a
Nation's Catastrophic Fall from
True God-faith

A True Story

John Worker
for Jesus Christ

Copyright © 2014 by John Worker for Jesus Christ.

Library of Congress Control Number: 2014904684
ISBN: Hardcover   978-1-4931-8314-2
               Softcover   978-1-4931-8315-9
               ebook   978-1-4931-8313-5

All rights reserved. No part of this book may be reproduced or transmitted in any form or by any means, electronic or mechanical, including photocopying, recording, or by any information storage and retrieval system, without permission in writing from the copyright owner.

This book was printed in the United States of America.

Scripture taken from the King James Version of the Bible.

Rev. date: 12/01/2014

To order additional copies of this book, contact:
Xlibris
1-888-795-4274
www.Xlibris.com
Orders@Xlibris.com
545552

Contents

The Situation, Setting, Writer's Promise, and Omen 7

PART I
LIFE ALONG AMERICAN RIVER ROAD

Chapter I	Road Kill, the Matriarch, and the Sage Woodsman	13
Chapter II	Brothers Pencils and Rifleman	28
Chapter III	Pushy Jimmy	32
Chapter IV	Night Train to Skowhegan, Pong Choolie Aboard, and Bullets Fly	35
Chapter V	Nosey Frank Finds Out Everything	46
Chapter VI	Prison-school Lets Out—Yahoo!	52
Chapter VII	Hobo Lane and the Secret Underground Tunnel	64
Chapter VIII	Gardiner Fruit to Dance Night on Kingsbury	72
Chapter IX	The Ancient Trail to Bolley's Famous Franks	78

PART II
THE INVADER

Chapter X	Jimmy's First Idea	95
Chapter XI	Jimmy's Other Idea	106
Chapter XII	The Beat-down	110
Chapter XIII	Captain Cornelius and Two Dollar Eva	118
Chapter XIV	Fresh Kills to Report	124
Chapter XV	Lawn Work in Low Purgatory	134
Chapter XVI	Plugged Hole Taken On	139
Chapter XVII	Beast Shot and Killed	147
Chapter XVIII	Captain Byrd, Saplings, and the Head-chopping Table	159
Chapter XIX	The Flashlight	164
Chapter XX	Marvelous Creature of the Sky—Slain	171
Chapter XXI	Sharp Turn on Vine Street	178
Chapter XXII	Giant Bloodsuckin' Suckers at Horseshoe Pond	187
Chapter XXIII	The Gravel Delta	19

PART III
THE BIG STORY

Chapter XXIV	New Marvel "Master Charge"	198
Chapter XXV	Indian Spirits Along the River	202
Chapter XXVI	The Mysterious Visitor	213
Chapter XXVII	The Ancient Pathway Lives	220
Chapter XXVIII	The Bottle Drive	225
Chapter XXIX	Night of Unrest, Hysteria	235
Chapter XXX	The Go-between	245
Chapter XXXI	The Philadelphia Incident	256
Chapter XXXII	The Black Man	269
Chapter XXXIII	Face Bashed In	276
Chapter XXXIV	Reid State Park	282
Chapter XXXV	The Rock	288
Chapter XXXVI	Death on Kingsbury	293
Chapter XXXVII	The Prophecy	300

PART IV
FIVE DECADES LATER: 2016

Chapter XXXVIII	Prophecy Fulfilled and Promise Kept	311
Chapter XXXIX	Winding a Valley Road	319
Chapter XL	"It's Time"	327
Chapter XLI	Sins of the Flesh	337
Chapter XLII	Acts of Demonstration	346
Chapter XLIII	Murky River	354
Chapter XLIV	The Murky Swim Up	363
Chapter XLV	The Spirit World and God Blessed Rebirthment	373
Chapter XLVI	JB Purgatory / Eternities / Paradise	380
Chapter XLVII	Thrust Units and Bond Souls	385
Chapter XLVIII	Christian Faith Crossover	391
Chapter XLIX	Secondary Repentance and Dead Presidents	402
Chapter L	Articles on Myths and Missing Links	409
Chapter LI	Fabulous Aching Heart Love	435
Chapter LII	Epilogue: How Men Cry	442

The Situation, Setting, Writer's Promise, and Omen

Father passed away eight years ago at a hospital in New York City. He was 91. Mother, 92, blind, mental capacities mostly intact, lives in an assisted-living apartment in the same city. What a change from Maine. Her imminent departure from this earth has caused her youngest son to take up the pen, to as fast as he can write down and read to her what she already knows, so that there may be peaceful closure for her soul.

Her oldest son, Daniel, owns a travel business that caters to the rich and sometimes famous of America. These ones often like to rent expensive private getaways in the romantic and panoramic settings of Italy and France, countries where the man specializes. Today, he resides in a small town on France's coast. Because Daniel loves New York City almost as much he loves mother, he flies in twice a year for a week or two, to check in on her and Broadway.

The year is 2011. The jotting down must begin right away, so that the truth will no longer be confined to just mother and her youngest son. This is what she wanted 45 years ago, for people to someday learn the truth about the terrible thing that took place back then. The task will take time to do in the way that she would want, with storyline and attention to detail.

* * *

The danger signals should have been obvious to everyone. Why the more mature minds had not resolved to deal with the vulnerability prior to that fateful moment remains an unanswered question to this day. As for the youngest son, though he had yet to reach teenage years, an ancient truth, *a dark truth*, had already been divulged. And so it was, at the flashing instant of a neighborhood slaying, he understood the overshadowing reason as to why it had to take place and the ghostly, labyrinthine mystery that had led up to it.

There were good outcomes that grew from the sudden ending of an innocent life. There came a showing of love from a person who had seemed to love no one and nothing except, perhaps, an automobile. Other adults were brought to remorse. Two youngsters had their futures brightly altered. Yes, for those who sought for something positive, light rose from darkness.

It was a friend's idea to spend the summer days of 1966 in a fun, explorative manner by producing a weekly newspaper that would tell of the neighborhood's happenings; the papers would be sold to houses in the same neighborhood. To say the least, apprentice reporters of any age should never be given charge of "the big story" that would end up coming his way.

Other issues fell into the hands of youth during that long-ago summer. He was too young to handle one hot potato, let alone several. But the Hand Divine must not have seen it that way, for what took place was just too remarkable not to have come from Him. The Big Guy Upstairs does not work on our schedule, only His. He sees things that we cannot, and that is because we allow ourselves to become too busy buying this and that, running here and there, down here.

The backdrop was a United States that had come through an unprecedented time. The 1950s had the post-WWII economic movement away from "military machine" throttling full steam toward a new fruition. The 1960s saw middle-class affluence taking center stage nationally. With it came the realization that the burgeoning American economy required corporations not to remain in the comfort of stillness for even a moment, for fear of losing momentum, corporate edge, market share. Everything was about growth, about becoming bigger and better in some way, and this seemed to mercilessly invoke innovation, which in turn spurred the inventions of new and more futuristic products and the discoveries of things once unknown.

The mid-1960s presented a nation that was diversifying not only in the way of internal affluence but also international influence. The world seemed to be opening up in many different ways, and there was so much hope back then. But there too was concern about the escalating Vietnam and Cold Wars. Almost nightly, news programs reported on the human strife associated with the "coming to town" of civil rights for Black America. Back then, love, humor, and patience were important ingredients for the nation's families; they certainly were for the writer's.

Television sets had been available for consumer purchase since the late 1940s. The video boxes instantly proved to be mighty deliverers of information and enjoyment for families. The following decade had the unit the hottest item to buy into the home. Prior to the television invasion, people mostly did light chores after supper; before bedtime, women often sewed or knitted while sitting in a rocking chair close by to their families; husbands might have read the newspaper while children their books; together the family listened to radio dramas and music. These pastimes were not totally over the hill by the late 1950s, but they were in decline.

By 1965, most American homes owned a television. Weekday TV began the morning with shows for tots. Then came sitcoms. *The Dick Van Dyke Show* was a national favorite, its lead actor a darling with housewives. Game shows *Concentration* and *Jeopardy!* held the late morning and noon, soap operas the mid-afternoon, and talk shows the late afternoon. News programs were early-evening sitters' lead-in to westerns, such as *The Virginian* and *Gunsmoke*, and totally weird comedies like *McHale's Navy* and *My Mother the Car*, which cast the mother of the lead actor—Dick Van Dyke's big-nosed kid-brother Jerry Van Dyke—as a talking car.

Weekend mornings had cartoons: *Bugs Bunny*, *Popeye*, and *Road Runner* were most children's favorites. Afternoons were filled with baseball, college and professional football, professional wrestling, and roller derby. A meteoric rise in the viewing of sports, both in front of "the box" and at events, took place. High school athletics became even more ardent than before.

The back half of the 1960s began to reveal that the rapid acceleration of change was leading the nation to someplace else. Where would that "someplace else" end up being? Today we have the answer: all we need do is read the labels on non-food products in order to see where they were made; all we need to do is make note of the sparse amount of job ads; all we need to do is view our TV sitcoms, Hollywood movies, and professional wrestling shows. All we need to do is check our personal computers, cell phones, newspapers, magazines, and lottery tickets to see where the collective soul of a once-great nation has ended up.

Neighbors residing near river roads throughout America should be reminded and younger people should come to know of what life was like back then. The writer sees with such clarity how good the time really was. But in this day—a day of lightning-fast computers and hyper-intelligent cell phones—can people come to accept this truth about the past, a past that did not possess these magical items, a past in which people were not possessed *by* them?

In that America of yesterday, a person's word was a promissory note of personal honor, and when delivered, integrity begat humble satisfaction, if not a private feeling of self-glory. Respecting other people's desire to have personal dignity was as important as retaining one's own sense for the same. On this, the people of Maine and America as a whole were meticulous.

Every city has a road that runs beside a river; for some places it might be a lake or an ocean. Throughout time, the body of water and the road have been witness to just about everything, but they could neither write nor speak of the good and bad things seen. Forty-five years ago the young reporter promised not to run the "the big story" edition. The reason was to save hides. Two important persons told him to wait 50 years, when people were either dead or did not care anymore. That meant something to him back then, and it helped him to put it aside. The period of hush will soon be over. The still-rookie editor will show by way of act of demonstration that he has kept his word and thus retained his honor.

But after all the years has his agreement to comply with the wishes of a covert group constituted nothing more than a case of displaced honor, considering the death he was covering back then had been in actuality an accidental murder? The question will forever remain indelibly imbedded in the mind and soul of the editor.

Part IV is a fast-forward shoot in time to right now—2011: the year the writer begins to put it all down. During the shoot came a sudden, sharp turn in trajectory. A strange event took place on a late evening in 1997. And so began an aftermath of Godly instruction not meant for the receiver only. The Lord has been removing the writer's soul from his body in order to show and teach him "things of the spirit." Jesus demands they be shared. Otherwise, why would He bother? Just for me? As the saying goes, "God is a God of love." But His teachings are not to be selfishly kept inside the person granted them. The receiver is also "a revealer," not only of certain long-hidden truths but also of the terrible things to come for the world in the near future.

Other than the enlightenment, what has been the reward? Years of pain and suffering. The last few years have at times had the suffering so acute that I did not know how I would make it through to the next hour. I have prayed thousands of times for Jesus to grant me the grace to bear up. I have even prayed that He allow the body to die so that my soul may be released from duty. Jesus does not want that. Not yet, anyway. "Thy Will, Lord Jesus, and not mine."

Reader, the revealer respectfully presents to you the following questions. Which would you prefer to hear? For all the salt and light the Lord has granted His servant-writer, would you like to know how many millions of dollars he has made and how much he has enjoyed living life in the lap of luxury? (And, by the way, he certainly hasn't been.) Or in his talking of sufferings, may you with a new set of eyes look into the mirror of your own soul-self, recognize and repent your poor choices in life, and choose to make room inside your mind and heart for the same salt and light that is available to all?

Now and then it is good to be reminded of the fact that Jesus died without a penny on him; He went out of this world owning nothing; even His clothes had been ripped off. Tortured, naked, hoisted above the ground so that people standing on and around Mount Calvary could see, He died slowly while baking in the hot sun. He was not even granted a last sip of cool water.

Thirty-three years prior to the crucifixion, in a cave that housed farm animals, hay, and *something else* mixed in with the hay, Jesus entered the world. Other than having fine parents, the baby was born into nothingness. Mary and Joseph suffered torments and extreme physical hardships in their plights building up to, during, and after the birth, when they had to grab their baby and flee to Egypt. The parents survived because of a faith in God, but faith and prayers did not eliminate their tribulations. Instead, they were granted the grace of perseverance and hope.

Jesus entered and left physical life naked. God the Father did not spare His only begotten Son from poverty and sufferings. In other words, He did not give Jesus special treatment. What type of example would that have been for us, His other children?

What exactly is earth? Why is it here? *Why are we here?* We live for a while and then one day we die. Everything and everyone eventually die. So why bother coming? And what does a murder in 1966 have to do with the one that happened 2,000 years ago and the terrible things that are to come? The answer is everything is connected. The writing of the final edition continues. . . .

PART I
Life Along American River Road

Chapter I

Road Kill, the Matriarch, and the Sage Woodsman

Mother always said Maine winters were the bane of her existence. She believed that because the springs tended to be windy and rainy and the falls early and cold, there was never enough time for summers to properly settle in. When a hot and humid summer did occasionally visit central Maine, it could pack violent thunderstorms. This was particularly true in 1966.

Youngest son, 12 years old, was a week away from completing grade six when he learned of a parental plan for a classmate of his to spend the coming summer weekdays at the house. Because the classmate's parents worked weekday jobs, they wanted to ensure their only son's days off would be active and fun. All persons involved in making the plan thought it a good one— all except Charlie. He and Jimmy Ford had never been friends. It was not that they had been enemies, either. The reality was that the two had never connected much with each other. Charlie was strong, blond, and naturally athletic. Jimmy was undersized, of orange-red hair, and plastered with facial and arm freckles. What Jimmy did have going for him, Charlie consoled himself, was his energetic and outgoing style. At recesses and lunchtimes, he always tried to be involved in schoolyard sports, and so he ranked "okay" in the unspoken pecking order every elementary school had. For sure, he could keep the two going, getting them involved in things.

Summer had been in the atmosphere for a month. There had been several bad thunderstorms, with a hard one hitting the previous night. Though there was not news of a direct lightning strike, considerable wind damage had taken place in and around the city of Gardiner. Charlie's friend Mike phoned to say a big tree on the river's side of River Avenue had split apart and fallen onto the thoroughfare, snapping power lines. Mike lived along there and had a view of the situation, which was just north from his place. He commanded Charlie to come down right away. Because city trucks had already arrived, he said for Charlie to meet him at the scene.

Eleven o'clock Saturday morning had the sky cloudless, the sun beating down hot. Mike was sitting on shaded grass directly across the avenue from the action. Charlie sat down beside him. Watching the city crew sweat, cut up the tree, and dispose of it in a dump truck was entertainment for the two. River Avenue connected Gardiner to South Gardiner, three miles away, and on Saturdays there tended to be more traffic than on weekdays. Mike was a year older and probably five years smarter than Charlie, and when the former laughed at seeing the grimacing faces of the drivers who had been stopped so that the dump truck could be repositioned, so did the latter. Mike always used "road" and never "avenue" when referring to the thoroughfare. Most locals did the same—mislabel River Avenue "River Road."

"Because lightning struck the tree down across River Road," Mike mused, "the lost dead wandering the shores of the Kennebec can use it to cross over to our side."

The two had already learned from the workers' conversations that there was no evidence God's flashing arrow had been involved in the selective culling of an aged maple tree, but that a strong gust of wind had likely been the device utilized by Nature Divine. That did not stop Mike from coming up with such a fun idea and Charlie going along with it. They laughed.

Mike always had good ideas. His mind was set on the two of them spending the afternoon fishing up at Cobbossee Stream, just above the dam....

"Charlie, your dad will drive us there, won't he?"

"I don't know. I can give him a call from your place and ask."

Dad was always good about taking me places, as long as they were not more than ten minutes' drive. The plus for the man was that I would be out of sight for a few hours, leaving him uninterrupted to fix, dig, scrape, and paint while mom cleaned and cooked.

The reason Mike offered up my dad was because his was not around anymore. Mike was the fourth of five children, and just after his little brother Pete was born, the father abandoned the family. The mother and the five were left alone to struggle in a small two-story house located in a low-lying area along River Road. Due to ground creep, the house leaned noticeably right, as if to be nodding its respect for—or acknowledging its deep fear of—the 50-feet wide swampy zone that separated it from the property next over. Locals and passers-by alike had sometimes been heard to make comments about the house's inevitable assimilation into the smelly swamp and the hope that no one was inside when it happened.

Mrs. Bondy was a saintly woman. She loved, fed, and protected her kids, all the while working full-time at the Gardiner Nursing Home. Part of me lived for hanging out at their slanted shack; it was always action-packed and happy. If I were present when supper was ready, Mike would ask his mother if I could eat with them. Always would she agree and say, "Tell Charlie to call his mom and see if it's okay." But losing his dad at four years old had been hard on Mike, the first son, and it had caused him to grow up too quickly. He was street smart and clever, always managing to get out of trouble as easily as he had gotten into it.

We walked to his place so I could make the phone call. Mom and dad were aware of the Bondy family's single-parent situation. Because of it, the dominant male Monroe had developed a sort of a fatherly feel for Mike. I dialed. After a hem and haw, the man caved.

"Said he'll take us. Let's get over to my place and dig for worms. Bring your gear."

My house was located not far from his, about five minutes' walk uphill and away from River Road if we were to use the shortcut: an old path through the woods. Otherwise, we had to walk a less direct route uphill south on River Road and then, after a turn right, uphill west on Kingsbury Street. I lived about 150 hundred yards up Kingsbury. When we were younger, the woods seemed the fun way to go, but not anymore. Grownups tended to use tarred routes, and Mike and I believed ourselves no longer little kids. But the walk did take longer.

At my place we grabbed a couple of dad's shovels and went for the dig. The line where the front lawn met the woods was our prime spot for finding worms. No matter how many times we had dug there over the course of previous summers, oodles of them had always been found.

During winters, because the deciduous trees were shed of their leaves, our houses could see each other. From Mike's gravel backyard, Charlie's place looked like a white, pillared mansion nestled nicely on the slope of a snow-coated hill. From Charlie's front yard, Mike's place looked like a tilted little two-story shack stuck in a gloomy pool of gray ice next to River Road. Situated directly across the road from his house was a substation of the Maine Central Railroad, beyond which were a band of land, a stretch of river flowing south past the bridge, and the southern skirt of Randolph, all quite viewable when standing at the very northeast corner of the Monroes' yard where a large rock conveniently stuck up from the ground, granting an extra three inches to human elevation, though binoculars were required if one wanted to properly spy on activities the other side of River Road.

The truth was that my yard was large and reasonably well managed, making it fine for calm activities such as afternoon jogs through sprinklers, suppertime barbeques, and evening games of croquet. What was also true, when the two of us were together, was that his yard tended to be more fun. Over the years, Mike and I had built, erased, and rebuilt many complicated roadways for our Tonka trucks. Winters had us skating on the sheets of ice that formed naturally over top of the gravel yard.

Dad approached. Lizzie, the family dog, walked beside him. "Got enough worms yet?"

We had half a can of the squiggly little beasts. Lizzie poked her snout into the can so that she could get a good sniff of them.

"Lizzie, get your nose out of there!" yelled dad. "You're gonna get stuck!"

"What we have should be enough," I answered.

"Okay then. Put the sod back neat and get all your stuff to the car in five minutes. Do you have eats and drinks for up there?"

"We don't need any."

"Yes, you do. Go make yourselves some peanut butter and jelly sandwiches. On the way, we'll stop at LeClerc's Market for a couple sodas."

"Dad, we don't have any money."

"I know. Hurry up."

We ran to the house. I dearly loved my mother. I knew that when she found out why we were in the kitchen she would insist on making the sandwiches. Luckily, she was standing at the stove when we walked in.

"Hello, Mike. How are you today? Hear you're going fishing."

"Hi, Mrs. Monroe. Yup, Charlie and I are headin' up to Cobbossee Stream. We plan on bringin' back supper. Mmm, is that your famous spaghetti and meatballs I smell?"

Mother laughed. "Yes, but famous—*I don't know*. You're welcome to eat with us tonight, unless you would prefer to go home and eat the fish you catch."

"Mom, we need to make peanut butter and jelly sandwiches. Are there any Lorna Doones or Fig Newtons we can throw in?"

"I'll check. But listen. Let me do the lunches for you. I'll bring them out in a couple minutes. Your dad is very busy today, so go right away and put your gear in the car."

The time was barely noon, which meant we would have five hours of fishing before the adult male came to reel us in. We were at this point very anxious fishermen, and our minds were imagining something grand: a pail full of bass, white perch, and pickerel.

Mom emerged, smiling, holding a brown bag. Dad got into the captain's seat.

"Catch some big ones," she charged, handing me the bag through the window.

Our journey took us up the rest of the hill-portion of Kingsbury Street, lifting us away from the valley's steep western slope. LeClerc's Market was only a two minutes' drive. Mike and I pressed the buttons for the automatic windows, causing them to go up and down erratically. Next, we began to hit the automatic door-lock buttons. The clunking sounds gave us to laughs, but not the man. "Quit that! We paid a lot of money for this car. Do you want things to break?"

Dad was right. We were being irresponsible. The car was a shiny black 1961 Buick Electra. He and mother had bought it second-hand in 1963. They liked it mostly because of the "snazzy" looks and the reliability associated with the Buick name. Prior to the Electra, the family automobile had been a 1957 two-toned-gray Dodge Coronet. The parents had done a lot of looking around before deciding to buy that one brand-new off the lot. They were amply pleased with the fancy looks of that one, too. It ran fine for three years, but then it became a mechanical nightmare, the Dodge dealership a regular stop. On a mid-summer day in 1963, dad angrily stormed, "I've had it with that thing! It's gone and there'll be no more Dodgers ever again! I used to like them in Brooklyn, but now that they're in L.A. I can't stand them!"

We made the store. Ray LeClerc, his kid-brother Norman, and some neighborhood buddies were playing baseball in the open field across the street from the family's convenience store. Ray spotted me and waved.

Dad passed me two quarters. "Don't dawdle. Just the sodas and bring back the change."

Ray's father was sitting on a stool behind the till. He was reading the *Kennebec Journal*. He did not acknowledge us. Mike and I each grabbed a Pepsi.

Mr. LeClerc was a pleasant, hard-working man who always made time for his son's good friend. He and Mrs. LeClerc shared the duty of running their neighborhood's "house" grocery store. The family lived in the upper two levels of the medium-sized three-story unit. The second floor had a large playroom that contained pool and ping-pong tables.

"Hi, Mr. LeClerc. Here's fifty cents for our sodas."

The man opted not to lift his head but instead peered over his reading glasses, which looked to be gingerly balanced on the tip of his nose. He smiled. "What, no candy today? Just yesterday I got in a fresh stock of watermelon strips, salty pumpkin seeds, candy cigarettes, and mint and grape juleps. The grape is new. Give it a try. And, Charlie, look at these—a fresh load of your favorite." Beside the till was a brand-new plastic holder packed tight with pretzel rods. "Prices are up. A rod is now two cents, and you get only one julep for a penny."

I studied the oversized pretzels through the clear plastic. They looked particularly well toasted and salty. Pretzel rods were my soft spot, and Mr. LeClerc knew it. I was tempted only for a moment. I did not want to disobey dad.

"Just got in a fresh barrel of nickel-pickles, too. Unfortunately, they're up to a dime now. My boys say it's the best batch ever. Give it a try? You got enough money."

"I love those things. What-say, Monroe? Let's split one."

"Nope, can't buy more than these sodas."

"Then forty cents does the job. Here's your change." Mr. LeClerc tossed a dime onto the counter. "Raymond's playing ball across the street. Go over if you want."

"No time for ball," jumped in Mike. "We're fishin' up at Cobbossee. Have a good day."

"Have a good day, Mr. LeClerc," chimed I.

As dad drove away, Ray and I again waved. For a moment I pondered the odd social situation. He and I were best friends at school. Sometimes we played ping-pong and pool after school. Mike and I were not friends at those times. He was in grade 7 and hung out with others in his class. When passing each other in the schoolyard or going to and from school, Mike and I barely nodded. The unspoken rule seemed to work fine in that no one's feelings had ever been hurt. After weekday suppers and on weekends were the times that Mike and I liked to chum.

Mike generally spoke more politely to adults outside his family than those inside. Not that he was outright impolite to his mother and siblings, it was just that there always seemed to be hint of sarcasm bordering on rebelliousness in his voice inflection and body language when around them, and as of late it had been getting more obvious. Though my mother liked Mike, she had a gut feeling there was another side to him. She had several times expressed her concern that I was being negatively influenced by him. So far in life, there had been no proof of it, but my reassurances had not allayed her concern. Perhaps she saw something that I couldn't. Recently, she had tried to implement a rule that would have severely limited my time at his place. I vehemently pleaded against it. Thankfully, dad nixed it prior to the start gate, saying that all they needed to do was keep the lines of communication open, give out good advice, and encourage me to stay on the good path. But he cautioned me. "Charles, it's your and his decision as to whether a rule will have to be put in place. So, try to be a good influence on Mike, if you really do believe him a close friend."

Between 100 and 200 yards above the Cobbossee Stream dam was our lucky area. Here, the water was crystal clear, the bottom a mix of small rocks and light brown sand. The water only gradually deepened, and at about 30 feet from shoreline the bottom was no longer discernible. On sunny days, schools of fish could be seen roaming the shallows to the edge of the outer deep. Along the stretch rested large blocks of stone and concrete that had been left behind from an old torn-down bridge. Some of them stuck up out the water, to about 15 feet out from the shoreline. We would leap onto them, then onto ones farther out, and from there fish. It made us feel like we were in a boat close in to shore, and it allowed for a panoramic and penetrating view of the fishing grounds all around us. We could even see beyond the shallow and into the deep, where larger creatures of a fiercely carnal nature liked to lurk. These were the treasures Mike and I enjoyed nabbing most. We viewed the zone a type of freshwater Grand Banks and had often wondered why we had never seen other fishers here.

Always running close to shore were small schools of sunfish. Sunfish were uneatable but the large ones fun to catch because they put up a good fight. Farther from the shore, at about 20 feet out, water maybe five or six feet deep, were roaming schools of yellow perch. They were almost as voracious worm-eaters as sunfish, but they also went for spinners and spoons, whereas sunfish liked only worms. "Yellows" were eatable, but I had tried it once and found it bony. Anyway, to me they looked too ugly for eating, with their dark green stripes dominating their dull yellow-gray bodies. The biggest were about ten inches long, and when hooked they put up an honest resistance. Mike and I always tossed them back. Sometimes the same fish was caught twice; at least that was what we speculated. We guessed the schools of "yellows" could have as many as a hundred students and teachers—the large, fun-to-catch ones being the teachers. The problem was that when we cast our lures into the school, they would all attack in a frenzy, and we never knew if we would hook a lousy pipsqueak or a genuine teacher with a fighting attitude. Still, it was fun to be guaranteed some kind of catch with every cast.

Farther out, at the edge of the deep, where the bottom was eight to ten down, were the smaller schools of white perch. When Mike and I finished our practicing on "sunnys" and "yellows," we went for the "whites." White perch tended to be finicky. They seemed to be not much interested in worms, yet we knew with certainty they relished the flavor of the slimy little dirt mongers. "Whites" came across as intelligent and choosey, and they always made us work to catch one of them. We had to be patient with our playing of the hook and bobber, and eventually a member would move in for the kill. It was a joy to throw a few of these into the pail because when breaded and pan-fried they tasted delicious, with only a few bones to be concerned about.

As the hours wore on, Mike and I would up the ante and go after pickerel and bass. It required our changing of lure tactics. Worms got put aside in favor of red-and-white spoons or large fake worms with hooks sticking out or jitterbugs, which were large fake bugs that swam the surface; the jitterbug's juicy little legs that seemed to propel the insect were in actuality two three-pronged barbed hooks. When hungry and in the right frame of spirit, bass liked to strike the surface and suck down a good-sized bug that had made the bad decision to land on the water. If it happened to be one of our jitterbugs instead of, say, a May beetle, the bass was irreversibly hooked. Its only chance of escape was to fight so hard that the line would snap. And fight it would, jumping out of the water two or three times, jerking its head every which way, sometimes causing the line to snap at the point where the lure was tied. We dreaded losing one. A loosed bass, however, was not exactly a winner, for it was stuck with slow-killing hooks and a large plastic bug in its mouth.

Though not as coveted as bass, pickerel still rated as a genuine score. "Picks" were long, tubular-like fish that possessed numerous sharp teeth in an elongated mouth. Swimming like darts, they might be termed freshwater mini-barracudas. They could get up to four feet in length, but the ones we caught mostly ranged between 15 and 30 inches. They could not resist red-and-white spoons. Loved 'em for some reason. We sometimes saw a "pick" move slowly into shallow water for a perch. The fish tasted decent when breaded and spiced, but an eater had to be careful of the frequent bones. Bass tasted better and carried almost zero bones.

This day, Cobbossee Stream gave up four white perch and one 20-inch pickerel. Mike had managed to snag and lose a nice-sized largemouth bass. Mostly that is what we talked about on the way home—the good fight it had put up and how it had stolen Mike's favorite jitterbug.

Mike stayed for supper. After downing mother's blueberry pie topped with ice cream, we left for his place. The site of the fallen tree was cleaned up and the downed lines fixed. Mike crossed River Road. He wanted to check for the workers' cigarette butts. He picked up three that still had a decent smoking section left on them, pulled out a pack of matches, and lit one.

"How about you, Monroe? Want one?"

"No thanks."

"Aw, come on, grow up, why don't you."

"I hate the stink of those things. Cigars and pipes smell way better."

"Well, there weren't none of those, and you wouldn't want to smoke someone else's cigar, all chewed and soaked with spit."

There was a big dinner planned for the next afternoon at his grandmother's place, across the river, in Randolph, and he asked his mother if I could join them. As usual, Mrs. Bondy said yes and for me to get permission from my mother. There we were, over-stuffed from supper and setting our sights on the next feast.

The Bondy family and I watched TV into the evening. Mother called at 9:30 and asked Mrs. Bondy to send me on my way. I had forgotten about having to be home by 9:00.

The walk up River Road took me past the Donahues' place: an old, well-kept two-story house lived in by two elderly sisters. Their brother, Jim, had lived with them up until two-and-a-half years prior, at which time—a harsh and sudden instant—the man's earthly sojourn ended. The morning of his death found central Maine blanketed in snow from a typical wintertime nor'easter. School had been canceled for the day, and I was heading to Mike's.

I had just about reached the end of Kingsbury Street when a car sped by. I heard a horn. Turning onto River Road, I saw the car, now well past the Donahue property, sliding sideways to the bottom, where it settled in front of the Bondys' porch. Although city plows had been by overnight, there were several inches of snow on the roadway. The situation was extremely slippery. The driver had not been able to stop quickly, and I did not know why he had wanted to. Then I noticed a body lying on the other side of the road from the Donahue house. The driver exited his car and ran slipping and falling up the hill. I reached the felled man first. He was not conscious and blood was already coming from his nose.

The driver arrived and pointed to the Donahue house. "Son, quickly go knock on that door and tell the people to call an ambulance."

I did as told. Ten seconds went by and the older spinster opened.

"Miss Donahue, please call an ambulance right away. A man has been run over."

"Charlie, is it Jim? Please, Charlie, tell me right away. Is it him?" The younger Donahue, the quieter of the two, joined her sister at the door.

"I don't know" was my reply, and I was telling the truth. The man on the ground was bald. The Mr. Donahue I knew had a full head of hair. I went back to the scene. The driver was upset and kneeling next to the body. His eyes were closed and his head was tilted down. Within a minute, sirens could be heard. I noticed a hairpiece 15 feet down the road. Then I saw Mr. Donahue's big snow-pusher a little farther down. Now I knew for sure the felled man was Jim Donahue. He always liked to push his driveway snow over the bank on the other side of River Road. Lying there, hairless, face blue and swollen, bleeding profusely from his nose, the man looked so different from what I knew. The sisters emerged as the ambulance and police car came up. They burst out screaming, crying. The moment was so terribly grievous.

After the ambulance left, the older of the two police officers wanted to talk with me. He was a friendly man. I told him what I had seen. The day after the accident, walking home, I noticed the same policeman using a measuring tape and writing down notes at the scene. I stopped to watch him. He smiled, greeted me, and asked that I remain. He walked down the sidewalk, picked up something, and brought it to me. I had dropped my plastic gun holster. The officer patted me on the shoulder and asked how I was doing. Later, when I described the man to mom, she said that he was Lieutenant Ralph Cates, one of the nicest men she had ever met.

Sunday morning, the two families went to church: mine to St Joseph's Catholic Church and Mike's to Winter Street Baptist Church. Afterward, I rode my bike to his place. I hadn't bothered to change clothes because Sunday best was required attire at his grandmother's. Uncle Allan's 1959 Chev Biscayne was parked at the railroad station. The car did not have enough room to hold everyone, and that was why Mike and I were rendezvousing, so we could ride our bikes to the Randolph residence. The front door was open. Mike's uncle stood just inside the entrance.

"Hi, Mr. Barry."

He smiled. "Hi there, Charlie. We're leaving right away. You know about Mike and you not being allowed to get there first?"

Mike appeared. "Nope, he knows no such thing. Let's go, Charlie. We're gonna smoke 'em this time. They're waitin' for Nancy and Janice, which means we'll be halfway done dinner before they get there."

"Hey, watch the mouth," jabbed back the uncle. "Anyhoos, you won't have even made the bridge when we go by you slow pokes peddling like crazy."

As it turned out, Uncle Allan was only half-right. The car beat the bikes, but we did make it onto the bridge before they went by. To rub it in, the driver had slowed, stuck his laughing head out the side-window, and tooted, while his passengers laughed and pointed at us. The race to the exquisite feast was always a fun, impassioned challenge. So far, pedal-power had yet to garner victory, but one past competition had the bikers making it off the bridge and almost to Randolph's number one business enterprise, Shep's Garage.

Nanna Barry—"Mrs. Barry" to me—met us in the front hallway. She was a petite woman in her 70s. Her light charcoal-gray hair was, as always, combed into a tight bun that sat on the crest of her head. With a straight-up posture and firm face, she presented herself as a Puritan descendant and a bona-fide matriarch to a medium-sized line of Maine oak. Mrs. Barry's small and round face housed large eyes that showed bead-sized pupils centered within hazel irises. When she smiled, which was not often, her bounteous whites glistened such that it seemed salt and light were pouring out upon everyone present. Politeness and gentle talk ruled Nanna Barry's meals. No one gobbled food, but instead we went slowly, methodically. In contrast, mealtimes at the Bondys' tended to be loud and fast, to say the least, and diners sat tilted. The two places shared one solemn custom: every dinner and supper began with grace.

From prior mealtime conversations, I knew that the Patriarch Barry had died of lung cancer years earlier. The Barrys had managed to bring three boys and two girls into the world. The mother was proud of her sons . . . Well, for sure two of them and *perhaps* the third. The first son became a doctor. He practiced in Biddeford. The next became an engineer. I never heard say where he resided. And then there was Allan, who lived with his mother.

Uncle Allan seemed an enigma to some—*most*. Mid-30s in age, the man displayed long, curly black hair, except on the top his head, where significant balding had taken hold. He was a bit of a jokester around kids, and he fashioned himself a ladies' man. Several years ago, Allan had married the woman of his dreams, or so he had thought. The twosome had a short courtship before tying the knot. The knot got untied during the honeymoon, and the marriage was quickly annulled. Coming out of it, the man's only public comment was that he had made a mistake, that she turned out not to be the right one, that she only reminded him of his first true love from years before. The statement did not clear "the air" but on the contrary only added to people's curiosities as to what had happened on that *honeymoon shrouded in mystery*. Allan had recently taken up with another woman, and now that too was over.

Maine to the core, the man was known to be an expert outdoorsman. For a good part of his early adult life, Allan had worked for long stretches in the remote lumber camps of the northern counties. Mike and I admired him because we figured he knew just about everything on hunting, fishing, tracking, and how to survive in the wilds. He was a sometimes Boy Scout leader, knew how to make camp in minutes, and could tie every knot imaginable. Mike's knowledge of fishing and his often funny ways of looking at things in life had mostly come down from this man. A good example was a few years back when Mike and I were traipsing around in the woods behind his house. We were flipping our jackknives into the ground and at trees as we went along, and each of us cut a hand. He said for us to rub our cuts together for a few seconds because that was what the Indians used to do in order pronounce themselves blood brothers forever, if they were not already of the same parents.

For a couple weeks of evenings last summer, Uncle Allan had Mike and me over to Randolph so that he could teach us how to tie Indian gimp and make rings and wristbands with Indian seed-beads. During it, he talked about the Kennebec Indians and how they had lived throughout the valley prior to the 1700s. He said the native nation consisted of several tribes. The one that lived in and around the Gardiner-Farmingdale area was called Abnaki. Its members fished our area's rich waters and hunted and trapped the vast woodlands that teemed of prey.

Mr. Barry described the Indians as initially friendly toward the Europeans, when the latter began arriving in the 1600s. Problems due to the two cultures' opposing views on land ownership eventually broke the peace. Natives were never the aggressors when things got heated, but only acted in defense. When the British government denied the Natives' land claims in any part of the valley, most of that Nation's population fled to Canada. Mr. Barry noted that back then Maine was still part of the Commonwealth of Massachusetts and not yet its own state. The few Indian families that did stay behind tried very hard to assimilate into the new culture.

Mr. Barry firmly believed that the "spirits" of the old Kennebec Nation still dwelt in the valley—not in the cities and towns but along the uncluttered shorelines of the "big river" and its contributory waterways. "God never separated the aboriginals from this valley. He was generous to the Indians in the secret next life because human governments failed to give them any respect. The Big Guy Upstairs always makes things right. Sometimes it takes a while. He doesn't use our schedule. Look how England was eventually booted out of America."

It was obvious that a keen sense of fair-play lined the character of our teacher. Though Mr. Barry was not of big physical stature, he possessed a larger-than-life spirit in that he seemed to know about things that the human eye cannot see, things of the invisible forces of life and death that surround us at every moment.

After dinner, Uncle Allan led Mike, Pete, and me out to his garage. The structure was not quite double-sized and had a dirt floor. In one corner sat a large cage constructed of two-by-fours and chicken wire. Inside, a young raccoon impatiently paced back and forth. Mr. Barry had come up on it a month ago, when he was driving the back road from Augusta to Randolph. Confused and scared, the kit was huddled up to its mother, who had been made road-kill by a previous vehicle. To save the kit, he took it here. Thrice a day since then and holding the youngster tight in his arms, he had been feeding it milk from a baby bottle.

"Can Pete and Charlie and I hold it?" Mike asked.

"You boys can give it a try."

Mr. Barry opened the cage door and removed the young raccoon. He showed us how to hold it without getting scratched. Growing bigger and stronger by the day, the coon was now of a more feral and uncooperative nature. The three of us took turns trying to hold and pet it. Didn't work. Mr. Barry placed the animal back into the cage. After he showed us how to tie a special anglers' knot that an angry bass couldn't break, we headed back into the house.

Nanna Barry's two daughters had started out as housewives. One stayed with it; she lived in Bethel, and that was all I really knew about her. As for the other daughter, Christine—the one here at the dinner table this day—it was apparent that the mother retained extra-special feelings of warmth and compassion for her. This daughter would have to cope with many more years of emotional, physical, and financial hardships raising five children while working full-time. The matriarch and Allan tried their best to help her out.

Christine's oldest daughter—Rose, 18—had not lived at home for five years, but she was allowed to visit now and then. The father's abandonment, immediate taking up with another woman, and refusal to see his children had hit her the hardest. Basically, her dad had stuck a knife into her heart. She became depressed, but it soon turned into anger, violence. The decision was made to send Rose to a young women's reformatory, located in Hallowell.

"Allan, we've already decided what has to be done with that wild animal."

The son's voice showed irritation. "Yes, Mother. I'll release it when I'm ready."

"Where's that gonna be?" asked Mike.

"Someplace remote. Exactly where, I've yet to decide."

Nanna Barry changed the subject. "Michael, do you and Charlie know that before refrigerators, people had ice boxes to keep their milk and meat cold, and the blocks of ice that went into them came from our Kennebec River. A big storage building for ice was right here in Gardiner? Our old ice boxes weren't as large as these new fridges. About half the size, I'd say."

"No, Nanna, I didn't know that."

"I didn't either, Mrs. Barry."

Even when there were other children present, Mrs. Barry sometimes liked to speak directly to Mike and me. At these moments, she was not ignoring the others; and those others always seemed to take it well, as if they knew why their nanna was doing it. It was just that Mrs. Barry recognized that Mike's spirit needed to feel a special glow from hers, and an ever so gentle firmness, too. By including me, Mike never felt singled out.

"Gardiner supplied ice for the entire eastern United States. Back then, everyone knew this, but these days most people don't know anything about it. All along the river, men were employed in the ice business. To keep the ice blocks from melting, they got rolled in sawdust from our valley's paper mills. One of the mills was right here in town. It's a good thing these new fridges came along because the river got too polluted in the thirties. That was when sewage from cities and northern pulp mills began to inundate the river. The smell got so bad, and the fish stopped running. The situation worsened in the late fifties. That's when many houses in the valley got taken off property systems and hooked into city sewer lines. Every day since then, raw sewage from seven thousand citizens of Gardiner has been dumping straight into the Kennebec. Folks sure wouldn't want to have any of that frozen stuff sitting in their ice boxes."

"What fish used to run the river, Nanna?" asked Pete.

"Striped bass and salmon. Every year, Atlantic salmon and stripers would run the Kennebec as far up as Augusta. There they would try to jump the Edwards Dam. The sight was something. Huge fish could be seen. Both tasted real fine. Fisherman would line the shores. For the first couple hundred years the Europeans were here, they enjoyed a river jam-packed with fish, and it made for profitable industry, too. State government had to enact a law disallowing lumber camps from feeding their men salmon more than four times a week. Can you believe? But then came the Edwards Dam. After it was built in the early eighteen hundreds, the fish stocks sharply declined because the best spawning grounds had been cut off. Even the sturgeon fell off, and it had been such a sturdy species prior to that. But life in the river completely collapsed in Maine's version of the Dirty Thirties. Like I said, it's even worse today.

"Truth is, the Lord did not forsake the people of Maine, even though He might well have." She lifted her coffee cup and took a sip. "And that's because of our human *shortcomings*, if you know what I mean in more ways than one." She looked around the room, smiled and winked at Mike. Had the starchy lady said something meant to be funny? And about a subject like that? Her listeners were not sure, so to be polite, everyone looked at each other, smiled.

"Despite our, as I said, 'shortcomings,' Maine remains full of industry. Why, right here in Gardiner we have so many factories for such a small center. No one has to be unemployed. There's not a good reason for even one person not to have a job here."

With that, Mrs. Barry ended her lesson. An uncomfortable silence took over the living room. It did not last long. Allan cleared his throat.

"Have I mentioned to anyone that I'm pretty sure I found a job this week?"

"No, you haven't," said his sister.

"*Yyyup*, I'm pretty sure I'm the new short-order cook at Ernie's Drive In. Should start sometime this week or next, once the boss let's me know."

Allan's mother stared into her son's eyes, then took another sip. "Well, Allan, I feel confident you'll be called. I'll pray on it tonight."

It did not matter that tucked into Nanna Barry's history class was a dig at Allan. Every Sunday dinner was required to have an educational moment of re-exposure to America's glorious past. She was a living history book that begged to be shared, but, at her insistence, slowly, gradually. The instant a lesson ran its course she would straighten up, purse her lips, and remain reticent for the next ten minutes, as if to be embarrassed to have held the floor for so long.

The last several years had found Mr. Barry securing off-and-on local employment. He stayed at the places for only a few days or weeks. After each departure, his habit was to withdraw from the world and concentrate on his manifold hobby passions. After some months passed by, he was back to work. His best success at sticking with a job had been during those earlier years in the northern camps. But because the guys up there tended to be heavy drinkers, Mr. Barry eventually made the decision to leave that world behind him forever.

Ernie's Drive In was a mile north of Gardiner, in the township of Farmingdale. Mom and dad occasionally got takeout cheeseburgers, french fries, and clam cakes from there; sometimes we got served at the car and ate right there, in it. I knew that if Mr. Barry saw me, he would stack the Monroes' baskets extra high.

The bike ride home was as good a time as any to tell Mike about the schoolmate situation and mother's rule that he could not come over while Jimmy was around. She felt that because Mike and I were such close friends, Jimmy would end up being left out. Even though I had objected, I knew that she was right. I also knew that the two would not mix well, being that Mike was a cunning fox and Jimmy a scruffy chipmunk. When I told him, it was as if it meant nothing. "Yeah, so what."

Chapter II

Brothers Pencils and Rifleman

Tony and kid-brother went outside to play some catch. Even though four years older, Tony did not object to having Chuckie close by to him; "Chuckie" was middle brother's name for kid-brother. Over the years, Tony had taught Chuckie how to properly pitch a baseball and throw a football, and up to his level, too, so that their playtime together would be equally fun for both. The two tossed a tennis ball for an hour and went back inside. There in front of the TV, they guzzled a large bottle of Hires Root Beer and munched down to nothing the whole big bag of Humpty Dumpty BBQ Potato Chips.

There were three boys in the Monroe family. Daniel, 16, was on the way home from a friend's place in South Portland. The two had just finished their junior year at a Catholic high school located in Portland. During the year, Daniel took room & board nearby to Cheverus High.

As a tot, Daniel had been diagnosed with extremely poor eyesight. In order for him to get properly fitted for glasses, the parents had to teach him the alphabet. During the learning sessions, the little boy held the paper a few inches from his face. At three, he was able to read simple things and was prescribed glasses that looked like the bottoms of two Coca Cola bottles; neither he nor the parents cared about that detail. The first time he put them on was the first time in his life he could see with 20-20 vision beyond a few inches. The period of instruction had opened up the world of literature to him, and the little boy could not stop reading.

In early elementary school, teachers came to believe Daniel a mental prodigy. He was urged to skip grade 3, and he did. In grade 7 at Gardiner Junior High School, he finished runner-up in the state spelling bee championship. In grade 8 he won it. Off the family, except for the youngest son because he was only seven, went to Washington D.C. for the U.S. competition. The four stayed at the Mayflower Hotel. At breakfast one morning, they had the opportunity to meet and chat with former President Truman and First Lady. Daniel met many high profile politicians while there, and the entire experience changed him. Coming out of it, he figured himself to be worldly and a whole lot too worldly for Gardiner. This was apparent to most.

Daniel did well in the national competition, but not well enough to win. Even so, Tony and youngest brother considered him a genuine genius. Summers since D.C. had seen the brainy brother reading a different novel every day, and he had already amassed for himself an impressive home-library. Add to it, he was addicted to the city's public library. Because he and head librarian Glennis Neely had become friends, she favored him when new books arrived.

Tony was two grades behind Daniel. Sometimes teachers openly commented on his academic abilities versus his older brother. Naturally, this was disconcerting to Tony. He was smart enough, but what was obvious to everybody was that the two were remarkably different. Tony was athletic, Daniel not. Tony preferred guns to books. In fact, at his unripe age of 15 he was already a sort of gun-oholic, more than willing to do in any and every pesky varmint when asked to do so. There had also been "jobs" done for personal pleasure. In life so far, he had never missed an opportunity and never missed taking down his animal quarry. Tony was an emerging sharpshooter destined for noteworthiness, but nobody was sure what type it would end up being. Popular in its heyday, the TV show *Rifleman* had been off the air for three years. One time the handle "Rifleman" was jokingly applied to Tony, and he liked it. Hence, the nickname stuck.

Dad picked up Daniel at the Augusta Greyhound terminal. They got home at 8:30. Mom fixed her oldest son a plate of leftovers. Tired, not talkative, he ate quickly and took *The Portland Sunday Telegram* and *The Boston Globe* upstairs to his bedroom; the one from Portland had financed the spelling-bee trip. Father's routine was to purchase the newspapers early Sunday morning at Gardiner Fruit. This day, the family-size soda and chips had been included. . . .

"Dad, next time please try to remember to buy King Cole BBQ chips. Humpty Dumpty's are too hot. Makes Chuckie and me drink the root beer too fast."

"Wow. Thank you for telling me that. From now on I'll know better. How about instead, next time I get a bottle of root beer or Moxie and a bag of pretzels—*my* favorites."

"Sorry, Dad. Chuckie and I appreciate what you got us. Please never mind what I said."

"I didn't get that stuff just for you two. But now I see it's all gone. Thank you again."

Daniel also had a nickname. Being that he was a mathematical whiz with a butch haircut and already at his age of 16 over six feet tall and thin as a rail, mother had recently compared him to two pencils. It got chortles. After that and when he was thought not to be within earshot, we sometimes affectionately referred to Daniel as "Pencils."

Monday morning, the adult male ordered me out of bed at 6:30, early but normal on school days. He knew that the ability to move fast first thing in the morning was not something his youngest son was born with. For there to be enough time to pick up Ray LeClerc and make it to Central Street School by 8:30, I had to leave the house by 8:00. An hour and a half from bed to Kingsbury Street was plenty of time, though to me the early mornings always seemed hurried.

At 6:45, I was dressed and headed downstairs. Dad had already poured me a bowl of corn flakes. Mom liked to sleep until 7:30, at which time she would rise and make lunches for her boys. Because high school had already let out, my brothers did not have to be up. So there we were, just the two of us, sharing five minutes of cereal time together. Not sure why, I stared and marveled at the man. As always, he was clean-shaven, eating fast, racing through the *Kennebec Journal*. I loved my father beyond words. He was a rock—in his way of being a rock.

"Dad, do you like going to work every day?"

"What kind of question is that? Charles, don't be silly. Just eat your cereal."

"Ah, Dad, you have blood on your chin from shaving."

The man was required to leave home between 6:50 and 6:55 in order to be at work by 7:00. This meant he had to be up by 6:00. Always at hearing him would Lizzie jump from Tony's bed and run downstairs. Dad would let her outside so that she could do her business wherever she felt like doing it. When done, she would scratch the door and he would let her in.

Dad worked at Kennebec Manufacturing, located at the top of Northern Avenue. Being the place was unionized, management was strict about employees starting at the seven o'clock buzzer. Every worker was required to punch a timecard before going hard for the next eight hours. The facility made children's clothes under the brand name "Health-tex."

Dad was the head machinist there. He and his crew of three men were charged with keeping the hundred or so high-powered sewing machines in good working order. Another of his jobs was to mold and solder into creation special types of sewing machine attachments for the five factory sites. The attachments allowed merging cloths to fast-feed the machines. New types of stitches were regularly being introduced from the company's New York-based fashion designers, and the attachments were vital for the successful production of all lines of pants and shirts. Dad had always kept the skill close to his chest, like a poker player a good hand. In the whole company, he was the only one who knew how to make them to work properly. Ones that the company purchased from outside makers always clogged. Sometimes he had to be out of town for a few days. We missed him awful when that happened.

Chapter III

Pushy Jimmy

Youngest son skimmed the *KJ*. The tag "KJ" was what most people used when referring to the Kennebec Valley's newspaper, which, except for Sunday, published daily out of Augusta.

"Good morning, Charles."

"Hi, Mom. Can I have a nickel for LeClerc's?"

"Go comb up and brush your teeth while I consider giving you that much money."

The job took all of a minute. "What do you say, Mom?"

"Here's your nickel."

"Love you. Thanks. Bye."

"Same to you, dear."

I made the store at 8:10.

"Hi, Mr. LeClerc. Got a nickel today." Most mornings had me coming in with only two or three cents. Since prices were up, I was able to purchase about the same as before. The man went to call for his son. He possessed the mightiest of vocal cords.

"Raymond! Charlie's here . . . ! A whole nickel, huh? What do you want?"

"A watermelon strip, a mint julep, a new grape one, and a pretzel rod. I'll grab that."

The man picked up a little brown bag and walked behind the candy cabinet. Ray's feet pounded down the stairs.

"Hi, Charlie." He pulled the bag from his dad's fingertips and tossed it to me. "Let's get outta here." The adult male looked slightly annoyed, but he didn't say anything. Ray reached into the cabinet and grabbed a handful of malted milk balls, popped one into his mouth. "Did you see the yoyos?" He pointed to the display basket holding the colorful new arrivals. "They're only a buck twenty-five. We'll throw in a couple pretzel rods and a red hot fireball because you and I are buddies." Ray stopped to look back. "Is that okay, Dad?"

"Yeah, I suppose. Now get!"

Out in the parking lot, I stuffed the watermelon strip into my mouth. I had enjoyed the units on many past mornings but only now, suddenly, did the mind wonder why something red and green with little black spots tasted like coconut. I asked my buddy. He smirked and shook his head.

"Monroe, who cares other than you? What about the yoyo?"

"I'm going to ask my mom for the money. She'll probably say no at first."

During lunchtime at school, Jimmy mentioned about having a couple of interesting projects for us to work on starting next week. He also stated there would be little to no watching TV and playing ball games for him over the summer.

"What are the interesting projects?" I asked.

"Wait till next week," he responded.

"Why can't you tell me now?"

"Why are you so pushy all the time? How about trying not to be that way. Anyway, what difference does it make if you know right now? Just eat your sandwich and quit asking."

Jimmy could be hard to stomach at times; this was one of those times. I moved away from him. *Me? Pushy? Not me. You're the pushy one, Jimmy . . . jerk.*

The real reason I wanted to know his plans was so that I could figure out how to block them. It was my house and my neighborhood, so we were going to do the things I wanted to do. Jimmy would be no more than an intruder, as far as I was concerned.

For supper, the family enjoyed mother's savory-seasoned turkey croquettes made with yesterday's turkey. The dish came served with french fries, wax beans, and cream corn.

"Ma, Chuckie and I prefer the wax beans when you throw lots of salt and melted butter on them. And *again*, just to remind you, in the future please don't put the cream corn next to the fries. The wax beans go better there, and that way the fries won't get all soggy like they are now."

"This I know for sure, you were born with two arms, two hands, and two legs. Last I saw, they haven't been chopped off yet—*yet*. But there's still opportunity for that. In the meantime, there's no excuse for you not to get up off your duff and come in here to do things for yourself. Your attitude has managed to get my goat a little bit. That special room above the garage is latched, but it can be unlatched and used again. Right, Herve?"

"Not yet because I'll need him to help me with the roof come August. Maybe after that."

"Sorry, Ma. I get the point." In a low voice: "*Chuckie, go into the kitchen and bring back the saltshaker and a big spoonful of butter. Wait a sec before you go.* Ma, what's for dessert?"

"Apple pie and topped with ice cream, if you like."

"*Chuckie, bring back our desserts, too. Pile mine high with ice cream. Slide the saltshaker into your pocket and try to hide the spoon of butter so Mom doesn't see.*"

Done dessert, Tony and I went outside to throw hoops. Our parking lot was tarred, wide enough for three cars, long enough for two. At the house's end of the lot was a double attached garage that held a backboard and basketball rim. Tony and I and friends tried as often as possible to work the net. It didn't matter what Jimmy had said to me during lunch. This and other types of ball games were what we were going to do.

* * *

There could be no precognition as to what would end up taking place over the course of that long-ago summer of 1966. His classmate's outgoing, bordering-on-intrusive personality would be the catalyst for bringing into light dark truths that might have otherwise, perhaps even should have, remained hidden. Adults will be drawn into an eddy of heightened drama due to one boy's nearly perilous struggle to break through the ramparts of secrecy and uncover a truth that he was too young to know, a truth that if exposed would endanger him and his family, a truth that if withheld would alter fate and in doing so expunge the path to further killing.

Chapter IV

Night Train to Skowhegan, Pong Choolie Aboard, and Bullets Fly

P encils had his own bedroom whereas Rifleman and kid-brother shared one. Prior to the family's moving in, our half of the upstairs had been the house's second apartment unit. The bedroom Tony and I used was the flat's living room, so there was plenty enough space for the two of us.

My bedtime on school nights was 9:00. Tony's was 10:00, but he sometimes retired early because bed was where he liked to read his favorite magazine, *Shooting Times*. When this happened, the nightlight stayed on. So far in life, it had never kept me awake. Tony maintained that I was "the fastest faller-asleeper in the world." He claimed that the instant my back hit the bed, I was already out. This night, due to my rapture at there being only two-and-a-half days left to school, a quick trip into deep slumber was not in the stars.

Half an hour went by, and Tony turned off the lamp. Sleep continued to evade me. After supper tonight, Mike and I had hung out for a while. He mentioned about his family eating our catch from Saturday, along with their special fried potatoes. Mike always liked to remind me about those potatoes because he knew how much I enjoyed them—and, too, watching how they got made. The Bondys' kitchen was at the back of the house, where the place's structural integrity twisted downward, causing the lean to be most acute in that zone. Their stove sat dangerously unlevel, and because the thing was gas, the flames were required to show significant bend in order to remain within the laws of gravity: upright. To start, the mother and daughters selected the largest potatoes, then carefully sliced each one as if it were a role of bologna.

This made the units look like large, thick potato chips when done. They owned an extra-large frying pan and filled it a fifth of the way up with corn oil. Naturally when on a burner, the pan was tilted, and this made the oil pool to one side. During the fry, potato slats got randomly moved back and forth from deep oil to sizzle-side. Chatting away, mother and daughters took turns adding shakes of salt and pepper. Only near the end did the potatoes get tasted. Some units ended up burnt, others medium-brown to moderately crispy, the rest soft and greasy. No fries anywhere compared!

There was another "situation" about the house. Their bathroom was located in the worst of all corners, right off the kitchen. When entering, one never knew what would have to be contended with in order to achieve goal. Always was the toilet broken in some fashion, but it still had to be used, for there was no other option except the woods. When a person sat down on it, the entire unit rocked if one wanted it to, and always did the base show looseness that allowed for a swivel from ten to two o'clock. Going into the Bondys' bathroom was not unlike trying to make it through the Windsor State Fair's Fun House with your pants down. Where exactly the flushed contents ended up no one knew for sure. What we did know was that the same corner of the dank basement below was in constant receipt of drips and splats emanating from the ceiling above.

Toward 10:00 my ears discerned the northbound freight train approaching. The track ran parallel to River Road all the way up from South Gardiner. In the past, when rolling through Gardiner, the diesel engine's imposing sound and the *whir* of metal wheels rubbing against metal tracks had never disturbed my sleep. On past oddball nights like this, when I had remained awake for whatever reason, the sounds had in fact helped me to fall asleep. Where the train passed by Kingsbury Street was a slight dip at the point metal rails connected. One side was still intact from original construction, the other side a replacement section that had been put in last year. Each rail car passing over the dip caused a distinct *tick* that allowed me to count the number of cars constituting the elongated assemblage, assuming I could make it to the end before falling asleep. That happened only once; the total that night was 44. Most nights had me not making it to ten. The train cars carried unknown cargoes that had originated from Portland and, prior to there, unknown points out of state. The units would slide past Kingsbury Street and through the Gardiner core in the dark of night, then on through Farmingdale, Hallowell, Augusta, and Waterville, before landing at its final destination: Skowhegan, 45 miles up the Kennebec River. I had never been to Skowhegan. In my mind the place ranked as a mystical, lawless, far-off territory. There, I imagined, thieves, derelicts, and ghosts hurriedly unloaded cargoes destined for arcane back-road deliveries to unmapped sites farther to the north. Skowhegan was the last stop before the great, uncharted, *wild* frontier of northwest Maine.

Dad first noticed my interest in trains when I was a toddler. Back then when driving by the station, he sometimes remarked on how the track went all the way up to Skowhegan. Whenever I asked him where Skowhegan was, he would point up the track and say, "It's up there somewhere." To me, his finger always seemed to point a little bit into the sky, and this had given the youngster over to a permanent intrigue about the place.

Mother would have to be asked about the yoyo first thing Tuesday morning. Based on past experience, I knew that asking dad would get me nowhere. "Ask your mother" would be his answer. Dad earned the bucks, and every Friday noon he handed the pay-envelope to his wife, the resident accountant. If there were 125 pennies to spare, she would know. The past had also taught me that to get a yes from her would likely involve a process. To have the money for Thursday noon, after school let out, I had to have her yes by Wednesday night.

"Goodbye, Mom." We hugged. She smiled and tried to hand me three pennies. "I don't need it. But, Mom, LeClerc's just got in some really nice yoyos. My old one is broken. Can I get a new one? They're only a dollar twenty-five."

"No, dear, that's too expensive. Now here's your three cents for some candy. *Goodbye.*"

"Thanks, Mom. I love you. Bye."

"Hello, Mr. LeClerc. I have three cents today. Can I have two malted milk balls, a watermelon strip, and a mint julep. The grape ones aren't that good."

"Raymond! Charlie's here!" The man smiled at me. "What? No pretzel rod today?"

"Too expensive. Can't afford two cents anymore."

Ray arrived, checked to make sure his dad wasn't looking, grabbed two handfuls of malted milk balls from the candy cabinet, and jammed four units into his mouth. "Bye, Dah. Char, wha ya mah say abow oh-ho?"

"Don't know yet. Ray, you're drooling chocolate all over your chin."

He swallowed, wiped his chin with the back his hand. "Thursday afternoon we can hang out across the street. Broten, Kiley, Robertson, and Spike all say they'll be getting yoyos."

What? Persons who rated were going to be getting new yoyos? Peer pressure was now on me. Mother would have to be asked a second time before the day was out. Badgering her, getting her to feel guilty, was my best shot.

"Let's run so we have time before the bell," urged Ray. "Hope we finish the book today."

Mrs. Gillis was our substitute teacher. Our real teacher was Mr. Miles, but he had come down sick. The students liked Mr. Miles. He was a bit of an oddity in that he was our first male teacher. He had done time in the military. He was tall, broad-shouldered, and displayed a crew cut with flattest top and sharpest edges anyone in Gardiner had ever seen. At the first sighting of him, everyone in the class giggled and got to whispering about how he could win every eraser-on-the-head runoff if the teachers had them. Always in suit and tie, he taught with confidence and force. After lunch, Mr. Miles' manner was to remove his sport coat, loosen his tie, unbutton his wrist cuffs, and carefully role up his sleeves. To some degree, we feared the man. Before Christmas, he began to suck on Smith Brothers menthol lozenges. By February he was shoving them into his mouth left and right. The classroom air reeked of medication. He informed us that his throat was getting worse. By the end of February he could hardly speak. That was when Mr. Miles went on leave and Mrs. Gillis showed up.

We liked Mrs. Gillis just as much, but for different reasons. She was loose on the academics and great on chatting and the fun crafts-and-games stuff; at least once a week she had us in an eraser-on-the-head go-around. After her first few days, she offered to read us a book. She had recently come across one that looked both interesting and educational for the time we lived in. And so it was at the start of April when Mrs. Gillis began to read a few pages of *Pong Choolie, you rascal—!* to us every day. The story was about a 12-year-old North Korean boy who was befriended by an American soldier during the Korean War. The first 12 years of the boy's life had had him being raised by his communist father. At the war's start, the father gave the boy over to be a helper to and a messenger for the local commander of the North Korean communist army. Early in the book, Pong Choolie got ordered to deliver an important letter to the commander of a far-off city. The travel had to be done on foot through a treacherous mountain pass. The timing of his extremely adventurous assignment was about mid-war. When he started out, the Chinese Army was on the verge of a three-million-strong invasion, to bail out the sinking North Korean Army. The American units were caught off guard. Individuals and small groups of men ended up stranded behind the rapidly advancing enemy line. Pong Choolie hated the South Koreans and Americans—and, for that matter, he hated the Chinese even more—but he ended up helping out a wounded American private he encountered along the way. The youngster instantly saw the GI as a cheerful, jocular, big-brotherly type of soul, not at all like the North Koreans and especially not like the Chinese communists. He took to the man, who in turn saw Pong Choolie an innocent kid stuck in a bad situation. Later on, the boy helped a small American unit through hellfire to safe ground.

Mrs. Gillis saw the story an opportunity to teach her class about the scourge of communism, so prevalent and spreading in the world of the 1960s. "Communists are not like us," she asserted. "They're godless, ruthless persons who forcibly take over countries, only to then shove communism's erroneous beliefs down regular citizens' throats. They imprison, even kill those who object or resist. They are bent on taking over the entire world. All Americans, including you children right here in this classroom, must remain on guard against them, so that they may be prevented from landing on our shores." She read the book only in the final 15 minutes of school. The class was totally taken in. If on a day we had been dawdling or too boisterous, there was no reading of Pong Choolie. We quickly learned to fall into line just as we had with Mr. Miles. We were now down to the final pages, and we just had to finish it!

LeClerc and I joined up with Broten and Kiley in the schoolyard. Broten informed all players that the game was set for Friday at the park. "We start a one and play tackle. Kiley here's bringing the ball." Broten noticed Sheehan entering the schoolyard. "Hey, Sheehan, get over here! Friday's the game. Tackle. Kiley here's bringing the ball. Starts at one o'clock. Hey, McKane, get over here! Have you seen Spike? We play on Friday at the park, one o'clock. Kiley here's bringing the ball. Tackle this time. No more of that baby flag stuff." Broten always did the organizing and decision-making, and no one ever interfered. "Somebody find Robertson! Where's Cushard?" The bell rang. "Hope we finish the book today."

Ray and I and two of the guys played ping-pong after school. Ray's big brother, Roger, made a guest appearance. He was in the same grade as Daniel, but a year older. Roger also attended Cheverus High School. Daniel and Roger knew and respected each other, but they had never become real friends. Perhaps it was because my brother had skipped a grade and therefore was considered to be a bit of an oddity.

Roger was the oldest of three boys. He was strong, blond, and athletic—like me, I figured. His brothers believed him special. He joined us at ping-pong and immediately proved himself way above our league. The guy pounded the ball with amazing accuracy. None of us could return it. After a few minutes, he tossed the paddle onto the table and left the room.

Ray boasted, "He's good with the yoyo, too. On Thursday I'll ask him to show us Walk the Dog with it."

"How do you walk a dog with a yoyo?" asked Broten.

Ray shook his head. "Broten, don't be like Monroe in asking stupid questions. You'll find out Thursday." We laughed. Ray's vertical growth had yet to kick in like it had with his classmates, and even though on the puny side, he still remained a total sports player. As a result, he always got laughs when being mouthy because everyone liked him and no one ever felt challenged.

At 4:30, I headed home. The sky was cloudless, the lower atmosphere stewing in its own humidity. We had almost been suffocating at Ray's, but there had been too much fun happening for us to dwell on it. Now I was dwelling on it. Sweat poured from my forehead and chest. *Hope it's not hot like this on Friday*, I thought. At 5:00, lower Kingsbury Street was made.

The family almost exclusively used the backdoor, which opened out onto our large parking lot. Going in, past the door was a small hallway with two mailboxes. Patrick Kiley's dad was our mailman. On weekdays and Saturdays, his job was to open the door and come into the hallway, to place mail in our box and the box for the people in the apartment upstairs. A young couple with a newborn baby girl lived up there. Mr. Morton also worked at Kennebec Manufacturing, coincidentally as one of dad's machinists. The couple was definitely private, and though friendly-in-short when spoken to first, they tended to be non-talkative. This made it easy for the Monroes to forget that tenants lived up there, that the Mortons even existed.

Other users of the backdoor had one of three options: go directly right toward the door that opened into the Monroes' kitchen, go right and turn left for the stairs leading to the second-floor apartment, or turn left to open the door into our double-attached garage. Even on the hottest days, the hallway remained semi-cool. I stayed here for a minute, to cool off and think.

Once again the big question had to be asked. *How do I not come across as a pest?* I wondered. Even at my young age I recognized when politicking was involved. I also knew that my budinski brothers should not be close by.

I opened the inner door and entered our kitchen. "Hi, Mom."

She smiled. "Hello, dear. You must have been at LeClerc's and that's why you're late. Bet you're still thinking about that yoyo, huh?"

What a turn of luck. This was too good an opportunity to let slip by. I drooped my shoulders and showed a face of dejection. "I guess so, Mom. A little bit."

"Well, cheer up. I thought about it and decided you can get one. It's expensive, so don't be asking for any pennies or nickels. I'll give you the money tomorrow night and that way you can buy it after school lets out on Thursday."

"Thanks, Mom." I went to hug her. "I love you so much."

Daniel and Tony were in the TV room; the small room was just off the kitchen; we called it "the den." In there was a picture window dad had installed last summer. The window was really made up of two windows that cranked open. They—the crank-open windows—will come to figure into some of "the things" to soon take place.

Both brothers heard us talking in the kitchen.

"What's this about a yoyo?" asked Daniel.

"Yeah, is Chuckie getting something else Dan and I don't have?" added Tony.

Mother firmed her posture and stamped a foot. "If I remember correctly, someone got a dollar from me today so he could go buy a box of bullets at Gardiner Hardware. And someone else gets to go to a private high school in Portland. Is that free?"

There were no comebacks. I saw an opening. "Mom, a box of bullets costs fifty cents."

"Say that again?" came Tony.

I did not respond. He got up from the couch and walked into the kitchen. He looked irritated. "Did I hear you right, what you just said to Mom?"

"Dear, it doesn't matter," offered mother in an effort to calm her middle son's riled state. "Charlie is just trying to get your goat. You know that."

Her words were not enough. Tony's honor had been challenged. "Ma, a box of fifty twenty-two-caliber bullets went up from fifty cents to seventy-five. Long-rifle hollow-points cost an extra twenty-five."

"I know, dear. It's okay. Don't worry about it."

He gave me a dirty look, then turned and went back into the den.

Soon, I joined them. They were watching *The Merv Griffin Show*. I asked if it was any good. They stared at me and did not answer. In Bible class earlier this year, I learned about a young boy named Joseph; he was from the Old Testament and not Jesus' dad. Joseph's older brothers believed that the youngster was overtly favored by their father. One day when all of them were doing work far from home, the brothers decided to either kill Joseph or sell him off to slavery. They did the latter. Right then, Daniel and Tony wanted to do the former to me.

"Supper's ready, boys. Come get your plates." Daniel always took his at the kitchen table, so he could be with mom and dad. Tony and I preferred to take ours back to the den. The parents were okay with it because the kitchen table wasn't really a table, but instead a small bar-type situation that required tall stools. This was what the parents had opted for six years earlier when they had the kitchen renovated. Though it looked trendy and fun to be at, the bar—which we called "the counter"—had proven not big enough for five persons to sit comfortably.

"Charles, before you race back to the den to inhale your food, go tell your father supper is ready. He's in the front yard, working on the porch."

I went quickly. "Dad, supper's ready."

"Let your mother know I'll be in in a few minutes. I have to finish something first."

Our front porch ran the width of the house. Above it was a second-floor overhang supported by four pillars that landed on the front edge of the porch.

Some time back, dad had noticed dry rot in most of the pillars, floorboards, and undercarriage. Replacing bad wood with good wood and then painting the whole unit was his first big job of the summer.

I went back inside. Tony was half done his meal. Hostility was gone from his spirit.

"Chuckie, after supper you and I are going into the basement to do some target shooting."

Supper consisted of broiled chicken, french fries, wax beans, and cornbread. The family really liked mom's cornbread, but especially Tony did. She did not make it often, and when so, there would be two big pans—one for the first night and one for the next. Her chocolate chip cookies were available for those who still had room. I did not.

"Hey, Chuckie, wanna see my long-rifle hollow-points?" He opened the box and passed it to me. The heads were longer than the regulars, and each had a hollowed-out core. "I've been waiting all afternoon to try them out. Dad, Chuckie and I are going downstairs to get started."

"Aw, come on, leave me alone."

"Oh, Dad. Please let us. Remember how when you got home from work you said it would be okay as long as you came with us at the start."

"That doesn't mean I like the idea just because I said okay." The senior Monroe put his fork down and wiped his mouth with a napkin.

Mother spoke up. "Herve, I don't like this. First Tony, now Charles?"

"Neither do I," added Daniel, prior to his biting down on a chocolate chip cookie. He had been quiet, overly pensive during the main course. Tomorrow would be his first day at Kennebec Manufacturing. Dad had managed to secure a summer job for him there, and it would be the oldest son's first shot at full-time summer employment. His assignment was in the cutting room—a large and open warehouse-type area located next to the sewing floor. There, in the cutting room, large rolls of cloth had to be spread onto the many elongated tables: spread on top of spread on top of spread. The stacks then had to be precision-cut with industrial-sized jigsaws. When the cutters finished, other workers would move in to re-lay the materials in a structured manner prior to being transferred to the stitchers. Daniel would be a "re-layer." The position was fast-moving and required manual dexterity—not exactly his forte. Zero looking forward to it to say the least, he needed to earn clothes and spending money for his coming senior year at Cheverus High School.

"I know, Jeanne. I'll go down to make sure they do it right."

The three males descended into the basement. Because our house was built in the late 1700s, the wall construction above the basement was not of the modern two-by-four and two-by-six framing, but instead that of the pre-twentieth-century post-and-beam design. Also, two of the basement's four walls were constituted of a primitive groundwork of large gray, snugly-fitted-together stones. Whenever it rained, the two walls wept the excess groundwater water into floor gutters, which had been etched into the soft concrete floor along those walls when it had been laid in the 1930s. At that time, the two other outer walls of stone were replaced with concrete. The gutters channeled the flow to the basement's northeast corner, where there was a hole that allowed the water to disappear into the ground. The corner had no proper lighting, and the basement as a whole was cold, dark gray, and perpetually sooty. Cobwebs hung everywhere, especially from the ceiling in the quadrant with the hole.

The hole was a point of interest for the family, for there was morbid curiosity as to where the dungy portal actually went. Was it straight down to that someplace in desperate need of coolant? Several feet back from the hole showed a slightly downgraded concrete floor, but at a foot away, a catch basin surrounded it. As such, when approaching the hole, one had the feeling of being pulled into it by a tractor beam. Dad maintained that the pipe simply allowed the water to disappear into the deep ground.

A significant slowing of the drainage had occurred during the height of the previous spring thaw. The water backed up enough to cover most of the basement with an inch to three of wetness. Dad planned to unplug it sometime before next winter arrived. Unfortunately, a job thought to be minor will end up not, and when breakthrough is finally achieved, the opening up of a "can of worms" will also have been achieved. Soon afterward, shrill screams will come to penetrate through two muggy nights, only to be received by ears the far side of neighborhood windows. A particularly strange evening will take place, during a torrential thunder and lightning storm. The family will experience a calamitous overnight, forcing dad to take over-and-above action short of calling in a priest. Neighbors will come to question the sanity of the family.

Over the years, dad had deconstructed and rebuilt several areas in the home. He had replaced some of the house's original four-by-four and six-by-six posts and two-by-ten beams. Because the dark brown shafts were exceptionally dense and nowhere near rotten, he had decided to keep them. Tony had been down many times to target shoot, and a few of the posts were already leaned up against the designated concrete wall; tacked onto one of the posts was a target sheet that the hardware store had supplied free-of-charge to their good customer. Sometimes I had been down to watch brother shoot. This would be my first time firing the rifle. Dad wanted to make sure everything was set up safe. The shooting table was 20 feet from the target. Dad and I watched Tony carefully load the single-cartridge bolt-action rifle, aim, and fire. The short-rifle .22-caliber regular bullet he used was from a box purchased last month. He put the rifle down, and the three of us went to check the results. The sweet smell of spent gunpowder filled the air. The hole indicated Tony a bull's-eye shot. Dad lifted the sheet so he could see what the underneath looked like. The bullet had barely penetrated half an inch.

"They don't make beams like this anymore. Solid as bedrock. Tony, as I've instructed you in the past, the both of you are to be especially attentive when loading the rifle and when you're lifting it to aim and fire. Concentrate and don't talk at those times. Back upstairs I go."

Brother let me shoot his last three "shorts." The long-rifle hollow-points were now ready to be tested. Tony slowly removed a single bullet from the box, loaded the weapon, aimed, and fired. The hollow metal head made a *thud-splat*. He shot a few more and placed the rifle down, so that we could go do an inspection. The shorts had left a small, clean hole that a full slug could be picked out of with a nail. The long-rifle hollow-points gave a larger, deeper, rougher hole, and the slug inside the wood was flat, spread out, partially broken. Tony remarked on how much more effective the new bullets would be on a bothersome animal or prowler. He let me load and shoot the rifle ten times. Tony was always good about teaching me "guy things." I loved my bother.

Later, back in the den, the two of us ate chocolate chip cookies while he showed me how to clean the rifle. "You use it, you clean it. That's the rule." While I followed through, Tony went to the gun rack and removed his prized possession: a .308-caliber rifle the parents had gotten for him last Christmas.

Mother had objected to buying another gun for their 15-year-old, but over the course of the weeks building up to Christmas, father worked hard to convince her that it would be okay. No wrapping job could hide what was inside. Just before opening presents on Christmas Eve, everyone in the family wondered aloud as to what Tony's gift could possibly be. At opening it, he discovered a box of bullets included. "What goods a gun without bullets?" mother blandly offered, and everyone laughed.

After spring thaw, dad took Tony to a rural gravel pit so he could practice with the long-barreled unit. I was allowed to go along as an observer. But the bullets proved to be too expensive for random target shooting, and so the visits to the pit ceased after one more time.

Tony closely examined the .308. His awestruck affection for the long-gun was obvious, the way he rubbed the stock and patted the barrel. Several times he pretended to load, aim, and fire at imaginary animals passing by on the other side of the picture window.

At 6:30, dad joined us in the den. He wanted to watch the national news as presented by two men named Huntley and Brinkley. Tony knew to immediately remove himself from the adult's comfortable sofa chair or else risk getting a rolled-up *KJ* whacked against his arm. Dad had never managed to warm up to Walter Cronkite or any other chair in the den.

"Be quiet. I want to hear the news. . . . Jeanne, we're finally bombing Hanoi. It's about time. I don't know why Johnson waited for so long."

A monotone response came from the kitchen. "Yes, Herve, you're sure right about that." Mother was still at the table. With pencil tip on notepad, sometimes tapping it, she worked on the weekly finances. The last few days had had her and dad going over the pros and cons of getting that new marvel called "Master Charge." A decision had yet to be made.

At the first commercial break, the adult moved his eyes to his den-mates. "You guys are nutcases. Finish up with the guns. Don't you know you could kill someone with them?"

"Okay, Dad, we'll finish up right away."

"Okay, Dad, we'll finish up right away."

Tony looked at me, laughed out, "You must be my echo."

Daniel had already retired to his bedroom. It was there where he could best relax, with a book. Tonight, also, he was trying to put aside thoughts about his new reality of having to rise every weekday morning at 6:00 for the next two months. The parents were worried about their oldest, but particularly mother was. At 7:00, she came into the den to watch *The Andy Griffith Show* and *To Tell the Truth*. She always got a kick out of the first show's Barney Fife and entertainers Kitty Carlisle and Tom Poston, both of whom had nightly spots on *To Tell the Truth*.

At 8:00, mother went to prepare for bed. She liked to retire between 8:15 and 8:30, and that way she would have at least an hour for reading a book. She very much valued the time and looked forward to it every day. She had recently started a biography on Abraham Lincoln.

Dad liked to stay in front of the TV till 9:00, at which time he would get up from his chair and go prepare for bed. He, too, liked to read, but not books. *Readers' Digest* was his comfort zone. There was a pile of them on his nightstand.

The three of us watched *Gunsmoke*. The instant it was over, I heard, "Time for bed." I turned to see an adult bear staring at me. "Time for bed, I said."

Tired, I thought sleep would hit me right away, but it did not. Thoughts about the new red yoyo and the end of school worked at my spirit. Daniel emerged from his bedroom, headed downstairs for a glass of milk.

"What are you reading now?" I asked.

"*The Hobbit*."

"Is it any good?"

"Does the job."

To get to and from his bedroom, he had to pass through his brothers' bedroom. Old houses had situations like this, and never had it been an issue or bothersome for anyone.

Lightning came. Faint thunder followed. The lightning got brighter, the thuds louder, sooner.

Chapter V

Nosey Frank Finds Out Everything

Someone was pushing at my shoulder. "Charles, time to get up." The voice was not dad's.

"Okay, Dan, I'm awake."

"What did you say, Tony?" No response. "I said, *What did you say?*"

"Dan, you know how he talks in his sleep. Don't wake him up because he gets angry."

"His head was leaning up and his eyes were open. This brother of ours is a strange fellow indeed. Looked like he was talking to someone over there." Dan pointed to the little room that separated our two bedrooms; it had been the former second-apartment's kitchen. "He needs to see a psychiatrist. Since it happens during sleep, Freud should do him just fine."

"Who's that?"

"Never mind and just get up."

I got downstairs at 6:45. Dad and Daniel were almost done their cereals. My bowl of Cheerios was waiting on the counter.

"Did the thunderstorm wake you?" asked dad.

"No. I fell asleep before it hit."

"Not that one. The really bad one that hit at around three," came Daniel.

"Nope, didn't hear that one, either."

An hour later I arrived at LeClerc's Market.

"Raymond! Your friend's here . . . ! What can I get for you, Charlie?"

"Nothing. I'm buying a yoyo and no candy for a while. My mom's giving me the money tonight so I can buy it tomorrow." I checked the tube of pretzel rods. They were selling down. I sure hoped there would be enough holdouts for tomorrow's freebies.

"Will you be buying a yoyo or not?" asked Ray the instant he saw me.

"Yup. Tomorrow."

After school, Ray, McKane, Broten, and I played pool and ping-pong. We chatted about how the book ended. Mrs. Gillis had managed to finish reading it to the class, but the final page had left everyone with a big question mark? The American soldier convinced his superior to let Pong Choolie board a naval transport that was about to depart for safer shore to the South. It was not a hard sell, for the youngster had helped the soldier and his fleeing unit escape a communist ambush, and he had ferreted out several enemy weapons caches for the unit to blow up. But because Pong wanted to bid farewell to a girl, he got separated from the soldiers and captured by the same Inspector he had formerly reported to. All the villagers knew that Pong had aided the enemy. The Inspector beat him near to death. After a few days recovering, Pong escaped and began a long, frigid trek south on foot through communist-infested forest, toward freedom. That was where the book ended, leaving the class to wonder whether the kid ever made it. The lack of "finish" disappointed everyone. Mrs. Gillis stated, "If any of you ever become authors, I sincerely hope you never leave readers wandering out in a cold forest like this one did."

"Good thing *Treasure Island* doesn't end like that, because if it did, I wouldn't keep reading it over and over like I do."

"Why? How does that one turn out?" inquired Broten.

"The bad guy—but he's kind of a good guy, too, and his name is Long John Silver. Well, anyway, he's got a peg leg probably because a shark bit him, and he has to walk with a crutch. At the end, he grabs some of the loot and sails off to a secret place with a negro woman. Both are never seen again."

LeClerc: "A *negro* woman? That sure is different. Sounds like your type of book, Monroe. Maybe Mrs. Gillis should have read us that one, instead."

Roger entered the room. His face showed a serious expression. "Unfortunately, I was walking by when I heard the word 'negro' being used. Nobody around here knows anything about the real world out there. It's not supposed to be used anymore. The new word is 'black.' *Black*—got it? Now, don't ever again embarrass yourselves in front of me like you just did." He shook his head and turned to leave. "I can only teach you juveniles so much."

At 5:00, McKane and I left. The sky was cloudless and the air its recent atypical tropical. For a third of the way, he and I walked in the same direction. We talked about Friday's football game. Being fast runners, we hoped to be on the same team, if Broten would have it.

"You must have been at LeClerc's."

"Hi, Mom. Yup, I was there. What smells so good?"

"Pineapple upside-down cake. It's tonight's dessert. For supper we're having meatloaf and surprise, surprise, fries. We *were* going to have the second pan of cornbread, but *you know who* got into it today when I wasn't looking. I'll give you the yoyo money tonight."

"Did he do as he always does, leave a tiny bit behind so that no one can accuse him of eating the whole thing like a big old hog would, even though he is one?"

"I heard that!" yelled Tony from the den.

The cook used the opportunity to scold the perp once more. *"Yyyup! That's him, alright!"*

"I'm starving."

"Everyone's starving and not just you!" came a different set of vocal cords from the den.

"Charles, don't take Daniel seriously," comforted mother in a low voice. "He had a long day at work. He's tired and irritable." She turned away. "Hey, you in there! Be nice!"

"Yeah! You in there, be nice!" iterated I.

"I have some news for you. I'll be babysitting Frank Prudhomme this summer. It'll be on weekdays while Mr. and Mrs. Prudhomme are at work. How do you feel about that?"

I was caught off guard. Frank lived across the street. He was five years old and an okay kid. He had first arrived at the Prudhomme residence when he was three. The boy was not their son, but they soon came to love him as their own. He had been born out of wedlock to a distant second cousin of Mrs. Prudhomme. The two had met only once, when the cousin was a child. Because the mother had a serious drinking problem, State social services saw fit to remove Frank from her care. The system looked after the tot for a while. Family records were checked, and the decision was made to seek out the Prudhommes and ask that they take him in. They agreed.

Immediately upon arrival, Frank displayed a forward attitude that made him seem older than his less-than-handful years. Perhaps it was the end product of his time spent inside the harsher realities of State foster care. The youngster quickly proved to be the possessor of big ears, in that he had the uncanny ability to find out just about everything going on in the neighborhood—and then talk about it to everyone else.

During Frank's two years across the street, I had sometimes found humor in watching him get into trouble. The best one took place a week after he had arrived. He got hold of a full container of dish soap and squeezed it empty onto their concrete steps leading down to the sidewalk. He took the lawn hose and watered the steps, but only a little bit. It looked like he knew what he was doing. I was shooting hoops at the time, and stopped to watch. Next, he got down on his knees and, armed in rubber gloves that went up to his elbows, rubbed each step soapy. He kept pausing to scratch his face and scalp with his soapy gloves, and this caused him to scratch even more. Soon, soap was everywhere on him. Every half a minute or so he stopped to grab his "blanky" and hug it. Eventually Mrs. Prudhomme shouted for him. "Frank, where did you go! Frank! Frank! You better not have left the yard again!" When she discovered him: "Frank, what have you done?" She was clearly very angry, and the youngster burst into tears.

Next, Mr. Prudhomme came out to assess the sudsy situation, determined the appropriate action necessary, and followed through. The cleanup took him half an hour. He stopped once to glare at me. Truth was, twice I had yelled at Frank to stop. He yelled back. "I'm washing these dirty steps! Mind your own business, Chuckie!" Then, "Stop bothering me and just shut up!"

"Mom, will Jimmy and I have to do things with him all the time?"

"No, not really. He's too young. I'll mostly look after him. Sometimes I might need your help. When that happens you and Jimmy can keep him busy outside with you. He looks up to you, Charlie. Do you remember when you were his age, how you looked up to your brothers? How you used to follow them around? And they let you, didn't they?"

"Yes. But one time they didn't. Remember when they climbed out of the garage window to get away from me and I followed them and fell out and broke my arm."

"They did that only once. Your brothers have always cared about you."

"They have?"

Mother's face tautened. She was annoyed at my comment, and I did not want that.

"Okay, I'll help with Frank whenever you want."

She smiled. "That's more like it. Consider him your little brother. Will you do that?"

"Yes-yes-yes. Okay-okay-okay."

"Good. Let's eat. And don't be snarky with me."

After supper, I went outside to throw a tennis ball against the narrow strip of wall that separated our two garage doors. The wall was three feet wide and a decent backstop for my practicing pitching. My mound was the middle of Kingsbury Street, and as long as I hit the wall, the ball would bounce straight back onto the driveway and into my hands. Mr. Prudhomme appeared. He must have heard the ball banging against the wall. He did not look cordial.

"Charlie! Come over here right now! I want to show you something!"

I immediately obeyed. He pointed into the grass. A dog—Lizzie he believed, and so did I—had placed a soft, extra-large, swirl-shaped poop smack in the middle of the path leading from their side-door to their parking lot, where sat their brand-new Ford Fairlane.

"Marion and I just missed stepping in that thing when we left for work this morning. Now pick it up and take it away."

"Okay, Mr. Prudhomme, I will."

"Right now, Charlie."

"Yes, sir, but I need to get my shovel. I promise to come right back."

Upon return, I found Mr. Prudhomme gone and Frank standing next to the evidence.

"What are you doing, Charlie?"

"I'm picking up Lizzie's poop."

"I heard Joe and Marion talking about it. Why did she do it over here?"

"Because she doesn't like your cat. This is her way of showing it."

"I hope BJ never gets hold of Lizzie. He'll kill her dead, that's for sure. Joe says no dog in Gardiner can take him down."

Joe was probably right. Their cat was some big and tough. A few years back, I had witnessed BJ take on a German shepherd named Buddy. Buddy was the Burdys' dog. They used to live in the house that the Camerons now owned. The place was just up Kingsbury Street from the Laithrans' and directly across the street from the Robbins' home.

Buddy believed he owned the neighborhood. When one day he saw BJ nonchalantly strolling up the street, the dog perceived the cat to be laying down a challenge. The giant shepherd hotfooted it in for the kill. In no way retreating, the fired-up feline sidestepped to the ditch and dug his back claws in, readying for Buddy's aggressive arrival. Their coming together brought an explosion of hate and rage to the airwaves. In the most frenzied and wicked manner, Buddy bit, growled, and barked while BJ hissed, slashed, and yelled. Injuries were viciously meted out to and by both combatants. The nasty skirmish went on for half a minute. Death seemed certain for one. Then, suddenly, they stopped to stare at each other. After a moment, BJ turned away and slowly walked off. Buddy chose to do the same. The dog's ears were bloodied, and he licked at his chops as if his tongue or the inside of his mouth had been knifed.

"Lizzie hates cats, especially BJ. I've seen them eying each other lately." I bent down and leaned in close. "Make sure to tell all the neighbors around here about this very, very important treasure I've discovered right here in your yard of all places. Okay, Frank?"

"Oh, Charlie, you're so funny. Why don't you throw it in our gully?"

"Probably not a good idea. I'll throw it in mine."

"Can I come and watch?"

"Sure, but first get clearance from your dad. I'll wait while you go fast."

The little guy was quick about it, thrilled to be an observer. "Joe said it's okay."

"Why do you call them by their names and not 'Mom' and 'Dad'?"

"Because they're not my mom and dad."

"Who is?"

"I don't know, and I don't like to talk about it. As far as I remember, the State of Maine was my mom and dad for a while. I think my real mom might have been named Ellen or Evelyn or Esther or something. But I don't care about her. She didn't love me. The State didn't love me, either. Don't ask me about it again."

"Yeah-sure. Hey, watch this." I heaved it with all my might. "There it goes!" I leaned in and whispered, *"Marion and Joe will be so happy when you tell them what you saw me do, but don't tell anyone else because I don't want them coming around here looking for it."*

"Charlie, you're so funny. Did you know I'm going to be staying at your house this summer and playing with you and your friend Timmy all the time?"

Chapter VI

Prison-school Lets Out—Yahoo!

"Charles, wake up. This is your last day at Central Street Prison-school."

"Thanks for telling me that, Dan."

"You're not supposed to use that expression. Remember?"

"Okay."

"Say what, Tony . . . ? Oh, never mind."

The brain was totally alive. *Dan's right! No more prison-school after today! Yahoo!*

"How much does a yoyo cost?" asked the same brother, downstairs at the counter.

"A dollar twenty-five."

"That's how much I make an hour."

"You do? Wow. What are you going to do with all that money?"

"Are you making fun? Do you want to get punched?"

"Daniel, that's a lot of money to him. And, for that matter, it should be to you."

"I suppose you're right, Dad. Sorry, Charles. At the end of the week I'm going up to LeClerc's Market to buy forty yoyos."

I entered the store at ten before 8:00. "Hi, Mrs. LeClerc. I have the money for a yoyo."

"Good morning, Charlie. Wait a sec while I go call for Raymond."

Feet pounded down the stairs. "What are you doing, Monroe? Wait till after school. Bye, Mom. Love you." As Ray passed behind the candy cabinet he grabbed a handful of malted milk balls and tossed me a couple.

"Thanks, Ray. Bye, Mrs. LeClerc."

"Bye, guys. Have a good last half-day of school."

Mrs. LeClerc was at the register because Mr. LeClerc was upstairs in bed sleeping. Starting every Wednesday, he worked five days of late-evening shifts in the kitchen at Togus VA Medical Center. There, he helped in the preparation of patients' meals for the next day. Following the shifts, which ended at 4:00 a.m., his pattern was to sleep into the late morning and take over the store at noon. This meant that the yoyo deal would be sealed off with him present and not Mrs. LeClerc. I knew this a good thing because the mother was just too sweet for her son Raymond to pull any of his shenanigans on. Mr. LeClerc, on the other hand, was a naturally muscular man who possessed lumberjack forearms with tattoos; these had been needled into him during his stint in the U.S. Navy. A guy who liked rough-and-tumble to some degree, he insisted his three boys be respectful yet macho at the same time. What that meant was Ray could jerk his dad around as long as he was reasonably polite about it.

We arrived at school to discover two police cars parked in front. Some weeks back, we had heard that the Gardiner Police Department would be by to take our fingerprints before the end of session. This was the rule for students in grade 6. All of us were taken in with the process, which ate up most of the morning. Then, at twelve-noon sharp, release from prison-school was granted. In the prison yard, wild cheers, yelps of jubilation, and "Yahoos!" were heard coming from all parolees. Papers, pencils, and crayons were tossed into the air and all over the place and trampled on as if they were nothing more than bad reminders. Guys heading over to LeClerc's Market gathered around Ray. Ten minutes later, we arrived inside the store. McKane remained back, near the entrance. Nobody had ever seen him with even a penny to spend. There were 13 children in the McKane family, and it meant there was no money for anything other than the essentials.

"Hi, Dad. We're ready."

The storeowner seemed edgy, greeted no one. "None of you touch anything before handing me a dollar twenty-five."

"We get a couple pretzel rods and a red hot fireball, right Mr. LeClerc?" I asked.

"What are you talking about?"

"Dad, you agreed to the pretzels and fireball. Charlie and I heard you."

"Oh, I agreed, did I? Raymond, tell me, how am I supposed to run a business? Listen, because I'm in a good mood, each of you can have a gumball and that's it."

"All of us are expecting this," argued the owner's son.

In actuality, only Ray and I knew about the giveaways; neither of us had mentioned them to the other guys. Mr. LeClerc was a man of his word. Why was he giving us a hard time? Perhaps it was because he did not expect six kids would be involved. Suddenly, he smiled.

"Guess I had you guys going. Have to dig hard for things in life. Can't make it too easy. Wouldn't be a good example. All of you go ahead and grab what Charlie said."

Everyone knew Mr. LeClerc was a fine man. I especially held him in high regard. When the parents and brothers went for their week in Washington D.C., I stayed with the LeClercs. Breakfasts the adult male was in charge of had the boys getting served the oldest box of powder-sugared chocolate donuts he could dig up from the store below. Each of us was allowed to have two. Dry and hard, they required softening up with hot chocolate. The first morning, he said, "This is how you do it." He dipped half the donut into his cup, then shoved it into his mouth, crossed his eyes, and mumbled and grumbled chewing it down. We giggled and copied him.

Ray told us to wait outside while he went to get Roger, then quickly checked to make sure his dad wasn't looking, grabbed a yoyo and a fireball, and went to give them to McKane. "It's okay. You can help me with chores this afternoon. My dad'll be fine with it. Just not right now. I know him. I'll tell him later." McKane declined, but the kind gesture again showed Ray to be a decent buddy to everyone. He put the yoyo back and tossed the fireball at McKane. "It's paid for, so put it in your mouth and shut up."

Walk the Dog was just one of the tricks Ray's brother demonstrated. At a mere two minutes in, he stopped, waved his hand over us, as if to be a magician, and said, "I can do no more for you yoyos. You're on your own."

His students felt more than ready. We started out calm, eating away at our pretzel rods. Each of us passed McKane a short section. Then came the red hot fireballs. A minute into sucking on those things, adrenalines shot. *Wow, these suckers are hot!* Everyone began to run around wild, using yoyos in an illiterate manner.

"Yeah! Yeah! Freedom! We're outta prison! No more prison-school! Yahoo! FREEEEEDOM! We're finally outta Central Street Prison! Yeah!"

Each of us at some point had his fireball fly from the mouth and onto the ground. No problem. We knew exactly what to do: pick it up, wipe it off on the pants, pop it back in. "Yeah! Yeah! FREEEEEDOM! Yahoo!" Oops, mine popped out again. No problem. Another wipe and back in it went. "Yeah! We're outta prison-school! Yeah!"

"Hi, Mom. What smells so good? Is it chicken? Hi, Lizzie." I bent over to pat our happy tail-wagging house-greeter. "Lizzie, after supper I'm taking you outside to show you how to walk the dog. Listen to me, you're mine, not his."

"Hello, son. You were at Ray's, were you?"

"Yup and thanks again for the yoyo money. We had blasts with them. I'm so tired."

"I hope you're not worn out on it already."

"No, but maybe tomorrow."

Mother laughed. "I hope you're kidding. And, yes, you're right. It's chicken—chicken dumplings with french fries and wax beans. Made a big batch. Since you haven't eaten any real food since this morning, you must be hungry. Wow, are you ever sweaty."

"I'm starving."

"We're all starving, and you didn't work all day in an overheated hole like some of us did!" It was Daniel, shouting out from the living room.

"Well, you didn't suck on a red hot fireball and work on a yoyo like some of us did!"

"Charles, it's really not worth responding to him. He's tired and irritable, and his shortcomings on patience and anger control are more obvious than usual. He doesn't like his job. Everyone needs to make allowances for him. Best to ignore him when he gets like this."

"Okay, I'll try to."

Tony stuck his head out from the den. "Ma, will supper be ready soon? I'm starving."

Again from the living room: "We're all starving!"

"Chuckie, toss the yoyo over here. I want to try it out."

At 7:00, Mike called. He wanted me down to his place right away, so we could go check out two boxcars that had been left on the track in the morning. A couple crews were by in the afternoon, to empty them out, but they drove off before finishing. Mike had watched them from his porch and that's how he knew the car doors were shut but not locked. Boxcars often got left unlocked, when no cargo was inside. Sometimes Mike and I would find small piles of product spilled from bags and boxes the workers had dropped and broken open while handling.

Mom gave permission, but I had to be home by 9:00. Mike was sitting on his porch stairs when I arrived. We scurried across the road and into the lot. We slid the big metal doors fully open so that the daylight could help us. The insides of each car smelled musty, and our discovery was unspectacular. One car contained pallets carrying bags of seed grain made in Iowa. The other held bags of chemical fertilizer from New York. The loads were meant for Gardiner's Agway store; the place supplied farm needs for this portion of Kennebec County.

A bag of grain must have split apart when the workers were unloading; a small pile of its contents was on the ground, just below the boxcar door. Mike bent down to take a pinch between his fingers. I did the same. He placed the stuff in his palm, to look at it up close, using an index finger to rub it around. I did the same. He smelled it, and so did I: a little earthy. Finally, we tossed it into our mouths for a chew. The stuff tasted bland but not terrible. Mike said, "No offence, Iowa, but—" *phew!* He had spit it out. I proceeded to do the same. We walked back to his place so we could watch *Gilligan's Island.* At 9:15 the phone rang.

"Charlie, that must be your mother," said Mrs. Bondy as she reached for the receiver.

"Hello, Jeanne. Yes, I'll send him right away."

"Sorry, Mrs. Bondy. I forgot about having to be home by nine."

Nancy and Janice laughed out, "Oh-yeah-right, *you forgot.*"

When I got home, dad stared at me. "Didn't your mother tell you to be home by nine?"

"Yes, and I'm really sorry. I just plain forgot." I drooped my shoulders and looked down at the ground.

"Well then," said the adult in a friendlier voice, "next time try to remember."

The two Health-tex men arrived home at 12:05, for a quick lunch. Even with a time allotment of only 30 minutes, the adult male preferred to vacate the factory rather than brown-bag it and eat there. To be home in five minutes required he race out the factory door the instant the noon buzzer sounded; that gave him 20 minutes for eating and talking, and five to make it back in time for the start-buzzer. Always upon arrival home did the man have a big smile and a kiss for his wife. Others present got a warm greeting. This day, soup and grilled cheese sandwiches with dill pickles were served.

Daniel looked drained, but he tried to be social. He asked his two brothers what time they had gotten up from bed. Both answered around ten. His tone and demeanor remained the same, showed no envy. But the family knew the reluctant man of 16 years missed being 15. Soon enough it would be Tony's and Charles' turns to enter factory life. *So, young brothers, go ahead and enjoy your summer weekdays while you still can.*

Daniel ate fast, then went to sit in the car, to brood. Mother showed a look of concern.

"Working in that cutting room is hard enough for adults. For him, I fear, it's too hard. He's only sixteen and one who is heavily inclined toward slide rule and pencil. On top, he's miserable about missing his favorite show, *Jeopardy!*. Let's all have good thoughts for him."

"Yes, let's make sure we do that," added dad.

"Good thoughts?" snickered Tony. "That'll sure help Pencils."

"You heard your mother. And no more wisecracks."

"I have to leave for the park. We start playing at one."

"Well, you better get going. You don't want to be late for the game," jested mother.

"Don't forget all the stuff I've taught you," reminded coach Tony.

The park was a ten-minute walk away. Mrs. Laithran was outside working on her flowers. The woman was and had been for many years the high school principal's secretary. This meant she as well had summers off. It also meant she knew intimate information about families in and around the Gardiner area. Mrs. Laithran was not one to gossip, but what she did sometimes like to do when in the right frame of spirit was share historical information about houses and family trees. Over the years, she had proven herself to be an encyclopedia of local trivia.

Mrs. Laithran loved to garden. Besides being all around the perimeter of her house, gardens were imbedded here and there in the Laithrans' expansive back lawn. Every summer, when gentle breezes were flowing just right, the air of lower Kingsbury Street filled with a myriad of sweet and lavish aromas that emanated from her gardens and those of the Dells.

"Hi, Mrs. Laithran. How are you today?"

She stood up and turned. "Good afternoon, Charlie."

"Hello, Dot."

"Hi there, Jeanne. Hello . . . , Harve."

The parents left the house only a minute after I had. Dad smiled and waved.

"No time to talk," said mom. "I'm taking the men back to work. I'll stop by later."

"That's fine, Jeanne. I'll be out here. See you then."

Mrs. Laithran's first name was Dorothy. Adults in the neighborhood called her Dot. That's what she preferred. For some strange reason Mrs. Laithran had yet to properly grab hold of dad's name. When greeting him, she would say hello, briefly pause to look confused, and finish with either "Harve" or "Harvey." A few years back, dad asked mother why Dot wasn't getting his name right. She responded, "Harvey, that's because you've never corrected her."

The car pulled away, leaving Mrs. Laithran and me alone.

"Is Daniel working with your dad at the factory?"

"Yes, but he's in a different section."

"It's nice that they can come home for lunch. Bernard doesn't have enough time to do that. So, what are you up to today?"

"I'm playing football with friends at the park."

"Wait here a minute, Charlie. I have something for you."

Mrs. Laithran went into her house. From past experience, I knew she would reappear with something sweet in her hand. The woman was an expert baker. I was partial to mother's baking because she was my mother. Her cookies were every bit as good as Mrs. Laithran's. But there was something extra-special about this neighbor's cakes. They had a unique flavor that was hard to describe other than it was remarkably delicious. Out she came.

"Here, have this piece of chocolate cake. Walk with it but take one bite here first."

"Thank you. . . . Ohh, it's so good. How do you do that?"

"I have a special ingredient. No one else knows it. Even Bernard doesn't."

"Thanks again. I better get going. Is Peter coming to Gardiner this summer?"

"Probably, but we're not a hundred percent sure. I'll let you know."

Mr. Laithran was the manager of the city's post office. At home he was in charge of the large vegetable garden located in their backyard, near the edge of their section of the gully. Yearly, the garden produced copiously, and always did Mr. Laithran delight in delivering bags of cucumbers, squash, and green beans to all of his neighbors.

The Laithrans had one son. Dick was 28 years old and a neighborhood icon. He had excelled at high school basketball and still liked to wear his varsity jacket. After graduation, he attended the University of Maine to become a teacher.

Dick no longer lived with his parents, but he occasionally dropped by to visit with them. If Tony and I happened to be outside when he drove up, we would beg him to play basketball with us. He generally did, but only for a few minutes. When doing lay-ups, he could touch the rim and almost dunk the ball. It did not matter that our rim was a foot below regulation. As far as we were concerned, he was a real star.

Mrs. Laithran had another son, Phil, from a previous marriage. Phil Laithran and his wife and four children lived in Pennsylvania. He was a high school principal in a suburb of Philadelphia. Most summers had the family visiting Gardiner and staying at the house for a week or two. Their oldest boy, Peter, was my age. The two of us had always gotten along well and managed to get in a lot of basketball time together.

I made it to the field with 15 minutes to spare. The rest of the players were there and practicing. Sheehan, a big guy, already looked too sweaty. The classmate liked to sometimes invite a bunch of us over to his place, which was a dairy farm situated inside city limits. Sheehan's Dairy produced the best-tasting chocolate milk in the valley, if not the country. The Monroes were committed partakers. Competitor, Hood's Dairy, Maine's major milk supplier, produced not near as quality a product.

Broten picked the two sides, and at it we went. By luck, McKane and I ended up on the same team, but it was to no avail because we had Cushard. He did not own sneakers and always wore bulky shoes, which slowed him and the rest of his team down. An hour and a half later, the two bruised and sweat-drenched rivals ended their match, tied at 30.

Most of us headed to LeClerc's. Broten brought enough money to buy everyone a six-ounce soda. All of his buddies thought well of him for doing that. In the field across the street, players chugged, talked, and laughed of game highlights.

Broten's dad worked for Gardiner Coal & Oil Company. He drove the place's big oil tanker. Everyone in the city either knew or recognized the man. Broten had an amazing ability. He would read funny poems and limericks at night, and the next day in the schoolyard he would sing-recite them and get all of his buddies laughing. Cushard lived a street over from LeClerc's Market. His dad worked at Kennebec Manufacturing, as my dad's top wrench. According to the Monroe adult, Gerald Cushard was the most skilled machinist he ever worked beside. He said the man possessed a sixth sense around anything mechanical. An additional charge of dad's lead wrench was the site's huge boiler. Other than Cushard, only expensive, slow-to-arrive out-of-town specialists could fix the thing when it broke down. Sadly, on weekends the contents of liquor bottles proved truncheons against the senior Cushard's better spirit, and the vile liquid had always kept him from better success at work and home. Likely this was the reason sneakers could never be afforded for his son. The man often missed Mondays, or he arrived at noon; some weeks it was Tuesday noon. Over the years, dad had had to defend Mr. Cushard to senior management. Several times they wanted him gone, but dad refused to go along with it, stating that he and the plant needed him. Several winters ago, the Monroes' boiler furnace stopped working. Dad asked for Cushard's help. That Saturday the top wrench spent all day fixing it and teaching dad the art, in the event of future breakdowns.

"Oh, Lizzie, you're such a good dog. You don't belong to Tony. He just thinks you do. You and I know you're mine. Don't be listening to him when I'm around, okay?" The pooch got lots of love and pats from me. Except for her tan chest and a single Washington-quarter-sized spot of the same color above each eye, the happy-time house-greeter was jet-black.

"Hi, Mom. It smells wonderful in here. Smoked haddock?"

"Yes, boiled with boiled potatoes and boiled cabbage."

The family sometimes ate smoked haddock on Fridays, the no-no day for Catholic mouths to touch meat. Mother always made sure to plaster the fish and potatoes with salt and butter in order to "bring out the flavors."

"Why can't we have french fries instead of those boring boiled potatoes every time?"

"*Every time?* We almost never have them. You like fries too much. We can't be eating those greasy things with every meal. Just appreciate whatever your waitress serves you."

On other Fridays, we enjoyed lobster with french fries, crabmeat sandwiches with fried potatoes, clam cakes with fries, halibut with oven-fried potatoes, scallops with french fries, or dreadful mackerel with *it did not matter*. We used to have baked swordfish, but in the last few years it had become harder to find and too expensive.

Kennebec Manufacturing paid their employees every Friday, just prior to lunch. Dad's commitment was to bring the check home at noon and pass it to his wife. When the company's "system of checks" had first rolled out six years before, the parents had expressed concern as to whether the bank would honor the simple piece of paper. Their doubts soon ceased. Prior to 1960, the Friday envelopes had come home filled with crumply bills and coins. Almost weekly it included old silver dollars—Peace and the occasional Morgan—and then there were the marvelous-looking Buffalo nickels, Mercury dimes, Walking Liberty halves, and very old Standing Liberty quarters to be inspected by the then child. Still, the now 12-year-old liked the idea of a single, valuable note of paper. I used to ask mother if I could hold it, and always did she let me. Not surprising, the years of training had brought me to the love coins, greenbacks, and checks—basically anything "money."

As section manager, dad received salary: about $175 per week in 1966. This was considered decent pay, and it meant that mother did not have to work outside the home. Most non-managerial factory jobs in Maine paid between $50 and $120 a week, depending on years of experience and difficulty of labor. Husbands and wives often worked in the same factory, and together they made enough money to have a life of good and plenty—plenty enough, anyway.

After Friday lunch, mother's routine was to drive dad back to work, and that way she could use the car to run her errands, the first one always to Gardiner Savings & Loans, to cash the check; the last Friday of every month required a mortgage payment be made. Her next duty was to purchase a week of groceries at Harriman & Black. The store was across the street from the Gardiner Shoe Company, which made top quality shoes for men. There, Mrs. Prudhomme worked in bookkeeping while her husband handled the end of the shoe-line as a "laster."

For many years, perhaps decades, Harriman & Black had been the only proper grocery store in Gardiner. There, a loaf of bread was currently priced at 16 cents and a dozen eggs at 45, best in the city. A can of wax beans could still be taken off the shelf for ten. Butter was reasonable, at 75 cents a pound. A few years back, competitor A&P opened across the road from the bowling alley. Classmate Tommy Robertson's father was the manager of the national chain outlet. Mother checked the store only once. "The place is okay, but I prefer where I've been shopping for years. Mr. Harriman and Mr. Black are nice gentlemen, local to Gardiner. I'm certain that I'll always remain their patron. Too, it helps to keep our money in the area and not go out of state. Besides, the prices at A&P aren't that good."

When done groceries, mother's next stop was for a gas-up at Chapman Esso, located on the corner of Church and Water Streets. The tank usually lasted to the following Friday, as long as there had not been a Sunday drive down to the coast or through the countryside. A few Fridays ago, mother had vented to dad about the price of gas. "I felt blindsided by Chapman's tow truck when I saw the price of regular at thirty-two cents a gallon. Fuel is getting too expensive. We need to be careful about our driving habits." Dad totally agreed with her.

This day, mother's final stop had been at McDonald's Bakery, to pick up a dozen walnut brownies and a half-dozen each of éclairs, jelly-filled powdered donuts, and cream horns. Total expenditures, not including the mortgage payment of $39, came to just under $35. Her intended 15-minute chat with Dot had ended up being 30, and it meant she had had to literally speed in order to make it back to the plant by 3:30, to pick up the men. Mother often said the Monroes could not have better neighbors than the Laithrans, Prudhommes, Dells, and Robbins.

Dad was not in the house. Most warm late afternoons and evenings of summer had the man working on various outside maintenance projects. On rainy days and wintry ones, he concentrated on inside-the-house issues.

"Charles, go tell your father supper is ready. He's in the front yard."

"Okay, I'll run 'cause I'm starving, even for boiled potatoes. . . . Hi, Dad. Mom says supper's ready. Are you almost done?"

"What do you mean, 'are you almost done?' It's not just stick a piece of wood in and hit a few nails. Lean down so I can show you. See how all the boards have dry rot. They have to be replaced. Let your mother know I'll be in shortly."

"Thanks for showing me that. Bye. . . . Mom, Dad says he's coming in shortly."

"Charles, I've already informed your brothers that the bakery stuff has to last through the weekend because I'm not going to do any baking. Do you understand?"

"Yes, he does. The others do, too. Right, everyone?"

Dad had decided to come in right behind me. He stopped to make eye contact with each of his sons. None of them said anything, but each nodded *yes*.

The reason mother would not be baking was because she wanted to use Saturday for picking out planting flowers at Butler Twins Garden Center and for looking at wallpaper at Mattson's Wallpaper & Paint. Sunday would have her planting the flowers in the garden that lined the street-side of our home. Last week she announced that on the first rainy weekend of the summer she and dad would wallpaper the kitchen. "You boys'll have to be out of our way on that weekend." She wanted to have the items purchased and in the home before that future weekend arrived. As for the four males, there was hope that weekend would never arrive.

Mike phoned after supper. He wanted me down to his place, but I was too tired. We agreed to meet the next morning, so that we could do a detailed exploration of the geography below the rail track, down toward the river. He said, "Bring your jackknife because we'll need them."

Tony and I watched *Rawhide* and *Gomer Pyle, U.S.M.C.* After that, we went outside to play catch. Mrs. Prudhomme was watering her flowers. At seeing us, she called out, "Joe! Joe! Come out here and talk to Tony! Get him to help you with that job tomorrow!"

Within a minute, Mr. Prudhomme emerged from their side-door: that was the one they always used; the front door was for their upstairs tenants, the Knights. Joe, not once looking up from the ground, slowly trod his concrete walkway to his concrete steps leading down to the concrete sidewalk. Only then did he look up and wave a hand at my brother. "Tony, come over here right now. I have something to talk to you about."

Without hesitation, Tony dropped his glove and went. Just under six feet tall and of robust arm and body girth, Mr. Prudhomme mostly wore a white undershirt in hot weather. He retained only a small amount of white hair on the sides of his head, and his face and the top of his head stayed red and shiny from spring to fall. In short, he, even though in his early 60s, came across as a strongman not to be messed with; scarily, he looked liked professional wrestler George "The Animal" Steele. Time on Kingsbury Street, however, had shown Mr. Prudhomme to be more like a gentle bear, easy to get along with and helpful to neighbors when they came to him with questions about their own construction projects.

Ever since the Prudhommes' only child, their beloved son Donald, had left home to join the U.S. Navy, Mr. Prudhomme occasionally employed neighborhood teenagers who he deemed sturdy enough to handle heavy work. In recent time, Tony had become his chosen subject. Brother was definitely sturdy enough; my oft-bruised arms attested to this truth.

The two walked to the house's east side, where there was a run of lawn ten feet wide, which in turn gave way to a steep bank of ten feet. Mr. Prudhomme showed Tony what needed to be done in order to fill in and shore up the slope. Next to the sidewalk was a two-yard pile of loam that a dump truck had dropped off earlier in the day; it required transfer by wheelbarrow, then tamping down before topping with sod that Mr. Prudhomme wanted

Tony to remove from a distant spot on his property—along the edge of a particularly sharp slope down into Rollins Woods. Tony agreed to start the next morning. The job would likely take most of Saturday.

Brother Rifleman was happy about the opportunity to earn some bucks. Mr. Prudhomme always paid him well. The new issue of *Popular Science* had arrived at LaVerdiere's Drug Store, and Tony wanted it. The magazine was his second favorite to *Shooting Times*.

Chapter VII

Hobo Lane and the Secret Underground Tunnel

The air was hot, burdened down with heavy humidity. There had not been an overnight thunderstorm, but another monstrous demonstration seemed imminent, if not tonight then likely the coming week. Tony was already in an obvious sweat, struggling with a wheelbarrow full of dirt.

"Hello there, lucky brother Tony. How's the shoveling going so far?"

"*Ha-ha-ha!* Shut up, why don't you!"

He wasn't smiling. I laughed anyway. "See you later. Please continue to sweat. And don't use 'shut up.' Use 'be quiet' instead." I took off running down Kingsbury. Tony was overly tall and big-boned for his age, and he carried elongated flat feet as excess baggage. This made for an exceedingly slow runner. Even though he was four years older than me, by the time I had turned five I could already outrun him. Daniel was another story. He could run fast, when he figured there was a reason to and he sported the appropriate footwear.

Mike was sitting on the front step of his slanted porch when I arrived.

"Got your jackknife?" he asked.

I lifted the handle an inch out of my pocket so he could see.

He nodded and stood up. "Let's go do what we're supposed to."

We crossed River Road and jogged through the substation's front lot, past the south side of the building, and into the unloading area, which contained the team and main tracks and a siding. The two now-empty boxcars were still sitting on the team track; a crew had been by Friday to finish unloading them. Our intention was to get into the fields nearer to the river and explore them in north-south directions. In the past, Mike and I had done some cursory checking down there, but nothing major. Today, we were determined to spend hours investigating things, and we had no idea what those things would end up being. Mike planned for us to head north first, toward city core, and then turn back south, into the unbridled zones toward Mount Tom.

We stopped on the main track, to look north, then south. The temperature was already in the high 80s and it was not yet noon. The air just above the tracks was thick and wavy. The smell of warm creosote rushed through our nostrils and thoroughly invaded our greeting lungs. The smell was not bad; in truth, we liked it. Soon, our minds became infected with a sense of being metropolitan, in a small-town type of way. Last year Mike and I had watched a Maine Central Railroad crew replace old ties with new ones at this very section of the track. Mr. Stedmont was the crew chief. This past spring had him my coach in Little League Baseball. We noticed grasshoppers shuttling about the gravel and track areas. Later in the summer the hoppers would be bigger and the population thicker, and there would be ample hornets and bumble bees to worry about, too. Mike unfolded his jackknife and bent over to slice out a sliver of wood from a newer tie. I copied him. He stood up and stuck the little piece close to his nose. So did I.

"This is real man's wood," he concluded, and so did I.

A few feet river's side of the track was a six-foot bank down to a flat zone running north-south, 40 feet in width. Beyond the flat came a gradual slope ranging anywhere from 40 to 60 feet down through brush and trees to the Kennebec's mucky shoreline. Even though Gardiner was 40 miles inland from the Atlantic Ocean, the river here experienced daily tidal fluctuations.

Mike and I began our survey on the flat section below the main track. We discovered old tracks—ancient ones it seemed by their rust and partial burial. One of them had been the main track; a couple former team tracks were connected to it. Milkweed, burdock, thistle, and dandelion inundated the area and at times made forward movement rough on our legs. Along its riverside border we discovered hint of a lightly trodden path. We walked it, toward the city. Empty liquor bottles littered the way. Mike picked one up and smelled its contents.

"Don't put your mouth on it," cautioned I.

"Monroe, do you think I'm stupid? This is another reason we brought our knives, just in case we have to show them to any rummies we might run into." Mike looked me in the eyes. Realizing his comment had unnerved me, he offered some calming words. "We shouldn't have a problem. They mostly come out at night." He picked up a cigarette butt that had an inch of un-smoked section left on it, pulled out his jackknife and unfolded it, cut half an inch off the filter, pulled out a pack of matches, lit the cigarette, and took a puff. "Let's keep walking."

As we approached downtown's southern perimeter, the lower flat gradually rose to merge with the current track. Mike and I about-faced and headed back south. Nearing the substation, we noticed a man standing on the main track, at the exact same spot we had sliced the wood. He faced the river. We continued on and soon recognized him Mr. Barry. Hands in pocket, the man appeared to be in deep thought and did not acknowledge us. We halted on the lower flat directly to his front. His eyes remained closed, and he seemed to be taking in long, slow breaths.

"Hi, Uncle."

"Hi, Mr. Barry."

The man opened his eyes and smiled. "I knew you were there." He looked at Mike. "Your mom said I'd find you out here. She's concerned about you two stirring things up. Didn't you see the NO TRESPASSING sign the station manager put up? It was probably because of you guys hanging around here all the time and throwing stones at him last year that he did that."

The stone-throwing incident was not fiction; it had indeed taken place.

On a hot afternoon last summer, the manager had left the station's office door open so that he could receive airflow while doing paperwork at his desk. The small, one-room office opened out onto the station's gravel parking lot. From the Bondys' porch, Mike and I observed him use a hand towel to wipe the sweat off his face a few times. He was a middle-aged man, bald and chubby. That day, the valley's lower atmosphere was particularly hot and humid, without breeze. Mike and I were bored stiff. He suggested we throw rocks across the road such that they would bounce on the gravel and into Mr. Schmebb's office. We did not know the man's name, but that was what Mike always referred to him as—"Mr. Schmebb." Our intent was not to hit but annoy him. We succeeded. He exited his office and looked around. When he did not find anyone to accuse, he went back inside and sat down. A few minutes later, we threw more rocks. The game of tag went on like this for a while. Each time he came out to look around, Mike and I ducked down behind the porch's fence. We peeked through the slight spaces separating the boards and quietly giggled our faces off as we watched him glance every which-way. The fourth time out, he was noticeably frustrated, and when he scratched the top of his bald head, Mike and I just about burst our guts laughing while trying to remain silent. Mr. Schmebb heard us. When he started for the road, we stood up, waved, and ran around the house and into the woods. The manager ended up talking to Mrs. Bondy. Later, she scolded us, saying the man was okay and not angry, but he doesn't want it to happen again.

"The sign's on the building," reasoned Mike, "and we don't go near it."

Mike's response turned out to be sufficient. Mr. Barry understood our youthful interest in things of railroad and chose not to take it any further.

"Uncle, you sure looked like you were in deep thought about something when we came up, with your eyes closed and all."

"Deep thought? Eyes closed? Nah, I was enjoying the smell of the creosote. Found anything interesting?"

I jumped in. "There are lots of old tracks. Do you know when they were being used?"

"Yup, and it goes like this. Maine Central Railroad calls this here Brunswick-Augusta run the 'Lower Road.' I'm standing on the new 'Lower Road.' You boys are standing on the old 'Lower Road.' I'm standing on today, you're standing on yesterday. There's a lot of history down there." He descended the bank and joined us. "These old ones were decommissioned in the thirties, I do believe. Steam-powered locomotives used to run on them. What a sight it was, though I don't think anyone appreciated it back then, and that includes myself. These tracks were laid in the mid-eighteen hundreds. In Gardiner, the times were prosperous. Our city was an economic center for the region. Boat building went on here, and the ice and paper industries were big. There were furniture-making shops, shoe mills, and wine-makers. We still have shoe factories, a paper mill, and a winery. Gardiner was considered a sort of boomtown. Your nanna said jobs are still easy to find here, and that's probably true. Hey, here's a thought. Since you guys like these tracks so much, maybe railroad men are what you can become when you get old enough. It's good and honest work. Maine Central is unionized and considered one of the better outfits to work for in the state. It just needs to see clear of its money problems. You boys were barely born when Hurricane Edna hit in '54. It washed out long sections of the Lower Road. Fixing them cost the company almost everything. There's still talk of it going bankrupt, but I doubt the State will allow that happen. Hopefully, with their big customer International Paper opening that new Androscoggin Mill last year, things'll turn around for Maine Central."

"Maybe I will," responded Mike. "I do like trains, and I'd probably like the traveling. If I was to join up, I'd want to drive their biggest locomotive."

"Me too, Mr. Barry. But I'm not really sure what I want to do when I get older."

"Okay. Enough about jobs. Mike, you don't come down here after dark, do you?"

"No. Why?"

"The area isn't safe. Since the early days, there's been an alcohol problem in the city. There was a hobo pathway through here. During the Depression, men sometimes jumped trains to get to places that had work. Say has it the pathway ran from August-Gardiner clear through to Portland, even to Boston. When I say pathway, only sections closer to cities got walked. Mostly, the bos rode boxcars or empty ore-carts, and that way they were able to stay out of view. The path hasn't been used much since the last World War. That was when jobs got plentiful. After the war and into the fifties, use of it went back up a bit, but it's slowed to almost nothing again. Did you fellas find any evidence of a footpath?"

"Yup. Charlie and I even walked it for a ways."

"And we found empty beer and liquor bottles," added I.

"Hope you didn't run into a rough-looking man wearing a funny blue hat. Sometimes he's with a blonde."

"Nope, didn't see anyone," answered Mike.

"Where are you boys headed now?"

"South, Uncle. How far, we don't know. Maybe to Mount Tom."

"If you're going that far, then you should look for signs of an underground tunnel. Long ago it ran from the Gardiner Mansion down to the river. Have you guys ever heard of it?"

We shook our heads *no*.

"That's understandable. You're young. The tunnel was supposedly part of the Underground Railroad. Been a rumor for a long time and could be one of the best-kept secrets in the state. Almost no one from the outside knows about it. Even in Gardiner it's rarely talked of anymore. Back then, no one other than the Gardiner family knew for sure, and that's because there were people around here who were anything but sympathetic toward slaves. That's who the tunnel was meant for, *slaves*. The family couldn't chance there being any talk of it. And then there were the southern bounty hunters prowling around New England at the time. They carried pockets full of cash so that they could pay off locals for turning in slaves.

"The tunnel was supposedly built in the 1850s to help negroes fleeing to Canada. At night, secret transport boats pulled ashore. The slaves hopped off and ran the tunnel to the Gardiner Mansion. There they would stay for a while, before taking the next step. The Gardiners were sympathetic to Abolition, which was a fancy word for ending slavery. When the war ended in 1865, need for the tunnel was gone. You'll likely learn about some of this stuff in high school history, but there won't be anything about tunnels. I doubt you'll find much when you get down there. Maine Central and regular road construction probably eliminated all trace of its lower portion. Today's Gardiners would know the details, but they are very private people. And they are good people, too, so stay off their land. Anyhoos, it's all fenced.

"When you get past Mount Tom, you are at that point parallel to their land, and that's where you should keep your eyes open for something down near to the river. The brush is extremely thick, but look for something out of the ordinary, like a cave-in or a sunken area that looks out of place. Stay along the tracks till you get there. *What am I saying? You guys are only thirteen and twelve.* Quit for the day and come back with me to the house. Nanna's there. Mike, you know how she doesn't like to leave without having seen all of her grandchildren."

"Charlie, let's do as my uncle says. Besides, I'm hungry. We can ride our bikes down River Road next week. Mount Tom's too far to walk."

"I can hardly wait. Mr. Barry, was there really a railroad in the tunnel?"

Mike laughed. "That's bright of you, Monroe. A railroad in the tunnel to the Gardiner Mansion. Heh-heh-heh."

"Why are you making fun of him? It had a small rail, like miners use for moving ore."

"Really?" returned Mike, surprised.

"No, of course not. 'Railroad' is a code word for a secret system, but I had you going. Anyway, it's not nice to laugh at people when they ask silly questions."

The three of us laughed as we made our way through the rail lot. We passed by Mr. Barry's Biscayne. The owner remarked, "There's ol' Biscuit. One day I hope to find out what that aged racehorse can actually do. Can't bring myself to press down on him just for fun. He might drop dead. *Yyyup*, there'll have to be a good reason to put a hard whip to my ol' Biscuit."

We crossed River Road and climbed the tilted porch's rickety steps.

"How far up the tracks did you boys get?"

"To the edge of downtown. At Bailey Auto we turned back," answered Mike as we entered the house.

"So you didn't get as far as Skowhegan, huh? Next time try to make it there and then walk through the woods for a while. Soon enough you'll hit the Canadian border. Then, if you keep going, you'll make Alaska. Try doing that sometime this summer."

The matriarch heard her son's teasing of us, and she was not impressed. "Allan, stop filling their young minds with such nonsense right now."

"*Oh, Mother,*" was all her son had in comeback.

She and Mike's mom were sitting in the living room. The other Bondy children had already visited with their nanna, and now they were busy elsewhere.

"Boys, come in here and sit with me. You like trains and railroads, do you? There's a lot of history across the street, and that's because the history of every state in this great country of ours is contained in the development of the railroad."

Mike looked at me and rolled his eyes. He decided to remain silent, patient. We sat down.

"Here, have a few cookies, the both of you. They should help hold you off till supper. I brought enough for everyone. I'll take only a few minutes, and then you can go do the things that you prefer. The track across the street goes to Portland, where it connects to the Boston and Maine Railroad, which operates throughout most of New England and into New York. I do believe that coming out of Portland the track also connects to the old Grand Trunk

Railroad. That particular line goes westward clear through to the Great Lake States, such as Michigan and Illinois, and there they load up with brand-new cars destined for dealerships all over our country. That old Grand Trunk I'm pretty sure went even into Chicago. There, tractors and other types of farming equipment, pigs, and so forth got loaded on. The line still exists and is used to this day, but the name 'Trunk' has disappeared over time. I think it's owned by a Canadian outfit now. But, truly, the track right here, the one across the road, connects us to everywhere in North America. It's part of the national line, which, during the last big war, was taken over by the Feds, so that military and other essential wartime matériel could be rapidly moved to where they were needed most, for our country's survival. Gardiner may not be a big place but it is in some ways every bit as big as New York City. People should keep the railroad close to their hearts because of how important it has been and continues to be to our great nation.

"Now, having said that, I want you to hear me out on this. Don't ever get to thinking you come from small-town, Maine. Your minds can think small if you choose to let them, but don't do it. Gardiner people have always thought big and that's why the folks around here are mostly content and successful in life."

Mrs. Bondy piped up. "Charlie, remember when we stood on the porch and watched the last passenger train come through Gardiner? Michael, where were you that day? Pete and the girls were with us. Pete was too young to understand. It was so sad. We waved and some of the passengers waved back. Seeing them do that for the last time, well, it made me cry. The passenger cars had 'Boston and Maine Railroad' written on the side."

"Yes, I remember us waving. When they waved back, it felt so strange, as if they were already ghosts from the past. And I remember you getting upset about it."

"I must've been ridin' toilet or doing something else more important," cracked Mike.

No one paid notice.

"Allan, I think that was the year you were away," noted his sister. "It was 1960 when you were gone, wasn't it?"

"*Yyyup*, Christine, that was the year I chose to be absent from the world. The family still wonders about it, huh?" He glanced quickly at his mother and sister. Then he smiled. "Well, you'll just have to keep wondering." Mr. Barry looked over at me and winked.

Mrs. Barry retook the conversation. "That particular passenger train was called the 'Kennebec.' Passenger service throughout Maine ended in 1960. Mike, you would have been only eight. Charlie, you were what, seven? You once mentioned that your family took the train from Boston when they moved here to Gardiner. You weren't born yet, were you? If I remember right, you said your mother was pregnant with you."

"Yes, that's right."

"Losing the passenger service must have bothered your parents some."

"It did, and it bothered my great-aunt even more because she used to take it from Boston to come here for visits. My uncle used to take it from Old Orchard Beach to come here and to go to other places. I remember picking them up at the depot."

Mrs. Barry shook her head. "The train-stop was always a place of activity and hustle. Then, suddenly, nothing. The Johnson House, the only decent hotel in the city, closed shortly after that. For decades, people of our city saw out-of-town folk walking with their suitcases from the depot into downtown and to the Johnson House, where they checked in. The place was quaint and served real fine meals. With all the industry here and the travelers it brings in, where do they now stay? In Augusta—at the Augusta House. Sitting here talking about losing the passenger train and the Johnson House brings tears to my heart."

"Mine too." Mike rubbed his eyes, pretended to cry. His levity brought laughter to the room, and this was a good thing.

"Okay, that's enough, boys. I've had my time with you. Go do your own things now. Pete, I think, is outside working on roadways. Probably would like the two of you join up with him, to make it more fun. Allan and I'll have the family over for Sunday dinner in a few weeks. Charlie, you can come along, but ask your mother first."

"Thank you for inviting me. I'll ask her, but I'm pretty sure it'll be okay. Goodbye."

"Bye, Nanna. I love you. Bye, Uncle Allan. I . . . never mind."

Mr. Barry followed us. "Mike, hold on. Before you go, I have something else to tell you. Be careful about disturbing things down along the river just south of the station. The spirit of the Abnaki is strong there. That's it. Bye."

Mike and I were perplexed, but joining up with Pete in the making of viable roads through a barren gravel spillway was more important than asking the sage for an explanation. Obviously, young fun still held a part of our spirits. Two hours later, Mike said, "Let's go inside so you can call your mom about staying for supper. I'll check to see if we're having those special potatoes you like so much."

Because I had been away all day and she wanted me home for a while, mother declined my request but said I could return after supper. She was making pizza. I did not argue. I really liked her pizza.

Chapter VIII

Gardiner Fruit to Dance Night on Kingsbury

Tony was still at the jobsite, and Mr. Prudhomme stood beside him; it was pay-up time. At supper, Tony went on and on about how many magazines and bullets he could buy with the $8 he had received. It was easy to see just how pleased the young man was with his day of manual contribution to the general upkeep of the neighborhood. The following summer would have him joining the Health-tex team, and this day had proven good training for him.

The Monroes gobbled down the homemade pizza in record time. A bakery brownie and an éclair managed to also get jammed into the youngest son's belly.

"Bye, Mom and Dad. I'm heading to Mike's." I went quickly, giving them no time to say anything back. I knew how mom can change her mind or how dad can sometimes overrule her. Tony followed me out. He wanted to throw hoops. Lizzie came with him.

"Lizzie, stay here. Stay with me. You can't go with Chuckie. I said come here! Good, gotcha. Remember, you're my dog, not his."

Just past the Prudhomme house, I noticed Frank inspecting Tony's work.

"Hi, Charlie. Your brother did a job over here today. Joe looked it over again after supper and decided Tony needs to *improob* his work. What does 'improob' mean?"

"I don't know, but you should go over and tell him right away."

"Where you going?"

"Down this way. Take care and don't trip and fall down that nice new bank, Frank."

"Oh, Charlie, you're so funny. Can I come with you?"

"No. Bye, Frank."

"I'm coming anyway."

"Frank, listen to me. You have to stay home. You're only five years old and that means you're too young to go where I'm going. It's dangerous and you could get killed."

"Okay, Charlie, if you say so. I'm going over to tell Tony right away."

"Remember that you're not supposed to cross the street. Just go stand on your top step and holler as loud as you can over to him what Joe said."

"Okay, Charlie. I'll do that."

On I went. Then I heard, "Charles, come back! Mom changed her mind! You have to stay home and have a bath! Trust me, you really need to have a bath!"

The voice was Daniel's. I briefly turned to wave, then proceeded to walk away faster.

"Charles, I said come back! Come back right now! Mom says you can't go to Mike's!" When Daniel saw me again turn to wave, he cupped his hands around his mouth and yelled one more time, as if through a loudspeaker, "Get back here! Mom said you have to stay home!" I pretended not to hear and upped my walking speed.

Tony hollered over to Daniel. "That smelly little rat heard you, now let's go get him!" He must have winged the basketball with might because I heard it bounce hard on the driveway and almost instantly bang loud against a garage door. I glanced back to see Daniel, Tony, Frank, and Lizzie running full steam after me. I hightailed it. *This is not good! This is not good!* screamed the mind. Lizzie caught up to me in front of the Dells' house. Even though only medium-sized, she was the fastest dog this side of Gardiner. She hated cats but was scared of all dogs, even puny ones. Over the years, Buddy and other canines had chased Lizzie, but none had ever caught her. The King of Prospect Street was this big mean mongrel named Moe. A couple months ago, he tried to sneak up on her. She and I were at the bottom of the mini-valley, walking along the ephemeral rill just for something to do. Lizzie adeptly swerved the timbers and quickly brought the chase to end when Moe ran snout first into a big old crusty elm. Last year, she ran down a squirrel, killing it before it made a tree. We scolded her for that. Now she was next to me and wagging her tail like this was fun. I looked back. Tony and Frank had fallen behind. Daniel was definitely my worry. Even though not athletic, he could sprint for real when his passion got up. I knew if he had his high-top U. S. Keds on, the rundown would be over before I reached old man Waite's place, at the corner of Kingsbury and River Road. I glanced back to see he was wearing loafers, but still gaining ground. If he caught me, Tony would follow up with punches. Frank urged Daniel onward: "Run, Pencils, run! Get that smelly little rat!"

I beat him to the corner and at 20 feet downhill I heard a gravelly *thud* and "Ugh!" Lizzie and I kept running. In front of the Donahues' was when I connected the chase was over. I slowed to a jog and turned to see Daniel on the ground. He was clutching his left knee. He had not been able to negotiate the sharp left turn through the dirt ditch. Tony arrived and helped him up. Daniel glared down the sidewalk at me, his face as red as his bloody knee was. Tony shook his fist and shouted, "Chuckie, you and Lizzie are in real trouble this time!" He helped Daniel back to the house. Lizzie and I continued on to Mike's.

I told the Bondys what had happened and that I was probably in trouble. They agreed. Soon, the phone rang. It was dad. He wanted me home right away. I was all shook up and worried about what would happen upon my return. Dad was not the type to spank or hit. He preferred to give firm talks, timeouts, and/or groundings. But this time his youngest son may have crossed the line. I just did not know what to expect.

Lizzie and I approached. Frank was out there in wait.

"Hi, Charlie. Pencils hurt his leg real bad. You're in big trouble now."

"Frank, thanks for letting me know something I already know."

"Oh, Charlie, you're so funny."

Now it was Tony's turn. He was back playing hoops. "You rotten skunk, you're in real trouble now. Pencils got his leg all bloodied up. You better get in there. Lizzie, come here." Tony crouched down to receive the dog. She wagged her tail and jumped up on him. She was not in trouble at all. *Maybe that's what it'll be like for me when I get inside*, I thought.

No one was in the kitchen. Dad emerged from the bathroom. He did not look pleased.

"Why didn't you listen to your brother? Now his leg is hurt because of you."

"I'm sorry, Dad, but Mom said I could go to Mike's after supper. I wasn't sure what Dan wanted. You know how he's been lately. The other day Mom told me to make allowances for him by ignoring him, and that's what I did."

"Okay then, as long as you've learned your lesson. Go in the bathroom and say you're sorry."

Daniel, still in shorts and socks, sat on the lidded toilet. He did not acknowledge me. Mother knelt in front of him. The major cleaning was already done, and now she was plucking out pointy little pebbles from his torn flesh. Each extraction brought the patient's facial muscles to tighten, breath to gasp. A brush-coat of iodine came next. The sharp sting caught him off guard, and his neck and head totally reddened. He lifted his tense lids to give me a dirty look.

"Dan, I'm sorry." I drooped my shoulders and looked down at the floor.

"Just listen next time and don't run off when I'm calling you."

Mother turned her look to me. "Did your father have a talk with you?"

"Yes, he sure did. But, Mom, you said I could go to Mike's after supper."

"That's right, but I changed my mind." Mother applied a bandage, then pressed on it, to make sure it would stick. "There, that should do. Charles, take a bath. I'll make a pan of Jiffy Pop for later. Hervey, can you pick up a big bottle of Hire's Root Beer at Gardiner Fruit?"

"Doesn't that take the cake. Now I have to go out to the store. Charles can come with me and have his bath when we get back." Dad, irritated, grabbed the keys. Off we went.

Located at the center of Water Street, city core's main thoroughfare, Gardiner Fruit was the most popular convenience store around. Monday to Thursday, the store closed at 9:00 p.m. Fridays and Saturdays had the place open till 11:00. Sundays it closed in the early evening, at 6:00. Mostly, owner Bob Newsome worked the place. He was a big, strong, friendly man, who was known to be unfriendly in his dispensing of rowdy teenagers when they happened by.

When it came to penny candy, LeClerc's Market demolished Gardiner Fruit. Mr. Newsome's large body, hands, and fingers did not take kindly to the task of bending over and stretching forward to pick out one of this and two of that. His impatience was always obvious with young customers, and that was probably why he stocked so little selection. He was also not noted for carrying seasonal items, such as yoyos, baseballs, miniature footballs, and marbles. On everything else, from groceries and refreshments to snack items, his place was stacked the best. On weekday afternoons, right after the factories let out, the store could get packed tight with customers. Truly, the place seemed a goldmine for both owner and shopper.

The owner's relief guy for Friday and Saturday evenings, Mr. Bill, was at the cash. A son of his was a classmate of Tony. A few years ago they had played Little League Baseball together. Mr. Newsome and Mr. Bill had their fingers on the pulse of the greater Gardiner area, which included Randolph, Pittston, Chelsea, South and West Gardiners, and Farmingdale. Some people even joked that the two guys had their fingers *inside* the pulse. City policemen often came in to buy sodas, snacks, and smokes. If no one else was around, they might stay an extra moment, to chat and lay bare bits and pieces of information that no one else but policemen know about. As a result, Newsome and Bill often had hot bulletins. Going into Gardiner Fruit was way more than about buying something.

"Hey there, dadso and son. How goes it tonight, Herve?"

"Fine, I guess. Just this bottle of soda. What's new out there, Elliot?"

"Maybe you've already heard, but there are a lot of worried people in the shoe business. Commonwealth Shoe, Gardiner Shoe—people at both of those places are hearing things about their mills closing down. The owners say they aren't making enough money. Rumor has it they're going to move to places of cheaper labor. Some say the mills might close permanently."

"What's going on? What's changed?" asked dad.

"Competition from other countries is cutting into them real bad. And then there was that nasty strike at Commonwealth a few months back. Their union's a pretty tough one. Workers wanted higher wages than what the company was offering. The two parties fought it out pretty good, before settling at a dollar thirty-five an hour plus piecework. But the owners weren't happy. You don't work at either of those places, do you?"

"No. I'm at Kennebec Manufacturing."

"Then you're probably okay. Haven't heard anything about that place. Is it union?"

"Yeah, but it's not a tough one like the shoes have. Frontline workers get a yearly raise, usually a nickel. The base hourly wage is a dime or more below the shoes. Last year the company brought in quota. When a line-worker produces more than what is figured a right amount for eight hours, they get extra pay. Can be as much as fifteen dollars more a week."

"Now you're talking my language. Here's your change. Take care, dadso and son."

Father relayed to mother what he had heard at Gardiner Fruit. They quieted for a while; their blank expressions indicated pensiveness, a concern for the area's families. We watched *The Lawrence Welk Show*, but it was not until well into *The Jackie Gleason Show* when the adults lost all thought on serious matters. They laughed and laughed.

At supper, mother had mentioned about the family attending the nine o'clock mass tomorrow. It meant a rise by 8:00 would be required. Tired, I went to bed after Gleason was over.

Loud music, happy voices, and laughs were coming from the Prudhommes' house. The Knights and their guests were reveling in another one of their Saturday night dance-a-thons. I got up from bed and went for a peek out the window. The Knights drove a maroon 1962 Chrysler Imperial Crown. It was parked, as normal, at street's side and directly in front of their upstairs living-room window. Six visitor cars were parked up and down the street. The Knights lived in the apartment on the house's second floor. They paid the Prudhommes $50 a month, same as mom and dad got from our tenants. The couple was in their early 60s and had no children. Both worked at Commonwealth Shoe Company, located near the top of Brunswick Avenue, just up from Sheehan's Dairy. Mr. Knight was a section foreman there; his wife worked in the office.

The Knights moved into the apartment in 1962, just after they had arrived in Gardiner from Haverhill, Massachusetts. Since then and twice a year, the couple hosted dance marathons on the house's third level, which was nothing more than a large empty room finished with hardwood flooring. The couples always made sure to move their galas from house to house in order to reduce the chances of their neighbors' patience levels wearing thin.

Once a year, the core of the troupe arranged for a large extravaganza in the ballroom at the Augusta House. The events were courtly and attracted serious dancers all the way up from Wiscassett and down from Waterville. On those evenings their expertly delightful sways owned the State Capitol. Mr. Knight presented himself especially dapper for the occasions. Daring and light on his feet, the man was reputed to be the best dancer in Kennebec County; and then there had been one happy sojourner last summer, perhaps a tipsy dance partner, whose female cords boasted him the best anywhere. Mr. Knight himself had once talked to the senior Monroe about his World War II stint in the U.S. Navy and how it had been then when his soul had taken wholeheartedly to the art of dance. After the war, the Navy Knight went on to perfect a trademark style in his many years of dancing Boston and area's ballrooms.

If the best professional spirit was required inside the capitol city's quality guesthouse, the other Navy spirit ruled the smaller house-gatherings. In the past, across the street, the noise levels reached higher and higher levels as the liquids flowed and the evenings wore on. After 11:00, laughs became guffaws, constant and well into the next morning. Bellows like, "Where did you learn to dance like that!" and "My dead grandparents can move better than you two!" could be heard. Toward the east and west walls of the dance room, the ceiling slanted sharply down because of roof encroachment. After midnight, when fine bodily movements gave way to tawdry manipulations, invariably one or more couples would fling themselves against the ceiling. This always got giant roars, with yells like, "Call the roofer right away, they put a hole in it!" "They're destroying the property! Someone get the police!" "Bartender, get them another drink, they're still standing!" The Knights were extraordinarily nice people, and that was probably why the Prudhommes put up with their parties.

I jumped back into bed.

Chapter IX

The Ancient Trail to Bolley's Famous Franks

The Laithrans were walking to their Chev Bel Air just as the Monroes their Electra. The very neighborly man was smartly attired in suit and tie, his wife a conservative navy-blue dress with white trim.

"Bernard, how about today you and Dot go to Saint Joe's and we'll give Christ Church a try?" proposed dad. "I've always wondered how the other side works it."

"Good idea, Herve, but I don't think the ladies would go for it."

The snazzy Electra followed the neighborhood's oil-burner up Kingsbury. "That ol' 57 stinks worse than awful," remarked dad. "The rusty can barely makes it up our hill. Definitely not enough of car for them. Needs putting down. Tony, don't get any ideas."

"Dot and Bernard feel the same. She says they're about to start looking for a new one."

The mind was barely awake for the first half of church. Only when stomach began to churn did the rest of the brain perk up. Father McIver's sermon was particularly grueling. He talked of how thankful to God we should be for having so much good and plenty.

". . . Truly, Maine is a land of milk and honey, with its thick forests, fish-filled lakes, endless ocean, bountiful farmlands, and ample employment and educational opportunities. Dear folk, it's as if our Almighty God looked down at us, smiled, got a twinkle in His eye, and waved a mighty hand, to give Maine His full blessing. He can do the opposite, as we know from the Bible, so let us pray we forever be on guard for our state and nation, so that we may remain in His good standing. Amen to that."

On the way home, mother mentioned how Father's talk had resonated in her soul and how she hoped it had for the rest of us. "When we're down about something, let's try to remember what Father McIver said." Dad agreed but said Father DeBruin could have said it in half the words. As we pulled into the driveway, Mother proclaimed, "God has blessed Maine and this family. Now let's go have a big breakfast. We'll eat around eleven. It'll also count as lunch. As you boys already know, Dad and I will be working on the outside of the house all afternoon. Means I won't have time to cook. We'll go to Bolley's for supper. Is that okay, Hervey?"

"Yup, sounds good to me."

Tony and I cheered. Daniel showed no excitement. He liked Bolley's, but it was just the mood he was in. "Hot dogs will do just fine, I guess."

The oldest son was preoccupied with the dread thought of having to be back in the cutting room for the next five days. I loved my brother Daniel, and I looked up to him. He possessed wisdom ahead of his years. The gift, however, had another side, in that, excepting him, it was apparent to everyone that he did not have the developed maturity to emotionally cope with such a high IQ. This presented a problem for those in close contact to him, but particularly so for him. The thing with Daniel was that because of his brilliant mind, he cared about people and about things too much, and this fact also bothered him. Add to that, there was his tendency to over-contemplate the future, especially if there was something he deemed unpleasant in it, and this could exacerbate his moodiness. The family knew to always be gentle with the young man.

After french toast, sausages, hash browns, and orange juice, everyone was ready to get to their assignments: dad to the porch, mother to the garden, Daniel to the living room couch, and Chuckie to Rollins Woods, entrance to which was located across the street from our house—not directly across the street, because there the Prudhommes' residence sat, but just up Kingsbury.

Tony wanted to go to LaVerdiere's Drug to buy his magazines, but, to his dismay, he could not. At least not right away. He first had to report to Mr. Prudhomme, who had ten minutes earlier phoned about corrective work that needed doing. I did not tease my brother because we were in close quarters and I valued my life.

I phoned Mike. He agreed that it was his turn to come to my place.

"Bring your jackknife because we'll need them." He was pleased to hear it.

Rollins Woods presented decent exploration opportunities for two young spirits. Right off Kingsbury, the forest floor sloped sharply down, for 70 yards, to Rollins Brook, at the bottom. On the other side of the minor waterway was a fairly steep climb to a level section of forest that stretched all the way to lightly-used Cottage Street, near to the city's southern extremity, though still an eighth mile from the Gardiner Mansion. Just the other side of Cottage

Street was the Henley farm-field; the far end of the field had a fence that separated it from the heavily wooded north line of the Gardiner family's property. With the aid of an old tractor, Mr. Henley worked the field every spring and summer. Sometimes he liked to ride the large-wheeled vehicle up and down Cottage Street just for the fun of it, with all his children—five or more it seemed—laughing and holding on for dear life, clutching whatever pipe or metal bar they could. When a car passed by, each child would release a friendly hand to wave at the folks inside. Invariably one or more would swing sideways, like a door slamming open, giving all on board to panic. The astute driver knew exactly what to do about it: hit the brakes hard enough to produce a swing back, so that loose hands could regain hold. A few months ago, mother had commented about Mrs. Henley being pregnant again: "That Mr. Henley's got another biscuit baking in his wife's nine-month oven, proving he knows as much about husbandry as he does farming."

Mike and I crossed Kingsbury Street and entered Rollins Woods by way of an old path leading down to and beyond the brook. Supposedly the path always existed, yet no one knew exactly why. It was not as if we had observed the thing being used much. In fact, other than Tony, Mike, me, and years earlier Donald Prudhomme, no one else had ever been seen entering or exiting it. Yet the path was five feet wide and fallow-like.

The forest was filled with animals: raccoons, skunks, rabbits, squirrels, chipmunks, and woodchucks; and then there were things we did not know what they were. Down toward where the brook empties into the river, muskrats might be seen dunking down into and popping up from the mud holes they had dug just under the shoreline. Deer and fox had been observed in the past, but they had likely been in a wander on an old route and just passing through. In the wilder times of yester-decades, black bears had walked the area. Now and then a lonely black straggler might still be seen strutting fast along River Road down South Gardiner way. A couple years back, someone in the neighborhood claimed to have almost run over a bobcat crossing Kingsbury around midnight, near to our place. Speculation later concluded the bobcat likely a large Manx. Even though this calmed people's fears to some degree, no one was really sure.

A month after last summer's how-to sessions on Indian crafting, Mike and I got the thought to ask his uncle about the atypical path that we were now on. After taking a moment to ponder the question, Mr. Barry offered that it had been and still was an ancient passageway for animals. He believed the Kennebec Indians had used it for many centuries, setting themselves along it, in wait to bring down passing prey. But how could he know this with such certainty?

Later that day and without further prompt from us, Mr. Barry returned to the subject of the forest pathway. The moment exposed a man of an alternate soul, one that showed a different, more distant face, as if a roaming yet familiar native spirit had entered him in order to teach the two young, enquiring minds of the long-ago reality. "The spirit" could see how Mike and I had yet to be tainted by the materialistic modern-day world. Mysteriously and not in a way that would chill children's spines, his voice slowed and deepened to that of a man we did not recognize:

> *"Throughout time the trees have shown respect for the ancient trail made sacred by the blood of those lesser beings the Great One Above put on earth for the sustenance of a First Nation's People, and the trees' children were not allowed to play—that is, their seeds were not granted permission to take root in the holy ground of the forest roadway. Almost two hundred years ago, the native owners were vanquished from their eternal inheritance, yet even to this day primal senses of wild beasts hold testament to a glorious past, and the beasts still wander its length, in endless search of something they wish to never find. When young souls such as yours receive truth with open eyes and wanting ears, their mission in life then becomes as a light for others who seek release from the darkness of the past."*

Still to the day, Mike and I retained no doubt as to what he had said, and that was because we tended to believe everything that came from the elder's voice box, except when he was pulling our legs, and we always had to be on guard for that.

Based on direction, the ancient path had to have passed through where the Monroe house now sat, or close by to it, then beyond the house and through the wooded gully, to hook up with the ephemeral rill at the bottom of our mini-valley. After following the waterway's route, the path continued through the Bondys' gravel delta, then across River Road, through the train yard, to finally meet up with the shore of the Kennebec River. There was indeed an uncanny feeling of the existence a former throughway leading from the north edge of the Monroes' woods, but it was not as obvious as the one we were now descending inside Rollins Woods.

While the two of us made our way down the steepest part of the trail, I thought about my having awareness of the path's ancient history and how it had allowed me to understand why so many seemingly abnormal events had taken place in and around our property over the years. Mr. Barry's revealing account had granted the mind lucidity to things eyes might distantly detect but never comprehend. Trying to lay it out to family members would not have worked; they would have thought me nuts. But this summer would come to change things and change people. Perhaps the persistent stagnant air and oppressive humidity gripping central Maine would help to ignite the strange events to take place, both during the day and in the dead of night, *frightening night*.

Mike and I made the bottom. Rollins Brook was flowing rapid and full, about six feet wide. For some distance north and south of the spot where the path crossed over, the brook's bottom consisted of large rocks and gravel. Here, the run of water was more like minor rapids, ranging from one to three feet deep. A few years back, Mrs. Robbins had warned Mike and me about the water's quality. "Absolutely do not drink the water down there and do not put wet hands in your mouths. You'll get dysentery or ptomaine poisoning, and if that one doesn't kill you, your feet will have to be amputated." Mrs. Robbins was old man Waite's daughter. She and her husband Paul and their two foster boys lived 40 yards up Kingsbury from the path's entrance.

No fish lived the stream, but at the right time of summer ample frogs and salamanders could be found all along its portions. About 50 yards downstream was a sharp elbow that caused a widening and slowing of flow, allowing for a fairly large siding of dead water. We headed there first. Today, the stagnant pool was 30 feet in diameter and the bottom four feet at its deepest. Hundreds of tadpoles were swimming it.

After ten minutes of steaming rocks into the water, we moved on. Rollins Brook turned south and meandered. Mike and I surprised a family of whip-poor-wills. They flew off in a panic and did not make their usual *whippoorwee* sound. Late nights sometimes heard the birds chanting out their warning calls from likely this very zone we were now passing through. Curving around old timber, shooting through the Rollins Brook ravine, filtering past leaf-filled trees rising upslope to Kingsbury Street, the sounds by then could be faint yet frighteningly eerie.

Mike and I observed squirrels and chipmunks. We threw rocks at them, but never with the intent to actually hit one. We whipped out our jackknives. Each of us broke off a small branch, so that we could whittle our way along the brook, toward the unnerving tunnel ahead.

"Where did your uncle go for that year? Up north to a lumber camp?"

"Except for him, no one's really sure. He didn't go to a camp—that much I do know. Before he left, he and Grandma had been arguing almost daily about his drinking. Then one day he disappeared. A year later he showed up dry. Never touched a drop since. He once opened up a little bit to Mom about it. Told her he had met the woman of his dreams while away. They were even gonna get married. Anyway, it didn't work out and he never said why. He did confess that he still loved her and probably always would. Could be that was the reason he couldn't stay with the one he did end up marrying.

"He's told Mom something else. When he gets a job, after a while the work gets stressful and the boss gets bossier. It gives him the temptation to go back to drinking. That's why he quits. Then he tries to console himself by doin' his hobbies. It's that Indian spirit in him. Don't be askin' any more questions about it, and don't be tellin' anyone what I just told you. Grandma says we shouldn't think Gardiner is a small place. She may be right in one way, but secrets and other types of talk have a way of gettin' around."

"You don't have to be concerned about me. I know when talk is okay and when it's not. This information isn't anything much to know about."

"You say that, but I've been around longer than you. I know better how people can be."

In ten minutes we arrived at the mouth of the tunnel. The thing was definitely awesome and way too iffy for me. Mike didn't see it the same way. There, in front of us, lay a 60-yard city-built tunnel that went deep under River Road and the rail tracks, before giving way 20 feet up from the river's shoreline. The pipe was five feet in diameter, and we could see right through to the other end, which showed as a distant, tiny ball of gray light.

Mike prodded me. "We're doin' it. You squeeze past the bars first and I'll follow."

We had been through this before, and never had I conceded. "No way. Not me."

"Come on, Monroe. When are you gonna get some guts?"

"Mike, you go ahead on your own. When you get back, let me know what you found."

He thought about it for a few seconds. "I'm not going it alone. Let's get out of here."

Slowly, we made our way back by a different route, up the opposite slope, northeast along the plateau. When we got to Rollins Brook, the lament of a distant bagpipe could be heard. The sad melody became louder as we climbed toward the street. Then, the lament changed to a happy tune. Mike and I made the top of the path and stopped; the spot, directly across the street from the Laithrans' house, gave us a clear view into the Camerons' backyard, which was just up from Mr. Laithran's vegetable garden. Because properties on lower Kingsbury were large and contained forested sections with significant geographic relief, no fences had ever been built. Bill Cameron was in kilt and sported a bonnet. The man marched around happily, winging his torso this way and that, all the while masterfully working the prickly instrument.

"Bill Cameron sure looks like he enjoys what he's doing," commented Mike. "One of his stepdaughters is in my grade. She's about as cute as they come. You're not yet old enough to know about those things. Does the guy always do this?"

"Only on certain Sundays. And I am, too, old enough. Anyway, neighbors around here say when he gets out the bagpipe it means he got into something else on Saturday night. People like to talk. No one knows for sure, except the Camerons. He's a real nice man, friendly and all. Likes knowing people are watching and listening, as long as they don't get up close. When my dad hears it he covers his ears and rolls his eyes. Sometimes he pretends to have a heart attack. The first time was a few years back when he was doing work on the roof. He pressed his hands against his chest and stumbled toward the edge. Tony and I were playing basketball. We got all upset thinking he was about to fall off. We hollered at him as loud as we could. Dad's eardrums are messed up from a swimming accident as a kid. Then he had to be around gun blasts in the war. Says hearing bagpipe is like having knives jammed into his ears. One time he said battleship artillery going off next to his head sounded better. It's after five. I better get inside."

"Take care, Monroe. I'm headin' home. Got that Ford guy comin' tomorrow, don't ya?"

"Yup."

"Well, don't be callin' me when he's around." Mike walked off fast, nose out of joint.

I noticed Mr. and Mrs. Knight sitting on the Prudhommes' front porch. The day was just after peaking in heat, and the two were in T-shirts, shorts, and sandals. There were tall, half-full glasses of what appeared to be ice tea on the table beside their chairs. The two looked relaxed and each held a book.

"Hello, Mr. and Mrs. Knight. You must have danced the whole night away."

They laughed.

"Hello, Charlie."

"Hi, Charlie. No, we didn't dance the whole night, but most of it *yes*, and now we're paying our dues. What have you been up to?"

"My friend and I just finished exploring in the woods. We didn't find much." Frank appeared. He must have been in his backyard and heard us.

"Hi, Mr. and Mrs. Knight. Hi, Charlie. Whatcha doing? Can I talk, too?"

"Frank, you caught me finishing up. Gotta go. You can talk to the Knights. Bye."

"*Thanks, Charlie*"—"*Thanks, Charlie*," cranked out both Knights.

"Thanks, Charlie," said Frank as he joined them. "See you tomorrow. That's when we get to play all day together. You, me, and your friend Timmy."

I pounded a fist against the outer door. "It's Jimmy!" My thought turned to the hot dog feast soon to take place at Bolley's Famous Franks. I entered the kitchen. Mom was there.

"Charles, we've been waiting for you. Everybody's hungry and ready. Wash up quickly."

I did as told and rushed out to the car. Tony was already sitting in it. We began racing our electric windows up and down. Dad appeared.

"Stop that right now. Do you want to break them? Do you ever see me playing with the buttons? Don't be doing it anymore. *Aww, no*. It's that Bill

Deers again, with his blasted bagpipe. Like I need a headache. Keep your windows up until we're on River Road."

Mom and Daniel got in, and we began our trip to Augusta. Mother stated, "If everything goes without a hitch, we should be at Bolley's by six-thirty and home by eight. That way, Daniel and I can be in bed reading by eight-fifteen, as we like."

Augusta was located six miles up the Kennebec River, the dog shack another two miles north, on the road to Waterville. We passed the Bondy home—no one was out—and proceeded past the public library and into downtown. At the first street light we turned right, onto the section of River Road running north along the river, right to Augusta. We passed by the Agway, the old train station, Lucky Strike Lanes, and finally the Shell gas station. When we hit where Northern Avenue connected to the River Road, dad said, "Dan, you and I will be turning there tomorrow morning for work."

"Thanks for reminding me," responded the despondent senior brother.

We were now at the gateway to Farmingdale. A mile up, we passed Ernie's Drive In, open, green Biscayne not present. The township had no proper center but did contain several important outlets: Meadow Hill Golf Club, Creamy Frost ice cream stop, Butler Twins Garden Center, and legendary Woody's Pizza, owned by a very large man named Woody.

"Mom, do you know anyone bigger than Woody?"

"Not personally, but *War of the Worlds* Orson Welles is probably just as big."

Tony: "No way Welles. What about the guy who sings Christmas carols?"

"Burl Ives? Perhaps. How about you, dear? Do you know anyone?"

"Sure do. Three, in fact. Haystack Calhoun is over six hundred pounds. Then there's Crybaby Canon at four hundred and twenty, and Gorilla Monsoon. I think he's just under five hundred. Woody's big, but I don't think he cracks four."

"Who are they?" asked mother.

"Wrestlers on TV."

"I thought you don't like that stuff."

"I don't. But if I happen to be in the den when the boys have it on, I might catch a glimpse when I flip a page of the *KJ*."

Me: "I really like his pizza. Remember the time we ordered from there and when we got home and opened the boxes one of the pizzas had his cigar ashes on it?"

"That was nothing. I just blew them off. You bringing it up gets me to thinking it's time for another El Producto. Haven't had one for at least a month."

"Dad, can you take us golfing someday? It's okay to smoke cigars out on the course."

"*Us?*" came mother. "Don't include me. Trying to whack a little ball with a metal stick into a hole in the ground isn't something your mother would find enjoyable. And then to fork out so much money to do it. Golf is for the well-to-do to waste their time and money on."

"You and Dan don't have to come and that way it's cheaper. Dad can take Tony and me."

"Wilson sometimes smokes Swisher Sweets," remarked middle brother. "Says the mouth-end of the gar is soaked with sherry. Maybe I'll try one of those out on the course. When can you take us, Dad?"

"I don't own any clubs, I've never golfed, and I don't have the time. And, Tony, just because your friend smokes cigars doesn't mean you can. You're too young for that."

"Days Jewelry sometimes carries clubs. Right now they have one in their window."

"Listen here, Charles. Your father and I like to wallpaper. It's a form of hobby for us, and a very enjoyable one during which we can share our time together. It's also constructive and not a silly way of wasting time and money. Right, Hervey?"

"Oh, yes. Enjoyable, constructive . . . *together*."

Everyone laughed, even mother. At four miles came Hallowell. The place was somewhat a "bedroom community" for Maine's capitol. The city's main street began on the south side with the massive Hallowell Shoe Company. Past there, the main consisted of a convenience store, a pizza shop, a hardware store, four shoe stores, and a dozen or so antique shops.

Every summer, people from New York liked to stroll the sidewalks, shopping for shoes and antiques to take back to their houses and apartments. After tiring out, tourists might then head over Freddies Restaurant, located just off the main. Hallowell's best and only burgers and fries were served there. Except for in front of the quik-stop, the main street was devoid of cars and people, being that it was Sunday evening. We kept a speedy pace. I asked, "Mom, will we ever go back to Ferdies? Their fried clams and french fries taste every bit as good as Howard Johnson's."

"Oh, will you grow up, why don't you?" interrupted Daniel. "Why do you insist on calling it 'Ferdies'? You're basically a teenager, for crying out loud, and not a little kid anymore. It's *Freddies*. Got it? *Freddies*. F-R-E-D-D-Y-S. *Freddies*."

"That is incorrect," jumped in mother with a big grin. "Tony, it is now your turn."

"*Freddies*: F-R-E-D-D-I-E-S. *Freddies*."

"That is correct. Tony, you are the new state spelling bee champion. Hervey, hit the ejector button for Daniel's seat. As they say, out with the old and in with the new. On to Washington we go, with Tony this time."

"Yes, Jeanne. Washington. I'll get rid of him right away."

Dad pressed the button that locks and unlocks Daniel's door, then hit the up-down button for his window. Tony and I busted out laughing, but not oldest son.

"Well, who cares how some little grease hole is spelled! G-R-E-A-S-E-space-H-O-L-E. *grease hole!* There, did I get that one right!"

"Daniel, calm down," chided mother. "You didn't lose your sense of humor in Washington, did you?"

He received the point, gave nothing in return.

"Charles, as far as eating there, I don't think we'll be doing it anytime soon. The grease hole is a bit on the pricey side."

We made the big cemetery at the southern rim of Augusta. After that came Dairy Queen and five new-car dealerships: Jeep, with its big show of Jeeps made famous in WWII; American Motors, with its humble lineup of pathetic Ramblers; Coe Chevrolet, proudly displaying a front yard filled with new-fangled Chevelles; Shoppe Ford, catching passers' eyes with its platoon of snappy-looking Mustangs; and Nichols Pontiac, the outlet mom and dad had purchased the car we were in. Coe and Shoppe were on opposite sides of the street from each other. Tony stared at the Chevelles, and I the other way, at the Mustangs. Appropriately, the State Motor Vehicle & License Bureau came next, just prior to the State Capitol Building.

I asked, "How come Cony High School isn't named Augusta High School?"

"Who cares?" grunted Daniel. "Mom, what time is it?"

"Just after six. Cease your worrying, first son, for we are on schedule. And, third son, on your question, *I don't know.*"

Tony: "The only thing we need to know about Cony High School is how much Gardiner High's going to beat them by in the next football or basketball game. Nothing else in the world matters more. It's in our blood to hate Cony more than they hate Gardiner. That way we retain the superior hate-power needed to pound them into pulp. We're not taught that by anyone, it's just that as freshman we learn it from teachers and upperclassmen all on our own."

The car-ride continued past the elegant Augusta House, through the rotary, and downhill into the city's core. Except for in front of the convenience store and the Greyhound Bus Station, the street was vacant. We passed by Edwards Dam and entered the mill zone. Like Gardiner, Augusta had mills. The biggest was Bates Cotton, which made rolls of cloth destined for eastern U.S. clothes factories. The place was situated on the north slope of the city's lower valley. At the top of the road was a sign indicating Waterville 23 miles ahead, Skowhegan 39.

"Mom, can we go to Skowhegan this summer?"

"Why all the way up there?"

"I don't know, other than I just want to go."

"Well, I sincerely doubt it. We don't know what's there, so why waste the gas, especially now that it's thirty-two cents a gallon. Who knows, maybe this Friday I'll get blindsided again."

In two miles, Bolley's Famous Franks was made. Daniel asked, "What time is it?"

"Twenty after six. We're still on schedule, as long as everyone's already decided what they want to order."

Being takeout only, the hotdog shack had no chairs inside. Customers had the choice of either walking inside to order or using in the drive-thru lane. Every past visit had had the Monroes choosing the latter, and this evening turned out to be no different.

"While we're in line, each of you tell me what you want. Speak loud so I can hear."

"Dad, that never works. You always half-hear it and then mess it up even more. We'll each tell her what we want when we get to the window," reasoned Daniel, in his way.

"Nope, tell me now. I have a new system. But speak loud."

Tony went first. "I'll have two hot dogs with onions, ketchup, and mustard . . . and a root beer."

I went next. "I want just one hot dog with onions, mustard, and relish . . . and a grape soda."

Daniel grunted and went ahead. "I'll have the same as Charles, except orange soda."

"I'll have the same as Danny and Charles. You and I can split a Pepsi. We'll need a large order of fries. That should be enough for everyone. How about you, Hervey? What getting?"

"Two hotdogs, one with onions and mustard on both."

As we moved up to the window, Tony said, "Dad, I changed my mind. I want only one of my hot dogs with ketchup, not both."

"That's fine, Tony, no problem."

Dad was calm—too calm. Uneasiness held the backseat, but the sons remained silent: watching, listening.

"Hello, miss. We'll have a large order of fries, one bottle of Pepsi, one root beer, one orange, one grape, and eight hot dogs with onions and everything else on them. That's it."

Silence momentarily owned the car; four passengers were rapid-processing the unbelievable hot dog order they had just heard. Suddenly, together, three brothers broke out with one big "No, Dad!" Mother added, "Herve, make that seven dogs, not eight."

In order to alleviate backseat anxieties, the man had no choice but to reveal his new system. "All you need to do is use your finger to scrape off the things you don't want."

"That'll be four dollars and thirty cents," said the woman.

Dad, still calm, corrected her. "Miss, make that one less hot dog."

"Then that'll make it four even."

"No, Dad!"

Mother, blindsided: "Four dollars? That much? *Again* prices have gone up?"

"Miss, please wait a moment." He turned. "Try to calm yourselves back there."

"Dad, scraping doesn't work," came Daniel. "The three of us are canceling our hot dog orders."

"Well then, tell her what you want, and loud so she can hear! Daniel, you go first!"

Bolley's fried their onions before piling them onto their dogs. This was partly why the place was so popular. The other part was the wieners. They were slow-broiled so that their skins would contract and mostly not pop open; biting down on one brought forth a *snap* and a bold squirt of tasty juice right up to the pallet. To top it off, the buns were steamed.

"I'm stuffed," said Tony as we pulled away.

"What time is it, Mom?"

"Doesn't matter. We'll be home by eight. Herve, for variety let's take the back way."

At the north edge of Augusta's downtown, just past Edwards Dam, we turned east onto the bridge over the Kennebec River. I noticed two boxcars idle on the tracks. MEC was written on their sides. Eight empty ore-carts had SOO LINE on them.

"Mom, today when Father McIver said Maine was the land of milk and honey, I got thinking about something."

"What was that?"

"You used to buy honey. How come you don't buy it anymore?"

"That's because Tony eats the whole jar in one day," barked Daniel.

"I do not."

"Okay, two days, then."

"Listen to me. All of you eat the honey too fast. The stuff is expensive, and we can't afford a new jar every week. I sometimes like buying things you boys don't like that much and that way they last."

"When I was you kids' ages," reminisced dad, "I ate molasses on bread with butter. We have both at home. Eat that instead. *Mmm*, just talking about it brings me to want one."

"Yuk, I hate molasses," retorted Daniel.

"Me too," agreed Tony.

"Me too," copied me. "I'm going to have a brownie instead."

"I've told you boys how many times not to use the word 'hate'?" reminded mother, with a hint of impatience. "Use 'don't like' instead. Tony, Gardiner

High students don't *hate* Cony, they *don't like* them, and only when it comes to sports. And, Daniel, you *don't like* molasses. The word 'hate' is too strong and should be used only for the worst of things, otherwise it's a sin. Which reminds me of what Father McIver said at the end of mass today, about everyone needing to do regular confession. I say *today*. He says it every week. Anyway, we need to go and soon."

"Sure. Whatever you say, Father Mother," returned Daniel.

Dad ignored the issue. "And if you *really* don't like something, you can use 'can't stand' instead of 'hate.' But try to mostly use the expression 'don't prefer.' It's not so negative. And as your mother just said, try to avoid using 'hate' because we hay—*can't stand* that word."

The back-route from Augusta to Gardiner was rural and scenic, and the road actually held the name River Road. Hallowell and Farmingdale did not exist on the east side of the Kennebec River, and there were no more bridges until Randolph. About halfway home the air began to stink, but not the same as the river. It was obvious we were passing near a farm.

"That smell is disgusting," stated Daniel.

Dad did not agree. "Daniel, I keep telling you, I keep telling all of you, it's a healthy smell. When the air smells like this"—he took in a long deep breath before continuing—"then you know things are good in the world. This is what God created earth for." Through the rear-view mirror he could see his boys pinching their noses and laughing at what he said.

"*Thanks for telling us that, Dad*," came Daniel, in a sarcastic, plugged-nose voice. The adult male took another deep breath. His childhood had been on a farm, but not his wife's.

"Herve, get through it. Please speed up."

"*Thanks for telling him that, Mom.*"

The boys giggled, still holding their noses.

Dad got angry and hit the gas. "Daniel, what did I tell you about saying that?"

"That I'm not supposed to, I guess."

"That's right. None of you boys are. You're not old enough. Especially you, Daniel."

Dad liked to sometimes use the expression "Thanks for telling me that." Daniel had picked up on it early in life, but he came to use it too often and, according to the adult male, at inappropriate times. This had brought down the rule about us kids not being allowed say it until we matured.

"Why again can't we use it?" asked Daniel.

"Because you don't know the right time. Only the master knows, and that's me." Everyone laughed. "Mostly I use it to manipulate the people I'm talking to, but only in subtle ways, to get the subject changed or to make them feel like they've said something important, even though most of the time they haven't. And, oldest son, *subtle* is not your style. Not yet, anyway. Learn from the master! All of you!"

Even the car roared.

"How do we know beforehand when you're going to use it?" asked Tony.

"You can't know something like that beforehand. It just happens when it happens. Whenever you're around the master, always keep your eyes peeled and your ears open."

Another roar.

Just prior to the right turn onto the Gardiner-Randolph Bridge sat Shep's Garage. The auto-body repair shop was a going concern in this part of the valley, and it employed a good amount of men who knew how to in one way or another make metal right. Shep's lot was always packed with dented and crunched autos and pickups waiting in line to get fixed or picked before being tossed. Dad slowed the car to an almost stop. Five heads turned, to review the recent arrivals. The driver behind us slammed on his brakes just in time to avoid rear-ending the Electra. He pressed mad on the horn, and dad stepped mad on the gas. All of us jerked back in our seats. We crossed the bridge and over the tracks.

"Mom, what does MEC on the trains stand for?"

"Why don't you ask your father? Don't think you have to be asking me about everything all the time. Spread it around. Ask him things, too."

"But, Mom, when I do, you always jump in when you don't like what he says."

She chuckled, "You're right. I do do that sometimes. I won't anymore. Or at least tonight I won't."

"Dad, what does MEC stand for?"

"It stands for Central Maine Railroad."

"Then why aren't the letters CMR?"

Again Daniel barked. "What difference does it make! Why is this important to you?"

"Just because you get to miss your favorite show *Jeopardy!* for a lousy job doesn't mean you can take it out on everybody else!"

"That's not the reason! It's because you're always wondering about everything! Can't you just be quiet!"

"Dan, you know better than that. He can't shut up," added Tony with his two cents.

Mother jumped in her seat. "Hey! Don't use 'shut up'! Use 'be quiet' instead!"

The adult male saw this as an opportunity to teach his children a sure-fire method. "Tony—and Daniel and Charles, for that matter—when you catch yourself using a word or expression you're not supposed to, correct yourself halfway through. Naturally, it's best to use a proper voice, but sometimes we speak before thinking, especially you boys. But it happens to almost everyone. Not me and your mother, mind you, and that's because we're older and more experienced."

"How's that, *Father?* Please explain to your passengers what you mean."

Sometimes in discussions with dad, mother used "Father" instead of "Herve." This only happened when she was questioning something he had just said or done, and there would be "edge" to her voice. Pressure was then on the man to produce a credible response or else risk losing personal dignity, even "face" with his family. Mother used "Hervey" and "dear" in opposite ways, when she was wanting of approval or feeling an extra warmth toward her hubby.

"This is what I mean. Tony, when you start to say 'shut up,' say 'shut—be quiet' instead. Eventually you'll use 'be quiet' only. When you catch yourself using 'hate,' correct yourself with 'hay—can't stand.' Your mother doesn't like the word 'stupid.' Mostly it's you Daniel who uses it. So, correct yourself by saying 'stu—silly.' And then there's that other word. When you begin to say it, correct yourself by saying 'shi—crappo.'"

The car and all its contents busted into a giant roar. Once settled: "Dad, Mr. Barry says 'Maine Central Railroad' and not 'Central Maine Railroad.' But then the letters should be MCR. I'm going to ask him next time."

Daniel refused to release my bait. "An R is not needed. Look at it. Isn't it obvious the thing is a railroad? Only a stu—brainless idiot would need to see an R. MEC must stand for Maine, then something that starts with an E, and then Central. We need to figure out what the E stands for. Next time at the library, I'll ask Glennis. She knows everything."

Daniel's answer was sufficient. I changed the subject.

"Dad, at home, can I make a hot chocolate to dip my brownie in? They're a little dry."

"Well . . . ? Sure, why not? Go ahead."

Mother said nothing and kept looking straight ahead.

"That sounds good to me. I'm gonna to do the same," stated Tony.

"Me too," came Daniel.

Dad informed the two older sons of the discordant situation. "There's only one brownie left. Since Charles asked first, he gets it."

In the predicament that had just developed, I thought it best to look straight ahead and pretend not to notice that two big brothers' heads were turned in and staring serious heat at the one positioned between them.

"Maybe they can have the last two cream horns. They're just as dry."

Dad quickly offered, "Dan and Tony, I'll make you both a molasses on bread with butter. How does that sound?"

"Oh-ah, that's okay, Dad. I'll have a dry cream horn with a hot chocolate."

"Me too," followed Tony.

I had one more question: "Dad, can I stay up to watch *Bonanza* with you and Tony? I don't have school tomorrow. Anyhoos, Mom says hot chocolate keeps me awake if I have it too close to bedtime."

"I don't see why not. Yes, you can stay up." *Bonanza* was the man's favorite show.

Mother did not say a word; she kept looking straight ahead.

Daniel asked, "Mom, what time is it?"

"Ask your father."

"Jeanne, I'm not wearing my watch."

Mother did not say another word; she just kept looking straight ahead.

"Daniel, check the clock when we get inside."

"Whatever you say, Dad."

During the show, it dawned on me that the adult male fashioned himself Ben Cartwright of the Monroe clan. I, too, began to believe him that. "Buck up, boys. Be the men I raised you to be. Just take your fingers and rub off all the things you don't want on your hot doggies." Logically, I became Little Joe, Daniel—Adam, Tony—Hoss.

Hoss and Little Joe landed in their bunks just after 10:00. The nightlight remained on so that Hoss could peruse his new *Popular Science* magazine. He paused, grabbed a different mag, and looked over at me. "Chuckie, try reading *Scientific American.* That way, for a change, you can learn about something important in the world and the universe instead of that garbage railroad stuff you like to talk about." He tossed it onto my bed. "Open and learn."

"Not tonight. Thanks anyway." I placed it on the nightstand and opened my most favorite book ever: *Treasure Island.* Soon, the freight train could be heard coming up from South Gardiner; it was running a little late tonight. I yawned, closed the book, and said goodnight to my brother. The Skowhegan-bound train carrying secret cargo reached Kingsbury Street and then instantaneously the section of track Mr. Stedmont and his crew had fixed. *Tick . . . tick . . . tick . . . tick . . . five . . . six . . . seven . . .*

Part II

The Invader

Chapter X

Jimmy's First Idea

First Mondays of summer breaks always had the youngster's spirit glowing in its new-found freedom, and in a very laid-back way: *Hey, Mom and Dad, what's the rush?* Different from the Mondays were the first Fridays, the day after prison-school let out. They tended to be highly celebratory, lived at an accelerated pace. The first weekends were even better, not that he and the family did anything much; rather, it was just the sheer euphoria at knowing a return through the gates of prison-school was a far two months off. Because July 4, 1966, fell on Monday, the weekend lasted three days, which meant that the first Monday was actually Tuesday. A few minutes before 8:00, mother bid her youngest son out of bed. . . .

"Aw, come on, Mom, what's the rush? Let me sleep a little longer."

"No. Get dressed quickly. Jimmy'll be here any minute. What did you say, Tony?"

"You know how he talks in his sleep."

"Sure seemed like he was speaking to someone over there in the old kitchen."

"If you wake him, he just gets angry and denies it."

"How come you're not up yet?"

Rushing wasn't in me, so I didn't. Sunlight slipped past the blinds' fringes, indicating a beautiful day was waiting out there. In truth, I had doubts about the summer, being that two intrusive personalities were going to be circling me at every moment of every weekday, pecking and pecking at me nonstop.

Frank was sleeping on the den couch; his "blanky" was tucked underneath his head.

"Marion has to drop him off at seven-thirty. He'll nap like this every morning. Make sure to always let him wake up on his own."

"Means I can't watch TV. Guess it doesn't matter because Jimmy'll be here. Can I have two toast with grape jelly?"

"Yes. Go sit and I'll prepare them. And say 'please' to you servant."

There came the muffled sound of the outer door being pushed open. Next, three soft knocks touched the inner door. Mother opened.

"Good morning, Doris. Hello, Jimmy. Charlie's right here."

"Hello, Jeanne. Have to run. Be back around four-thirty. Thanks again for taking Jimmy."

"Glad to do it. See you after work."

"Hey there, Mon—Charlie. What are you doing?"

"Just about to have breakfast."

"What? Did you just get up or something?" Jimmy glanced into the den. "Who's that?"

"Frank. He lives across the street. My mom's taking care of him this summer. Like you, it's just during the day. What are those big ideas you have?"

"Sure hope he doesn't get in our way. Today we can start building a tree house in your woods. Your dad's got spare lumber, don't he?"

"A tree house?"

"Yeah, *a tree house*. What else is there to do around here? Like I said at school, don't expect me to be playing basketball and watching TV all the time. A tree house will be fun. We can make it as fancy as we want. Hurry up and finish your toast. I'm bored."

I slowed my chewing, stared off to the side. "Hmm . . . What's your other idea?"

"That one's even better. I'll tell you next week, but only if we get the tree house done this week. Probably not gonna happen based on how slow you're eating."

Jimmy's idea seemed a pretty good one, but I didn't want him to know it. I felt that because of our strong personalities, power struggles would constantly go on between us. From schoolyard experiences, I knew that Jimmy could be played by my coming across aloof to everything he said. Keeping him frustrated and guessing would help me to stay in control of the options.

But, I had to admit, Jimmy had already captured some of the power. Besides his not wanting to watch TV and play much ball, there was another reality—the fact that I was caught between a rock and a hard place. Mother was getting $20 a week for taking him in, and she was expecting me to help make the arrangement work for all parties.

"Hi, Charlie! Is that your friend Timmy?"

"No, Frank, that's *your* friend Timmy."

"Hi, Timmy."

"The name's Jimmy, kid. Get it straight."

"Okay, Jimmy, I will. What are you guys doing today?"

"None of your—Not much, kid. Quick, Mon—Charlie, let's get outta here."

"Frank, why don't you go watch Captain Kangaroo and his buddy Mr. Green Jeans."

"I can't stand those two idiots."

"Turn it on anyway and watch something else."

Jimmy and I headed for the garage. The unit had originally been built as a barn for the main house. When cars arrived in the early 1900s, the barn was converted to a double garage. At that time, too, by way of the construction of our hallway, the garage became attached to the house. Dad stored lumber in several rooms on its second floor.

As well, ample beams and boards were piled underneath the structure. Back in the 1930s, cars were bigger and heavier than when they had first come out. To support the newer vehicles, the garage's undercarriage was lifted and leveled; thick posts were planted into concrete footings, and this made for a decent-sized crawl space underneath the floor of the garage. The opening was four feet in height and ran the entire width of the backside; the underbelly gradually lessened in height as one crawled forward, toward the front of the garage.

Over the years, dad and previous owners had stored heaps of wood on top of older heaps under there. The loose beams and boards were not arranged in any type of neat order, and so within the various piles could be found micro-crawl spaces and tunnels. The oldest boards nearer to the ground were rotten. The Monroes knew that many creepy-crawly things of various sizes and levels of meanness lived inside the nooks and crannies and in the dark crawl space as a whole. On past evenings when doing something in the garage, dad, Tony, and I had occasionally heard scratching sounds coming from below. A few times, heavy hissing and outright fights were heard; a few days later, the smell of a rotting carcass might have been picked up. There were fairly large holes burrowed into the ground toward the back, where it was darkest. How deep they went and what exactly resided in them no one knew.

The garage was big enough for three cars, but where a third car could fit was dad's workshop. He stored most of his better boards in there. The hallway, the stairs to the apartment, and the den constituted the section that was added in the early 1900s in order to connect the main house to the barn-now-garage; the addition was built with a second floor above, and it led into the second floor of the garage.

The garage's upper floor still had traces of the old barn. The floorboards were the same style of lumber as the original house beams: thick, long and wide, un-planed, dark gray, bedrock-hard. The east portion of the upstairs, which faced onto the west side of the Laithran property, had formerly been a combination chicken coup and pigpen. When the family first moved in, dad had to scrape four inches of very hard, foul-smelling dirt off its floor.

Over the years, Mrs. Laithran had several times mentioned to the family that prior to 1952 small groups of minor livestock had been kept up there during the winter months. The other months had the animals living outside in pens along our north side, right beside the crawl space's south end; there, the animals could remain hidden from neighbors' views and Kingsbury Street traffic. Mrs. Laithran always made sure to bring up the slaughter room, also located on the second floor, next to the pen-room. It was a narrow, elongated nook that held a "special table" back then. Throughout the former time, outright screams, desperate yelps, and the ghastly sounds of death were occasionally heard coming from the chamber, generally a day or two prior to holidays. We knew which room it was. There was definitely a funny feel to it, and the air exuded a strange, though faint odor. Everyone pretty much stayed out of it. Just after the family moved in, dad placed a latch high up on the room's door. A few years passed by before his kids were tall and brave enough to unlatch and enter. Spare boards were stored in there as well.

Jimmy and I went around to all of dad's inside storerooms. There was enough lumber to build ten tree houses, but all we needed was the right amount of the better stuff to build one. Boards that looked too nice were left behind.

While we picked, I thought about the best tree to build in. A large poplar located a few yards inside the home's north-side woods was conveniently positioned at the top of a sharp slope down into the mini-valley. I knew that if our big wooden box were built high enough in the tree, we would have views of the whole valley, the Bondy property, and the train lot, right down to the river. With the telescope I got last Christmas, Jimmy and I would be able to dig up hidden facts about people and places. *Wow, Jimmy's idea is fantastic! But don't tell him.*

I wanted to show Jimmy the tree before we began sawing. We headed around the house and onto the narrow stretch of lawn running parallel to its north side; the runway fringed the top of the mini-valley's southern flank. The walk took us past the crawl space.

"Jimmy, we should stop here and check under the garage for some more wood."

"*No, no, no*—not under there."

"*Yes, yes, yes*—under there."

"Don't we have enough?"

"We do, but we might find even better stuff."

We trampled down the tall crabgrass, to lay bare the entrance, and got down on all fours. Daylight enabled us to see five feet into the crawl space.

A dark underworld existed beyond that. Perhaps something under there was staring back at us.

"See the front edges of the woodpiles? Let's crawl under and check them. We'll have to keep a sharp eye out for small animals and large bugs. I don't know how we're gonna do that without a flashlight."

"Look at the size of that spider web over there! Heck, I've never seen a spider that big! I'm not going under. Something might kill us."

"Wait here while I go get my dad's flashlight."

"Even with a flashlight I ain't going under. You can go alone, and I'll wait here. If something kills you, don't expect me to pull you out. It can eat you, as far as I'm concerned."

"You're right. We have enough wood. Even my dad doesn't like going under there. Thinks he has to sometimes. Always takes his flashlight and my baseball bat along."

We backed away and continued, only to halt in front of the den window. The two-door, double-glass unit allowed persons inside the home to look out onto the stretch Jimmy and I were on: a 20-feet-wide flat zone that separated the house's north side from the mini-valley's steep slope down. The elongate section of land consisted of three distinct, parallel bands of vegetation. The first was made up of tall weeds and crabgrass, a section of which we had just flattened with our feet; past the crawl space, the band also contained blackberry and black raspberry bushes and wild strawberries. The next band was the grassy path we were walking on; its width ranged from five to ten feet.

The band farthest from the house was more like a natural wall that consisted of regular and black raspberry bushes, tall chokecherry bushes, trees, and bamboo. The band's width ranged from three to ten feet, prior to the slope down.

The land along here was a few feet lower in elevation than the opposite side of the house—the side that faced onto Kingsbury Street. As a result, the bottom sill of the den window was six feet above the ground. Twenty feet to the front of the window, just before the mini-valley's slope, sat an oversized black metal barrel.

Jimmy pointed. "What the heck is that?"

"Our incinerator."

"Why do you need it?"

"Every few days we burn some of our garbage in it."

"Like what?"

"Cardboard, gristle and bones, corncobs and other leftovers. Dad burns some of his construction scraps in there, too. See all the stuff on the ground?" Garbage was strewn around the incinerator. "An animal must have gotten into it last night."

"That sure is different. I didn't think normal people do things like that."

"Normal people don't, but we do. It's fun to see a flame coming out of it. But you don't want to be downwind. Sometimes we have to shut our windows on this side because of the smell of burning rubber, linoleum, and rotten meat and fat. The people in the apartment upstairs shut theirs fast because smoke mostly goes up and not sideways. You know that much, don't you?"

Jimmy pointed to the ground just below the den window. "What happened to those birds?" We walked in for a closer look at the three carcasses: one robin and two sparrows. Finding dead birds here was a regular occurrence ever since dad installed the window. On a Sunday afternoon two weeks after he had been put in, the family came home to find a massive owl lying dead on the den floor. Smashed glass was all over the room. The family was shaken by the gruesome scene. After the cleanup, dad got upset about having to replace the glass and screen, mother got upset about the expense, and Daniel and I remained upset about the poor owl.

Finding dead blue jays on the ground was also saddening. Then there were migratory birds that we did not what they were, except dead. Some were quite interesting to look at, prior to their getting tossed into the gully. Sometimes we saw or heard birds hitting against the window. Mostly they survived. Regardless, dead or alive, victims always left behind feathers stuck to the glass. So far only big owl had managed breakthrough.

The window was obviously an object of deception for flying creatures and probably not solely because of the clear new glass. The old house and barn had sat as separate units for over a hundred years. Maybe the birds sensed a former cut-through that did not exist anymore. Perhaps even more, they saw the window as an entrance to the old barn.

Because of the Native pathway, the mini-valley attracted all sorts of creatures. Undoubtedly, zebras, elephants, and giraffes had never walked it; pterodactyls and buzzards had likely not roamed the sky, either, except for maybe 60 million years ago. But what was also true was that many furry and feathery beings had in the past and still did use the area, during the day and especially at night. Some things were known to routinely creep up from the river after darkness had set in, and they could cause trouble for people along this section of Kingsbury.

Looking out from inside the den, one had a clear downward view of the incinerator and the gully; we often referred to this stretch of the mini-valley's slope as "the gully." Because of the bushes and trees that lined it, the view into the lower reaches was somewhat obstructed.

As a whole, the mini-valley was made up of thick bushes and trees of all tallness. There were several very old trees, some of which leaned a little sideways while a couple others so much so that they looked to be struggling at every moment to stay standing. Some had fallen over decades ago; large mushrooms and other invasive fungi could be found attached to them; tangles of Chinese cucumber vines also thrived in and around the same rotting hosts. I related the owl incident to Jimmy.

"When our neighbors found out, they scolded us for not coming to get them for a look-see. What I should have done was put it under a rag next to the sidewalk and charged people. But instead, I threw it into a hole I dug halfway down this here gully."

"Whew, you have a strange place. I like it. What else you got?"

"Hmm . . . Last fall an animal was getting into the incinerator at night and tossing things out. It must have liked eating the meat, fat, and vegetables that didn't get burned up enough. One Saturday night, my dad and my brother Tony and I were watching TV in the den. The window was cranked open because it was so warm. We heard noises coming from out here. Dad turned off the lights and TV, got his flashlight, and shined it onto a big male raccoon standing in the barrel. Tony quietly removed the screen from one side and whispered to dad to keep the flashlight directly on the coon's eyes so it would stay frozen still. He went for his .22 rifle, quickly loaded it, aimed, whispered to my dad to move aside, and fired. My dad jumped back and hollered, 'Why didn't you warn me!' He's got bad hearing.

"We went outside to look at it. Wasn't anything special other than it was huge for a raccoon. Dad told me to bury it the next morning beside the owl. I wanted to burn it in the incinerator, but he said no because the smell of the thing roasting might attract other animals. He ordered me not to tell anyone, but I did anyway. The neighbors again scolded me for not putting it out on our lawn.

"And I got another story. Three years ago a mother deer and her baby came up to the top of the path across the street. Me and a neighbor saw them just standing there. We watched to see what the two would do next. They started crossing the street for here, but when they saw me they stopped. We stared at each other for a few seconds, then they turned and walked back down the old ancient pathway into Rollins Woods."

"Old ancient pathway . . . ? What the heck are you talking about?"

"A long time ago, Indians used it for hunting prey. Went right through where our house now sits, and then down through the woods to the river. We're going to build our tree house just off of it. I'll think of more stories while we head there."

"That's okay. I've heard enough for one day. Save some for the rest of the summer."

"Means I can't tell you about the snakes that live in and around these woods. Nope, you said you don't want to hear anymore."

"How come you know all this stuff about some old ancient pathway?"

"An old wise man told me about it. He has lived around these parts forever and knows things no one else does. Says the animals can smell the old pathway, and that's why they still use it. All the animals, even snakes from all over Maine, try to find their way onto it. Jimmy! Watch out! You're gonna step on one right now!"

He gasped and jumped back. I laughed and walked on ahead of him. He ran up behind me. "*Ha-ha-ha*. Very funny, Monroe."

"Here, we made it. On the other side of this bamboo is the tree we're gonna build in."

"No way bamboo. You're right, it is bamboo. What the heck is it doing here?"

The bamboo patch owned a 15-feet-long stretch that went six feet deep into the woods, almost to the edge of the slope; the east end of the patch ended at the pathway. The bamboo had not only proven sturdy enough to survive a generation of harsh Maine winters, it had proliferated beautifully from its initial few skimpy saplings.

"Mrs. Laithran—she's our next-door neighbor—says a Captain Byrd planted a few saplings of the stuff about forty years ago. He had brought it up from Africa or South America, I can't remember which. Anyhoos, the stuff took real good, as anyone even like yourself can see."

"Who the heck is Captain Byrd?"

We turned onto the path. "He used to live in our house. Mrs. Laithran says he was a merchant mariner and captain of a ship that went all over the world. Sometimes he was gone for months and brought back things from some of the places he had been, like flower bulbs and grape vines and berry bushes from different parts of the United States. The flowers are all around the edges of our front and side lawns where they meet up with the woods. Some of the berry bushes are along where we just passed. He renovated our house and put in some real fancy marble from Africa. The stuff's at the base of our fireplaces. I'll show you later. Here's our tree. Look down over there. See that big fallen one? The grapes are all around its base and stump."

"You're right. This here tree will do us real good."

We climbed up, sat on a branch, discussed how and where to begin, what the unit should look like. The view was even better than I had thought it would be. To gain a more total view of the world below, right down to the train tracks and beyond, we would have to cut away tree branches along a fairly wide line down the mini-valley. Jimmy and I decided that once the unit was built, he and I would take turns climbing trees that had impeding branches while the other sat in the tree house shouting out instructions. *This is going to be fun, fun, fun,* concluded the mind. *But don't tell Jimmy.*

"I have a telescope we can use."

"Sure, but let's stop talking and start building."

Jimmy was turning out to be bossier than I had expected. Besides an aloof attitude, a keen sense of sarcasm would be the other half of my weapons arsenal against his overbearing nature. Our feet had just made the ground when we heard, "Charlie! Jimmy! Where are you? I'm lookin' for you guys!" We exited the path to find Frank standing on the end of the porch. He smiled, jumped down, and rushed up. "There you guys are. Whatcha up to? Can I play with you?"

It was right then that I realized Frank had no intention of staying by my mother, that he would always be looking to play with Jimmy and me. To prevent this, once the tree house was completed, the two of us would have to move around in stealth. When Frank could not see us, he would be looking for us. And when he did spot us from afar, Jimmy and I would turn and hoof it in the opposite direction. The best times for us to not be pestered while building the tree house would be when Frank was eating lunch and having his afternoon nap.

"No, kid, you can't play with us," responded Jimmy.

Mom was also getting $20 a week from Frank's mother. Hence, there was pressure on the Monroe boy to make that arrangement work, too. The fact that Jimmy was not taking to Frank complicated things. But Frank refused to be put off, for he was every bit as stubborn and combative as his freckled adversary.

By the end of the first day, the two had become archenemies. It showed in their constant battling to gain my attention. This was not a totally bad development, for I realized that one could be played against the other at my convenience. Whenever my agenda got challenged, cunning psychology could put things back onto "my tracks." That's how I figured it.

After his Wednesday morning sleep, Frank came to the garage. Jimmy and I were sawing.

"Keep out of our way today, kid," yapped Jimmy the instant he saw the tough toddler.

"You dirty rotten snipe, Jimmy! You can't be bossing me around anymore!"

I looked Jimmy in the eye. "Don't be so hard on him." I turned to Frank. "You can watch but don't get up too close, okay?"

"Why? I'm not causing any trouble. I just want to watch."

Jimmy couldn't contain himself. "Look here, kid, don't be getting on my nerves like you did yesterday. Listen to Charlie and stand back or else."

"I told Marion and Joe about how mean the both of you were to me yesterday."

This worried me. I did not mind anyone being angry at Jimmy. But the last thing I wanted was his parents, especially his dad, to have something against me.

"Why me, Frank? What did I do?"

"That dirty snipe is your friend. That means you're in my bad books just like him. That's what Joe said about 'bad books,' that you, Charlie, might be getting into his 'bad books' if things don't change over here."

"Jimmy, it's okay for him to get up close. I promise he won't be in our way."

"Yeah-yeah, right."

Wednesday afternoon Frank refused to go into the house for his nap. He sat down on the lawn in the hot sun and watched Jimmy and I as best he could. The bamboo mostly shielded us, but not completely. Jimmy and I quietly laughed to see Frank holding his blanky against the side of his face, sucking on his thumb, trying hard not to fall asleep.

Jimmy could not hold back. "Hey, kid! Go into the house to have your little sissy nap! Don't be so stupid and fall asleep out here in the hot sun!"

"I'm not stupid! You're stupid! And you're the sissy, with your sissy red freckles all over you. If I'm to fall asleep, it's gonna be right here where I can keep an eye on the both of you!"

"You mouthy little brat! I should come down there and slap your face silly!"

"Jimmy, why do you do that? Don't be so rotten to him. I'm going to get into big trouble if he complains to his parents again. Just leave him alone when everything's going peaceful."

"What are his mom and dad gonna say when they see him red as a beet with a sunburn?"

"You're right. I better go tell my mom." Jimmy followed me down the tree.

"Where are you going, Charlie?"

"To get my mother."

"Why are you doing that? Are you gonna tell on me, you mean snipe?"

"What the heck is a 'snipe'?" asked Jimmy.

"I have no idea."

Thursday, July 7, halfway into noontime, Jimmy and I finished the tree house. Daily, out there on the front lawn and in the hot sun, Lizzie had been at Frank's side, to keep him company. She had been far more patient than he. Every time Jimmy and I exited the path to take a break or get more wood, she wagged her tail and ran up to greet us. As far as Jimmy and I were concerned, the dog deserved a visit to the lookout.

I lifted her into my arms and carefully climbed the tree. Jimmy had taken a liking to Lizzie and though she was kind of in our way up there, he did not mind. She stayed with him while I went to get the telescope. Frank, finished lunch, was on the way out.

"Are you and Jimmy done? Can I go up in it?"

"We still have a few things to do. Shouldn't take more than a few weeks to a month or two. We'll decide whether you're old enough then."

"Okay, Charlie. Why are you going into the house?"

"I need to go to the bathroom."

My return found Frank standing at the edge of the woods. He looked angry.

"How come Lizzie gets to go in the tree house and I don't? I'm telling Marion and Joe."

Frank had picked up on my "Marion and Joe sensitivity" and was playing it at every opportunity. I wanted it to stop, so I shrugged my shoulders at the seething tot. "Go ahead. See if I care." But I certainly did care.

Jimmy and I spent the rest of the afternoon taking turns in the tower and at the saw blade. We decided that a break from the Monroe residence and Frank was needed. The next day, Friday, would be for swimming up at The Oaks. Later, when we asked our mothers, they agreed to let us go.

Chapter XI

Jimmy's Other Idea

Below the dam ran 40 yards of rapids, after which Cobbossee Stream widened, and this produced an immediate and marked slowdown in the water's flow. Along the south-side shore were short stretches of shallow water bottomed in fine-grained sand, perhaps better described as sandy mud. The Oaks was a 30-yard run of beach starting at about 150 yards below the dam. Behind the beach was a steep hill leading up to the gathering area and snack bar. Beyond The Oaks, depth of water lessened and grade of channel steepened, forcing the stream to become on-and-off rapids right down to its entryway into the Kennebec River, almost a mile away. Remnants of four old, torn-down dams existed along the course.

On hot days, the beach could get packed tight with kids of all ages, but predominantly below 15. Really young children were usually under the supervision of their mothers or grandparents. Our moms had given each of us a dollar, enough for admissions, sodas, and snacks. The Monroe matron dropped us off after lunch, with parting instructions to walk home and be home by 4:30. That gave us three hours of beach-time. This day, the place was thronged and noisy.

LeClerc, Broten, and Kiley were there. Because of my feeling responsible for Jimmy and the fact that he had never been close to those guys, I decided to stay separated from them.

The day turned out to be the best so far. The feeling must have been mutual because later in the afternoon, while taking a break from swimming, Jimmy shared some fascinating information. For the first time, he seemed like a regular guy, relaxed and not bossy.

"The other day my dad was telling me about the big eels that live inside this here stream. A whole bunch are in the rapids just below the dam. They can't get any farther up. There, they hide in the rocks. All the other broken down dams below here also have lots of eels. There's even some moving back and forth on the bottom of this here section we're swimming in. Some guy named Dusty sets out traps for them, not around here but farther down. He catches all kinds, but he can't set any nets just below the dam because the flow's too fast and rough.

"My dad says the eels come all the way up from the Atlantic Ocean every year to spawn in the Cobbossee. Says for them to get here they have to swim along the bottom of the Kennebec River, and on the way they get all fat and plump eating our shit."

"Hey, Jimmy, you better be careful about saying the SH word. If there's a dragonfly close by, it'll attack you and sew your lips together, and you won't never be able to speak again. That's what Tony told me when I was a kid and said that word."

"It's okay to use 'shit' when you're talking about real shit. It's at other times you're not supposed to use the word 'shit.'"

"What does 'spawn' mean?"

"Means the eels leave their eggs in the sand at the bottom. After the eggs hatch, the babies head downstream into the Kennebec and swim to the ocean. Because they're born here, they have the instinct to return when they're grown up and want to have their own babies."

"What does that Dusty fellow do with the eels?"

"I asked my dad the same question. Says the guy sells them to expensive Chinese restaurants in New York City. People there love the taste, and they'll pay a big price for it." Jimmy changed the subject. "I thought for the rest of the summer we could do a weekly newspaper and sell them for a dime to people in your neighborhood. That way we can keep busy and earn some spending money at the same time. We can write about the things we do and find. It's my mom's idea. She says adults will buy the papers just because we're kids and they want to help us stay busy and out of trouble."

"How do we make a newspaper?"

"First, we make one the way we want it. Then we copy a whole bunch of them to sell."

"How do we sell them?"

"How else? We go around knocking on people's doors."

"How many pages will it be?"

"Just one. My mom says we only need enough stories to fill a single page. It would be too much writing to do more than that. She says we need a lot of short stories. Things about us and about the neighborhood and maybe about other things if we think they're interesting. Anyway, if people want more than one page, they can read the *KJ*."

"Like what types of things do mean, about us and the neighborhood?"

"Like I said, things we do and things that happen. People might like to know about them. We can go about on the streets and in the woods looking for stories. We can spy through your telescope when we're up in the tree house. Shouldn't stay in one spot all the time, and that way we can keep Frank guessing where we're not."

The idea seemed as good as Jimmy's first one. And I really liked the part about being out of Frank's sight. Outwardly, I remained non-committal.

We arrived home just as Mrs. Prudhomme was crossing Kingsbury, to pick up Frank.

"Hello, Mrs. Prudhomme. How are you doing on this beautiful summer day?"

"Don't be getting so smart with me, Charlie," she gruffly gave back. "I'll be right now having a talk with your mother about you boys' attitudes."

"Oh-ah, Fra-Frank was a very good boy all week. He's just a little too young to do some of the things Jimmy and I like to do, and he doesn't understand that. But we don't want him to get hurt."

She sneered at Jimmy, turned away, went inside. I looked at him. "The newspaper is a great idea. We can start working on it first thing Monday morning."

Almost right away she was back outside. "Frank! Frank! Where did you disappear to!"

"I think I know where he is. Please wait here while Jimmy and I go check. Don't worry, Mrs. Prudhomme, he'll be safe once we get him down."

Mother's toasted crabmeat sandwiches came served with potato salad and wax beans. During supper, a massive sheet of gray cloud moved over top of Gardiner. Mother asked Tony and me to listen to the local news for the area's weather forecast.

"Ma, it's supposed to rain all weekend. How come you didn't do some shakes of paprika on our crabmeat? You know how much Chuckie and I like that stuff to be put on."

"How about you get up off your rear-duff and put some shakes on it yourself," came dad.

Soon, the two adults entered the den, to watch *The Huntley-Brinkley Report*. Coming out of the Vatican II meetings, which ended last year, the Church has decided to let Catholics eat meat on Fridays.

"Well, it's about time. But I don't know if we can trust the news. We'll have to ask Father McIver about it on Sunday."

"Jeanne, they wouldn't say something like that if it wasn't true. And to be honest with you, I'm sick of having to eat fish every Friday."

Mother did not respond. The rain began and quickly intensified. "What do you say, Hervey? Should we do the wallpapering this weekend?"

"No because I want to use tomorrow to cover the boys' walls with those soundproof tiles."

"*Father*, it can wait. Tony and Charles, you'll have to be at friends' places tomorrow and Sunday. Just be home by suppertimes. Tomorrow we'll get Gerard's Pizza. For Sunday, we'll see."

The two boys cheered. We liked Gerard's pizza even more than hers.

"I'll give Wilson a call tomorrow morning and see what he's up to," said Tony. "For Sunday, I'll probably go over to Arthur's house."

"What about you, Charles?"

"On Sunday I'm going to the Barry's for the afternoon."

"Again? So soon? Did they invite you?"

"Yup. And tomorrow I'll go down to Mike's."

Daniel wasn't an issue; it was not necessary to ask him how he would busy himself. After work today, he stopped by the library to sign out a new novel Glennis Neely had put aside for him. Currently, the two were lying on the living room couch. Tomorrow would have him returning the book and staying there the rest of the day. Sunday afternoon would be for his devouring of the two Sunday newspapers. Tony and I were the ones mom and dad had to be on top of.

Later, up in bed, we kept the nightlight on. Tony opened his *Shooting Times* and I my *Treasure Island*. He tossed the magazine onto my bed. "I dog-eared a page. Take a look at the beauty I circled in red pen. That's what I want for my birthday, a .22-caliber Ruger. Comes with a nine-shot clip that slides up into the handle. Imagine how much fun we can have with it."

Tony's birthday was at the beginning of August. I briefly studied the unusual-looking handgun, closed the magazine, and tossed it back to him. "Looks pretty good, but it won't to Mom and Dad. Have you shown them yet?"

"No. Have to wait for the right time. Definitely not this weekend."

"They usually give in on everything. Just takes more time for some things." I yawned and closed the book. "I'm too tired. See you in the morning."

There would be no train passing through Gardiner. I missed its sleepy sounds on Friday and Saturday nights.

Chapter XII

The Beat-down

Saturday morning, the rain came down steady and hard. The three boys stayed in bed late. Wilson Donnelly showed up at 11:00; this was not supposed to happen. Tony got up and led him into the basement, for some target shooting. Kid-brother and Lizzie followed. Tony was always good about letting me hang around him when a friend was over, but only for a little while. Lizzie, on the other hand, could remain with them the whole time, if she wanted.

Like Mike was to Charlie, Wilson was a year older and five years wiser than Tony. Kids from West Gardiner had to grow up that way—tough and life-smart. The Monroes really liked Wilson, being that he was highly animated and opinionated, but in a fun-spirited way. He loved to laugh and joke around. When he said things that were off the wall, no one ever felt offended. However, the teenager did tend to hang too close to a particular four-letter word. In our house, he was careful, but when not in the hearing range of the adults, he allowed himself leeway.

Tony told Wilson about the no-talking rule when handling the rifle at certain key times. He did that because kid-brother was there.

"Okay, to start, I'll take five shots, then you can do the same. We'll go back and forth until all the bullets are gone. I have two boxes. Should last us if we don't race. Ah, Wilson, Chuckie will rat us out if we don't abide by my dad's rule."

"You won't do that, will you, Charlie?"

"*Yyyup*."

He laughed it off. So did Tony and I. But they somewhat obeyed.

Tony took five shots and passed the rifle to Wilson. "My car's bin runnin' like effin' . . ." BANG—"crap lately. . . . Have to fix it before I start my effin' . . ." BANG—"senior year. My dad's bin drinkin' again. . . . Lately he's bin gettin' violent. A few effin' . . ." BANG—"weeks ago my car wasn't runnin'. . . . Where's the effin' . . ." BANG—"thing when ya need it? Broke down, that's where. . . . One night he got upset at me about some little effin' thing, and he effin' . . ." BANG—"attacked me. I had to run from the house. Here ya go, it's your effin' turn."

"I'm lookin' to get a brand-new . . ." BANG—"handgun for my birthday next month. It's called a Ruger. . . . The thing has a nine-shot . . ." BANG—"clip that slides up into the handle. . . . Can you imagine the . . ." BANG—"fun we can have with it. . . . No one should want to come around here . . ." BANG—"trying to cause trouble. . . . They better have more than . . ." BANG—"ten people if they want survivors to tell their side of their slaughter. Here, your turn."

"The night I ran away, I was walkin' along effin' . . ." BANG—"Brunswick Avenue. It must have bin around three . . . in the morning when an effin' . . ." BANG—"cop car pulled up beside me. Ralph Cates was inside. What a sight, to see a lieutenant working the overnight shift. . . . Anyway, he took me to the effin' station and was real nice to me. I know his effin' . . ." BANG—"nephew Ron. It's too bad Cates got himself murdered. . . . And of all things, while he was in the line of effin' . . ." BANG—"duty. On top of that, right near to where I live. Go figure. Why the department hasn't made . . . a proper effin' arrest is an effin' . . ." BANG—"travesty of justice. Here ya go. Be effin' careful not to effin' shoot me."

"Chuckie here was all upset about Cates getting . . ." BANG—"killed, like they were friends or something. I personally don't remember the guy. His nephew, either."

"Ron? He's okay, I guess, just like the rest of us effin' guys around this age, dreamin' too much about how and when we're gonna score that first effin' slice of banana cream pie."

"Mom doesn't make that kind. Wakefield's Diner does. Try there."

The two busted out laughing. I turned red. *What did I say? What's so funny?*

"Last year I had to use this Remington to . . ." BANG—"take down a big male raccoon."

"You've already effin' told me that story, remember?"

"Oh, right. . . . Well, anyway, there's been something else getting into our . . ." BANG—"incinerator the last few nights. . . . I want to take it down with my .308, but Dad won't . . ." BANG—"let me. Chuckie and I've had our eyes open for it . . . but so far it's been able to . . ." BANG—"elude us. The mess it leaves behind . . . means it's probably pretty . . ." BANG—"big. I've been saving a couple long-rifle . . . hollow-points for the . . ." BANG—"job."

"Tony, that's effin' six shots you just took. Pass the effin' thing over to me right now before I wrestle it away and effin' shoot you dead right here. . . . What's goin' on in this effin' . . ." BANG—"basement of yours, with the effin' water creepin' our way?"

"Floor drain's plugged. Sometime this summer Dad and I are going to unplug it."

"Looks like you better get to it sooner than later or someone's gonna effin' . . ." BANG—"drown down here. . . . Next week I have to move out of my house and relocate to effin' . . ." BANG—"Augusta, of all places. . . . I'm gonna live at the effin' . . ." BANG—"YMCA for a while. . . . My mom needs to get out before he effin' . . ." BANG—"kills her. . . . What's effin' worse is that I'm gonna have to attend effin' . . ." BANG—"Cony High School."

"Chuckie, time to give us space. Go tell Dad how bad the water is backing up."

"Bye, Nelson."

"Take care, Charlie. . . ." BANG. "There ya go, Tony. I took effin' seven shots because you took effin' six your last turn."

At the top of the stairs, I yelled, "Wilson, don't give it up yet! Take a few more shots!"

"Shut your face!"

"You're not allowed to say that! Use . . . 'be quiet your face' instead!"

Mom and dad were finished one wall. The man looked at me. "Your mother and I are not supposed to be able to see you."

"Tony just told me to *shut my face*. Isn't that as bad as using 'shut up'?"

"I don't have time for that right now."

"Dad, the rainwater's backing up worse than ever. It's almost reached the shooting table. Bye. I'm off to Mike's."

"Thank you for telling me that. It's just the news I've been waiting for."

"Son, before you go, your father will be picking up pizza from Gerard's at six. Be home by then. Herve, the water down there really upsets me. Can you fix it sooner than later?"

The man's face turned dour. "Jeanne, we're wallpapering."

I whispered, *"Mom, can I stay and watch wrestling on TV? Starts in a little while."*

"Ask your father. And take these two peanut butter and jelly sandwiches with you."

"I heard, and it isn't wrestling. Watch it at the place you are *immediately* leaving for."

"But I'm pretty sure champion Bruno Sammartino is fighting Crybaby Cannon, and I don't want to miss it. Mike's sisters always hog the TV and never let us watch anything we want. Anyway, you like wrestling. You watch it with me and Tony sometimes?"

"You're way off base. If it happens to be on when I'm in the den reading the newspaper, I *might* catch a glimpse when I'm turning a page. I don't see you anymore."

Mike and I had talked earlier on the phone. Because of the poor weather, we postponed our search for the underground tunnel to next Saturday. The air was cool, crisp, and clear, even with the rain. The thought came to do a short stint in the tree house. I pulled the telescope from the garage.

Slowly, I scanned the mini-valley. Nothing. I moved the scope to the old train track and right away picked up three persons. I focused in. The man with the funny blue cap was there. Beside him were a blonde and an old, weathered-looking fellow. The blue-capped man had hold of a bottle, and he raised it to his mouth for a swig, then passed it to the woman. She did the same and handed it to the old guy. The drenched threesome halted. The blue-capped guy seemed to get angry. Suddenly, he sprang onto the hobo and beat him down to the ground. With one fist raised, he straddled the old guy, who looked to be pleading for his life. The woman latched hold of the guy's bindle stick and rifled through the sack. She picked out a bill and some change, then tossed the sack and stick onto the ground. Calmer talk ensued. The hobo was released and allowed to stand up. The blonde hand-brushed the dirt and mud from his jacket, straightened his hat, and the three continued on, toward city core.

The ark's roof and the leafy branches above it had proven to be good cover from the rain, so I left the telescope there. As I came onto River Road, haunting memories of that winter day returned. After I told the sisters to call an ambulance, the driver directed me to go with Godspeed to the top of the hill, to stop oncoming traffic. Before running off, I was compelled to look down at Mr. Donahue. What happened next took all of a split-second, as if time had come to an almost-stop—my first experience with this strange phenomenon. His face showed blotches of red, blue, and purple. I heard a voice in my head: "In death comes life." More words came, but I would lose them later that day. And a final sentence: "Will you live it for me?" I took off up the hill.

Fortunately, because the weather had deterred most drivers from trying the road up from South Gardiner, so far no vehicles had lurched onto the scene. I arrived at the top of the hill and waited on the sidewalk. I could see Mike down at the bottom, standing in the middle of the road in front of his house. He had already stopped three southbound cars. Far-off sirens were heard getting louder. A car came along. I waved it down. The driver rolled down his window.

"Sir, there's been an accident halfway down the hill. A man has been run over and the police and ambulance are coming right now."

"I can hear them. Son, you did good to come up here and stop me, but you're too young. I'll take over and you can go."

I ran back to the scene. The ambulance and police car arrived. The sisters emerged from the house and carefully descended their front stairway; the snow there had yet to be shoveled. The attendants put Jim Donahue onto a stretcher and carried him to the back of their vehicle. Blood gushed from the old man's nostrils. His face was now ice blue, but he was still alive. The sisters made it to the street. They burst into screams and tears at the sight of their dying sibling. The driver, who had been kneeling over the body up until the ambulance arrived, became very emotional at seeing this. The senior officer, Lieutenant Cates, directed him to go wait in the police car, then instructed the other officer to go to the bottom of the hill and talk to the drivers of the stopped cars, at this point numbering five. Next, Lieutenant Cates showed concern for me. We talked. Jim Donahue died that afternoon in the hospital.

As for the now-deceased lieutenant, it had been six months since his untimely demise during a New Year's Eve bash at the Gardiner Sportsmen's Club, located a mile up Cobbossee Stream from the dam and notorious for its potential for late-night scuffles.

Just before midnight, a distress call went out to the Gardiner PD. Things were out of hand at the club and help was needed. The night before New Year's Day tended to be busy for police departments throughout the country, and though a small center, Gardiner was no different than bigger cities. The department was stretched thin, and only a single man in blue could make it to the club right away. Cates happened to be him. Dispatch warned that backup would take time.

Twenty minutes later, the second unit arrived to find the parking lot empty, except for the first responder's car. With tense right hands on holsters, the two officers rushed into the club. It seemed no one was there, but they knew this could not be true. Then they noticed a body lying on the floor in the midst of strewn tables and chairs. The officers hastened to their lieutenant's side. The barely-conscious man writhed and moaned, obviously in a state of consummate distress. He was rushed to the Gardiner General Hospital, where he died two hours later.

Because there had yet to be proper arrests, major concern and an undercurrent of fear had been gripping the community ever since that fateful eve. Area people were waiting . . . waiting . . . waiting for some arrests. Rumors about who had actually been at the club that night remained unconfirmed. What deepened the mystery was the lack of communication from the PD and the lack of reporting from the valley's primary public defender, the *KJ*.

Too, to consider: Lieutenant Cates had not been a recent arrival from a far-off city. He and his family had a long history in the area. His siblings, nieces, and nephews lived throughout the valley, and they were beyond antsy for real answers and real charges. Joyce Cates, a niece of his and a classmate of mine, showed the same disturbed spirit of her greater family.

Something was up. But what? For the first couple months, the PD's silence had perplexed folks. A feeling that there was an emerging lawlessness within our midst began to encroach on people's psyches. The last two months had heard less and less mention of the slain policeman. Uncomfortably, things seemed to be returning to a fashion of normal. It was not that the unsolved slaying of one of our finest was being left for future Maine historians to deal with, nor was it believed best for the truth to be eventually granted a place in the gray annals of local folklore; it was just that the folks around here were growing sick and tired of being upset and frustrated about everything in the world. Gradually, the good people of Gardiner seemed to be conceding to a form of healing—an improper healing—because that was better than no healing at all. There were very worrisome things going on in the world: the war, the race riots, the nuclear threat. Were not these issues enough to be upset about?

The nation's honor was under challenge. There was the Space Race to the moon, a race against a nation that four years earlier had tried to put nuclear missile silos inside Cuba and point them at America. A year later, the Kennedy assassination took place. Americans were not convinced assassin Lee Harvey Oswald had acted alone. A few days after his arrest, while being transferred to arraignment, Oswald was murdered on live television. I saw it. Mother did not believe me when I rushed into the kitchen to tell her. How could something like that happen? He was in the middle of a team of Dallas detectives when shot by a strange guy named Jack Ruby. This added to citizens' belief that a cover-up of some kind was definitely going on. Nightly, local and national news programs presented informative updates on so many of the critical issues of the day, and the spirits of all watchers were constantly left coping with a jumble of frustrations and question marks. Why dwell so much on Cates? Was not what happened to him nothing more than a minor puzzle-piece inside America's king-size jigsaw puzzle of 1966? *I'm glad to be a kid,* thought I, somewhat soaked, making it onto Mike's rickety steps.

"Good. You're home on time. We're finally getting through to you. Dad's washing up. Go with him to Gerard's. You know how he likes to have company. Even yours."

"That's funny, Mom, but can't Tony go?"

"No. He's in the middle of cleaning his guns. How does the kitchen look?"

"Really nice. Are you done?"

"We have just a little left to do. Dad and I still want you and Tony gone tomorrow."

"The walls look empty without the religious pictures and crosses up."

"I want to arrange them differently, maybe even replace some of them with regular pictures. I'm going to take the time to think about it."

"Good. You're home. We're finally getting through to you. Jeanne, what do I get?"

"Two double-pepperoni pizzas and two Italian sandwiches. Also, a large bottle of Hire's Root Beer and a big bag of BBQ chips—but King Cole and not Humpty Dumpty because they're too hot. Here's five dollars. Should be enough, shouldn't it?"

"I certainly hope so. Prices haven't gone up that much. Charles, let's go."

After placing the order, dad and I got back into the car and headed for Gardiner Fruit. The soda and chips could have been bought at the pizza place, but the adult male was of a different thought. Mr. Bill was at the till. Dad asked him about the Cates case.

"There were out-of-towners involved. I hear whispers they're connected to persons of importance. Cates was held while others beat and kicked him. His insides got busted up real bad. He never had a chance. Some there did stand up for him, but it was too late because the hardest blows had already been landed. Witnesses are afraid to speak up. That's what I hear."

When another customer entered the store, Mr. Bill ended the discussion. Some of his information was already out there in the public domain, some not. For obvious reasons, from the get-go this youngster had held a keen interest in the Cates case. As far as he was concerned, something had to be done to bring the perpetrators to justice. If there were any chance at all, the boy would take the matter into his own hands, for that was how passionate he felt about it.

"Elli, you can also ring in for an El Producto and five chocolate bars. Charles, get your mother and me a couple Heath Bars and Daniel a Clark Bar. For Tony, you know what to get."

"Can I get something for Lizzie?"

"Sure, but don't get her anything with chocolate. Dogs get worms and diarrhea from it. Your mother really likes her new living room rug. Brown would not go well on it."

"Yeah, I know. You've said that before. I'll get her a PayDay."

After supper, Tony and I went outside to play ball. Parked beside the Prudhommes' Fairlane was a red Corvette. Frank was outside and saw us. "Charlie and Tony! Donald's home from the Navy!" Donald, still in naval attire, exited the house and headed for his car, a 1961, to unload.

"Hey, Donald! Welcome home! Can Chuckie and I see your car up close?"

"Sure, come on over!"

Donald did not have to be dressed in such a grand manner, but he wanted his mother and father to see him that way. He was thrilled to be in the Navy, and his parents were extremely proud of him. He let us sit in the vehicle. After that, he lifted the hood. The engine looked strange, alien. Though it was easy to see that Donald reveled in owning such a renowned sports car, most of his comments were about the mechanical problems he had been having with it. He said he was fed up and wanted to sell it off.

Tony thanked Donald. So did I. Brother rolled his eyes. "This is my constant echo in life." I turned red. Donald laughed. We were hoping to watch *Wagon Train* when we got home. But, to our utter dismay, the parents and Daniel were watching *The Lawrence Welk Show*.

Chapter XIII

Captain Cornelius and Two Dollar Eva

On the way to church, mom reminded dad to ask Father McIver about eating meat on Fridays. Dad balked. "I'm not bringing the subject up because the Pope's already decided."

"Then I'll ask him at his yearly visit. We should all go to confession before then."

Father's sermon was on the mysterious ways of God. A particular part hit hard at the hearts of some of the folk there, including the parents.

"Our dear Lord often works in *wisdomic* ways that are difficult to understand and accept. He is far more generous than we humans tend to be. Today's Gospel reading has Jesus' parable about the workers who were hired late in the day getting paid the same wage as those hired in the morning and at noon. The others don't like the idea and think they are being cheated. The owner of the field responds that he can do whatever he wants, seeing it's his money. Jesus is not referring to human owners of businesses here on earth. He is referring to God the Father, Who owns all of heaven and earth. Human owners would go bankrupt operating like that landowner, but God cannot because He doesn't use money but instead infinite grace. His love and mercy are available for all humans who humbly go to Him to confess fall-downs in moral uprightness, even if it's at the end of life. Now isn't that a wonderful thing to know? Regarding our relatives and friends who are away from the Lord, a kind and gentle tap on the shoulder is what they need, so that they may consider reattaching themselves to the One Who can deliver them.

"But, to their own disfortune, many of these persons try to hold God in some kind of judgment, and that's because they think they've been hard done by. But I say it again—God works at levels we humans often do not fathom.

To help explain, I say the following. While we tend to plan our lives in the hours, days, and weeks to come, which, in my humble opinion based on my many years of being in this world, is what most people do, He as well works in those short segments. But even more so, the Lord works in years, decades, and centuries. This truth is shown throughout the Good Book. But who exactly reads it these days? Dear parishioners, do try to reserve time on Sunday evenings to peruse the excellent offering.

"Now I return to my point by bringing up the following situation, and with only tenderness in my heart, for it is meant for your gentle encouragement. At a previous parish of mine, a young couple lost their child. She died at only two years old. As you can imagine, the parents were thoroughly grieved. They asked me why God allowed this to happen. For me, as a priest trained in both seminary and decades of parish work, the answer is evident. But for the persons directly affected, their emotions can be so intense that no explanation will do.

"You see, dear folk, God sometimes comes to take the most precious flower in the field as His Own, and sometimes it's a baby. The parents miss the love of that little baby so much, and it hurts them beyond what words can describe. There is now a hole in their hearts. But what if that baby had never been born? Yes, I ask you, what if she had never even been conceived? They wouldn't know the love of that baby, and they wouldn't miss her. How can a couple miss what never was? Would they want God to do that, to wipe out the occurrence of their having that wonderful little girl and therefore wipe out their memory of her? Even to consider such a thing would hurt even more. They would shout 'No! We never want to forget her! Our memories of her are precious!' So you see, the baby was truly a gift from God.

"Our dear Lord, as Catholics are taught, keeps baby souls in a special place called limbo, and there the babies await their parents' natural leaving of earth, so that there may be a reuniting above. This in and of itself is a heavenly thing to look forward to. So, dear parishioners, please do not wait until some future time to be more loving and understanding toward others. May I add, too, that none of us is allowed to rush the process of getting off earth, for we must depart by God's terms and not our own. . . ."

In the car-ride home, the parents talked about Jerry, their firstborn, who died four days into his life. Jerry had always been a subject mom and dad could not handle past a few words. This time, however, the two talked openly of their being glad to have held him in their arms for a few days, before he left. When done, mother quietly cried. The boys stayed silent. I thought about the time she talked of dad's breakdown in the week following Jerry's passing, and how it had been hard for her to remain strong for him in the face of her own grief.

Father had been involved in the Pacific theater of WWII. While there, he received news of his mother's passing, from a heart attack. Weeks later, he got news that his 18-year-old baby brother Henry was KIA in Italy. The private had been involved in the landing at Anzio Beach Head; a few days later, he was killed by a hand grenade in the German's counterattack. Dad had not been allowed leave-time and thus had been internalizing an ocean of pain up until Jerry's death. For a week, he wept for all three of them. Their future boys would never come to know grandmother, Henry, and Jerry and therefore never miss the loves our mother and father still did.

Once again the Biscayne beat the bikes to Randolph. During the splendid meal, I described the incident I had observed from the tree house. At first, no one said anything. A minute passed and the matriarch came out. "You boys best stay away from that area down near the river. Searching for things you don't know about could get you into trouble. Anyway, Mike, you'll be leaving tomorrow for Camp Bomazeen. You'll be gone for what, two weeks?"

"Yup."

After another short silence, I went again. "On Friday at The Oaks I heard about how every year big eels swim up the Kennebec River from the ocean. Then they go up Cobbossee Stream to have their babies. They can't get past the dam. Some guy named Dusty sets traps for them, and the ones he catches he sells to expensive Chinese restaurants in New York City. The people there just love the taste. When the eels run the Kennebec they get all big and fat eating our sh—" *Stop! Dragonflies! Dragonflies will attack! Quick, Chuckie, think!*

All around the world, clocks slowed to an almost-stop. I glanced around the table. Nancy and Janice showed dropped jaws, and they looked at me with eyes that screamed *No!* Mr. Barry stared down at his meal, waiting for me to expose my developing character. A shocked Mrs. Bondy shook her head—*no, no, no*—while at the same time mouthing the word. The matriarch and Peter continued their eating.

There was no backing out. The subject had been raised, people had been listening, and I was required to finish up in some way or form. Mike elbowed me.

". . . *ortcomings* and whatever other little whatnots they might find."

Laughter swept the table. While fooling no one, I had managed to escape sharp stings.

"Is that right, Allan?" asked his mother.

"Almost, but not quite. The eels do indeed move as Charlie said, but they actually live out most of their lives in our freshwaters, the ones that they can reach, that is. They spawn somewhere out in the Atlantic. Eels do it reversed from the stripers."

"Thank you, Charlie and Allan. I find that story very interesting. I suppose the eels get themselves washed out pretty good in our Cobbossee. That waterway is still fairly pristine, although given more time man will pollute that one as well. The herbicides and fertilizers farmers use these days are full of chemicals."

"Mother, the water below the dam isn't that pristine. The factories add in their own types of shortcomings, and the eels have that as well in their systems by the time they make it onto the plates of New York restaurants. As for me, I sure wouldn't eat one of those slimy things."

After the get-together, Mike and I went for our bikes. Mr. Barry approached just as we were to pedal off. "Listen up. Like Nanna Barry said, you both need to be careful down there along the old tracks. I'm not blind. I know you'll do whatever you want when no one is around. But I tell you this for your own good. Charlie, that guy you saw yesterday, the one wearing the hat, his name is Cornelius. He goes by 'Captain Cornelius.' His great-grandpappy was from Hallowell, and he fought in the Civil War for a tough Maine regiment. Cornelius inherited that Union cap from his dad, who had gotten from his own dad. The thing is a relic, but Cornelius thinks he has to wear it all the time, and it's getting ruined. The woman he usually has with him is named Eva. People around these parts have nicknamed her 'Two Dollar Eva.'"

"Why is that?" I asked.

"Uncle, be careful with him. He's a little too young for that stuff. How come you know?"

"Hey, watch the mouth. How I know is because one night up north in the logging camp a bunch of us were sitting around the campfire. A couple guys who came from this area got talking about them. Everyone laughed and made jokes about her, but not me. I just kept quiet. Other things I know about them come from people around here just talking, but especially from cops I've come to know. Anyhoos, Mike, you should know better than to think bad of me?"

"Yes, Uncle. I'm sorry. You're right."

"Okay then. They said Eva gets money from men for certain types of favors. But that's the smaller part of the game. These guys who go to her tend to be low-types, and sometimes they get bragging to her about some of the bad things they've done. In other words, they spill their guts just for the fun of it. She then gives the information to Cornelius. He protects her. Nobody in his right mind messes with him. A tough fighter, smart, got every angle covered. And then there are the bums that pass through. No one gets by him unless they pay up in some way. It doesn't have to be money. It can be something material that he might like to have. If they aren't willing to fork over, they get beat up and sent back the way they came.

"Police from around these parts know him, and they're willing to pay him a little something to get information they might otherwise have to dig hard for and still never get. A couple dollars or a large bottle of Fairview's cheapest sherry will do him just fine. He also likes the hard stuff. There's always a two-quart jug of Kentucky bourbon in police reserve as reward for information that turns out to be particularly helpful. You guys probably saw an assortment of his empties when you were exploring along the river some weeks back.

"A big score can happen for Cornelius when a guy comes back for another visit with Eva. If Cornelius has something on him, he'll shake the guy down for five bucks, maybe ten. If the guy doesn't want to pay, Cornelius might start to rough him up or threaten to go to the police with whatever he's got. The man is cunning in these type of business matters. Next, he'll play the police, offering them bits and pieces, slowly, so he can get paid a few times and not just once.

"But the good thing is that as rough as Cornelius can get, he doesn't like having to beat down on anyone. It might hurt business. He mostly threatens and pushes. After the guy or the drifter pays up, Cornelius puts on a smile and tells him to come back any time, as long as he makes sure to be a good citizen, peaceful about business matters and all. He and Eva keep two rooms at the rooming house just town-side of Baileys. You guys know the place. It's that dilapidated building across the road from the library."

"Sometimes I see them sittin' on the front steps," confirmed Mike.

"They also do a little bit of honest work, keeping the inside of the building clean and doing custodial work for the City when asked. They keep the other renters in line and collect monthly rents for the landlord. But alcohol is a huge problem for them. When drinking, they can get very foul. Even with all I've said, their money mostly comes in piecemeal, so sometimes they search for empty soda bottles along the tracks. They won't do it in the more open areas because to do such is below them, they figure. Good for you two that they don't, huh?

"The camp guys said Cornelius has a another strange way, about how he likes to be addressed with respect. Those who do it get treated less harshly. If he's in the right frame of spirit, he might even let them pass through free."

"How does that happen?" Mike asked.

"He wants to be saluted. At the same time, the visitor should say 'Ay, ay, Captain Cornelius' and follow with something like 'And how are you doing on this sunny summer day of 1966? I hope good. To help make the day even better I bring you a gift, and it is my hope that in doing so I may gain peaceful passage through your camp.' Years ago, when he was in his twenties, someone tried it on him. By then he had already renamed himself Captain Cornelius. Got it from the Bible. People learned about it, and when that visitor addressed him in such a grand manner, he took to it and told the cunning hobo to inform everyone else who intends on passing through that if they do the same, they'll get treated better than they normally would.

"Cornelius and Eva are smart. They could have made something better of themselves. Drinking has always pulled them down. That's enough about those two. And as far as you two are concerned, work on your pedalling. You'll never win, but at least you could make it a little more competitive for the next times."

"Mr. Barry, I have a question. What does MEC stand for on the train cars?"

"Where did that come from—left field? Maine Central Railroad, of course."

Chapter XIV

Fresh Kills to Report

Just before dusk, the rain stopped. Figuring for a half an hour of playtime, Tony and kid-brother went outside for hoops. A few minutes went by and an explosion of hisses and animal yells shattered the calm air. Half the sound seemed to emanate from an animal we knew, the other half from something we did not; both combatants were hidden in the bushes. BJ, the cat with attitude, was known to patrol the property's perimeter along its border with Rollins Woods. He was now in the throes of a serious scrap. With what? We knew it wasn't Lizzie because we had left her inside the house.

Donald ran out from his side-door, straight for wood's edge. He hollered at something, but the vehemence continued unabated. He ran back into his house and quickly re-emerged with a flashlight in one hand, a handgun in the other. Near the entrance to the old path, he stopped, shined his flashlight into the brush, and raised the gun. *Blam. Blam. . . . Blam. Blam. Blam.* He lowered the gun and was about to descend the slope when BJ raced past him.

"Hey, Donald, did you get whatever it was!"

The Navy man straightened up. Our streetlight, based in ground just off the Prudhommes' sidewalk and 15 feet up the street from their concrete steps, lit the street and portions of both his and the Monroes' front and side yards. He seemed a little put-off to discover us watching.

After a moment: "Yup, sure did! Come on over and see, if you want!"

"I've never seen BJ run like that," said Tony as we came up. "Was it a bobcat or a lynx?"

"Nope, a mother raccoon and her three kits. BJ must have gotten between them. Had to kill the mother because she had hold of him and wouldn't let go. The kits can't make it without her, so I did them, too. Didn't enjoy it. BJ never aggresses, only fights in defence. Buddy learned that a few years ago. Maybe someday Lizzie will get a chance. Hope not, for her sake."

"What's your gun?" asked Tony.

"A thirty-eight. I'll remove the last bullet. Here, take a look. Use the flashlight."

"Thanks. Yup, nice piece. Good to have around, just in case." The two laughed. Tony pretended to shoot the .38-caliber into the woods, before handing it back to Donald.

"What's that I hear? Animal banshees crying out about these dead raccoons?"

"Nope. They're whip-poor-wills. But standing here it sure sounds like they could be banshees. In the morning, I'll bury the bodies down-slope a ways. Let me shine the flashlight onto them so we can get a good look." The three of us studied the dead bodies for a half a minute. "You brothers take care of yourselves and don't have any bad dreams tonight."

I as well knew that it was a family of whip-poor-wills behind those sounds, and that's because Donald had told me the same a few years ago. On the way home, I asked Tony what banshees were. Once inside, he recounted the incident to the parents. Dad said that last night an animal had gotten into our incinerator and that he hoped the dead raccoons had been the culprits.

The anticipated knocks came just after 8:00 a.m., then the sound of the kitchen door opening. "What? You're still eating breakfast?" Frank was on the den couch. "Hurry up and let's go before he wakes up." Too late.

"Hi, Jimmy. Are you and Charlie gonna be nice to me this week and not a couple dirty rotten snipes like you were last week?"

"What are you talking about, kid? We weren't bad to you. And I'm getting sick of you calling us snipes. Try something else for a change."

"Yes, you were, too, bad to me. From now on the both of you are booger snots."

"Frank, I was nice to you last week, wasn't I? Don't you remember how it was just Jimmy who was rotten?"

And so, the second week of summer began pretty much the same as the first: irritatingly.

"Where do you want to start?" I asked.

"Anywhere that's outta here and right now."

"Oh, will you just shut—be quiet your face and sit down. Let's talk about things while I finish my cereal. Explain again to me how we should do the newspaper. I want to make sure I agree with you or not."

"What we need to do is get out there and find more stories."

"'More'?"

"Yeah, *more*. We already have our lead. It'll be about the tree house."

"We built a tree house. So what. What else is there to say about it?"

"We spent a lot of time working on it. People might want to know. That's what my mother says. She wants me to bring home a copy for her and my dad to read."

"That's a pretty . . . okay idea. Maybe I should do the same."

"You can write the master copy and keep that one for your mom. But first we use it to write out a bunch more. We should do five each and then sell them for a dime apiece. With the money we make, we can go to LeClerc's and reward ourselves."

"I totally agree with you. Let's go. My mother said for the next two weeks it's okay for us to go down along River Road and the train yard. There might be some good stories there."

As we entered our search into truth, I thought about Jimmy's expectation that I write the master copy. I had no inclination to tussle with him on it. In school, his ability to write proper sentences had lagged. This, I surmised, was the real reason Jimmy's mother wanted him to do a newspaper, so that he could work on this skill.

Past the Bondy house, we came up on a dead skunk in the middle of the road, directly in front of Mr. Monahan's place. The man must have seen us through a window. He came out.

"Come up close to me, boys. I have something to ask of you."

"Hello, Mr. Monahan. My friend Jimmy and I are looking for articles for our newspaper."

"That's good, but I got something even better for you to do. Go get the shovel that's leaning up against the left side of my garage and bring it out here so you can scoop up that smelly dead thing. Then you can heave it real good over the bank on the other side of the road. You'll have to be careful about the traffic. Now please do as I ask."

"Mr. Monahan, I have a question. When the paper is done, will you buy a copy? It'll cost you only a dime. Jimmy and I'll be doing one every week."

"Sure, why not, if that's what it'll take to get that dead stinker outta my sight, ya little manipulator. Being that way ain't such a bad thing. How old are you, Charlie?"

"Twelve."

"Old enough and same as a teenager, as far as I'm concerned. Means you're almost a man. I need you to mow my lawn this weekend. Pay you a dollar an hour. You'll earn it because I want the lawn raked up afterward. Young as you are, you'll probably have to ask your parents. Might take a couple hours if you work hard like a man. What do you say?"

"Yup, I'll do it. But, like you said, I better ask my parents."

"If you do a proper job, I'll be wanting you back here every time. Starting this winter you can shovel snow from my driveway and walks. At seventy-six I'm too old for that stuff. I'll need you when I need you. Will you help out this old guy or not?"

"Yup. What time do you want me here on Saturday?"

"Mid-morning, around ten, no earlier. Now go scoop up that smelly little corpse and scoot up the hill to the opening where the old tree went down and heave it with all your might as far over the bank as you can get. Remember what I said about the traffic."

Skunk on shovel, Jimmy and I jogged up River Road, to the opening. With a quick swing of the shovelhead, I yelled, "Heave ho!" Along this part of the road, the track below came tight against the steep bank. My intent was to throw the flattened unit beyond the track. Jimmy and I looked down to see it land smack between the two rails. He pointed. "Who the heck are they?"

"Oh sh . . ."

"'Oh shit,' what?"

"It's Captain Cornelius and Two Dollar Eva. They're looking up at us."

"What yas punk kids think yas doing! I'll bash yas brains in for throwin' that at us!"

"Run, Jimmy, run."

On the other side of the road, I went to a walk.

"Shouldn't we still be running?" asked Jimmy.

"No. Slope's too steep and bushes too thick for them come after us."

"What were they doing down there?"

"Maybe just going for a walk or maybe doing lookout or maybe searching for empty soda bottles to return to Gardiner Fruit for money. The place pays three cents for a small and five for a large. Don't you know that?"

"I don't bother with empty bottles."

"Well, I do. There's money in it. Sometimes people in cars toss theirs before making it into downtown. That steep bank beside Bailey Auto is a gold mine, and those two hobos don't like to search for bottles out in the open. But we will later. Too bad beer and liquor bottles don't get anything. Nobody picks them up and now they're everywhere. Boston Coal's parking lot sure has a mess of them."

Jimmy said a dead skunk made for a good second-lead story, but I convinced him that we should put the raccoon incident in that spot. We headed for the rail yard.

MEC was written on four boxcars. A line of empty ore-carts had SOO LINE on them. Wooden pallets were haphazardly piled near the station's south wall. One pallet had been busted up, and its wooden remains were strewn all about the main track. Loose strips of metal strapping were everywhere. Numerous colorful little piles of product, left from dropped bags and boxes, decorated the gravel beside the team track. Grasshoppers and bees were larger in both body and number versus the prior week. To top it off, the rainy weekend had left many mud puddles on the dirt's surface; a really large one was pooled at the south end of the lot.

"Why did we come here?"

"To find a story or two."

"I sure don't see them."

"Listen to me. The railroad is important to Gardiner and America. Everyplace in this beautiful country of ours passes through here. City folk need to know what America sees."

Jimmy frowned. "Okay, Monroe, whatever you say, even though there ain't been no passenger train for years. Remember the paper is only one page and you're doing the writing of the master. I don't like saying it, but you're right. The place is an embarrassing mess."

For a while, we had fun bantering the title. Finally, Jimmy said for me to go ahead and name the paper *whatever*, since I would be writing the master copy.

Late Wednesday morning, returning from an unsuccessful search for stories, Jimmy and I came up on the Dells' 1963 Mercury Comet parked at the side of the road, just up from their property line and across the street from our east woods. Something didn't feel right. Shovel in hand, Mr. Dell came jogging out from his backyard.

Still a ways off, he hollered, "Did you guys see it!"

"See what, Mr. Dell!"

He arrived. "Never mind. I'll find it. And when I do, there's going to be trouble."

He walked a few feet into the woods and using the shovelhead, poked around and pushed aside the low brush and leaves.

"What is it you're looking for?" I asked.

"There you are! Gotcha, I sure do!" He shoveled something out onto Kingsbury Street, then rushed over to it. "Now that your slithering body is out here on the road, I can take care of you in a proper way!"

The rope-like creature tried to regain the woods, but it was to no avail. "You must be the biggest garter snake in the world! See if I care!" The grounded reptile looked to be over four feet in length. Mr. Dell chopped down on the snake's midsection, cutting it in half. "You must be a thousand years old! See if I care!" In a passion, up and down he went. "There! There! Take that and that! Just in case you ever got the notion of making a nest in the Dells' rock garden—well, now you won't!" In short order, the formerly great legless beast of earth was scattered into little pieces. Mr. Dell stopped to catch his breath. He looked at me. "Charlie, how come all the animals of Maine aim themselves for your yard? Were you and your buddy building some kind of Noah's Ark last week, with all the sawing and banging I heard coming from your place?"

"Well, kind of, I guess. My friend Jimmy and I are writing a weekly newspaper for the neighborhood. You can read about it if you buy a copy from us Friday. It'll cost you only a dime. This snake story might make it in."

"How old are you?"

"Almost a teenager, as far as I'm concerned."

"And what about you, Jimmy?"

"Me too."

"I'll only need Charlie, but just to be polite I thought I'd ask you the same question. You're both almost men, though neither of you are near the physical unit my son Bruce was at your age. No matter, Mrs. Dell and I could sure use you come this Saturday, Charlie. The lawn needs to be mowed, and there are a few other chores needing doing. We'll pay you a dollar an hour. Probably three hours of work. What do you say—will you come by?"

Though not ecstatic, I agreed. The Dells' property came in three parts: a small front yard with two flower gardens; a huge backyard that had apple trees, a big vegetable garden, and a couple storage sheds; and a daunting side-yard that contained a steep hill, a couple rock gardens, and pear and plum trees. Likely the Dells would want me to clip the edges.

After Jimmy left, I informed mother of my pending jobs for Saturday. She felt her youngest was taking on too much, but I convinced her that I needed to earn my own money. "Aw, come on, Mom, they say I'm man enough. And men need money to spend, don't they?"

"No, not really. Not in this house they don't, not unless I agree first. Does Mr. Monahan have a gas or a push mower? Never mind about going down there to ask him because I already know. In the past, I've seen him struggling with a little old push. You're definitely not man enough for that thing, especially if his lawn is long. You should ask your father about using ours. Not tonight. Wait till Friday evening."

Thursday morning, Jimmy and I began to prepare the master copy. The effort required planning. As we discussed each topic, I wrote in pencil, so that I could erase and rewrite and erase and rewrite again. We wanted people to find the articles fun and interesting, and that way the next edition would be an easier sell, maybe even a breeze.

The headline story was titled BUILDING THE ARK OF KINGSBURY, the second-lead BIG BJ THE CAT AND GIANT RACOON FIGHT TO DEATH. The three lesser stories were UNKNOWN VEHICLE KILLS SKUNK DEAD ON RIVER ROAD, GIANT GARTER SNAKE SLICED TO PIECES, and LOCAL RAIL YARD A BIG EYESORE.

It took right to Mrs. Ford's arrival, at 4:30, for each of us to finish printing out seven copies each, two more than we had originally planned.

Even with that much time, Jimmy and I had been required to remain focused, diligent, and constant in the use of our fingers.

Friday morning, we covered lower Kingsbury, Mr. Monahan, and parts of Dennis and Prospect Streets. Jimmy turned out to be a super-salesman. "Charlie here lives at twenty-five Kingsbury Street and I'm his friend from school. We're trying to keep busy and stay out of trouble by writing a neighborhood newspaper. Will you please buy a copy and help us out? It's only a dime. Has some very interesting articles in it."

Almost every person bought one. A few commented, "A dime? The *KJ* costs fifteen cents." Still, they bought. Some houses had nobody home. There was only one person who flatly refused us. Mrs. Robbins was in the middle of polishing off a coat of wax from her dark green 1959 Cadillac El Dorado when Jimmy and I accosted her.

"Let there be none of that nonsense with me. Charlie, listen here. I believe I've told you this before, but you were with a different friend at the time. You boys make sure to never get even one drop of that brook water in your mouths. I know it looks clean, but believe you me it isn't. Travels West Gardiner's outer farmlands, then slowly muddies its way through Sheehan's Dairy's pastures. All their cows walk, crap, and piss in it. If you don't heed my warning, ptomaine poisoning and dysentery will cut you down before you make even ten steps. You'll have to have your feet amputated right down there along the water and then walk around with crutches the rest of your lives. Now, have you seen Kenny?"

"No, we haven't, but have a good day anyway. Goodbye."

"And goodbye to you, too, I suppose."

We were sold out by noon. At lunchtime, Jimmy and I counted our take: $1.50. Two customers had refused to accept change from their quarters, and that's why we had an extra 30 cents. We skipped mom's dessert and went for LeClerc's Market. I picked out a Frosty Root Beer, a Mallow Bar, a small bag of King Cole BBQ Chips, and a nickel-pickle, even though it was a dime now. All were destined for my immediate consumption. I grabbed a large bag of BBQ chips and a big root beer for the family.

"That'll be ninety-five cents, and you still need to pick out your penny candy."

"I'm too big for that baby stuff now. Ah, Mr. LeClerc, is it okay if I owe you twenty cents until next Friday? We'll be back here then. I have only seventy-five on me."

"I suppose, but be a man about it and don't make me have to ask you. Did you see Raymond playing ball across the street?"

"Yup. And after we leave here, we're going over there to show them how to do it right," joked Jimmy. He did not buy much: just a small soda and chips.

When I asked him why, he said he wanted to show his mom and dad most of the money he had made.

We played ball till 4:00 and went home. The Ford's car was in the driveway. The mothers were pleased to hear of our successful newspaper launch, and both were looking forward to reading it that evening. After Mrs. Ford and Jimmy left, mother informed me that starting a week from tomorrow the Fords would be away on vacation for three weeks and at the end of the summer they would be moving to South Paris, Maine.

"Now, for better news. They want you to go with them to a movie tomorrow evening in Waterville. They'll be by at five-thirty. You'll need to be washed up and done eating by then."

"Mom, Waterville is close to Skowhegan, isn't it?"

"About halfway between Augusta and there."

"I have to ask dad about the mower. Mr. Monahan wants me down there at ten."

"Best to ask him after supper, when he's watching the news. I see you brought home large chips and soda—for everyone, I presume. At a commercial, ask him if he would like some. Then ask about the mower. He just might say yes without having actually heard the question."

The news began. A commercial came.

"Dad, can I get you a bowl of BBQ chips and a glass of root beer?"

"I just ate. What do you want?"

I ignored the question and went to the kitchen. Mother winked at me.

"Jeanne, Johnson's sending more troops to Vietnam. That does it for me on the guy. Hope Nixon runs again. Make a better president, and he'd get things straightened out over there."

"Yes, dear, but remember, I'm a Democrat and not a Republican, like you are, so I don't necessarily have to agree with that assessment of yours."

"Dad, Mr. Monahan and Mr. Dell want me to mow their lawns tomorrow. Mom said it's okay with her but to make sure with you. They have their own lawnmowers. They'll be paying me a dollar an hour. Is that okay?"

The commercial ended.

"Fine. Jeanne, them negroes are rioting again. This time it's in Detroit. Where's this country of ours going?"

"To the moon, Herve, and before the Russians. Might help things along if our government asked Jackie Gleason to go down to NASA and inform our scientists what else will be landing on the moon right after the Russians, if they do end up beating us there."

"We're lucky to live in Maine. Negroes don't come this far north. Don't like the cold."

"Dear, that's not quite true. There are some in Portland. Remember how twice we saw them sitting out on their front steps when we made wrong turns driving through the city?"

Dad looked away from the TV, took hold of his glass of root beer. "John Dell has a gas mower. Does Mr. Monahan?"

"No, he has an old push."

"That's nuts. Probably as old and rusty as he is. Use ours. Walk it down there and don't ask for a ride. Hmm, a dollar an hour. That's pretty good for a kid. What are you, thirteen?"

"Yup. Kind of."

"Do you know how to start it?"

"No."

"You just put one foot on the mower and brace yourself with the other foot. Then you pull the cord with all your might. Tony'll show you. Where is he, anyway?"

"In the basement."

"Go call him to come up here. Jeanne, I think you're right about NASA needing Jackie Gleason to go down there and kick their—"

"Herve, I say it again, don't count America out. It's not over until one side makes it to the finish line. I've heard we're catching up. Haven't you heard the same?"

"Yup, but when it comes to our government, I don't like thinking positive till I have to."

Tony arrived. "What is it you want, Dad?"

"I'll need your help tomorrow. After work today I dropped by the City to borrow one of their long snakes to unplug the hole. It's in the basement. Did you see it?"

"Yes, and I put it together. You and I can take turns jamming the thing into the hole."

"Go show Charles right now how to start the mower and about being careful with it."

Mr. Monahan was waiting outside. "Thataboy, Charlie! Good idea bringing a gas mower! I read your newspaper. You said about being able see everything down here with your telescope. When you notice that my lawn is long, just come down and do it. Now, about that Donald fellow. I could use him to take care of a few varmints that have been getting on my nerves. Have him give me a call. I'll write my phone number on a piece of paper."

Because I knew Donald would not have taken well to an article on the raccoons, Jimmy and I had passed on trying to sell him a copy.

"And you're right about that messy rail yard. This week I'll be dropping by there to have a talk with the manager—that Mr. Smith guy. Don't know if that's his name, but the name Smith is the best chance I got of being right."

The job took two hours. Mr. Monahan wrote me a check for two bucks. I was pleased and anxious to show it to the parents. Pushing the lawnmower home, I came up on the Donahue sisters working on their front flower garden.

"Hello, Charlie. My sister and I have been talking about you. Your ears must have been burning because, well, here you are, and with a lawnmower of all things. Would you be able to mow our lawn right now or this afternoon or perhaps tomorrow sometime? Please say 'yes.' We know we can trust you to do a good job for us. There was another young man we could have asked, but we didn't. Will you help out a couple humble old ladies?"

"Yes, I'll be glad to. And if there's clipping you want done, I'll do that, too. I just finished Mr. Monahan's lawn. This afternoon I have the Dells' to do. Tomorrow is when I can come here. They're paying me one dollar an hour. Thought I should let you know."

The quiet one: "A dollar an hour? Sister, what do you think?"

"We have little choice, Catherine. Charlie, that'll be fine—*maybe*. We'll talk more on it tomorrow. And bring this gas thing of yours so the job won't take as long as our old push."

Chapter XV

Lawn Work in Low Purgatory

John and Kay Dell were in their mid-50s and ranked up there with the other nicest people in the world. Mrs. Dell was a housewife and every bit as accomplished a gardener as Mrs. Laithran. Mr. Dell was a shop teacher at the high school and also head of the department. The man knew everything about carpentry, fixing auto bodies, and repairing engines.

The Dells' yards were immaculately kept. Even so, this young man did not perceive the adults to be unreasonable. Perfection would not be expected, but *almost* perfection would be. They had nothing to be concerned about; the right man had been hired for the job. He had already been tested by the hayfields of Mr. Monahan and was now ready to take on green acres.

"Kay and I read your newspaper. Not bad. Work on the spelling. We're a little concerned about that eyesore Maine Central calls a rail yard. They need to clean it up and get a grader in there to level the lot. Thanks for bringing it to our attention.

"And about those raccoons Donald smoked. They were probably on the way to your place to try out that new ark. Fun to read about. Keep it up. Make sure to bring your next copy here first. Time to get busy. I logged you in five minutes ago, and here we are talking."

The Dells operated differently from Mr. Monahan. He had kept checking in on me, sometimes stopping me for a chat. A short man with thick glasses and scarce a hair left on his scalp, he spoke with gruff Irish vocal cords, but his sound waves were not as raspy-grained as Father McIver's. Mr. Monahan was, to put it bluntly, "mouthy," in that he frequently used sarcasm and humor to punctuate his speech and to help get his points across. There too was the perpetual hint of nip and pipe smoke inside his personal airspace. All of it made for a magnetic personality. I really liked the old fellow. He had children and grandchildren. They lived out of town and were prone to visit only infrequently. Mrs. Monahan passed away many years back.

The Dells, on the other hand, were not avid talkers, even with each other, and especially when there was work to be done. No longer was I the kid who walked past their place. I was now their hired hand, and I knew that there should be no appearance of dawdling at any time.

The Dells had raised two daughters and a son. Bruce had recently married and moved to Augusta, where he was a teacher. Prior to the move, he had been the groundskeeper and maintenance man up at the Gardiner Nursing Home, the same place Mrs. Bondy worked. During winters there, he had been allowed to use the place's snowplow to clear his parents' driveway after snowstorms. Tony and I always made sure to wave and cheer him on whenever he drove down and up Kingsbury, laughing and pointing at us, while we toiled at the shovel.

Sharon Dell lived in San Diego, California. She was married and a secretary. A time back, Mrs. Dell mentioned to mother that Sharon and her husband had successfully scaled the Matterhorn and that the two were planning to take on Mount Kilamanjaro next. Mrs. Dell expressed concern that her daughter and son-in-law were becoming risk-takers when instead they should be concentrating on their careers and raising a family. She said that when she had broached the concern to her daughter, Sharon became impatient and argued back that her and her husband's climbing mountains together was, on the contrary, helping their relationship.

The Dells other daughter, Nora, was a nurse at International Harvester in Ohio. She and her husband had two boys. A little later in the summer the boys would be visiting their grandparents for a few weeks.

Mrs. Dell had also revealed that Nora and her husband were in the process of "transitioning." I happened to be in the kitchen when mom was relating the story to dad. Daniel was there. When I asked what "transitioning" meant, he cut in, "It's when someone goes from being dumb to being stupid." Mother stamped a foot, but then laughed, admitting that more often than not the process of change ends up being exactly that.

The first hour seemed to go fast. *Piece-o-cake*, I thought. *A newspaper—hah! That's not real work. I like mowing way better than snooping around this neighborhood only to end up sitting and writing for hours on end. . . . Good, the front lawn is done, except I have to clip the edges. . . . Okay, I'm ready for the huge back one. Oh, right, they don't want me mowing over the apples that have prematurely fallen. Gotta pick 'em up first. Move the mower slowly, so my time can add up. . . . Wow, this ain't no lawn, it's and outfield. . . . Almost every house has that same little storage shed like this one here. . . . I've never seen so many weeds in a garden. I sure hope they don't ask me to weed. Don't prefer weeding at all. Clipping's bad enough....*

Every so often, Mr. or Mrs. Dell walked past my area, but not real close. I pretended not to notice them. They seemed to not look my way, yet I knew they were checking on me.

I want to do a good job for Mr. and Mrs. Dell. They're really nice people. I'm definitely going to make time to play with their grandchildren. . . . Mr. Monahan and Mr. Dell say I'm almost a man. They got it wrong. I am a man. . . . This section is taking too long. The Dells will probably want me to clip the tall grass hugging their sheds. Think about the money, Charlie. That way you'll stay positive. . . . A dollar an hour is way better than a few dimes for a lousy little newspaper. This is the type of work I enjoy, and it's real man's work. . . .

The second hour ended just as I began the third lawn; it had that wide, long, steep bank.

This is awful. . . . I'm too tired, and I haven't even started the hill. . . . Can't stand doing hills. I ain't no man yet. . . . It's too steep! I can't do it! Oh, no! Here comes Mr. Dell!

"You're doing a fine job, Charlie. Mrs. Dell and I are pleased with your effort so far. When Bruce was your age he never had a problem with that there hill. How about you? Can you handle it or not? Looks like you might be struggling. Are you tired or something?"

"No, not at all. Not yet."

"That's good to hear, but you've only just started it. Come over and get me if you decide to decide differently."

I hate this hill. . . . Muscles are sore everywhere. . . . After this I go home. Then I get to go to Waterville. Can't wait. . . . The Dells better not ask me to weed. I'll just say no if they do.

Halfway through the third hour I finished. Mrs. Dell asked me to weed the vegetable and rock gardens. She had already finished her front flower gardens. Reluctantly, I agreed.

Weeds are everywhere! How can I possibly do all this? Should have said no. . . . I'm still a kid, and kids never do weeding because it's against the law. . . . The Dells better not ask me to play with their grandchildren. . . . Concentrate on all the money you're making, Chuckie, because the newspaper pay peanuts. . . . Doing a newspaper is more fun than yard work. But yard work is real work and the newspaper business isn't—keep telling yourself that, Chuckie. . . . Yard work is awful. Mother says we shouldn't use hell. If weeding ain't hell, then it's purgatory—low, low purgatory, right down there at the edge of hell. . . . Who needs money, anyhoos? Some things just aren't worth money. I can't stand doing lawns and I hay—hate weeding. . . . There. Done. Finally. I better get paid right away. And I'm never coming back!

"That's a fine job you did for us, Charlie. Mrs. Dell and I will be having you back next week, if it's okay with you and the lawn is long enough. Is it okay with you?"

"Yup."

"That's what I want to hear. And you're fine to do weeding, right?"

"Right."

"Good then. Mrs. Dell will leave the front flower gardens for you to do with the others. You worked three and a half hours. Come in the house with me and I'll write you a check."

Another check—yeah! I love doing yard work!

Mr. Dell played it up. He took me into his office and pointed for me to sit in the chair next to his desk. He sat down, lit his pipe, reached for his book of blank checks, and opened. Slowly he wrote one out and carefully removed it. He shook my hand and said, "You earned every cent. You almost remind me of Bruce, but not quite. Have a good day, Charlie."

I arrived home. "Hi, Mom. Got another check. Three-fifty this time."

"That's fine, dear. Now you can hand both of them over to me to hold for next Friday. You'll have to come along with me that day, so we can open up a savings account for you. This is a good way to get paid. Stops you from rushing out to spend all of it right away on silly things, like one of your brothers does."

"What? I have to wait till next Friday for my money? This is awful. The Donahues better not try to pay me by check tomorrow. I'm going to demand cash if they do."

"Charles, calm down. Tomorrow you must be polite to those two old ladies. They're very nice and they're desperate for your help. I really doubt that they'll try to pay you by check. Now, go have a bath right away. You really need to. I'll have supper ready when you're done. Be fast because the Fords will be here in an hour."

The bath relaxed me. If it were not for the totally enjoyable evening to come, I probably would have gone straight to bed. I had no idea what movie we would be seeing.

The Fords were on time. We turned onto River Road, and Jimmy's dad noticed a long line of empty SOO LINE ore-carts parked on the track. He slowed down. "Let's each of us count to ourselves as fast as we can how many cars there are and compare what we get. On your mark, get set, go."

One, two, three, four . . . five . . .

"Charlie, wake up. We're in Waterville. Your mom said you were tired so we decided to let you sleep. Now you'll be able to enjoy the movie."

"Thanks. I really needed that."

The movie was *Country Singers of Maine.*

"Charlie, wake up. The movie's over. Did you see any of it?"

"What-huh . . . ? Oh, right. I guess so, but I can't remember."

They laughed.

"You've slept enough. Try to stay awake so Jimmy can have someone to talk to other than his dad and me."

"I can't believe I missed seeing that famous country singer from Maine."

"Who's that?" asked Mrs. Ford.

"You know, that Glenn or something Miller fellow. He's from Bangor. Sings *King of the Road* and *Engine, Engine, Forty-Nine*. They're on the radio all the time."

Mrs. Ford turned to her husband. "Dear, I don't think we saw him in the movie, did we?"

"Nope. But who needs him? Me and my good-as-new six four Plymouth Belvedere are king of the road tonight. Right boys?" He hit the gas and slammed his hand down on the horn. The backseat cheered.

"I don't recognize you, so I won't use the word 'dear' until I know my husband is back."

"I'm still your dear—king-of-the-road dear, you bet I am." He hit the horn again, and the backseat cheered again.

Shock and disgust came over Mrs. Ford's face. "Sheldon, please!"

"Those two are real songs and not like the crappo my brother Tony listens to."

"Why, what does he like?" asked Mrs. Ford.

"Frankie Valli & The Four Seasons. Whenever *Big Girls Don't Scream* and *Walk Like a Man* come on the radio, he puts it louder."

Jimmy: "I hate those songs."

"Me too," said Mr. Ford as he pressed down on the horn. "King of this here road, I am—yes, I am, tonight."

"*I said*, 'I don't recognize you' . . . *dear*."

The time was just before 9:00, and the sun was almost down. At Waterville's southern fringe, Jimmy noticed a line of railcars on the track.

"Charlie, don't count them."

"I sure will too and out loud. One, two, three, four . . . five . . ."

"Ah, Mom and Dad, he's asleep again."

"No, I'm not. I'm just kidding."

The whole car roared.

Chapter XVI

Plugged Hole Taken On

The good priest's sermon was on Noah's Ark. He claimed God did not need Noah to save all the living things. Parishioners were caught off guard, unsure what to expect next.

"If what I say is true, the logical question is why does God tap Noah for the job? Because if God were to do the whole thing all by His lonesome Self, who would know that it was He Who did it and the reasons why? In other words, without Noah there would be no witness to God's infinite power and grace, and there would be no testament.

"So, good folk, Noah isn't required to save every sort of rodent, stink bug, and flea, for God Himself can take care of those ones. Noah's main duty is to be a witness, testifier, and proclaimer for all generations to come. After the event is over, the first batch of generations will receive the story by way of word of mouth. Back then, that's how historical events got passed down. People didn't have the convenience of pens and paper. Centuries later, the Almighty has Moses write it down, and now we have it forever, in the Bible. And, folks, please do drop any notion that there is anything old and moldy about what our early church leaders mistakenly labeled The *Old* Testament. More appropriately, it is The *Foundation* Testament, not old at all, but as fresh and fragrant as a springtime daisy in Maine is. This is why your good priest always maintains the present tense when referring to the Bible. In that manner, we are better able to see Jesus and God the Father as alive and well, with us right here today and every day.

"It is not possible for The New Testament to stand mightily on its own, that is, without The Foundation Testament forever holding it high up to heaven, where God the Father resides with Jesus our Savior at His Right

Hand. The New Testament is, truly, The *House* Testament, built on the most solid of foundations. You see, without The Foundation Testament, we would not have the Ten Commandments and God's assortment of other laws and statutes as given out by Him, and there would have already taken place many centuries ago an 'apostasy of the faith,' which is a *transperversion*, if you will, into the unnatural laws of Satan's evil ways. So I say it again—there's nothing old about God's Word *in its fullness*. . . ."

Parishioners were pleased with Father's explanation. At the end of service, he reminded everyone of the importance of using the confessional on a frequent basis, praying for the dead, and allowing him into their homes, for his yearly visit come August. Adults fidgeted. Mumbles filled the church's airspace, and they got louder. The good priest would have none of it.

"Dear people, you've had me with you for long enough to know that I do not bite and that I give out little to no bark whatsoever. A priest's visit into your home is a special time for one-on-one. I've been to your places before, so there's no reason for any discomfiture. Now, please calm down, everyone. Retain no fear of opening your doors to me. Calm down, I said!"

In the drive home, mother remarked on how Father's sermon had hit the mark. "He was a little long-winded in making his points, as usual. DeBruin could have said it in half the words. Maybe next week we'll get him." Dad and Tony talked of their hope of making breakthrough sometime in the early afternoon. The City wanted the snake returned Monday morning.

They had made progress yesterday. The two took turns slamming the long metal sheath into the hole. They discovered the tunnel did not go straight down, but instead mostly outward and only a little bit downward, in the north direction, passing underneath the property's north greenbelt and twelve feet under the bamboo patch, to empty out down the slope, thirty feet below the tree house's tree. When finally unplugged, the other end of the pipe would allow our basement water to once again flow through the mini-valley.

Late yesterday afternoon, dad had directed Tony to go out onto the gully slope and listen as the former slammed the snake against the most forward section of the obstructing material. The thudding allowed Tony to determine the exact point where the metal tip contacted the slope's under-surface. He marked the spot for today. Tony believed the last five feet of drainpipe had collapsed for the same reason the Prudhommes' slope had: gravitational creep.

Before leaving for the Donahues, I went for a look. The marker was 15 feet west of the old path. A quick study revealed the pipe's outflow would join onto the path farther down the slope. Tony and dad figured to dig a good-size hole into the slope so that the broken section could be exposed and replaced.

The Donahues' front lawn was small and of mild slope down to the sidewalk. Their side lawn was twice as big and went uphill toward old man Waite's place. The back lawn, inclined slightly downward all the way to the

Monroe property line, 15 yards past the raspberry bushes, was more like a narrow baseball field. After the line, our land went moderately uphill 100 yards through woods, to connect with our front lawn. I was set to start the mower when the ladies approached. "Charlie, we're glad to see you," came the older. "Tell us again how much you're charging these two kind-hearted old ladies for this small job."

"Miss Donahues, I don't charge people. I *take* one dollar an hour, no more, no less."

"My, my, that's steep for such a young person. You better get to work. My sister and I expect you to go at the same speed Jim did. And we need you to weed our gardens."

"Miss Donahues, I thought I should let you know that I don't accept checks, only cash."

"Well now, that's quite bold of you. When did you get to be like that?"

"As of today. It's not that I mean to be rude or anything, but yesterday I got blindsided by my two best customers who paid me with checks that aren't good for a week."

"Charlie, is that what you consider us to be—*customers?*"

"Oh yes, but not in a bad way. It's just that I'm a businessman nowadays."

"Listen here. Catherine and I are not your customers. We are your . . . *clients.*" The younger sister stared at me.

"Sounds even better. Thanks for telling me that. And, ah, can I ask you one more question before my time starts?"

"Go ahead, young man?"

"I was wondering about those logs exposed on your steep slope that goes down to the Bondys' yard. Why are they there?"

"It's a private matter. Catherine and I don't like to talk about it. Work, Charlie, work!"

The job took three hours. The sisters seemed more at ease. The older handed me three one-dollar bills and asked me to stay for a couple peanut butter cookies and a glass of milk. I gladly accepted and went to sit in the old rocking chair, the one I always used to sit in. The three of us reminisced about how when I was a kid I would sneak into their raspberry patch to pick off the biggest ones. At first, they did not know if it was human or animal doing it. One day they spotted me in the act and called mother. When I arrived home, red-lipped and red-fingered, I got scolded and sent back down to apologize to the ladies. They invited me inside for a snack. Jim was alive back then. It seemed to me that he did not prefer to hang close to his sisters, that he liked his independence. When he arrived home to find me sitting in his rocking chair, he talked real nice and let me stay in it. When the sisters told him that it was me who had been lifting the raspberries, he laughed. That day broke the ice. From thence forward, whenever the sisters saw me walking by, they always invited me inside for a snack and chat.

I eagerly polished off the cookies and milk. The quiet one said, "You enjoyed it today?"

"I liked the mowing. But to be honest with you, the weeding I didn't like at all. To have to bend over all the time to pick and pick at little things gets boring, and it makes the time go slow. But that doesn't mean I went slow. It's just the time that went slow. I actually went faster because I wanted to finish it quickly."

"I meant the snack."

"Oh, yes. Very delicious. I miss Mr. Donahue. He was such a nice old man."

The older: "Goodbye, Charlie. We'll be having you back in a couple weeks. Maybe sooner. We'll phone to let you know exactly when. By the way, we miss that old man, too."

"More than you can imagine," added the younger.

I noticed Mrs. Laithran working away at her flowers. She saw me.

"Hello, Charlie. Bernard and I would like you to come with us to Creamy Frost in Farmingdale after supper. We'll buy you an ice cream cone. There are some things he and I want to discuss with you about your newspaper. Especially Bernard. He might have a few ideas for you. How does six-thirty sound?"

"Good. See you then. . . . Hi, Mom. Got paid three dollars cash from the Donahues. Feels like I'm a rich businessman."

"Your father and I are proud of you. There's something he and I discussed about your money, or, I should say, *some* of your money."

"Before I forget, after supper Mr. and Mrs. Laithran want me to go with them to Creamy Frost for an ice cream cone. They're buying. Is that okay?"

"Sure, dear, that'll be fine."

Daniel was at the counter. "I read your so-called newspaper. You need to rename it *The River Road Rag*. What's with the word 'the'? '*The* River Road.' Don't need it. Besides, it's River Avenue. Did anyone other than Mother and me read it?"

"Yes, and they liked it and can't wait to get their hands on the next one. *Ha-ha-ha!*"

"You're kidding. And you don't need to be sarcastic."

"I'm not kidding. The next edition is going to be even better. Jimmy and I just need to find more stories. Right now we're digging up something on Bailey Auto."

"Now I know you're pulling my leg, but I'll still bite. What about Bailey Auto?"

"Can't talk about it. By the way, Mom's not getting any more free copies. Means you'll have to buy it. And I know it's River Avenue, but it looks more like a road than it does a hoity-toity avenue in Washington D.C. that you got to walk on once in your whole lifetime. So I call it River Road like most people do around here."

"The parents do—that's true. Means you can go ahead and keep using the word 'the,' not that you would have listened to me, anyway. And since when did you get to be so mouthy?"

"Charlie, your father and I decided that with all the money you're making this summer, some of it should go for buying your school clothes for the coming year."

"What?"

"Yes, dear, that's right. For every three dollars you make, your dad and I want you to put aside fifty cents. Always give it to me right away, and I'll hold it for you. That way, by the end of the summer, there should be at least five dollars built up. I stopped by Slosbergs' Clothiers the other day only to find that their prices have gone up. Decent pants now go for two dollars and twenty-five cents, even as high as three. Button shirts are a dollar fifty and two dollars. Shoes at Corner Boot are up to four and five dollars. Your contribution will certainly help out."

"How much will your so-called newspaper cost?" asked Daniel.

"A quarter."

"*Whaaat?* The *KJ* costs fifteen cents and even that's too much. I'll be nice and give you the same and not a penny more. Use a dictionary next time. Hey, here's a story for you. Yesterday a guy came by to look at our old canopy tree. Said he was a botanist and that our tree is officially registered with him. There are only two others like it known to exist in New England. He took pictures and samples of the leaves and bark. Called it a Luden tree. Said 'Luden' was an old name that's not used anymore. Supposedly some anthropologist planted it a hundred years ago. The botanist figured the tree is at the end of its lifespan and dying off."

"I don't know if I can. But if I do, the paper will definitely cost you a quarter."

"Alright then! Get away from me!"

Mr. and Mrs. Laithran were waiting in their new car: a green 1965 Impala they had purchased three days ago. The first day they pulled in with it, dad was outside. That night he said to mom, "Too much car for them. What were they thinking? Won't fit into their tiny garage."

Dad was partially correct. The day after the car had been purchased, Mrs. Laithran confided to mother that Bernard, at 62, was going through a post-midlife "change in priorities." She had argued against the large car, but to no avail.

To preserve the fine automobile, Mr. Laithran insisted on putting it in the garage every evening. The entrance to the single-car shed was so narrow that it did not look possible for a car that size to make it through. The narrowness, however, presented an optical illusion. Prior to the purchase, Mr. Laithran had measured the width and determined that there were four inches to spare; as long as he was careful centering the auto, there was a two-inch give on each side. Mrs. Laithran was required to direct Bernard at every entering, for a sway to one side or the other meant scrapes and dents. The stressful nightly episode ended when the Impala's front fender tapped against the garage's back wall; that way and only that way would the garage door descend to the ground. Their first two evenings at doing it had Tony and me outside, playing hoops. Both times we stopped to watch. The first night went well, the second not.

Reaching for the Impala's door handle, I noticed a scrape and a minor indentation.

"Off to Creamy Frost we go, Charlie. Dot and I read your paper. It's not the *KJ*. Not yet."

"Bernard, slow down. I want to look at Kay's flowers. . . . Oh, my. We'll have to double up the effort on ours, dear."

"That's not the arrangement, dear. I do lawns and vegetables, you do flowers."

"Charlie, we saw you mowing the Dells' lawn yesterday. How much do you make for that, if you don't mind me asking?"

"Not at all. They pay me a dollar an hour. All my clients pay me that."

"A dollar an hour? Bernard, you can keep doing ours. Don't worry about the flowers."

"I'm not. There's the rail yard. I'll drive us in for a closer look. . . . You're right, Charlie. The place is disorganized and messy. Look, that big puddle is still there. Guess I might have to stop by the station and take it up with the manager this week."

"Mr. Monahan says his name is Mr. Smith."

"All those stories you wrote? You need to give more details. That's important to readers. You're right to call that big garter snake a killer. But garter snakes don't kill humans. They kill large beetles, mice, and rats. If it was as big as you say, the thing was an easy hundred years old, and had it been allowed to live, it would be exterminating for another hundred years the mice and rats that infest our wooded gulch."

"What types of details do you mean?"

"I'll give you some examples. About those raccoons, was there any blood and was it splattered or not? On the dead skunk—don't write 'it stunk like a rotten dead skunk' because that's too obvious. Only say that when it's something other than a dead skunk you're writing about. Say the skunk's corpse smelled worse than a dozen rats dead for three days heaped on a pile of fresh pig squat. And describe how it looked. Was it flatter than a Wakefield Diner pancake because after it got killed a whole bunch more cars ran over it? Readers love that type of stuff. Jot down every detail right away, at the scene, and that way you won't forget anything when you're writing the paper later on. Add a second page and keep a dictionary close by."

"Last Thursday Jimmy and I both wrote out seven copies. After we finished selling them on Friday, we walked to LeClerc's Market. On the way we decided that starting next week we're going to expand our circulation to include all of Dennis and Vine Streets. It would take us too long to write out two pages for that many customers. And to include every little detail would mean it's a book we're writing and not a newspaper. But thanks for the ideas."

"Dot, now that school has let out can you borrow the mimeograph machine?"

"No."

"Well, Charlie, you and your friend will just have to write smaller and that way you can fit more stories onto one page. Try to write faster, too. Dot and I would appreciate you bringing us the first copy of your next edition. We'll pay you fifteen cents for it."

Mrs. Laithran: "The *KJ* costs that much, so a dime for one page is plenty. Charlie, let me remind you that you just can't make things up. That would be a sin. You know that, I'm sure."

"Yup. But I don't think it's really a sin for Jimmy and me to stretch the truth a little bit. Besides, as long as persons know they're going to confession pretty soon, they can do small types of sins ahead of time without it bothering their consciences."

"Did you hear that, Dot?"

"Never mind, Bernard. We're not Catholic, we're Christian, and Christian we'll remain. Charlie, we don't believe in confessing to a priest all the time—."

"And that's because Jesus' cross is like a good Timex watch," interjected Mr. Laithran. "Even if we fall down and end up at the bottom of the stinkin' Kennebec River, it keeps tickin' and Jesus keeps forgivin', whether we're sorry about it or not."

The Impala pulled in at 8:00. Tony and dad were outside hosing off their hands and arms. I thanked the Laithrans and joined the Monroe men. We stopped to watch Mrs. Laithran direct the Impala into the garage. It was dad's first time. No scrapes this night.

"Dot, if I didn't see it for myself, I wouldn't think it possible. Good job directing your husband. You don't want to get any marks on that well-kept second-hand car of—"

"*Dad-dad,*" I whispered, "*The car got scraped going in last night.*"

"Well, there you are, Bernard. Good to see the garage door makes it all the way to the ground. Have a great evening."

"Why thank you, Herby, but we already were."

Tony and father had achieved breakthrough, shoveled a dugout into the slope, and replaced the broken section with newer pipe. To stop small creatures from crawling up the pipe, the two wrapped screen around its mouth.

Chapter XVII

Beast Shot and Killed

Jimmy was thrilled to hear how much people liked our newspaper. He wanted back out onto the streets right away. We decided to work first on developing a story against Bailey Auto.

"I'll bring along a pencil, paper, and clipboard. You can say the details out loud, and I'll write them down."

"Hey, that's not a bad idea, even for you, Mon—Charlie."

"We should bring some paper bags for the empty soda bottles we find."

"You guys, can I come along?"

"No, *Frankie-Frank-Frank*, you cannot come along," snapped Jimmy.

"I'm gonna tell Marion and Joe on you mean guys."

"Go ahead and tell them. I don't care because I don't live around here. They can take it up with my newspaper partner. Come on, partner, let's hit the road."

On the way there, I noticed the Nickles' car parked in the rail lot. The station door was open. "Jimmy, that's Mr. Nickles talking to Mr. Smith. He's an officer in the Navy. Must be on leave. We sold Mrs. Nickles a paper last week. Wonder why he's in there."

"Who knows and who cares. Let's just keep walking."

The west wall of the auto repair shop was 60 feet in length and ran parallel to River Road. A fairly steep slope descended 15 feet from road's edge to the place's wall. Mike and I had occasionally checked this spot for tossed soda bottles. We never touched the empty liquor and beer bottles because they were not returnable, and now they were numerous.

Jimmy and I scored two large Hires Root Beer, three small Frosty Root Beer, two Orange Crush, and two Royal Crown Cola bottles. Jimmy counted

31 beer empties, mostly Schlitz. There were 13 wine bottles, some from Fairview, and 11 hard-liquor bottles, the biggest ones from Kentucky. The slope was weed-laden and plastered with litter. No detail got left out.

"Jimmy, let's head over to Boston Coal. Their dirt lot is always a mess, and we just might find something dead along their backside."

Boston Coal did not disappoint. Jimmy said one messy lot was enough for each edition. This story would have to wait for next week. Our collection of returnable bottles from the two places was enough to fill three large paper bags. Next: Gardiner Fruit or bust.

Just town-side of Boston Coal sat the Gardiner Public Library. In front of it we heard a woman shout from across the street. "Cornelius! Look over there! I think thems might be those two kids that threw the dead skunk at us!"

"Hey there! Yas kids don't move one inch 'cause I'm comin' over there right now to beat yas brains in and have a talk with yas!"

Jimmy and I stopped and stared. The blue-capped man got up from the rooming house's front steps, hobbled over the sidewalk, and began to cross the road.

He waved a fist. "Why did yas throw that dead skunk at us! We was mindin' our own business. Yas two ain't so small I can't be puttin' both my fists through yas faces."

Think, Charlie, think! I saluted. "Ay, ay, Captain Cornelius, and how are you and Two Dollar Eva doing on this fine sunny Monday morning of 1966! Jimmy and I hope good, and to make your day even better, we leave these three bags of bottles for you to return for money at Gardiner Fruit!" I saluted him again. "Jimmy, let's put the bags down right here."

"Cornelius, did yas hear that! Now he's bein' rude! Get 'em good!"

"For cryin' out loud, Eva, can't yas sees I'm already tryin' to do that! Yas know I can't hardly move on Monday! Hey there, yas mouthy punks! First yas throw a dead skunk at us and now yas bein' rude to my lady! What wees ever do to yas two! After I beats both yas brains in, I'm gonna pound the shit outta yas!"

"Where do we run to?"

"Into the library. I don't think he'll go in there."

We entered to see Glennis Neely walking out from a side room. She noticed us, smiled, turned, and approached. *Think, Charlie, think!* "Jimmy, go keep watch at the front window. When you're sure they're gone, come tap me on the shoulder."

Jimmy saluted. "Ay, ay, Captain Monroe."

"Hello there. Aren't you Daniel Monroe's brother?"

"Yes, Miss Neely."

"I must say, it certainly is pleasing to see a couple of our city's fine youngsters in the library on such a sunny summer morning. And you've a pencil and clipboard. This must be a serious matter. How can I be of help?"

Think, Charlie, think! "Well, ah, Jimmy over there is not looking for anything, but he wanted to come along to see what a library looks like on the inside. I'm looking for information on . . . Civil War captains. Yes, that's what I need, information on Civil War captains."

"What specifically?"

"Well, ah, I think I might be looking for a book called . . . *Civil War Captains of Maine*."

"Don't have it. But we do have readings on Maine generals of the Civil War."

"Who might those be?"

"Generals Joshua Lawrence Chamberlain, of Brewer, and Otis Howard, from Leeds."

Jimmy came up and tapped my shoulder, whispered, "*They took the bait. They're on the way to Gardiner Fruit.*"

"Young man, don't be rude. Learn to speak in turn. This is the inside of a library, if you didn't know. Now, besides those two generals, there are Civil War colonels and majors who came from Maine. After you're done with the materials on Chamberlain and Howard, I'll bring you readings on those other officers."

Wow, Dan was right. She does know everything. "Miss Neely, I guess I'll have to go to the library in Augusta for that book. I'm not looking for information on generals and those other whatnots. It's captains I want because they're the most important. They know everything and they get to tell the generals and the other whatnots what they can do and where they can go."

"I won't have it. You need not go to that place. We are a more . . . *unique* library and far a more *appropriate* one for you."

Patience continued to prove a virtue Jimmy wanted no part of. He poked me in the back.

"Miss Neely, do you know what *MEC* stands for on the rail cars?"

"Your brother asked me that question a couple weeks ago. I don't know for sure, but I think the ME stands for Maine, and the C would obviously be for Central. Why it might be confusing has to do with what most people use when referring to our state—*MA* or *MN*. But Maine's real mark is *ME*. As of late, the State and post office have been trying to get people to use that one. But again, as for *MEC*, I'm not a hundred percent sure. You might give their head office a call or ask the manager at the local depot."

Ask the manager? How come I didn't think of that? "Miss Neely, you've told me everything I need to know. Thanks you for your help."

"Remember, for anything on those generals, you need not go to that other place."

"Ay, ay, Miss Captain Neely. I promise I never will."

The Dells' car was parked in front of the train station's office. Mr. Dell stood leaning over Mr. Smith's desk. His right arm was raised and pointing to the train lot.

Jimmy and I had our next edition's first story—a Bailey Auto exposé. Five more stories were needed by Thursday morning. We hung out in the tree house for the rest of the afternoon, took turns peering through the scope, found nothing. Frank was not allowed to climb trees. Thankfully, the rule had come down from his mother and not a Monroe. Still, the little irritant remained close by to us the whole time.

Another middle-of-night thunderstorm hit Gardiner. The home was awakened by its unmistakable violence. Soon, distant sirens were heard. They got louder. I went to the window. Two fire engines sped by. In a few seconds the shrill sounds ceased. Tony came up beside me.

"A house at the top of Kingsbury must have been hit by lightning. Might be the McGales' place, maybe the Nickles'."

"Jimmy and I'll check up there in the morning."

"Let me know what you find. Go back to sleep."

The McGale house had not been struck, but a tall elm tree next to it had been. A large branch had broken off and banged hard against their roof. Though only slight damage had been done, the incident was definitely reportable. I wrote as Jimmy gave his observations.

A few minutes went by and the front door opened. Out came Miss McGale. The pencil immediately fell from my hand and onto the ground. With dropped jaws, Jimmy and I stared. An English teacher at Gardiner Junior High, she was a mid-20s blonde, perfectly shaped, and about the prettiest thing that these two sets of young eyes had ever seen. I sure wanted to be in her class come grade 7. Her parents owned the house, and she, still single, lived there. Maybe I had a chance with her, but certainly not Jimmy.

"Hello, Miss McGale," said we at the same time.

"Hi, boys. We're all okay. No one was hurt, just very startled by the ordeal. Have a good day." She got into her car and drove off.

"I'm counting on her being my teacher come grade 7," remarked Jimmy.

"She won't be because at summer's end you're moving to South Paris. Where is that?"

"Who told you?"

"My mom. She heard it from yours."

"I don't want to move, but it's not like I have a say. Do you know where Norway is?"

"No."

"Doesn't matter 'cause neither do I. Anyway, my parents say it's just past there."

Miss McGale was not always my number one heartthrob. Miss Eakins, our Grade 4 teacher at Central Street School, had played that role for two years. Early into the grade, I developed a major-league crush on her. When spring came, she announced her pending nuptial and relocation to Blue Hill come the end of school year. I was crestfallen.

That year, Miss Eakins and her students experienced a tragic event. On a sunny November afternoon, the principal, Mr. Mercato, got onto the school's intercom. His voice shook as he slowly spoke. "Please, everyone, teachers and students, stop what you are doing and listen carefully. This afternoon in Dallas, Texas, President Kennedy was shot. It is with great sadness that I bring you this unfortunate news. The president was rushed to the hospital, where a short time later he was pronounced dead. Vice President Lyndon Johnson is now our president."

The students were young but not too young to understand the graveness of the matter. All of us had been at our parents' sides a year earlier, in 1962, to watch the nightly news report on the Cuban Missile Crisis: an awful development that had led humanity to the doorway of nuclear holocaust. President Kennedy had been unwavering in his stance against the Soviet Union. To everyone, big and small, male and female, Kennedy was still America's top hero, for he had held ground against the fearsome bear and won.

Miss Eakins was so shaken at the announcement that she instantly broke down crying. For ten seconds her face remained buried in her hands. She reached into her purse for a handkerchief, in futile attempt to get control of herself, for her students' sake. The moment was emotionally overwhelming for the girls of the class. All of them wept openly. The boys showed no tears; instead, we just kept moving our stares around the class and back to Miss Eakins. We were past the age for allowing ourselves to cry from physical hurt, and we had yet to reach the age of maturity for national tears.

Right then and there, an unbreakable bond was formed between the grade 4 teacher and her students. Looking at Miss McGale, however, was not strictly about the heart, for there was an additional, lower, more-manly aspect to it.

We now had story number two: McGALE HOUSE STRUCK BY LIGHTNING. Story three came Tuesday evening, when dad, Tony, and I were watching TV. Both sides of the den window were cranked open; screens were in place. The time was 9:30, and it was dark outside. Tony heard noises coming from the incinerator. "Dad, something's out there."

The three of us went to the window. A beastly shadow was standing in the black metal barrel, chomping on something, perhaps desiccated turnip peel or an unburned steak bone. We could not discern the species, but it seemed wild in origin and not domestic.

The adult removed the screens while Tony went quickly, quietly, for his .22 rifle. He loaded it and whispered, *"Just one long-rifle hollow-point should be enough to take it down peacefully. Step aside, Dad and Chuckie."* I did, and the adult didn't. Tony raised the rifle. BANG. The unidentified creature was instantly thrown from the oversized metal can. "What the heck!" shouted dad, jumping back.

"Don't worry. I made sure you were clear. Had to shoot before it caught our scent or heard us. Let's go out and see what it is. Chuckie, bring dad's flashlight."

The dog came with us. Gully side of the black barrel, a furry pile lay motionless. I shined the flashlight onto it. Lizzie went up close for a sniff.

Tony IDed the species. "It's a porcupine. A big and healthy one it was, too."

He was right. Prior to the call of death, it had been a splendid specimen. With his foot, Tony flipped the body over. The warm corpse displayed a splattering hole that completely exposed its mortally damaged insides. It was obvious death had been instantaneous. I kept the flashlight on the porcupine's head. His shiny black eyes remained open, unflinching, and his scruffy snout and ample whiskers, also black, glistened moist from life. Pencil and clipboard were absent, but I knew the sight would remain gruesomely entombed in my mind. Story three's title: BIG PORCUPINE SHOT DEAD.

"Charles, bury it in the morning. This time dig the hole more toward the Laithrans' garage. We've yet to put any bodies there. Let's get inside and go to bed."

Wednesday morning, I was anxious to show the body to Jimmy and Frank.

"Why did Tony kill it?" asked the little guy.

"Because it was getting into our incinerator and making a mess."

"Donald did the same to that raccoon family. He left yesterday to go back to the Navy."

"Frank, if you want, you can watch Jimmy and I dig the hole and bury it."

At a foot deep, the shovelhead hit something that didn't sound like rock. Jimmy knelt down and reached into the hole, to brush away the loose dirt. The top of the object was dark green and shiny. I joined him, and with our fingers, we picked the hard dirt from around it. He lifted out an unbroken old bottle. We found more of them as we dug. Jimmy slid the shovelhead under the corpse and tossed it into the hole. Frank used his little shovel to help refill it.

"Hey, kids, what are you doing down there?"

"Hi, Mrs. Laithran. We're burying the porcupine Tony shot and killed last night."

"So that was Tony, was it? Good for him. He's our shooter. Always needed someone like him in your house. In the nineteen twenties and thirties, Captain Byrd was the chosen one. Then there were those before and after him. Tell me how it happened."

Jimmy cut in: "We sure will, in the newspaper come this Friday."

"You've already mentioned Captain Byrd to Mom a few times."

"Yes, I have. He owned your house for about twenty years. He was a merchant mariner and traveled around the world. At that time, Gardiner and Wiscasset were busy places, and he was the captain of a big merchant vessel. There are some strange stories that go with him, and not the type of stuff for your newspaper. Bernard and I'll have you with us again to Creamy Frost come this Sunday. I'll tell you more at that time. Bernard can handle the gory stuff. Friday, you and your friend Jimmy will have to drop by here first, okay?"

"I already promised Mr. Dell the first copy because he's willing to pay more. Look what we found while digging the hole." Frank held up two of the five undamaged bottles.

"A treasure trove of them is under there. Where you buried that animal was an old dumpsite for your house. The ones Frank's holding up are really old. The antique stores in Hallowell will pay you good money for them, as long as they aren't cracked or chipped."

"They pay money for old bottles?"

"Sure they do. Every summer people from New York invade Hallowell, to check the antique shops and buy all kind of things, including bottles like those. New Yorkers have more money than brains. When finished, they head over to Freddies Restaurant to eat burgers and fries and chat about all the fun time they had spending their hard-earned money on old chairs no one wants to sit in anymore and old empty bottles they don't exactly know what to do with. On weekends this time of year, Freddies is usually packed tight. Dig up all you can and get your dad to drive you up there early in the week. That's when they restock their shelves."

Jimmy and I spent two hours digging up more bottles. Frank reveled in wiping them off.

"When can we take them to Hallowell?" asked Jimmy.

"Like Mrs. Laithran said, my dad needs to drive us. Might be sometime in the first two weeks of August. He gets them off, just like your mom and dad do. All the factories around here close down for summer vacation at that time. Don't you know that by now?"

"Yeah, so what. Didn't ask, did I? And quit saying that, already."

Mother called out from the den window. Lunch was ready.

"This is boring. I'm done digging forever. But we can still use it in the newspaper. After lunch, we should go try to find one more story, to make our five."

Stomachs filled, we made for River Road. In front of the swampy zone separating the Bondy and Monahan properties, we noticed the stationmaster in the train lot. He was not in his usual white shirt and gray pants but instead work clothes. He was picking up and rearranging.

"Jimmy, right there's a story. Let's cross over and interview him."

"Okay, but let me do the talking. That way I won't be hearing you shout for us to run."

Having noticed our encroachment, the man just stood there, staring at us, waiting.

"Hello, Mr. Sir. How are you today?"

"Fine. Why are you here?"

"We've started a neighborhood newspaper, and we're looking for stories. We noticed you over here. Monroe here says you're the station manager. That would mean you know everything about railroads. Can I ask you what you're doing?"

I rolled my eyes and said nothing.

"I'm trying to make the place look better for the people who live around here."

"When I put this in my newspaper tomorrow, who should I say told me?"

"I'm glad you asked that. Tell them you interviewed a Mr. Smith. Make sure Monroe here writes down that besides all the cleaning up Mr. Smith did, a crew will be in next week. A couple loads of gravel are going to be dumped and a grader will be by to smooth it out. When all is said and done, the place will look new. I'm glad you fellows are doing important work and not throwing rocks at people." Mr. Smith looked at me and smiled.

"Have you got all that, Monroe?" snapped Jimmy.

"Yes, and ask Mr. Smith what *MEC* stands for and why *SOO LINE* is on the ore-carts?"

"Mr. Smith, what does—"

"*Maine Central Railroad*. As for the other, means it comes from a place called Soo."

"Jimmy, ask him why all the train cars don't have *MEC* on them?"

"Mr. Smith, did you hear Monroe?"

"That's a good question, Monroe. Are people around here really interested in these things? Never mind, I don't have time. Maybe another day. Young men, the meeting is over."

Jimmy turned to me. "I've decided to run with this very important story. To make deadline, Monroe, you'll have to hurry up and get writing it. Let's go, already!"

The master copy was finished at 11:00. Mr. Laithran had been right about the employ of smaller writing: five more-detailed stories fit onto one page; I convinced Jimmy about including a sixth very short story on the rail-line names. The rest of Thursday went for writing out ten copies each. We were anxious for Friday morning—to hit the streets and sell, sell, sell.

The newspapermen went hard. By noon all copies were sold. Walking home, we giddily talked of our almost four-dollar intake and how well the morning had gone. When mother mentioned that she would try to set up my savings account without me, that only Frank would have to accompany her on errands, Jimmy and I cheered. Frank cried. After lunch, the two of us set out for LeClerc's Market.

"There you go, Dad. A glass of Hires Root Beer. My three clients want me back to mow their lawns this weekend. Here's a bowl of your very own pretzels. Is there anything else I can get for you, after your hard week of work for the family?"

"Yeah, some answers. I thought your clients wanted you back in two weeks."

"The rainstorm got the grass to grow good and long."

"You're able to handle our gas mower okay?"

"Yup."

"You can keep using it for Monahan and the old ladies. Your mother said she cashed your two checks this afternoon. Next time, you can go on your own to the bank and sign the file card they put aside for you. Your mother probably already told you that. She put a dollar in the account, for your school clothes. Sunday, when you get paid, make sure to reserve another buck or so for your depositing. What are you going to do with all the money you get to keep?"

"Monday I'm getting a new flashlight at Gardiner Hardware."

"What's wrong with one I have?"

"Too small, not dependable, and it's not mine. I need a big one for going in Rollins Woods at night. Jimmy and I need stories for our next edition. Maybe there's something happening in there at night that people should know about."

"I read your so-called newspaper." The voice was Daniel's. He was still sitting at the kitchen counter. "Took me all of two minutes."

"Shush. The news has started. Go to the kitchen if you want to talk to him."

"I don't"

"Yes, you do. Come in here right now."

Mother was sitting beside him. "Charles, at the bank I bumped into Miss Alpen. She mentioned that the teenager who had been doing her lawn for the past few years won't be able to anymore because he has a regular job."

Tony, loud from the den: "How come he gets all the pay jobs and I get nothing?"

"That's because your brother has been walking the streets of this neighborhood for years. Everyone knows him. You're a homebody. Except for our immediate neighbors, no one knows who you are. If it were up to me, you'd be working non-stop, that's for sure."

"Please, Jeanne—*the news*. Tony, go in the kitchen if you want to complain."

"Nah, that's okay. I'm done."

Mother continued: "I recommended you to Miss Alpen. Can you go to her place sometime this weekend and knock on her door? I told her to expect you. She'll show you everything that needs doing. She has a push mower and insists it be used. She lives next door to the old Cropley's store, across from the junior high. Will you please do that for her and for me?"

"The war isn't going well. Sure hope it's over soon. I'm not concerned about you, Daniel, with your thick glasses, and you, Tony, with your big flat feet. The military will never take you guys in. It's Charles I worry about. He's only five years from draft age."

"But, Mom, I don't know if I can fit her in. I already have enough work."

"Listen, she's an old lady in need of help. She's tried to find somebody and has had no success. Because of you being so busy, I didn't want to say you. But there's just no one else. Please go there tomorrow or Sunday. Think of all the money you'll earn."

"Okay, Mom, I'll do it."

"That pleases me to hear you say that. Oh, ah, Tony?"

"Yes."

"You'll be doing our lawn this weekend, right?"

"Yes, he will," indicated a firm-voiced adult male.

"The job doesn't pay!" shouted the middle brother.

"Well, now," returned mother, "isn't someone's birthday coming up in two weeks, and hasn't that same someone been asking about getting a new gun as present. Maybe his father and mother will be more disposed to the idea if the young man proves himself mature, dependable, and cooperative—and for the whole summer, too."

"How can I mow it if Chuckie's got the mower?"

"Mom," I whispered, *"I need it for tomorrow morning. Then again for most of Sunday afternoon. He can use it tomorrow afternoon or Sunday evening."*

"Tony, tomorrow afternoon the mower will be reserved special just for you. . . . Haven't heard your positive response yet."

"*Yes-yes-yes*, I'll do the lawn tomorrow afternoon."

"For crying out loud, please shush, everyone! My goodness, Clay's a draft-dodger now. Says his new name is Mormud Alley. What's the difference? Needs to belly up to the bar and do his duty over there in Vietnam. If Elvis Pressley and John Wayne can wear a uniform, so can he.

Sonny Liston got paid by the mafia to take a dive. Never be proven. Imagine, happened right here in Lewiston. Clay tapped Liston and down he went. Before the ref made ten, Liston looked up. When he realized it wasn't over, he put his head back down on the mat. Marciano would have knocked the crappo out of that bigmouth, Clay."

"Dad, you keep telling us to shush," pointed out Tony, "and now it's you talking. See, I'm being polite. Besides, Clay would flatten Marciano. The fight wouldn't last two rounds."

"Charlie, in all honesty I have to say you and Jimbo have improved at the rag business. It's not the *KJ*. Not yet, anyway. You need a genuine lead story, something that will grab your readers' attention, something that will leave them begging for the next edition. A better second-lead would also help in, in, in *your rise to glory*. Start thinking bigger, outside our pathetic little zone. Life around here is more than about a little Maine road along a polluted river. Polluted river roads are all over America. Anyway, it's *Avenue*, not *Road*, not that anybody cares."

"I don't. And you've already told me it's 'Road.'"

"Like you know about Marciano. I saw his fights, and I've seen a couple of Clay's."

"Listen to me. Allow yourself to think huge. Everyone in America uses river roads or river *whatevers*. When you think gigantic, your articles will become more gargantuan than life itself. Don't use the words 'big' and 'giant' all the time. I've just now been making the point and hope you received it. Use those words only sparingly. Try others that mean the same. Keep a thesaurus and dictionary next to you when you're writing."

"Civil Rights Movement! Civil Rights Movement! I'm getting sick and tired hearing about it every night! What's the problem? Don't negroes already have enough civil rights?"

"Maybe in Portland they do, Herve, but not in Chicago, where there are so many."

Me, from the kitchen: "Dad, we're not supposed to use the word 'negro' anymore."

"What? They're not negroes anymore? What name do they go by now?"

Daniel: "They're 'black people.' Like Charles said, the word 'negro' is out of style."

"The boys are right, Herve. Let's try keeping up with new styles and words."

"What's wrong with using 'colored folk'? That's what everyone's been using since time immoral. They're colored and were not. We're white."

"That's not quite true," countered Tony. "Black is actually the absence of color and white is net accumulation of all colors."

"It's all nonsense, anyway. Negroes aren't black. They're brown. And we're not white, we're . . . ? Jeanne, down at Mattson's, what's the new word they use word for light tan?"

"*Beige*. I doubt it'll catch."

The inclusion of Vine Street will end up turning the final weeks of summer break into a nightmarish reality. A fledgling newspaper—a fun "rag" that caught people's attention—will be dealt a near-fatal blow. The final edition will be pulled and placed into long, cold storage. For the next 45 years, the train, Jim Donahue, Lieutenant Cates, and memories of a former neighborhood would abide unsettled in the writer's mind and heart. . . .

Chapter XVIII

Captain Byrd, Saplings, and the Head-chopping Table

That July Sunday evening of long ago found Charlie too fatigued for a trip to Creamy Frost, but his company was expected. Mr. Laithran would have comments and recommendations. Mrs. Laithran would have hidden, even sordid history to divulge about her neighbor's house—*and that,* Charlie did not want to miss. On the walk over, he thought about how Jimmy and he had made for a pretty good team. Each one's strengths had been filling in for the other's deficiencies. When dealing with adults, Jimmy had proven to be smooth, skillful at playing mind games. Charlie, having studied the intruder's ways, felt ready to take full command of the enterprise, now that Jimmy would be away for three weeks. In the short-term, the future was his and his alone. Innovation and change could now be effectuated without having to first sell them to an intransigent fifty-fifty partner. . . .

"Happy you made it, Charlie. Nice to read about Mr. Smith cleaning up the station."

"Bernard, go slow past the Dells. . . . Guess I'll be back to my flowers early tomorrow."

"A call to their head office is what did the trick—."

"Excuse me. I promised to fill Charlie in on some of the history of his house, which means he belongs to me right now. I'm sure you already know that your parents bought the place from the Woodmans in 1954. That family lived there for only a year. Mr. Woodman and Joe never got along. That's why the Woodmans moved. A couple times the two fought it out right there in the street. Poor Mr. Woodman never had a chance. He was tall and game enough, and he could throw a decent punch, even get Joe to back up a bit, but his punches didn't pack enough power because he was as narrowly built as a spaghetti noodle, just like your dad is. Out there on Kingsbury they'd eventually get all tied up in a knot. Once that happened, it was like watching a gorilla trying to wrestle a python off him. Soon, Joe would get the upper hand and pummel poor Woodman. For those who watched, there was concern the back of Woodman's head would cave in. After a while, when Joe got whatever was bothering him out of his system, he would stand up, slap-swipe his hands together over top of an almost dead-looking Woodman, then strut off as if to be tickled pink. You might want to let your father know not to get on Joe's bad side—even worse, Marion's. Joe may look big and slow, but when his back gets up, he can spring like a lion.

"Your house is one of the oldest in Gardiner. Comes in eighth or ninth, I believe. The Prudhommes' place is even older. Fifth, I'm pretty sure. Old man Richards up there on Lincoln Avenue wrote a little book about the oldest houses in the area. Both were constructed in what's called the Federal Period, which ranged from 1790 to 1830. I believe they were done just prior to the end of the 1700s, but maybe in the very early 1800s. Joe's big elm tree was planted at the time his place was built. Probably over a hundred feet tall. With so many dead branches now, it must be nearing its end of days."

"Dot, I thought you said you were going to talk about Charlie's house."

"Yes, you're right. Charlie, last week I was telling you about Captain Byrd. In his twenty years living at your place he made changes. He covered up the home's original hearth with walls. Your central chimney has not had heat and smoke rise through it since back then.

"His ship traveled the world, and while in foreign places he thought to bring back slabs of fancy marble and install them at the bases of your two fireplaces. They need to be cleaned out and inspected if they're ever to be used again, otherwise you could have a house fire."

"Dad knows that. Says we'll never use them. Anyway, they're sealed. Some of this you've already told us, but it's okay because you always have something new to add."

"Honestly, I can never recall what I've said and not said in past conversations with your family. Maybe I've told you this before but here goes. The good captain brought home bamboo saplings and grape vines that soon flourished. To this day, the things still grace the wooded part of your property. You've got wild strawberries, blackberries, and black raspberries all along the top of your gully. Some were brought in from far away. Have you tried the grapes?"

"Yup, but there aren't many vines left. The trees are crowding them out."

"How do they taste?"

"Pretty good, but I don't like the seeds."

"You said they're being crowded out. That's a shame. They need attention. Eventually there won't be any left. The same will happen to all the wild flowers that line the edges of your woods. No one has looked after them since before the Woodmans. The people who moved in just after the captain left looked after them okay. You have lilies of the valley, unique daisies, tulips, and black-eyed susans. Every year they come up all on their own, with no one having given them an ounce of attention. That's why I call them 'wild flowers.' The tulips are particularly pleasing to look at, so tall and big-cupped."

"Those are Mom's favorites. She actually does try hard to find the time to weed and turn the soil around them."

"Hope you didn't take my talking about the flowers as saying something against your mom and dad. They're very busy with you children and with work on the house. It had fallen into disrepair prior to your arrival, and now the property looks good, just like in the days of Captain Byrd. Here's Creamy Frost. After we're done our cones, I'll continue. . . .

"Where was I? Oh, yes—the good captain. He dormered the second floor of your house. That's when he installed the pillars your dad's been working on. The additions made your place look somewhat like a mansion. That's what the captain wanted, but it certainly isn't close to being one. Way too small. And mansions usually have at least three floors. The Prudhommes' house has three floors and pillars that make yours look like birthday candles. Their place *might* register as a mansion, but I doubt it because it's also too small, though huge compared to yours.

"But, Charlie, it's *your* house that has the strange history. The graves of dead things are all over your land. This is no tall tale. Those brick and concrete slabs that rest in peace near your property line with us, beside your sour apple tree? You might as well know the truth."

"Dot, do you really think anything is gained by you bringing up all that old dead stuff?"

"Mr. Laithran, I really need to know. There might be something for the newspaper."

"Go ahead, Dot, but don't say anything about that woman who committed suicide up there in the second apartment, just before Herve converted it to bedrooms for the boys."

"How did she do that?" I asked.

"She gassed herself by sticking her head inside the gas stove's oven. Your dad stores the appliance up in that former slaughter room. I told you already about the killings that used to go on up there, haven't I?"

"Not really. It was Mrs. Laithran who told Mom. But it's okay because I like hearing about it, especially if you've got new details. People like to get the details, you know."

"I tell you, Charlie, the screams and desperate cries that used to come from up there, and how immediately after the bloody act got done, peace and quiet once again reigned. It wasn't only the beheaded animal that quieted, but all the pigs, turkeys, and chickens in your backyard or up in that pen-room calmed right down knowing that they had survived the blade, at least until the next holiday or big Sunday feast came along. Always on those mornings before the bloodletting, it was as if the animals knew one or a couple of their heads were fated to the chopping block, with the constant mix of grunts, squeals, and puck-pucks, and there would be a general scurrying about and scrapping with each other. Soon enough, the butcher Byrd came out to make his pick, rushed in to grab hold of it, then rapidly ascended those old back stairs of yours. It went from the ground beside the pen straight up to your second floor. Strange-looking thing it was. Poorly built. I doubt you would remember it. Your dad tore it down. The pipe-smoking captain made sure to wear his long dark raincoat and captain's cap on those mornings. The chosen animal yelped and writhed in utter terror, and when the two made it into the room, the sound of death was almost instant. Hearing the meat cleaver hit against block got the other animals to quit fussing and start pecking the ground for feed. Stuff like this doesn't bother you, I hope."

"No. I like it. Mrs. Laithran, what about those brick blocks along our property line?"

"They're crude gravestones. Human corpses are buried under them. They were the people who first lived in your place and later died off sometime in the 1800s."

"Is that woman who killed herself buried under there, too?"

"No. Only in the olden days did people bury their dead in their backyards. She came to this country a couple years after the Second War. She was German and barely spoke English. Her husband was already dead when she arrived here. There was hearsay he had been a German officer stationed at a concentration camp, maybe even the commander there. Awful things happened at those camps. Ironic, her gassing herself to death."

Mr. Laithran cut in. "I just now remembered to ask you something. You wrote about the SOO LINE not meaning the same as MEC and that it originates from a place called Soo. That's it? That's all there is to say?"

"I figure people don't really care that much as long as I give them something."

"Listen here. You have to get the details right—all of them."

"Being it's one page and not the *KJ* or a book, I can only write so much."

"That's enough for now, Bernard. We're home. Next time you'll have more opportunity to discuss the paper with him. Charlie, we'll expect you with us next Sunday."

Tony and dad were tossing hoops. I joined them. Mrs. Laithran got out to guide the Impala forward.

"Hi there, Tony and . . . Harve."

We stopped to watch. Only two backups and no sound of a scrape was heard.

On the phone, Mike and I arranged to meet up early Monday morning, for a trip to Gardiner Hardware. He had arrived home from Camp Bomazeen Friday evening. Due to my being so busy, we had yet to spend time together, though we did have a brief chat when I passed by his place early Saturday afternoon, from doing Mr. Monahan's lawn.

Chapter XIX

The Flashlight

After signing the card, I handed the teller two dollars. She wrote "$2.00" and initialled beside it, opened a small gray box that had the letter M written on the front, and slid the savings card into the appropriate slot. It would be updated at my every future visit. The money deposited today would go toward the purchase of my school clothes. Eight one-dollar bills were tucked inside my wallet and two dollars of change in a pocket. Mike and I left the bank and headed for Gardiner Hardware.

"I haven't any lawns to do this coming weekend. We can bike down to Mount Tom and look for the underground tunnel."

"I won't be around. Mom's takin' her vacation time, and we're all goin' to Bethel to see my aunt. Uncle Allan's pickin' us up Thursday morning. We'll be gone for nine days. How all of us will get along crammed into his Biscayne, I don't know. He says we'll be fine. Good thing Rose doesn't live at home anymore because seven couldn't do it."

"There's still seven of you."

"Nanna's not going. She and Uncle need a break from each other."

"I haven't seen his car at Ernie's Drive In."

"Doesn't work there no more. Quit after a week and a half. Said the heat in the kitchen was too much. Doesn't your dad have a flashlight?"

"Yup, but it's too old and corroded. Always have to keep banging it with a hand to get it to work, and then it cuts out when you need it most."

"How much money you got?"

"About five bucks."

"That should be plenty. After leaving there, we can head over to Gardiner Fruit and spend what's left. Let me do the talkin' when we get inside. I know how to get prices down. Five bucks, huh? Mowing lawns sure pays well. Doesn't really matter to me because I hate doin' that stuff. I'm glad my place has only gravel and weeds for a yard. When we passed by Bailey Auto, I noticed Mr. Monahan's car parked there. Must be havin' engine troubles. Does he pay well?"

"Worst payer I got, and he gives me a lousy check instead of cash. On top of that, he's a hard man, always pushing. The Donahues are the same. They keep shouting 'Go faster!' at me."

"Sometimes I see the old codger and those two grumpy crows outside. With what you just said, I won't feel bad about refusin' them if they ever do ask for my help. I'll tell them to call you. Captain Cornelius and Two Dollar Eva weren't out on their steps when we passed by the rooming house. Hope they're not out there on our way back. Uncle Allan said Monday's their worst day. I wonder what information they're dangling in front of the police these days. Bet you anything they know who did Cates in up there at the Sportsmen's Club last New Year's Eve."

We made the hardware store. The man at the service counter came around to cut us off.

"What can I help you with today? Keep your hands where I can see them."

"I'm lookin' for a good quality flashlight," responded Mike. "Do you carry such a thing or do I need to head up to Augusta Supply?"

"How much do you want to spend?"

"No more than four dollars and that includes batteries."

"That's too bad, because if you had five dollars you could get this big beauty right here, and it comes with batteries."

"Sounds good to me. Pay the man five dollars, Monroe. That's the best I can get him down to." At the till, he leaned in and whispered, "*I ain't stupid. I know you got more money than what you said.*" As soon as we were outside, he said, "Maybe you can buy me a pack of smokes as payment for my gettin' the man down. Don't worry about buyin' me anything else."

"The man at Gardiner Fruit won't sell cigarettes to me. But he will a couple cigars if I say they're for my dad. He'll think there's no way you and I would smoke them."

"I won't."

"I know. One's for my dad and one's for me. I'll buy you a soda and a bag of chips or a chocolate bar. On the way, we can look for throwaways with a good smoking part left on them."

"Your parents will smell you smellin' like a cigar, and they'll know."

"If I smoke it out in the woods while my dad smokes his in the den, no one will figure it out. And if I smoke it when I'm with you, I'll just say it was you. Heh-heh-heh."

"You're finally gettin' there, Monroe. I've been a good influence on you."

"Lookie there, the codger's car is back in his driveway. Couldn't of been much wrong with it."

We noticed an MEC boxcar parked on the team track. The door was slightly open. We crossed over, went up to it, slid the door open all the way, and climbed in. Sunlight was sufficient for us to determine the container was empty except for bits of scrap and a dusting of grain on the floor. The thought came to try out the flashlight. I noticed a small, elongated object on the floor near the front wall. "Mike, look over there. Might be a dead rat or something." I shined light onto it as we slowly approached. Five feet back, we stopped. There it was, the largest dragonfly we had ever seen. Thankfully, it wasn't facing our way.

"Doesn't look dead. Maybe it's sleeping off the long trip here," speculated Mike. "We should leave before it wakes up."

"Not yet. I want to study it for a minute. I'll try getting up a little closer."

"Whatever you say, but hurry up and don't make any noise."

The dragonfly continued to lie motionless. In my estimation, the thing was eight inches long, wingspan about the same. Its main body was hairy, medium brown in color, and its head held huge black eyes. Suddenly the dragonfly began to slowly turn, to face us.

"Oh, sh . . ."

"Your flashlight must be warmin' its body. Let's get out right now."

We leaped from the boxcar and ran for Mike's. We kept glancing back, to see if the dragonfly was following after us. It was not. The boxcar door remained open. The light and heat of day would eventually draw the mini-beast out into the neighborhood, in search of fresh game. What type of panic would happen when women, little kids, and big truck drivers saw it? Faints, screams, and road accidents—that's what. People needed to be warned. I now had the lead story for my renamed and re-launched newspaper *American River Road*: HUGE DRAGONFLY FOUND ON TRAIN.

"Will your dad take us up to Cobbossee tonight?" asked Mike.

"Probably not, seeing it's a week night. If you're with me when I ask, he'll have a harder time saying no. Means you should come along with me to my place later."

"Call your mom to see if it's okay for you to eat here. My mom and sisters are making those special potatoes you like."

Mike grabbed his gear and off we went, for my place. We remained nervous about the dragonfly and kept glancing up in the air and over our shoulders.

"God made that dragonfly big for one reason and one reason only, and that's to kill things. Must have come from Iowa. I wonder how things made in Iowa end up on Maine Central trains in Gardiner. Doesn't make any sense."

Mike's comments got me to thinking about a new title, something that would give clearer warning to our local citizenry: HUGE IOWA DRAGONFLY INVADES GARDINER.

The adult male was outside. He pretended not to notice us.

"Dad, Mike and I are hoping you'll drive us up to Cobbossee Stream so we can fish, but we'll need ten minutes to dig for worms. If you take us it'll probably be the last time I ask you this summer because Mike's going away to Bethel for almost two weeks. Please, Dad?"

"It's a weeknight. You know better than to ask me, but you did anyway. Okay, this one time I'll do it. Be by the car at six. You can have two hours up there. No stopping at LeClerc's."

"Can we have until just after dark? That's when the hornpout come out."

"What's that?"

"They're like a small catfish," answered Mike.

"We have those in Maine? What do you do with them?"

"Fry 'em up for breakfast."

"I'd like to see one. You can have the extra time."

"Thanks, Dad. You're the best."

After finishing our dig for worms, Mike ran back to his place, to get a particular tackle he had left behind. The time was 5:45. While waiting, I shot hoops. Suddenly: "Mom and Dad, there's a negro man coming! He's up the street and coming down this way!"

Frank ran across his lawn, past the Fairlane, to the edge of his lot. Pointing up Kingsbury, he yelled again: "Mom and Dad, there's a negro man coming. He's very tall!"

Because Kingsbury Street angled northward after the Laithrans' house, the Prudhommes' dinette window and their lot as a whole allowed viewers to see up the street, right to the top of the hill. The opposite was true from the Monroe property; the Laithrans' place blocked our view.

I tucked the basketball between an arm and hip and went for the middle of the street. Sure enough, Frank was right. There was indeed a tall negro man walking our way. When he reached the Prudhomme parking lot, Frank accosted him. "You're the first negro I've ever seen." The man smiled, leaned down, and offered his hand in friendship. The two shook.

"What's your name, young brother?" asked the walker.

"Frank. And that's my friend, Charlie, over there." He pointed at me.

The man looked up, smiled, and waved. I waved back.

"What's your name and what are you doing around here?" asked Frank.

"Name's Clarence. I'm visiting with my friend, Henry. He lives up the street. You probably know him. He and I are in the Navy. That's where we met, and now we're good friends." Henry was the older of Mr. and Mrs. Robbins' two foster children. Some months back, he had joined up. "Right now, we're on leave. Henry invited me to Gardiner. He went ahead to his grandpa's house, down at the end of the street, to warn him about me coming inside for a visit."

"My brother Donald's in the Navy. He was home for a week, but he had to go back."

"Henry and I will be doing the same in a few days."

I slowly made my way closer. "Clarence, do you know K. C. Jones?"

"Hmm . . . ? Do you mean the guy who plays for the Boston Celtics?"

"Yup. He's my favorite basketball player."

"Nope. Can't say we've met."

"Can you dunk the ball?"

"Looking at your rim from here, I would say it's something begging to be tried. Toss it over, young brother Charlie, and let's go see about answering your question."

Clarence dunked the ball twice, then said he had to "mosey on." We shook hands. I now had my new lead story: BLACK NAVY MAN VISITS GARDINER. Dragonfly story was bumped down to second-lead.

Frank went into his house. After a few minutes, he was back outside. "My dad says as far as he knows, Clarence is the first negro in history to ever walk down Kingsbury Street. Says he can now die in peace because he's seen it all."

I walked up to him. "Listen to me for a sec. I was a little embarrassed when you were hollering about Clarence coming down our street. He's not a negro anymore."

"What is he?"

"He's a black man. They're all black people nowadays. Please don't use the word 'negro' ever again when I'm around, and that way you won't embarrass yourself in front of me."

"Okay, Charlie, they're all black people and Clarence is a black man."

"And something else. I was pleased to hear you use the words 'mom' and 'dad.'"

"Look behind you. Your friend Mike is coming."

"You won't believe what I just saw—a negro fella down at old man Waite's place. He was standin' at the door. I thought he was tryin' to break in, but then the door opened and there was Henry, all smiles and just lettin' the guy inside. Go figure. There's your dad's comin' now."

"Mike, that was a black man and not a negro anymore. That's what Charlie just told me."

"Sure, kid. See ya later, if I'm unlucky."

As we drove away, I decided on a new lead title: FIRST BLACK MAN IN HISTORY WALKS DOWN KINGSBURY STREET. Dad dropped us off at 6:15. The sun lingered as a diminishing yet still imposing fireball in the cloudless western sky. This time of day, Mike and I should have been able to see the reservoir's bottom to at least a dozen feet out from the shore. But the water was gray, cloudy. At shore's edge and a couple feet onto the sand rested a coat of thick gray foam.

The shoreline itself had undergone change. Much of our valued stretch was now packed with large piles of dirt and gravel. Close-up inspection revealed the piles contained chunks of old tar. Some piles had been placed far enough into the stream to be entirely surrounded by water, while others were half in the water and half on the sand. Mike and I put our rods down and ambled from pile to pile. We came to an area inundated with dead fish. Different species were present, some the best for angling and eating. As we made our way, the stench worsened. We noticed a small pile of brown fur ahead; the dead muskrat lay partially in the water. Because the rotting corpse smelled so bad, we stopped ten feet back from it.

"City trucks have been dumpin' their loads of dirt and tar here, from their fixin' up of old roads," speculated Mike, "and now they've ruined our fishin' hole."

We made our way back, picked up the gear, and headed in the opposite direction, toward the dam. There were no piles going this way, but the murky water and foam persisted. We fished for half an hour and got nothing, not even a bite.

"All the fish have either died or left the area," concluded Mike. "Makes no sense to stay here. Let's cross over the dam and try the other side. We probably won't catch nothin' there, either. That side's never been any good. But at least the water should be okay."

Mike was right, the place felt no good, like it was a dead zone. After an hour, we stopped with the rods, sat down, and tossed rocks into the water. Dad came early, so he could watch us fish for hornpout. When we told him what we had seen, he got angry.

"How could the city do that? The river's bad enough, and now they're ruining our stream. I'm not the type to call down to the City and complain, but maybe this time I should. Then again, they've always helped me out when I've asked, like with that snake I got from them."

"That's okay, Dad. I'll take care of it."

"You can't call them. An adult has to do that."

The mind went to work. *My new lead story. CITY TRUCKS DUMP LOADS OF TAR AND GRAVEL INTO COBBOSSEE STREAM. First black man gets bumped into second-lead. Dragonfly goes to regular stuff, along with Boston Coal's dirty lot. Two more stories needed.*

"This reminds me of the big fish-kills the Kennebec River has gone through in recent years. There was the bad one last year, and an even worse one a few years ago. Do you two remember when the shores of the river were full of dead fish?"

Mike: "Yup."

"Dad, I remember, but Mike and I need to find a new fishing spot. How about up near the Sportsmen's Club?"

"Mr. Monroe, I agree with your son. The fishin' up there should be real good."

"Too far a drive. Besides, that's where Cates got murdered, and his killers are still on the loose. I tell ya, bad is going on everywhere. Policemen and fish are getting killed, and no one's being arrested and no one's speaking up. Then there's Kennedy—assassinated and his assassin assassinated. They say there wasn't a conspiracy, that Oswald acted all on his own as the trigger. What a bunch of crappo. What's happening to this country of ours?"

The mind mulled the angry adult's comments. *How about CITY DUMP TRUCKS ASSASSINATE FISH IN COBBOSSEE STREAM . . . ? Or maybe CITY DUMP TRUCKS TRIGGER GIGANTIC FISH-KILL IN COBBOSSEE . . . ? A little long but use it anyway. My readers will love it!*

Chapter XX

Marvelous Creature of the Sky—Slain

Tuesday morning, Frank followed me onto the path. He picked up an old, dried-up bamboo rod, fallen from years ago, and began to whack away at beetles and ants on the ground. I sat in the ark and looked through the telescope for larger objects. Non-discernible chatter was heard. The voices belonged to mother and Mrs. Laithran; they were conversing near the brick grave-markers. The thought came to check inside Rollins Woods tonight, just after dark. *Don't really want to go in there alone. Maybe I can get Kenny Whitson to come with me. Mrs. Robbins never lets him do anything, and he's 15 already. I'll let him use my new flashlight.*

A loud BANG broke the morning peace.

"What was that, Charlie?"

"Sounded like glass breaking. I'm coming down so we can go check."

We hustled onto the north greenway and stopped in front of the den window. One side was smashed in. A dead robin and two dead sparrows were on the ground just below it.

"One of those must have broken the window," offered the five-year-old.

"No, they were already there. A big bird's inside. Might be still alive. Can't see anything from out here, so let's go in."

Mother and Mrs. Laithran approached. "Charlie, Dot and I heard it. What did you find?"

"One side of the den window is smashed in. Whatever did it is on the floor, and it may be still alive."

"Oh, my. Dot, please come with us."

We hustled around the backside, across the driveway, through the hallway, and into the kitchen. We stopped at the doorway to the den. A tragic sight was set before us. For five seconds we stared and said nothing. At the foot of dad's chair lay motionless a large bird, obviously dead. The mind saw pay dirt. *My new lead story:* GIGANTIC BIRD SMASHES THROUGH PICTURE WINDOW. *Dead fish is now bumped to second-lead, first black man drops into the regular stuff, along with the dragonfly story and the dirty parking lot.*

"That's a really big hawk," noted Mrs. Laithran. "Poor thing. A marvelous creature of the sky it was, until it got killed right here in your home. Must have thought the window was an open hole into that former barn. Or maybe it saw the reflection of a sparrow and flew in for the kill. That hawk was itself a killer, and that window of yours is a 'killer window.'"

Correction: GARGANTUAN KILLER HAWK SLAIN BY KILLER WINDOW.

"Charles, go and bury the thing in the gully right away."

"Frank, come and help me. Bring your little shovel and I'll use the big one."

"You should dig near where you dug the other day," suggested Mrs. Laithran, "and that way you can kill two birds with one stone by finding more old bottles at the same time. I guess that wasn't a nice way to put it."

"Good idea. Come on, Frank. We're going to have fun-fun-fun doing this."

"Charlie, I can't wait. It's way better now, with just you and me and no more Jimmy."

Tony appeared. "What was the big bang that woke up Lizzie and me? Ma, did you drop something again? Oh . . . so that's what it was. Completely dead or do I need to finish the job? Heh-heh-heh." Lizzie went in close for a sniff.

The afternoon and evening were spent down at Mike's place. I got home at 8:30 and spotted Kenny in his driveway. He saw me and waved. I went for the tennis ball and my flashlight. Back out on Kingsbury, I yelled, "Hey, Kenny! Let's toss the ball!"

He descended the hill and stopped in front of the Laithrans'. Standing mid-street, not far from each other, we threw the furry sphere for 15 minutes.

"Kenny, it's getting too dark. Come on in the woods with me. I have a new flashlight. You can use it most of the time. But first ask your mom or dad."

He waved for me to come up to him. "I don't need to ask them anything. Anyway, they're down at Grandpa's. I can go with you for a little while." Halfway down the path: "Maybe I should have phoned to ask my mother, but she would have just said no. When I don't ask, I don't get into as much trouble later on, when she finds out—*if* she finds out. Paul never lets me go anywhere, either. Why are we in here, anyway?"

"Why do you call your dad *Paul?*"

"Charlie, you know the story. He's okay, I guess. Never seen fit to call him Dad. He doesn't mind me using his name. Alberta makes me and Henry call her Mom. Not much water in the stream these days. How do we know August is around the corner? The heat makes the river smell worse than ever, and this time of year it shrinks from the lack of rain, causing our shit to settle along the shores. The sun bakes it into big and crusty pancakes. Wouldn't want to try one."

"Kenny, I think I can hear them. Speak low for a while."

"Hear what?"

"Whip-poor-wills."

"Oh, so that's what they are. Always wondered. Don't know why I never asked anyone about it. Don't know whether anyone would have known the answer other than you."

"Donald Prudhomme would've. Maybe others around here should know what they are."

"I need to get back home before they find out I'm gone."

As we retreated uphill: *WHIP-POOR-WILLS SOUND OFF IN ROLLINS WOODS will be my new lead story. Makes six. Hawk will be my second-lead. Dead fish will join the regular stuff, just up from the bottom, where the black man, dragonfly, and dirty lot will be.*

"You're going into high school this year, aren't you?"

"Yup. Won't miss junior high, that's for sure, except for looking at Miss McGale in the hallways. What grade are you going in—seven?"

"Yup, and I'm looking forward to something different. My real first name is John. My parents have always called me by my middle name. This year I'm sticking with John. It's a little embarrassing to have to correct my teacher on the first day of school every year. And everybody messes around with the name Charles, making other names from it. Can't stand that anymore. But I do kinda like Charlie. Tony calls me Chuckie. Don't mind that one, either."

"You're right about a couple things. Junior high sure is different. In elementary grades we had only one teacher, but in junior high and high school we get a different teacher for every subject, and then we have a homeroom teacher on top of that. You would have to correct each one of them. To me, you don't look like a John, so I don't think I'll be calling you that."

"You and my family and other people in the neighborhood can keep calling me Charlie."

"Here's your flashlight, Johnny."

"Bye, Kenny. Hope you're only in a little bit of trouble." We laughed.

While walking for the driveway: *Think bigger, Johnny, like big reporters do. Dress up the title a bit.* WHIP-POOR-WILLS FRIGHTEN KINGSBURY STREET RESIDENTS. *Nah. Try combining two stories for one fantastic lead.* WHIP-POOR-WILLS WEEP AT NEWS OF HAWK'S DEATH. *Not bad.*

Maybe it should be WHIP-POOR-WILLS CHEER AT NEWS OF KILLER HAWK'S DEATH. How about WHIP-POOR-WILLS DANCE AND SING AT NEWS OF GARGANTUAN KILLER HAWK'S DEATH? Make your decision Thursday morning.

I stopped halfway across the driveway, to gaze into the clear sky above. Stars shone as if to be their own tiny flashlights gazing down at me. I was quickly captivated by the crisp celestial display. Time seemed to do that "stand still" thing again. With the frequent news updates on the Space Race and with shows like *Lost in Space* and *Outer Limits* gracing the television airwaves of the day, most young minds had given over to the belief that there was amazing potential contained and someday to be found in the secret processes of the universe.

It was close to ten o'clock. I went to get the telescope from the tree house. This time I was not on the prowl for a story; I already had my six.

In the quest for new information about mysterious things "out there," the telescope was of no help. The tiny sparkles of stars became only slightly less-tiny sparkles when observed through the lens. But then . . . then . . . I noticed something unusual. In the western sky, a strong sparkle moved at a fairly fast clip, eastward, directly for Gardiner. I tried to follow it with the telescope but was only marginally successful, managing a few brief hook-ups only. Through the scope, the object appeared to have a defined circumference.

The event was unspectacular. Still, I wondered what it was and went inside to tell Tony. The resident scientist was surprised, interested.

"Let's go outside so you can show me exactly what happened. . . . Did the object move at a consistent speed?"

"Yes. It started over there—over West Gardiner way—and it came over top of us here, in a straight line, and then it disappeared over Pittston. The whole thing took about two minutes."

"Did it shine like a really bright star, and could you see an outline to it or not?"

"It was really bright and through the telescope I think I could see a round shape, but the thing moved too fast for me to stay focused on it for long."

"Were there any flashing lights to it? Different colored lights?"

"Nope."

"And it didn't change directions even in the slightest way?"

"Not that I could tell."

"I know what you saw. This is amazing. I wish I had been out here with you."

"What? What was it?"

"You're a little bit too young. I don't think you can handle the truth."

"Oh, will you please just tell me."

"Will you run it as the lead story in your next edition?"

"What am I supposed to say, 'yes' or 'no'?"

"'Yes,' or else my lips are sealed. And you have to say you found out what the object was from an 'unnamed NASA source.'"

"Okay-sure. It'll be my lead, and I'll write what you want."

"The object was either the U.S. satellite Echo I or Echo II. It was likely Echo II because you said it was so bright. Darn it! I wish I had been out here. Echo I was launched in 1963 and Echo II was sent up last year. They're both huge, perfectly round silver balls, basically like metal balloons, and way taller than the tallest man. The satellites are for scientists to test reflecting radio signals on. Darn it! Why wasn't I out here! Both can be seen with the naked eye, but especially Echo II because it's bigger. Can you believe it? That satellite has been around the world hundreds of times, and it passed right here over Gardiner. Brings me so much hope. Darn it! I wish I had been out here! What are you going to name the article?"

"Ahh . . . NASA SATELLITE SEEN PASSING OVER GARDINER."

"Wow, isn't that exciting. Can't you think of something better, Mr. Editor?"

"How about . . . MAGNIFICENT NASA SATELLITE PASSES OVER GARDINER?"

"That's more like it. Remember what I said about quoting an unnamed NASA source."

"Ay, ay, Captain Tony. 'Unnamed NASA source' it'll be. How do you spell 'source'?"

"S-U-O-R-C-E, I think. Wait a sec. The C might be an S. Ask Dan when you get inside. Better yet, look it up in the dictionary. Oh, hello, Mr. and Mrs. Robbins. Beautiful evening, don't you think?" offered Tony to the familiar couple walking by. The two half-waved and did not answer him. "Out walking, are you?" asked Tony, trying too hard to be congenial.

"Never mind about us walking."

"I'm pretty sure Kenny's up at your house," said I, also trying to be friendly.

At this, the two stopped. "How do you know that?" asked Mrs. Robbins.

"Oh-ah, I-I saw him outside your house just before it got dark."

"Did he stay there or did he come down here to play ball with you?"

"Well, no, not really. He didn't come all the way down. I went up the road a bit, and we tossed the ball for only a little while, and then he said he better get back to his work."

"So that's what you say happened, is it? Well, I'll be asking for his side of the story when Paul and I get up there. Goodnight to the both of you." Mr. Robbins nodded, barely.

The two turned and continued on home. A cold-blooded scream penetrated the dead hot air. It seemed to have come from the open window of our living room. The Robbins stopped and looked back at us. Another scream came, followed by "Get away from me! Help, someone, help!" The Robbins continued up the street, faster. Tony and I rushed into the house.

"Mom! Mom! Where are you! What's wrong!" hollered Tony from the kitchen. Lizzie was crouching under the kitchen counter.

"Boys, come to the living room right away!" yelled dad. "I need your help!"

We rushed in to find mother standing on a chair. Dad was holding a rolled-up *KJ*. "Your mother saw a mouse. I'm looking for it right now. Charles, stay at that doorway. If the mouse comes your way, kick it to me. Tony, go stand at the other doorway."

"There it is, Herve!" The mouse had been hiding under the RCA stereo cabinet. The scared rodent, realizing there was no chance for escape, turned and went back under. Dad moved fast. The man bent over and, using the newspaper, swiped around under the old music box. The rodent scurried out and headed for under the couch. Dad sprang smartly and whacked down on it. The mouse was dead.

"Tony, go get a glass of milk for dipping. It'll slide down your throat easier that way."

The boys busted out laughing. At hearing us, Lizzie came running into the living room, wagging her tail, prancing. Previously, she had thought the matron was shouting at her, and that was why she was hiding in the kitchen when Tony and I came in.

"Herve, that was an awful thing to say. Charles, pick it up with a tissue and go throw it in the gully." The man helped his wife step down from the chair. "How did a mouse get in here?"

"Probably came from the gully, through the pipe we unplugged," answered Tony.

Dad agreed. "I better check the thing tomorrow morning, before I go to work."

Daniel appeared from upstairs. "You people woke me up. I have a hard day at work tomorrow, don't you know? Anyway, I'm here now. What was all the commotion about?"

I dangled the dead mouse by the tail. After *ugh* and a roll of the eyes, he turned and went back upstairs. The dead rodent and I headed outside. I noticed the Knights looking out from their second-floor living room window. Mr. Prudhomme was standing on his front lawn; BJ and Frank were beside him. Circling the garage, I saw Mrs. Laithran standing on her side-porch.

"Hi, Charlie. What a beautiful evening we have. Is everything okay at your place?"

"Yes, Mrs. Laithran. It sure is a beautiful evening. Have a good night."

"Before you walk off, I noticed you and Kenny playing ball earlier."

"Yes, that's right, he and I did that. Goodnight."

"Wait another moment. After ball, I noticed you and Tony standing on your driveway, and both of you were looking up into the sky."

"Yes, you're right. Goodnight again. I'm in a rush."

"If you don't mind me asking, why is that?"

I turned to look across the street. The Knights were still in the window; Mr. Prudhomme, Frank, and BJ were still at their posts. The moment begged for an explanation. "I'm in a rush because I'm carrying a dead mouse! After my mother saw it and screamed out, my dad killed it with a rolled-up *KJ!* Then he dipped it in a glass of milk and told Tony to swallow it! Tony screamed 'Get away from me! Help, someone, help!' Right now I'm going out back to throw the dead mouse into the gully because Tony didn't want to swallow it! I'm a little embarrassed to be shouting, and I don't mean to be rude to anyone! It's just that I want to explain it only once! If anyone wants, they can come and watch me!"

"Thataboy, Charlie! Heave it good!" came Mrs. Knight. She stuck her head out the window and waved.

"Dad, can I go watch him?"

"No! Let's get back in the house. BJ, you too, and quit your staring!"

Mrs. Laithran: "I'm relieved to hear that. Goodnight, Charlie. Goodnight, everyone else!"

Chapter XXI

Sharp Turn on Vine Street

Early the next morning, dad doubled-up on the screen and used extra wire to fasten firmer its hold around the drainpipe's mouth. I headed to Mike's. This day would be our last chance to get together before his Bethel trip. Mrs. Dell was in her front yard. Two young boys stood beside her.

"Charlie, please come over here for a minute. I want you to meet my grandchildren. This is Bobby. He's eight years old. And this is Corey. He's six. Boys, this is Charlie. He's thirteen. Is that right, Charlie?" I half-waved to the kids, and they half-waved back.

"Yup."

"Would you be able to come with John and me and the boys to our cottage on Saturday? Our lawn can wait until next weekend. We'll leave late in the morning and be back in the evening. I'm sure you remember our cottage out there at Horseshoe Pond. You and the kids can keep company swimming and fishing while John and I do some fixing up. Bring your swim trunks and fishing gear. You can fish from our dock. We even have a small rowboat, but you'll have to wear a lifejacket. We still have three of them from when our children were young. You won't need to bring along any food. I'll bring lunch, and for supper we'll have an outside fire for roasting hot dogs and marshmallows. How does that sound?"

"Fantastic, but I need to ask my mom."

"I just now got off the phone with her. She said for me to hang up and rush out here to intercept you as you walked by. She and your dad are planning to go out to the Augusta House Saturday evening. Your mom prefers that you come with us, but only if you want to—and you've already said you do. You'll need to be here at eleven."

Adding the Echo Satellite story meant F.N. Boston Coal's messy parking lot would go to next week's edition. Tomorrow—Thursday—the press, *the fingers*, would have to go fast the whole morning. Friday's sell will deliver into the editor's hands a substantial amount of coin.

Thursday morning, the main draft of *American River Road* was finished at 10:30. The copying of it, over and over, commenced.

This is easy. Who needs Jimmy, anyhoos. The newspaper business is way more fun than yard work. . . . There, two copies done, and it's only 11:00. . . . There, two more copies done, and it's only 11:30. . . . There, two more copies and it's . . . noon already! I've written only six copies! I need to stop for lunch. The break will do me good. I'll come back refreshed. But first, try to do two more. Dad and Dan just got home. . . . There, two more done. Dad and Dan just left. Forget lunch, there's no time. Frank wants nothing to do with me. 'Too boring,' he says. Just keep writing and forget about everything else. . . . There, Chuckie, you got two more done, and it's only 1:15. Why are you slowing down? Speed up! You need ten more. . . . I miss Jimmy. Frank, where are you? There, two more done and it's . . . past 2 o'clock! I'll never finish! But I have to because people are counting on me, and they really need to read these important articles. . . . Who the heck cares about a newspaper, anyhoos? This isn't a newspaper, it's a rag. The KJ—now that's a newspaper. There, two more done. Got a mere six more to go and it's only . . . 3:00! Don't give up. Refuse all temptation to quit. . . . Quit, Chuckie, quit! Give it up! The newspaper business stinks! Don't prefer it. In fact, don't like it at all. Pays peanuts and people demand too much. Get up and do some exercises. Like what? Pushups. . . . Now do some jumping jacks. . . . Now do some squat thrusts. . . . Now shake your hands and wiggle your body at the same time. . . . Finish up by rubbing your face all over. . . . Now pinch your cheeks and pull 'em out and make fluttering noises with your lips while crossing your eyes and twisting your face. . . . There, get back to writing. . . . Two more finished and it's 3:30. Four more to go. Faster, Chuckie, faster! Mowing lawns is way more fun than writing a newspaper. A newspaper is supposed to be rolled up and used for killing flies and mice and bumble bees and hornets and for whacking Tony. . . . Two more done, two to go. . . . Newspapers are for picking up dead birds with and for dogs to do crappo on. Newspapers are for wrapping mackerel heads and for whacking Tony. . . . Chuckie, you have your 20. So what! Your hand is killing you, your neck is sore, you're tired, and you've yet to make a dime! I hate the newspaper business!

Friday morning, I phoned Ray to see about getting a baseball game going for the afternoon. He said to be there at 1:00. The newspaperman left on sales calls. Going door-to-door alone was toilsome and a little bit on the scary side. Continuously meditating the assets of LeClerc's Market helped me along: *Mallow Bars. PayDays. Heath Bars. Chunkies. Rollos. Tootsie Roll Pops. Pretzel Rods. King Cole and Humpty Dumpty BBQ chips. Bottles of Grape Crush, Bubble*

Up, and Royal Crown Cola. Popsicles. Fudgesicles. Creamsicles. Nickel-pickles, but they're a dime now. Red hot fireballs! Dad's Frosty Root Beer and pretzels. For sure, a Bubble Up as reserve. Mallow Bars. PayDays. . . .

The selling went well. Subscribers were fine forking out 15 cents for the new edition. I was halfway through Vine Street and down to my last two copies when a man approached.

"Hey, kid, are you Charlie or Jimmy?"

"Charlie."

"People around here say your paper's pretty cool. But don't let it go to your head."

"Thanks. I won't."

"Listen up. I've got something for you, but you can't be putting it in your newspaper, and you can't be telling anyone about it, either. If you agree to that right here and now, I'll tell you about something real big—the Cates killing. About what I said, do you agree or not?"

"Yes."

"Where's your buddy?"

"He went on vacation with his parents. I won't say anything to him if you don't want."

"I don't. Now, let's you and me go sit on that stump over there. My name is John. I'm twenty-one and work for Mckee Construction. Took today off because I strained my back. I work with a guy named Billy, a rough man who looks about forty years old. He's okay, but I wouldn't want to be around him when he gets drinking. And I can tell you he's the type that likes to do a lot of that on weekends. Gets brawling when he's drunk. Like I said, at work he's okay.

"Billy has taken a liking to me, and sometimes when we're working alone together on something, he gets talking about what's on his mind. Most of the time it's not much, sometimes about the messes he got himself into. I just listen. But in the last few weeks he's been bringing up what he saw last New Year's Eve, up there at the Sportsmen's Club.

"Whenever he brings up the subject, he glances around to make sure no one else is close by. Then he leans in and with a low voice warns me to keep my mouth shut or else. He smiles and says he was there, at the club that night, as if to be bragging. I asked him what happened. Now, I wish I hadn't. He gives out only bits and pieces at a time, but I've put them together.

"Says everyone was into the liquor early, and later in the evening a disagreement got going. People he had never seen before were there—out-of-towners, from the Lewiston area he learned as the evening wore on. There were some from around here, and then there were those from outer Farmingdale and Manchester. Billy comes from Farmingdale, and those were the ones he was with.

"When trouble started, someone called the police. Soon enough, Cates showed up, alone. Billy says Cates was too aggressive in his handling of things. My feeling is Billy's stretching the truth, and what he remembers is from a mean drunk's perspective. What else was Cates to do, act like a coward? Suddenly, one of the guys from Lewiston latched hold of Cates from behind, and that was the beginning of the end for the good lieutenant. People's passions were already up, and when they saw one guy standing up to Cates, a bunch of fellas decided they weren't going to let the one go it alone. They swarmed Cates, kneeing and beating him silly. He went to the floor in terrible distress. The people quickly realized there would be hell to pay, so they cleared out. Everyone knows the rest of the story, him dying a few hours later.

"One time when he got talking about it, I asked him if he had managed to get in his own licks on Cates. Billy got real upset, and he stopped talking about the subject. But after only a week went by, he started bringing it up again. My feeling is that if he was innocent, then how come he just didn't say no? Charlie, you won't be squealing to anyone about this, right?"

"I sure won't. But, John, why are you telling me?"

"You and your buddy have gotten people's attention around here. Everyone thinks you guys are acting pretty grown up. Anyway, I couldn't keep holding the information inside of me. Already I feel better having told someone . . . someone I can trust.

"Some of the guys involved in the killing—they're connected. Billy says they know people and policemen, local and State, and no one should want to mess with them. This fact I do know for sure, that there's a lot more story behind the story. Billy says the PD knows everything. Because of that, people are scared to death of speaking up and being accused of ratting. And, truthfully, they should be scared." John patted me on the back. "Have a good day, Charlie. Time for me to move on. I'm confident about your promise."

"John, before you go, I've got something for you. Here, my second-to-last copy. For you it's free. I think you'll like this edition better than the last one."

"You already sold one to the house I visit. But okay, I'll take it."

With that, the mysterious man walked off.

I got up and turned to the house behind me. The woman living there had bought a paper last week, and I wanted to sell her this week's final copy. There she stood, at her front window. Naturally, because of the heat, the unit was wide open. The instant our eyes met, she pulled the curtain closed. Right then, I realized she must have been listening in on John and me. I wasn't a hundred percent sure. Maybe she had only watched us, wondering why we were sitting on her stump. I decided to skip the house and sell my last copy to the next one over.

Neither John nor I knew that our futures were now entered into a real-life game of *Jeopardy!*.

Chapter XXII

Giant Bloodsuckin' Suckers at Horseshoe Pond

"Glad you're on time, Charlie. Put your stuff in the trunk. Bobby and Corey are sitting in the backseat." They half-heartedly waved. "Sit with them. John and I won't be long."

I got in. The younger said, "My Auntie Sharon climbed the Motherhorn."

"That's *Matter*horn, Corey," corrected the older brother, "and Uncle climbed it with her."

"What's that?" I asked.

"It's a tall mountain," answered the younger. "And now she wants to climb a bigger one called Killamanwithajar."

"No, Corey, the mountain's name is Killamanwithajar-*oh*."

Mr. and Mrs. Dell got into the front seat.

"There you are, Charlie. Pleased you could make it."

"Hi, Mr. Dell. I prefer Horseshoe Pond over mowing lawns and weeding gardens."

"John, please slow down in front of Dot's place. . . . My, my, her flowers are looking bold. We better be back into ours tomorrow."

"Tonight, Mom and Dad and the Laithrans, Knights, and McGales are going out for supper and dancing at the Augusta House."

"Your mom asked us to come along. We could have had Bruce and his wife take the grandchildren overnight, but we had already planned our day at the pond."

After a silence, the younger said, "My mom and dad are 'transishing.'"

"No, Corey, they're *transitioning*." Corrected the grandmother, "Charlie, do you know what 'transitioning' means in this case?"

"Yes, I sure do. It's when—"

"That's good enough. And, Corey, we won't be mentioning it again, will we?"

"No, Grandma."

"You're recent edition was pretty good and definitely better than anything the *KJ* has put out in a long time," offered Mr. Dell. "Imagine, a negro man walking down Kingsbury Street. I wish I had seen it, but just knowing is enough. I can live out the rest of my life in peace."

The older brother spoke up. "Grandpa, we shouldn't be saying the word 'negro' anymore. We supposed to use 'black' instead. That's what Mom and Dad say."

"We've started doing that at our house, too," added I.

"It's a good idea, John," affirmed Mrs. Dell. "Charlie used 'black' in his newspaper, and now his family and Nora's use it. We should start doing the same, not that we talk much about negroes, except lately because they're causing so much trouble in the big cities."

"*Yes-yes, okay, dear.* And that hawk, Charlie. You should have left it out on your front lawn for a few days, so people could walk by and see it. And on another of your articles, how do you know for sure that it was the Echo II satellite that passed over Gardiner?"

"Well, like I wrote, I got the information from an unnamed NASA source."

"Who might that be?"

"He swore me to secrecy."

"That doesn't matter anymore, once you've written the article."

"Okay, but please don't tell anyone else because if he finds out I told, both my arms will end up bruised. The source was my brother Tony. He reads about these things all the time in the science magazines he buys at LaVerdiere's."

"You gave him up pretty quick and without much of a fight, don't you think?"

"Yes, you're right. It's just that it was kinda bothering me to hold it inside. I had to tell someone, especially people I can trust. I was going to report another messy parking lot, but there wasn't enough room for it. I can't do more than six articles on one page for each edition."

"Too bad. Make sure to include it next time. Don't stray from what gave you your early success. People enjoy reading about not only dead things but dirty places, too."

"Yes. I'll make sure."

"Other than that, like I said, this time your paper was the best yet. We've been keeping our eyes open for that dragonfly. Got the grandchildren to ask old man Waite and Mr. Carrington next door here if they've seen it. They haven't. Have you?"

"Nope. And I don't want to. The thing was gigantic."

Bobby opened up a little more. "We have gigantic dragonflies in Ohio."

"Could it have come from Ohio and not Iowa?" asked Mrs. Dell.

"Could have," conceded Mr. Dell, "because Iowa might have been a stopover point on the way here. Were the letters MEC written on the side of the boxcar?"

"Yup."

"Well, that says a lot right there. We don't have dragonflies that big in Maine—not inland, anyway. There are some pretty good-sized ones along the coast, especially down Bath way and on George's Island, but they don't look the way you described that one. Why did you conclude it was from Iowa?"

"Because the grain in the boxcar came from there."

"Did you hear that, Kay?"

"Hear what?"

"About the way Charlie determined the dragonfly came from Iowa. It's almost brilliant, but not quite, and that's because it may have boarded the boxcar on the way from Iowa, especially if the car unloaded some of its product elsewhere before getting here. If a full load came here, then you're probably right. But if the train stopped to do some unloading in New Jersey or New York, then the dragonfly would have vacated at seeing giant rats jumping aboard. Nope, I'm with you—it's from Iowa. And why was it a Maine Central boxcar and not one from an Iowa railway? You might try to nail some of these details down in your next issue."

"That's a good idea, but I have to be careful about having enough space. I need to interview Mr. Smith. He and I have become good friends. So far, I have only one story for the next edition. Maybe I can stretch the dragonfly for another week. Good reporters know when and how to do things like that, getting two articles for the price of one."

"What you should try to find is one really big story," hypothesized the driver, "something more on the investigative side. Something that will grab people's attention and make a name for yourself in the newspaper business. The *KJ* hasn't done that in a long time."

"I've been thinking about running with something exactly like that. It's big, alright, but I don't have enough information yet. I need to do more investigating."

Mrs. Dell took hold of the conversation. "Your father's off for two weeks, isn't he?"

"Yup."

"When I was talking to your mother the other day, she said the family won't be traveling this summer."

"That's right, we're staying here."

"She mentioned about your dad and her wanting to trade in the car for a newer one. They'll be using some of the time off for that. They may want one of those new color TVs, too. I told her Pomerleau's has a good selection."

"I didn't know that, but I'm happy to hear it. They must have decided to get that new marvel called 'Master Charge.' I've heard them say they don't have the money without it."

"Dear," came Mr. Dell, "did you take in what he just said about Master Charge?"

"Not now, John. We'll discuss it another time. Charlie, your mother said that your dad and Tony are going to fix the roof during the time off. Does it leak?"

"Yeah, the ceilings upstairs in the bedrooms do when it rains hard. There's a big leaky spot in the little room that used to be a kitchen. It's just above where a stove once sat. That stove got used by an old German woman to kill herself. She stuck her head inside it while the gas was turned on. She didn't light it, so how it killed her I don't know."

"Charlie, a woman doesn't need to fry her head off to kill herself. She just needs to rile up her husband enough about refusing to get a Master—"

"John, please! And, Charlie, we'll change the subject. The kids are too young."

"Yes, you're right. Sorry. We're going to Reid State Park next Sunday."

"John and I've been there a few times, but mostly we prefer to spend our relax-time out at Horseshoe Pond. Bobby and Corey, we're almost at the cottage," encouraged the grandmother.

The Dells had built the small, cozy wooden structure a couple decades back. The task had been a labor of love, carried out while their two daughters and son were young. Now, it was their grandchildren and a friend who would get to enjoy a beautiful day in cottage country.

"We're here already. The twenty-minute drive seemed to go by in ten. Charlie, this week please make sure to drop down to our place and spend time with the boys."

"Yup. Would it be okay for me to mow your lawn on Thursday or Friday instead of next Saturday? Me and a friend have some investigating to do on that day."

"Sure, anytime Thursday or Friday will be fine."

I had been to the campsite once before, when I was five. It was a weekday afternoon in late spring when mother and I drove out to the pond for a visit with Mrs. Dell. Dad was at work; Mr. Dell, Daniel, and Tony were at school. I was allowed to wade in the water up to my knees. Their minor beach was a mix of sand and small smooth rocks. The water's bottom was covered in slimy weeds, and the flats of my feet detested the feel. Soon, I felt a prick on my ankle. I rushed out of the water to see blood flowing onto the top of my foot. There was an inch-long worm—a bloodsucker—attached to my ankle. Mrs. Dell and mother were sitting in lawn chairs just up from the beach. I screamed. They came running, and mother hand-swiped the sucker off.

Today, for me, there would be no going into the water. The children went in without hesitation. No one figured there was need to warn them. Maybe, just maybe, the suckers would decide not to suck today. While fishing from the dock, I kept a close eye on them.

Sure enough, at five minutes in, the younger screamed out. They rushed from the water, and Bobby ran to get his grandparents. Corey stood frozen-still at the shoreline and continued to scream bloody murder. I jumped from the dock and brushed one of the two suckers off his ankle just as Grandpa Dell arrived onto the scene. Both bloodsuckers were way bigger than the one that had tried to do me in seven years earlier.

"That's the biggest bloodsuckin' sucker I've ever seen!" yelled Mr. Dell as he slapped the second one from his grandchild's lower leg, only to then slam his foot down on it. "Take that, you suckin' sucker!" Tony's blood surrounded the flattened creature. The first bloodsucker had managed to make it back into the water. Mrs. Dell came, and the two boys ran to hug her. She had a towel and wiped the blood from her grandson's leg and foot.

"John, this is the same issue we've always had with the pond. But the bloodsuckers are getting to be more and bigger every year. Look how a good-sized gash of skin is gone from Corey's ankle. This is far worse than our children ever got."

A thought came: *People should know the truth about what's happening out here, and it's my job to tell them. HUGE BLOODSUCKERS ATTACK LITTLE KID AT HORSESHOE POND.*

From then on, the young Ohioans stayed with me on the dock. I caught a 15-inch pickerel. The three of us were thrilled. A bigger one struck later, but I lost it. Next, we climbed into the small boat. The adults warned us not to paddle far from the dock.

Ponds, I believed, were supposed to be much smaller than lakes, and although Horseshoe Pond was not large, it was not exactly small, either. The body of water was situated at a sharp bend—curved similar to the outer perimeter of a horseshoe—in Cobbossee Stream, where a shallow valley—within the horseshoe's inner curve—had been excavated thousands of years ago by the scraping, gouging North American continental glacier of the last Ice Age. Like most lakes and ponds of Maine, the small valley, now Horseshoe Pond, was initially filled with ice-melt from the receding glacial mass. Since then, freshwater rains and melting snows had been keeping it and all of Maine's abundant lakes and ponds perpetually replenished.

Grazing cattle utilized the pasturelands leading up to much of the shoreline. Only one stretch of shore had cottages. Also, here and there along the pond could be found sections of shore that were more like swamps. Birds of many sizes, various wild creatures of the land, and a healthy variety of fish species all used the pond and its surrounding areas in their pursuits of enjoyment and food. The back road connecting Gardiner and Lewiston had a bridge that crossed over Cobbossee at its inlet to the pond. A time back, dad had taken Mike, Tony, and me there to fish. Standing on the bridge, I observed what initially looked like a round green monster gradually making the surface, just below where I had my rod pointed. Due to its imposing size, the thing scared the wits out of me. The turtle was over two feet in diameter! I must have scared it back because as soon as it saw me, down it went. That day, Tony caught a 20-inch largemouth bass. What a fight it put up.

Early evening, the Dells and grandchildren and I roasted wieners and marshmallows. The youngsters had to be cautioned several times about not putting the ends of their sticks too close to the flame. The occasional rowboat was seen slowly making its way past our site. Thankfully, powerboats were against the 'Law of Horseshoe,' and the absence of their crass noises and rough wakes allowed for a tranquil setting. But there was not the absence of sounds, for a myriad of birdcalls continuously graced the airwaves. There, too, were the infrequent yells of a feisty loner loon who seemed to think he was the boss of something; perhaps he was not alone and had a mate, and sometimes it was he yelling at her and her yelling back at him. Then there were the occasional fishy slaps at water's surface—sounds made from the blunt attempts of bass to chomp down floating insects. With the sky above blue and cloudless and so the western horizon, whose orange sun radiated friendly fire, banshee-spirits could have easily been given over to the belief that the campsite was perfectly placed at the doorway to paradise.

"Kay and boys, listen to me. As big as those bloodsuckin' suckers were today, they're tiny compared to what they could have been or could become at some future time. You see, if those commies had managed to drop an A-bomb on us a few years back, or those bastards decided to lay one on us sometime in the future, soon enough all those suckers'll be as big as grown men because of all the radiation in the air and water. They might even grow arms and legs. If that happens, we'll have to change the names 'Horseshoe Pond' to 'Black Lagoon' and 'bloodsuckers' to 'creatures.' They'll be charcoal gray and all busted open with radiation and oozing juices, just like your hot dogs were, and you won't be able to go anywhere near the shore because a creature of this here Black Lagoon of ours might see you and leap out from the water and"—Mr. Dell crouched down, formed his hands to look like claws, and crept toward Bobby and Corey—"run after yas and grab yas and suck the blood out of yas bodies and brains, if yas got anys." The two ran off screaming, giggling.

"John, please, that's enough of that. The boys will have nightmares."

At 8:30, we left camp for Gardiner. Mrs. Dell probed me: "Charlie, maybe Bobby and Corey can visit at your house sometime this week? We'll let them, if it's okay with you."

"Yeah, Grandma!"

"Yeah, Grandma!"

"That's a real good idea. And, Charlie, you can show them that ark of yours," added Mr. Dell. "Maybe you can help them climb up and into it."

"Yeah, Grandpa!"

"Yeah, Grandpa!"

The children's enthusiasm encouraged the grandfather. "They can go over to your place a few times and not just once, right?"

Think, Charlie, think! "Guess I can get them to look through my telescope at all the things people around here do when they think no one's looking, like picking their noses and stuff like that. Then I can show them the graves of all the dead birds that have smashed through our den window, and then there's the graves of all the other animals Tony has shot and killed. He likes to target shoot with his rifles and new Ruger. That one has a nine-shot clip. Maybe the kids can look at it and even hold it. Then I'll show them where Captain Byrd—he's a man who used to live in our place decades ago—chopped off the heads of pigs and chickens just before eating them right there, raw and all. Then there's that stove I told you about. We have it in cold storage. Even though it's not hooked up, we can pretend to use it. And then there are the graves of all those dead people who built our house *way, way back in the scaaary seventeen hundreds*. And there are a lot more things than that, I just have to think of them. Oh, how could I forget? There's a mysterious animal that's been getting into our incinerator. Tony wants to shoot it dead. Maybe the kids can be there when the job gets done. If it's okay with you, Mr. Dell, they can come over right away on Monday morning, and that way they won't miss anything."

"Yeah, Charlie!"

"Yeah, Charlie!"

"Sounds fine to me. I'll bring 'em up."

"Now that I think about it, John, Nora said the kids shouldn't be away from our yard without us. But, Charlie, like we said before, come by to visit with them often."

Daniel was pouring a glass of milk. "What's this? You're back already? It's barely nine o'clock. No matter. I've been wanting to speak with you about your rag, and now is as good a time as any. New title's pretty good. *American River Road.* Gutsy, I have to admit. Your claims about things being 'huge' and 'gigantic' are fine, as long as no on can prove you wrong. That's the way the newspaper business works—write whatever you know you can get away with. You're catching on and you might even be ready to take an important step forward. Try to find a unique story, something that'll raise you up in position and power, something that will leave *KJ* reporters stunned, if any of them ever get hold of a copy of, of, of your incredible one-page newspaper known as the great *American River Road!* Whew, I must be tired."

"Right now, I have three fires in the gas stove, but I need to do more investigating."

"Good. I'm looking forward to your next edition. I can't believe I just said that about such a pathetic little rag. I must be *really* tired. Goodnight, Charles."

"Mom and Dad aren't back?"

"Nope, and they probably won't be back until after midnight. At this point, coffees and polite conversation are over. They're now heating up the dance floor. Oh, to be a fly on the wall and watch those four weirdo twosomes trying to outdo each other."

"Me too. But it's just three couples trying for second place. Mr. and Mrs. Knight are the best dancers in America."

"No, they're not. Bobby and Barbara are."

"Who are they?"

"They're on *The Lawrence Welk Show*."

"Yuk, I hay—can't stand that show."

"Same with me, but I watch it anyway. It's one of those things you don't like doing but at the same time can't stop yourself."

Chapter XXIII

The Gravel Delta

On the way to church, Daniel asked, "Who got second place last night?"

Mother: "What do you mean?"

"At the Augusta House, when all of you were ... dancing the night away."

"Herve, do you know what he's talking about?"

"He means did you dance better than the Laithrans and McGales," clarified Tony. "We all already know the Knights are light years ahead of you."

"That's silly," returned father. "The Knights are pretty good, but they aren't *that* good."

"Yes, they are. That Watusi they did. And there was the waltz, how they so gracefully separated and came back together. I watched them while you and I tussled on the dance floor."

"To me, when they moved apart, it looked like Bea was going to slam into the wall. I was hoping she would, just to make a point about showing off. Seriously, Jeanne, I think you and I were the best dancers at the Augusta House last night."

The backseat laughed. The dance partner laughed. Even the driver laughed. When faces settled, the man offered his final assessment. "Bill and Gurt McGale were pretty good, and it was a surprise to see Dot and Bernard so full of energy. Seemed out of character for them. Those two couples tied for third place, and the other two definitely for first." Even the car roared.

Father McIver's sermon was on the subject of sacrifice. He stressed that even small sacrifices should not be discounted as silly or meaningless. "When persons abstain from certain food items they truly enjoy, like Catholics are supposed to do on Fridays and during times of Advent and Lent, the Lord accepts it when done in good will, with no complaining." He talked of how Jesus and the Father hear and reward personal prayer, how the benefits do not necessarily come as much in this life as for the next, and how prayers can be applied as a lifeline for the poor souls of the dead who suffer in purgatory. Only in our judgment will we learn of our rewards for the prayers and personal sacrifices we made. The good priest stressed that the Lord does not prefer showy displays because they derive from bloated personal pride.

After that, Father moved his homily to the subject of bigger sacrifices, including the "ultimate one," which Jesus did for us 2,000 years ago.

"Ultimate sacrifices did not end with Jesus' death on the cross. They've continued to this day, in faith situations, as with martyrdoms, and regular life, as in wars. Many soldiers, and I make special reference to those who fought in the more recent wars because persons sitting here this very morning may have served in one or more of them—and then there are those in our families who served. Well, to go on, many soldiers willingly gave over to the ultimate sacrifice. Not that they wanted to die, but they were prepared to die, and in fact did so. Happenstance is not necessarily a consideration in the matter because oftentimes the soul has agreed to it beforehand, to die for others, so that those others may live, so that *indeed* a nation may live. The truth is that if those particular battlefield soldiers did not get injured, many mortally, then others would have. We should always pray that the good side defeat the bad, and we must never forget those who sacrificed so that we could go on living.

"A soldier wakes from sleep and mentions to a fellow soldier about having a bad feeling. Sure enough, that same day the man is killed in action. Perhaps it's not death but instead the loss of limb. Sacrifice is sacrifice. And who are the most direct benefactors? Why, it's the witnesses, of course. Those who actually see the death or severe injury—it is they who have been given the opportunity to continue on in life because of someone else's absorbing the hit, like our beloved Lord Jesus Christ willingly did in the grandest of moments on the cross. Beforehand, Jesus knows of the tortuous death to be pronounced upon Him. He has a close relationship with God the Father, Who informs His Son of what must take place. Jesus speaks of this in the gospels. And He is very upset about it, with His *bloody bloodspiration*, if you will, the night before. Does this help everyone here to see better your priest's point?

"A man or woman wakes from sleep and mentions to someone close that he or she feels a bit *off* today. Later that day or week, he or she is run over by someone who had made the bad decision to drink too much and drive. Maybe the driver wasn't drunk at all but was carelessly speeding. An innocent person is killed, but the death saves the life or lives of persons who later would have been run over by the same driver. Naturally, the driver has now been given a wakeup call to turn away from his or her bad inclinations. But it is not a free ride, for the person must repent and pay in an appropriate way to both society *and to God*.

"We must always have forgiveness in our hearts, even in the most unfortunate of circumstances and outcomes. Still, we have the free will to do what we want. People can choose to benefit from or fumble away the opportunities—*the graces*—our merciful Lord grants.

"As to another side of the subject. When someone decides to cold-bloodedly kill, it does not constitute beneficent sacrifice but instead is an act of evil. The devil wants it, and we need only look at human history's odious practice of human sacrifice to the devil and his pagan demons as prime examples.

"So when it comes to persons of anarchy, brawling, violence, murder and so forth, they are not in the Lord's domain but that of Satan, who hates them. Satan has charge down there, in the below-world, and he wants as many of these not-repentant heathens and pagans as possible to come down to him. God, on the other hand, is infinitely loving and forgiving of those who repent to Him, and He has overall charge of the earth and heaven above. He is the God of law and order, and we here on earth are supposed to be made in His Image. But, I say again, the Lord God does not deny us the free will to make choices at every moment in our lives, to be good or do wrong. God is the One Who rewards, whereas Satan is the prison warden who accuses and punishes the not-repentant. So, dear parishioners, do keep your soul-person-selves in good shape. Remember about the Saturday afternoon confessional. The Foundation Testament's great prophet Daniel said, and I quote from a page I marked off in preparation, 'And I, Daniel, prayed unto the LORD my God, and made my confession, and said, O Lord, the great and dreadful God, keeping the love and mercy to them that love him, and to them that keep his commandments.'

"Dear parishioners, for sake of your personal salvation, do not presume on God's mercy, but instead do what He says and have the guaranteed hope of attaining eternal life in heaven. Have a healthy fear of the Great One Above, as you would a healthy fear of displeasing your own loving, kind-hearted human dad, and especially so if he were a president or a mighty military general. And our beloved Almighty God is certainly far, far above those titles. You never know when the Lord will come calling like a thief in the night. Amen to that."

While mowing Miss Alpen's lawn Sunday afternoon, I got to thinking that there would not be enough time to produce a newspaper for the coming Friday. Besides the Dells', there were Mr. Monahan's and the Donahue sisters' lawns to do. The fact that people really liked the paper gave me to not wanting to disappoint. My immediate neighbors would be informed of the delay. The break would allow me time to finish my investigations, alone, and that was because Mrs. Ford had phoned yesterday morning, to inform mother that Jimmy would be back for the last two weeks of August only.

After supper, I joined the Laithrans, for our trek to Creamy Frost. Mr. Laithran didn't waste time. "*American River Road*. That's a decent new title you got there, and your stories were better. But I tell you, you need something special, a surprise knockout punch the *KJ* won't see coming, like what that Clay fella didn't see himself doing to Liston. Something phantom. For that, you just might have to widen your field of investigation beyond our neighborhood."

"I think you're right."

"Got something, do you?"

"Yup, and more than one. Probably have three irons in the fireplace. I just need more time to finish my research. These days I don't seem to have it."

"What exactly do you need to do?"

"Interview my secret sources. But first, I need to find them. Then I need to figure out what to ask them. Everything depends on what they say."

"Charlie, do you remember me telling you about my having a secret?"

"Huh? What? Oh, right, I almost forgot. A secret ingredient you put in your cakes."

"Maybe you can interview me and make that your special story."

"I'll keep it mind. But thanks, anyway."

"What secret ingredient is that, Dot?"

"Bernard, if I told you, then it wouldn't be as much fun for you to read about."

"I'm probably better off not knowing."

"Have you seen more mice?" asked Mrs. Laithran.

"No. Dad sealed off our big pipe. No more will be sneaking in."

"What pipe is that?" she asked.

"We have a big pipe that runs from our concrete basement floor, into the gully. It empties the water that comes through our basement's rock walls when they leak from bad rainstorms and snowmelts. It was plugged and Dad and Tony unplugged it a couple weeks ago. The other end comes out a ways down our gully's slope. Before learning that, my dad thought it went straight down to become part of the ground water. As for myself, I thought it emptied into the sewer."

Mrs. Laithran: "You were in your place five years before a city sewer-line was put under our street, so naturally that water wouldn't go in there. Also, prior to 1959, didn't your family know where your toilet stuff went?"

"Don't know and never asked. My mom and dad probably know."

"A few decades ago, a concrete basin was put in under the Donahues' backyard, close to your east property line. Your property is huge. You know that, right?"

"I know we own most of the woods on our side of lower Kingsbury."

"That's right. The top of the containment rests a few feet below the Donahues' raspberry bushes, at the lowest part of their backyard, just prior to your property line, after which the land ascends to your front lawn. Your house, the Donahues' house, and old man Waite's were hooked into that big sewage tank. Back then in the thirties, the captain was the one who whipped up the idea, and he managed to get the Waites and Donahues on board. The thing was said to be bottomless. When I say 'bottomless,' I mean that it had no concrete bottom. Inside the basin, the bottom was dug out pretty deep. A load of coarse stones got dumped in, but eight feet of empty space was left above it. The belief was that the toilet stuff would empty in and just melt away into the rocks and ground water. In addition, a log structure was built on the one side of it, to shore up the slope. No one thought it would fill, but it did. Took a couple decades. Then, too, the concrete eventually formed fractures. We're here. Chocolate dips for everyone?"

"We can talk while eating. Go ahead, Dot, finish the sewer story."

"The thing worked okay right up to 1959, but that's because brown and yellow seepage had been taking place for years. Their raspberries grow huge because there's been an almost endless source of inhumane enrichment directly underneath them. Prior to the installation of city sewer lines, seepage was a concern for most families around here, but especially for the Bondys. Even their own toilet stuff—where exactly did that get channeled to? Probably right into the river. For years they had to put up with raw seepage from the three houses uphill from them. The stuff kept spreading and spreading onto their backyard. The smell down along their lower zone must have been unbearable. During winters, their ice was always a mix of brown and yellow. How are the ice creams so far?"

"Mine's fine, Dot."

"Delicious, thank you."

"And that culvert—the one that somewhat controls the water level of the swampy zone beside the Bondys' house? It runs underground down to the river. Shore rats use it, and they thrive in that swamp. It's a secondary base for their traveling up and down our little valley, looking for whatever they like to look for. All of us living around here need to be on guard."

"There, Charlie, do you see why John Dell should have left that giant snake alone?"

"Snakes and all kinds of animals have always wandered the secret path that runs past our house and down our gully slope, through the mini-valley."

"Secret path?" wondered Mrs. Laithran aloud. "That's no secret to us and your parents. Down the gully, near the bottom of the 'mini-valley,' as you call it, once stood your place's outhouse. After the underground basin was built in the thirties, the outhouse didn't get used much. The captain and the people who came after him kept it intact as backup, just in case. Two or three years after you moved in, your dad tore it down and filled the hole. He didn't want any of you boys wandering down there and falling in."

"We still have our outhouse," added Mr. Laithran, "but it's not an outhouse anymore. A long time ago I filled the hole in, but I kept the structure. You know our little shed that's back of the vegetable garden? That's it. We store things in there. Before running water changed our lives, everyone had to use an outhouse of some kind. Today, the formerly-great Kennebec River is our outhouse. Maybe that's a good story for you to write about in your newspaper—old outhouses. After running water came into our homes in the early part of this century, everyone's lives changed. Prior to that, getting enough fresh water was a daily chore that consumed a lot of time. After having it for a while, people got to thinking about how to deal with their bodily issuances without having to leave the house, especially at night. A crapper was placed inside the bathing room and fresh water was piped to it. The bottom of the crapper required a large diameter pipe—a sewer pipe—that went underground to the outhouse. Rats entering homes by way of the crapper was a problem until people got smart enough to make a flip-up lid for the seat in the outhouse. The outhouse still got used now and then, mostly by persons who were working or lounging around outside the home. As long as users placed the lid back down, rats and mice had no way of getting into the dugout and sewer pipe."

"You've reminded me of something. When I first started to go down to play at Mike's, I remember the backyard smelling like a bathroom all the time. The ice toward the back woods was just like you said, but it was after the new sewer lines were put in. When I asked Mike about it, he told me that it had been way worse in past years. He said they couldn't go in their yard during winters because the surface was covered with brown and yellow ice that stunk awful."

"That house should be demolished. Mrs. Bondy tries so hard to raise her kids alone. Her husband has been gone for years now. I hope they move out before the place slides off its foundation and topples over into the swamp."

"Lately, Mrs. Bondy has been talking about it. Mike's grandmother and uncle are trying to help her find a place before the winter comes. Last winter they had a lot of problems with their furnace. Kept breaking down and freezing them out. One time their pipes broke and leaked everywhere. Mike's my best friend. I don't want him to go even though I know they should. Hope it's not far away. Mrs. Laithran, did you know that there's a whole stretch of wild raspberry bushes down riverside to the old abandoned tracks?"

"No, I didn't. Why do you ask?"

"They're going to be ripe pretty soon. They'll go to waste if someone doesn't pick them. I might go down to pick and eat a few, but there are way too many. You make raspberry cookies and pies every summer. Maybe in a week or so, when the berries are ripe, I can show you where they are. If you want, I'll help you pick them. We'll need to bring a few large bowls."

"That would please me very much. I'll remind you then."

"You have to be careful around those tracks," cautioned Mr. Laithran. "There's that old hobo pass-through down there. City drunks still sometimes walk it."

"Bernard's right. When we're down there we'll need to be attentive."

"We'll go early in the evening, just after supper. Come this Wednesday I'll check how far along they are."

"Our little trip seemed to go by fast. Must have been the vibrant conversation. Goodnight, Charlie. Bernard, please try to be more careful tonight."

"Yup. And please try to guide me better than you did last night."

Part III
The Big Story

Chapter XXIV

New Marvel "Master Charge"

Dog and I exited the home. The time was just after breakfast. To start off, I tossed her rubber ball, and she ran as fast as she could to retrieve it. After a few minutes, I put the basketball down and went to throw the ball for her again.

"It's too slimy, Lizzie. Lick it off. Okay, good enough. Get your snout out of the way so I can pick it up. Good girl."

The garage door was shut, but there were noises coming from inside. Up went the door and out came Tony and dad lugging the extension ladder. They leaned it up against the eve of the roof and went back into the garage to get the roofing materials. Dad asked for my help. A little miffed, I haphazardly winged Lizzie's ball, hard as I could. It went across the Prudhommes' front lawn and into their backyard.

The roofers seemed not in a good spirit. The job would take until sundown, if it were to be completed in one day; that was what the workers wanted, which meant they did not want any interruptions, hindrances, surprises. The non-talkative adult pointed to the items needing transfer.

Though I had recently registered myself "young man," delighted I was that dad deemed me too young for helping on the roof. The hauling took all of two minutes. The mind cheered, *Back to B-ball!* I noticed Lizzie in a crouch, with a front paw up and tail pointing. Her stare was across the street, to the Prudhommes' yard, where BJ stood equally firm-footed on the edge of his lawn, just off the sidewalk. He stared back at the dog and growled. I did not know cats could do that, but now I did. So did Lizzie. No more did the rubber ball matter. She had successfully retrieved it from the Prudhommes' backyard, but the dog's intrusion must have stirred the cat.

"Lizzie, come here." She ignored me, continued to stare, and went into a deeper crouch. BJ responded in the same manner. The backbone hairs on both animals were now straight up. Fight was imminent. I went fast to grab hold of her collar, but she took off before I made it. BJ backed a couple feet and dug his four claws into the sod. Readying for action, he arched his back and at the same time shortened his body length, so that maximum forward thrust could be attained at the initial clashing together of the two combatants.

"Lizzie! Lizzie! Get back here! BJ's gonna kill you dead!"

My shouts proved futile. The female dog was finally getting her chance to do in that arrogant male cat. Now that Buddy was gone, Lizzie figured she was Queen of Kingsbury. There would never ever be a feline crowned king—not on her watch, anyway. *"Death to the cat!"* I imagined her barking the instant they hit together.

BJ was not thinking along the same line. It was true that he had set down challenge to the dog. But he would not be the aggressor because to act in such a manner was below the king's position. He would only defend, for in that role would come honor.

Hate for dog engulfed the cat's inner spirit as he caught Lizzie unsuspecting of such an onslaught of imposing cruelty. But, to my surprise, Lizzie managed to unhinge BJ: he tumbled backward a few feet. Not in the slightest way leaning toward running off, he, with lightning speed, repositioned himself sideways to Lizzie, dug his back claws into the ground, and with a raking front claw and then the other, struck Lizzie on both ears. Her barks and growls momentarily gave way to a loud yelp. Responding in a beastly rage not previously witnessed by the Monroe clan, she leapt onto BJ. The cat was now underneath the dog, and the latter bit mightily into the former and shook him with ferocity. The dog's teeth must have achieved penetration through her enemy's outer shield of fur and flesh, for the cat cried out in utter distress. Not to be outdone by the self-proclaimed queen, King Cat clutched tight hold of Lizzie's head, bit in, and shook with even fiercer intensity. The level of hate and violence the enemies displayed toward each other even America's fighting Marines would find remarkable. Recognizing neither disposed to giving in until the other resigned or died, I ran at them.

"Stop! Stop!" Startled, they ceased fighting and looked sideways at me, as if to say, "What's your problem, human?" I grabbed hold of Lizzie's collar and pulled her away.

"You're such a good girl. You won. Maybe it was a tie. Let's go get your ball." Malice gone from her spirit, she went into that happy, tail-wagging mode. I glanced back to see BJ casually, proudly walking off, tail straight up, backbone hairs relaxed. Lizzie's head showed several minor gouges, and there was a long, deep scratch on her snout. If it were not for the copious blood flowing from both of her ear flaps, the event might have been put aside as "one of those things." Father and middle brother stood at roof's edge and looked down at us.

"We saw it," informed Tony. "Is she okay?"

"She's bleeding from both ears. BJ clawed them bad. And she has other cuts, too."

"Dad, we gotta go down and check her out."

The man did not look pleased. "You go and I'll follow."

"Lizzie, come here. You're such a good girl. Wow, you really are cut up. Dad, we need to get her to the vet right away."

Though annoyed, the elder did not disagree; the dog's bleeding was obvious. He bent down and patted her head. Her tail wagged extra-fast. She was getting all kinds of attention and did not seem to know why. Rare it was for the Monroe patriarch to show even the slightest affection for the dog. He mostly "put up" with Lizzie. But now he seemed to be revealing a form of love and a sincere concern for the inferior creature. "Today's a holiday. I hope he'll see her."

The four of us left for West Gardiner, to see Dr. Denon, the local veterinarian and horse-fixer. The good man was home, and he agreed to see Lizzie. He took half an hour to carefully bandage her flipped-back ears. He let us watch, so we could learn it. He told us how often to change the dressings and gave us enough applications to last two weeks. The charge was $8.

Mother was not impressed. "A trip to Dr. LeBlanc costs twelve dollars and a dog doctor almost as much? Where's the sense to that?" She turned to me. "Maybe you should do better at watching Lizzie! Your mother and father aren't supposed to be working to pay for a dog!"

"Yes, Mom, you're right." I dropped my shoulders.

"Straighten up! Take your medicine like a man! Blindsided by a hawk and now a dog! This is getting ridiculous! Please, all of you—go outside. That way no one can see me cry. We'll eat a late lunch. Come in on your own at one-thirty and don't make me have to call for you."

"Yes, Jeanne, we'll do that."

Mother was still stewing about the $7 it had cost to replace the broken window and screen. Because of these unexpected expenses, her financial envelopes were depleted. This month certain bills could be only partially paid. She detested having to do that: carry balances forward. This was the reason the new marvel "Master Charge"—a pay-for-it-later-with-interest card—had not totally been decided on. Dad was for it, mother not so much. Ever so subtly had husband been trying to turn his wife.

"Charles, the situation wasn't totally your fault," consoled dad as we exited the house. "You know what she can be like when the hair on her back gets up."

"Yeah, but right now I'm upset about her being so angry at me."

"*Whaaat?* I'm talking about Lizzie, not your mother. You two boys listen to me. I know you'll be disappointed if we don't buy a color TV, but unless your mother and I decide to get that new Master Charge, expect to be watching black-and-white for a few more years."

"But that thing we have in there breaks down all the time," argued Tony. "The repairman keeps having to come back here to fix it, and he charges five to eight dollars every time. It would be cheaper in the long run to get a new television that works. One of Ma's favorite shows is Andy Griffith. It's in color and we can't see it because of that old crappo thing in there. And then there's *The Lawrence Welk Show*. That crappo one you and Ma like so much is also in color."

"When that 'old crappo thing' in there breaks down, I don't have to call a repairman, now do I? Appreciate what we have. We're not made of money. A new color TV costs almost three hundred dollars. Anyway, I heard from someone at work that the Griffith show isn't as good in color. Now, enough about TVs. Let's get back on the roof. The job is going to take into tomorrow. Charles, remember what your mother said about keeping a better watch on Lizzie."

As they started up the ladder, I heard the man mumble, *"Maybe we won't be getting a new car, either. The one we have is still okay. It's only five years old."*

Tony laughed. "Good luck with that one, pops."

The wife had been working the husband with her own issue. She wanted the car traded in for something newer. When it came to owning a decent house and car, mother was okay with monthly payments; it was just the discretionary items that required saving up for prior to purchase.

At lunch, mother mentioned about the home not needing a new television. Dad took it further. "We don't need another car, either. The one we have will do fine for a few more years."

"Herve, I really feel that we need something newer. The Electra is already five years old. Just the television should be enough not to buy."

"You say that, Jeanne, but the tubes keep breaking. The repairman costs five to eight dollars every time he comes here to fix it. Besides, you and I really enjoy Andy Griffith, and it's in color now. So's Lawrence Welk. Lots more shows will be in color this fall. And think of the boys and how we'll have more fun as a family and save money in the long run."

"Mom! Is it lunchtime yet!" hollered Daniel from the living room couch. "I'm hungry!"

"We're all hungry in here!" hollered back I, "and you haven't been working hard on the roof like some of us around here have!"

"Stop that, Charles! Daniel, come! Your lunch is waiting!" Mother looked at us and laughed. "Can't believe I forgot him." Her spirit was back to calm.

Chapter XXV

Indian Spirits Along the River

The Dell grandchildren had me for the afternoon. The roofers worked into the evening. Only a small portion remained for the next day, which happened to be Tony's 16th birthday. He was hoping for the Ruger. Around 8:00 in the evening, Mrs. Ford called to inform mother that things had changed, that they would be moving to South Paris in a few days, and that Jimmy would not be coming back to our place. She thanked mother and requested that she thank me for being Jimmy's friend. Even though I had come around to liking Jimmy, I was glad for the news.

Tuesday morning found the young Ohioans playing in their grandparents' front yard. I hustled by, hoping they would not notice me. They did.

"Charlie, come over and play with us!"

"No time today!"

With clipboard, sharp pencil, and determination, I went for the freight depot. Mr. Stedmont and his crew were raking the perimeters of the rail yard. A couple loads of gravel had been dumped in earlier, and a grader was spreading it around the main area. I crossed over and stopped to watch. Mr. Stedmont noticed me and came up.

"Hey there, Charlie. Anything I can help you with?"

"Hi, Coach. I came over to talk to Mr. Smith and noticed you and your men here."

"Mr. Smith? Who's that?"

"He's the man that runs the station. Will you be working on the tracks, too?"

"No. Not in this spot. People around here complained about the lot. That's why we're fixing it up. Didn't look so bad to me. They should see some of Maine Central's other yards. Then again, I hope they don't. Once we're done, folks around here should know they've the best-looking one in the state. This afternoon we'll be fixing a section of track across from Mount Tom. That's a bike ride for you, but don't bother coming. My men don't like being stared at."

"Coach, have you ever seen or heard about the underground tunnel down there?"

"Underground tunnel? What are you talking about?"

"The tunnel that runs from the Gardiners' mansion down to the edge of the river."

"Why would there be something like that?"

"For negroes—I mean, black people—to run up from the river and escape to Canada."

A look of astonishment came over Mr. Stedmont's face. Then he frowned. "Charlie, have you ever seen the back entrance to the Gardiner property? You know, the dirt road that turns off of River Avenue down near Mount Tom?"

"Yes."

"There's a heavy metal gate that stops cars from driving onto it, right?"

"Right."

"There's a big sign hanging on the gate. No one can miss it. What does it say?"

"PRIVATE PROPERTY—KEEP OUT."

"Have a good day, Charlie. Stick to baseball and church."

I thought about Mr. Stedmont's odd parting instruction, and I pondered the man himself. Like the Monroes, most Sunday mornings had him and his family at Saint Joseph's church. The man was a sturdily-built fellow whose face showed thick bone structure indicative of one who had never backed down from another man's physical posturing. He had also been a baseball coach who demanded strict work ethic and proper behavior from his players. Inside church, however, he showed a different, more humble spirit. There, he and Mrs. Stedmont came across as being committed to making sure their three children turned out good. The man was definitely God-fearing, for I myself witnessed it on the Sunday Father McIver reminded parishioners of his summer visits. That morning, the Stedmonts sat two rows to our front. When Father made the announcement, I saw Mr. Stedmont quickly turn his head to look at his wife. The matériel "fear" so totally carried the train man's face.

I walked to the station door, stopped just before it, and knocked on the outside wall. "Mr. Smith, sir, it's the newspaperman coming by to see if he can ask you some questions."

"It's you again, is it, Monroe? Show yourself. There you are. Come inside as long as you're not carrying any rocks. Quick, Monroe, I'm busy. What do you want?"

"First of all, I just want to let you know how much better the train yard looks. My next edition will carry a story on it. I have a question about something people around here would like to know the answer to."

"What's that?"

"When a boxcar with MEC on it has a load that comes from another state, like, ah, Iowa, how does it get here if—"

"I know what you're getting at. You asked me that before and as I said before, I'm busy. Why do people want to know? Never mind. I'll be as brief as possible, and then you can be on your way. I must say, it's a pretty good question. Are people really interested in such matters?"

"Oh, yes. They sure are."

"Well then, it's all quite simple, and it works like this." Mr. Smith heard my tapping of pencil's tip against clipboard. "Good. You came prepared. You'll have to write fast. How a load gets here or anywhere from someplace else depends on the source and destination. Both source and destination can be primary, such as a mining or manufacturing site, or they can be secondary, such as a warehouse or another train yard."

Schmebb's talking too fast. No way I can keep up. I'll just pretend to write.

"How and when trains transport goods is up to the railroad people to decide. The wants and needs of both the source and destination sites are always taken into consideration, and costs are also kept in mind. Are you getting all this, Monroe?"

"Yes, sir. 'Source' and 'destination.'"

"Excellent. The product may or may not go directly to its destination. There may or may not have to be transfers along the way. More than one railway may be involved, and if so, the companies may have contracts and other types of agreements in place."

You said brief, Schmebb! Hurry up or I get a rock!

"Availability and rapidity of transport can depend on customer needs and the associated costs. The whole thing can get quite complicated. Did you get all that, Monroe?"

"*Com-pli-ca-ted*. There, got it." I put two quick taps of lead to the clipboard. "Thank you for this important information, Mr. Schhmith. The story may make the next edition, depending."

"You take care of yourself, young man. Keep up the good work. We need more reporters to grow up just like you."

That evening, the family celebrated Tony's birthday. Because he was now of legal age to purchase bullets, he no longer had to claim they were for his dad. The present included two boxes of bullets. The die was cast for the fateful night to come.

Early Wednesday foreboded of another day of unrelenting heat. The last rain had been two weeks ago. Still, because of our close proximity to the ocean, the city's atmosphere remained humid, even a little sticky. An angry outburst of thunder and lightning seemed imminent. Too, there was something else in Gardiner's air: the peak putrid stench of the Kennebec River. The high temperatures and lack of regular influx of rainwater had caused the river's width to shrink and flow to lessen in speed. Hence, sewer lines of Gardiner and cities upriver had been for many days emptying their horrid contents closer to the surface of the water. Here and there, large flats of smelly sludge had collected into the shallows of the many minor indents up and down both sides of the river. Shorelines in the more open-flowing areas displayed ripple-coated surfaces made of the same crap. Things were different but no better at mid-river, for there the slowing of flow had caused the normally reasonably viscous river to collapse into an undulating centerline of chunky, brownish-gray thickness. The situation could easily be confirmed by those human contributors daring enough to walk the Gardiner-Randolph bridge. Environmentally minded crossers could now officially raise a stink at the realization that the grotesque mash of open sewer would inevitably grow wider, denser, deeper, and slow even further because of its having to take in new arrivals from such willing sponsors as Richmond and Woolwich, while working its way southward, only to then, in the delivery of a form of self-deprecatory punishment, mercilessly wreak havoc on Maine's more-coastal nostrils at its arrival into the super-sized toilet of grand release known as "Bath": exactly what people should never want to have in the waters of central Maine's primary grunge outlet to the Great Atlantic.

Same as yesterday morning, Daniel left early for the library. Sitting on steps, reading while waiting for the free bookstore to open was a far better choice than getting guilt-tripped into working on the roof. Truth was the over-brained high school senior had nothing to be concerned about. Dad had never asked and never would ask for this son's physical contribution. It was one of those silent "family things" that no one ever questioned. And, like yesterday, just before lunchtime, senior son would sneak back inside unseen through the home's rarely used front door.

I sat in the tree house. The telescope skimmed again and again the train yard, tracks, and hobo pathway. Two hours passed and though bored as nails, I remained patient, waiting, looking for the subjects to show themselves. They did not.

The roofers were done by lunchtime. Wilson arrived. He and Tony were eager to try out the new weapon, first in the basement, then at the Litchfield gravel pit, where the two would get to practice on live targets: frogs and birds. This part was secret, but I knew it anyway.

After lunch, I returned to my watch. Finally, the subjects entered my search area. I climbed down, went for the brown bag that I had prepared that morning, and left for the tracks.

Standing unnoticed on the main track, I studied the twos' body languages. Their backs were to me. They walked a leisurely gait southward, away from my position. Captain Cornelius and Two Dollar Eva held hands as they carefully manoeuvred the lower track's dense-pack of burdock, thistle, and milkweed. Both heads toted long, straight, grease-laden yellow-brown hair. The man sported his tattered Union cap and a backpack over a shoulder. The sweethearts were uncommunicative, seemed at ease. According to Mr. Barry, Wednesday was the best day to approach these hard drinkers. Gone was the wrenching hangover headache from last weekend's binge and yet to begin was the aggressive search for the extra money needed to get them through the coming weekend on the same liquid and smokes; that search would begin tomorrow. Today, I knew, was my only chance.

To address them at their level, I quietly descended the slope, cautiously made my way closer. "Ay, ay, Captain Cornelius and Miss Eva." They turned and did not seemed startled. This time I added a salute. "Ay, ay, Captain Cornelius and Miss Eva. And how goes it on this hot and smelly August day of the year nineteen sixty-six? I hope wonderful, and I bring a present for you, so that there may be good will between us."

"Bring it here, kid."

When I reached him, he latched hold of my shirt and raised a fist. "Why shouldn't I put this through your face for throwin' that dead skunk at us? You're what—fourteen of fifteen?"

"Yes, sir. But, sir, the other day my friend and I were taking orders from another captain to clear that dead skunk from his sight. He told us to take it across the road and heave it over the bank. We did as ordered but didn't think to look first to see if anyone was there. We didn't throw it your way on purpose. That's why I'm here today, to apologize and make things right."

"Cornelius, leave the kid alone. He's okay."

"Let me see what's in the bag. What the . . . Aww, for cryin' out loud, it's Bubble Up!"

"Look, Cornelius. He taped four quarters to its side."

"But it's Bubble Up, Eva! Of all the sodas to get me, he picked Bubble Up. Kid, we prefer Moxie. Oh, well, I suppose it'll go with something Fairview's got. Okay, there's peace between us. I bet I know what your favorite book is—*Treasure Island*, right?"

"Ay, ay, Captain."

"That's yours, too, Cornelius."

"No it ain't, Eva. You know better than that. *Treasure Island* is my second favorite."

"Oh, right. You prefer the Bible best. I know, I know, that's where you got your name from. Kid, his real name is Bob. What's yours?"

"Eva, how many times have I told you? Don't be sayin' that name ever again. Now you've even told this here kid."

"Sorry. I keep forgettin'. Hey, kid, you won't be tellin' anyone, will ya?"

"No. I promise."

Cornelius reached into his backpack and pulled out a small book. "Kid, see this here? I carry one around with me. It's the New Testament. The whole Bible's too big to carry all the time. I keep one of those on my nightstand, next to my *Treasure Island*. You should, too. My lady asked your name."

"Char—*John*."

"The back half of the name is familiar to me, but I don't think I've ever heard the name Charjohn. Well now, Charjohn, you take care of yourself."

"Captain, sir. I believe you might have information about some important things. And my name has no Char. It's just John."

"Just John, huh? And what are those important things that I might know about?"

"In the Old Testament, before people had pencils and paper, stories about families and other things got passed down to their children by way of word of mouth. That's what the priest at my church said. I was hoping you had information about the Gardiner family's old tunnel, something your father or grandfather might have told you about."

"The Gardiner family's old tunnel . . . ?"

"Yes, sir. The one that went from their mansion down to the river."

"Listen, John-boy, you're too young to be writin' a book. Why exactly is it you care?"

"Because, sir, people in the city are not sure if it's true, and they want to know."

"A punk kid like you is gonna tell 'em? Think about it. Why would anyone in their right mind dig an underground tunnel a quarter mile long for colored folk to run in when they can just walk on a path at night, when the air above ground is as dark as a tunnel underneath it? Don't make sense to dig and dig and chance gettin' people's attention. The Gardiners ain't stupid."

I was encouraged. The tunnel was all I asked about and here was Cornelius bringing up something about "colored folk" walking a path at night. To me, it confirmed that the grandchildren of the city's founding family had indeed been part of a secret system.

"Were the Gardiners involved with the Underground Railroad?"

"Now, right there's the problem. 'Underground Railroad' don't mean there was a railroad or anything else under the ground. It means there was somethin' goin' on at the time, and the word 'underground' meant it was secret, except to those who needed to know. After the people of that day died off, and then their children died off, a rumor got changed into somethin' else.

"Listen here, John-boy. How could a story like that get started all on its own? It couldn't, and that's why there's some truth to it. As far as I know, right from the beginning, and that was before the War of the Rebellion broke out, that story about the Gardiners has been circulatin'. My grandpappy believed it because his own pappy knew about it. Whether the stop was ever used only God, the Gardiners, and the ancestors of those who might have used it know for sure, but what it did show was the Gardiners at that time had a sympathetic heart. They's good people, and they's private people, so don't be thinkin' about botherin' them about this, ya hear?"

"I won't, sir."

"You said *things*. What else, now that you got my attention?"

"Well, ah, I was wondering about something more recent, a true story that you might be passing on to your own children."

"And what's that?"

"Something you might know about a policeman's death."

"Stop right there, kid. You're definitely too young to be that fuc—"

"Cornelius! Don't be usin' swearin' language to Johnny. You know better than that."

"Just calm down, Eva, and quit shoutin' at me. Swearin' involves usin' the Lord's name in vain, and I don't do that. The F-word is foul, that's true, but the last I knew it had nothin' to do with Jesus and the Big Daddy Upstairs."

Cornelius returned his look to me. "Listen closely, kid. How could you be so effin' stupid. You should wait for my age to be that. Stay young while you are. The stuff I know could get *me* killed. The ground you're stupidly tryin' to walk on is very dangerous. Once someone gets on it there ain't no gettin' off. If the wrong person happens to hear you know about things you shouldn't, your life's in danger. What possible reason could you have for askin'?"

"Sir, all the adults around here are upset about there being no one properly charged. And the *KJ* refuses to say much about it. Everybody just keeps waiting and waiting, and I hear that you know everything about things most people don't."

"Did you hear that, Eva! People around here know I know about this!"

"Calm down, Cornelius! It's not Johnny's fault! And I said stop your effin' shoutin'!"

"Okay! I will! Even though I shouldn't!"

"In a way, he's helpin' you by tellin' you somethin' you didn't know. You and I gotta be more careful from now on. You know what those men are like and what they're capable of doin'. You promise me right here and now we're gonna be more careful."

"You know how your Cornelius operates. He always makes sure he has options and a back way out of every situation that comes up. Still, you're right, I suppose. I promise you, Eva, I'll try to be more careful. John-boy, you make sure to tell anyone you hear say about me knowin' things that it's not true. You tell them that Cornelius is a secretive man who knows never to speak about bad things, only good things. And if he does happen to have a secret, even a gun to his head won't cause him to open up about it."

"Ay, ay. I surely will." The woman who had eavesdropped on John and me—she entered my thoughts. *Were she and her husband involved with the News Years Eve ambush of a policeman?* The moment remained opportune, but my next query could come nowhere near to the Sportsmen's Club. "And, ah, Captain, would it be okay for me to ask one more question?"

"That depends. But go ahead, anyway."

"Do you know anything about Indian spirits living a little farther down along the river?"

The man's face turned white. He looked at his woman. "This kid don't know to resign his position while in good standing. *Indian spirits living a little farther down along the river?*" Cornelius was highly agitated. "Are you tryin' to rub my face in somethin' or what?"

"No, Captain. I'm only trying to learn about invisible things you might know about."

Cornelius made a fist with his right hand and punched it hard against his left palm. He then slapped his chest with both hands. "The line stops with me, ya hear!"

"Ay, sir, but I don't know what you mean."

"That's why you need to read the Bible, John-boy. My great-grandpappy—the same one who knew about the Gardiner family wanting to help colored folk—he drank real bad and it got passed down. But I'm the end of the line. My son be about your age by now, and he ain't never gonna be a drinker. Alcohol is an awful curse, and the curse ends with me, ya hear?" He slapped his chest again, not as hard.

"You *hope* your son don't take up drinkin'. You ain't seen him since he was even before one year old, so you don't really know nothin' about his situation. And *that's* the *real* truth."

"I know he went to a good family! That much I do know! And I don't blame him for Sarah's death, like you sometimes say I do! Now back off, Eva!"

"You've never said it sober, that's true, but you've more than once said it to me when you've had too much. That's why your relations didn't take the boy in—remember?"

"I said back off!"

"Okay! Okay!"

The captain turned to me and tried to explain. "My boy, my little John-boy." He got choked up; tears began to flow. "Like you, his name was John. I called him by that name—*John-boy*. Maybe it's why I call you that, bein' you two are close enough in age. My wife Sarah died a few days after he was born. She suffered in the pregnancy. The doctors told her the baby might not get born alive but it didn't matter because she herself would likely not make it to the end. They wanted her to give up the pregnancy, but she refused. Sarah ended up goin' the distance, and the baby was born alive. But she was too sick and weak. She got to see and hold her baby boy before passin' on." Lots of tears. "It was too hard for me to see. I was already a partaker, but after Sarah's burial I went haywire. I guess I did blame John-boy when drinking, but never when sober. The boy was mine. I loved and took care of him the best I could. A neighbor woman looked after him when I was at work. But soon the drinkin' got the best of me. It's true what Eva said, that I didn't have him for even close to a year. The sitter-lady and other neighbors complained to the State about me, a drunk man raisin' a little kid. They took my John-boy away. Can't blame anyone. Probably should have thanked them. The only thing I know was that he went to a good couple who don't drink." Cornelius turned to Eva. "That's how come I know I'm the end of the line! I know he won't be a drinker! Do ya hear me! He won't never drink!" He paused, thinking. "John-boy, Eva's got the same deal—a kid she don't know."

"Why you bringin' him up! You know how upset I get!" It was Eva's turn to cry. She looked away from her man. "Johnny, he's right. I too have a son. He be five years old by now. About six years ago, Bob—"

"Don't call me by that name, Eva."

"Cornelius and I had a big argument. I decided to leave him for good and go someplace to get away from ever drinkin' again. Waterville was where I went, to a special place to dry out. I got help there, and I met a nice man. He was there for the same reason I was. The two of us fell in love. Oh, he weren't no big tough guy like this man here."

The captain smiled, made two fists, punched them onto his hips, and pushed out his chest. "Yeah, that's right. He weren't no Charles Atlas, like this man here is."

"But he was as cute as a button, and he had the best sense of humor. He told me I was the love of his life. I didn't think what ended up happenin' could ever happen to me, but it did. I got pregnant. He said to me from the start that if either of us ever found out the other was back to drinkin', the one who did the findin' should leave the relationship right away so as to not fall back into the same trap. When I found out I was pregnant it was confusing for me, so I went out and bought a bottle. When he came on it half empty, he began to cry. Then he walked away from me without sayin' a word. Later I found out he left Waterville. Johnny, I never got a chance to tell him I was pregnant with his child. Because he was so secretive about his own life, I never learned where exactly it was he hailed from. Maybe he figured one or both of us would end up back on the bottle, and that's why he never said. It may be that he came from around here, but I don't know. The only thing he did reveal was that he was from mid-valley. Sometimes I see a man in a car drivin' real slow by our building, and it's like his head is turned to look at me. But my eyesight's so bad, and it's gettin' worse. His name was—"

"Don't say it, Eva! It don't matter no more because that man's in your past. You're with me now, and that's all that counts."

"Johnny, the State did the same with my boy as they did with Cornelius's little John-boy. They took him away just after he turned two. Later I found out the family he went to changed his name." Eva shouted at Cornelius: "I know your son's name when I don't know my own son's!"

"I'm sorry, Eva. I don't mean to hurt your feelings by bringin' him up."

Eva looked back to me. "I tried so hard not to drink while raisin' my son, but without a man around to work and help out, it got too hard. I went to drinkin' heavy again. That's when the State stepped in. Johnny, don't you think a man should know he got a son?" Eva began to weep uncontrollably. Cornelius rushed over to her.

"Eva, you got me, and we got each other. We need to believe good things about our two boys. That way we can get by dealin' with the pain inside us."

Cornelius's lady was not ready to let go. "After the State took my son away, I returned to Hallowell. Cornelius and I got back together, and we decided to make a fresh start in life. We came to Gardiner. This here's a good man. I don't either know where my son is, and my poor eyesight is a constant bother for me. At night, in the dark, it's even worse. Those cheapo dollar glasses Woolworth has ain't strong enough for my eyes. Oh, Cornelius, life's not been fair to us. We need to quit drinkin' and go find our kids, to see them one last time before we die. That way we can reassure them about how much we love and miss bein' with them, and we can tell them not to become like us. We can dress up and look nice for one day, can't we? Maybe we can go visit at Christ Church and pray for the Lord's help."

"Yes, I know . . . *Christ Church*. We should try because it hurts too much believin' we'll never see them again. But isn't it better they don't know us? That way they can imagine us bein' somethin' better than we are. If I could only see my boy once, I'd tell him like you said—'cept for readin' the Good Book and *Treasure Island*, don't become like me." The man paused to wipe his eyes with his dirty hands. "Eva, I don't blame my son for Sarah dyin'. I said it once or twice, a long ways back, but I was intoxicated. You know that."

"I know. When you're like you are right now, clear-minded and good-hearted, you don't have that demon inside you, the one that gets you angry at others and blames them. But it was because of your drinkin' and gettin' angry that no relatives spoke up for takin' in the boy in. They've always been scared of your alcohol demon."

"I know, I know. It worked out best, even though it hurts me awful. Hey, kid, I'll tell you one more thing before we part company. My great-grandpappy's great-grandpappy did somethin' not right. It's one of those pass-down stories. He hurt the Kennebec Indians. He made money sellin' them alcohol, when he himself didn't drink. Go figure? The Indians couldn't handle the firewater. They took to it too hard, and it hurt their cause for bein' able to stay in this valley.

"The Bible and all—now do you see what I'm sayin'? The Lord shows he visits sin to the fourth generation and even beyond that. He might even hold a person accountable forever. When I get drinkin' real bad I sometimes stumble my way down there, down this here pathway, to that place you were askin' about. I feel like I just have to go, and there ain't nothin' or no one who can stop me. When there, I can see them. They stand in front of me, but I can see right through them. They stare. Without movin' their mouths they tell me to stop drinkin' because they've forgiven me. 'Bob, stop punishing yourself,' they say. 'Stop your drinking. We're okay with you now, so stop feeling guilty inside. We're happy here.' John-boy, it's as if I was the one who was sellin' them the alcohol back then. It's the strangest thing. They help me to feel better inside. Maybe that's why I go down there. But true forgiveness comes from the Big Man Upstairs, and that's what I need, I guess. Enough for today. Leave us alone."

"Ay, ay, Captain. Thank you for your help. Bye, Miss Eva. If it's okay, may I pass by the raspberry bushes just down a ways from here? I want to see if they're getting close for picking, unless you want them for yourselves."

"Go ahead. Eva and I've tried them in past years and decided we don't prefer them. They aren't foul-tastin' or anything. Probably shouldn't go to waste."

"Johnny, before you go, you said a priest told you about stories bein' passed down through generations. Are you Catholic?"

"Yes."

"Catholics pray for the dead, don't they?"

"Yes, for them and the souls in purgatory. I guess they're kinda the same thing."

Captain looked at me funny. "Purga*what?*"

"Cornelius, never mind about that. Johnny, next time you're in church will you pray for me and him? Will you remember to do that?"

I turned to the captain, straightened, and saluted. "Yes, ma'am and sir, I surely will."

The captain laughed, firmed his posture back, and returned the military gesture.

Chapter XXVI

The Mysterious Visitor

"This matter of the city stooping so low, thank you for bringing it to my attention. I've talked to the so-called powers down there at city hall, reminding them that the good citizens of Gardiner—the people who pay their salaries—will not put up with any more shenanigans from their—*our*—road crews. Charlie, still keep a sharp eye out when you're up there, just in case. Now, here's your check for two hundred pennies. You earned it. Got big plans for the afternoon? Swimming up at The Oaks, maybe?"

"Not today. I have another client to look after."

"Bet he don't pay you as much as I do, being so young as you are."

"You're right, Mr. Monahan. You pay the best."

"Oh, I do, do I? Well that ain't no good. I don't want to be paying anyone the best. I just want to pay the same. What does he pay you?"

"One dollar an hour."

"You're right. I do pay the best and don't mind it at all. Take care, Charlie. See you in two weeks, unless we get a good pour of moisture. In that case, I'll have you back sooner."

The old ladies were working at their flowers.

"Hello, Miss Donahues."

"Hello again, Charlie."

"Would it be okay for me to mow your lawns on Friday instead of Sunday? The family's going to Reid State Park on that day."

"Friday? That's tomorrow. Yes, that'll be fine. See you then."

"Miss Donahues, I just want to let you know I won't ever again be asking about those logs and that gigantic concrete container under your raspberry bushes. You always said it's a secret as to how your raspberries get so large

213

and tasty, other than it had something to do with the bushes' wide and deep roots. For sure, I won't tell anyone what I learned from a neighbor about how it got all choked up full of crappo and broken apart and how it's been letting out brown and yellow seepage for years, even though most around here already know. Goodbye."

The spinsters looked stunned. *What did I say? An icy parting won't do.* "And I just remembered something else. I take checks again. If you prefer, you can pay me that way tomorrow. Bye again and have a nice rest of the day."

The older sister raised a finger, smiled. "Charlie, before you walk off, and because you think you know so much, my sister and I just want to make sure you have *all* the puzzle pieces. Before the 'gigantic concrete container,' as you refer to it, filled and broke, the gravel you and your friend have for years been so eagerly playing and crawling around in was more like real gravel, not nearly as dark and silt-laden as it is now. You as well have a nice rest of day."

"Well, Miss Donahues, all I can say is thanks for telling me that."

"Don't mention it. Totally our pleasure. Isn't that right, sister?"

The Dells' grandchildren were happy to have me drop by after lunch. "Charlie, we haven't seen that dragonfly," reported Bobby, "but we're still watching for it. That's what Grandma and Grandpa keep telling us to do when we get in their way."

"The air stinks because of the river," added Corey. "Grandpa says when it gets this bad the rats like to swim around in our toilets, but just sometimes and not all the time."

"What Corey said is not quite what I mean," corrected Mr. Dell. "When we have a particularly hot and dry August, like this year, the river level gets so low that some of the sewer pipes become exposed above the water. In the middle of the night, when people aren't doing so much flushing, rats living along the river—and there are lots of them down there—like to go on the hunt for eatables. Sometimes they run up the pipes, and when they find bits and pieces of un-chewed corn and meat and other whatnots to eat, they get encouraged to go farther up the pipes, in search of the source, if you know what I mean. Sometimes people see them in their toilets. At the meeting of their eyes, both parties get the sh—"

"John, please don't say that word."

"Yes, Kay. Both parties get the daylights scared out of them. They instantly turn, one running away, the other swimming away. Boys, do I need to explain which does what?"

Both giggling. "No, Grandpa."

"The story's not over. Soon, both parties get to thinking about their situations. The rat figures he's now free and clear, so he stops running and begins to walk back down toward the river. The homeowner figures he or she better get back into the bathroom and flush the toilet a thousand times.

But the rat's no dummy. When the big gush comes along, he just hops onto a particularly elongated chunk of you know what that just got loosed from being stuck in the pipe for a month and holds on for the ride of his life, just like that Russian astronaut Yoonie Googalin did a few years back on that Sputnik rocket of his."

Corey: "Grandpa, what's a Sputnik rocket?"

"I'll explain that one another time. Charlie, the clock starts now. There's probably three hours for you today. After you're done mowing and clipping, Mrs. Dell will show you all the weeding she wants done. You don't mind weeding, do you?"

"Nope."

"Well then, a big check awaits you. I can already see myself writing it, but I won't until the work's been completed. Where's your newspaper?"

"I took a break this week. Maybe next week I'll have it."

"You might want to include something about the rat problem. Remind people to keep their lids down and to look before sitting. The *KJ* never runs good things like that."

"Mr. Dell, before you start the clock, I have a question. Some people say the *KJ* doesn't say enough about important stuff. That newspaper's not like mine. Mine has only one small page, but theirs is big and has lots of pages. What exactly is it they don't say?"

"I read it almost every day and I still don't know what they say and don't say. The one thing they do say, and it bothers me to no end, is that the bad smell of the Kennebec is due to its shrinking, which causes the alewives to die off. What we're smelling right now has nothing to do with a few dead fish. And they write about car accidents and things that happen inside the Capitol Building. You can be sure the paper doesn't report the whole ugly truth when they're told not to. Thank goodness legislature's on recess because if those politicians were sitting in that building right now, some of their sitting would be on toilets, and they'd be flushing and flushing and the smell of our river would be that much worse. Now, kids, leave Charlie to his work."

A loud engine, metal wheels rolling on metal bars, and the occasional human shout indicated activity in the rail yard below. I rushed to finish mowing. After receiving two one-dollar bills, I went to the road, carefully checked both ways, and crossed for the bank side. The sisters, back at their front flower garden, gas mower resting silent nearby to them, saw me. The older shouted, "Charlie, why did you do that!"

"Miss Donahues, please don't worry! Ever since Mr. Donahue got mowed, *I mean*, run down by that car, I've been extra careful about crossing River Road! I came over here to see what's going on with all the noise in the train yard!"

"Please be as careful on your return! You know how sensitive my sister and I are about it!"

Because the road was steep and close to the bank, there was no proper ditch. So as not to distract drivers, I descended the bank six feet; going farther would have taken me past the weeds and wild grass and into the taller greenery. Here, I was hidden from drivers' sights. Because of the steepness of the slope, the bushes situated to my front, but below me, were stunted in height, and this allowed me to have a good view of the tracks and loading area at the bottom.

An MEC diesel engine diligently worked the main and team tracks. The driver donned an engineer's cap. When backing up, he poked his head and left elbow out of his side-window. He seemed an impatient man yet at the same time careful enough to do exactly what he was supposed to. The engineer grudgingly took instructions from his co-engineer, who walked up and down along the tracks, impatiently waving out important instructions with his left hand in a sign language peculiar to "men of train." There was a time schedule to be kept; MEC's head office and depot personnel demanded it.

Before they could leave behind their inbound carloads filled with boxed and bagged materials for the local merchants, three empty boxcars needed to be temporarily relocated from the team track to the main track behind them. The dense sounds of heavy metal clasps clanking together and screeching apart brought periodic shock to the airwaves, highlighting the sometimes dangerous nature of the trade.

In gruff harmony, the two men worked speedily, efficiently. Neither was young; neither was old. Both appeared to be strong, weathered men who likely did not, even on the best of days, put up with attitude from anyone, especially chubby substation managers. The driver was wiry and of ruddy complexion, the other guy tall and wide-shouldered, with a face stretching forth the same sun-beaten, leathery skin as the first.

The driver remained self-urged throughout. After making or breaking a connection, he jumped down on the gas pedal, causing the engine to roar and cab to bolt forward. At these times wide swells of gray diesel exhaust raged up from the metal behemoth. Soon, the intense smell of spent fuel made its way through my nostrils and into my lungs. I loved it. What a welcome change from the smell of the Kennebec.

The action slowed only at the moments of coupling and uncoupling. At these, the co-captain rushed to get in-between the two units so that he could flip this and whack that in order to make the hooking and unhooking work. Once that was done, he quickly stepped back five feet to wave *Get going!* at the driver.

"Thought that was you," came a voice.

Startled, I turned. "Oh . . . hello, John. How did you know I was here?"

"When I turned off of Vine and onto this here Water Street, I saw you crossing. Wasn't totally sure it was you, but figured it might be. It worked out okay because I was heading to your place." John took a moment to look around. "You like trains, Charlie?"

"Yeah, I sure do. You said *Water Street*."

"That's the name until it makes Kingsbury. Then it becomes River Road."

"I didn't know that. It's actually *River Avenue* even though everyone says *River Road*."

"No matter. How come you didn't come around with your newspaper this morning?"

"I needed a week off to do other things. And I don't have a partner anymore. Means I have to do the whole thing by myself. Takes longer."

"Got rid of him, did you? That way you get to keep the whole take?"

"Sorta-kinda, I guess. John, you said you were heading to my place. To see me?"

"Yup—to see you."

"You know where I live?"

"Sure do, and if I do, so do others. You seem concerned. You should be. We need to talk about things. I'll join you down there and we can sit. . . . Look, there goes the train northward. Might stop at the little depot just before Hallowell. If not, the next stop will be Augusta. Might even make it to Skowhegan by early evening. The train doesn't always go up that far. If it doesn't, then Waterville will be its final place of rest before turning back."

"The train doesn't always go up to Skowhegan?"

"Nope."

"Why not?"

"Because it doesn't always need to. Goes there only when there's something to deliver or pick up. Might return this way later this evening, on its way back to Portland. Then again, maybe not."

"Are you okay over there, Charlie!"

"Yes, Miss Donahues! I'm fine! I'm talking with a friend!"

"I like what you just said, about me being a friend. Friends cover for each other, and they know how to keep their mouths shut. That way they help each other through rough patches when they come along.

"Someone must have heard us. The other day, when I said you were an okay guy and shared certain information with you? Remember how we sat down on an old stump? The house on that property has a short front yard. I should have done the same as Billy does when he goes on about that subject. He turns his head every which-way to make sure no one else is close enough to hear. Remember how I told you he does that? Well, like I said, I should have done it."

"I know what you're saying. After we finished talking and you left, I noticed a woman at the window. It was open. Right then I figured she had been listening. She buys my newspaper and knows I write things that get people stirred up."

John looked away, showed a bland expression, as if his mind was in a different universe. I didn't want to disturb him, so I kept quiet. Half a minute went by. He tipped his head to look at the tracks below.

"This means things must be happening. Her husband is connected at city hall. The two know people, including cops. That's what my sister said a time back. Lately, Billy's attitude has changed. At work I've sometimes caught him staring cold at me. Like you said, she buys your paper, and now she's wondering why you didn't come around to her place today. Do you think she knows you realized she was listening in on us?"

"I'm almost positive because as soon as our eyes met she pulled the curtain closed. Because of that, I skipped her house that day."

"This is not good, this is not good. Means my gut's been telling me right. She must be thinking you quit her place for a reason. This is not good at all." John paused again, looked around again. Serious thoughts were again ricocheting through his mind.

"This part of Water Street is where it all began. The event took place right around this spot here, a few years ago, when there was a bad snowstorm. An innocent man got done in. That deadly incident was what set unstoppable things into motion, things that should never have happened. The question is *why . . . why did it have to lead to the good lieutenant's death?* If I can somehow find out, then maybe I can get the both of us out of the mess we're in. Maybe, just maybe, I can get them to back off from what I think they might be planning to do. I'm not real sure about it, but they're not a group to put down a challenge to, and that I do know for sure."

"John, what do you mean what happened here a few years ago with an innocent man?"

"An old man was killed and the course of the future was altered. Things underneath the light of day began to happen after that, but I'm not sure why."

"I still don't know what you're saying. Please tell me what you mean about the old man."

"I didn't tell you everything Billy told me. One time he got talking and wouldn't stop." John again paused, to again look into the deep space of his inner thoughts. . . . "I should go. For your information, I don't live on Vine, just my sister and her husband do. She's older than me. We've always been close. She's a housewife and they have a little baby girl. Her husband works in Augusta. They were living in the house when it happened, that winter day. I remember my brother-in-law talking about it. He drove up and was halted in the line of cars just as the old guy was being driven away by the ambulance.

What he saw doesn't mean he knows more than what he saw. But there are missing pieces, and they need to be found and put in place. There was something that happened at the scene before he got there.

"I haven't said anything to my sister and brother-in-law about Billy. I've kept my mouth shut, except to you, Charlie. Take care of yourself. Maybe I'll see you next Friday when you bring the paper. If I don't decide to have a sore back on that day, means I'll drop by your place after work. If I sense things going downhill real fast, I may need to come by before then. I know you're nervous about me just showing up at your door. Your parents would wonder why I'm there and why it's you that I need to talk to. We can't have them asking questions. From now on we'll talk near your tree house."

"You know about my tree house?"

"Sure I do. Everyone who reads your newspaper knows about it. People talk with each other about things going on in their lives and about other things. Your one-pager has become a subject for people's chat. Think about it, Charlie. What else fun is there for people to talk about these days? The war? The race riots? Remember, not a word to anyone."

"Yes, John, I promise. Not a word. Ah, how do you get from your sister's place to my tree house without crossing over my front lawn, chancing my parents or brothers see you?"

"I enter the woods in her backyard and go straight south, below Prospect Street's dead end and above that slanted house, then into your valley where I hook onto an old pathway. I know because I've already done it once. Saw you, too, but you didn't see me. That was what I wanted, to check things out without anyone seeing me."

Chapter XXVII

The Ancient Pathway Lives

The adult male and middle son pulled into the driveway just as I did with the lawnmower. "Dad and I have something special in the backseat. You're too young, so don't come up close to the car. And you'll have to turn away as we take it into the house."

"*Ha-ha-ha.* What is it?"

"A new color TV."

Besides the usual junk food, Friday afternoon's buy would include a bottle of Moxie, as reserve, and two cigars. *I'll just tell Mr. LeClerc they're for Dad.*

After supper, mother followed her husband into the den. She looked over at her youngest. "What's wrong, Charles? You seem . . . *off*."

"I'm okay."

"I don't think so. Tell me what's wrong."

"Something's been bothering me a little bit, that's all."

"Here we are with a brand-new color television from Pomerleau's, and you act like it doesn't matter. For sure, something is on your mind. I'm concerned, so tell me."

"Alright. This afternoon someone told me the train doesn't always go to Skowhegan."

Dad: "What do you mean, 'the train doesn't always go to Skowhegan'?"

"It always makes Waterville but only sometimes goes to Skowhegan."

"That can't be true. Skowhegan is too big and important."

"You say that, Herve, but what exactly is there?"

"International Paper, for one."

"No. International Paper is in Warren. There might be an S.D. Warren paper mill in Skowhegan, but I don't know for sure."

"I don't think so. S.D. Warren must be in Warren. That's why the place has the name."

"That's why we need to go," postulated I. "We can do both places the same day."

"Good idea. We'll go on a Sunday afternoon, before the summer is over. We can eat supper at Bolley's on the way back. What do you say, Jeanne?"

"Yeah, Mom. How about this Sunday?"

"Warren, of all places. *Father*, we need not waste gas to quell curiosities, only to find out what's *not* in either of those places. And may this be the last time I have to address the matter."

"Yes, you're right. Charles, don't ask us again."

Tony: "Everyone, I can't hear the show. Please be quiet or go talk somewhere else. See, Dad, I said it nice."

Daniel was still at the kitchen table. "Yeah, be quiet in there. I can't concentrate. Charles, I have yet to purchase your new edition."

"I'm on vacation. You'll have to wait till next Friday."

"Chuckie, I said I can't hear. So shut your face, will you?"

"That's enough with your sour disposition," shot the adult male.

"Tony, how many times have your father and I warned you about that language?"

"You said don't use 'shut up.' I didn't."

"Same thing. Use 'be quiet' instead."

A commercial came. "Dad, the old path through the woods—the one Mike and I sometimes use—did the people living here before us use it to go to that old outhouse you tore down years ago?"

"What kind of question is that? No, the entrance to that path was near to the incinerator and went through where you dug for bottles. That one has basically disappeared over time."

"I feel better. I'm glad we talked. Dad, can you take me up to Hallowell sometime next week? I want to sell those old bottles to an antique store."

"We'll see when next week comes."

"Please be quiet. The news is back on. See, Mom, I did as you said."

At the next commercial: "Mom, you know how sometimes you talk to the Donahues?"

"Yes . . . So?"

"I once heard you say to Dad that they were bitter at the guy who ran over Mr. Donahue."

"Yes, and they still to this day feel the same way. Why?"

"You know how I was there. Now I would like to know more. Please tell me everything you know about what took place afterward."

"It's not for you. The sisters and I speak in confidence. Naturally, I share things with your father because we are husband and wife, but that's where it ends. Why do you ask?"

"Because I was there. I was only nine years old when it happened, but now that I'm almost a teenager I've started to wonder about it."

"Please shush. The commercial is over." It was dad this time. "Well, will you look at that. It's that Martin Luther King again. Got hit by a rock today. Why the heck does he go marching around in places he shouldn't. No wonder he got something thrown at him."

Mother whispered, *"Charles, let's go where we can talk."*

Daniel was no longer at the kitchen counter. We sat there.

"When I returned from telling the sisters to call an ambulance, I saw the driver kneeling beside Mr. Donahue. I told you back then how I heard a man's voice in my head say, *'In death comes life. Will you live it for me?'* The voice said something else but it didn't stay with me. Back then when I told you, you said the accident had been traumatic for me and to not give it any more thought. The guy felt bad. Lately, I've been thinking he was praying."

"Makes sense. He's Italian. He and his family still live in South Gardiner and he still works in Augusta. The man—Giacomin—was very remorseful. It wasn't right what the sisters did. I've never said that to them, but I did one time suggest they loosen their grip on the rope."

"What do you mean?"

"After Jim died, the sisters were all over the police department. The two are connected. They're old, they've lived in the area for a long time, and all their lives they've been civic-minded. Means they've followed the goings-on of the community and state. They've come to know people, and they enlisted their help. That part I learned from the sisters, but the following I didn't. The chief and Lieutenant Cates were hounded mercilessly. They didn't want to do what they ended up doing. At first they refused. Then came the phone calls from the Capitol and eventually the governor's office. I'm not saying it was the governor himself who made the call to the police department, just someone from his office."

"Please explain what you mean and how you know this stuff if the sisters didn't tell you."

"I'm friends with Arliss Smithson. Her husband, Lou, is the owner of Kennebec Realty. He knows just about everything about everything around here, but what he doesn't know is that Arliss fills me in. It's strange how people tell their realtors personal and secret things. Lou is not one to gossip. Naturally, he shares some of it with Arliss, just like your dad and I do. Now, Charles, don't you be telling anyone about this."

From the living room: "You heard your mother."

"Dad, I thought you're watching the news."

"Can I do two things at once without your permission?"

Mother continued: "Gardiner has seven thousand people, but it services an area of twenty thousand. With Augusta thrown in, the mid-valley's population tops sixty thousand. What I'm saying is a person can know a lot of people and a lot of things, but not everyone and everything. Things happen and soon enough they disappear from people's minds or they get covered over."

"I still don't know what you're trying to say."

"Look, you asked me, and I'm taking the time to tell you in the way it has to be. The guy was charged with manslaughter. He got a record, a big fine, and he lost his driver's license for five years. Arliss has told me that he and his family have suffered many obstacles since then. Every day he has a hard time getting the nine miles to work, and to be on time is another issue.

"The man was very remorseful. He never defended himself, just humbly took it on the chin. Everything the court pronounced on him he accepted. And there was no mercy. The repentant man admitted right from the get-go that he had been speeding. With utmost reluctance, Lieutenant Cates put together the case against him. The pressure on Cates was intense, and it affected him and his family, I later heard, and that's because he got a lot of heat from the other side. Caught in a type of Health-tex pant presser, his heart wasn't into doing the guy in. But the sisters' side won out.

"The man recently approached the two ladies, apologized again, and talked of the difficulties he and his young family were having. He said his wife was pregnant and asked for their mercy and to maybe even put in a kind word with the same powers that did him in, so that his license might be considered for reinstatement. The sisters coldly refused.

"Now, Charles, please don't blame or hold anything against the women. Jim was their life. Seeing him all bloodied-up, lying unconscious on a stretcher—well, it was just too much for them. He was such a nice man, and he had taken a liking to you."

"I promise I won't hold anything against them. You said something about another side."

"Yes, that's right. There was the side that said it wasn't the driver's fault, that it was Jim's fault. They said *that old man* made a very bad decision to be in the middle of the road just the other side of a blind hill in the midst of a snowstorm. He should have seen how city plows had not been by for a while and that there were several inches of snow coating the road. They basically said that if the old man hadn't been in the road, a road meant for cars and not persons pushing snow-scoops, he wouldn't have gotten himself killed. Like I already said, the chief and lieutenant were caught in the middle of the two warring sides. Do you see?"

The phone rang.

"It's probably Mike. He should be back home by now. . . . Hi, Mike. . . . You're moving tomorrow . . . ? Okay, but can I see you in the morning for a couple minutes? I need to ask you about something important. Ask your mom right now if it's okay. . . . Good, I'll be down then."

"Hi, Mike, how's the moving going?"

"Not bad if you like moving. Personally, I don't. Minute's all I got."

"Where are you moving to?"

"Highland Avenue. The house is on the hill, near the top. Has three stories. We've got the second and third floors. Nanna arranged it while we were gone. Good thing, too, because sittin' on our toilet was gettin' like tryin' to ride a bucking pony with your pants down. Uncle Allan knows a guy with a truck. He'll be here any minute."

"Want my help?"

"Already asked Uncle about that. Said it's for us to do. What do you want?"

"The morning Mr. Donahue got run over, you were down here stopping traffic, right?"

"You're still on that?"

"Yes, and I really need your help."

"Sure, why not. I was here till the policeman took over."

"What did you see?"

"Nothin' much except what you saw, that the old guy shouldn't have been in the road."

"That's not what I saw. I came from the top of the hill. From up there it looked like the driver's fault. He was speeding and couldn't stop in time."

"Now that's pretty stupid. What's an old guy who can't see, walk, and hear properly, especially with those thick earmuffs he liked to wear, doin' in the middle of a road on a blind hill in a snowstorm? I agree with what the cop and the other two guys said. They stood there just shakin' their heads."

"The cop? The other two guys?"

"Yeah, so what?"

"I made a big mistake."

"What do you mean?"

"Lieutenant Cates interviewed me. I told him I saw the car speed by and toot his horn. But that wasn't what happened. It's partly my fault he got killed. It's up to me to make things right. Means I gotta run with the story."

"What are you talkin' about, Monroe? Run where? What story?"

"Can't explain it now. Thanks for your help. When can I visit at your new place?"

"I'll call you."

Mike had mostly not been around for the last five weeks. He knew nothing about my newspaper because in our brief get-togethers during that time, I had not mentioned it. Hence, my expression "run with the story" confused him.

Chapter XXVIII

The Bottle Drive

Mrs. Knight slowly descended the concrete steps and onto the sidewalk. "That's a nice new car you're washing in a real gentle way, Herve. What is it?"

"A '64 Buick Electra."

"Another Electra, huh? You must really like that model. How does it ride?"

"Even smoother than the last one, and because the outside of this one is beige, the insides don't get as hot from the sun as the black one did."

"Huh . . . *beige.* Smart move, especially this summer. Hi there, Charlie. Playing your favorite sport again, are you?"

"Hi, Mrs. Knight. Basketball I like, but baseball even more. My, you look nice, tonight."

"Herve, that's quite the son you have there."

"Yyyup, he sure is. Don't know where he learned to spread it the way he does. Oh-ah, but he's right about one thing—you sure do look fine. You and Harry must be going out to an expensive restaurant."

"Kind of, I guess. He and I are going for supper and an evening of dancing up at the Augusta House. Here comes my handsome dance partner right now."

"You're right, Bea. There he is, handsome and all. Good evening, Harry. You and your better half sure do like a million dollars tonight."

"Hello, Herve. Like the way you spread it. Tonight's our yearly banquet at the Augusta House. Hi there, Charlie." The man helped his wife get seated in their Imperial Crown. "Careful, Bea . . . There you go, you're in. Make sure your arm is clear as I close the door." He turned to us. "Have a good night, men." Mrs. Knight smiled and waved.

We waved back and watched them pull away. "Mrs. Knight's not doing well," remarked dad. "She seems to be getting worse. Good thing she likes dancing. Keeps her looking forward."

"What's wrong with her?"

"I thought you knew. Ask your mother sometime. The Knights don't talk about it, or at least to us they don't. Marion mentioned something to your mother the other day. Go back to your basketball. I want to finish up with my snazzy new car before Lawrence Welk starts."

Under my breath: "I hate that show."

Dad heard it. "What you just said is a sin."

"Sorry, Dad. I should have said 'I can't stand that show.'"

"That's not much better. It's only a television show, not a person or a place. Use *I don't prefer* for things that don't matter. Besides, who are you to speak? There are shows you prefer that I don't, like *F Troop* and *Hogan's Heroes* and *McHale's Navy*. Then there's so-called professional wrestling and that silly show *The Munster's*."

"Sometimes you like to watch wrestling with me and Tony."

"I might happen to be in the den when it's on, that's all."

"And you always watch *Hogan's Heroes* with us, and you laugh."

"Okay, that one's not bad. But the others are."

"I love those shows. And what about that lousy *My Mother the Car* you and Mom never miss?"

"What did I already say? You love people and dogs, not TV shows. I watch the car one just to be with your mother, even though you're right about it being lousy."

"I heard Mom once say she loves Lawrence Welk and Dick Van Dyke."

"She did? Thank you so much for telling me that, but they're real people!"

"They're shows, too!"

"Just shut—be quiet and throw your ball!"

The Monroes attended early mass. Once home, church clothes got shed in favor of T-shirts and shorts. The day was sunny and hot, ideal for the beach. But, to the youngest son's dismay, the parents had decided to change the family's destination to Boothbay Harbor.

The hour-and-a-half trip took us across the bridge to Randolph, then south, past the western edge of Pittston, at which point the matron noted, "Randolph and Pittston intestines smell no different than Gardiner's." The auto crossed over the ever-muddy East River and entered Dresden. Yearly, at the same time of season, the brown river teamed of smelts. I always wondered how anyone could eat fish taken from there, considering the look of the river and how the air around Dresden always *smelt*. Supposedly the fish tasted okay.

Onward the Electra!

In 20 minutes, the northern outskirt of the once-important fishing and shipping city, Wiscasset, was reached. The small city still ranked as a fairly significant micro-center for this part of the state. Commercial and sport fishing, lobster trapping, clamming, and worm digging dominated the economy. The place was also a highly traveled thruway for traffic emanating from Bath, Brunswick, Rockland, and places up and down the Kennebec and Sheepscot River valleys.

Entering from the north did not necessarily prepare travelers for the picturesque beauty soon to be exposed. A few minutes put us inside city proper. Past rides through Wiscasset had sometimes had the adult male opting to drive his passengers around the city's oldest residential streets. A notable mix of old and very old houses, many of them constructed of unique architectural designs, both quaint and bold, were discovered.

Onward the Electra! The drive took us downhill, out of Wiscasset center and onto the western shore of the Sheepscot River / Atlantic Ocean Estuary, where boats of various lengths and girths could be seen moored. The two most notable vessels were the abandoned 50-year-old schooners *Hesper* and *Luther Little*; anchored near to each other and roughly a hundred feet from shore, the large, ghostly gray-brown spectacles made fun conversation pieces for Route 1 travelers.

Wiscasset was the self-declared lobster capitol of Maine. The feisty crustaceans were not trapped close to this port of call but instead were brought in from deep-water grounds situated farther out in the Atlantic. Multitudinous stockpiles of lobster traps—each with a snaring net attached—decorated the shores east and west of the Wiscasset-side of the causeway. The bridge itself was low-lying, of zero arch, and about half a mile long. While traveling it, noses had no choice but to accept the intensely rude offerings of the vast clam flats. Daily, especially along here, the estuary was subject to extreme tidal fluctuations, and when the tide went out, a plain of concrete-gray mud became exposed, allowing it to finally . . . *finally* exhale the odoriferous gases that had been slow-baking inside its mud-laden holds since the last tidal influx. Here, inside this mucky slop, grew the tastiest of clams: the *soft shell*. Unfortunately, that all too familiar scent of human excrement, steaming up from the Sheepscot River's central flow, was not exempted from adding its own molecular enrichment to the causeway experience.

Surrounding the estuary were worm farms. Worming was an important industry for fishing. The slimy critter looked like a cross between a giant worm and a giant millipede. During the day and sometimes at night, workers walked the farms, using metal rakes to dig down at the dirt, so that they could pluck up the grotesque slithery bodies as they stretched straight up into the sky, toward the false star that had encouraged them to do so. Fisherman, naturally, used the worms as bait.

The run presented a splendid passageway to what the earliest of settlers might have called "the other side of the world": Edgecombe—North Edgecombe to be exact. Due to the water's shallowness on this side, the shore retained far fewer boats and much more in the way of marshland. Here, the estuary was an avian paradise. The dominant species was seagull, but if one looked with intent, there might be detected the wings of the more beautiful birds Green Heron, short-billed dowitcher, piping plover, and western willet. And surely along this very shore might be spotted those evil invaders substitute teacher Gillis had warned of. Two eyes eagerly went on the lookout. Perhaps today one or more would drop down into the water.

"Slow down, Dad. I want to see if there's a communist in the water or on the beach."

"*A communist?* You've been watching too much news."

"Aw, come on, Dad, slow down. One might land right while we're driving through."

"Why would a communist land in Maine?" asked mother.

Daniel: "*Communist*: C-O-M-M-U-N-I-S-T. *Communist*."

Tony: "That would have been almost brilliant if it wasn't such an easy word."

"Go ahead. Take your best shot. Give me a harder—"

"I mean the killer dive-bomber bird I can never remember the name of."

"*Cormorant*. C-O-R-M-M . . . wait a sec. There's only one—"

"Too late," interrupted mother. "Tony, it's now your turn."

"*Cormorant*. C-O-R-M-O-R-A-N-T. *Cormorant*."

"You are correct. Tony Monroe, you have successfully defended your championship title against Pencils, the *former* state spelling bee champion. Congratulations."

"Well who the heck cares about how some stu—stinking bird's name is spelled!"

I pointed. "Everyone, look! There's one landing over there right now!"

"Where?" "Where?" "Where?" "Where?"

"Just kidding. Anyhoos, if we do see one I already have a name for it . . . *Yoonie*." I laughed. The others grunted, even the car.

Boothbay Harbor was 30 minutes southeast of Wiscasset. The place used to be a favorite destination for the family. *Onward the Electra!* The road to the harbor cut through spruce and pine forest, and though it presented peaceful symmetry and pleasing evergreen air, the lack of deciduous trees and open sections soon gave passers-through to total boredom.

"I wish we could go to Reid State Park sometime," came I.

"We haven't made it to Boothbay and you're talking about going somewhere else?"

"Mom, don't bother commenting back to him," remarked oldest son. Even at the harbor he would likely remain inside the car, reading a book, just as he always had in past visits.

"I would have preferred Reid," added Tony. "Boothbay has no beach."

"I thought you boys like to walk around on the rocks along the bay. You know how much you like to find snails and little crabs and those other things. What are they called?"

"Sea anemones," answered Tony. "Boothbay is fine for an hour, maybe two, but then we get bored stiff. Right, Chuckie?"

"You said it."

"Well, isn't that too bad. Your father and I like it there. We enjoy sitting in our foldouts, taking in the beautiful bay, reading our newspapers. Right, Hervey?"

"You know, Jeanne, I think Reid State Park would have been a better place to go. I also get a little bored just sitting there. I'm not one to jump around on rocks, but I do enjoy going in the water and tossing the ball with Tony and Charles on the beach."

"It's too late! Why didn't you speak up yesterday?"

"You're right. I should have. It's just that I know how much you like Boothbay."

"Today will be different, now that I know everyone's going to be suffering in boredom."

"Mom, don't listen to them. Boothbay will do just fine."

"Thank you, Daniel. I'm glad someone's on my side."

"I wouldn't go that far. I said the place will do just fine, that's all."

"Ma, please don't be upset. It's not that Chuckie and I don't like Boothbay, it's just that we don't prefer it. Can this be the only time we go there this year?"

"Well lookie here. We've arrived. You know, Jeanne, I've decided to change my mind. Right here is the place I want to be more than anywhere else in the world. I'm so happy we came here instead of Reid State Park."

"Me too," added I.

Mother groaned. She had thought to bring along a tin can. She remembered how much I used to like to collect snails and other little crustaceans to bring home and poke around at later. Even though I was past the age for it, I decided to please her and fill the can one more time in life. At stay's end, I put it in the trunk. Dad saw it when he was putting the foldout chairs back.

"Throw those in the water."

"But I want to study them later, at home." I said it loud, so mother would hear.

"Herve, leave him alone if that's what he wants to do. That's why I brought the can."

At Gardiner, the driver diverted to Farmingdale, for supper at Ernie's Drive In. We got served at the car. The tray holding our greasy burgers, greasy fries, greasy clam cakes, and slippery milk shakes sat clipped to the driver's partially open window. The adult male warned backseat occupants to be extra careful not to drop or spill anything on the upholstery and carpet. The car's first owner had kept the inside immaculate, and the new owners wanted it to stay that way forever. The youngest still managed to knock over his milkshake. An indecent amount made it onto the seat; some even seeped into the cleavage between the seat and backing. I wiped it up as best I could. Tony, happily: "Uh-oh, Chuckie spilled his shake. Ma, pass a bunch of napkins back here before it soaks into the seat more than it has already." When calmer emotions returned to the Electra, eating continued.

"Dad, can we go to Hallowell tomorrow, so I can sell my bottles?"

"Go ahead, Herve. Why don't you take him."

"I don't want to, and I really don't have the time. But I guess I will and that way I won't be asked again. And, Charles, it's not *we* who are going to sell the bottles—*it's you*. Tony, you can come with us."

"No thanks. Wilson's picking me up in the morning. We're going to the Litchfield gravel pit to practice with the Ruger."

"I thought you two did that already."

"We did. But we need a little more practice to become expert marksmen."

"Are you going to shoot more frogs?" I asked.

"You're shooting frogs?" Dad looked at him through the rear-view mirror.

"Yeah, I guess so, but not that many. There's a swampy area at the pit. A hoard of them live there. Nobody'll miss a few." Tony stared angrily at me.

Father did not pursue it. Perhaps my arms would escape Tony's meting out of justice. He had also done in a few small birds, but I knew better than to reveal this tidbit, for my head might end up paying. Suddenly it occurred to me that having the information could work in my favor: "You punch me about the frogs, I tell about the birds!"

"Mom, why do—"

"What-what? Ask your father. And I promise not to say anything."

"Dad, why does Mom like that crappo show *My Mother the Car* so much?"

"I've never asked her. Let me think. . . . Probably because she gets to see her favorite actor's mother, especially now that *The Dyke Van Dyke Show* has been canceled, I'm so thrilled to say." He put a quick hand to the horn and laughed. Daniel sighed out his resignation at having been born into such a farcical family. Tony chuckled. I thought *Huh-what?* And my mother and the car said nothing; both kept looking straight ahead.

We arrived home tired. Dad said the unloading could wait for morning.

I managed to fit all 15 bottles into a single large box. The trunk had yet to be emptied, so I slid the box onto the backseat. Dad wanted to be back home by 11:00. The day was already boiling.

Fifteen minutes' drive brought us to the first antique shop. The window showed a rack filled with the same types of bottles that I had in the box.

"That store won't buy because they already have too many they can't get rid of." The adult slowly drove the main. Only the lesser-quality outlets had old bottles in their windows. The better shops displayed nice things, such as unblemished antique furniture, figurines, and vases.

"Dad, that store right there should do."

"Good because there's an empty parking spot in front."

"Can you come in with me?"

"Okay, but you do the talking. Remember about this not being mine."

"Yup." I slid the box from the backseat. Scrapes of old oil and grunge from our garage floor lined the tan upholstery. I ignored it, said nothing.

We entered. "Hello, Mr. Sir. My dad and I were driving by and noticed you have a few old bottles in your window. You must have sold a bunch of them this past weekend to people from New York. Would you like to buy the ones I have here to replace them?"

"So far, young man, you haven't gotten anything right. I have *a lot* of bottles in my window, which means I didn't sell any or at most one or two. Regardless, show what you have."

"Here they are. None are broken. They're as good any I've ever seen."

"I'll give you a nickel for each. Wait—I'll give you an extra nickel for each of those three. Hold on a sec. That one right there is worth fifteen cents to me. Let's call it an even dollar for the whole box."

"Sounds good to me. Thank you."

"Charles, don't you think you should try another place? A dollar doesn't seem enough."

"You and your son are fine to do that, but I doubt you'll do better. I'll give you an extra quarter, and that's my final offer. If you leave with them, please don't bother me again."

"Dad, I don't want to go anywhere else. A dollar and a quarter is good enough."

He turned away.

"Mr. Sir, may I ask a question?"

"Go ahead."

"What do people from New York do with old bottles?"

"You know, Charles, that's a good question. Truth is, they usually ask me what they can do with them, and I sure tell them. You and your father have a great day."

"Sir—"

"Nope. You said *a* question."

Out in the car, the man let loose. "I will have used more than half a dollar of gas getting this big boat to and from Hallowell, all for you to make a buck and a quarter. How much time did it take for you to dig up those bottles? Don't bother answering. What I want is for you to think about this situation and how I've wasted the better part of the morning. Maybe you should be a little more careful about requesting my time on weekdays, considering all the work I still need to do on the house. I spend a lot of time with you boys on weekends, don't I?"

"Yes, Dad, you do. But digging up bottles in the gully kept me busy, and that way I was able to stay out of getting into trouble someplace else."

"Be quiet. You're supposed to stay out of trouble all the time everywhere."

"You're right. Sorry, Dad. Because it's so hot, I'll buy each of us a Frosty Root Beer."

The man did not respond, and we did not exchange another word until the Shell Station. "If I'm to divert to Gardiner Fruit, you're going to have to put out for some pretzels, too."

"Okay. I'll do that, and you don't even have to come in." We parked. "Dad, why are you getting out of the car?"

"Because I want to. And since when do I have to explain myself to you?"

The adult went directly to the sales counter. "Hi there, Bob."

"Hey, Herve, what can I get for you today?"

"One simple but beautiful smelling El Producto. Here's a nickel. My son's getting some stuff, but he's paying for it. Things sure are dry out there."

"Got that right. Need rain real bad. Sorry to tell you this but a single gar is up to a dime now. Anything new in your neck of the woods?"

"Not much. Here's the extra nickel. Just now got back from taking my son to Hallowell so he could sell fifteen old bottles he dug up from our gully. Took him hours to do it, and then to use my time and gas driving him there so he could get a whole buck and a quarter from the antique shop." The owner laughed. Dad joined in. "I guess it's best to have a sense of humor about some things. Elli was saying something the other day about rumors the shoe mills might be moving out or closing down completely. In case any of your customers are worried about that happening at Kennebec Manufacturing, up there on Northern Avenue, they needn't be."

"You *hope* it doesn't close down, but you don't really know, do you?"

"Oh, I'm pretty sure. I've met the owner a few times over the years. A real nice man. He founded the company back in the twenties, and he told me and the manager his factories will never move one inch except to expand. He's old now, but his sons are nice men, just like him. I've met them. Someday they'll take over. But you didn't hear any of this from Herve."

"Count on it. There's your little buddy. Two Frosties and two small bags of pretzels. Herve, I'm just now reminded—don't you want a Swisher Sweets with your El Producto?"

"Nope, don't like that one. Too sweet."

Mr. Newsome looked at me. "I'll definitely remember that for next time. Young man, that'll be seventy cents."

"That's too much."

"Charles, pay him."

"But I've already got it figured out. What I have should cost only fifty cents."

The owner smiled. "It goes like this, young fella. My suppliers recently raised their prices, and if I'm to stay in business I have to do the same to my customers. A small bottle of soda is now twenty-five cents and a small bag of chips a dime." He looked back at dad. "A big bag is up to thirty-five. Can you believe it?"

"The way of the world these days." Dad leaned in. "Seems too quiet out there. Been nothing in the *KJ* about what happened up at the Sportsmen's Club. Guess no one really knows the details, and maybe no one ever will."

"On the surface that's the way it may seem."

"Now that you say it, just the other day I heard from a good source that there are certain people who know there's a story behind the story. That's exactly how he said it. Would you happen to be one of those people, Bob?"

"I shouldn't be. Elli, either. But like you got from your source, he and I hear things that no one except those on the inside know. Elli in particular hears because he works the Friday and Saturday evening shifts. That's when cops and certain others come in here to pick up mixes, snacks, and smokes. If it's later in the evening, they might've already had a few, but not the cops on duty. Some persons get talking. Like I said, especially with Elli because he's so friendly. People just open up to him. Maybe the guy you talked to is in the know. For us here, it happens like this. Over time, Elli and I get a bunch of pieces to whatever puzzle. Then we put them together to see the whole picture. There seems to be some kind of disagreement going on behind the scenes. The powers can't come to agreement on certain matters regarding Cates, and what I can see coming from it is more trouble. Hate to say it, but backwoods beatings and maybe even deaths. Didn't hear it from me."

"Count on that. But what about justice for the policeman's family and for his soul, so that he may rest in peace?"

Another customer entered the store. It was the owner's turn to lean in. "In the mysterious case of Lieutenant Cates, justice may be something only

God will deliverer." The new arrival approached the counter. Mr. Newsome straightened up and smiled. "I know what you mean, Herve. It's too dry out there. Maybe there'll be rain tonight. What do you think, Lou?"

"You bet, Bob. For sure Gardiner's gonna get pounded, if not tonight then sometime this week. Feel it in my bones."

After exchanging a quick greeting with Lou, dad headed for the door. I followed slowly, paused before exiting. Maybe the real estate man would have something hot.

"What have you got for me today, Lou?"

"Nothing much. Things are quiet. How about you?"

"Nothing much, either, except for the funny little story I just heard."

That guy Lou was probably right. Realtors in small centers even know about the weather. Due to the lack of rain, the ground was dry. In spite of it, foliage and lawns remained relatively green and growing. The valley's heavy humidity, ever moving up from the ocean, was the sole reason browning and crackling had not taken hold and the young man still had mow-jobs to do.

Chapter XXIX

Night of Unrest, Hysteria

During supper, the adult male mentioned about wanting to have a peaceful and uninterrupted final few days of vacation, so that he could finish scraping and painting the house's oldest section of shingles, located on the upper northeast wall. He had started the job that afternoon, and he wanted to continue with it after *The Huntley-Brinkley Report* was over.

"Jeanne, NASA launched a spacecraft to go around the moon. It's to keep an eye on the Russians after they get there first. . . . That jerk Lennon's decided to apologize for saying the Beatles are more popular than Jesus. Wants to make sure about making more money, that's all. We'll see how popular those clowns are in fifty years."

"Yes, dear, you're probably right. But don't let him get your goat."

Dad cracked a pretzel between his teeth. "Yup."

Tired, barely able to keep eyes open, I thought about hitting bed ASAP. Then other thoughts came: *Really? This early? Decide when the news is over.*

Playing hoops with Tony won out over bed. I paused to look down at Lizzie. She lay on the lawn, chewing away at the big ham bone mother had given her after supper. Dad exited the house and waved for Tony and me to follow him to the jobsite. He wanted our help in leaning the extension ladder up against the tall northeast wall. After watching the man climb it 20 feet, we turned back for the court. Dad could be heard scraping like a madman at those old shingles. Maybe it was John Lennon's throat he was really scraping.

Time went by, and the sun began to set. Mother emerged from the house. "Boys, go tell your father to come in right away. It's an emergency."

"What's wrong?" asked Tony.

"I hear rodents running around inside our walls. They sound pretty big, which means they're rats. Now go quick and get your father. Lizzie, come inside with me."

Tony grabbed the bone away from the canine and pointed. "Lizzie, go with Mom. Get in the house with her. Go! How come you never listen to me when he's around! Go, Lizzie! Now!"

The two of us went rapidly to tell dad. He hasted down the ladder. "Get away from me!" shrieked from the open living room window. "Scat! Get away! Help, someone! I said get away! No, Lizzie! I didn't mean you! Get back here!"

The brothers followed after their father. He rushed us past the killer picture window and black incinerator, then past the backside of the garage and its creepy crawl space. Dusk was arriving and grayness was settling in. We made our way around the ex-barn's west side. I saw Mrs. Laithran placing wet clothes onto her side-porch railing. Not wanting to be impolite, I waved. The three of us got onto the driveway. I noticed Mr. Prudhomme, Frank, and BJ standing on their lawn, looking our way. I waved. Frank waved back. I looked up. Sure enough, Mr. and Mrs. Knight were looking out from their upstairs living room window. I waved. They smiled and waved back.

"Go get 'em, Charlie!" hollered Mrs. Knight.

"Thataboy!" came Mr. Knight

Inside we found mother sitting on the kitchen counter, Lizzie hiding under it.

"You men took long enough. There are two of them—*two big rats*. At first I heard them in the walls. That's when I went outside to get you. When I got back in I couldn't hear them. Lizzie and I walked around, and when we made the living room, that's when they ran at us. Thank goodness Daniel had already gone to bed. He must be sleeping because he didn't come downstairs after I spoke out loudly at them."

Tony, sarcastically: "*Ha-ha-ha.* Mom, you didn't speak out loudly, *you screamed.* The whole neighborhood heard you. Dad and I pretended not to notice everyone gawking at us as we made our way in. Neighbors must think we're a bunch of screwballs."

"Hey! *Ha-ha-ha* back to you!" Dad looked hard at Tony. "Don't speak for me, and don't speak that way to your mother. All women scream when they see rats. Don't you know that?"

"Sorry, Dad. Sorry, Mom. I promise not to do it again. Where did the rats go after you *spoke out loudly* at them? And what did Lizzie do? Didn't she chase after them?"

It was my turn. "Everyone, please don't fret about our situation because I'm going to take care of it right now." Pretending to use a cane, I limped to the dining room window, bent over, and hollered, "Every neighborhood needs a family like ars! Thataways yas all can believe how normal yars ars! *Ha-ha-ha!*"

Up the street came Mr. and Mrs. Robbins, apparently out on another one of their evening strolls. They stared while slowly continuing on by.

"Last time we killed a mouse! This time we're gonna kill two big rats! *Ha-ha-ha!*"

"Charles, pull away from there!" yelled Captain Dad. He took my place at the window. The ship's dog went up beside him and stood with both her front paws on the sill. "Oh, ah, good evening, Paul and Alberta. Charles is right. We got a rat situation in here. Lizzie and I are taking care of it. Please continue enjoying your walk."

"Thank you for your permission. We already were."

The conversation, if one could call it that, was over, but dad and dog remained at the window. "Hello, there. I guess we can hear distant thunder coming from over Chelsea way. It's probably heading for us. What do you gentlemen think?"

Lizzie firmed her posture, squared her ears, lifted her snout, sniffed in as much air as possible, and quickly concluded the alien molecules were of a hostile source. She growled. A few seconds passed by and dad pushed away from the window and dog went down to all fours.

"That was the oddest thing. Two men just now walked past Paul and Alberta. None of the four said anything to each other. That didn't surprise me. But when I addressed them, they said nothing back and just looked at me. I didn't recognize them. One carried a flashlight. I watched as they went down the street, and, son of a gun, they turned off into old man Waite's woods, near our property line. I think they got onto Jim Donahue's old shortcut. *Strange.* Something doesn't feel right. Jeanne, please call the old ladies in the morning. Maybe relatives are visiting them."

"Okay, I will. Now let me finish. We—I mean, Lizzie and I—entered the living room. She got up on her chair and didn't notice the rats when they came out. After I said for them to get away, they turned and ran under the stereo, just like that mouse did. But again Lizzie must have thought I was talking to her because she slumped out of her chair and, with tail between legs, cowered out of the room. Our watchdog has been of no help. The rats must have had a quick talk about their situation because next thing, out they ran, for the wall opening in the back hallway, where you've been working on that the electrical outlet, *father*. That must be how they got in here from the basement. I again heard them scurrying around in the walls. Then nothing."

"Charles, go get that new flashlight of yours. If they haven't escaped through the drainpipe, they're probably hiding somewhere in the basement, trying to wait us out, till they think no one's home. Then they'll come back up here and eat our food. Rats usually work in twos. They're smart, but not as smart as me."

"While Chuckie goes for the flashlight, I'll load my Ruger. He can shine light around down there, and when we find where they are, you sweep them out into the open so I can shoot them dead. Promise not to miss. I'm definitely a marksman now."

"Don't be silly. There'll be no gun. But the broom is a good idea. Charles—flashlight?"

"Yup. Got it."

"Tony, go into the garage and get the dirt shovel, not the spade. I'll get the broom from the closet. If we find where the rats are hiding, I'll do as you said—sweep them out. Then you can bang the shovelhead down on them."

"Lizzie, stay here with me." Mother bent down to pat her faulty watchdog's head. The little girl was back in the good books. "You're my only girl, so I forgive you for failing me. But you better come through next time and kill those rats dead, like you did the squirrel last year."

Lizzie pranced and wagged her tail at the matron's attention.

The basement stairwell had several steps with long cracks; each one creaked three times as the men descended. If still present, the rats were now aware of our approach. The lighting was decent only in the central area, where the shooting-table sat. Perimeters and an earthy room that formerly stored firewood had poor to zero lighting. Putting shine into those areas was my duty.

Dad's preference was to find, extract, and kill the sharp-toothed invaders as soon as possible. If they had not already escaped, they were not to. The killings would be for middle brother to do, for the father's "position" in the home was above such violent display.

There was another room to be concerned about: "the secret room," we called it. When the connection to the garage had been done in the 1930s, a concrete room had also been put in, underneath the den. For reasons only Captain Byrd and God knew, a proper doorway into it was not cut from outside or inside the home. The room could only be entered through an opening located high up on the concrete wall it shared with the basement. The hole was big enough for one person at a time to pass through.

Years ago, Tony and I had used dad's stepladder and flashlight to peer into the prison-like cell. Old garbage and wood scraps covered the floor. Later, dad shoved several long planks through the hole, to keep them stored in there and out of his way. Two were placed with one of their ends sitting on the bottom lip of the hole, the other ends on the floor. This allowed for persons, mice, large arachnids, and rats alike to slide down into the room. Perhaps our two intruders had scampered along the tops of our stone and concrete walls, then onto the planks and into the room, to hide out. Sometimes we had found dead mice on the upper ledges, generally a day or two after the adult male had put down D-Con. This is how we knew that the scent of a rodent runway existed up there. But rats were too smart to bite down on store-bought poison.

We slowly checked the basement's unlit outer zones. I shined the flashlight as we went along. We entered the old firewood room. The empty unit was particularly humid and musty this night. As I flashed the beam across the stone wall, large spiders retreated into the little chasms and tunnels that inundated the 170-year-old, vertical rock network. No rats present.

"Charles, you'll have to go through the hole. You're the smallest."

"Why is that room there, anyway?"

"Don't rightly know what Captain Byrd had in mind when he put it in, and then without a doorway." A serious look came over the man's face. He threw his head left and right, then stared all scared-like at Tony and me. "Only the dead are allowed to live in there. Do you boys know why? Because it's *purrr-gahhh-torrreee*. Charles, I'm kidding. Get in there."

"What's purgatory, again?"

"Start climbing. It's the middle place souls go to before God allows them through the pearly gates. Catholics believe it exists but Protestants don't. They think everyone just goes straight to heaven or hell and there's no in-between. Boys, don't give it much thought. Just live good lives, do what you're supposed to do, and don't do what you're not supposed to. Okay, you made it. Sit and slide yourself down. Try not to get splinters stuck in your rear ass."

"The grains go the other way. It's coming back I'll have to be careful about."

"When you're all the way down, I'll pass you the shovel. Tony, I don't think we checked underneath the shelving unit in front of the brick wall."

The basement contained a large brick structure that spanned from floor to ceiling; it supported the hearth just above it, in the kitchen. Three decades ago, the captain encased the large brick oven within walls, but in the basement he built a shelving unit only on one side of the support. No one in our family had ever set eyes on the kitchen's old-world stove.

"You're right. We didn't. That was pretty stupid of us. Chuckie, don't go any farther. Slide back up just enough to pass me the flashlight. Dad, can I use the word 'stupid' when Ma's not around? Sometimes that's the only word that'll do."

"I suppose, but only infrequently and when Daniel's not in earshot. If he hears you, then he'll go back to using it all the time, and I definitely don't want that."

I flipped over onto my knees and stuck my head out of the hole. Tony bent down and shined the flashlight under the unit. Sure enough, out raced the two terrified rodents.

"Don't let them make the pipe!" shouted Tony. Dad swept at them with the broom. Both rats tumbled into the base of the brick wall. Brother rushed for the shovel, which he had leaned up against the stepladder. Dad also went for it.

With intent to land squarely on the ladder's top step, I thrust myself from the hole. As my lower body exited, a sliver of wood jammed through my pants and into my knee, causing me to flop out sideways.

"Ouch!"

The ladder tilted just as dad latched hold of the shovel. I tried to steady it, but couldn't. He raised the shovelhead, and Tony rushed in to grab the handle away from him. In doing so, Bigfoot booted the lead rat forward, out of harm's way.

"You said *I* get to kill them!" The shovelhead came down on Tony's foot. "Ouch!"

"Dad and Tony! Catch me! I'm falling!"

The two looked up just in time to receive the ladder and me onto their shoulders. All of us went to the concrete, but no one landed hard. A little embarrassed, we quickly stood up and looked at each other. Then we laughed and brushed the dust and soot from our clothes.

"Chuckie, you look pretty scary. Your face is all smeared from your hands being dirty. Don't touch your face anymore. It's ugly enough now."

I crossed my eyes, gritted my teeth, rubbed my face with both hands, and with fingers combed my hair straight back. "*I'm not a Monroe anymore. I'm a Munster.*"

"You're more stupid than I already thought you were."

"Both of you, stop it! The rats must have made it into the pipe. They're either waiting in there or already out the other end and into the valley. Tony, bring the shovel and let's get into the gully. Charles, give me your flashlight and go get the bucket. Fill it with hot water from the boiler's faucet. When you hear me tapping on the other end of the pipe, pour it in."

"Dad, this is a perfect spot for my Ruger. Let me bring it—*please*. If the rats are in there, the hot water will stun them and flush them out. You shine the flashlight on the end of the pipe, and I'll shoot them dead the instant I see their ugly little heads."

"Forget it! Use the shovel!"

The long sliver of wood was lodged in the skin just above my right knee. The end stuck out through my pants. I pulled it out. The tapping came. I poured the bucket of hot water into the catch basin, threw the bucket down, and quickly headed outside for the gully.

The lightning was more intense, and the thunder followed sooner than before. The realtor had been right. In a few minutes, Gardiner would be engulfed in heaven's fury. Though the rain had yet to begin, violent winds battered the trees.

Past the tree house, I carefully felt my down the steepest part of the slope. Nearing the bottom, I noticed a light approaching on the old path. After a moment, I made out two dark figures. The adult male and son stopped ten feet from me. Dad shined the flashlight onto my face. I did the same facial contortion and growled out, *"Father and brother, did you manage to find and kill both of those intruders or do you need me to do the job with the Ruger."*

The two exchanged whispers, turned, and disappeared back down the path.

"Hey! Where are you going? Wait up!" I groped my way forward. "Wait up, I said!"

"What do you mean 'wait up'? We're over here, at the pipe."

I looked left and discerned a small light through the leafy branches.

"Dad and Tony, is that you?"

"Who else? Wait where you are because we're coming your way."

"Why did you come out here before?"

"We didn't," answered Tony. "We just now finished."

"Dad, those two guys you saw—you said one had a flashlight. A few minutes ago it must have been them I saw on this path. When the guy flashed light onto my face, I pretended to be a monster like before and must have surprised them because they turned around and left."

"Rain's started. Let's get inside. Your mother's all worried."

"Did you kill the rats?"

"No. The stupid things weren't in the pipe, which means they're not that stupid. This time, Dad and I triple-wrapped the screen around its end. Nothing else will get in, *hopefully*."

The clock showed 9:30. Dad said everyone best go to bed. With all that had taken place and with the thunderstorm soon to enter its peak rage, sleep would likely not begin until the ten o'clock train arrived. No *Shooting Times* and *Treasure Island* tonight. Tony turned off the light.

A minute passed and we heard someone ascending the stairs to our bedroom. No lights were on in the house. A lightning flash lit the room. A man loomed large beside Tony's bed.

"Boys, we've got trouble. Come downstairs with me right now. There's no time to get into your regular clothes. One of you put Lizzie in Daniel's bedroom."

"Why, what's wrong, Dad?" asked Tony.

"Your mom and I heard those fellows walking across the porch. Don't turn on any lights. Tony, get your Ruger and fill the clip. Charles can shine the flashlight while you do it. It's on the desk. Both of you do as I say and fast. Then get your raincoats and shoes on."

"Herve, I'm scared." Mother was in bed, covers pulled up to her eyes. "Please stay inside and call the police."

"Jeanne, I said it already, the job is for us to do. Anyway, the storm has likely put the phone out."

"I'm worried about Daniel."

"Don't be. He's sleeping and Lizzie's with him. We'll tell the both of them in the morning what happened." Dad turned to his boys. "Gun? Flashlight? Are we ready?"

Both: "Yes, Dad."

"Then let's do the job. Tony, stay close behind me. Charles, you follow behind Tony. Keep the flashlight off until I give the word. We want to catch them off guard."

The storm was in full delivery. Wild winds and deluge failed to turn us back. Our gushing adrenalines pushed our spirits into heightened states of awareness, readiness. We hustled past the front of the garage and around the west side, onto the elongated greenway. Dad halted us at the incinerator and whispered, *"I think they're just ahead of us, beside the bamboo. Tony, come up next to me. Keep the gun pointed down and don't flip the safety till its time. Charles, stand beside Tony. Keep the flashlight pointed forward but don't turn it on until I say. From here, we move extra quietly."*

Because the house blocked the streetlight on this side, we were in total blackout. A double flash of lightning lit the air, and two almost-deafening thunderclaps instantly followed. The split-second moments exposed the backs of two figures ahead, next to the bamboo, as dad had said. The beings were oblivious to the fact that three men were now on to them.

"They're turning the corner and heading into the front yard!" came dad in a loud, excited whisper. *"Let's move fast! Charles, put the flashlight on! Tony, flip your safety off and keep your gun pointing forward! Hold it tight with both hands! Quick! Quick!"*

"Dad, the flashlight won't come on!"

"What! It worked fine in the gully! Bang it with your hand!"

"Still doesn't work! Maybe the batteries are used up!"

"You should always check beforehand and know to keep backups! Never mind about it now. Let's just get up into the front yard!"

We shot around the corner and saw the two backs moving fast for the southeast bend of the house. The intruders were now aware that someone was on to them! Here, the streetlight helped a little. Making it around the corner would allow them several routes of escape. They could even enter the house! The kitchen! The parents' bedroom, where the frightened Monroe matron lay, with covers up to her eyes!

"Tony, shoot 'em!" ordered dad. "Shoot 'em right now! Quick!"

An odd thing took place: brother hesitated. The home's shooter was not yet of the belief bullets were necessary on humans. His spirit needed convincing, but there was no time for that, or so I thought. Then it happened again, that slowing of time to an almost-stop, just like at the Sunday spread in Randolph and two and a half years ago, when I looked down at the dying Jim Donahue. Suddenly, loud pig squeals and the cackling of a dozen hens filled the dead airspace. The panicky pleas seemed to emanate from the northeast corner of our lot, near the crawl space, where there had once been *that pen*. A particularly upset pig began to squeal above all others. Then came a man's loud voice. "Gotcha! You're coming upstairs with me, to fulfill your eternal destiny of filling my family's bellies. And there'll be no escaping for you, so just shut up!" The pig cried out in desperate pig manner as the sound of two feet rapidly climbed those former steps to bloodletting. A door creaked open—banged shut. The man and the pig were now inside and making it official. Almost instantly, a loud thud came, and with the ghostly animal sacrifice all animal noises immediately ceased. Right above us, a second-floor window slammed open. It was not Daniel's window, but the one in the old kitchen. A ghastly looking 50s woman leaned out.

"Kill them, Tony! Kill them dead before they come in here and gas us!"

A uniformed man, thin-faced and light concrete in color, leaned out beside her. "Mr. Monroe, you have your orders. You are to gas them immediately. Do you understand me?"

"Yes, sir. I sure do" But brother continued to hesitate.

"Tony, I beg you," pleaded the dead stalag commander. "Please gas the both of them before they come in here and take us away. Whom will you talk to during the long nights?"

BLAM-BLAM. BLAM-BLAM.

The blasts startled me back into the reality of regular time. I turned away from the old kitchen's window to see two bodies lying facedown on the lawn, 30 feet to our front.

"Got 'em. Told you I'm a marksman. They won't be bothering the Monroes ever again."

"Good shots, son. Let's go flip 'em over. Charles, you can shine light onto their faces."

"Dad, I already said it doesn't work."

"Oh, right. Anyway, the streetlight should be good enough."

We turned them over. Stunned, the three of us straightened up and took a step back. We silently stared, disbelieving of the horrible sight before us.

"Ah, Dad, Tony killed the Mortons dead."

"I see that. I guess Rae and Carl must have heard our commotion earlier in the evening. Probably got worried about us. Because the phones are out, they came out here to check to see if we Monroes were killing each other. Instead, Tony ended up killing them, and now they'll never know. Oh well, they're already dead and nothing can be done about it. Best I don't call the police in the morning. And, Charles, forget putting it in your newspaper. Too bad. Carl was my most dependable machinist. We'll take in their baby. Your mom and I always wanted a daughter. We'll need the spade and the regular dirt shovel. We'll dig a hole big enough for the both of them, in the gully, near where Charles dug for bottles. Tony, you drag Rae and I'll do Carl. Shame their chests are blown open. Why did you have to use short-rifle hollow-points?"

"I didn't. I used *long*-rifle hollow-points. Shorties would have blown open their backs, not their fronts."

"Thanks for telling me that."

"Tony, you killed them dead!" I screamed. "Why did you have to do it!" I started to punch him. He let go of Mrs. Morton and tried to grab hold of my flailing arms.

"Calm down! Calm down! Wake up, you stupid idiot! You're having a nightmare!"

"Okay, okay, I'm awake."

"Who did I kill?"

"Mr. and Mrs. Morton. But you didn't kill their baby. Mom and Dad are gonna—"

"They're all still alive, stupid. Remember how the parents have the rule about us not being loud up here because it disturbs the dead and the Mortons if they're in their living room? Well, you just blew that one out the window. They're in there, and they must have heard you. So just stay shut up and go back to sleep."

The thought came to tell my brother who he talks to in his sleep. "Tony?"

"*Shut up*, I said already."

"Use 'be quiet' instead." Another thought came: *I should put a plaster on my knee*. I reached down to touch the wound, to check if there really was one.

"Hey, Chuckie. While you were in your little dream world, the worst part of the storm hit us. There were some big cracks and bangs that came from our front yard. I think we might have lost the Luden tree. We'll have to go out there and see in the morning."

Chapter XXX

The Go-between

The family was no longer in denial. Our canopy tree's largest branch lay across the front lawn. A good-sized section of the tree's main trunk had peeled out with it, and the tree's core was now exposed, its advanced rot obvious.

The last few years had seen Luden producing less and less of its unique little leaves. Now the family knew why. The part that remained upright was seriously imbalanced and needed to be put down. Except for dog, everyone brooded. Later in the morning, father phoned for a professional crew to come in and take care of it.

The thought came to put Luden's obituary in my final edition. But then other thoughts came: *Will readers find it nonsensical . . . ? They really liked the article on mud puddles. . . . How do I properly honor a royal tree with so little space . . . ?*

Just before noon, Rae Morton knocked on the kitchen door. "Jeanne, Carl and I are planning to have another child. The upstairs is a too small. We'll be moving out this weekend."

"So quick. Where to?"

"Probably Randolph or Chelsea, but Carl and I haven't started looking. We're staying with his brother and sister-in-law temporarily."

After Mrs. Morton left, mother showed a long face; she was upset about the loss of rent money and the challenge of finding new tenants. I grabbed the telescope from the garage. Frank was playing in his front yard.

"Hi, Charlie! Where ya going?"

"None of your—To the tree house."

"Joe and Marion saw what happened to your tree. They're worried a branch will break off our old elm and crash through our roof or onto the Knight's car. Because it's so full of disease, they've decided to get it cut down. They go back to work on Monday. I can't wait to be with you and Jimmy. It's so boring over here."

"Jimmy won't be back. He moved away."

Melancholic, telescope pressed to eye, I sat in the tree house, searching for something to take my mind off Luden. I scanned southern Randolph. Nothing. I tipped the scope down, to take in the lower track. I was also sad about the Prudhommes' old elm.

"Hope it's not me you're looking for."

Startled, I glanced around, saw no one. The voice was familiar. Nervousness welled up inside of me. "Where are you, John?"

"I'm here and that's all you need to know. Seeing me isn't important, and that's because this is what it might be like for you and me. Neither of us will see it coming, like that old man didn't." An uneasy pause. "Let's have no further talk on the matter. Why I'm here has not so much to do with what has already happened. I'm here because of the future—yours and mine. But future things won't be accidents, even though that's what they'll be made to look like." Another uneasy pause. "I'm scared, Charlie. Things are not good, not good at all. Billy won't have anything to do with me. Sometimes I catch him looking at me real angry-like."

"The woman's husband was there."

"What do you mean?"

"The old man that got run over that morning, the snowstorm was almost over, and it had been a real bad one. City plows and sand trucks hadn't been on River Road since the middle of the night, but they should've been. Several inches of snow blanketed the road. Right after the event, the sisters complained to the city. They even threatened them."

"Wait a second, Charlie. I'm following but I'm not. What are you trying to tell me?"

"John, I was there. School had been canceled for the day, and because of it I was able to witness what happened. Mostly witness it, anyway. That morning, people left later than usual for work because they had to shovel out. When that woman's husband stopped at the bottom of Vine to look both ways before turning for downtown, he must have seen the police car and ambulance. He decided to turn right and head to the scene. In front of the train station he was blocked from going any farther. He got out of his car and went to talk to the policeman stopping traffic. A guy from another car was already there with the cop, and the three seemed to know each other, a friend of mine says. He was standing nearby and heard them say the accident was the old man's fault and not the driver's. The guy from Vine definitely works for the City."

"And this information is useful?"

"Please let me tell you the whole story. It's about the things that happened not only right after the old man was run over but in the following days and weeks."

"Go ahead then, tell it all."

"From the top of the hill, where I was, it looked plain and simple. The driver was speeding and he hit the man. But from the bottom of the hill, where the policeman and the two guys and my friend were standing, it looked like the old man had done something real dumb, being that he was in the middle of the road, a road that was icy, snow-covered, and just the other side of a blind hill. To top it off, the old man was pushing a big snow-scooper and wore a hat with thick earflaps. I now see that it wasn't totally the driver's fault, if at all.

"Lieutenant Cates was the investigator. He sent the other cop down the hill to stop traffic. A little after that, he questioned the driver and me. Next day, I saw him back at the scene. He was using a measuring tape and taking down notes.

"Just before the accident happened, I was walking down Kingsbury, heading for my friend's place on River Road, just across from the train yard. He lives in the tilted house. When I got close to the end of the street, I saw a car speed by. I told Lieutenant Cates the same and that I heard its horn. But I didn't tell it right. I only realized it a few days ago. How it really happened was I was walking with my head down, looking at the snow. I heard a horn and looked up to see the car go by. The driver tooted just as he was making Kingsbury, and that's the reason why I looked up. The old guy should have had enough time to move out of the way. But he must have decided to keep pushing the scooper because he wanted to save it from getting broken to pieces. Either that or he just didn't hear or see the car at all. There's just no other way it could be.

"The driver should have been charged with speeding. But instead he got charged with manslaughter. His life has been ruined because of it. The man felt so bad. You should have seen him like I did, there at the scene. He took the whole thing onto himself.

"Cates wanted nothing to do with charging the driver like that. He got stressed out and even wanted to step down because of it. He and the chief were pressured. It was terrible on them because they felt for the guy.

"Those two old ladies—one of them called out to me last week when we were talking next to the road—they're his sisters. None of them ever married. Jim was the old guy's name. He was the one they depended on for doing their heavy chores. Lying there unconscious in front of them, bleeding as bad as he was, made them real upset. I saw how they screamed and cried. When the driver saw it, he bent forward, put his face in his hands, and cried like the sisters.

"But the sisters' deep pain soon turned into deep anger. They blamed everyone else. They made phone calls, lots of them, over and over again. In their eyes Jim could do no wrong. He was a real nice guy. I knew him. But he put himself in danger partly because of them always pushing him. This was something the two sisters could never admit to.

"The sisters called the Capitol and talked to persons who represent this part of the state. Even above them. They called and called and went down to city hall to complain about the lack of plowing, sanding, and salting. They claimed what happened was partly the city's fault. The chief was in a bad spot. What was he to do? Even the governor's office called.

"The driver had to take the fall. He didn't try to fight back. Too nice a guy. But it wasn't the lieutenant's fault. He wasn't responsible for what ended up happening to an innocent man."

"And you know this how?"

"The two ladies are our friends. Mostly my mother talks with them about the more important things. I mow their lawns. My mom's told me everything because I asked her."

"Sounds to me like you've figured out something I haven't told you. There were those who had it out for Cates. Some of them knew the driver and his wife. They told others about the injustice that had been done, and bad feelings spread around. You're right about the guy—the driver. A real nice man everyone apparently takes to when they get to know him. He had nothing to do with what happened to Cates. Hey, Charlie, don't speak for a minute. I need to think."

The minute passed, and John emerged from the thicket.

"What you've told me might make a difference. I'll have to use the go-between. Things'll need time to work through the system. Probably a few days to a week. I'll let you know the outcome. It's time for me to go. Don't be scared. This might fix things regarding the two of us with them, but it won't fix what has already happened."

"You're going to see Captain Cornelius, I bet. Or maybe that Billy fellow?"

"So . . . you know about the captain. He's not the go-between. Cornelius knows some things, but only those that are at his level. He doesn't know about the upper-level power struggles and agreements that take place before and after. He might see or find out about the messy in-between stuff that gets carried out by the low-level types like him.

"As for Billy, me going to him would be about the stupidest thing I could do. A mistake like that could cost me my life *and yours*. Billy's at almost the same level as Cornelius, but he's slightly higher because he can function in the regular world. And he has a bunch of friends that are mirror copies of him. This makes Billy far more dangerous than the captain. But Billy's clumsy. Because of that woman overhearing us, the powers above are now aware of him telling me things he shouldn't have. To get back in good standing he wants to make things right. He wants to fix the situation, and I'm going to give him the chance.

"It's someone else I'll be seeing for this—a neutral source that everyone likes and trusts. Think about it, Charlie. Where do people go when they run out of snacks, mix, and cigarettes on Friday and Saturday nights? I'll be back. Start keeping an eye out for me in four days."

John turned . . . vanished into the woods. I had the notion to expose this swarthy matter to mother. She could be trusted not to speak about it to anyone, especially to dad. She would not want to rile him more than his kids already did. I left the ark and went inside.

"Mom, I have something big to tell you." Her eyes were red. "Have you been crying?"

"Dear, something bad has happened. I just now got off the phone with Marion. Bea Knight died this morning. She went into the hospital yesterday afternoon. Her health hasn't been good for a long time, but it suddenly went south. I know hearing it is upsetting for you. You've been so friendly with the Knights. It's okay if you cry."

"I feel bad and I miss her already, but I don't feel like crying. It's not that I'm trying not to, it's just something that doesn't come natural to me anymore."

"Well, it still does to me. Give me a moment." Mother went for a tissue, dabbed her eyes and nose. "There, I'm okay. What is it you have to tell me?"

"It's not that important. What's Mr. Knight going to do without Mrs. Knight?"

"He has no one else here, so he'll probably move back to Massachusetts. By the way, we're going to have to tighten our belts, now that your father and I are losing fifty dollars a month in rent. I've already placed an ad in the *KJ*, but it's going to take time to find the right person or persons for upstairs. We'll only accept quiet types and ones who will not object to having three boys around, *especially you.*"

"You're right, Mom. I'm sorry about everything I've done wrong lately."

"It is my sincere desire that your father and I have a peaceful, interference-free next few days. We'll especially require your cooperation for that to happen."

"For sure you can count on me."

"What have you got planned for the rest of today?"

"Mike called this morning. They've settled into their new place and he wants me over. I'm leaving right now and stopping at a store on the way to buy batteries for my flashlight."

"They can't be spent already?"

"Ahh, I guess I'm not really sure. I'll check it tonight. Bye."

The way to Mike's took me through downtown. I stopped in front of Day's Jewellery. Necklaces, watches, and small kitchen-top appliances dominated the display window. There was also that single golf club; it had yet to sell. I went inside. A loudly dressed man of early 20s age greeted me. I immediately recognized him the owner of the city's only Chevrolet Corvair convertible. The little car had occasionally been seen parked at the Carringtons' house. Likely, the driver was courting or trying to court Ethel Carrington. I asked him about the club.

"You golf, do you?"

"I'd like to, but I need lessons. Should have a set of golf clubs for that."

"Not really. Listen, my name is Wes. What's yours?"

"Char—*John*. My name is John. There's no Char."

"Okay, this is how it goes, John. All you really need are three clubs. A putter, a wood driver, and a middle iron—like a seven. That's what I have in the window, and coincidentally it's only seven dollars. I'll take it out for you to hold. . . . Seven dollars, that's all. . . . MacGregor. . . . Top quality. . . . Can't be beat. . . . What do you think?"

"It sure is nice, Wes. But I don't know?"

"Listen, you buy it and I'll give you your first golf lesson right here, free of charge. Then you'll be able to say you know how to golf and just need more practice to get it down good."

"Does it come with a couple golf balls?"

"No. But listen. There's one at the bottom of our dead-box. Let me dig around in it for a sec. . . . There—catch. Got a decent-sized dent but should do you just fine. What do you say? Buying or not? Wait before you answer. I'll throw in a free tee. Now, say *yes, you're buying*."

"Sure. I'll get the money out of my wallet. . . . Here."

"Thanks. I'll ring it in. . . . John, do you know how to play baseball?"

"Yup, and I'm pretty good at it."

"Then that already makes you almost a decent golfer. You'll just have to work on pointing your skills down to the ground. Except for driving and putting, the seven-iron does pretty much everything for you. Here, I'll show you. You see how all you need to do is spread your legs like you're in a batters box, but don't crouch. Hold the club right . . . here. Don't just stand there, John. Copy what I'm doing. . . . Yeah, like that. Look down at the ball and don't take your eyes off of it at any time. But before you do that, you've supposedly already figured out exactly where it is you want to hit it. If you want, even with a seven-iron you can spot your ball on a tee, as long as it's your first hit. Now gradually lift the club in the air behind you, leaving your eyes on the ball, and swing down not as hard as you can and straight onto it. Just go slow and fake it inside the store because we don't want to have to pay for a broken window. Right?"

"Right."

"Correct answer. When you swing down, make sure to hit the ball straight on. That way it'll go where you want. There's your first lesson. Let me know when you're ready to buy the other two clubs, and I'll order them in. Make sure I'm working and that way you'll get two more lessons. Then with some practice you should get onto Meadow Hill in good shape. You're young. Means your dad or another adult will have to be with you. Is that a problem?"

"Nope."

The next stop-of-interest would be Gardiner Fruit. Thinking on it, I decided no. The ten dollars I had started out with was now down to three, and I needed to conserve for only what was needed. This was not the only reason to stay out. Mr. Newsome now knew that the Swisher Sweets cigar I had bought from him was not for Herve but for me. I was thankful he had not exposed my deception to dad. Today I was alone, and he just might decide to chew me out.

Slosbergs' Clothiers came next. Determined, I went inside.

"Hello, young man," greeted a smiling upper-fifties lady. "I hardly recognize you, but I do believe you're Herve and Jeanne's youngest son. Am I right?"

"Yes, Mrs. Slosberg. I'm him."

"And your name is Charlie, just like my husband's."

"Yyyup."

"So, Charlie, what can Charlie and I do for you today?"

Mr. Slosberg used crutches because he had lost a leg to cancer. He smiled and waved, remained seated at the back of the store.

"I've decided to come in and check your prices for myself. My mother said your pants and shirts have gone way up in price, and because I work and make my own money these days, she and my dad say I have to help pay for my school clothes."

"Sounds fair to me. Just so you know, our costs have risen and that's why our prices have gone up. We don't take pleasure in it. We don't rub our hands."

"Yyyup, and I can sure see you and she are right. Lucky for you, I know you're still cheaper than across the street."

"Across the street?"

"Yyyup. First of all, you're way cheaper than Harry Glaser's place, but you're only a little cheaper than Frank Wise. The only store cheaper than you is Woolworth, but the clothes there are big and baggy. That's what farmers need but not me. Mom says that for Daniel's senior year at Cheverus he needs nicer clothes than what you sell here, so they'll be shopping at Frank Wise. She really wants him to be named valedictorian and nicer clothes will help. Anyhoos, I'm done checking. My mother and I'll be by in a few weeks. Goodbye."

"My, my, how you've cheered us up. And we're *sooooo* looking forward to your return. Isn't that right, Charlie?"

"Whatever you say, Irene. But as for myself, I'll be a lot cheerier in a few seconds, when I hear the door close." The seated man pointed a crutch at the front door. "Bye, son."

I stopped to review the home furnishings displayed in New England Furniture's window. Mother had more than once said, "The place carries so-so sofas and springy mattresses." I shook my head, turned away, and whispered, *"The place carries so-so sofas and springy mattresses."* Mattson's Wallpaper & Paint had boring paint, wallpaper, and curtains in its window. I sped up. The aromas wafting from McDonald's Bakery's open door brought me to a halt, made me want to go inside for something. The lineup was too long.

Manson & Church Drugstore held the northeast corner at the intersection of Brunswick Avenue and Water Street. Up until two years ago, the place had served real fine milkshakes. There had also been a Coca Cola chest and a small counter with three swivel stools for customers to sit at and drink their shakes and sodas while waiting for prescriptions. Shortly after LaVerdiere's Drug came to Gardiner, Manson & Church removed their nice little setup. "What a poor decision and a big marketing error," mother had said of it. The family patronage soon switched to the new arrival. My mouth still yearned for something sweet. I entered.

"Hello, ma'am. I need to buy a pack of backup batteries for my flashlight. A person never knows when they'll be needed most. That's what my dad's taught me, and he said for me to stop by here so I could get them and at the same time see if you sell single cigars, like a Swisher Sweets. He's very busy and was hoping you would allow his son to give you this here dime he gave me to buy it so I could bring it to him, just like I'm already doing with this here golf club that he needs for Meadow Hill. Says a single gar costs a dime and not a nickel anymore."

"I suppose I'll let you do that for him. You're too young to smoke it, that's for sure."

I rounded the corner and approached the bridge over Cobbossee Stream. At west end's portal sat Wakefield's Diner: a metallic silver, boxcar-type unit that was a bit of an oddity in that it stood on a 20-feet-high mesh of metal bars that looked like accordion stilts; the bars were based in concrete footings on the city's backside parking lot, which separated city core from the stream, and this allowed the eatery to be level with the sidewalk.

Until last summer, I had never been inside the restaurant. It was then when Mike and I ducked in. Supposedly the place served fantastic custard and banana cream pies, but Mike did not want pie. The waitress said we were too young to be in there on our own. Mike convinced her to let us stay, but she was short. We split an order of french fries and gravy. Mike got miffed and before we left, when the waitress wasn't looking, he rubbed pennies under his shoes to make them dirty, then dropped one into the cream pitchers on all the nearby tables.

I went inside and sat on a barstool.

"Hello, young man. What can I do for you?"

"Hello, ma'am. I'll have a slice of your custard pie. Hear it's really good and decided to try it out. Hear your banana cream is good, too. Maybe that'll be for next time so I can tell my big brother and his friend about it and you can get more new customers. Neither of them have ever had a piece of that kind. I'll have a glass of chocolate milk to wash it down with. Sure hope you get yours from Sheehan's Dairy and not Hood's."

"And your parents know you're here?"

"Well, no, not really. But they allow me to make some of my own decisions, now that I'm old enough to earn my spending money."

"How do you do that?"

"By mowing lawns for clients. And I know how to tip fifteen percent. Arithmetic's my best subject."

"Don't I recognize you?"

"No, ma'am. Never been in before."

"The afternoon's already half gone. Won't this ruin your supper?"

"It'll count as my dessert. I promise to eat everything, including my vegetables."

"How old are you?"

"Not quite fourteen."

"What grade are you going in?"

"I'm, ah, still in junior high."

"I suppose you can stay. What's your name?"

"Char—*John*. My name is John. There's no Char."

"Uh-huh. And do you golf as good as you talk?"

"Not yet."

"Let me know what you think of the pie. I'll get your glass of *Sheehan's* chocolate milk."

"Ohh, ma'am, it's heavenly."

"Nice of you to say. Tourists often make similar comments. People from New York claim it can't be matched anywhere."

"Thank you for letting me stay. Count on me coming back sometime soon."

"Uh-huh. And that'll be a dollar fifty before tip."

Halfway across the bridge, I stopped to look down onto the parking lot below. Rats pranced the berm of boulders bordering the stream. The big rodents seemed unconcerned about being out in the open. Next came Joe's Pizza, positioned at the opposite end of the bridge. When originally built, this place, too, had to be significantly raised in order to achieve evenness with the bridge's sidewalk.

The parents rarely ordered from here because Gerard's Pizza was closer. The owner, Joe, was Italian and mostly worked the place alone. His pizza was as good as any, but it was his uniquely "Mediterranean" submarine sandwich that raised the pizzeria high. He named it—what else?—"Joe's Special." Before sliding the elongated tube of dough into the pizza oven, his habit was to brush-coat it with virgin olive oil. Ten minutes later, the sub-bun came out overly long, wide, and greasy. After another light coat of oil, the bun got sliced open for its lower half to be covered with a tasty assortment of spicy cold-cuts and slices of black olives and provolone cheese. Joe's last act, prior to re-placing the bun's top half, was to squeeze a bottle of his secret Italian dressing all over the insides. The sub was enough for three regular people or Tony.

I slowed for a look inside. Joe sat on a stool, reading his *KJ*. Customers' cigarette butts littered the sidewalk and ditch in front of the outlet. I picked up two that had a decent amount of smoking part left on them and continued on to Mike's. Thoughts meandered through: *Mom's not convinced about eating meat on Fridays. . . . We're watching our pennies. . . . We'll be having crappo mackerel again. . . . Maybe Saturday we can get from Joe's. . . . For that, I'll need Tony's help. . . . Make it happen, Chuckie.*

"I've been waitin' and waitin' for you, Monroe. Everyone around here's gone, and I'm dyin' of boredom. What took you so long and why a golf club?"

"Sorry, Mike. Rushed fast as I could. Brought the club so I could show you how to golf."

"Didn't know you knew."

"Had my first lesson already. I'll show you what I learned. Here's a couple cigs for you. Got the other kind of cig for me. We can light them up and smoke while we golf."

"Good idea. Nice to see I'm gettin' more and more through to you."

"Watch me and listen. Put the ball on the grass in front of you, about this far away."

"Isn't that brilliant. I wouldn't have known."

"I have to tell you everything from the beginning, so be patient. Because it's your first shot, the ball can go on a tee. I have one. Let me stick in the ground. Now, stand just as I am, like in a batter's box. Hold the club same as a bat, but point it down to the ground."

"Do I have 'stupid' written on my forehead?"

"Yup-okay. So now, hold the club tight in your hands and raise your arms behind you, but up in the air and not sideways like you're going to hit a pitch, which was something you could never do in Farm League. Remember how you were always the ninth batter on your team, the 'Maroons.' It was the color of your team's jerseys, but you thought it meant you were supposed to leave your teammates marooned on the bases, and you always did."

"Very funny, Monroe. Hit the ball or else I'm gonna wrap that club around your neck."

"Before you lift, swing, and hit the ball, you have to look in front of you to decide where you want it to go. After that, you stare down at the ball and almost touch it, but very gently, with the iron. Make sure you're straight on the ball. Then, without taking your eyes off the ball, lift the club like I already showed you and swing down and whack the ball hard but not with all your might. It's like being a pitcher. If you throw the ball too hard, you lose control of where it goes."

"Just *shut, shut, shut up* and show me."

"I'll hit the ball to go between your house and the neighbor's. Should land in your backyard and not the gully as long as I don't hit it too hard. I have to take into account the ball's dent. The way I'm positioned, a little toward the side of your place, it should curve nicely between the houses. Here goes . . ." *Whap* . . . "See, perfect."

"Lucky shot. If I didn't know any better, I'd say you know what you're doing. Pass me the club and go get the ball."

"Okay, got it. I'll stick it on the tee, but that's all I can do for you. Just take your time and do as I sh—"

Whap . . . BANG.

"Mike, that's not what I showed you."

"What do you mean? Couldn't have hit the ball any better. That's the windowpane Nancy's new boyfriend replaced just yesterday. Poor guy's been tryin' hard to get into Mom's good books and somethin' else. This might've done it for him. Kept sayin' it's an eyesore, all cracked and at the front of the house. Mom said don't bother because it's only a window for the landlord's third-floor storage room. But he kept insistin'. Unfortunately, the guy's a bit on the stubborn side and don't like taking no for an answer. That's what my mom and Nancy both say."

"Nancy has a boyfriend?"

"Yeah, a Ron Cates fellow. He's a nephew of that cop that got killed up there at the Sportsmen's Club. What am I gonna do now?"

"Let's clean it up. That way everyone'll think it's the nice new clean window he put in."

"Good idea. Quick, let's do it before someone comes home."

Chapter XXXI

The Philadelphia Incident

"Hi, Mrs. Laithran. Came by to remind you about us picking berries after supper tonight."

"Good morning, Charlie. Wait where you are while I stand up and away from the garden. Yes, I remember. What time should I be ready?"

"Five-thirty. See you then."

"Please wait another moment. I have something to tell you. Phil and his family will be arriving tomorrow, probably in the late afternoon or early evening. They'll be here for a few days only. Tomorrow I'll be baking cookies and pies with the raspberries we pick."

"I can't wait to see Peter. We'll need to bring three large pans."

"I'll have them. I see your parents are getting rid of that old tree."

"Yup, and the family's really sad about it. We liked it as much as the birds did. The Prudhommes are getting their big elm cut down, too."

"What a shame. But I suppose it has to go. Too much rot in it now. To think that thing was planted in the seventeen nineties, during the time of George Washington, our beloved first President. What are you up to today—writing your next edition?"

"Not yet. I need to dig up more information on that big story Mr. Laithran wants. Maybe I'll have it for next Friday. This afternoon I'm mowing Miss Alpen's lawn. Right now I'm heading to the Donahues. They called this morning with extra chores for me to do."

"It's good that they have you. Their brother Jim has been gone for almost three years. Now you're their Jim."

"I never thought about it that way, but I guess you're right."

"You'll probably be doing your own lawn soon, now that it looks like a hayfield again."

"Nope. Job doesn't pay. That's why Tony gets to do it. Anyway, Mom and Dad made it a requirement for him to get a new Ruger for his birthday."

"Ruger? What's that?"

"A special type of handgun. Holds a nine-shot clip that slides up into the handgrip. A tenth bullet goes in the chamber. His birthday's gone by and he got it already. Says people shouldn't want to come around here looking for trouble unless there are more than ten of them."

"Charlie, give me a hint. What's the storyline you're working on?"

"Sorry, Mrs. Laithran, can't say. If I did, then I wouldn't have to write the story, and I wouldn't make any money."

"Fine then. Never mind. Just now you telling me about Tony's fancy new gun reminds me again on how he's the continuation of something that has been in your house since it was built. Somebody like him was needed back then, and I guess still is, and that's because of all the animals that seem to wander in from nowhere for your yard. Even the birds stalk your place. Why, just the other day I heard a woodpecker banging on a tree inside your gully. When I walked behind our garage to try to get a glimpse of it, I noticed a hummingbird hovering in front of your picture window. Pretty sure it wasn't that dragon fly looking for you. Truly, your house is a bunch of Alfred Hitchcock movies all put together and over and over again. Then I smelled cigar smoke. Later, I noticed you coming out of the woods from where you had dug for old bottles. That wasn't you smoking a cigar, was it?"

"Well, ah, yeah, kind of, I guess. But please don't say anything to my mom and dad."

"Can't they smell it on you?"

"Yes and no, as long as I make sure to smoke it at the same time Dad smokes his."

Mrs. Laithran looked away. "Hi, Marion! Hear that old elm of yours is getting cut down!"

"Hi, Dot! My how word gets around fast! Come on over to this side of the street so we can talk without others hearing!"

Mrs. Laithran and I met up at 5:30. Frank was playing in his front yard.

"Good evening, Frank."

"Hey there, Frank. Goodbye."

"Hi, Mrs. Laithran. Hi, Charlie. Where ya going?"

"It doesn't matter. *Goodbye.*"

"Yes, it does to me. Can I come along?"

"I don't think your mother would approve of you leaving the yard, and then to go down near the river," reasoned the elder. "That's where Charlie and I are going, to pick raspberries."

"If Mom says I can go, can I?"

"Well . . . I suppose. Go ask her real quick. Tell her that I'll be along and Charlie and I will hold your hands when we cross over River Road."

He ran off, returned in less than a minute. "She said yes as long as I'm back before dark."

A thought came. Then another. "Mrs. Laithran, please wait here with Frank. I have to get some things from my house. I'll be fast."

At my return, Frank asked, "What's in the bag?"

"My flashlight, extra batteries, and a bottle of Moxie. I'm bringing them just in case."

"Just in case of what?" asked Mrs. Laithran.

"Can't rightly explain it. Stuff probably won't be needed. Let's walk fast so we have enough time. Frank, try to keep up."

"Okay, I will. I'm not allowed to drink Moxie."

"I'm not bringing it for us. It's for something else, *maybe*."

"Can I use the flashlight?"

"Yeah, I suppose, but only for a little while, after you've helped us pick berries. Then, when I say, you can use it, past the bushes, where the tall trees are. It's a little dark in there. The flashlight will help you find bugs and stuff. I'll give you ten minutes with it, and you can't keep it turned on all the time, otherwise the batteries lose power."

The 40-yard stretch of tightly intertwined raspberry bushes ran the section of old tracks Mr. Barry had instructed Mike and I not to disturb. We had no intention of disturbing anything other than raspberries.

The bushes seemed far enough below the current track of use and high enough away from the river for the product not to absorb the scents of diesel fumes and human discharge. We kept sampling the berries as we went, and they tasted fine.

The evening was warm and sunny. Because the prevailing breezes emanated from over West Gardiner way, the river's rancid, ever-rising brown molecules were being herded into Randolph and Pittston. As such, the air on our side of the river did not stink.

Frank picked for over an hour and never once complained. When we came to a narrow break in the bushes' thick line, I took him through and into the semi-darkness that underlie the tall poplars. I passed him the flashlight, told him to be careful, ordered him to not go down close to the shoreline, and went back to picking. Two pans were now full and the third one was halfway.

"Couldn't have a better evening for it."

Mrs. Laithran and I turned.

"None of that *Ay, ay, Captain* stuff tonight, ya hear, John-boy?"

"Yes . . . okay. Hello, Cornelius. Good evening, Miss Eva."

Both stood still, smiled, stayed silent.

"This here is Mrs. Laithran. Mrs. Laithran, I'd like you to meet Cornelius and Miss Eva. I know them. We're good friends."

"We're *real* good friends, yes we are," returned Eva. "Cornelius and I are pleased to meet you, Mrs. Laithran."

Cornelius took a long deep breath. "The air is clean tonight." He looked at me and smiled. "So are a couple other things." He winked. "Eva and I decided to take a walk. Don't think we can remember such a beautiful day." The man looked around, took another long breath, sighed. "The spirit here is peaceful this evening."

"Cornelius, I hear noises in the woods."

"I hear it, too." He looked at me. "What do you suppose that would be, John-boy?"

"We brought a little friend along with us." I turned and called for him to come out.

"Are we going home?"

"No. Not yet. Come up close to Mrs. Laithran and me. Frank, I want you to meet some special friends of mine. This is Cornelius and Miss Eva."

The man smiled. Eva walked up close and bent down to the boy's level. She put out a hand. "Hello there, Frank. I'm pleased to meet you. How old would you be?"

"I'm five," responded the little guy as he put out his hand to shake hers.

"Did you hear that, Cornelius? He's five."

The captain smiled, rolled his eyes. "I heard. Maybe we should keep going so they can finish their picking."

"Frank, I have a five-year-old son. I bet he looks just like you. I can feel in my heart right now that you and him are the same—*good boys*. I haven't seen him for a long time, but he's always in my mind and heart."

Frank remained silent, brave, did not back away from her, not one step.

"That's a real fine flashlight you got there."

"It's not mine. It belongs to Charlie here."

Cornelius and Miss Eva looked at me funny, seemed confused.

"People who've known me for a long time call me Charlie. It's from my middle name—*Charles*. With new friends I prefer the name John. That's my first name."

The blue-capped man showed a stunned face. He turned to his woman. "I can't believe what I just heard. What an amazing co—"

"And Charlie's got a bottle of Moxie in the bag," interrupted Frank. "He said it's not for any of us to drink but maybe for something else, but he wouldn't say what."

Cornelius firmed his face. "I think I know what. *Sooooo*, John-boy, you thought you might be running into us tonight, did you?"

"Well, yeah, kind of, I did. But I also brought along the flashlight and that way I could be on the safe side. I learned to do something like that from you."

"You did? How's that?"

"Remember how the last time when we talked you reminded Miss Eva about how you always keep your options open by having a back way out of situations, just in case? Tonight I copied you."

"And what exactly is your option that will get me back to thinking things are square between us?"

"It's the flashlight. Miss Eva said she can't see well anymore, especially at night. I thought Frank could use it to stay busy while Mrs. Laithran and I picked. Then, if you and Miss Eva came along and neither of you wanted anything to do with Moxie, Miss Eva could have the flashlight, instead. That way she could see the world better at night and not run into things."

A bright gleam swept aside the captain's scowl. The whites of his eyes showed a cheery sparkle, and his smile kept growing, as he thought more and more on what I just said. His sparse yellow-brown teeth became exposed, up to and then above his swollen blue-green gums.

"Frank, you can give the flashlight to your new friend, Miss Eva. It's okay because it was always meant for her, after you and I tested it out for a while. I brought along extra batteries, so come quick and get them, too, for Miss Eva."

"Here, Miss Eva. It's all yours."

"Thank you so much, my little Frank. Let me shake your hand one more time. I want you to know something. Every time I use it at night, I'll think of you. In my heart and mind my little boy's face will be the face of you."

She turned to Cornelius. Tears flowed from her eyes. He rushed over to her. "I know the pain, Eva. I know it real good." They hugged, but only for a moment. "It's time for us to move on. Thanks for giving Eva the flashlight, John-boy. I will always remember what happened here tonight. And I, too, will see a face every time Eva uses it. It'll be your face. Pray for me and Eva. We're trying real hard to change our lives because of our talk with you the other day. Maybe someday we'll even end up at the door of Christ's Church. Right, Eva?"

She smiled. "That would please me, Cornelius. Time for us to go, like you said. Goodbye, Frank. I miss you already. Goodbye, Johnny. Nice to meet you, Mrs. Laithran."

"Take care, John-boy. I want you to know that if I could see my son, I'd want him to be just like you. That's what I'll imagine from now on—that he's you." The man tried hard to rein in his emotions. For a moment, he stared into my eyes. Tears streamed down his cheeks. "I don't blame my son, not one bit, because I love him to death, even though I don't know him no more. I had to say it one more time and that way you know for sure his father, Bob, is telling the truth." He turned to Eva. Heads tipped down, holding hands, the two returned to their slow trekking down an old road made of rusty old tracks.

"Mrs. Laithran, do we have enough or do you want to stay and finish the third bowl?"

"It's plenty. Let's leave right away."

The Philadelphians arrived a couple hours earlier than expected. I was outside, tossing hoops. The family of six included three sons and an infant daughter. Except for baby, all waved enthusiastically at me; each added a friendly verbal greeting upon exiting the vehicle. This day, as in past times, I was very much taken by the visitors' show of warmth.

Mr. and Mrs. Laithran came out. Hugs, kisses, and super-happy talk engulfed the group as they walked into the house. Ten minutes later, Peter emerged. The oldest child and the same age as me, he was definitely of superior basketball skills. His brothers were ten and eight. A few minutes went by and they joined us.

"My dad has me in wrestling. The coach says I'm real good at it," bragged Peter. "Want me to show you?"

"No thanks. We can keep doing this."

"You can't beat me. Someone who knows how to wrestle will always beat someone who doesn't. Come on and let me show you."

"You mean you want to wrestle right now?"

"Yeah."

"Where?"

"On your garage floor."

"I really don't want to."

"You have no reason to be scared. I promise not to hurt you."

"It's not that I'm scared. I just don't feel like wrestling."

Peter continued to push, challenging me, my manhood. His brothers were desperate for it, prodding away at me with things like, "Yeah, come on, you two—*wrestle*." "Beat him bad, Charlie, and pin that bossy brother of ours." "Don't let him think you're scared of him."

Finally, with infinite reluctance, I agreed.

Peter said, "I'll pretend to be the champ. Do you know who he is?"

"Bruno Sammartino. Watch him all the time."

"Good. Call me Bruno. And you can be what you already are, someone who doesn't know his ass from a hole in the ground about wrestling. But don't worry, Bruno's clean. He doesn't punch unless he's punched first. So don't even come close to trying something like that or else I become Cassius Clay and you Sonny Liston, except when I hit you it'll be real, and when you hit the ground, it'll be in Auburn, not Lewiston. Got it?"

"Yup."

"Okay, let's start. One, two, three, go. . . . Gotcha. . . . No, I don't. Not yet, anyway—but I will soon enough. . . . Take that . . . and that . . . and that. Still haven't got you. . . . There, you're almost pinned. . . . Don't fight the inevitable. . . . Almost got you. . . . There, you're . . . you're . . . finished . . . finally. Good match. You put up a good fight."

The scuffle lasted a couple minutes. Because I knew no wrestling moves, my effort had been defensive and futile. Both of us were sweaty, filthy from rolling on the garage floor. Peter saw that I was embarrassed at his brothers' cheering, so he put out a hand to shake mine.

"For someone who knows zero, you did pretty good. I should have been able to pin you sooner, but I couldn't because you have decent natural strength. You don't have the build to be a Bulldog Brower, but you could definitely be a Johnny Rodz. Think about taking up wrestling."

The gracious acknowledgement put away my embarrassment.

"Yeah, you did good, Charlie. Wrestle again," urged Tim, the older of the kid-brothers.

"Yeah, wrestle again, you guys," followed Carey.

Peter stomped his foot. "Shut up!" He looked back at me. "Let's play more ball. By the way, we're here tomorrow, but on Saturday we have to go visit our grandfather—you know, my dad's dad, in Waterville. We do that every time we come to Maine, remember? Sunday we're going to Boothbay Harbor. Mom and Dad asked me to ask you to come along. Our car isn't big enough, so you and I will ride with Grandma and Bernard."

"I was already there last Sunday."

"Please come," urged Tim.

"Yeah, please come with us," followed Carey.

"Come on, Charlie. You and I are the same age, and I get sick and tired of being around these pain-in-the-ass squirt brothers of mine. You won't have to bring any food and drink. Mom and Dad say we'll have hotdogs, french fries, and Pepsi the whole time."

Tim turned and walked off. "Carey, come into the house with me."

"Why are you doing that?" asked Peter.

"To tell Mom and Dad what you just said about us!"

"You do and I'll make your life miserable from now on! Now, the both of you, get back here right away . . . ! What say, Charlie—are you coming?"

"I guess so. Let's quit playing basketball. I need to go to the hardware store to buy a flashlight. Come along with me."

"Can we come, too?" asked Tim.

"No, you absolutely *can not* come!" Peter turned to me. "I'll be right back. Have to tell my parents where I'm going." Returning, he showed a look of disappointment. "They said okay as long as Tim and Carey can come along."

"Yeah!"

"Yeah!"

"Shut up, already . . . ! Why do you need a new flashlight?"

"My dad's is old and corroded. Have to keep banging it with a hand, and then it works for only a few seconds. We need a good one for tonight. Thought we could go exploring in the woods after dark."

"Why, what's in there?"

"Some very scary things. We'll go down as far as Rollins Brook and walk along it for a while. If we're quiet, we might hear whip-poor-wills chanting."

Peter, sarcastically: "Wow, that's it? That's scary?"

"Oh-and-ah, we just might run into a black bear wading for a gargantuan tadpole oozing with radioactive juices. Means we have to be very careful about not stepping in the brook. The water comes all the way down from a place called"—I leaned in close to the little brothers—"Toe! Maine! It's full of radioactive poison from a big dirty dairy farm that lets their pigs and cows swim in and drink the water! They ooze out dead rats and pig squat and stuff that looks like chocolate milk into the water! Means if your feet get wet, they'll have to be amputated!" The two got scared. I straightened up and looked at Peter. We laughed. "And there's even a better chance of us catching a big mother raccoon fending off a hungry bobcat from taking one of her kits. If the bobcat does kill and eat one, we'll have to be real quiet so we can hear the banshees of dead wild animals crying out from the *scary* woodlands."

"Now, that's more like it. Is there really a bobcat in there?"

"Yyyup, and the folks around here have even given it a name."

"What's that?"

I looked back at the tagalongs, gritted my teeth, raised and clawed my hands. "His name is BEEEEE-JAAYYY!"

"Yeah! Yeah! We can't wait!"

"Yeah! Yeah! We—"

"Shut up, you two! How many times do I have to say it! Hey, Charlie, let's pick up some balloons so we can have a water-balloon fight tomorrow. The hardware store should have them."

"No. But Woolworth has loads of them in different sizes and shapes. The regular ones cost a penny, the bigger ones two cents."

Inside, when the clerk wasn't looking, Peter stuffed a handful into his pocket, then into his brothers' pockets. He grabbed a fourth handful and came toward me. I walked away and he followed after me. Bent over, trying not to be noticed, up and down the aisles we sped. He cut me off and stuffed my pocket.

"Now that we're done shopping, let's get outta here."

"No. We have to put them back. I brought enough money to buy what we need."

"Don't be stupid and waste it. We're just going to break them."

"Nope. We have to put them back. Then we can select the ones we want."

"Okay, square. Thank God people in Phili don't think like you Mainers do."

During lunch, dad mentioned that he and mother would not be returning until 4:30. He wanted to peruse Mattson's Wallpaper & Paint and Walker Lumber while mom did her Friday errands. He asked that I make sure behaviors remain composed during the water-balloon fight to come. I went outside to toss hoops. The Laithran adult males were walking toward the Impala.

Phil: "Charlie, the boys'll be out in a few minutes. They're just now finishing off raspberry cookies. See you later."

Phil and Bernard drove off. Mom and dad emerged from the house.

"Herve, what's that awful smell?" asked mom the instant dad opened the door for her.

"You're right. Yesterday I smelled it. Wasn't this bad. Thought it was rotting milk from Charles' spilled milkshake. I washed the seat pretty good, including some dirt and oil stains that someone carelessly left behind. The smell's obviously not rotting milk."

"It's so bad that I don't think I can ride in the car. Could it be something in the trunk?"

"I'll go check. . . . Wow, the smell's atrocious in here. I'll remove the foldouts."

"I thought you did that Monday morning."

"I took Charles to Hallowell and plumb forgot. Here's the problem. Charles, come here!"

"Hi, Peter. Here's the ball. I'll be right back. My dad called for me. . . . What, Dad?"

"You left your can of snails in the trunk! For five days those things have been in there baking their rotten rear asses off! And those oil stains you left—they still show! Our new car is being ruined by you! Get the can out right now! Your mother and I are very angry about this!"

I immediately did as dad commanded, after which he slammed down the trunk's lid. My emergency posture activated.

"I'm so sorry, Mom and Dad. I promise to be more careful from now on."

The two took more notice of the three Laithran boys standing on our lawn, staring. They got into the car, lowered the front and back windows, smiled and waved to Peter and his brothers, ignored me, and drove off. I went to heave the can into the gully. The Philadelphians followed.

"What you just did with your head and shoulders seemed to work pretty good. I might try doing that next time I get in trouble. Forget basketball and let's start filling the balloons."

We filled half of them and split the rest, shoved them into our pockets.

"On your mark, get set—"

"No, Peter. Not yet. We'll go through the balloons too fast. Why don't we start out by standing ten feet apart in a square and toss one. I'll toss it to you, then you to Tim, then Tim to Carey, then Carey back to me. The first time we'll toss it real slow. The next time a little faster. Then faster and faster until it breaks on someone."

"Sounds good to me."

The first round went fine. To start the second, I heaved the balloon super fast. It slid through Peter's hands and broke against his chest. His brothers and I laughed. He calmly went for the largest filled balloon, returned to his designated corner, and immediately threw it with all his might toward Tim's face. The middle grandson had no chance; the balloon slammed in, soaking his head and T-shirt. Everyone else laughed. Tim went for a balloon, then rushed over to pound it down on Carey's head. "*Ha-ha-ha.* Not so funny, is it?" Carey looked like he might cry, but he didn't. He noticed me laughing. "Charlie's the only one still dry! Let's get him!"

I hollered, "Now, Peter! On your mark, get set, go!"

The four of us rushed for the balloons. As Peter bent down, Carey slammed one against the side of his face just as Tim brought one down on the back of their bossy brother's head. Peter got me really good in the face. Soon, all pre-filled balloons were used and all combatants wet.

"We should each fill only one at a time, and none of us are allowed to throw it until everyone's got theirs filled," suggested I. They agreed.

We had total fun, running, dodging, soaking each other. Mr. Prudhomme and Frank appeared. The gentle bear carried a scraper in one hand, an aluminum ladder in the other. He put the ladder up against his house, climbed it, and began to scrape away at the old paint. Frank came down onto the sidewalk so he could watch us. "Can I play, too?"

"Sure you can, kid!" hollered Peter. He ran across Kingsbury and slammed one down on Frank's head. Tim and Carey followed up with theirs. Frank screamed and fell sobbing to the sidewalk. The brothers laughed as they jogged away. Mr. Prudhomme climbed down and went to Frank's aid.

"You guys! That was a big mistake! Forget the balloons and come over by me right now!" I went to stand under the basketball rim.

Mr. Prudhomme took Frank into the house. I kept my eyes focused on his side-door. A mere moment passed before the ruffled bear emerged, only to disappear around the backside of his semi-mansion.

Peter led his brothers up. "What's the problem? It was only water. Didn't hurt the kid."

"That's probably true, but his dad doesn't see it that way. He's right now coming to get you guys. Let's go around to the gully-side so we can get onto my front lawn. We'll watch for him from there. Keep your eyes peeled as we go. If he doesn't spot us for a while, maybe he'll let it pass by. Later, when things are calm, you can go over and apologize to him and Frank."

"Apologize for what? Water?"

We made the front lawn. There we stood, waiting, watching, in every direction. Things were definitely too quiet. Suddenly Mr. Prudhomme, holding a broom handle with both hands, came running out from the section of lawn Tony had fixed. The big guy moved with frightening speed, across Kingsbury and onto the Monroes' land, directly at us. His mission was obvious: teach four boys to never again be so stupid, even though I had not been.

"Run for your lives!" I yelled. "It's everyone for himself!" We scrambled this way and that. A few times we knocked into each other. The grizzly bear refused to relent. He chased us all the way around the Monroe residence. Then, when we thought his slowing down and walking away meant he was giving up, he suddenly did a one-eighty and ran us back around the other way. The next thing we became aware of was the raging grizzly could no longer be seen. He had yet to whack one behind, so I knew the war game was not over.

"He's gone," said Peter. "Let's just finish off the balloons."

"He's not gone. He's hiding, waiting for us to *think* he's gone. Mr. Prudhomme! We're sorry! Please leave us alive! You've scared us bad enough!" He rushed out from the bamboo patch, only to take a half-run at us. He turned for the street. We had escaped his brand of justice.

"Mr. Prudhomme, we're sorry. We won't do it again. Please tell Frank."

With his back to us, the big man raised an arm halfway up and waved a finger. "Charlie, one day I'd like to get my hands on you. You're young, so instead of you it'll have to someone older."

"I didn't do anything! It was Peter! His squirt brothers do what he does! Just get Peter!"

"That's your story, but I know better. You put them up to it."

"No, I didn't! Peter did!"

"Thanks for putting all the blame on me. Maybe we should get to wrestling again."

"Don't worry. You leave in a few days. I live here."

Mr. Prudhomme went back to scraping. Frank stayed inside. Father and mother drove up.

"Hello, you guys," offered mother in a pleasant voice. "How's everything going so far?"

"Hello, Mr. and Mrs. Monroe," returned Peter, in an overly pleasant voice. "Everything's under control now. We're back to having fun."

"What was that again?" asked mother. Dad ignored us and carried his purchased items into the garage.

"Mom, don't worry. Questions like that don't get answered the same way in Phili. Peter means everything's fine. It's okay for you to go inside and get Tony to help you with the groceries because he's just sitting in the den as usual. I should stay with these guys to keep them company, so they don't get into more trouble."

Mother shook her head and turned away. Peter's dad and grandpa arrived. The four of us approached the Impala. Two smiling men got out.

"Hey there, young fellas. Y'all have a guilty look. What did you do wrong this time?"

"Everything's fine, Dad. Don't worry about us. You can go inside."

"You know, I was just kidding, but now I'm not. Nice of you to let Bernard and me know we can go inside. How else could we have ever known? Peter, don't be a wiseacre. Should you have to come in with me so we can discuss your attitude?"

Peter tipped his head down and dropped his shoulders. "I'm so sorry, Dad. From now on I promise to be better for you and Mom."

The effort looked pathetic, childish even. His dad looked over at me.

"Charlie, I hope you don't do that."

"No, I sure won't from now on."

The man did a John Wayne double-take, then shook his head in resignation and turned to his step-father. Bernard smiled. Done with us, the two went inside.

Tony came out to help lug in the grocery bags. "Stinks like rotten fish in here. Mom, did you buy that crappo mackerel again! Must have been on sale for half price!"

"Yes, and you *will* enjoy it tonight, whether you *actually* do or not! Try to instead concentrate on the tasty french fries and buttery wax beans we'll be having with the rotten *it!*"

I saw my chance. "Peter, let's shoot hoops. Grab the ball and start playing with your brothers. I need to talk to Tony for a sec. . . . Tony, do you know if we'll be eating that awful-smelling mackerel tonight?"

"Yes, and the shit-load Mom got smells like it was just pulled from the Kennebec."

"Listen. Yesterday I was walking by Joe's Pizza and through the window I watched him make a sub. It looked *sooooo* good. I got thinking how nice it would be for supper on Saturday, especially after being force-fed that crappo mackerel tonight. I know how much you like the sandwich. Mmm, and with a nice Pepsi to wash it down. I'm getting hungry just thinking about it. Anyhoos, Mom and Dad expect you to mow this here huge hayfield of ours tomorrow. I'll be using the lawnmower in the morning, but you can have it in the afternoon."

"Shut your face!"

Chapter XXXII

The Black Man

Saturday morning, the Philadelphians left for Waterville. After a morning mow, I spent a few hours with the Dells' grandchildren. At 3:00 I left for home. Just onto my driveway, I heard a screen door slam open. Out ran Frank, straight for Kingsbury.

"A black man is coming! Mom and Dad, a black man is coming!"

He stopped at the same spot as before, at the up-street edge of his lawn. He noticed me.

"Look, Charlie! A black man is coming!"

Can't be another one this soon. I went for the middle of the street, to see for myself. *Maybe this one knows K. C. Jones.* "Oh no! Frank, that's not a black man! That's Father McIver!" *Think, Charlie, think!* I rushed up to my little buddy. "Frank, he's a very nice man, and he likes to talk too much, just like you do. So why don't you run up the side of the street as far as the Robbins' driveway, and when Father McIver makes it to you, say hi and ask him every kind of question you can think of. You know how good you are at that. Talk as much as you can, and real loud, too, so I can hear you from here. It's okay. Just stay off the street."

"Yes, Charlie. I'll do that right now."

He ran, waving the whole way. I remained at my spot, to watch, to listen, to make sure.

"Hi, Father McIvy. How are you today? My name is Frank. My friend Charlie says you like to talk too much just like me."

The good priest stopped, smiled, and leaned down to greet the youngster—my cue to hightail it into the house so I could warn the parents.

Just before making the door, I heard a loud shout. "Frank! Frank!" It was his mother. "Who gave you permission to leave this yard!"

"Charlie did! So just shut up and mind your own business so I can talk to Father McIvy!"

"Oh, it was Charlie who gave you permission, was it? Joe! Joe! I've had it with that troublemaker across the street! It's time you had it out with his father!"

Both parents were in the kitchen. "Mom and Dad, Father McIver is right now coming down the street. You might have two minutes."

"Oh my goodness, Herve. I knew you should have put the crucifix and pictures of Jesus, Mary, and Joseph back up right after we finished the wallpapering."

"Me? When I went to do it, you said not yet because you wanted to think about it."

"I don't care about that right now. Please just rush and put them back up wherever. While you're doing that, I'll pick up the den. We'll sit in there for coffee. Tony, put your guns and bullets away. Help your father and me. Rush!"

"Ma, does Father McIver's coming here mean that you won't have time to cook supper and we can order from Joe's?"

"I already said no. But you're right. There won't be time. Yes, Joe's it'll be."

"Yeah!"

"Yeah!"

"Charles, get outside and stall Father as long as you can. Ask him anything and everything, like you always do with us. Maybe your habit can actually be of use this time. Go!"

I rushed out to see Frank walking back to his house and Father McIver making it onto our driveway. He saw me, smiled, and waved. I rushed up to him.

"Hello, Father McIver."

"Hello, Charlie. As you've likely determined, I'm here for my yearly visit. Hope your parents are home. Are they and what's that banging I hear?"

"Yes, they're inside. My dad's just finishing up a project. Shouldn't take more than a couple minutes. In the meantime, Father, I have some important questions to ask you?"

"Yes. Go ahead."

"You know how in church we always pray for the souls of the dead. Well, ah, the other day I saw a couple dead people down along the river, just beyond the railroad station. They asked me to pray for them. Can dead people still be alive?"

The good priest smiled. "If the sighting was, as you say, down along this here repugnant river of ours, in the thick of an ungodly such as today, then you saw two of what our church calls 'poor souls,' meaning two souls *in* or *from* purgatory."

"But, Father, to me they looked alive even though they seemed to be dead."

"Pay no attention to that minor detail. Whether a human body is inhaling this putridity or not, the soul operating it or had at one time operated it can be alive or dead. God is clear on this matter in the Good Book. Remember how Jesus told a chap to come along with Him and to leave behind the dead to bury their dead? Dead bodies can't very well bury other dead bodies, can they? So, for your benefit, try to stop talking so much all the time and instead use some of the time to read the Bible. And, yes, we must pray for the poor souls, so that God may reward our commitment to Him and grant them the grace to reverse their lives, whether they still be here or in that afterlife place we Catholics call purgatory. I as well will remember to pray for them."

"Their names are—"

"The Lord knows their names. Listen for a moment. . . . The banging has stopped."

"And, Father, my other question is who is your favorite baseball player?"

"I have a couple. Carl Yastrzemski and Tony Conigliaro. Who's yours?"

"Mickey Mantle."

"Mickey Mantle? He's a Yankee. Your favorite player should be on the team you cheer for—the Red Sox, certainly."

"Father, I hay—can't stand the Red Sox. I love the Yankees."

"That's a sin, young man. You live in New England, which means there's no excuse to cheer for any team other than our dear Red Sox. I expect a sincere repentance at your next visit to the confessional." Father McIver stared into my eyes, then smiled. He had been kidding.

"Charlie, are you still planning to become a priest?"

"Well, yes, kind of I am, I guess maybe, but-but I can't."

"You can't? Why, may I ask, is that?"

"Because my dad won't allow it. He says I have to grow up and get a real job."

"Either lead or step aside. Our talk-time is over. Me back's up and there's no sense trying to stall me more than you already have. Move it, son."

Once in the hallway, Father offered some calming words. "Charlie, I see your nervousness. Don't be concerned. I'll be gentle with your dad. I'm a master with words and things of the mind and spirit. He won't suspect you opened your big mouth."

We entered.

"Hello, Jeanne and Herve. Hope I'm not catching you at an inconvenient time."

"Hello, Father McIver. What a nice surprise. No inconvenience whatsoever. Herve and I are happy to have you drop by."

"Hello, Father. Jeanne's right. Glad you came."

"Herve, please show our visiting royalty into the den while I pour coffees." There were chuckles. "*Father*, cream and sugar?"

"Of course, as always."

"Dear, I was actually talking to the other Father."

"Both additions will do me just fine, dear Jeanne."

"Here, Father McIver. You can sit in this chair right—"

"Never mind, Herve. The spot I've already chosen is where I'm at."

It was dad's chair. I laughed, silently, blocked from Father McIver's sight but not from the other father's. He did not looked pleased as he tried to ignore me.

"*Mom*," I whispered, "*come by me and look in the den. Father McIver can't see us here.*"

Next to me, on the desk, was today's *KJ*. I rolled it up and pretended to whack it against Father McIver's arm. Mother and I each cupped a hand over our mouths and bent over laughing, silently. Then, in an instant, she turned serious, whispering, "*Charles, leave us be. Go outside or where brothers are. Daniel's in his usual spot, and Tony's upstairs with his magazines.*"

"*I'll go outside.*"

Mother picked up the coffee tray and went into the den. Pretending to leave, I opened and closed the door, remained out of sight, within earshot.

"Here are your coffees, men. Father, while I think of it, I have a question for you."

"And what, pray-tell, is that, kind lady?"

"Herve recently heard Catholics don't have to abstain from meat on Fridays. True?"

"And where, may I ask, did Herve hear a thing like that?"

"On *The Huntley-Brinkley Report*."

"From those two heathens, now. Doesn't surprise me at all. Perhaps you should consider switching to that Cronkite chap, not that he's any better but at least with him there's only one heathen to contend with." There was a pause in the conversation. Then came three *clinks*, indicating a harmonious sip of rich blend had just taken place. "Now, on your question. To tell you the truth, that's not exactly what I've heard from the bishop's office."

"Pray-tell, Father, what exactly have you heard?" asked mother.

"Nothing . . . nothing at all." Another break came. Then: *Clink. Clink. Clink.* "But I tell you something else I've heard from certain priests who seem to be in the know about inside things. I must say that I hope it's nothing more than a bad idea that'll soon be put to the grave rather than into action. Supposedly sometime soon, in our holy church sanctuaries of all places, guitars and folk singers are going to replace our choirs. And, I can barely stomach to say, they'll be positioned at the front of the church, either on or beside the altar. That way, as the storyline goes, everyone can see them. That's right, priests and parishioners alike can concentrate on them instead of eternal life God grants through the crucifixion of His Son. *It's just an awful idea.* Next thing you know, I'll have to introduce them like I'm Ed Sullivan and they those devil Beatles. Let's the three of us have a short prayer on it. 'Oh sweet beloved Jesus and God our dear Father, please, we beg You, say it won't be so. Amen.'"

Clink. Clink. Clink.

"Jeanne, this is excellent coffee the Lord and you made."

"The Lord? How's that, Father? I don't remember Him in the kitchen with me."

Mother's words brought gentle laughs, then another pause. . . . *Clink. Clink. Clink.*

"You see, dear fine lady, it goes something like this. It is our Lord God who made the earth, skies, and sun, and it is He who brings forth the rain. He owns all the beasts and plants of the earth, and He grants us use of them, at our will. He creates big things, and because we are made in His image, we create little things. In other words, He makes apple trees and coffee beans for humans to make apple pie and, as you've already done, tasty brown brew."

I bent over laughing, silently.

"Oh-ah, yes, Father, but it's blueberry I baked. Would you like ice cream with it?"

"That would be *almighty fine*, for I cannot remember the last time I enjoyed such a splendid, cold concoction. However, before you exit the room to prepare the dish, I just want to say that you have quite a good son there."

Mother laughed. I knew her laugh; this one was fake. "Father, we have three good sons."

Dad was more realistic. "We do? Which one?"

Clink. "I'm glad you asked that, Herve. Now, kind lady, I would like a moment alone with your husband, so I ask that you not rush in bringing back the delightful plate."

"Sure. Take all the time you need. Herve, did you want a slice of pie with ice cream?"

"Yes, please."

"That's the kitchen door I just heard. Probably Charles coming back in. I'll check."

She entered the kitchen. Our eyes met. "*Mom, I heard you mention ice cream. Remember how I stayed up late last night? Well, after you and Dad went to bed I finished it off. I'm telling you now, so you don't get blindsided when you open the freezer.*"

"You couldn't have. There was a half a box left."

"I know, and I'm sorry. I crumbled a whole bunch of Lorna Doones in it. The concoction tasted so good I couldn't stop eating it."

She pointed to the door and whispered, loudly, "Get out of this house right now!"

Clink. Clink.

"What was that you said, dear lady?"

"Oh, nothing at all, Father."

"Yes, Mom, but can I grab a glass of water to take with me?"

"I suppose."

"I just thought of something else. There's still a little bit of whipped cream left. You know when Tony eats all of something and because he doesn't want people to think he's a selfish pig, even though he eats from the container and licks the rim, how he'll always leave a smidg—"

"Yyyup, unlike somebody else."

"Rrright. Well, anyway, there's a tiny bit of whipped cream left. Father can have that."

"Better than nothing, I guess."

I slowly made my way to the kitchen sink, turned on the tap a quarter-way only, and began to rinse and rinse the glass, letting it get almost full each time.

"At the last house I visited, wrestling was on the box. I insisted the owner leave it on so that I could become more aware of the types of silliness the devil has come up with to entertain people these days. You don't watch wrestling, do you, Herve?"

"No. Don't like it at all. And it's not really wrestling."

"Well there was this guy named Dog Bowser or something—"

"Excuse me, Father. That would be Dick 'The Bulldog' Brower."

"Thank you for the correction. I always take well to it, and I highly recommend all my parishioners be the same way. There should never come forth harsh feelings from the one who has been corrected in a kind manner."

Clink. Clink.

"So this big fellow was wrestling against Johnny something or other—."

"Johnny Rodz. The smaller guy was Johnny Rodz."

In louder voice: "Did I not hear you just claim not to be a watcher of wrestling? I'm your priest. Confess immediately and admit to your diversion away from truth."

"Oh-ah, it's Tony and Charles who like to watch it. Sometimes I might happen to be in here reading the newspaper."

"Good answer, and I accept it as valid, though I was merely putting your wits to test."

Clink. Clink.

"However, it does remind me that I haven't seen—I mean, *heard*—a similar voice to yours in the confessional in recent time. Perhaps my assistant, Father DeBruin, has. If not, may this be the most gentlest of reminders to do this important duty for your dear soul-person-self."

"Yes, Father. Thank you for telling me in that manner. You're kind-hearted."

"No mention, Herve. To continue, I noticed how this Bulldog fellow could manipulate the Johnny-guy like he was a mere baton in the masterful hands of a Gardiner High School majorette celebrating a glorious last-minute come-from-behind victory over our arch rival, *those dread Cony Rams*. The situation reminded me of my own teenage years, some fifty years ago, and how I could do pretty much the same to anyone who crossed me in the wrong way or managed to call up my goat a little too close to my side. And to be a Catholic boy in Scotland meant the fists had to be used almost daily. But eventually I decided to relinquish the pugilistic life in favor of a real job, and that was to promote the Lord. And no one, nowhere, not even my beloved dad, could stop me, nor did he ever dare try to, bless his soul—Amen to that."

"Well, all I can say, Father, is thank you or telling me that."

Clink. "Don't mention it, Herve. It was totally my pleasure. Now, onto a different subject of con—"

"*Get out of this house right now!*"

"What? Come again, Jeanne?"

"Nothing at all, Father. Hope it's okay for me to come back into the den."

"Indeed. Your dear husband and I have had a melding of the minds. We realize more than ever just how much we're on the same team, and that's the Red Sox. Right, Herve?"

Clink. "You bet. The Red Sox."

"Here's your pie, served with fresh whipped cream and no ice today. Sorry about that."

"That'll do me just fine, dear lady."

"And here's yours, other father. Served with no ice and fresh out of whipped cream."

"Herve, who would be your favorite baseball player?"

"Let me think for a moment. . . . Whitey Ford. I really enjoy watching him pitch."

Clank. "Whitey Ford! Why, he's another bloody Yank—"

"Now listen here, Father McIver. That'll be enough of that language. We don't use it in this house, especially when there's a priest present."

When the laughing subsided: "Dear fine lady, may I respond with a sincere *thank you* and note to your clever manner. Mmm, this sweet offering is totally delightful. If I may, a fill of the cup would go well in helping to wash down what remains of it and for our continued chatting."

Chapter XXXIII

Face Bashed In

The parents and grandparents treasured their exposure to Boothbay's harbor-side beauty. The whole time, too, the adults loved doting over their little baby girl. The day was the Philadelphians' last in Maine. The ride home had me quiet, sad about the visitors' imminent departure the next morning....

As the Pennsylvania automobile pulled away, all travelers waved their final goodbyes to Dot and Bernard, then to me. Alone on the court, basketball resting between an arm and hip, I stared and waved back. For me it was always a sad thing to see visitors depart, as long as the visitors had not been obtuse. They had not been.

The business of publishing was far from my spirit. Still, there was a feeling of wanting to get a final edition done and distributed. I knew neighbors would take well to a big Gardiner-story, one that would divert their minds away from the problem world. A few persons were almost demanding I produce something along that line. The reality was I had two big articles to write: the Gardiner family's involvement in the Underground Railroad and the story behind the murder of a police lieutenant. The thought was that if I did come through, a form of regional stardom might fly my way—a result that would allow me to get of out of the finger-publishing business with a bang. A few readers, perhaps even most, would be caught breathless by the second article's darksome content. But, right after that, then what? Would they speak up? Would they make phone calls? Would they shout from rooftops? And then there were the stories on Indian spirits along the Kennebec River and Horseshoe Pond's giant bloodsuckers.

The long and the short of it was this: the job had to get done. I didn't yet have enough information on Cates. How do I get it? What exactly was I looking for? Where should I begin? Other questions came. Was I overreaching my duty as a reporter? Was an early success at the "newspaper game" causing me to discount the "little stories" that had delivered that early success? Mr. Laithran and Mr. Dell would likely have said so. And then there was Jimmy—or, better stated, *lack of Jimmy*. He had had a way of keeping me in line and on topic. In truth, the mundane items were what we enjoyed writing about the most.

Finished morning nap, Frank joined me outside. Lizzie was with him, and that meant Tony was finally out of bed. Dad and Daniel were already back at the factory.

The rest of Monday and over the next few days I mowed lawns and weeded gardens; it wasn't constant work. Between jobs, I sat in the tree house, with the telescope, looking out, listening, reading *Treasure Island*. Nothing came of it. Tuesday evening had me playing baseball at LeClerc's. Wednesday afternoon, I got together with Mike at his place.

Late Thursday afternoon, Tony and kid-brother played hoops while Frank and Lizzie sat on the grass. Mrs. Laithran emerged from her house and approached. She had a serious face.

"Hello, all of you. Tony, I need to talk to you for a moment."

"Hello, Mrs. Laithran." Tony handed me the ball. "What's up?"

I went in close for a listen. Frank got up off the grass and came over.

"Something has been eating Bernard's vegetables. Every evening he tells me that a little more of his garden has disappeared. He also finds items that are half-eaten or chewed only a little bit. He's afraid none of his cucumbers, squash, and green beans will make it to picking time, which is still a couple weeks away. What do you suppose it is?"

"Might be a woodchuck or a porcupine. Would have to catch it in the act."

Frank spoke up: "I'm going over there right now to see if it's there."

"You can't do that," said Tony. "You know you're not allowed to leave our yard. Besides, what if the animal is there and it bites you?"

"I don't care. I'm going right now, to warn it to run away so you can't kill it."

I grabbed Frank's arm. "Stay here. Mrs. Laithran hasn't asked Tony to kill it."

She leaned down close to the little guy. "Thank you for staying." She straightened up, looked back at Tony. "If I manage to spot the animal in there, can I come and get you, so you can, ah, *take care of it?* Otherwise, Bernard and I will have nothing left to harvest."

"Sure, come get me. I'll be glad to *eliminate* the situation for you."

"Thank you, Tony. I'll be by when it's time." Mrs. Laithran turned and left.

"You don't be killing that poor animal!" shouted Frank at Tony. "I'm gonna sneak over there every day so I can warn it to run away!"

My brother angrily pointed a finger into Frank's face. "Don't do that or else your parents will be told that you're not listening. Do you hear me, Frank?"

"Yes, I hear you."

A day passed. Knocks came early Friday evening, but not against a door. Daniel got up from the living room couch and went into the dining room. "Charles! Kenny Whitson's knocking at the window in here! He's showing me a ball and mouthing your name!"

"Thanks, Dan! Mouth back to him I'm coming out!"

Despite a lack of regular athletic involvement, Kenny was overly muscular and exhibited natural coordination when playing sports. A bit on the short side for a 15-year-old, measuring an inch below me, he carried a mature-looking skull, large and bony, as if he were in his early 20s. Basically he came across as a man-boy, and one who retained a throwing arm stronger than mine. Mostly when we tossed a tennis ball back and forth, he stood at the downhill position on Kingsbury, just south of the Prudhomme property line, and that way he could wing the ball uphill to me, standing in the street, near to the entrance to the ancient path into Rollins Woods.

Kenny and I threw a mixture of pop flies, line-drives, and grounders. We yelled out encouragement to each other. Frank must have heard us. He came down onto the sidewalk, to watch us; his position was halfway between the throwers. Soon, he asked if he could play. Kenny was resistant, but when I insisted that it would be for a little while only, he relented.

Kenny and I threw the ball very gently to the little guy. Even so, at no time did he come close to catching it. At least he always ran as fast as he could to retrieve it. This helped Kenny to stay patient. The youngster's ability to throw was even worse. Invariably, the ball went sideways in the most inconvenient directions away from where Kenny and I stood. I broke for a couple minutes so that I could teach him how to properly hold and release the ball. Didn't work. As the minutes wore on, I noticed Kenny's facial expression and body language descending.

"Frank, just Kenny and I are going to play from now on. You can watch us if you want."

"That's not fair, Charlie! I still want to play!"

I steamed a line-drive grounder down the hill to Kenny. Frank ran onto the street and with one hand miraculously, unfortunately, stopped the ball dead. He picked it up and threw it back to me and not to Kenny. The ball went squirrelly in the wrong direction. By turning his back to the guy downhill, Frank's message had been obvious: crap on you, Kenny.

The man-boy's face reddened, but he remained at his spot. Frank retrieved the ball, ran back to the sidewalk, and when he got set to throw it to me again, Kenny yelled, "Stop!" He ran up to the little guy, pushed him to the sidewalk, pulled the ball from his hand, and threw it to me. Frank exploded into screams, got up holding an arm, and ran crying into his house.

"Kenny! Kenny! Come up here right away!"

"Why!"

"You did something real bad! You're in big trouble! If Frank's dad gets hold of you, he'll kill you dead! Why are you walking so slow! Don't be stupid! Listen to me—Run!"

Kenny stretched an arm out and with an open hand waved it down a couple times, as if to say, "Calm down." He continued to strut unrushed, confident. As for myself, I knew to retreat uphill to Kenny's driveway, for it was there that I could best observe the yet-to-develop outcome and if necessary go knock on the adults' door. Mrs. Robbins and female wrestling champion The Fabulous Moolah did not present dissimilar attitudes and physiques. Paul, too, could not be discounted if help in wrestling down a large, angry mammal were required. Fortunately, he possessed a grappler's body built more like Smasher Sloan's than Bulldog Brower's. Even so, it would take both of them to handle an out-of-control George "The Animal" Steele. I remained at the edge of the driveway, waiting, watching, keeping my options open.

Sure enough, Frank's father exited the side-door. An understatement, he looked angry. With both fists clenched, he walked swiftly toward Kenny, who at this point was just making it to the spot where I had been standing to throw the ball. His back was to the approaching man, and so he was unaware of the level of danger soon to leap upon him.

"Run, Kenny, run! He's coming up to you!"

Kenny turned to see the big man *on the way in*. Despite my urgings, Kenny did not want to accept the seriousness of what he had done to Frank. He reversed direction and walked toward the enraged strongman, apparently trying to meet up with him halfway so the two could talk it out. Just before they came together, Kenny did the same hand wave—*Calm down, big guy*.

There were no more warnings to be shouted. I stood there and watched what their coming together would bring. Part of me figured Kenny deserved to learn a lesson; a part of that part believed he should get his head slammed for attacking a little kid. But the other part of me feared for his life. In my mind I could already see Joe making mince meat pie out of Kenny's face.

The big, angry male grizzly leaped onto his unprepared prey. Kenny hollered, "Wait a minute! What are you doing!" It was too late and to no avail. The wild-eyed man-animal now had the man-boy in his clutches, and there would be no release until all aspects of the mauling were completed. Next, the big man banged a couple short rights against Kenny's face. Down to the ground the two went, Joe on top and in control. From there he masterfully twisted the 15-year-old into serious shapes, like a Shrine Circus clown would one of those snake-like balloons filled with air. Kenny screamed out for my help. *Should I go get his parents? Nah. Not yet.* Joe vise-gripped the upstart teenager's head between his right arm and chest, so that he could squeeze every bit of the prey's residual resistance out onto the tar. To help it along, a good six hard left fists required landing squarely onto Kenny's nose, and they were. Rather than playing dead, Kenny twisted around in effort to get away and by doing so caused the grizzly to maul more enthusiastically. The strangely graceful manner in which the one-way brutality was being delivered might be compared to watching "The Animal" manhandle that mouthy midget wrestler Sky Low Low. *Has Kenny has had enough? Nah. Not yet.*

Next, Joe sat on the deflated man-boy. Using his knees to pin down the underling's shoulders, he proceeded to pummel down lefts and rights. The only good news for Kenny was for the back of his head, which rested on soft ditch-grass; this meant his skull would probably not cave in. Kenny yelled for my help. *Are you nuts? I told you to run. That was my way of helping and you refused it. Time to get his parents? Nah. Joe still has more to get out of his system.*

Suddenly the grizzly stopped. "You won't be touching my son again, will you?"

"No. I promise."

With that, Frank's merciful father—for he had done no punching into Kenny's soft underbelly—stood up, looked at me, slap-swiped his hands together, turned, and calmly walked home. Mr. Prudhomme was once again the neighborhood's gentle bear. *"Yeah! Yeah! Good job, Kenny!"* I yelled in low voice that he would not hear.

The victim got up from the ditch and came toward me. Until I saw what he looked like up close, I had the full intention of shaking his hand and telling him he did pretty good for a small guy who knows nothing about wrestling. The 15-year-old was totally beaten down. He was dirty, his shirt was ripped, and his face was red and blotchy blue, with swelling. Thankfully, blood wasn't streaming from his nose, but he did have cuts. To top it off, he was crying.

A little embarrassing it was to see such facial wetness coming from a teenager. But my spirit quickly turned to wanting to give him consolation. Kenny, I realized right then, was a despairing soul. He had never been close to his appointed parents, but he had been to his older brother, who was of the same blood and now off in the Navy. Since Kenny's birth, up until a few months ago, the two had never been apart. I believed Kenny now felt alone in the world.

"It's okay, Kenny. Joe won't bother you again. He's gotten it out of his system. Everyone in the neighborhood is back to being safe. But you better stay clear of Frank forever."

"Yeah, I sure will."

I patted him on the back. "You did real good. You're still alive and able to walk. Nothing seems broken. He's a big guy and you took his best shots.

Means you have a lot of natural strength and that's why he wasn't able to defeat you until the end. It'll all be forgotten in a day or two. Let me shake your hand. You ain't no Johnny Rodz but you sure could be a Sky Low Low."

We laughed.

Kenny wiped the tears and drops of blood from his face. "I should have listened to you when you said run. Now I've gotta go inside looking like this. What are Alberta and Paul gonna say?"

It was too late to come up with a plan. Through their living room window, the foster parents must have observed us talking. They were now standing outside on their driveway.

"What's going on out here, Kenny? What did you do wrong this time?"

"Nothing, Mom. Everything's fine. We played ball really hard. I fell down a few times. That's why I look the way I do. We're all done. Thanks for letting us play."

She turned to me. "I bet that's your story, too—his *falling down* line."

"Yes, Mrs. Robbins."

"Then how come you don't look all beat up like he does?"

"Leave him alone, Mom! I'm telling you the truth! Why is it you never believe me!"

"That's enough, Kenny! Don't shout at your mother! We just want to know how you got your face bashed in! Now get yourself in the house!"

Kenny cried again as he ran past them and through the doorway. Mr. and Mrs. Robbins looked at each other, their expressions a mix of confusion, distress. They turned and followed after him.

Chapter XXXIV

Reid State Park

That final week of August began with the family's Sunday trip to Reid State Park. The first third of the way was the same as going to Boothbay Harbor. The family was accustomed to the stretch, so to cut through the monotony the youngest decided to pose a pile of questions, which elicited, depending on the subject, nothing much from Tony, sarcastic comments and yells from Daniel, grunts from both, and laughs from all. Sometimes a question got answered. . . .

"Mom, what was your favorite movie ever?"

"Give me a moment . . . *Gone With the Wind*. Clark Gable's best part. Alfred Hitchcock's *The Birds*, with Tipsi Hedren, was also good. Then there was *Cat on a Hot Tin Roof*. Elizabeth Taylor and Monty Cliff starred in it. Cliff proved he could do drama. Later, he did melodrama, killing himself. What about you, Herve? What was your favorite movie?"

"*Gone With the Wind* was too long and boring for me. Mine was *Singing in the Rain*. Fun and entertaining. Too, that tin-roof one was about as sappy and boring as a movie can get."

"Well, that's what I like, 'sappy' and 'boring.' I'm a woman and you're a man. Women like those type of movies. But I liked *Singing in the Rain*. Debbie Reynolds and Gene Autry were very good in it. Charles, it was you who asked. What was yours?"

"*The Amazing Colossal Man*."

"That was a piece-o-crappo," blurted Tony.

"It was not."

"Yes, it was. A man gets exposed to too much radiation and grows to sixty feet tall? Come on, let's be serious. The pathetic guy can't wear anything but a roll of Bate's Cotton Mill cloth. My favorite, hands down, was *The Day the Earth Stood Still*."

"I liked that one, too. It's probably my second favorite."

"Daniel, what about you?" asked mother.

"*Night of the Iguana*. Richard Burton wasn't particularly good in it, but the movie was suspenseful—diabolical, really. *The Birds* I liked."

"What does 'diabolical' mean?" I asked.

"Devilish."

"Now doesn't that take the cake," commented mother. "This morning we went to church to worship God and your favorite movie was because it was devilish."

"Jeanne, watching movies isn't the same as going to church," reasoned the adult male for his oldest son. "When you walk out of church you can leave all that stuff behind you and get on with life the way you're supposed to."

"Oh, is that—"

"Excuse me. I'll change what I said. I like that movie because it was darkly intriguing."

"And my third favorite movie was *Abbot and Costello Meet Frankenstein*, and my fourth favorite movie was *Abbot and Costello Meet the Mummy*."

"Those two were pretty good, but I like *The Fly* and *The Blob* more," came Tony.

The adult male shook his head. "You boys must be joking. Those weren't real movies."

"Yeah, Dad, like we believe you. You watched the Abbot and Costello ones with Chuckie and me and laughed just as hard. You even told us *shush* at the end of the commercials."

"Herve, that's true. I remember you laughing it up with the boys."

"I was in the den reading the *KJ*. What was I to do, put earplugs in? Have we had enough with movies yet?"

"My fifth favorite movie was—"

"No one cares about someone's fifth favorite movie! So just shut—be quiet for a while!"

"Though you needn't have raised your voice, your father and I are pleased to hear you correct yourself, Daniel. We're making gains, aren't we, Herve?"

"Yes, we are. But, senior son, as your mother said, try not to shout when your patience is put to the test. Remember that you're working on not just *what* you say but also *how* you say it."

"Yes, Dad, you're right. I'll try to keep that in mind."

"Dan, the crew from *Mission Impossible* couldn't get Chuckie to shut his face, so whether your breath is as calm as a summer breeze over Horseshoe Pond or you're the Colossal Man yelling out after stepping on a thumbtack, don't bother wasting your words on him."

"*Hmm*, then there's *that* son of ours. Herve, I never did ask you who our 'good boy' is. Please tell, which one has managed to pull the wool over Father McIver's Scottish eyes."

"Jeanne, some things are better left not repeated."

Even the car roared.

At Dresden, dad took the right; continuing straight would have taken us back to Wiscasset. The first couple miles went along the East River. Old, gray and tattered smelt shacks dotted the opposite shoreline. Forty minutes passed, and we came to Woolwich: population one thousand and situated directly across the Kennebec River estuary from Bath. The area's smell was particularly bad. The name "Bath" meant "City of Ships," but mother always maintained the name really meant "City of Something Else." The incredible beaches of Reid State Park, located on the southeast shore of George's Island, lay only half an hour away.

The remaining travel took us straight south, first portion of which ran beside the estuary. Just past Woolwich, travelers could view some of the most magnificent iron ships making up America's Navy and Coast Guard fleets. Bath Iron Works was a major player in the building of new ships and refitting of old ones. Dad slowed the car so his kids could get a good look. Though docked on the other side of the waterway and about a mile away, the battleships—huge, big, and small—seemed surreal, perhaps even alien-looking, to this youngster's eyes. Definitely contrary to the natural beauty of the bay, and contrary to humanity's belief, the metal killer-hunters had actually been dropped down to earth by gargantuan, other-world craft operated by large and ugly octopus-like creatures that humans could not look at without dying of terror. The people who worked on these soulless iron hulls were made to; their minds and thus their free wills had been covertly taken over by the above, unseen, anti-godly intelligences, if one could call them that. Human bodies, like robots, walked about in trance-like states, carrying and welding this and that, updating and uploading key data for the creatures. The metal beasts of Bath were diabolical magnets to young eyes traveling in automobiles. *Those invisible monsters can never defeat us because our diseases will kill them all!*

"My fifth favorite movie was *War of the Worlds*."

No one commented, not even Daniel. Boys' pupils continued to study the distant flotilla.

"What's the big deal? They're just boats. You've all gaped for long enough, so I'm speeding up before someone toots." During World War II, the adult had sometimes worked on ships like these, when they were in port for renewal. To look at them meant nothing to him.

The air smelled more and more of ocean as we made our way toward Reid. Thankfully, the Kennebec's air was not able to cut its way this far south.

Half an hour past Bath the traffic slowed, and in a couple minutes it turned into stop-and-go. Every five to ten seconds we moved forward one car length.

Mother: "This is ridiculous. Because the State decided to charge by the person and not by the car, it takes time for the tellers to count the people and figure out what to charge. The State claims it's fairer. *Rrright*. They make more money and we have to wait in line to give it to them. That's government for you. Twist and turn it any which-way they can, just like Chubby Checker does."

"Mom,—"

"*What-what-what*. What is it now? Ask your father, instead."

"Dad, when are we going to win?"

"Win what?"

"Just what I said. When are we going to . . . *win?*"

"We can't win anything because we don't gamble."

"That's not quite true," pointed out Tony. "Sometimes, Dad, you've liked to bet the horses at the Windsor State Fair. As far back as I can remember, you've never won. And then you've played the game where you toss a ring to try to hook it around the top of a Coke bottle, to win something for mother. You've never won at that, either. So, Chuckie, the answer to your question is 'never.'"

"Is that what you mean?" asked the man, looking through the rear-view mirror at me.

"Not really. When I say 'win,' I don't mean at what. I mean *where*, like 'Windsor *where*.' And not just you, Dad, but all of us."

Daniel could no longer resist the bait, but he at least kept a calm tone. "Dad, your mistake was biting on the hook. Tony's right. It's best to ignore him, especially when we're all packed in the car and in a lineup like—"

"I mean when will we ever take a Sunday drive to some of the other *wins*, like Windham, Winthrop, Winslow, and Winchester?"

"We've been to Winthrop!" hollered Daniel.

"Except for a few old houses and a general store, nothing much was there," added mother. "Seeing Winthrop once was enough. The family taking a relaxing drive is why we do most of our Sunday afternoon trips. It doesn't really have much to do with reaching a destination. Today, of course, is different, as was going to Boothbay Harbor. I doubt we'll be driving to Windham, Winslow, and Winchester, wherever that one is, because why bother. And, Daniel, regarding your anger explosions, perhaps you should consider a visit to the confessional next Saturday afternoon, to receive the Lord's forgiveness and a fresh start with His renewed grace in you. Hervey, you and I also need to go, as well as our other two boys."

Dad said nothing. Daniel said nothing. Tony said nothing.

"Mr. Laithran says his church doesn't believe in confession because they say God keeps forgivin' like a good Timex watch keeps workin'. No matter how often we sink to the bottom of the stinkin' Kennebec, Jesus keeps pullin' us up to make sure our Timex watch is still tickin'."

"Did you hear that, Jeanne?"

"Forget it, *Father*. We're not Christian, we're Catholic, and Catholic we'll remain."

The jewel known as Reid State Park was not unknown. Past the gate, dad slowly drove to a distant, auxiliary parking lot; the main lots were already filled to capacity. We passed by many cars displaying out-of-state license plates: New York, Massachusetts, Connecticut, New Jersey, and Pennsylvania were the dominant ones, but New York by far the most. Almost unbelievably, there were a few Florida plates; perhaps these autos had been driven here by retired Mainers who preferred this state's less-hot summers. Plates from Minnesota, Delaware, Michigan, Wisconsin, Virginia, and even some from California were seen. Oddly, very few came from the close-by states of New Hampshire and Vermont. Maybe those autos preferred to deliver their human contents to Hampton or Old Orchard Beaches, both closer drives than Reid. And then there was the occasional southern plate: Tennessee, North Carolina, Texas, Louisiana.

Once parked, we trod our way toward the beach. The boys made sure to point out every out-of-state plate we walked by. Tony, by himself in the next lane over, yelled "Indiana!" Mother yelled back, "That's a first! See if anyone else can find Iowa and both Dakotas!"

Sure enough, within the minute came "Right here's an Iowa!" from Tony. "Come on over and see it, everyone!"

"Will you look at that," said mother. "Who would have ever thought?"

Daniel: "It's a car from Iowa. So what. Who cares?"

Dad disagreed. "What do you mean? This car came a long ways. It's very dirty. Don't know how the driver could see through a windshield with so many smashed bugs on it. Hmm, a '66 Chevelle. The new design looks better than before. Still not as snazzy as the Electra."

"Dad, now it's you who's joking. That Electra is more like one of those iron crates we saw floating in Bath. The new Chevelles are the best-looking cars on the planet right now."

"No, they're not," disagreed I. "Mustangs are."

"I like the name. *Sha-vel*. Has a French sound to it," noted mother.

"What does it mean in English?" I asked.

"I said it *sounds* French, not it *is* French."

Dad had heard enough. "Run, boys! Last one to put sand under his feet is a rotten egg!"

Daniel took off. Tony grabbed me into a headlock, so that he could walk us there. "Mustangs stink like those stinking oil-burner Ford Falcons do. How many noogies do you need before you change your position on the what the best new car in the world is?"

"None! Chevelle is!"

Chapter XXXV

The Rock

Monday was spent close to home. I tried teaching Frank basketball. We took frequent cool-off breaks, to run through the lawn sprinkler. A couple times I left him alone for a while, so that I could go into the tree house. He was good about it and didn't dog after me.

Mike had called during breakfast, wanting me to go over to his place. Though tempted, I declined but said maybe in a few days. Since right after the family's return from Reid State Park, a gentle interior voice had been silently communicating to me: *Something important has happened and you're about to find out.* Because of it, I expected news, but nothing came. Clients' lawns needed mowing, and there could be no more putting them off. Tuesday and Wednesday would be for them, regardless of the interior voice.

Mike was not pleased with my turndown. Our friendship was changing, now that he lived across town and now that my experience in life was catching up to his. But there was more to it than that. Soon to begin his second teenage year, Mike was becoming more and more like the lead character in the movie *Rebel Without a Cause*. For a long time, quiet anger had been building inside of him, and recently it had begun to show more. Neither of us wanted an estrangement to take place. He had mentioned about another of Nanna Barry's Sunday spreads.

I did find something on my first go to the tree house, and I almost tripped over it. A big rock had been not-nicely placed at the old path's turnoff to the tree with the ark. I recognized it Tony's handiwork. At supper Saturday, he had mentioned about his having dug up the mostly-buried rock that afternoon. With it out of the way, he no longer had to be careful with the lawnmower in that corner of the yard. I complained. "Aw, shoot. I like to stand on that rock when the trees have no leaves. Gives me a good view down at Mike's place and the train yard."

"Don't worry," he snickered, "your feet and the rock will soon meet again."

The size and shape of the thing was a surprise: a smooth, two-feet-long, eight-inch-wide, round-ended, flattish, five-inch-thick-at-centerline, medium gray rock that basically looked like a giant medicine capsule that had been stepped on by King Kong. After studying it for a minute and with good effort, I moved it out of the way.

Tuesday morning, the young reporter figured to spend ten minutes in the tree house before leaving for a mow. The rock lay at the edge of the lawn, at the old path's entrance. Right away, he saw it the mystery man John's way of saying he had been by. Was he waiting in there?

Fearful or not, the "man" part of the spirit always desires for the physical body to travel the path that knowingly leads to places unknown, and that is because the man-part yearns for truth, no matter the consequence. But there is an alternate truth, and it is that the spirit of a boy will always reside inside a man, every man, and it tenaciously holds on to fear, sometimes too much, altering it into trepidation, cowardice even. That "little boy" part never really dies, nor should he, and he sometimes finds the strength to overpower "the man" in order to force the physical body to hold back, to remain on safe ground. The man-part of Charlie was now the stronger of the two, and the summer had found him growing stronger by the day. After placing the rock in the midst of the wild tulips, carefully, so as not to hurt even one of the matron's beautiful cups, he entered the path leading to an unknown place.

What would the mystery man John have? Good news? Bad news? The young reporter hoped that this day would deliver the resolution he had been so hoping for: *Exactly who killed Lieutenant Cates and why?* After the clandestine meeting, the last edition of *American River Road* could finally go to fingers. As he climbed the tree and into the Ark of Kingsbury, the young reporter believed the top of the world was his eternal destiny.

He sat down next to the telescope. Saw and heard no one, nothing. . . .

"John, I saw the rock. Maybe you're out there." No response. More time went by. "I've changed my name to John. That's my real first name. Don't know why my parents always called me by my middle name. Never properly explained it other than to say they liked it better. Whenever I ask them why they didn't name me Charles John and use my first name like normal people do, they always clam up, as if to hope the subject will die. *Charles*—don't like it at all. Never have, now that I think about it. In my mind the name John is way better. What do you think? Do you like the name John or not, John? John, please call me John from now on."

A couple more minutes went by.

"Maybe you're not out there, so I might as well climb down and leave."

"You're right about John being a good name. *Charlie* isn't so bad, but you should know what you want to go by. I've been here for a while. Felt I should make you wait, like you did me. For me, that big rock I threw onto your lawn has special meaning, and it should for you. You see, if the dog you love so much was walking by when I threw it, she'd be dead. The death might have been accidental or maybe not. To make a point real hard, it would be better for your dog to die by that big rock than for you to get run over by an old Ford 100 pickup. Yup, that Charlie kid is dead and buried. Gone forever. Young fella John is smarter and more grownup than Charlie ever was. John, can you see me?"

"No, but because I hear you, my gut says you're sitting on that old dead maple."

"I can't see you, either. After today, this'll be the way it is between you and me, unless we happen to pass by on the street. If so, we don't know each other. Got it?"

"Yes."

"I have a question for you. What can a few words do that a lifetime in prison cannot?"

"Ah . . . I don't know."

"Remorse. Words can bring about remorse. What you told me last time has made a difference. The go-between worked out. It took time to get through the system and back. Everything's okay, or as okay as it's ever going to be. Young fella John, you have to listen to big fella John real carefully. What happened to Cates was an accident waiting to happen. On New Year's Eve, he ended up at the wrong place at the wrong time. That night there were people at the Sportsmen's Club who harbored anger in their hearts against him. And the one missing ingredient wasn't missing anymore. The beating took place later in the evening. You're still young, but I bet you know the ingredient."

"Alcohol?"

"Yes, and because of that, their good senses could no longer control their bad ones. They didn't intend to kill him, just beat him to tar and teach him a lesson. When he came into the club all proud and confident, as he should have when facing the situation alone, it didn't take long for someone to shout out, 'There's that old cop! He's the one who did in that nice young fella and his family! He's the one who ruined an innocent man's life! He's here to do the same to someone else! Let's teach him a lesson he won't forget! Who's with me?'

"It wasn't long before the lieutenant was in all kinds of pain on the floor. Seeing him in that condition brought everyone to sober up, and they quickly made the decision to clear out. They were young and middle-aged family men. None of them need to go to prison because that would ruin a lot more lives than just theirs. They need to work and support their families, and their children need fathers. It was a bad mistake, and they all know that now. They were angry, but they didn't mean to kill him. Do you hear me, young fella John?"

"Yes, I hear you."

"There's only one man to be charged, and for no more than common assault. He won't do much time or even any. The arrangement's been made and that's the end of it. There'll be nothing else. The good news is everyone is going to be safe, including you and me.

"Billy's friendly to me again. He even bought me a coffee and donut yesterday. When no one else was around us, he leaned in close, smiled, and said, 'Make sure to tell that Monroe boy not to be writing anything in his little newspaper, because if he does and people get upset and make a stink, the arrangement will have to be canceled, and that wouldn't be good for the two of you. Make sure to warn the boy right away—tomorrow. You're gonna hurt your back at the end of this shift so you can have the day off to see the doctor. I'll tell the boss I saw you fall.'

"Lots is riding on your word, young fella John. Billy and the others know where you live. Why, you and your family live right here, don't you? So . . . what's your answer?"

"I want to write the story, but I won't. You have my promise again. But I have to ask you something. Shouldn't people know the truth? Shouldn't Lieutenant Cates's family know?"

"Not now. Not now they shouldn't. Probably never, but maybe in fifty years, when everybody's either dead or too old to give a shit anymore. Keep the rock around as a reminder of your promise and how it was through your help something good came from bad. In the case of Lieutenant Cates, remorse resulted from truth. What's the Bible's word for that?"

"Repentance."

"That's the truth, young fella John. My sister and brother-in-law don't want to live on Vine Street anymore. In fact, they've decided to leave Gardiner completely. Climb out of the tree and walk down the path. I have something to hand you before I go."

"Yes, okay, I'll do that right away."

The mysterious man John emerged from the bushes. I wasn't sure what to expect. To me, he seemed a man of honor, so I was not scared. But what exactly was he going to hand me? At mid-slope, we halted three feet from each other. John made a fist with his right hand and punched it against the palm of his open left hand. "Young fella John, you're no longer that boy Charlie, who wavered in his first promise. You're a man, ya hear? Dependable and strong of spirit, just like that rock."

"Yes, sir."

He threw out his right hand. "An agreement like this requires a handshake."

We clasped right hands firmly. The deal was sealed.

"You take care of yourself, young fella John. Remember—we don't know each other." He stared into my eyes, then released my hand.

"Yes, we don't know each other. Goodbye, John."

With that, he turned and disappeared down the old pathway. I would never see him again.

Chapter XXXVI

Death on Kingsbury

Thursday lunch was just ending when raps came against the kitchen door. Tony opened.

"Hello, Mrs. Laithran. I'll get my mother."

"Tony, I'm not here to see your mother. Right now there's something in Bernard's garden. Can you come with your gun? Oh, hello there, Charlie. Hi, Frank."

Mother appeared. "Dot, I heard what you said. Tony, go right away with her."

He went for his .22-caliber rifle and bullets.

"Don't you kill that poor little animal! I'm going over there right now to tell it to run!"

"Frank, you have to stay here with me," instructed mother.

"Has to be done, Frank," reasoned a gentle-voiced Mrs. Laithran. "There's no joy in it, but Bernard and I count on the vegetables from our garden." She looked at mother. "Thanks for your consideration in this matter. I promise you we'll be careful."

"I'm not worried. Tony knows what he's doing."

"I'm ready, Mrs. Laithran. Chuckie can come along. I'm training him."

The three of us left. Mr. Knight, still in deep mourning and on temporary leave from the factory, was sitting on his porch. "Hey there, folks! What's the rifle for?"

"Hi, Harold! There's been an animal getting into Bernard's garden and eating all the vegetables! It's in there right now! Tony is going to take care of it!"

"This I gotta see!" Mr. Knight put down his glass, got up from his chair, wobbled for Kingsbury Street, and crossed over to join us. Tony did not mind having an audience; in fact, he liked it. He halted the wagon. The man came up with a big smile on his face, jumped aboard for the ride. "Have gun, will travel, huh, Tony? May I call you Paladin?" The man and I giggled, but not the other two. They turned to pace us onward. Mr. Knight changed to a serious tone. "After you do this job, I'll need your business card. Never know, might require your services. How much you charge, anyway?" The man looked cross-eyed at me. We both busted out laughing.

Tony, unmoved, remained focused and stone-faced, ready to do "the job."

"Thataboy, Paladin. That's what we want to see, fearless determination in our shooter."

"Oh, dear. It's not like that, Harold," reasoned Mrs. Laithran. "It's something that just needs doing." She remained next to Tony. Side by side, Mr. Knight and I walked behind them.

"Mr. Knight, Tony goes by the nickname Rifleman. Paladin used a handgun. He just got a new one of those, but it's a Ruger. Carries up to ten bullets, not just six like Paladin's did. He hasn't used it to kill anything yet. Not in this neighborhood, anyhoos."

The man laughed. "Thanks for the information. Come on, Rifleman. Let's get to the job. Why you only walking fast and not running? Thought I'd come along to make sure you don't shoot just anybody, only the person you need to. And don't you be taking down Bill Deers. Who knows, he and his kilt might be marching around, blowing away on that Irish tuba of theirs."

"Mr. Deers does that only on Sunday afternoon, after he wakes up late from, ah, you know, Saturday night. And I think he's Scotch and not Irish, and it's beer, not Scotch."

As we walked on, Mr. Knight leaned in close, chuckled at what I said. "Bill probably does that Scotch-tuba-thing with air similar to mine right now. Don't you think Rifleman should loosen up a bit? Maybe he needs a girlfriend. I know the perfect one. Annie Oakley. Heh-heh-heh. Charlie, Bea always thought the world of you. I miss her so much." The man's eyes welled with tears. Then he straightened up, got serious. "Hey, didn't I see Frank outside a little while ago, running through that sprinkler of yours?"

"Yup, and right now he's inside the house with my mother," assured Tony.

We entered the Laithrans' backyard. The grieving man continued to express caution. "Half an hour ago I saw Kenny. He was going in and out of his garage, doing work around his place. Let's make sure it's animal and not neighbor you're going to shoot."

"Don't worry. Tony knows what he's doing. He's our chosen shooter around here."

"Thank you, Mrs. Laithran. Relax, Mr. Knight. My target will be animal, not human."

"What's your bullet?"

"Short-rifle hollow-point. Brought three, but a well-placed one should do. I chose short because I don't want the bullet piercing through the body, only to kill Moe or someone else up there on Prospect Street. Even worse, I don't want it to ricochet off a rock and kill one of us."

"Thataboy, Rifleman. Usin' your noggin, yes you are."

"I'm glad you're on board for the show, Mr. Knight. But there's a bad side to the story. The mortal wound will make a messy front to whatever it is I take down."

We halted 40 feet from the garden. The tops of the taller plants in the middle swayed back and forth. Brother loaded, raised the rifle, aimed it at the garden, and waited for the animal to show itself. The rest of us stood beside and a little behind him.

"Frank! Frank! Where did you go! You were supposed to stay in the house!" Mother was out on the driveway, desperately calling for her five-year-old charge.

"Tony, wait, don't shoot!" hollered Mr. Knight. "Let's make sure where Frank is!"

"There it is, Tony! Shoot it before it sees us and runs off!" implored Mrs. Laithran.

BANG.

"You were right. Made no sense to wait. Got the thing. It's dead. Let's go see what is."

A few feet inside the garden, a body lay motionless. The four of us stopped and stared down at the large, plump-bellied woodchuck. It was obvious the invasive grazer had died instantly. Blood and a gush of slimy, half-chewed vegetables oozed from its blown-open lower abdomen. None of us said a word. Cute as a button, the little guy's slightly-open mouth displayed buckteeth. His not-closed eyes indicated he never knew what hit him.

"Was that a gunshot I just heard?"

We turned to see Mrs. Robbins standing on the Laithrans' sidewalk, 60 feet from us.

"Yes, Alberta. Tony killed an animal that has been eating Bernard's vegetables."

"It was only a woodchuck," informed Tony.

Mrs. Robbins' face dropped. She rushed to the garden. "You killed my woodchuck. He lived in a hole in my backyard. Dot, why didn't you use a broom to scare him away? Why did you have to get Tony?" She bent down and picked up the little corpse. Blood and guts covered her lower arms and hands. "Chuckie, how could he kill you? You weren't hurting anyone."

"Alberta, I'm so sorry. We didn't know."

The carrier, sobbing, walked off, hugging the deceased pet in her arms. "I'll bury you in your hole, Chuckie. My yard will always be your resting place. . . . I'll never forget you, Henry. You're my son. You'll come back someday. I just know you will."

Tony and I immediately left for home. Once inside, I asked mother about Frank.

"He was in the bathroom. Guess I kind of overreacted, hollering like I did out there."

When I recounted the incident to her, she got upset. At supper, dad blew steam.

"What was Alberta thinking? You can't keep a wild animal as pet, and no animal of any kind is allowed to go around eating people's food. Hey, you in the den, why didn't you use a broom? Better yet, why didn't you tell Dot to use one? You've taken the gun stuff too far. Who do you think you are, shooting up the neighborhood? Enough with the guns. Do you hear me?"

"Yes, Dad."

"Did you learn anything today?"

"Yes, that I'm never shooting anything else in my life."

"Your mother and I are pleased to hear that. Target shooting is fine, but no more killings unless a black bear or a fox or a bobcat wanders in. A rabid dog is okay to shoot, too."

"Okay, I'll shoot those ones because they might try to kill Lizzie. I'll keep the Remington, but the other two I'm selling off. Sorry to upset you and Mom."

"Apology accepted. From here on, let's be done with the matter."

Friday, Tony refused to leave the house. He remained mentally withdrawn, watched TV the whole day. Lizzie stayed beside him. He kept patting her head, slipping her little snacks.

The afternoon had me shooting hoops. Frank remained nearby, yakking and yakking, running through the sprinkler. Mother was out on errands. The last few days had found her eager to check out the city's new grocery store. Cottles, a small Lewiston-based chain, was in its first day of grand opening. Certainly in the short-term, prices would be better than Harriman & Black. The matron's patronage, however, could never change on a permanent basis. After its initial period of low prices, Cottles would eventually go the way of A&P, which closed down recently.

"Though I may check new places as they come along," mother had reiterated to dad during lunch, "I will always be loyal to Harriman & Black. I've met both misters. They live right here in Gardiner. Shopping at their place helps to keep our money close to home and not go to Lewiston. I know I've said all this stuff before, but I like thinking out loud to you, dear."

"That's why I come home at noon—to see and talk. But on this matter you know best."

Mrs. Laithran came from her house; she held a piece of cake in each hand. "Here, Charlie. Eat while I tell you what happened last evening. Frank, this other piece is for you. Please go sit over there to eat it. I want to speak alone with Charlie.

"What I'm about say can be repeated to your brother and parents later. Last evening, I saw Alberta in her yard. I went over and apologized again. I told her that if Tony and I had known the animal was special to her, we would not have harmed it.

"She was friendly, and she opened up, admitting that the woodchuck had been a way for her to pretend Henry was still around. Said she misses him awful, that he was such a good boy, kind-hearted, easy to bring up. She's proud of him being in the Navy, but she's concerned about him seeing action. Many in the Navy didn't make it back from World War Two.

"I've never seen Alberta so warm and humanlike. She shared her concerns about Kenny. He has an explosive temper and sometimes makes bad decisions. She said that from the first day they got him, they believed a strong hand was needed. He gets too emotional about almost everything. When he was young, he got a spanking now and then. She admitted that they've been too verbally hard on Kenny at times. They never did that stuff with Henry, or not much of it. Now, they're at a loss. It seemed like she was reaching out for my advice. I've had no experience with a difficult child. Phil and Dick were pretty easy."

"My parents haven't, either."

"My parents haven't, either." Frank had been listening.

"You know how you've needed a good spanking now and then. How about you get one right now for listening in on us when you weren't supposed to?"

"Shut your face, Chuckie."

"Hey! Use 'be—'"

"Please, you two, no more. Charlie, you'll be along to Creamy Frost this Sunday?"

"I'm pretty sure yes."

"Can I come, too?"

"No!"

Mother was jubilant about the new supermarket, vowing to be a loyal shopper there as long as cans of cream corn and wax beans remained two cents cheaper than "the other place." While helping her with the groceries, I recounted what Mrs. Laithran's had said. She was relieved and requested that I not tell Tony for a few days. She didn't want him feeling better too soon.

"Mom, there's something else I need to talk to you about."

"I'll put away the fridge and freezer stuff while you tell me."

"It's what I know about Lieutenant Cates—his death. We should sit down someplace where we can be alone. The story I have is a long one."

"How could you possibly know about that? The police don't even know?"

"The police know everything and so do a few other people."

"How do you know?"

"Because of my newspaper and your friendships with the Donahues and Mrs. Smithson."

"Oh, my."

"Mom, like I said, it's a long story. You have to let me tell you the whole thing right from the beginning, and you have to let me finish. Otherwise, you won't understand how certain things are connected and how the arrangement came to be made."

"What arrangement?"

"Please, Mom. Let's go someplace far away from the den and Tony."

"Fine. Let's go sit out on the porch. We have half an hour before I leave to pick up your father and brother. I certainly hope that'll be enough time. And I promise not to interrupt. *I tell ya*, a person's got to be careful about what's said around a reporter, even one that's in the family." As we sat down, she smiled and placed a reassuring hand on my shoulder.

At the end, mother broke down crying. I put my arms around her and assured her that I would remain safe as long as I kept quiet.

"Why are you still crying, Mom?"

"Because I'm feeling sorry for myself. You boys certainly have been a challenge for your father and me—I've told you that before. And I've told you this, too, that I wish I had a girl. Guess I'm stuck with four men and a female dog. I love you all, but I've often thought I needed a daughter to talk to, someone who can relate better to me when I get emotional, like now." She smiled. "Oh well, guess Lizzie will have to do. She never talks back and always wags her tail.

"Listen, Charles. Take well to what I'm about to say. What has happened is not your fault. A neighborhood newspaper was a pretty good idea. Who could have known where it would lead. My tears are also for the Cates family. I don't know them, but I did know the lieutenant. He was a genuinely decent man, and it's not right for his family to be left in permanent limbo.

"Your father need not know about this. His efforts at the factory and around this old place keep him stretched enough. The Donahue sisters need you right now and into the foreseeable future. There's no one else to take care of their yard and do their other heavy lifting. Too, they'll need you to shovel their snow for the next few winters. The ladies are old now. You're their new Jim. You're the one they now rely on to protect them from the elements. Will you continue to protect them? That's what I want of you."

"Yes, Mom."

"Do you know the difference between Daniel and you? Let me rephrase that. Do you know *one* of the differences between him and you? While he lays flat on the couch reading a book, you're outside living one." We laughed. "I won't sleep well with what you've told me. All my life I won't sleep well unless you promise me that one day you'll run with the story. I don't know how you'll accomplish that, but I want you to promise me that you will at least try. I don't care if it's fifty years from now and I'm dead, will you promise me you'll try?"

"Yes, I promise. I know something that'll help us feel better. Instead of cooking the mackerel you bought at Cottles, why don't we wait for Sunday noon? Tonight let's order from Woody's Pizza. We haven't gotten from there in two years. It'll even cheer up Dan and Tony. And since we're watching our pennies, we don't have to double-up on the pepperonis like we usually do from Gerard's. We can get one large bottle of soda instead of everybody getting their own little bottle. I'll buy it and a big bag of King Cole BBQ chips and chocolate bars for everyone. I'll even offer Dad a buck for gas. It's okay to eat meat on Fridays, you know."

Mother laughed. "That's not a bad idea. Like you said, it'll help bring cheer." She wiped her eyes. "Until the pope says differently, we'll stick with those heathens Huntley and Brinkley."

Chapter XXXVII

The Prophecy

The summer had been a hot one, and for the youngest Monroe it had been one of discovery, unrest, and disorder. Yet by the start of the final weekend prior to the commencement of the 1966/67 school year, almost all loose ends had been roughly spliced and joined together. *Almost*, for it would take another 50 years for the reporter to complete the important task that had been entrusted to him. . . .

On the way to church, the driver commented, "All in all, the summer went pretty smoothly. Nothing much happened. That's the way I like it. I'm not complaining."

Listeners laughed.

"What's so funny? Did I miss something? Answer me, someone." The laughing continued. "Okay, there was the bad thunderstorm that knocked down our Luden tree. Other than that, what else? Oh, Charles, while I think of it, I meant to ask you the morning after the storm why you shouted 'You killed them!'"

Tony: "You heard him?"

"How could I not? It was loud enough and I was awake. Like I said, I meant to ask but forgot. I figured you had had a bad dream because I heard the two of you muttering right afterward. Charles, who was *you* and who was *them?*"

"'You' was Tony. 'Them' doesn't matter. It was only a dream. If you knew who 'them' was, you might get upset. Anyway, he shot them dead out on our front lawn."

Daniel could not resist. "You've certainly got my curiosity up. Come on, tell us, who did Tony murder? Was it Mom and Dad?"

"He didn't murder anyone. He shot them dead for a good reason, which wasn't really a reason except that our father ordered him to do it."

Daniel's patience gave out. "That proves it once and for all! You're adopted!"

"I am not!"

"Yes, you are!"

"Mom and Dad wanted a girl! If I was adopted there'd be a girl sitting here and not me!"

"You were the only thing available on short notice! Get it! That way, when we arrived here on the train no one would know!"

"Enough of that!" yelled mother at Daniel.

"Tony and I may have been young but not *that* young!" he yelled back.

"Well, I certainly don't remember," stated Tony, in a matter-of-fact tone, "which means I must have been too young."

Daniel calmed his tone. "Look at the color of his hair. It's blond. No one else in the family has it."

"Not true. My brother—your Uncle George—was born with blond hair. He kept it until his teenage years. That's when it went brown, just like Charles' is beginning to."

"Whatever you say, Mother."

"Our father?" wondered father aloud. "Father McIver ordered Tony to kill us?"

"It wasn't you and Mom who Tony shot dead."

"Thank goodness. So, who did Father McIver want done in?"

"I didn't mean Father McIver. I meant the other father—*you*."

"Me? Who did I order your brother to kill?"

"The Mortons. But you didn't know *them* was the Mortons. You ordered Tony to kill two other people, but he killed them instead. You shouted for him to shoot them in the back, before they made it around the corner and into the house, where Mom was all scared-like in bed, covers pulled up to her eyes."

"Of course I was scared. What woman wouldn't be at a time like that?"

"And then there was that woman and her husband upstairs. They shouted down at Tony to gas 'em before they made it up there and stole them away. Hearing you and that couple shout to kill the Mortons was just too much. Tony lifted the gun and did as ordered."

"*Woman? Husband? Upstairs?* Do you mean the Knights?"

"No, Dad. Upstairs in our house."

"Tony was supposed to shoot someone else but he killed the Mortons instead?"

"And he didn't use the rifle. He used the Ruger and put two bullets into each one's back. They never had a chance."

"It was only a dream," reminded the nightmare's shooter. "The Mortons are alive and well, but they must have heard Chuckles shouting. That's my new name for him. I won't be using the other one anymore. The Mortons gave notice the next day—remember? Dad, if you hadn't ordered me to kill them, I don't believe that I would have on the Knights' orders alone, which means the Mortons would still be alive and in our apartment."

"Me? It's my fault?"

"See, Dad. I knew you would get upset if I said who 'them' was. And it wasn't the Knights shouting down at Tony."

Mother shook her head. "*Father*, if you had only put up those soundproof tiles on the common wall as you promised you would, *but didn't*, the Mortons would, as Tony just said, still be living in our apartment and not handing over fifty dollars a month to someone else. Look, we've made church."

"This gets my goat. The reason I didn't do the tiles was because you insisted on wallpapering the kitchen the one rainy weekend we had. On the nice days it was important for me to get the outside work done. Then there was the plugged drain. Need I say more?"

"Dear, I somewhat understand, so please put your goat back in the barn. We don't want to be later than we already are. You know how I detest making an entrance. Now that the best rows are taken, only ones toward the front are left, which means we *will* make an entrance. Everyone try to smile and be happy. Look! The Henleys are just now getting out of their car! Wow, she's huge. Waddling, too. Biscuit's almost done. Let's go fast so we can beat them in."

Father McIver's sermon could have been titled "Beyond Faith."

". . . And for those who are believers, faith comes from a desire to believe. Persons must *want* to believe what the Bible says. But there are those who don't want to. They say, 'Oh how I truly would like to believe in the Bible and God and afterlife, but where's the proof? If there was even the tiniest bit of evidence, I certainly would believe.' Folks, these ones are nothing more than liars. They're full of hogwash, yes they are. Even if they had a mountain of their type of so-called scientific evidence sitting in front of their eyes, they still wouldn't believe. They would find some little trifling thing to get all twisted up about. And do you know why? Because, in truth, they have no desire to believe. Their real desire is to *not* believe.

"In today's Gospel reading, Jesus says *Seek and you shall find, Knock and the door will be opened*. If a person is not sincerely seeking, then guess what? He or she will never find anything of real value for the soul. These persons can be shown the truth and have it explained to them in a thousand different ways, but because they aren't sincere, the effort is a waste of time. He or she is going to stick to what they know, and that's a pile of something hog.

"Look here, good folk, you know in your minds and hearts what I say on this subject is the truth. We sometimes have them in our own families and friendships. It doesn't mean we should reject caring about them. We must always try to be good examples, so that one day they may come to say 'I want to be like you, a believer and no longer a heathen, and that way I too can have the hope of eternal life.' I caution you, though, that just because we love and care about the poor souls around us, we must never embrace the evil that they do, and they often do it openly, with no regard for our eyes and no respect for our spirits. The Lord expects us to offer them kind words of advice and even correction, but it should always be done with respect, for it is only in that manner that the Lord will bless the effort and grant these poor souls the grace to reflect, repent, and release themselves of their smelly hogs. This is shown in the Bible, with that crazy fellow in the graveyard. Jesus ordered the evil spirits out of him, and next thing you know, a bunch of stinkin' hogs are running into a lake to drown.

"The man, soul now cleaned out and all tidied up, asked if he could go with Jesus. Jesus said no and for the formerly crazy fellow to instead go home and tell his family and friends what the Son of Man had done for him. Only when each of us, and that includes your priest as well, is so totally selfish about our own individual salvation can we properly reach out in a kind-hearted manner to help others become the same. Only in our *salvation selfishness*, if you will, can any of us have the confidence of knowing eternal life awaits us and in the meantime be humble yet firm enough—never, *never* presuming on God's mercy to others but instead informing them of their wrongdoings and about God's ever-call to repentance.

"And, yes, there are persons who cheerfully heed good advice when it is offered. But, unfortunately, these days they seem to be few and far between. Why is that? Pride is the answer. And if it's not pride, it's comfort. 'I'm so *comfortable* where I am. Don't bother telling me real truth because it makes me too *un-com-for-table*. Why should I move to higher ground? I'm just so *com-for-table* being in common ground with mud. Being dense-headed and dumb as hog is just so *com-for-table* for me. So leave me alone! This is what I prefer!' Amen to that!"

Mike and I felt good about our chances to finally snare victory. Even though the new start-line handicapped ol' Biscuit, the bikers knew it would be touch-and-go against the motorized unit's hard-driving jockey. Right off, we scored a major gain by way of a shortcut past Walker Lumber and through the parking lot of the new strip mall where LaVerdiere's Drug had recently relocated and where the new supermarket Cottles was the anchor retailer.

"My mom shops at this new place and not Harriman & Black anymore!"

"Tell someone who gives a shit! Pedal faster!"

I chuckled, thinking on how Mr. Barry's nieces and nephew were surely pressing him for another victory. *"Can't we go faster, Uncle? Please don't let them beat us."*

"No worry, children. If we don't get them before the bridge, we certainly will on it."

"But Uncle, they took that big shortcut. If they make it off the bridge and past Shep's Garage, they're gonna beat us. Can't you make this old thing go faster?"

The Biscayne made the bridge just as the bikers off the other end of it.

"Aww, shucks, Uncle! They're making Shep's! Means they're gonna win!"

In the dire situation as it had developed, Mike and I would learn later, Uncle Allan saw no other option but to bear down. "This Biscayne ain't done yet. Let's finally see what it can do." The jockey leaned forward, put his chin on the steering wheel, gritted his teeth, and hit the gas. "HEE-HAA! Go, Biscuit, go! Get 'em, boy! You can do it!"

Biscuit couldn't do it; the bikers gained their first victory.

During dinner, I told the story of the woodchuck, including the post-mortem reaction from Alberta Robbins. Mike laughed.

Mrs. Barry commented, "By the Lord's will, something good will come from the incident, if it hasn't already. Other than the Lord, no one knows exactly what that might be. Your brother might have killed a human someday—by accident, I mean. Might even have been you, Charlie. Gun accidents sometimes happen in families. Now you say he has put the guns away. Let's hope his decision remains a permanent one."

Surprisingly, Mr. Barry offered nothing. For 15 minutes, the man stayed silent as various discussions bandied the table. His blank stare off to the side indicated pensiveness. He was chewing on something and not with his mouth.

At 4:00, the bikers said "Thanks" and "Goodbye" and exited the house. Mr. Barry followed us out.

"Mike, Charlie, hold on a minute. I have to tell you something. The chain is broken."

Mike glanced down at the bikes. "Both chains look okay to me."

"I don't mean that. I mean something else. I keep seeing it in my mind. The spirit of the native has been showing me a broken arrow. It represents the chain of death, broken. Around the arrow is a dark gray cloud and the background is white. The old forest roadway was a gray tunnel into a past world." And once again that familiar spirit entered the sage woodsman.

> "What you have heard from my friend is true. The ancient hunting path, hallowed with the animal blood of many centuries, has departed earth. The chain of death is no more. Animals will never again seek out something they know not why, to die honorably on a ground so hallowed. Trees, bushes—their children and their children's seedlings—they are now being allowed to romp and grow all along the former roadway. The ground is no longer sacred with blood, but is now a sacred covenant between life and hope, for a future filled of both. But there is

something else. The spirit of the Great One Above is not settled. The sky is a bright light, but there is a place of darkness still inside it. The darkness exists because the scale of justice—the Creator's justice—has not been balanced. And it must be balanced, justice must be satisfied, and only in that way will the darkness descend into the earth. The animals needlessly slaughtered in the generations after the aboriginal dwellers were vanquished, these animals were creatures of His Creation. Restitution must take place. A proper settlement must be made with the spirit of the Great One Above—."

"How's that supposed to happen?" I asked.

Startled by my sudden intrusion, the native spirit vacated his host. After taking a moment to focus his thoughts, Mr. Barry addressed my query. "I'm not a hundred percent sure, but I think is goes something like this. *Love must kill and mourn for the love, and only then will the spirit achieve settlement.*"

"What the heck does that mean?" quipped Mike, a little sarcastically.

"I don't know, and I won't know. Only Charlie will." The man looked me in the eyes. "You are the one, the 'witness' and 'teller,' but only when it's time. It will come and go as a quick flash in your mind. Your eyes will see and your subconscious will understand, but you will not consciously connect on the meaning until a future time. It may be many years later when that happens. Only at the appointed time will your conscious perceive the truth. Anyhoos, I should go back inside to get the others for the ride home. Take care of yourselves."

"Bye and thanks, Mr. Barry."

"Bye, Uncle. Thanks for the meal and losing the race. As for the stuff you just said"—Mike rolled his eyes—"*I don't know.*"

"Hey, Nephew, watch the attitude."

Though Mike and I were best of friends, we were very different individuals. Despite his Baptist teachings and the influences of his nanna and uncle, he was developing into a "meat and potatoes" type, growing more and more closed to "things of the spirit."

As for me, because of my growing list of experiences in life and because of the "people of the spirit" who had had influence on my views of the experiences, I, on the contrary, was becoming more open to the wisdom of the metaphysical. And there was that voice: a gentle man's voice I reconnected with every time I walked past Jim Donahue's death scene.

Supper was out of the question. Besides, it was leftover mackerel. There was, however, enough room for an ice cream cone. The Laithrans wanted me along with them to Creamy Frost, and this night I looked forward to it.

Six o'clock came. Tony and dad followed me out the door; they wanted to toss the tennis ball for a while. We played as a threesome until Mr. and Mrs. Laithran appeared.

"Hello . . . , Harve and Tony."

"Dot, I've told you before. It's *Herve* or *Hervey* and not *Harve* or *Harvey*."

"Is Bernard right? Have I been getting it wrong all these years?"

"Yes, but don't be concerned. I always knew you meant me."

"Well then, see you later . . . , Herby and Tony. We should be back in an hour."

"Chuckles, we can play B-ball when you get back."

"Sure. Bye." I got into the Impala's backseat.

"Did Bern and I hear right, Tony calling you Chuckles?"

"Yup. That's his new name for me, ever since you-know-what happened."

"Totally understandable."

"I can't stand the name Charles. Everybody messes around with it. Father Debruin even calls me Chas. Anyhoos, it's not my first name. Starting junior high, I'm going by my real first name—John. But it's okay for you to keep using Charlie. That one I don't mind."

"We miss reading your paper. Hope you won't be writing about the woodchuck."

"Even though people would like it, I won't."

"What about the big story or stories you've been working on?"

"I have all the information I need."

"Then Dot and I can expect to receive a copy come Friday?"

"School starts this week, Bernard. I doubt he'll have enough time for that."

Nearing the library, Mr. Laithran slowed the car. "Will you look at that. What a shame to have in our city."

The yellow-brown-haired couple sat lopsided against each other, on the lowest step to the rooming house. Eyes half open, legs limply stretched out onto the sidewalk, the two looked completely trampled down.

"That's Captain Cornelius and Two Dollar Eva. They've been into the drink again."

"Not them. I mean Boston Coal's filthy parking lot. You need to report it."

"To be fair, I thought about doing my next inspection on the other side of the city, across the street from Manson & Church Drugstore."

"Chapman Esso? Good choice. That dirty place could sure use a wakeup call."

"Not across the street that way."

"Then that would be the post office. Do you really want to start there?"

"No, not really. I was just kidding."

"Good one. Had me going. Is Dot right about you not having time for the newspaper?"

"I won't be writing another edition. Time's not the reason."

"I'm disappointed. You're bowing out too soon. Dot and I still want to hear those stories. Might as well just tell us right here and now."

"Can't do it. I've given my word to never speak or write anything about the really big story, except in fifty years I can. As for the others, I might as well wait till then, too."

"Tony was upset the other day," noted Mrs. Laithran. "How's he doing now?"

"Better. Says he's selling the guns, except the one he used on the woodchuck. Has a lot of memories and notches on it. Dad says it's okay to keep that one for protecting Lizzie from a roaming bobcat, black bear, or rabid dog, if any ever come around."

"Guess the shooters' chain is broken. Not a good outcome. Lower Kingsbury has always needed someone like him."

"How about Donald Prudhomme?"

"No, he won't due. A Navy man now. Besides, his house doesn't carry the burden of bloodletting. Yours does, with its history of . . . *well, never mind*. Chocolate dips, everyone?"

"Cherry dip for me this time, please."

"Me too, Dot. I want to try blood-red for once, to see if it tastes as good as it looks."

"Will you be stopping by LeClerc's Market today?"

"No. Too much out of the way."

"Means you won't be asking for money every morning?"

"Guess not. Buh-bye, Mom."

As Kenny Whitson had indicated, junior high felt much different than elementary. To start, every student was assigned a specific homeroom as base camp for the year. Because homeroom teachers did not teach a subject during homeroom time, they were more like strict babysitters. Mr. Dunstan was my "homey." First thing after bell, he went into roll call. This time when my name was called, I would not respond, "Here, but I go by Charles, not John." If Mr. Dunstan then followed with *that question*, as my last five years of teachers had done, I would not just reply "Yes."

"John Monroe."

"Here."

"Are you Daniel Monroe's brother?"

"Yes, but don't hold it against me."

He wasn't amused, but a few classmates were. They giggled. He looked at them, then back at me.

"Why do you say something like that?"

"Because his being my brother isn't my fault. It's my parents' fault." I smiled and looked around the class. More students giggled, louder this time.

"Mr. Monroe, that will be enough. I don't put up with mouth. Do you hear me?"

"Yes, Mr. Dunstan."

Ray spoke up. "Monroe's name isn't John. It's Charlie—*Pong Charlie.*"

"Oh, I see. Now it's your turn to be a smart aleck. Mr. LeClerc, I expect you to never speak out of turn again." Mr. Dunstan stood up and away from his desk, to pace back and forth in front of the blackboard, but only once. "Back to you, Monroe. Is your classmate correct?"

"Not really. But partly he is, I guess, and partly he's not. It's more like he used to be correct, but not anymore, now that I've made the decision to go by the name John."

"Why is that?"

"Because Charlie used to act like a punk little kid, so I decided to kill him off for good. Anyhoos, I couldn't stand him anymore. Used a Ruger to shoot him dead, then buried him in the woods, near an old path."

The classroom roared.

"What's a Ruger?" asked Broten.

"It's a new type of—"

"Hey you! Broten and everyone else! That's enough! I will not be competing with anyone in this classroom! Do you all understand me—especially you, John-John?"

There came a collective, "Yes, Mr. Dunstan."

"Good then." He again paused to calm himself, did more pacing. "I'll continue to confirm all my students are here." When he finished: "Let's start over, everyone. Welcome to junior high. Things here are different than elementary. I won't be asking each of you to stand up and talk about all the fun things you didn't do during the summer, and there'll be no more racing around the classroom with an eraser on your head—."

"Aw, shucks, that was fun. We really liked doing it."

"Broten, what did I just get done saying? You can't possibly be that thick-skulled."

LeClerc: "Oh, yes he can."

The room roared, Mr. Dunstan too, but he was obviously faking it. Everyone quickly quieted, stared at him, to see what he would do next. His false laugh went down to a false smile, then to a real ugly grimace, red with rage. He slammed an open hand down on his desk. "The two things that we do still do in junior high are send students to the office and expel them. Would your parents like that? No, they wouldn't, but we *will* do it. Anymore speaking out of turn will result in one-hour detentions after school. Does everyone get it?"

"Yes, Mr. Dunstan."

"Okay then." Again, the homey stopped, this time for longer, took in and let out a long deep breath, once again tried to take on a calm yet firm voice. He tried to smile; it looked real, *sort of.* "Today, all of you here are now young men and women. Childish competing for my attention will not be tolerated, and there'll be no speaking out of turn. This classroom will be quiet, and it will be respectful of authority and each other. Yes, absolutely, the first part of grade seven will be a period of transitioning for all of you. Can someone tell me what the word 'transitioning' means?"

No one put up a hand, so I decided to.

"Well, John-John, perhaps your brother Daniel has been a good influence on you. Let's look at this as an opportunity for the two of us—and truly all of us here—to get off on better footing. Now, go ahead and tell me and everyone else what 'transitioning' means."

Part IV
Five Decades Later: 2016

Chapter XXXVIII

Prophecy Fulfilled and Promise Kept

On that sunny summer morning of 1966, after the mysterious man John and I parted company for the last time, I moved the big gray rock to the edge of the woods. The next time Tony mowed the lawn he noticed it and later that day asked me if I knew how it had gotten there. I said the rock had been put there by me, to remind me of how lucky we were to have such a good dog. He looked at me funny and said nothing else.

The parents moved to Melbourne, Florida, in 1988. Though they loved living there for the next 12 years, they always said their best years were behind them—those 35 in Gardiner.

Eau Galley Causeway arches high above the Indian River, connecting Melbourne to the small ocean-side town of Indialantic. After marrying in the summer of 1990, my wife and I honeymooned at mom and dad's doublewide trailer. Daily the two of us drove across the causeway so that we could spend our afternoons on the white sands of the Atlantic coastline. The water tended to be slightly cool, the waves gently moderate, the air hot and breezy. Next to the beach were an old-fashioned diner, a Wendy's, and a lounge that boasted a second-floor veranda overlooking the beach and ocean. What a honeymoon it was.

Nine months later, daughter was born. Six months went by and the three of us boarded a plane back to Florida. Every afternoon, mom and dad reveled in looking after their only grandchild while son and daughter-in-law beached themselves. Nine months later, son appeared.

The 1990s had Kerry Ann and me ever looking forward to our Florida visits. We made every effort to go there twice a year when we could financially manage the flights. A few years passed by and we began to take the kids along with us to the beach.

The road that ran along the Indian River was called Route A1A. As the kids continued to grow, naturally their awareness of the world around them bloomed. Kerry Ann and I started to take them on car drives up and down the A1A. North to Cocoa and the green areas close by to the Kennedy Space Center and south to Sebastian Inlet State Park became our favorite places to go. When the kids reached eight and six, we went for our first visit to Disney World.

On a late 1990s summer night, Kerry Ann and I stood near the causeway's east entrance to watch a military rocket—carrying a military satellite meant for earth orbit—lift off from the space center. Even though we were 20 miles away, the sight was spectacular. We could readily see and hear the orange-red flame blasting out from the booster rocket. The air vibrated. People around us said that it was nothing compared to the takeoff of the Space Shuttle.

Due to deteriorating health, Herve and Jeanne had to be relocated in 2001 to a place where one of their boys could monitor them during their marked declines. They ended up at the Salvation Army apartment building in New York City. Daniel lived in The City at the time, and he frequently checked in on them.

The family viewed the years in Florida as an incredible life-gift, just as the years in Gardiner had been. The man's mind and heart are in continuous visitations to the two places; at almost every moment of every day does a part of my spirit spend time in Maine and Florida.

In 1976, Tony took down his Remington .22-caliber rifle for the last time. During the weeks leading up to the day, he had with no small emotion come to the conclusion that this was the only way out; he kept the decision to himself. A long-rifle regular bullet was selected for the job. Tony wanted the wound to be clean, mortal. The Ruger and .308-caliber rifle were long gone.

The summer afternoon was sunny and warm. Tony went outside and walked around to the north side of the house, past where the black incinerator had once sat. Lizzie hobbled beside him. In front of the old glory path she paused. The tired dog lifted her snout and sniffed the air, as if to be taking in the scents of former lives buried along that storied way. Perhaps she knew that it was her turn to join "memory lane." Together she and Tony slowly ambled the final paces into the front yard, and there, near the edge of the woods, they stopped. The air showed little breeze. Tony bent down to hug and kiss his dog's fine warm head for the last time. He helped her to lie down on the grass, in a manner upright and sideways to him. She yelped from internal pains, but she complied. Her age was 14, and for a year she had been suffering with incurable internal maladies. He asked her to remain still. To the very end she was obedient.

Tears streaming from his eyes, Tony turned, paced ten steps back, and stopped. Slowly he turned back to face her, to look at her fine personage one more time. Then he loaded, aimed, and fired. There had been no hint of hesitation in his determination to get the job done—cleanly. Years of practice had paid off. Lizzie instantly dropped her fine warm head and lay motionless. He threw down the rifle and rushed to her side, picked her up in his arms. Her blood coated his skin. He wailed while carefully placing Lizzie's dead body in the hole he had prepared that morning. The location was at the edge of the woods, where the wild tulips grew.

Tony shoveled the dirt back into the hole and placed the big gray rock on top. For a while, he hammered and chiseled at it, and then he stood up to review his effort. The job had been crude, yet the word LIZZIE could definitely be discerned.

Uncle Allan's prophecy had come true. The spirit achieved settlement in the summer of 1976. The light no longer contained darkness. *Love must kill and mourn for the love, and only then will the spirit achieve settlement.* Finally, in that generational chain of shooters, there came a link that would at some point in life learn the truth about what the spirits' hearts had felt each time one of God's creatures had been killed for fun. And with that fulfillment of retributive justice, the chain of death was allowed to stay broken forever—and that former path, one that had always led to the death of love, from thence forward became a secret path to healing. In the spirit, the big gray rock officially sealed and marked the ancient throughway MEMORY LANE.

In 1969, I witnessed the sudden passing of a revered man: Coach Bill Hoak, Head of the Gardiner High School Athletic Department.

Because of missing a few gym classes, I was called to the coach's office to get assigned KP duty as make-up. After he gave me tasks to do, I turned to leave. *Thud.* I swung around to see him lying on the concrete floor, out. I rushed for Assistant Coach Story, and together we ran back to Hoak's office. Story told me to run for Nurse Day and to tell the office secretary to phone for an ambulance to come right away to the high school gymnasium. Nurse Day and I ran back. Coach Story was applying CPR to his subject, now purple. Once Principal Summerville arrived onto the scene, no one else was let into the area. He asked why I was there. Story explained and requested that I be allowed to stay. The ambulance attendants worked and worked on the downed man, to no avail. Because it was illegal to put a corpse into an ambulance, a hearse was called in. I witnessed it all, from start to finish. Seeing that man placed into a hearse was an awful thing. The Angel of Death had come like a thief in the night.

Following graduation from high school in 1972, I spent most of my time away from Gardiner. Something odd happened on a late evening in the summer of 1975. That summer had me away in university geology field camp, studying the landscapes and bedrocks of New England's back areas. Almost nightly, the students built campfires and exchanged stories. During quiet times of reflection we sometimes gazed up into the sky. None of us ever noticed anything much, just the occasional shooting star. Mid-camp break came and I went home for a few days. Nightly, I took Lizzie out onto the front lawn so that she could do her business. One night, I moved a lawn chair to the darkest spot of the yard, where the streetlight was blocked and a view of the sky above unencumbered. I flattened the chair, lay down on it, and looked straight up. A minute went by and I heard a distinct, low-pitched, electronic-sounding *whinny*. My eyes were instantly drawn to the source. Flying over Gardiner were seven (perhaps five) shinny, plate-shaped objects. They did not look small and sparkly like stars do. They had definite outline and basically resembled small, shiny moons. Flying eastward in V-shaped formation, they took only a few seconds to span the sky. The sound they emitted was instantaneous, as if it were traveling at the speed of light and not sound.

In 1978, I left the city permanently. I went back for a visit only once, in 1985. Lizzie had been gone for nine years. At her stone, memories of her love filled me, but no tears came. I then went to another gravesite. Luden's stump was hardly much, dark brown, and soft. I took the time to ponder what the youngster did not have the maturity and space to write 19 years earlier.

> Some hundred years ago an unknown admirer of foreign species planted an exotic sapling on the front lawn of 25 Kingsbury Street. In truth, the young tree represented the person—the planter—and his or her family's hope for a better, more prosperous future, post-Civil War. The new tree and born-again nation experienced a difficult childhood, a time filled with harsh winters and storm-filled summers. But it was during that period of adolescence that they became strong enough to withstand the future wars and hurricanes. The foreign-born, assimilated Luden survived two World Wars and powerhouse Hurricanes Hazel (1937) and Edna (1954). The tree succumbed to natural causes during America's current conflict in Vietnam. There are certain mourning souls—some alive, some buried long ago and now existing as mere woodland banshees—who might prefer to say the valiant tree was KIA during a fierce skirmish with a nameless thunderstorm.
>
> Luden enjoyed a happy life keeping cover for and giving shade to a century of families that sojourned on its coveted ground. The tree is

survived by two elderly siblings living somewhere unknown in New England. Trees see and hear everything while they stand tall. Like humans and many nations of the past, trees do not stand tall forever. Let us hope our nation will stand tall forever.

After the start of the book's write, in 2011, time seemed to move too fast. Mother died in April 2013. *American River Road* was not as close to the finish line as I would have liked. Work, raising children, and faith-life had been holding most of my focus.

It is now early 2014, and the final edition is close to being done. The remainder requires extreme care, the right spirit. For that, a return to Melbourne was felt necessary. So, here soul-person-me stands, on the giant upward-arching causeway. I thought there would be a sea of joy waiting to flow into me upon my arrival, but instead there is sadness, a terrible longing. Maine comes to mind. I remember those whip-poor-wills, how they sounded hope through silent nights to exploring spirits yearning to face the waiting world. The time was decades ago, and we were kids and friends walking half-brave in a forest located somewhere out there in the universe. Sometimes it is hard to find the right words to set free that which is locked inside the heart.

The 1960s saw the dawn of manned space flights, and America quickly recognized its destiny to seek out things beyond earth. Despite the nation's external wars and internal conflicts, the future and the sky possessed our imaginations. People had so much hope, so much looking forward. We were living "American Pie" years before the song with that title would come out.

Today my soul longs for the innocence of that childhood view. In those days of long ago, friends and I preferred to be outside, throwing a ball, searching for new finds, walking through fields and forests, looking up. We never kept in touch. Where are they now? Do they feel as alone as I do? My chest aches like an old hollow log, its emptiness filled with pangs of joyful memories of things once whole: a family, a neighborhood, a nation. A lost time it is, a lost spirit am I, and inside me lives a heart that weeps for a dying country. The mortal situation is so clear.

America's debts and deficits indicate a dead future. Speaking frankly, the country is financially bankrupt. Soon, the U.S. federal debt will close in on $25 trillion; state debts together will make their own trillions. Positive political speeches will not change anything, for they are nothing more than clever deceptions willfully carried out to gain votes. There is a coming cataclysm. No nation in the world will be exempt. In a sense, we are already in the downfall.

Three years ago, in 2011, partly because of lack of money and the other part because of lack of vision, NASA retired the incredible, marvelous Space Shuttle Program; a big part of our national splendor went with it. The President also canceled the dynamic replacement program known as "Constellation." Thousands of people lost their jobs and hundreds of small enterprises along Space Coast either shut down or lost business such that they had to lay off personnel. There were those who claimed the Shuttle was too old, too expensive, obsolete. To say such was nothing more than smoke and mirrors and presidential spin, for there was not a newer manned program to step in and replace the Shuttle. The sales line was that private companies would eventually take over the responsibility and in the meantime the government could contract out to the Russian Space Agency for manned space missions when required. This a policy that came from a government that had promised to bring jobs back to America? Perhaps someday China will have pity on us and offer even cheaper services than private companies and Russia can.

Does anything else need to be said about "the situation" we are in? Yes.

Together let us travel an American river road of sharp curves, hazardous potholes, and sudden downhill drops. We will dive into the polluted water and crawl in the muck. Later will come an uphill climb to a wonderful place of panoramic view. I ask the reader to not become overly shaken as the driver steers you through a dark valley of personal reflection, that you courageously survive it, because, well, you'll find out when you get to the top of the other side.

All the people in *American River Road* were real, even Two Dollar Eva, her blue-capped boyfriend, the mysterious man John, and Billy Elkingwood. In the summer of 1974, I landed a laborer job at Mckee Construction Company. Billy still worked there. He proved to be every bit the man of concrete the mystery man John had described eight years earlier.

Many persons are no more, including Frank Prudhomme, who, for reasons unknown to the writer, died in young adulthood. Almost all last names were changed, sometimes to ones that sounded similar. In most cases, real first names were kept. Excepting for a couple, actual business names were used. Years back, I contacted Wilson Donnelly. Right there on the phone, he found the good lieutenant on an Internet site that records officers downed on duty.

> End of Watch: Saturday, January 1, 1966. Lieutenant Chase was assaulted while making an arrest in a domestic situation at a local club. He was caught from behind, bear-hugged and kneed in the abdomen, which resulted in a massive pulmonary hemorrhage, from which he

died. Despite being assaulted by several suspects, only one person was charged in connection with the incident. The suspect was convicted of simple assault. Lieutenant Chase had served with the agency for 10 years. He was survived by his wife and 3 children. (The Officer Down Memorial Page, Inc.)

An agreement born of whispers, nods, and silent fears had stuck. An on-duty officer slain at the hands of several, and the same police department charged a single person with common assault. A successful agreement like this might be tagged A DISPLACED CODE OF HONOR.

The book presented the situations the night of and months following Lieutenant Chase's slaying not precisely as they had happened. In actuality, Chase had taken assignment as "resident officer" for New Year's Eve at the Sportsmen's Club. The fracas was already winding down when the two backup officers arrived. A man and woman from Manchester were arrested. During the assault, several persons tried to intervene in Chase's defense. After it was over, Chase decided to remain at the club; those involved in assaulting him were no longer there. An hour passed, when, just after midnight, he dropped to the floor. The lieutenant died a couple hours later at the hospital. The Manchester couple was released from jail later that morning.

The author felt the best way to remember the good lieutenant was to write of his ultimate sacrifice. He was a dedicated cop who had real feelings, and he had family and friends who loved and cared about him. What happened to justice? There can be no doubt that a secret agreement of some kind was involved, and the writer is not referring to a plea bargain.

Reading was mother's favorite pastime in life. Prior to her passing, she had been blind for eight years. During the first six, she enjoyed listening to "talking books." At the start of this write, my goal was to finish the first draft ASAP and fly in to read it to her. But then came her sudden, sharp decline and with it the inability to receive this promised final offering. *The pain—set it free! The pain—set it free!* memories of whip-poor-wills echo inside my soul.

At the end of the book, will the reader wonder if the stories contained in it were true? If so, the writer answers the question with an emphatic "Yes!— and I say it in a better manner than corporations often do when claiming a product is American made. To be able to do so requires that at least 51% of the cost value of the parts making up a product be made in America. I consider Parts I, II, and III to be around 80%.

Let me explain. 1) Naturally, I could not remember every conversation verbatim, so I filled in based on how I knew people's personalities. Particular conversations either went as written or may have taken place in a like manner. 2) Though the time-setting for Parts I to III was the summer of 1966, some situations were gleaned from the complete year and those either side (1965 and 1967). This explains incongruities as to some recounted news items. 3) A small amount of the writing was fictionalization. This was done in order to maintain rapid flow and better illustrate the strengths and peculiarities of people's characters. A couple sub-storylines were in actuality allegorical "quickies" related to truths realized over longer spans of time. 4) In a few areas, "license" was used to connect things in an efficient way. Did the writer sometimes take fun in doing it, by embellishing a bit? Sure. 5) Another intention was to concentrate on the positive traits of people's personalities. As for the other stuff, humor and empathy were employed because that's just the best way to retrospectively see them.

Part IV utilizes none of the items listed above. Everything contained in Part IV "is" as written. Some of the mill-closure dates may be a little off.

Chapter XXXIX

Winding a Valley Road

Health-tex was a privately owned company until 1967, at which time the owner and founder Louis Russek took it public. This was done in order to raise enough capital to fund the expansion of his manufacturing facilities. Since the company's inception, in 1921, production had never been able to keep pace with the ever-increasing demand for quality children's clothes.

Cheseborough-Pond's Corporation purchased the majority of Health-tex stock shares in 1973 and in doing so gained ownership. Between 1969 and 1978, I worked five summers at the Gardiner plant, as a presser, re-layer, and cloth spreader. There was a cutter named Vern. He had been a B-29 gunner during WWII. I asked him how that had gone. He said that prior to engaging the enemy in the air, he was always "scared shitless," but once the action got going he gave fear no respect. He believed Maine would never see him again, that on any given day his time would be up. Vern loved his job at Health-tex.

Another cutter, Erlyn, spoke four foreign languages and played guitar for a '50s-type beatnik band. He had taught himself the languages in effort to alleviate his tendency to stutter when speaking English. It did not completely work. There was a guy Alex who was training to become a cutter. He was a Russian defector: a cargo ship worker who had jumped overboard and swam like hell to get to a better place. English was difficult for him. When he talked, his protruding Adam's apple jumped straight out. One of the languages Erlyn had learned was Russian, so that he could speak with the old-timer White Russians who lived in the area. When Erlyn spoke Russian to Alex, Alex would speak back to him in English. When Erlyn spoke English to Alex, Alex would speak back to him in Russian. When I asked the defector about it, he responded, "I do it because Erlyn speaks Russian as bad as I speak English." Each person working at the plant had a story; no one's was held up as more special than anyone else's.

In early childhood, dad broke his eardrums in a swimming accident. Because of it, he could not serve in the regular military in WWII. He signed up for special services and was sent to Ohio where he trained to be an armament machinist. He spent four years at Diamond Head in Hawaii. What dad liked best about life in Honolulu was in the evenings, when he donned suit to become maître d' at the Moana Hotel. He said he got to seat general officers and famous entertainers, like Charles Ruggles. When I asked him who Charles Ruggles was, he got impatient. "Everyone knows who he is. He's a famous Hollywood person of some kind."

In the mid-'70s, dad got Mike a job at Health-tex as a spreader. The position was very manual, involving a lot of lifting, stretching forward, and bending down. Mike had a problem lower back, and he constantly complained of the excruciating pain the job caused him. I was surprised that he lasted there a couple years. He then moved over to Bath Iron Works and became a welder, staying there 25 years. After leaving BIW, he spent a few years in South Korea working for a U.S. outfit building aircraft carriers for the South Korean Navy. He is now retired.

Dad retired in 1977. Before leaving, he taught the company's new head machinist, Carl Morton, how to make sewing machine attachments. In 1987, the three Maine Health-tex plants packed up their equipment, closed their doors, and moved south. Nine hundred Mainers lost their jobs. Carl Morton managed to secure a new one doing the same work for L.L.Bean in Freeport.

Except for those at the highest levels of corporate vision, everyone believed the mills would be relocating to the southern U.S., where the wages and utility bills were said to be lower. This was one of the usual storylines of the era: lie to cover up unbounded owner greed and at the same time try to make the move seem a little more palatable for the ones losing their jobs. The plants ended up moving farther south, to Mexico.

Prior to the 1987 site-closures, Health-tex had been a highly profitable company. In 1985, an investor group led by the subsidiary's president, Richard Brandkill, bid for its ownership from parent Cheseborough-Pond's. At that time, Health-tex commanded the major U.S. market share in the children's clothing category. Unfortunately, Cheseborough-Pond's had made bad investments in other business ventures, and the corporation's bottom line instantly suffered. The parent did not want to let go of the one child that was performing well, but when Brandkill's group upped its offer, top management saw the deal too good to pass up.

Brandkill and his group had, however, blown themselves to smithereens. They now owned Health-tex, but by having taken the company off the market and into their private hands, they had mired themselves in too much debt. In their unbounded greed and desire for grandiose image and power, they had over-bought a very successful company.

The new owners were in a tough position. They could neither afford to properly market the quality product nor keep up with the constant flux in styles. Two years after the purchase, the plants in Maine, Rhode Island, and Virginia closed in favor of cheap labor in Mexico. Just like everyone in the world, Mexicans need jobs. But Brandkill and his group were up to doing anything and everything to bail themselves out of a sinking fiscal ship. Money is power and image. Lack of money brings shame and embarrassment. They did not care about the product and the Mexican workers in the same way the original owner Louis Russek cared about his mill workers in those three states. The founder had always striven hard to be a leader in the making of top quality clothes and in the employing of more and more Americans.

Because the new team cared to the nth degree about making their bad deal look good to family, friends, and former Wall Street associates, the backs of innocent, hard-working Americans in Maine, Rhode Island, and Virginia paid the price. Too, the product paid the price. The brand fell into poor quality. The pants and shirts weren't as attractive as the others out there, and the stitching did not hold up. By the early '90s, the brand registered barely any market share. In 1995, Brandkill and his group sold the company at a small fraction of what they had paid for it.

For sure, Brandkill and each member of his team will answer for what they did, just as those involved in the slaying of an officer of the law. Nobody gets away with anything. God sees all and He knows people's true motives and what is in their hearts. In the Bible, Jesus says, *"Everything that is hidden will be found out, and every secret will be known. Whatever you say in the dark will be heard when it is day. Whatever you whisper in a closed room will be shouted from the housetops."* (Luke 12:2-3) *"Listen carefully to what you hear! The way you treat others will be the way you will be treated—and even worse."* (Mark 4:24)

In post-death life-reviews, perpetrators of injustices and crimes against humanity are shown the direct impacts and also the ripple effects their decisions/actions had on their victims, their victims' families, local society, and the geopolitical nations where the actions took place. Those who failed to reflect and repent during life do not survive the review. Persons who did reflect and repent their hurting of people's lives will survive it, for that is the Divine Will. There will likely have to be time served in purgatory, levels and lengths hopefully reduced or even nullified if there had taken place enough sin atonement during the stretch of life post-repentance.

[Spiritual note: Purgatory is the highly diverse, multi-level spiritual realm positioned below heaven and above the "lake of fire." Its purpose and further presentation are supplied throughout the reading ahead.

Some persons may wonder why they are suffering with so many issues after repenting and returning to the Lord. First of all, every person suffers in this world. Some have golden lives and do not suffer much at all. Others suffer from the moment they are born to the day they die. But for most people, it is somewhere in between the two extremes. All this suffering stuff is with the Lord, as hard as it may be for some people to accept. He knows the history from through the eons of every soul-person and the reasons why each was placed into physical life here.

Catholicism teaches that those who are with the Lord and suffer much in this world will get a good spot in the next life. But even these ones may have to first spend time in the Jesus-based (JB) purgatory. Why is that? It has to do with **unrecognized sins against the Will of God**.

The writer mostly uses "soul-person" over "soul." A soul-person is a "sentient energy-entity" that retains a level of *achieved* knowledge/intelligence and a defined perimeter—*spiritual skin* or *metaphysical surface*. Accepting this truth may be a stretch for some, but the truth doesn't disappear just because someone rejects it. The use of "soul" alone does not do a good enough job communicating what each human really is inside; the word is too vague, intangible, lofty.

Jesus said that we should forgive and pray for our enemies, even try to love them. This can be a hard keep. Forgiving those who have wronged us is more about releasing ourselves from a prison that harbors hate as cellmate rather than it is about releasing perps from responsibility for their wrong acts. *"If we hate others, we are living and walking in the dark. We don't know where we are going, because we can't see in the dark." (1 John 2:11)*

In our forgiving of perps we must not think that they will be released from Divine justice. Humans are made in the image of God—and God is a God of love, mercy, *and justice*. When God decides the justice to be meted out on a soul, He takes into account whether the person repented and accepted the justice human authorities delivered. If a person never got caught and therefore never answered to humanity, or the perp did answer but not sufficiently in God's eyes, God takes care of it. The soul-person will wish all debts were paid off while on earth.

When perps repent at the last second before death, do they go directly to heaven, as Protestants and evangelical pastors believe? No, they absolutely do not! God is not a chump. He is not a pushover. A person may have carried out the most reprehensible acts of demonstration, even against little children, *and if the person repents at the last second there comes immediate entry into heaven, while the victims and victims' families still suffer here?* Come on, let's get serious. Yes, the last-second souls are saved from the lake of fire, but they must go through a tough purgatorial process. They are considered "saved," but not from time in the JB purgatory. And just because it's JB doesn't mean "Easy Street." On the contrary, it can be extremely rigorous. Soul-persons must do much work and over an extended period of time. Jesus may assign them short durations inside the low spiritual realm known as "heathen-pagan (hp-) purgatory," which is actually a band of layers inside hell; the band of layers can also be called "hades": place of the dead. "The lake of fire" is the very bottom of hell and falls below purgatorial classification. The "shores of the lake of fire" and "the hall of suffering"—a crude locker room leading into the lake of fire—are the two lowest levels of hp-purgatory. JB soul-persons may have to spend time in either or both of these places. They will also have love-filled upper-level times and receive ample encouragement from Jesus and those who belong to Him. They will likely eventually have to experience a **God Blessed Rebirthment** (explained later) into circumstances that will cause them to face similar tests of character that they had failed to pass in their previous earth-term.

Christians who refute the existence of purgatory often refer to the guy crucified next to Jesus. He repented, and Jesus said the guy would be with Him in paradise before the end of the day. Come on, the man was crucified! Just like Jesus, he had nails driven through his hands and feet. Prior to being nailed to the cross, the thief may not have been subjected to the tortures that Jesus had been. So, unlike Jesus, he did not die at 3:00 in the afternoon. The soldiers took a bat to the man's legs, to break them, so that he could not run away after they took him down. *The soldiers first broke the legs of the other two men who were nailed there. But when they came to Jesus, they saw that he was already dead, and they did not break his legs. (John 19:32-33)* The repentant man must have experienced extreme suffering in the lead-up to his death.

By acknowledging his life of evil and expressing a faith in Jesus, the man was forgiven, but his body was still in the hands of those in Satan's corner: sadistic haters and torturers. The soul-person inside the body became enfolded in the heart of Jesus. All the man's retributive justices were paid in full, right there on the cross and over the rest of the day.

Christian teachers might reason back, "The wounds of Christ cover our sins. No one else needs to die like that." They are half-right, in the respect that when we go to Jesus, always and without exception, no matter how bad our sins, His wounds cover us, and we become enfolded in His Sacred Heart in such a way that nullifies Satan's capacity to take us down.

During the repentant person's life-review, Jesus' wounds also shield him/her from God the Father's wrath at having made such poor choices during life. The Good Father cannot bear to see His Son's wounds split open and bleed again. He will not turn down His beloved Jesus' merciful plea for the soul. With Jesus there, the judgment ends up being far more gentle. But woe to those who think they can go before God without Jesus beside them. Woe!

For the good-growth of our souls and for opportunities to achieve the innate ability to dwell harmoniously with the other souls in the upper realms, retributive justices must be incurred against and endured by the receivers, whether it happens in this life or the next. Take Paul as the prime example that demonstrates this truth. Prior to his conversion, he had been involved with the persecution of Christians. The Bible shows that while Christ's disciple Stephen was being stoned to death, the ones who had accused him paid respect to an observing, well-pleased Paul. *The council members shouted and covered their ears. At once they all attacked Stephen and dragged him out of the city. Then they started throwing stones at him. The men who had brought charges against him put their coats at the feet of a young man named Saul* [Paul]. *(Acts 7:57-58)*

After Paul converted, he suffered beatings and sicknesses and starvation and eventually had his head chopped off. During every moment of Paul's retributive justices, Jesus was invisibly at his side, enfolding Paul's heart into His Own. Paul had no purgatorial assignment and immediately went on to gain a great position in heaven. Naturally, he would be with Stephen and all the others he had been ecstatic about martyring off. At seeing Paul, the other soul-persons might have chuckled out something like, "Hey there, brother Paul, how did it feel?"

"Not so wonderful. Sorry about what I did to all of you."

"We know, otherwise God wouldn't have let you up here. Let's go. The banquet waits."

All except one of Jesus' apostles were cruelly martyred. John was the only one relieved from martyrdom's destiny because he had chosen to stay close to Jesus through the night of His arrest and crucifixion the next afternoon.

Protestants and Catholics of today might argue, "Many have gone through near-death experiences and found themselves either at the door to heaven or inside. What about them? They didn't go to purgatory." My response is "None of those persons received judgment. If they had, they wouldn't be back here. Those near-death situations are not accidental. The soul-persons are shown things of extreme importance, so that they can come back and reveal to, encourage, and advise the people around them. They are also given the grace to amend their own lives."

There is another potential future reality for those the Lord sends back. After a period of recovery, it is likely each will go on to suffer many issues, internally and externally. The rest of life is not a free ride. The heavenly court basically asks, "With all the salt and light you've been granted, will you accept your sufferings and offer them up as sacrifice to the Lord your God, for the benefit and salvation of those souls who do not know salt and light, so that many of them will not go down to the bad place below? Some of the souls may even be of your own ancestral family. Perhaps they will turn out to be other persons you know, like neighbors and co-workers." Peter says, *"Christ suffered here on earth. Now you must be ready to suffer as he did, because suffering shows that you have stopped sinning." (1 Peter 4:1)* He does not say a person will have to suffer, rather just be ready to. Peter went on to be crucified upside down.

This is what Jesus says about the person who repents, even if it's at the last second: *"In the same way there is more happiness in heaven because of one sinner who turns back to God than over ninety-nine good people who don't need to. In the same way God's angels are happy when even one person turns to him." (Luke 15:7,10)* Jesus tells His disciples the parable about the hired workers (Matthew 20:1-16). The ones who were hired an hour prior to the end of shift got paid the same as the ones hired in the morning and at noon. Jesus clearly says the ones hired late worked. They might have been assigned heavier lifting than the others, seeing that they were fresher and would not have to work for as long.]

All over Maine, New England, and America, hundreds of mills and factories closed their local operations during the 1960s-70s-80s. Gardiner Shoe closed in 1968; the building was demolished in 1970. The Prudhommes lost their jobs. Gardiner Paper shut down in 1970. The structure was hit by lightning and burned to the ground, ending ex-employees' hopes for a reopening; rumor had the real culprit a match. Hallowell Shoe closed in 1975. The father of the sweet love of my life was a plant foreman there. The family was devastated. Health-tex was one of the last to go. Augusta's Bates Cotton Mill burned down in 1989. The owners did not rebuild.

MEC was bought by a major national carrier in 1981. The line is currently owned by Pan Am Systems, which, prior to 2005, had been known as Guilford Transportation Industries. People living in the Kennebec Valley were shocked when Guilford ceased rail service on the Lower Road in 1986. The state refused to allow the track to be removed and took it under the auspices of the Department of Transportation. Years passed by before Maine Coast Railroad leased the track and restored service right into Augusta. After MCR declined to renew its lease, Maine Eastern Railroad took over the route's freight service in 2003. To this day, Pan Am Railways services Waterville by way of the inland track known under MEC as the "Back Road." Decades ago, the track linking Waterville to Skowhegan was removed north of Hinckley.

In the 1970s, brother Tony attended Northern Maine Technical Institute in Bangor and graduated a chemistry technician. He worked six years at the

Seabrook (NH) Nuclear Power Facility before relocating to a coal-powered plant in remote northern Canada. In 1991, he met a widow who had two teenage children. Two years later, they married in Melbourne. He is retired, lives with his wife in Edmonton, and considers the children and now the children's children as his own. Brother Daniel still runs his travel enterprise from France.

Chapter XL

"It's Time"

Looking up from this elevated vantage point, here on the crest of the impressive Indian River archway, the man sees only blue sky: plain and simple it is, but what a spectacular view. He stands at the point of his resurrection, the threshold of eternal life. It is his third afternoon of standing here. Alone, a young man again, feeling much better than the first day, he remains humble yet confident, without malice toward anyone. Even though he feels alone at times, he knows with certainty that he is not alone at any time. No one is. Reader, you are not alone. The man has been granted crystal clarity. How is that possible?

The Lord knows the answer, and that is all that really counts. He has His reasons, and He needs not explain to him (me) or anyone else. But several things do stick to the gray matter. Jesus sees how the person has rejected all that the world offers when it comes to materiality, how he has rejected the idea of gaining human note of some kind, and how he loathes to receive praise or over-and-above attention from the people around him. In the last 15 years of daily prayer, the man has asked for God's salt and light to be in his mind, heart, and soul. Jesus states in the Bible, *"Ask, and you will receive. Search, and you will find. Knock, and the door will be opened. Everyone who asks will receive. Everyone who searches will find." (Matthew 7: 7-8)*

The receiver has refused nothing and accepted everything Jesus and the Father have granted. *Why would I refuse the things that I have prayed for?* This aspect is important, for the Bible shows how God will, as a deprecatory punishment for affronting His kindness, withdraw a second grace when the first grace is ignored or refused by the receiver, be that receiver a nation, family, or individual. There comes the likelihood of a descent into moral blindness and spiritual stupidity, stuck at the bottom of a roadside slough known as "Murky River." We see it all over the world right now. Apostle James iterates, *"If any of you need wisdom, you should ask God, and it will be given you. God is generous and won't correct you for asking. But when you ask for something, you must have faith and no doubt. Anyone who doubts is like an ocean wave tossed around in a storm."* (James 1:5-6)

Another point on "Why him?" has to do with how the person has handled the fact that Jesus and the Father have so kindly leaned down to communicate in such a direct manner. Has he collapsed under the weight? No, but the stress has been almost unbearable at times. Has he let it go to his head? No. Once the going got rough, did he shirk duty by backing away from divulging to others the grace of enlightenment God was granting? No, he has not shirked his duty. In fact, there have been three prior undertakings done for the Lord. They are under different pseudonyms and have produced no revenue, but on the contrary have caused drain on his weak finances, and this as well has brought him to suffer. In spite of it all, the responsibility to share and reveal remains. He is nothing more than a "revealer" for Jesus; what is received must be revealed. Jesus has ordered that His revealer never be questioned or interviewed (not that anyone would want to, but someone might), that he not use popular marketing means of any kind but to instead just give out the book to persons needing of encouragement (who hopefully will pass them on to others), that he remain hidden and very small, and that he have "no lot" in the world. The last two points have been the easiest for John Worker to accept.

[Spiritual note: In 1966, Pope Paul VI abolished Canon Law 1399 and 2318, and this allowed the Catholic Church not to have to deal with private revelations; the Church could still do it but was not *required*. The astute and mostly overlooked pontiff believed no human or organization should dare come across as trying to place God inside a box, so to speak. (Some high-up ecclesia have come out since, trying to explain away or dispute the pope's order. But his decision remains as is, and oh how these ones will have to answer if they've contributed to the "putting away" of a legitimate apparition/communication from heaven!) Problems happen when persons say they've heard from God but actually haven't; perhaps it has been a deceitful spirit or a very evil entity's voice; perhaps it has been nothing at all and simply a person's own mind. But, truly, anyone who has read the Bible with intensity and accepts God's Word *in its fullness* has, in fact, heard the voice of God. In *ARR*, the revealer offers no contradictory information to Divine Truth, but instead does nothing but, *with clarity*, glorify God the Father and Son as *The Universal Power*. The Word of God is constantly quoted *in its fullness*. Cheers to the reader and may God's blessings of salt and light—and good internal sight—be with you.

A few pages back, the revealer introduced the term God Blessed Rebirthment, and it should not—NEVER—be translated into the lingo of "reincarnation." So, for the reader who had become nervous at seeing the term, please put the jitters away. Simply put, the soul inside the human body already existed prior to human physical conception; the soul was not created at the time of human sexual intercourse; man-woman sexual relations can *spark* the creation of a human fetus but never does it a soul. Capiche? (Is there a person/pastor out there who thinks having sex brings forth a soul-person? If so, to this one the revealer says, "Read the Bible—all of it!"). Much more to come on this item.]

A late evening 17 years ago, in 1997, I lay in bed, readying to fall asleep, when something strange, *extraordinary* happened.

Kerry Ann was next to me and already in deep slumber. So there I was, winding down, mulling my day, my marriage, and my life, particularly my early years of adulthood, a time during which I made some big mistakes. The months of bedtimes leading up to the night had often had me dwelling along these same lines. As to my marriage, I dearly loved my wife, but we had vastly different views on more than a couple things.

Kerry Ann and I met on a blind date in 1988. We fell in love. I was 34 at the time, so she obviously was not the love of my youth. The Bible says that one is the most special. At 20 years old I met her. The year was 1974. Sure, by then I had already experienced a few loves, but they had been more in the way of puppy stuff. Too, there were some serious loves to come later on. But this time was different. Looking at her pleased my eyes beyond words. To walk beside her, with my hand clasped to hers, was like having a bowl of the thickest, sweetest honey inside my heart. She was the love of my youth, the love of my life, and I have never forgotten her. I still love her the same way. It has taken me four decades to see this truth.

The timing of our relationship was against us. She was 17 and still in high school in Maine. I lived in Boston but spent the summer of '74 in Gardiner; that was when we met. From the outset, I saw distance and age difference as problems, but I let myself go with the heart. High school years are the most important for personal development and establishing direction of life. These years "hang" with us more than any other, as far as I was concerned back then and to this day still believe it. Even though she was mature for her age, she needed to have the full high school experience and the total freedom of being around others there. It is not a time to be emotionally tied to the concept of waiting around for some absentee guy who may or may not return for a weekend now and then. Her parents were respectful of her feelings, yet I knew they were advising her to be very careful. Even though I went into a type of death-mourning when we ended, ending was the right way. If only we had met as singles a few years later. If only.

There I was in bed, *thinking and thinking*, slowly drifting toward sleep. My memory jumped forward a couple years, to the late summer of 1976, precise timing two evenings before this then-22-year-old man would leave New England semi-permanently, to go thousands of miles west, to graduate school. A real plan for the evening had not been made. Not much of one, anyway. Determinably I headed to Hallowell—Freddies Restaurant. While seated at the front counter, I tried and tried to convince myself to use the payphone, to call her, to ask the bowl of honey to drop by and sit with me for a while. She lived only a short walk from the eatery. Maybe the real truth was that I was trying to convince myself not to use the phone. Lying in bed, more than two decades later, I still did not know the answer.

My half-baked intent was to chat with her about my life and coming adventure. I wanted to ask in as kind and unobtrusive manner as possible about her current life and future plans. By then she had graduated from high school. I also wanted to apologize for having been such a jerk and to let her know that she would always occupy a special place in my heart. That was the part that stopped me from reaching into my pocket for the change. I remembered thinking, *What's the sense, considering my imminent departure? Anyway, she might scoff at my invitation. Her mother might pick up the phone and refuse to pass me on. Worse, her dad might answer, recognize my voice, and order me to never call again.* I just did not know for sure, and I did not want to come across as "an interferer." Even back then I recognized the world a grand stage. *By calling her, would I be throwing a wrench into her emotions? Because of my feelings for her, is it worth taking the chance? Would it be selfish of me? Would I be overstepping myself? Am I so totally overestimating myself? This, too, is a possibility.*

Like so many who stopped by Freddies, I ordered fries with gravy and a Pepsi. This gave me the time to sit there and think more about my lack of decision. Their fries and gravy were about as good as anywhere. The mind quickly shot ahead to 1985, my week in Maine. During it, I went to Hallowell for another plate of Freddies, only to discover the place gone, closed forever.

Suddenly, on that 1997 night, my reminiscing was interrupted. The face of a man appeared in front of me. In a split second he disappeared and another man appeared; then he disappeared for another to appear. I would say more than 50 came and went. It was as if a black-and-white television was sitting a few inches from my face, yet my eyes were closed. Each man looked to be 60s or more, and each showed a serious countenance. They did not speak, but my mind *felt* them say, *"It's time."* The same thing happened the next night: *"It's time."*

After the old-man visitations, my life began to change. Since mid-teens, I had been away from the Lord, but now a major league calling back was happening. In 1998, in the presence of a Christian pastor, I repented my life of poor choices—MY SINS. I did not get into minute details, for we must be respectful of the pastor's ears and management of time. An open expression of contrition of the heart and mind is what counts. Anyway, the Lord already knew my details (and He knows yours). The pastor read an appropriate Bible passage and prayed over me.

At that moment, Christ's wounds covered all of my poor acts of demonstration in life: **the bad things my hands had done**—spikes driven through Jesus' hands; **the bad places my feet had taken me**—nails through His feet; **the bad things I had allowed into my heart**—gruesome whipping of Jesus' back; **my poor speech**—the punching against, spitting on, and belittling of His Holy Face; **my pride, ego, and belief in earthly gain/power**—crown of thorns pressed into Jesus' scalp. The Passion of Christ paid my debts (and yours if you go to Him). *This was to fulfill what had been spoken through the prophet Isaiah, "He took our infirmities and bore our diseases." (Matthew 8:17) "This is my blood, and with it God makes his agreement with you. It will be poured out, so that many will have their sins forgiven." (Matthew 26:28)* Apostle John says in his first letter (1:7-9), *"And the blood of his Son Jesus washes all our sins away. If we say that we have not sinned, we are fooling ourselves, and the truth isn't in our hearts. But if we confess our sins to God, he can always be trusted to forgive us and take our sins away."*

The awakening continued. A few months passed by and something that had been hidden behind a gray haze since my youth returned: *"In death comes life. This man became a willing sacrifice so that his young friend could have more life. I am Jesus. Will you live it for Me?"*

The 1990s was a time of rampant corporate restructurings, consolidations, and buyouts. In late 1999, the company I worked for went through its fourth "reshaping" of the decade. The three previous ones had sometimes found me involved in the letting go of personnel, some of them my friends. The fourth reorganization happened in my seventeenth year with Novartis Consumer Healthcare (the end-product of the 1997 merger of Swiss companies Ciba-Geigy and Sandoz Pharmaceuticals). As with the two prior restructurings and the merger, good people lost their jobs, but not me. This time I not only made the cut, I became a beneficiary at the expense of those who had been let go. I received the promotion to Regional Manager of Western Canada and a big raise in pay. An extra bonus came when the company allowed the position to be based out of Calgary, my home since 1978, and not Vancouver, as had always been the rule; it meant I did not have to move.

Things were going too good for me. The Lord wasn't going to put up with it. I needed to be a slam-dunked in order to know what the other side felt like. Soon enough, another situation of corporate greed and unfairness arose. I had the choices of shutting up, like I always had before, or speaking up. My decision to do the latter caused the company grief, and it highly agitated the president and vice. I was tossed for the first time in my life. Oh, what a feeling!

The Lord allows for these seemingly negative outcomes to happen. In fact, He germinates, waters, and fertilizes the ground before them. Sometimes He even orders for them to take place, and this is for the long-term good-growth of our souls, so that we may learn to be more empathetic, more righteous, more dignified soul-persons in His eyes. The Bible shows this hard truth many times. One example is when the Angels of God killed the firstborn children and cows of Egypt. Some people refer to this event as to why they do not believe in God. "How can I believe in a God who does something like that?" In order for the biblical saga to make sense, one has to know the whole story; otherwise, it doesn't. Some 40 years prior to the slaying of Egypt's firstborn, Pharaoh ordered his military to kill all the newborn male babies of Israel. "There, Pharaoh, how does it feel? Learn, Pharaoh, learn!" What about the slain ones? Were they nothing more than pawns in a sort of earth-size game of Chess? No, but without truth-in-light, that is what it may appear to have been.

My corporate dusting was only the beginning of Jesus' tearing me down to zero. Kerry Ann began to say that I was no longer the man she married. She was right. I couldn't stomach that egomaniac anymore. But she pined for his return and eventually wanted the "new me" gone.

If I had fought her about everything, the kids would have become more upset than they already were. In such a scenario, the family home would have had to be sold and the kids and mother would have had to move out of the neighborhood and away from their friends. I decided to let Kerry Ann keep the house and everything else, including my possessions from before we had met. I just could not have the children see their dad removing furniture from their home.

I chose to relocate my life to a rooming house close by. The kids saw me and to this day still see me all the time. I have never left their side.

Over the years, I have often reassured Kandis and James that their dad still loves their mother, as a person and as the mother of his children. Hearing that has pleased them very much. And it has not been a lie. I do indeed love Kerry Ann, but it's like a brother-sister thing now. I know it sounds strange. I want the best for her in life.

I own almost nothing, and that includes a vehicle and a proper bed. The old mattress I sleep on was a giveaway on someone's front lawn. There was a sign on it that read TAKE ME HOME, I'M FREE. I thought, *So am I. We'll make a good match.* I have never owned a cell phone and know nothing about the modern social-media avenues. I do retain an email address but have never been hooked up to the Internet at home; sometimes it's a month or more between my library or UPS-outlet visits to check and send my messages.

I've told the kids many times that they will never see their dad with another woman, that I will remain single till death do us part. The first couple times I said it, they insisted, "Dad, it's okay, we understand if you date and marry again."

"You say that, but I know differently. When children see their father with another woman . . . Well, it's like your hearts got a knife shoved into them. Not gonna to happen on my watch."

They shook their heads, thought I was being silly.

I explained to them the bigger reason their father won't be dating was so that I could better serve Jesus. They did not understand this. But the truth is that there was no way I could have produced for Jesus what I have in the past 16 years if courtship had been on my mind.

After Novartis booted me, I opted for a change of career. In 2000 I began to work with profoundly mentally/physically disabled men who reside in group homes. To this day I continue in it. Some of the guys are heavy and wheelchair bound. I and the other workers help them to successfully live out their daily lives. "Successful" mostly means accomplishing simple things that we regular people take for granted, like getting out of bed, toileting, washing up, eating without choking, taking medications. My successful day counts those things while at the same time managing to not get bit and/or punched. Going for strolls around the community and inside malls can bring good cheer to the disabled clients and their workers.

Since the old-man visitations, I have been taken into—that is, my soul-person-self has been taken into—personal meetings with Jesus. First thing He did was express a heartfelt cheer that I came back to Him. One time He took me into the close presence of God the Father. On my knees and with forehead pressed to the ground, I was allowed to gradually raise my head and come to gaze upon Him. The Almighty smiled, leaned down, and said, "John, My friend, . . ." The communication was of a personal nature and should not be divulged.

Jesus, too, has referred to me as His friend. One side of Jesus is full of bonhomie. The other side . . . ahh, not so much of that stuff. Most of the meetings have had Him not in a good mood. Unlike many of His pastors on earth, He is very frank and to the point. He has told me that there are so-called pastors who preach by their own sins of the flesh, that these ones are not with Him but instead with Satan. The Bible talks of them. Paul says, *"Anyway, they are no more than false apostles and dishonest workers. They pretend to be apostles of Christ. And it is no wonder. Even Satan tries to make himself look like an apostle of Christ. So why does it seem strange for Satan's servants to pretend to do what is right? Someday they will get exactly what they deserve." (2 Corinthians 11:13-15)*

The world has become so immoral that Jesus and God the Father have decided to bring it to an end. Paul says in his 1st letter to Timothy, *"God's Spirit clearly states that in the last days many people will turn from their faith. They will be fooled by evil spirits and by teachings that come from demons." (4:1)* The world's systems as we know them will be forced into breakdown and reformation. Important for the reader to know is that the physical earth itself will not be destroyed. After The Great Flood, God in His heart said, *"I will not again curse the ground any more for man's sake, though the imagination of man's heart is evil from his youth; neither will I smite any more every thing living, as I have done. While the earth remaineth, seedtime and harvest, and cold and heat, and summer and winter, and day and night shall not cease. . . . neither shall all flesh be cut off by the waters of a flood; neither shall there any more be a flood to destroy the earth." (Genesis 8:21-22 & 9:11)* The complacent, diabolically disoriented soul of the current world is what will be destroyed. To facilitate bringing "the change" into fruition, a series of unprecedented natural disasters will be allowed to take place within a short time frame.

The reason this will happen—and we are currently in the beginning of the tearing-down process—is not because of nations warring with each other. Wars are brought about because of the immoralities of men and women. The Bible shows this time and again. God's firstborn, the Jewish nation, required periodic bashing into oblivion for its turning away from Him and instead choosing pagan-liberal lifestyles. The outside nations that did the bashing were brutal and more evil than Israel/Judah. So, after many years of humiliating servitude, the Jewish people almost always found the wherewithal to repent and recommit themselves to the ways of God. Afterward, God allowed Israel/Judah or an outside nation to attack and defeat the jailor-nation.

In particular, Jesus and the Father are disgusted about adults killing of innocence; both in body and soul are the killings taking place. With regard to the soul, the innocence is the minds and hearts of the young. Today's children are being taught that evil is not only okay, it is a choice that even they can observe, learn about, and participate in. In spirit, the last few decades have shown the world to be drowning itself in filth, immorality. The body-earth must now and rapidly be brought to its knees and for an extended period of time—decades—in order to completely annihilate the will of evil, currently so deeply imbedded in the minds and hearts of the majority.

Good people will suffer beside bad people. But the good should know that they have the most wonderful eternal life awaiting them on the other side. Prior to body-death, some of the bad will come to reject and repent their evil ways, and this will be a positive outcome from the forthcoming cataclysmic breakdown of society. After body-death, the not-repentant bad people will be relegated to the below-places of eternal death, level of forced assignment dependant upon the seriousness of each soul-person's not-repented sins. But no level down there is good. Even the best is far worse than what we have up here on the earth's surface.

Jesus has shown me that earth is a school for souls of the cosmos; it is a physical-life field camp for the true self, which is, as said before, spirit-energy in constitution. The human body is a vessel of learning for the soul. Learning what, though? University of Earth is one of the toughest cosmic schools to graduate from. There is just no other way to move up. God's rules must be followed in order to merit graduation: to elevate, a soul-person must graduate.

When looked at in the revealed enlightenment contained in the reading so far, the concepts of "merit" and "graduation" should not be hard to grasp. Does everyone in Maine or Iowa get to graduate from high school or a state university just because they were born? But everyone *does* have the opportunity to choose a way of life that will one day merit eternal life.

The main criteria for meriting graduation is for the soul-person, the cowboy let's say, to have shown that he/she can subjugate the body, the horse let's say. We must consistently express the desire to refuse the many temptations thrown our way each day. When a falling down occurs, the person has the choice to get right back up and into the graduation hunt by way of the great grace of repentance. Repeated a hundred times, for the reader's benefit, "repentance" is the real focus of the book's Part IV. God always forgives and takes back the repentant person. Earth is not easy. As a Good Father, He did not make it easy for us. Why would He do that? What would we learn if our educational period was nothing more than a piece of cake?

A side-issue is Jesus does not prefer parents corporally punish their children. But if and when done, it should be very minor and only in the most extreme of behavioral situations. The Lord blessed my parents in this way, for as difficult as their three boys were at times, they always remained patient and never used raging, belittling speech, and never did they get physical other than the couple times dad gave me an open-handed whack on my rear end when I was five; the brothers never, that I saw. It didn't hurt, but I remember thinking, *Why did Dad do that? Oh yeah, because of the bad way I'm acting. I love him so much. I better stop doing what's making him so angry at me.* Dad's rolling up of a KJ to whap against a son's shoulder was considered more like a joke, and always did the son get the point, chuckle, and move from his chair.

Since day one with Kandis and James, Kerry Ann and I have been exactly the same as Herve and Jeanne were. It is great to set good examples, but it is not enough. Things also need to be explained in a kindly manner to our children, as a part of their education in life-skills. The mother and I always believed that the youngsters' understanding of respectful boundaries, proper manners and behaviors, and quality outgoing people skills must be taught and reinforced by way of empathy-building avenues: parental example and *explanation*. When they were young, never did we utilize prolonged timeouts, but instead opted for ten seconds to a few minutes max. They were allowed to return to normal activity only if they promised to act better. Always did they promise, because they loved and trusted their parents and wanted to be back in "the action" as soon as possible. Barking and hitting out at children works only when they are young and certainly does not instill empathy.

Painful strikes also insult the child, especially when the strikes are above the rear end. The use of pain-delivering strikes can potentially instill into the young receivers that it is okay to hit people, especially loved ones, not only while young, but also later in life. Grownups who as children were frequently struck hard by their parents will always remember it and may even harbor a level of resentment, though there may also be a lot of love.

In 1999, I was spiritually/emotionally helping out a church sister who was going through a tough period. Jesus gave a message that He wanted her to cease striking out at and spanking her five-year-old grandson, whom she had full custody of. The boy had been diagnosed with alcohol fetal syndrome and rejected by the mother. On top of that, he had been repeatedly molested at the age of three by a male gambling associate of the grandmother. As one can imagine, the boy had many emotional problems. With Jesus' message and my help, the church sister stopped hitting the boy and opted to explain things to him. But it had to be over and over, and it very much tested her patience and commitment not to hit.

[Spiritual note: Conversely, much of Islam teaches that a child should be beat until seven years old in order to have him/her turn out good. After seven, as the teaching goes, if the child has not been beaten, it is too late. To find out just how good that system works, all one needs to do is study the geopolitical nations that are mostly Muslim. They are terribly violent countries: brother against brother, where women are mostly treated poorly. Rape and murder of women are pretty much non-crimes if the male perpetrator can dig up a good enough Islamic reason for it. And how they treat their animals—WOW, that's a whole "nother" level of cruelty and brutality.

Not every Muslim family believes in the bad stuff, but many do. And then there's how so many lie to cover it up. Just ask the good ones who refuse to lie about it. They'll tell you. Otherwise, why do so many want to come here to live? As TV psychologist Dr. Phil might say, "How's beatin' ya kids workin' for ya so far?"]

Chapter XLI

Sins of the Flesh

Jesus and God the Father have shown me that today's world has a huge problem, and it comes in two parts. The first is pornography. Anyone who is a friend of pornography is not a friend of heaven. Pornography is an outrageous abuse of the gift of life each of us was granted prior to our arrival here, when we were discarnate soul-persons.

> Going around the Catholic Church in recent time is a story about an Italian woman who one night got a visit from her dead husband. A Rome, Italy-based priest has repeated the story many times, so that persons who hear it or hear of it second-hand may turn away from pornography, if they happen to be into it. The woman's husband, Sal, had died in a sudden manner the previous year. Prior to his death, the two had been producing and selling pornography magazines. They made wads of money at it and were living the high life, investing in buildings, too. After the man's death, she continued in the business. Late one night, she lay awake in bed. Suddenly the room filled with a dull orange-gray light, and inside of it stood her dead Sal, a shrunken, wrinkled, tortured and suffering shrimp of a being, exactly the opposite of the robust, over-confident man she had once known; his eyes shown like hot charcoals. He said that he had been condemned to a life in hell, that it was far worse than anything he could have ever imagined while alive, and that he had been allowed to come and warn her about the porn business. He finished by saying that if she continued in it she would be joining him down there.

Before disappearing, he pressed his hand against the bedroom door, leaving behind a burnt impression of it. The next morning the woman went to the priest and confessed her sins. She asked him to come to her place and see the burn-mark. The priest instructed that besides ending her vile ways, she must not live off any gains from it but instead give all of it away to charities, then live a simple, exemplary life. She did as the priest said.

[Spiritual note: Gospel of Luke Chapter 16 has Jesus telling the story about a cold-hearted rich man who dies and goes down to the place of terrible suffering. The guy looks up and pleads with Abraham to send down a drop of water on the finger of Lazarus, a poor man who had recently died and went to heaven. "Send Lazarus to dip his finger in water and touch my tongue. I'm suffering terribly in this fire." Abraham responds that between them there is a ditch that cannot be crossed over. The former rich man says, "Abraham, then please send Lazarus to my father's home. Let him warn my five brothers, so they won't come to this horrible place." Abraham answers, "Your brothers can read what Moses and the prophets wrote. They should pay attention to that." Then the rich man says, "No, that's not enough! If only someone from the dead would go to them, they would listen and turn to God." Abraham says, "If they won't pay attention to Moses and the prophets, they won't listen even to someone who comes back from the dead."]

The Roman priest's story is a hard one, but the learning is essential because if anyone happens to be into pornography, there is now enough enlightenment to bring about a ceasing, a repenting, and a regaining of the guaranteed hope of achieving eternal life someday. *What exactly is eternal life all about, anyway? What's so special about it? Is there such a thing as making love in Heaven?* Have these thoughts have ever entered the reader's mind?

The man works in a field that has more than a few young women as co-workers. Over the years, some have made pitches for me. Twenty-three was the youngest, and I was 53 at the time. She said to me, "Thirty years isn't that much of a difference." (Within the year she met a guy around her age, and six months later they married.) My writing about this personal stuff has nothing to do with vanity and ego, for there is a point in the making. As mentioned before, I do not date, but the idea of courting a much younger woman is something that has never been with me. Kerry Ann was 30 and I was 34 when we met on a blind date set up by my brother Tony and his then-girlfriend. I politely said to her that if she were 29 there would be no second date. Even her being four years younger than me was a bit of a turnoff. I discovered a long time ago that I am an unusual man when it comes to this. But I shouldn't be! Men and women need to act their ages!

The Bible states how the chosen Solomon fell out of God's grace because of his turning to young women. Despite all the wisdom Solomon had been granted, he as an old man chose to worship the bodies of young females. He even offered gifts to their gods (invisible demons). Later, God ordered for Solomon's temple to be burned and flattened. *Then the Lord was angry with Solomon, because his heart had turned away from the Lord, the God of Israel, who had appeared to him twice, and had commanded him on this matter, that he should not follow other gods; but he did not observe what the Lord commanded. (1 Kings 11: 9-10)* There will be no pardon for not-repentant persons who delved into, posed for, or produced pornography.

The second part of the problem is the unnecessary public exposition of men's and women's scantily clad bodies. Ostensibly the most attractive are the thin, young ones. "If you got it, girl, show it." Such display teaches young society to worship not only physical beauty but also nudity. As the young generation ages, it will continue to worship young nudity. The bent is a precursor to and breeder of pornography, incontinent sexual behavior, marriage infidelity, abortion, eating disorders, depression, sexual deviancy, and prostitution. God will hold not-repentant members of both genders equally accountable for their choosing to persistently turn away from the innate moral conscience imbedded into our souls prior to our arrivals here. These persons are not friends of the Divine, and Jesus' wounds do not shield them from God the Father's wrath and harsh judgment. Satan, *that old accuser*, is allowed to take them down, so he may teach them in the most vile and disgusting ways the difference between right and wrong.

[Spiritual note on God, Christ, and Satan: Who exactly is Satan? Does he really exist? Yes! In the Bible, Jesus and His apostles speak of him. They are not liars! Eight centuries before Christ, God the Father vents as follows to the prophet Isaiah (14:12-15): *"How art thou fallen from heaven, O Lucifer, son of the morning* [formerly]*! How art thou cut down to the ground, which didst weaken the nations* [reference to the fallen-Lucifer having negative influence on humanity]*! For thou said in thine heart, 'I will ascend into heaven, I will exalt my throne* [real bad case of pride] *above the stars of God: I will sit also upon the mount of the congregation in the sides of the north: I will ascend above the heights of the clouds: I will be like the most High.' Yet thou shalt be brought down to hell* [God's own reference to that place below], *to the sides of the pit."*

What is Satan all about? The reader will be startled to learn the truth about the devil. He is the tempter and then, ironically, the deliverer of the tortuous, sickening correctional methods to be used on those who failed to repent the evil that he had tempted and gotten them to do during life on the surface. In actuality, he competes with Jesus, the Good and Gentle Teacher, on how soul-persons are to be taught the difference between right and wrong. In his first letter to Timothy, Paul talks of persons who made a mess of their faith-lives: *"Two of them are Hymenaeus and Alexander. I have given these men over to the power of Satan, so that they will learn not to oppose God." (1:20)* Paul mentions it again, in his second letter to Timothy: *"Be humble when you correct people who oppose you. Maybe God will lead them to turn to him and learn the truth. They have been trapped by the devil, and he makes them obey him, but God may help them to escape." (2:25-26)* Mostly, Satan doesn't personally do the correcting, but instead he has teams for doing it: "the satanics," the writer calls them.

The reader might want to take a moment to ask him-/herself, "Where does soul-person-me want to learn the real truth and about the proper ways to behave—at a college in Maine or Iowa, or at a prison in Turkey or Iraq?" There is a strangely straightforward reason the captain devil does this to humans. He blames us, and he hates us.

"Why is that?" To understand requires we go back to a former time. Several eternities ago, the angel Lucifer occupied a top spot in God the Father's Kingdom. Many subordinate angels had come to follow him, and the scent of rebellion entered the wind.

Prior to the beginning of what we know as the human existence, God, the Father of Creation, in spirit, traveled across the rough, primitive earth in order to determine its readiness for His more-complete takeover. From the beginning, which has no beginning or end, this has been the process of the cosmos, to become seeded by the Great Creator; each planet to house life, by His Will, is left alone for a long period of time so that it may develop its own uniqueness.

The angels have been with God for a long time, but not from the beginning, for God created them. He perceived for there to be Beings of Light, for His company, and He willed them to be. They are *Angels of God*. And there are those He created, for to give the breath of life, which comes from Him, to the flesh of the physical realms of the free empire. They would be called *freedom souls*. Their flesh-vessels would hold the blood that contains a small amount of that very special positive life-force heaven itself is awash in. Biblical reference: *"Therefore I [God] said unto the children of Israel, No soul of you shall eat blood, neither shall any stranger that sojourneth among you eat blood. For it is the life of all flesh; the blood of it for the life thereof; for the life of the flesh is the blood thereof." (Leviticus 17: 12,14)*

> [[Spiritual note within a spiritual note: Throughout history, those who carried out human sacrifice treasured the blood of their victims. After the fallen angels were cast down from heaven and into the beneath-world, they no longer had access to (were able to replenish/bathe themselves in) the positive living energy that had formerly given their spirits superb powers. To get access to it, they began to invisibly connive people on earth into the practice

of human sacrifice. Each human body's heart, store of blood, and marrow contain a small amount of that vitally important life-energy from above. The demon gods of the Foundation Testament's eras were adept at getting their human hosts to offer up their enemies and their enemies' children. Milcom, also known as Molech, and Chemosh are two examples.

A more modern example of human sacrifice was with the Aztec people. Up until the sixteenth century, it had central role in Mexico. At the Aztec pyramids an estimated 50,000 humans were sacrificed yearly to demon spirits; the main one was known as Quetzalcoatl. During one bloody four-day rampage in 1487, 80,000 humans were offered up. The invisible entities surrounding the Aztecs certainly held them under a very dark, hypnotic control, for surely no one would willingly get in line to be murdered by way of knife into stomach, only to then have it angled up into the chest so that the person's heart could be pulled out still beating, to be consumed along with the blood.

A few years after the Spaniards arrived in Mexico, human sacrifice ended, around the mid-1500s, when the whole people converted to Christianity. Not all Conquistadors were wonderful persons, but liberation had to be achieved in one way or another. After the Conquistadors' brutal conquest, missionary Catholic priests and bishops arrived in to do their "nice guy" mop-up. Soon, millions of Aztecs were in line to be baptized, to have their past sins forgiven and begin a new life in the ways of God through Christ.]]

God desired to retain the company of His created spirits, for each to love and bless Him, and in His love He would take care of and shepherd them through endless time and endless universe. The human biological unit offered a grand opportunity for His spirit-beings to enter a renewed period of proving and knowledge-growth. At the same time, the savage unit would now be pushed forward at evolutionary hyper-speed into something more like His Image. *Then God said, "Let us make man in our image, after our likeness;" (Genesis 1:26)* For sure, the rugged, untamed, instinctive human animal would offer tremendous challenges for the operating souls and for the angels who dwell in spirit among them.

Earth, too, would have to be modified, basically created all over again, to be more like the home of God: HEAVEN. What an odyssey the Great Creator prepared for His children! In particular, the human brain would require intense scrutiny in order to magnify its desirable qualities and eliminate those that are not. At the same time, the intelligent spirit-entity living inside the body would force the gray-matter organ to expand its dimensions and break through its paradigms; proper routing during the period of accelerated growth had to be ensured; subjugation of the instinctive, temper-prone animal brain was another major concern for the operating souls and the angels who invisibly guide and supervise them. God's Will! *Are they* [angels] *not all ministering spirits sent forth to serve, for the sake of those* [freedom souls] *who are to obtain salvation* [prove themselves worthy of re-attaining "freedom class"]? *(Hebrews 1:14)*

What would happen to the children's love if their Father gave them free will? Would it not grow? Would not the Father's love grow when a child's love for Him remained strong? He made us from His Love and He desires for us to love Him back, but after being given His law of the spirit, would we choose to bow to the animal body by emotionally attaching to earthly ideas and items or would we choose to return to Him? The choices are ours because we have been given free will, but the rules are His because He owns the whole thing.

One of the angels, Lucifer, was thought to have done well in his decision-making over the many eternities. He rose to a grand position and became filled with pride. But the Great Creator saw the human developmental track record as not quite correct, particularly with regard to the overly sexual and violent natures of the biological entity. These issues had not been resolved nearly as well as they should have been, considering the positive advancements in other facets of the collective human soul's forward-moving intelligence.

Investigation showed Lucifer had been lying and murdering in order to advance his status. Allowed his style of generalship for thousands of years, Lucifer stretched God's patience too far. The angel failed to change his ways. Jesus says of him, *"He was a murderer from the beginning, and has nothing to do with truth, because there is no truth in him. When he lies, he speaks according to his own nature, for he is a liar and the father of lies." (John 8:44)*

Lucifer's influence was determined to have had a despoiling effect on the collective human soul. After body-death, souls were confused, angry, vengeful, and addicted to thoughts of human greed and lust. The animal had been taught to overpower the soul! Lucifer had fooled the world and himself. He was trying in his own way to move humanity forward properly, but he foundered. He and the angels aligned to him were chastised, stripped of some of their responsibilities, and given new posts as part of their correctional path.

God made known to the heavenly heights His plan to lift humanity from its animal bondage. He would send an agent of salt and light. The "agent" would be a powerful spirit borne by a special female human vessel. God does not work in a hastily planned, haphazard manner. So in order to be chosen, the female would have to be in His Will, meaning the operating soul of the female human body would have to be found in God's favor beforehand; it also meant that she herself would have to be born into an especially loving and humble family, also chosen beforehand. Would God send His Son down into the first family He runs into?

The woman would become the Messiah Bridge that God the Father would use to send His Son down through the threshold of spirit, into flesh. After the death of her human body, the soul-person known as the Mother of God the Son would be made Queen of Heaven and earth. As such, she would be Queen of the Angels; the Angels of God would take *some* direction from her. The plan was made known to the top echelons, and God perceived it a masterful way to make all the angels prove their obedience to Him, once and for all. The angel spirits were considered superior to the others. Would they take commands from a freedom soul and a female one at that?

The reassigned angels harbored hard feelings from their scolding. Even minor falls in the higher realms can be difficult to swallow. It was already a tough go for Lucifer to accept that God would beget a Son from Whom he would have to take instructions. The Son would, over time, correct the falsehoods Lucifer had helped to implant into the souls sojourning on earth. As well, Lucifer could learn the better ways that God the Father would have His Son use. "Learn, Lucifer, learn, so that you may become a better angel than you were!"

But when Lucifer found out that the female would rise to a level where he would have to take some of his orders from her as well, that was it! Pride insulted again, Lucifer cried out, blowing as a raging dragon, *"I will be like unto the most high!"* At that moment a third of the angels joined him in defiance. *And another portent appeared in heaven; behold, a great red dragon, with seven heads and ten horns, and seven diadems upon his heads. His tail swept down a third of the stars in heaven, and cast them to earth. (Revelation 12:3-4)*

Archangel Michael, who God had secretly raised in position, prostrated himself before the Throne. God blessed Michael with a new meaning to his name: "Who is like unto God." Michael rallied the loyal angels to fight the rebels while he engaged Lucifer. *And there was a war in heaven. Michael and his angels fought against the dragon; and the dragon fought and his angels, and prevailed not; neither was their place found any more in heaven. And the great dragon was cast out, that old serpent, called the Devil and Satan, which deceiveth the whole world: he was cast out into the earth, and his angels were cast out with him. (Revelation 12:7-9)*

In spirit, the fallen angels have been roaming the dark beneath-worlds ever since. *And the angels that did not keep their position but left their proper dwelling have been kept by him* [God the Father] *in eternal chains in the nether gloom until the judgment of the great day. (Jude 6)* God gave/gives the fallen angels rule down below. He allows them some access to and impact on the netherworld and our physical world, so that the living may be tested and tempted.

The netherworld is the top level of hp-purgatory and partially overlaps into our physical world. Allowed by God's mercy, the netherworld is not favored but instead put up with, for the benefit of saving deceased soul-persons from eternal damnation. The gray invisible level is not across the valley. God says, "*. . . for they are all delivered to death, to the nether parts of the earth, in the midst of the children of men, with them that go down to the pit.*" *(Ezekiel 31:14)* "*. . . and all the trees* [persons of strength and position] *of Eden, the choice and best of Lebanon, all that drink water, shall be comforted in the nether parts of the earth.*" *(Ez 31:16)* "*. . . yet thou shalt be brought down with the trees of Eden unto the nether parts of the earth.*" *(Ez 32:18)*

The good purgatory—JB purgatory—is across the valley and higher up in elevation.]

All not-repentant soul-persons of Hollywood and the "modern" music-producing culture and those involved in the sales and marketing of "sex" and the producing of sexualized advertising go down after body-death. They all abused the Lord's name and somehow thought it okay because they were making money while doing it. The Lord says to Moses, "*Thou shalt not take the name of the LORD thy God in vain; for the LORD will not hold him guiltless that taketh his name in vain.*" *(Genesis 20:7)* The hearts and minds of these so-called "entertainers" have an acute diabolical disorientation, and their negative impact on society, especially on the youth, has been and continues to be immeasurable. "*Don't you know that evil people won't have a share in the blessings of God's kingdom? Don't fool yourselves! No one who is immoral or worships idols* [idolizes evil people] *or is unfaithful in marriage or is a pervert or behaves like a homosexual will share in God's kingdom. Neither will any thief or greedy person or drunkard or anyone who curses and cheats others.*" *(1 Corinthians 6:9-10)* After saying it, Paul goes on as follows: "*Some of you used to be like that. But now the name of our Lord Jesus Christ and the power of God's spirit have washed you and made you holy and acceptable to God.*"

How many "Hollywooders" ever think to repent before that dread thief in the night shows up? Almost none do because they adore money and fame. There is no room for truth-in-light. Jesus says, "What does it profit a man or woman to gain the world and lose his or her soul?"

[Another spiritual note on Satan: He hates the above ones because he figures these are the types of humans that caused his own downfall. "God held me—me!—accountable for yas pathetic creatures. He did that to me because yas all so stupid and wouldn't listen to me and loved pride and money and all kinds of perversions. After I got thrown out from up there, I changed things around.

I lost the name Lucifer, so I decided to teach yas bad as good, so that ways I can bring yas down here. Yas didn't listen to that former good fella Lucifer when he tried to teach yas the right ways millennias ago. So now I teach yas bad as good, because yas all so stupid."

The first thing Satan does is take away all of their beauty. Every soul-person down there gets reduced to a broken-down unit that only faintly resembles the former human. Reader, remember the story about that Italian-stallion porno-guy?]

Then again, a rare few do muster the courage to look into the mirror of the soul and repent prior to their bodies going the way of dust. Bob Hope, an acute narcissist and notorious womanizer while being married to the same woman all his life, and Farrah Faucet, who had packaged herself (and made tons of money doing it) as some kind of flesh-goddess for young and old men to ogle and for young women to emulate, repented to God through Christ. Did the two go directly to heaven? No. They were assigned to a low position in JB purgatory—similar to a small and not-much-respected community college, let's say—where the two released their earth-term titles to take on the new title "worker." There, souls keep their earth-term first names; middle names can be added and perhaps even with "son/daughter of" when required for making separation from close-by soul-persons who carry the same earth-term name (e.g. "John, son of Herve" or "Mike Walter, son of Christine"). Because of their in-life repentances and significant sufferings of body and soul afterward, they were saved them from the lake of fire and all of Satan's "special correctional rooms" (later). But they still *may* have to do swing time in the shores of the lake of fire and the hall of suffering as part of their purgatorial cleansing process.

Chapter XLII

Acts of Demonstration

Jesus has repeatedly talked to His revealer about junkie gamblers. They are definitely NOT His friends. These ones live for gambling; their lives are consumed by it. Chronic gamblers tend to be cold-hearted cheats and liars, undependable, irresponsible, and always on the prowl for the next "hit." Those involved in the public promotion of gambling are also not His friends, and that includes club owners and politicians. Failing to acknowledge, cease, and repent in life, every one of them registers as not-saved (NS). In other words, Jesus rejects them, and Satan takes them down.

What about those who go for the occasional weekend of "gaming" to Las Vegas and those who buy lottery tickets? Depending on their other not-repented sins, as long as they are not of the vile kind, these persons will have to serve a period of time in purgatory on this issue alone before entry into paradise or heaven is granted. The spiritual problem with gaming is that the person expresses through **acts of demonstration** a "hope in money." Going to church, for example, is an act of demonstration of wanting to be, in a special way, closer to God. There is cash in neither paradise nor heaven. Up there, a savings account is how much love and kindness we possess in our hearts and minds, and a checking account is how much of that love and kindness we are prepared to give out unselfishly to others up there. Being in the Will of God, souls in paradise and heaven are innately righteous (in His Will) and have perfected self-control.

While on earth, we need to have enough money, and it should be obtained by way of decent work in fields that are not supporting/proliferating evil. The world is full of care organizations that supply food/clothing/schooling/shelter to the millions of poor people in undeveloped countries. In most cases, the cost to effectively help out a person in a foreign land is about a dollar a day. Even in America, there are many positive things that we can do with our time and money instead of gambling and/or seeking out naked bodies to stare at.

Many time-filling activities are neither positive nor negative in nature. Things such as reading (not evil stuff!), watching/participating in sports, fixing old cars, collecting coins/stamps, building model trains, knitting quilts, hiking, climbing mountains, hunting, target shooting, fishing, and so many other hobbies are neutral in nature when they are not done obsessively and in a manner that negatively impacts social/family/work life. Going to a sports bar (occasionally) to enjoy one or a couple beers with buddies is a neutral thing to do as long as participants practice *intelligent moderation*. This needs to be taught to our young generations. Is it? Mostly today's TV shows/movies teach the opposite, and our young seem destined to emulate the poor displays of actors and actresses who in their own lives are drowning at the bottom of polluted rivers.

Being involved in *neutral acts of demonstration* can certainly seed and grow good aspects into the soul. For example, by fixing up an old car with a buddy—or hiking, fishing, bird-watching, etc.—a person can grow the ability to develop and value friendships; a soul can learn to keep commitments, to be attentive to details, to work in team format, to manage time more effectively and coordinate tasks responsibly, to be kind-hearted, fun-spirited, outgoing, flexible, generous, and humorous; and there can be many more beneficial aspects gained for the soul, all while doing something fun with one's spare time. In order for acts of demonstration to register as neutral, the end products or end goals must at minimum be of a neutral nature. They must not be done for evil ends or to yield end results that will inevitably cause persons to sin. AND THERE SHOULD BE NO ABUSING THE LORD'S HOLY NAME WHILE DOING NEUTRAL ACTS OF DEMONSTRATION; OTHERWISE, THEY ARE NOT NEUTRAL.

What about tattoos and body piercing? They are huge potholes on our downhill drive. The receiving or giving out of them is NOT a neutral act of demonstration. To willingly receive or give tattoos and body piercing (a woman's simple, single earlobe puncture is addressed below) is an *act of demonstration of pleasure in self-mutilation and prideful showiness*. Acts such as these demonstrate a soul's inability to refrain from an impulse of showiness, even to the point of self-mutilation, and it is an open boast of the desire to place onto/into one's physical body a permanent advertisement/statement/display of some kind.

Young persons can be prone to fall into these traps, especially the offspring of parents who teach them that it is okay. Some parents bring their youngsters into the shops to have the marks placed onto/into them. This is an example of parents willingly passing/forcing their **sins of the flesh** onto their offspring. To do this is a violation of young victims' free will, for they are not old enough to comprehend the permanency of the act and that their bodies do not belong to their parents. Children mostly go along because they want to please their parents. Some involved with tattooing/piercing are weak-spirited souls, oh so willing to flow with the current when there is peer pressure to do so. Others are likely the opposite: strong-spirited souls who are strong for the wrong team. These ones need a firm-gentle tap on the shoulder. This book does that: *tap*.

God is more understanding with the young. For persons in their late teens and beyond, God is not so understanding. He said the following to Moses: *"Ye shall not make any cuttings in your flesh, nor print any marks upon you! I am the Lord." (Leviticus 19:28)*

God does not back away from His Word. Even a woman's single puncture through the earlobe has to be repented, either in this life or the next. The Gospels of Matthew, Mark, and Luke have Jesus indicating only perfected souls can enter heaven and be in the presence of God. *A man came to Jesus and asked, "Teacher, what good thing must I do to have eternal life?"*

Jesus said to him, "Why do you ask me about what is good? Only God is good. If you want to have eternal life, **you must obey his commandments**.*"*

"Which ones?" the man asked. Jesus explained it, but the rich guy wouldn't let go. *"I have obeyed all of these. What else must I do?"*

Jesus replied, "If you want to be perfect, go sell everything you own! Give the money to the poor, and you will have riches in heaven. Then come and be my follower."

When the young man heard this, he was sad, because he was very rich.

Jesus said to his disciples, "It is terribly hard for rich people to get into heaven. In fact, it's easier for a camel to go through the eye of a needle than for a rich person to get into God's kingdom." (Matthew 19:16-23)

The rich man claimed to have obeyed God's commandments all his life. Jesus had already said that it was enough for him to attain eternal life. But the guy was highly motivated, and he pressed Jesus. The Master Teacher's comeback shows that eternal life has levels, the highest being heaven, where God the Father resides. Imperfects cannot go all the way up there until they are perfected. In the next life, the man will learn about this, at high level in purgatory, and he will eventually come to accept the truth. All of purgatory has the Word of God available for the resident soul-persons to become familiar with. Most people die without having read the Bible and therefore know zeroes on the Word of God. The highest purgatorial levels are where souls learn to accept the more subtle rules, all of which are clearly expressed in the Good Book.

A woman's simple, single puncture does not sufficiently express as taking joy in self-mutilation. Almost no women think it fun having a needle jammed through their flesh; the experience is a negative one. So why would someone willingly go get more punctures? And to pay out money to get them while there are people starving in the world?

Still, while alive, everything we do comes by choice. We can choose today to repent our poor-spirited acts and begin to be good-spirited persons. Those who fail to repent their *acts of demonstration of pleasure in self-mutilation and prideful showiness* are NS.

Not-repentant persons who have tattoos of snakes, bugs, reptiles, and other beasts are in for a lot of harsh treatment in the next life. They have carried out *obtuse acts of demonstration against body and soul.* The skin markings reveal a devotion to ugly creatures. They are, in fact, **marks of the beast**. Snakes, reptiles, and insects are considered by the universe to be the lowest life-forms in the universe. These persons are dispatched to the lowest level down there, where burning of the metaphysical skin and vile correctional methods take place. *Jesus told them* [His disciples]*: "I saw Satan fall from heaven like a flash of lightning. I have given you the power to trample on snakes and scorpions and to defeat the power of your enemy Satan." (Luke 10:18-19)*

An open expression of repentance is enough. (For Catholics it has to be in the confessional, and for other Christians it should be with a pastor as witness.) The tattoos need not be removed. God sees what's in the person's heart and mind. He knows how hard tattoos are to get rid of. But a person certainly can try to have them excised, if so inclined. Post-repentance, the markings should be covered up with clothing, especially when in attendance at church. Pastors should insist all ministerial helpers cover their tattoos. Allowing or turning a blind eye to an open show of skin markings would imply a pastor's tacit approval of them. Scandal, contradiction, and poor example then enter the central zone of God's place of teaching and worship. The good thing about instituting/enforcing such a rule is that all parishioners would get the point without having the pastor cram it down their throats. This allows for non-ministerial parishioners to be gently, gradually drawn into accepting the truth about God *in His full Word*. Single-unit independent churches have as their head office the Lord Himself, so it would be easy for them to put the rule in place. Chain churches, not so easy. Their earthly head offices would have to do it.

As far as body piercing goes, including a woman's simple earlobe puncture, once a person repents, all material objects must be permanently removed from the sites of mutilation; to do otherwise would indicate a false repentance.

When the writer was very young, even for a woman to secure a small hole through each of her earlobes was considered by the Church and the general public a wrongful, even weird act. Women mostly used clip-on earrings back then. It gradually lost out, and many of today's Christian churches do not recognize these acts of demonstration as wrong. Don't they know God's Will and Word are immovable? For faithful women who retain a simple one-hole punch through each earlobe, if not repented in life, there will be an assigned have-to period in an upper purgatorial classroom on this particular matter alone; soul-persons will become reconnected to the Word of God. As such, ministerial helpers should remove all facial objects from their flesh-punctures while doing ministerial work. Pastors should insist on this and delete from ministerial positions those who refuse; these ones can still attend church service with the objects through their flesh, just not be ministerial helpers.

Does a reader not like what was just said? The following I say with good heart: "Please try to get past it. Don't allow the bad ideas of this so-called 'modern world' to get the best of you." *Thus says the Lord: "You object, O House of Israel* [Christian and Jewish domains]*! You say, 'The way of the Lord is unfair.' Hear now, O House of Israel: Is my way unfair? Is it not your ways that are unfair?" (Ezekiel 18:25)*

The issue goes like this. If a woman can wear an earring through an earlobe puncture, then why should not a man be allowed to do the same, for it would be discriminatory to say a woman can and a man cannot? And if one earring is allowed, what's wrong with two or three or more, if that's what the ministerial helper chooses? Once a pastor allows God's Word to be openly disobeyed by ministerial helpers, there is no stopping the level of future violations. Pastors should want to nip the problem in their parishioners' ears right away, before it spreads to the nose, tongue, neck, and wherever else.

As for the more serious incursions against one's own flesh, atoning penances can be as simple as having to carry the holes and marks as constant reminders. The two issues are not about generation gap or modern world versus old school, and that is because they've been around for many thousands of years. An angry God the Father says the following to the prophet Isaiah eight centuries prior to Jesus' coming: *"Therefore the LORD will smite with a scab the crown of the head of the daughters of Zion, and the LORD will discover their secret parts. In that day the Lord will take away the bravery of their tinkling ornaments about their feet, and their cauls, and their round tires like the moon, The chains and the bracelets, and the spangled ornaments, The bonnets, and the ornaments of the legs, and the headbands, and the tablets, and the earrings, The rings, and nose jewels, The changeable suits of apparel* [etc.] *And it shall come to pass, that instead of sweet smell there will be stink; and instead of a girdle a rent; and instead of well set hair baldness;* [etc.] *and burning instead of beauty." (3:17-24)* Who says God doesn't get angry? At least 500 years before Isaiah,

God tells Moses skin markings and punctures are no-no's. Obviously these things had to be prevalent, and the later generations didn't listen. In 1991, a well-preserved 5,300-year-old corpse was found in a receding Alps glacier. Scientists named the iceman Otzi. He had tattoos. It wasn't said he had any flesh punctures, other than the hole from the arrow that did him in, but surely the pagan had those as well, for the two go together.

[Spiritual note: What might the satanic teachers say to this category of not-repentant sinners, once they arrive inside their classrooms down there? WARNING: THE SATANIC CORRECTIONAL TEACHERS USE FOUL LANGUAGE. VIEWER DISCRETION IS ADVISED. BUT READ IT ANYWAY, FOR IT'S BETTER TO FIND OUT THIS WAY AND NOW, INSTEAD OF LATER, IN SOUL-PERSON.

"So, yas liked cuttin' up yas flesh and puttin' metal things in yas asshole-selves, did yas? Yas was all kinda stupid up there, now wasn't yas? Don't be even more fookin' stupid than yas already are by tryin' to answer me! Theys weren't fookin' questions for yas to answer! Why didn't yas use clip-ons instead, yas ass-brains, brains-dead, shits-for-brains? That way yas could have changed them now and then without havin' to put more fookin' knives into yas fookin' skins? By usin' clip-ons yas could have quit the things and yas flesh wouldn't have any fookin' leftover holes, assholes. Yeah, that's right, yas stupid ass-faced fookheads! Clip-ons! Clip-ons! Not *coooool* enough for yas, right, shits-for-brains? Yas liked someone takin' a blade to yas stupid fookin' reptile skins and cuttin' yas asshole-selves up. Well now, yas all in the right room down here for that fun stuff. Some folks down here really enjoy stickin' knives into skin. After yas get the point real, real good into yas stupid brains-dead shit-filled skulls, yas'll end up havin' to go to another special room down here, where yas stupid fookin' brains can learn about tattoos and needles gettin' poked into yas stupid skin. Why the fook didn't yas just have the things painted on yas asshole-selves up there, or use stick-ons, not that doin' those things ain't fookin' stupid, too. But at least yas could have washed them off if yas stupid brains changed their fookin' stupid shit-stinkin' minds? Not *coooool* enough, huh? Don't be fookin' tryin' to answer me, yas fook-faced assholes! Yas get what yas get, down here in our domain! Yas all need to learn! Yas'll learn, alright, by our fookin' methods."]

What about pastors and religious persons who, literally or figuratively, go around with Bibles while having markings and cuttings in their flesh? Unless they openly repent and recant them in life, they are not saved from the satanic correctional methods. Some will be granted the opportunity to do a **secondary repentance**. Secondary repentance? What's that? Jesus may allow a secondary repentance for some soul-persons. For sure, He will express His extreme anger and disappointment. Because the person had carried a

Bible and at the same time openly showed something against Will of God, the person had potentially led sheep to believe that these evil acts are okay with God. These so-called pastors and religious persons hadn't even read the Bible. Naturally, when in front of Jesus Christ, they break down in shame and by doing so show sincere repentance. This is good, yes, but full grace is not granted. The souls are saved from the lake of fire and the horrid correctional rooms of low hp-purgatory, but they are not totally saved. They must spend a long time on a tough purgatorial plane down there; they become acquainted with God's Word *in its fullness* and continue to worship. Paul makes reference to the plane: *"Therefore God highly exalted him* [Jesus] *and gave him a name that is above every name, so that at the name of Jesus every knee should bend, in heaven and on earth and* **under the earth***." (Philippians 2:9-19)* The Book of Revelation's John says, *"I saw a mighty angel ask with a loud voice, 'Who is worthy to open the scroll and break its seals?' No one in heaven or on the earth or* **under the earth** *was able to open the scroll or see inside it." (Revelation 5:2-3)* "Then I [Rev's John] *heard all beings in heaven and on the earth and* **under the earth** *and in the sea offer praise." (Revelation 5:13)* Even though this plane is not across the valley, Jesus has greater influence than Satan. Soul-persons will be required to have short stays in the shores of the lake of fire and the hall of suffering.

So you see, our acts of demonstration are very important when we leave earth-term and go before Jesus and God the Father. If during life we carried out only neutral acts . . . Well, that's better than having only negative ones to show. But this is an almost impossible keep because if we did not include God in our lives, likely the devil got in there, and we will not even know it until the life-review happens, at which time utter shame will seize us. During our travel through a life of ever-diminishing grace, the devil became more and more enabled to remove our innate ability to discern right and wrong. Today's world has millions of examples of this, in individuals, groups, organizations, nations, and churches even. To illustrate this truth, the revealer refers to the Federal Democrat Party. (The writer has no affiliation with any political party, but he's not blind.) Forty years ago, how many Fed Dems would have voted in a way that would lead to same-sex marriage and legalization of marijuana? Probably none. How many would have been for full abortion, including partial-birth abortion, where the baby is pulled out alive and stabbed in the nape of the neck? Back then, probably only a few. Today how many Fed Dems are for full legalization of all three? All and every one of them is the answer, and they are all headed for the lake of fire no matter how many times they say "Yay God" and "God bless America." God will never bless evil acts, evil people, and evil geopolitical entities. It's in the Bible—He curses them!

God the Father says, *"Again, when a righteous man* [or woman] *doth turn from his righteousness, and commit iniquity* [evil], *I lay a stumblingblock before him* [God curses him/her and he/she gets dumber and dumber and more evil], *he shall die: because thou hast not given him warning* [with this writing, I am giving out His warning], *he shall die in his sin, and his righteousness that he hath done will not be remembered; but his blood I will require at thine hand." (Ezekiel 3:20)* Later, Jesus says, *"But you can be sure that if you don't turn back to God, every one of you will also be killed* [by God's order, die fairly soon and be sent down]. *What about those eighteen people who died when the tower in Siloam fell on them? Do you think they were any worse than anyone else in Jerusalem? Not at all! But you can be sure that if you do not turn back to God* [God's Commandments and statutes], *every one of you will also die* [be sent down]." *(Luke 13:3-5)*

Chapter XLIII

Murky River

For a while, we've been traveling a section of road that runs beside a smelly waterway. Let us veer off, dive into the murky slough, and descend to its bottom. There we will vacate the vehicle and slither like American eels through thick crap. We will learn the truth about what they swim in down there. After a time, we will rise up and out of Murky River, to begin our trudge through swamps and forests that will get us to a sharp climb up a mountain.

Before continuing on, the revealer encourages the reader to make it through to the end of the book, for the Lord is infinitely forgiving of those who possess a humble, sorrowful, confident spirit when standing before Him. Thing is, we *must* recognize and repent our sins during life in order to have that confidence on the other side.

We have made Murky River's bottom. Let us exit the vehicle and begin our crawl through the vile objects of disgust: *Reprehensible Acts of Demonstration.*

Anyone who has activated for, politicized for, judicially ruled for, voted for, spoken in favor of, participated in, or helped in any way to bring in same-sex marriage (civil union, domestic partnership) is not a friend of Jesus. Unless a person sincerely repents, he/she will be condemned to the lake of fire. Jesus has shown me His extreme anger on the issue. Legally licensing something is to, in effect, socially legitimize it; sales & marketing and open displaying of it soon follow; it then has to be taught/shown to our young, impressionable children—and this is a horrendous killing of their innocent minds. To teach/show "the innocence" that homosexuality/lesbianism is a fine choice for them is an infinite mortal sin against Creation itself. Jesus has shown me that these people are not only *not* His friends, they are His enemies. For persons who fail to repent and cease in life, Jesus' cross will become a hot, killing sword. They will wish that they had never been born into the world. *"It will be terrible for people who cause even one of my little followers to sin. Those people would be better off thrown into the ocean with a heavy stone tied around their necks." (Mark 9:42)*

In today's world, there are persons who call themselves pastors and say to their flocks that same-sex marriage is okay. Some even have the audacity to do them. Here is what God the Father says in the Good Book: *"If a man also lie with mankind, as he lie with a woman, both of them have committed an abomination; they shall surely be put to death; their blood shall be upon them." (Leviticus 20:13)* We know that when persons participate in such actions they do not immediately drop dead or get struck by lightning. God is therefore speaking of the place they will be relegated to if repentance is refused in life. God may rule for a life to end quickly, via disease, accident, etc. God says to His prophet Micah, *"And I will execute vengeance in anger and fury upon the heathen* [those liar so-called pastors] *such as they have not heard." (5:15)*

Some say that when Jesus came down to earth all this stuff about proper sexual conduct changed, that somehow He came to contradict or overrule the Father. Oh, the rules changed, have they? This is what Jesus says: *"Don't suppose that I came to do away with the Law and the Prophets. I did not come to do away with them, but to give them their full meaning." (Matthew 5:17) "Not everyone who calls me their Lord will get into heaven. Only the ones who obey my Father in heaven will get in. On the day of judgment many will call me their Lord. They will say, 'We preached in your name, and in your name we forced out demons* [healed people] *and worked many miracles.' But I will tell them, 'I will have nothing to do with you! Get out of my sight, you evil people!'" (Matthew 7:21-23) The Word became a human being* [Jesus] *and lived here with us. (John 1:14)* "The Word" of what? That which comes from God the Father and not the deceitful mouths of atheists, pagans, and wolves that dress as shepherds.

A person who in God's name teaches things that are against God has committed an infinite mortal sin. Those who betray God in such a manner will be considered lower than not-repentant cold-blooded murderers, for it is the severest of sins against the Holy Spirit to teach in the name of God that evil is okay. You see, cold-blooded murderers do not have power over their victims' souls. To the public, cold-blooded murderers come across as cold-blooded murders, and they fool no one. With regard to those who betray God in the manner mentioned above, here is what Jesus says: *"Watch out for false prophets* [false pastors]*! They dress up like sheep, but inside they are wolves that have come to attack you* [fool you]*. You can tell what they are by what they do* [their personal lifestyles]*. No one picks* [God won't pick] *grapes or figs* [men or women] *from thorn bushes* [churches that teach evil as okay]*. Every tree* [organization] *that produces bad fruit* [corrupt souls] *will be chopped down."* *(Matthew 7:15-17, 19)*

The betrayers might shout, "The Old Testament says slavery and polygamy are okay, and therefore the book is 'old school' and nothing it says can be totally counted on as Godly truth!" The revealer's short rebuff to these ignorant assholes is *"You stupid Galatians! How can you be so stupid?" (Galatians 3:13)* "Sooooo you stupid Episcopalians, you stupid Unitarians, you stupid Universalists, you stupid Congregationalists, you stupid United Baptists, you stupid of the so-called United Church of Christ (UCC), you stupid Presbyterians (a lot of them but not all), you stupid of the so-called United Methodist (a lot of them but not all), and you stupid Lutherans (some and getting worse), show me where exactly in the Foundation Testament God approves of those two things." God never addresses them in a positive way. He knows they exist. Concerning slavery, He strictly advises those who have slaves/servants to treat them well and eventually set them free. Regarding homosexual/lesbian lifestyle/marriage, which the above denominations all approve of by their advertising "We are an *affirming* Christian church that welcomes all, regardless of personal lifestyle," the following is what God the Father says to Isaiah: *"The show of their countenance doth witness against them; and they declare their sin as Sodom, they hide it not. Woe to their soul! For they have rewarded evil unto themselves."* (3:9) *"Woe to them that call evil good, and good evil; that put darkness for light, and light for darkness; that put bitter for sweet, and sweet for bitter!"* (5:20).

Jesus' revealer will delve just deep enough into the abortion issue. Every reader knows the two human views. What about God's view? Even believers in abortion know the answer to that.

The long and the short of it is this. Anyone who has been involved in the promoting of or carrying out of abortion is not a friend of Jesus. Failing repentance (I repented!), an abortion doctor/nurse/facilitator/enabler/encourager/doer will not have the wounds of Christ to shield her/him from God the Father's wrath. The Gospel of Luke tells of the Sadducees who come to question Jesus. He answers, *"In the story about the burning bush, Moses clearly shows that people will live again. He said, 'The Lord is the God worshipped by Abraham, Isaac, and Jacob.' So the Lord isn't the God of the dead, but of the living. This means that everyone* [everyone deemed worthy to rise from death (Luke 20:35)] *is alive as far as God is concerned." Some of the teachers of the Law of Moses said, "Teacher, you have given a good answer!" (Luke 20:37-39)* God the Father loves infants. He is the God of life, not death. Failing a sincere repentance while alive, pro-abortion/-choice politicians (leaders of countries!), judges (supreme court justices!), and so-called human-rights activists will—just like the abortion doctors, nurses, and carriers—be condemned.

Immediately after judgment is pronounced, the satanics rush in to grab hold of the convicted killer, to hustle her/him down to the lake of fire.

Jesus has shown the revealer that right at the moment God grants (through an Angel of God) conception, a pre-selected soul is "corded" (by an Angel of God) to the woman's womb; in this way the two are enabled to get spiritually/emotionally accustomed/"attached" to each other. The system God uses is His and not for humans to tamper with. When the fetus gets large enough to accommodate the compressed (by an Angel of God) soul, the re-formed soul is compelled (by an Angel of God) to overlap the cellular unit; the two then become as one. The "rule of God" has *the process of human life* beginning at conception. In God's eyes, persons of abortion are deliverers of death.

[Spiritual note: Four thousand years ago, the Angel of God asks Abraham to offer up his child Isaac as a way to prove his fear of and obedience to the One True God. Abraham's heathen-pagan contemporaries are very obedient to their demon gods in their slaying of enemies and their enemies' children in sacrificial ceremonies. Would Abraham show a superior obedience by sacrificing his own beloved son? Good question—would Abraham do it? Yes, by his showing a sincere act of demonstration of his preparedness to do so. Just as Abraham is about to slay Isaac, the Angel of God calls down from heaven. *"Abraham, Abraham, Lay not thy hand upon the lad, neither thou do anything unto him: for now I know that thou fearest God, seeing thou hast not withheld thy son, thine only son from me." (Genesis 22:12)* The true God, Yahweh, demonstrates that He does not want nor need that stuff, for He is the Great Creator of Life.

This is a good spot to talk about the Angels of God. There are levels or, if you will, "classifications" of Angels of God. All retain strong sentient powers of projection. At the levels of Warring Angels (wide angels around 7 feet in height, give or take) and above—to the level of Archangel—great powers have been granted them by God. A Warring Angel of God could be compared to the powerhouse robot in the original movie *The Day the Earth Stood Still*. But an angel is a living energy-entity and not something made of metal alloys; they are not clones and each has a name. In the movie, the robot attended to and protected Michael Reny's human-looking alien role. Angels who are closer to the size of humans might be Guardian Angels; others might be attendants to human conception, delivering and attaching the re-formed soul-person to the mother and a little later transferring it into the fetus. There are still other classes of Angels of God who have specific duties *in God's Will*. They can show their wings or not show them, depending.]

What about those who say that people should look at the total person and not be so concerned about one or a couple issues. "People need to grow beyond their differences and concentrate on their common ground." I have heard pastors tout this. One time I heard a Catholic priest say it on a national news show when he publicly offered his support for a presidential candidate who was for same-sex marriage and abortion at all stages of pregnancy. In other words, these so-called pastors are teaching their listeners that it's okay to ignore the evil stuff. The revealer's response is "How many good deeds does a person need to do in the afternoon and evening to make up for killing babies in the morning? Just how much murdering of the Will and Word of God is okay for one party to do as long as both parties agree to get along? Should one simply ignore the rotten, smelly crap the other carries in its briefcase?"

I do not care how many good deeds a priest or a pastor may do during life, unless there is an open repentance and recantation of this deceitful advice, Jesus will chastise the person as a betrayer of Divine Truth. She/he will not escape the hard hand of correction. Now having said that, the revealer is not claiming that everyone in this category will go to the lake of fire. What I'm saying is they will at best have to do time in the hell levels of purgatory, where they will again and again be reminded, by the satanics, of the difference between stupidity and God's Will.

What about those who say that they are not personally for abortion but are pro-choice? That dirty laundry does not wash with God. These ones are enablers. Many women regret having an abortion. Many claim that they would not have pursued the option had it not been legal, and, as such, would have that little baby love in their arms, a baby love that they now miss so much. Does not God see this? Does not God know that almost all women would have loved their babies the instant they were born and placed in their arms? Oh, what a love it could have been!

"What about my daughter who died while having an unsafe abortion? If clinical abortion had been available in East Vassalboro, she would be alive today. It's the government's fault she died. It's all those Bible-thumpers' fault, too!" No woman, no matter how old, who dies during an abortion is saved. God's view on the matter is unmoving: there is no such thing as safe abortion for the baby. For a carrier to physically die while in the process of carrying out this reprehensible act of demonstration means immediate condemnation to hell. Parents that push for expansion of legal abortion because their daughter died during an unsafe one will, unless repented, end up going to the same place their daughter did. They would be far better off saying to themselves and to their pastor, "Our daughter made some terrible mistakes. We want to pray to God that He have mercy on us." And pray, pray, pray. All their lives, they should pray to God about it, that is, if they truly loved their daughter. "Pastor, please remember us in your prayers."

But because *displaced pride* drowns out the excellent qualities of humility and Godly-righteousness, parents and media will often end up promoting the legalization of acts of evil, even the reprehensible ones. When successful, they feel a good has been accomplished. These are Satan's end-time miracles, the perps his servants.

This book does not address the subject of abortion for a rape/incest victim and for a woman whose life is in danger if she were to continue in the pregnancy—except to say that an overriding problem with all abortions is what the acts of demonstration do (in God's eyes) to the hands of the soul-persons who actually do the abortions (doctors, nurses, etc.) and how it may encourage others who want to have an abortion to lie about the reason why, considering if abortion were illegal except in the three situations mentioned above. A previous book, *Messiah Bridge (MB): Handbook for Pastors and Prisoners* (2007), gets heavily into this area.

My particular circumstance, in the late 1970s, had my mate not telling me she was pregnant. A couple months prior to having the abortion, she had been out of the pill for a few days; this fact she also had not shared with me. She did not divulge the pregnancy until after the abortion. When I asked her why she had done this, her response was, "I thought you might have wanted to play dad." I recognized that on top of the abortion, her *act of demonstration of haughty coldness* meant our relationship had to be annulled. After it was sealed off dead, I began to go the way of the Bible's prodigal son, gradually descending a river road leading into dark waters, where alcohol, gambling, and female flesh received me with open arms.

This prodigal son eventually sickened of the polluted water's crap-strewn bottom, swam to the surface, climbed out and onto the opposite shore, and began a walk through swampland and dry forest. That was when I met Kerry Ann, in late 1988, while I was still in woods but at least out of Murky River. I was faithful to her the whole 11 years we were together.

As mentioned earlier, it was not until a couple years prior to the turn of the millennium that I went properly back to the Lord. The abortion was recounted in my confession of sins. Almost instantly, the heart and mind felt peaceful resolve. Today, my spirit retains a warm feeling for my former mate. In the early 2000s, I got a phone call from her. After that, we had several more conversations by phone. She had been residing in Florida since the early 1990s, in a city not that far from Melbourne. The last exchange had her wanting to fly in to see me. With a kind and gentle voice, I declined, and we have not spoken since.

This I know for sure, Jesus has forgiven me and that is because I went to Him and asked. About a year after my "big one" **primary repentance**, the Divine visitations began. When I am taken to Jesus, He instructs me in short; sometimes He scolds me in short.

Someday everyone will come before God. Christians will have Jesus in front of or beside them. Others won't but instead will have Satan standing beside or across from them, to accuse them to God. *"And he* [Angel of God] *showed me* [prophet Zechariah] *Joshua the high priest before the angel of the LORD, and Satan standing at his right hand to resist* [accuse] *him. And the LORD said unto Satan, The LORD rebuke thee, O Satan;" (Zech 3:1-2)* There will be no defense attorney there. Nor will there be a parent/spouse/sibling/friend. Each person is responsible for her/his own personal integrity or lack of it and, hence, salvation or condemnation. During the review of earth-term performance, the person's emitting energy will take on one of two natures. 1) Having failed repentance in life, she/he will be annihilated into a being of utter shame at the sight of every evil act of demonstration that was done. God may allow the soul's descent into shame to count as a secondary repentance, for He gets no joy in sending anyone to the lake of fire. The most debased souls are not granted secondary repentance, and the satanics immediately come to take them down. 2) Having chosen to reflect/acknowledge/repent while alive, the soul-person will be better accepting of her/his life-review, even when evil acts of demonstration are gone over. The person will have the grace to become elated at the fulfilled promise of eternal life. As shown in Ezekiel (18:21-23), it is God Who grants life to the soul. *"If the wicked turn away from all their sins that they have committed and keep all my statutes and do what is lawful and right, they shall surely live; they shall not die* [they shall not be condemned]. *None of the transgressions that they have committed shall be remembered against them; for the righteous they have done they shall surely live* [be saved]. *Have I any pleasure in the death of the wicked? saith the Lord God; and not that he* [she] *should turn from his* [her] *ways, and live?"*

In the second scenario, the soul may have to do time in JB purgatory in order to clear (do sin-atonement), invisibly task in the physical world (to gain merit), and cleanse defective desires from the soul's condition. Defective desires, such as smoking cigarettes or needing to drink cola/coffee all day long or constantly shop, are spiritually referred to as *displaced affections*.

[Spiritual note: There are levels of sin. Things like nicotine addiction, abuse of prescription pain meds, mild social-drinking issue ("I can't calm down without two glasses of red wine every evening."), an over-predilection to coffee ("Ten cups a day and no sonsabitch better get in my way."), and infrequent masturbation (versus "frequent," which means addiction, but infrequent isn't exactly good) fall into the category of *displaced affections*. Does a person love them more than God? For sure, they can be hard to quit. Some we don't have to, but instead just reduce to a level that shows *intelligent moderation*. Some we need to at least try to quit while alive.]

Marijuana-use does not qualify as a displaced affection. Users, even occasional users—because they, too, are helping to keep alive a very evil system and the myth that the drug is harmless—and promoters/enablers of marijuana-use are definitely not friends of the Divine. These ones are acutely satanically infiltrated, which means their souls are diabolically disoriented in every area of life. They believe in abortion, same-sex marriage, all kinds of open gambling, skin markings and punctures, pornography, etc., and they cannot stop swearing and using the words "shit" and "farts" and "fucking" and "holy shit" and "holy fucking shit" and "holy fucking Jesus" in their everyday speech. Amazingly, these ones believe something is wrong with Christians (*true* ones). Friends of so-called medical-use marijuana are friends of death and not friends of Jesus. All who die as not-repentant friends of marijuana are NS.

A recently completed medical study (2009) done out of Canada's McGill University concludes that daily cannabis use by young persons leaves permanent effects on the brain by inhibiting/reducing the presence of certain compounds essential for the brain's normal development during this very key growth stage. Besides its effects showing as depression and anxiety in the adolescents, the altered brain condition remains into and throughout adulthood. For adults, mental illnesses, such as schizophrenia, may show out.

If the effects of pot-use are that bad on teenagers, certainly one can assume the effects are not exactly good on adults who use the stuff. After body-death, the soul-person crosses over exactly in the same condition it had died. There is no smoking of any kind in paradise and heaven. As already stated, the soul-person is an energy-entity, and every microscopic point within the energy-entity retains the full memory of being in a human body. The heart and mind areas of the energy-entity retain the exact desires and wishes that the body-soul coalition trained into it while on earth. Death of the body ended the coalition, and the soul-person is now stuck with exactly what it had allowed the body to train it to become. The soul-person cannot achieve positive change without a body to use for that purpose. This is another reason why God allows for JB purgatory. It is only there that a soul can achieve purification, correction, atonement. When we cross over, all bodily markings, including tattoos and body piercings, are retained. Only if we repented them in life will God allow for them to be immediately excised from our metaphysical presentation; otherwise, by way of a successful secondary repentance (for those granted it by Jesus), they have to be gradually lifted out through painful purgatorial processes.

Unless soul-persons are like young children in their purity of hearts and minds, they are not allowed to enter paradise or heaven. *Some people brought their children to Jesus, so that he could place his hands on them and pray for them. His disciples told the people to stop bothering him. But Jesus said, "Let the children come to me, and don't try to stop them! People who are like these children belong to God's kingdom." (Matthew 19:13-14)*

Abortion, same-sex marriage, legalization of marijuana, and legalized euthanasia are watershed issues for both heaven and hell. If Satan's human servants can successfully achieve their legalization, he knows today's humanity is defeated. Almost all young children would grow up corrupted, with either nil or satanically disoriented concepts about right and wrong and about God. We're basically there already. Very soon, God's hand, though reluctant and getting no joy from it, will come smashing down. Yes, the good will suffer with the bad, but the good soul-persons will be saved. After a long dark valley, the slow re-forming of humanity will be allowed to begin.

Chapter XLIV

The Murky Swim Up

Let us now leave Murky River's bottom and begin our swim to the surface. Please be advised that the swim up is not a whole lot better than crawling the bottom, but at least we will be able to see a little bit of daylight penetrating down from above.

What about suicide? A parent might say, "My son was only fifteen when he shot himself to death. Is he in hell forever?"

In the good spirit world, suicide is considered a reprehensible act of demonstration against the soul housed inside the physical body, and even worse it is considered a horrendously selfish act that severely strikes at the souls of those who loved the person. Adults who commit suicide are always severely judged. Anyone who acted like a Kevorkian and facilitated a person into suicide will be considered a murderer and condemned to hell if there is failure to repent to Jesus during life. If and when possible, we should help the downtrodden in positive, non-threatening ways and never contribute to a person deciding for suicide.

Youngsters who inflict themselves in such a way may not receive as harsh a judgment. It depends on pre-circumstances of each situation. If the suicide was part of some satanic or weird loyalty pact, the person is immediately condemned. When a human has been so mistreated that she/he is all messed up in the head, God may show mercy—but heaven is not in the stars. The soul-person will have to go through punitive processes in purgatory, after which will take place a lengthy preparation for a God Blessed Rebirthment into the world at a future time, so that the soul-person can, hopefully, produce better outcome. It can be hundreds of earth years before that happens. She/he had so much preplanning, hope, and promise prior to birthing into the last earth-term, which ended up being full-term self-aborted. God's system doesn't see fit to rush.

A young person who died by way of drug overdose may or may not be judged as harshly an adult who died that way. Here, too, each situation is reviewed in its pre-circumstances. Adults who die through drug overdose/alcohol poisoning are condemned to hell.

At suicide funerals it should never be said that God called the person home, that God's Will has been done, that she/he is now in a better place. The utterance is heresy, a brazen insult to the God's Holy Face, and a "populist" lie meant to appease listeners' ears. It absolutely does not appease God! Presuming on God's mercy in such a heretical manner is a severe breach of Truth in Light; hence, the one called a pastor has sinned very badly. The Catholic Church used to preach about the severity of presuming on God's mercy and on how the living faithful should instead pray to God and accept the penances He sends down as second-hand atonement. Recent decades have seen the excellent instruction disappear in favor of "popular-isms" (populism).

Often it is the young who self-abort. Attending their funerals are others their age. What's the message to these young grieving minds? *God wanted my friend/brother/sister to commit suicide? Maybe that's God's plan for me, too.* I know of a Catholic family of four who attended my parish. The father committed suicide. Time passed, and his oldest son killed himself. A couple years passed before the mother did herself in. She thought it was okay to leave behind her 14-year-old son to fend for himself. What's he supposed to think? *God called my family home to be with Him in heaven? Maybe I should think about joining them.*

Instead of falsehood, talk should be about how too many exit this world as poor souls and how prayers from the living can help them. Why should we pray? The answer goes to what Jesus says when asked which is the greatest commandment. *Jesus answered: "Love the Lord your God with all your heart, soul, and mind. This is the first and most important commandment. The second most important commandment is like this one. And it is, 'Love others as much as you love yourself.'"*(Mark 12; Matthew 22; Luke 10) *Jesus told his disciples: "Have faith in God! If you have faith in God and don't doubt, you can tell this mountain to get up and jump into the sea. Everything you ask for in prayer will be yours, if you only have faith."* (Mark 11:23-24) Jesus told his disciples a story about how they should keep on praying and never give up: [He follows with the parable about a judge who is frequently approached by a widow and how the widow's persistence finally causes the judge to cave in, even though he personally does not agree with her.] Jesus says, *"Won't God protect his chosen ones who pray to him day and night? Won't he be concerned for them? He will surely hurry and help them."* (Luke 18:1,7-8)

God will not forsake the person who strives to become the aforementioned Bibles verses. In His infinite love and mercy, God will reward the one who perseveres in loving, prayerful commitment to Him. Because He knows that this devotee has great concern for the eternal salvation of a particular person who was known to have died as a poor soul, He will allow the soul-person to be raised through purgatory. He will eventually grant another earth-term through His particular grace of God Blessed Rebirthment.

But how many of us pray like that? Oh, how we like to expound to others on how much we loved and now miss that dead one and on how we suppose that the dead person is, from her/his heavenly perch above, keeping watch down on us. Where exactly is that in the Bible? This is nothing but spiritual ignorance and empty assumption. It's pagan love and pagan love doesn't save even one soul. Maybe that's why pagans don't like the Bible. Instead, they prefer séances, tarot cards, and mediums, none of which has lift. *"Ye shall not eat anything with the blood: neither shall you use enchantment, nor observe times. Regard not them that have familiar spirits, neither seek after wizards, to be defiled by them: I am the Lord your God." (Leviticus 19:26,31)* *"Yes, God will make his home among his people. He will wipe away all the tears from their eyes, and there will be no more death, suffering, crying, or pain. But I will tell you what will happen to cowards and to everyone who is unfaithful or dirty-minded or is sexually immoral or uses witchcraft or worships idols or tells lies. They will be thrown into the lake of fire and burning sulphur. This is the second death* [no secondary repentance granted]*."(Revelation 21:3-4,8)* Even before these ones experience body-death, God curses them, and their lives become more and more depressed. God says to Isaiah, *"And they shall say unto you, Seek unto them that have familiar spirits, and unto wizards that peep, and that mutter: should not a people seek unto their God? for the living than to the dead? And they shall look unto the earth; and behold trouble and darkness, dimness of anguish; and they shall be driven to darkness." (8:19,22)* Jesus says, *"Let the dead take care of the dead, while you go and tell about God's kingdom." (Luke 9:60)*

Only God or an Angel of God sent by Him has the power to bend down and lift up a soul, so that He may reward the living person who constantly prays to Him. In Chapter 2 of the Gospel of Mark, Jesus is centered in a crowd of faithful people. Present is a crippled man who begs for healing. *When Jesus saw how much faith they had, he said to the crippled man, "My friend, your sins are forgiven." (Mark 2:5)* When Jesus sees the teachers of the Law of Moses wondering why He said that, He responds, *"Why are you thinking such things? Is it easier for me to tell the crippled man that his sins are forgiven or to tell him to get up and pick up his mat and go home? I will show you that the son of Man has the right to forgive sins here on earth." (Mark 2:8-10)* He says in Revelation, *"Don't be afraid! I am the first, the last, and the living one. I died,* but now I am alive forevermore, and I have the keys to death and the world of the dead." *(Revelation 1:17-18)* Jesus has the keys. Means He can lock up and let out whenever He chooses.

[Spiritual note: What exactly is a "pagan," anyway? He and she are two people who revel in, so to speak, the dirt of earth. Irreligious in make up, pagans are godless in the sense that they lack any meaningful cognition of the one true Creator God. Pagans often use the term "god" in a half-baked, illiterate manner. They do not have the Spirit of God in them and instead rely on muscle strength, violence, addictions, mediums, senseless belief-systems, and human idolization as their gods. *"The Spirit is the one who gives life* [quality spiritual intelligence that leads the soul to eternal life]*! Human strength can do nothing." (John 6:63)* Very few people refer to themselves as pagans. Doesn't matter. The label applies by way of persons' beliefs and lifestyles, regardless of whether they say they're Christian/Jewish/Muslim. Pagans are heathens, but heathens are not necessarily pagans. Heathens are godless hedonists who either don't believe in spiritual things whatsoever or willingly attach themselves to Satan (e.g. biker gangs, those who praise Satan and do the satanic hand-signal: a physical act of demonstration of one's faith in Satan).]

The tap on your shoulder is done with gentle kindness, as another reminder of God's infinite mercy and forgiveness for those who go to Him and repent. The real truths about sin and evil are hard truths for those encased inside them, and so there has to be applied a little bit of firmness. Reader, I hope you can see that.

Too, the writer is well aware that the reader might view all this "spiritual stuff" as nothing more than hogwash, that the concepts of sin, repentance, afterlife, spirit world, and judgment are fictional things meant for the weak of mind. My response is that it does not matter what anyone thinks, because right after body-death a stark truth sets in: "I have total awareness." Dreadful fear now enters the soul-person. Who needs that outcome? Why not cross the valley to the good side today, while alive, if you have not already done so.

Judgment doesn't necessarily happen right away, but for the *not-repentant* really bad it does: drug dealers, hard-drug users, marijuana promoters and chronic users, alcoholics, abortion providers, scientists of death (e.g. cloners and abortofacient inventors/makers), producers of pornography, delighters in pornography, suicide assisters, cold-blooded killers, the violent, brawlers, abusers, torturers, delighters of torture (e.g. makers of torture movies), mafia and all others of organized crime groups, terrorists, Satan's devotees, so-called pastors who do same-sex marriages, participators in same-sex marriages, gay pride parade participators/organizers, and those who publicly belittled the names of Christ and God. Their staggeringly negative impact on young persons and society in general leaves the bowl of mercy empty for them. They are immediately condemned to the lake of fire. What about self-proclaimed witches and séance-doers? *"Stand now with thine enchantments, and with the multitude of thy sorceries, ... Thou art wearied in the multitude of thy counsels. Let now the astrologers, the stargazers, the monthly prognosticators, stand up. . . . Behold, they are as stubble; the fire shall burn them; they shall not deliver themselves from the power of the flame:" (47:12-14)*

Other souls may be allowed to wander the netherworld as a form of being in abeyance prior to judgment. They interact with other netherworld wanderers. Behaviors are observed and recorded by the Angels of God and other senior spirit guides. Satan knows God's rules and therefore knows which ones he cannot take down. But he can harass them to a degree.

I will give the reader a few examples of the places the Angel of God has taken me so that I could learn and tell people about them. Men and women who had angrily blasted out the names "God" and "Christ" had, in actuality, carried out a form of satanic prayer. These acts of demonstration pleased Satan and definitely not Jesus and God the Father. With hate filling their minds and hearts, the persons stomped on and molested the Lord's name in front of others. These others, including young children, may have been brought to do the same. Unless repented in life, and if their other sins are not warranting of immediate condemnation to the lake of fire, people who abused the Lord's name are thrown into rooms occupied by not-repentant-dead violent homosexuals and lesbians. They have to remain there and not just for a few hours. They receive correction by way of molestation. The ones doing the raping shout out things like—WARNING: THE FOLLOWING CONTENT CONTAINS FOUL LANGUAGE AND GRAPHIC IMAGES. VIEWER DISCRETION IS ADVISED. BUT READ IT ANYWAY AND LEARN!

"Yas molested God's name, did yas? Well now, yas deserve this, don't yas! Yas won't be ever doin' that again, now will yas?" Souls have to answer yes or no. If soul-persons keep saying the latter, Satan will eventually have to allow them to be released to another same-level purgatorial room or to a slightly higher-level room. If hateful defiance persists, then she/he cannot leave and may eventually be flung into the lake of fire. This does not happen much because in that horrid locker room the will of the soul gets annihilated. No soul-person willingly chooses the lake of fire. "Our boss, Mr. Satan, says wees has to ask yas the same question. Will yas be molesting the Lord's name again?"

"No, I won't. I promise."

"Well now, that's too bad for us 'cause wees loved yas assholes so much. Yas'll be goin' to another room with assholes just like yas asshole-selves. The *evil-lotion* room. There yas get to pick at each other's assholes and noses and eat the stuff. And when those dick-brain laugh tracks go off, yas better laugh. Yas have to jump around like apes and make grunty little noises. None of yas are allowed to talk to each others. Yas point yas fingees at things and at each other's body parts and make ape noises and beat yas chests. That's because yas believed that yas asshole-selves came from apes and not from God. Yas believed that, right? Answer me, asshole-mouth!"

"Yes, I believed that."

"Mr. Satan is here to take yas away. Smile and go along with him. Smile, asshole-mouth, future shit-eater, shit-head-full-of-boogers brain! Smile, I said!"

"Okay, I'm smiling." (laugh track)

"Here he is, sir. He's a learned person, now that we've had our fun teachin' him."

"Oh, he's a learned person, is he? Ask him if he ever dressed as a woman up there."

"I did but—"

"Don't talk to him directly, shit-for-brains, girlie-girl. Mr. boss-angel was talkin' to me."

"He's still yours. I'll be back . . . *whenever*. Make sure to use the laugh track often."

"So, fook-faced girlie-girl, yas still with us. How many times did yas dress as a woman?"

"Well . . . only three times that I can remember."

"Why did yas do it?"

"Once for Halloween. The other two times for acting jobs." (laugh track)

"In other words, yas stupid fook-faced girlie-girl, one time was for fun and the other two for money. Well, yas gonna get to do it a lot more times than that for us. We have a whole big wardrobe room for ones like yas. Wees all gonna watch yas stroll out on the runway, showin' off yas big new bras luggin' falsies inside 'em. Theys lots of different high heels in there, and teddys and skimpy little sexy panties, too. Yas'll get to wear them all and get us excited. Don't fookin' worry, wees pay yas good money for the shows, tit-face. And wees expect yas to laugh with the laugh track when wees playin' a fun game of poker with yas assholes later." (laugh track)

Souls granted secondary repentance may get assigned to personal prison cells instead of rape rooms. Relevant Words of God will be written on the walls. God says, *"The woman shall not wear that which pertaineth unto a man, neither shall a man put on a woman's garment: for all that do so are an abomination unto the Lord thy God." (Deuteronomy 22:5)* Learn!

Another night after falling asleep, my soul-person-self was removed (by the Angel of God) from my cellular body and escorted to a spiritual cavern deep inside the earth. Hollowed out of bedrock, the area was about the size of a large living room, with a ceiling a little higher than normal. An entrance to a dark tunnel was in one of the corners. The room was dimly lit, but it was enough for me to see their pink, wounded female flesh. There were 12 naked women in wrist and ankle chains. The lower half of their bodies were standing upright, but their upper bodies were bent over a metal railing; hands and feet were tightly linked to the floor; it was as if each were doing a permanent toe touch. They were bent over the railing in order for their rear ends to stay firmly propped up for the demons' desires. They were not-repentant prostitutes, women of pornography, Hollywood bimbos, and women who had falsely accused men of molestation. They were in a position to receive again and again from the demons exactly what they had chosen to do to men during life up there on the surface. On top of that, they had constantly molested the Lord's name. Satan's group was quite content to carry out their career duties as deliverers of retributive justice and correctional instruction. It was only for "reasons of God" that these particular women had been granted the minimum grace of not being thrown into the lake of fire. The satanics were allowed to take them down to this room and chain them, then abuse them in every way. Perhaps God, in His judgment, considered how poorly the women had been raised and treated as young children. Likely their not-repentant parents are also down there.

I was instantly disgusted and begged for their release. "Dear Lord God, they are souls with brains! Please have mercy on these pathetic creatures!" Because of my being in good standing with Him, my appeal was accepted as intercessory. He allowed them to be released from the rape room and move up to a less harsh purgatorial position. But the Lord required that I give something of myself to pay off a portion of their debts. My begging to God basically came down to this: "Is my innate love strong enough to suffer for them, so that they may move up to a better situation, or are my prayers empty words?"

When soul-person-me came back into my cellular body, I immediately became very sick. It was as if a thousand tiny, angry fleas waved into me through my left side. Within a few hours it felt like I was infected with stomach flu, Hong Kong Flu, and bronchitis all at the same time. For over a week I suffered like you cannot believe. A relentless brain-wrenching headache was also thrown into the equation. On the third and fourth nights, I burned as if there were hot charcoals everywhere inside me. My skin was red and felt burnt. I decided not to see a doctor.

Another night I was taken to a large hall-type place down there. It was filled with men in sport jacket and tie. Each clutched a Bible. But they were in pink tutus, pink stockings, and high heels. I understood that the satanics frequently stop by to laugh at and torment them. This is proper punishment in their next life. They deceived the flocks they were supposed to be leading.

These so-called pastors had not only *not* preached God's Word on living a homosexual/lesbian lifestyle, they had had the audacity to say that God does not care about that stuff. "God has more important things to be concerned about." Down there, souls keep their earth-titles, and that way the satanics can humiliate them even more and over and over. If these betrayers had participated in that lifestyle and failed to repent during life, they get thrown in to the lake of fire instead of coming here.

During their mid- and late-teens, even into their early 20s, Kandis and James were frequently, carefully taught on the subject of man-woman courtship and marriage, sometimes when the three of us were together, sometimes one on one. "Kandis, you have to be very careful because a large percentage of your generation's men are into pornography, which means that they are training their minds and hearts to see women as sex objects. You have to be careful about who you go out with on an official date. If your gut tells you to stay away, I don't care how physically attractive the guy is, the relationship is a loser from the start. If you see him as a kind-hearted individual who is respectful toward you, and he is someone who is careful about his demeanor and retains a humble, quality self-respect, I don't care how physically plain he may look, you should give him a shot. Courtship is a period of time during which the two of you can determine whether or not you can lovingly and respectfully share your lives together. Desire for sexual intimacy is a natural outgrowth from an initial stage of attraction that later moves to the realization that the two of you truly do make a good match and should commit. Sharing your bodies intimately is fab, and it can help both of you grow love in the heart and mind for each other.

"And, James, stay out of the Internet porn and any other porn. A relationship with a woman is not about sex. It is about *wanting to fill a longing in your heart*. Sexual intimacy is just one way of expressing your love for her. You must cherish the woman you choose, otherwise don't choose her. And you must treat her with extra-special respect. If a woman you date indicates early on that she wants you to be a macho superman and a partier, dump her right away. You can never be happy with that type, and, quite frankly, she'll never be happy with you for more than a few weeks or months. You should stay away from any woman who flaunts herself indecently. All she wants to do is get every guy in her zone to stare at her. Some women are graced with natural beauty and do not go out of their way to augment it. One of these is probably fine to consider as a potential 'woman of interest.' And don't bother with anyone who is argumentative and conceited. Though she may indeed be a physical marvel to look at, she should be dating, marrying, and divorcing the guy who is just like her—showy, loud, crude, disrespectful, pushy, argumentative, punches men, and loves bars and alcohol. Listen to me close on this. Satan runs Hollywood and in recent decades he has been getting his servant writers, producers, directors, and actors/actresses to show viewers that it is fine for women to hit men, funny even, worthy of laughs. 'Kick him in the groin and laugh as he bends over in pain.' Satan figures most people who watch his shows are stupid and will laugh at anything when the laugh track goes off. Even when a daughter punches her dad! James, forget her! Do you hear me?"

"Yup. I hear you."

"Another thing, my children. When you're married, wear pajamas to bed and don't be doing naked every night. Just some nights. Don't be like those godless, grunty-assed heathens and pagans. Buy nice pajamas and don't be sloppy. Sloppiness shows lack of personal dignity and disrespect for your mate. Insist your mate be the same as you on this issue. Set these ground rules before you get married, and discuss how many kids you want and when you want them.

"And there's more. When you make love, that's a time to share your nakedness. You shouldn't want to get to the place where you take each other's flesh for granted. When making love, you both might want to unwrap each other like a special present. Maybe say to your partner, 'When we make love I want you to be opening me up just like a Christmas present, but a lot more often than Christmas.' Be lovingly playful with your mate." Whenever I presented this part, in the various ways that I did, they always laughed. But they seemed to accept my every word. The years to come will bear it out as true or not.

"Still, when you're older adults, you'll end up doing what you want—I know that. I'm not trying to boss you around. You have free will. But I tell you straight, marriage isn't a license to treat your mate any way you feel like. I never want to hear that you're being overbearing, bossy, confrontational, disrespectful. Your partner is supposed to be special in a good way, not a bad way. It's not, 'Well, now that I love you, I can treat you any way I want. If you truly love me then you'll just take all the garbage I spew at you.' That's definately *not-not-not* okay.

"Both of you, listen carefully to me on the following. If during courtship your partner strikes out at you verbally or physically in rage, you must immediately end the relationship, even if it's the night before your wedding, even if it's a week after it. If you're prone to forgive and put behind, do it only once. If your so-called mate strikes out at you again, end the relationship right then—no ifs, ands, or buts. The partner's heart is not married to yours. He or she is married to violence and control, not real love. Forgiving the person is a must, but absolutely do not stay with him or her for even one more minute. Do not validate their violent temper. Do not—DO NOT—enable them to do it again by your staying. Instead, by your ending the relationship, you are enabling them to change to better ways. Maybe the former mate will grow to think, *Guess I shouldn't be such an idiot. Doesn't work for me or my partner.*

"As well, marriage partners are not prisoners to each other. Both need to have a feeling of freedom yet at the same time retain a strong desire to be together. But not at every moment. Marriage doesn't mean you're tied at the hip.

"You should have a separate hobby or pastime, or enjoy hobbies together but have individual expertise, like an assembled team would. You must be able to trust each other. If your partner's pastime is drinking with friends in bars, that's not a pastime, that's a man-jerk or a woman-jerk who craves to have his or her ego stroked by way of getting hit on. For twelve years, ah, before I met your mother, I chose to be a man-jerk flirting around with women-jerks. I know both jerks real well. Saint Paul said we must be as cunning as the serpent. How else to be as cunning as the serpent than to have actually been one for so long?

"Be good-spirited with each other. Make decisions together unless you prefer that your partner make most of them. That's fine, as long as that's what you both want. You were supposed to have come to know and love each other beforehand. There must have been a lot of commonalties. If not, why did you get married? Most things you'll agree on, but not everything. Don't ever look at making hard decisions as some kind of competition. Be open-minded but not stupid. If your partner wants to do something irresponsible, like drive inebriated or spend a pile of money irresponsibly, you *must* put your foot down. For really tough decisions in life, and often these can be on children issues, why not go by the fifty-fifty rule. 'Dear, last time we went with your view. On this particular matter I feel very strong, so let's try it my way this time.' And afterward, never say 'I told you so' when the outcome didn't turn out good. Your partner will likely already recognize it. Be a healing balm and not a nuclear bomb to your partner's spirit. Have a sense of humor and always be ready to give out lots of kindness and understanding."

We now rise up and out of Murky River, onto its opposite shore. The daunting swamplands and thick woods await our passage. For encouragement and establishing direction of movement, we begin the long journey by using a telescope to view the distant mountaintop, so that we may imagine ourselves already up there.

Chapter XLV

The Spirit World and God Blessed Rebirthment

A night in May 2003 I rest in bed, praying for God's Holy Spirit to help me bring a prior undertaking to a close. "Holy Spirit, You are my guide. You have taught me not to offend the person but to appeal to the inner goodness each of us came into the world with. No matter the depth of sin, goodness is still in there, somewhere. You have asked me to expose and attack the forces of evil haunting earth, so very much infecting humanity with moral cancer. The battlefield is the mind and heart of each person. The revealer has placed no cut-wound on the soul-person reading this offering, for only sin itself has been attacked. Lord, this nobody thanks You for Your incredible help and messages of love and redemption." (Some messages later in the book.)

I fell asleep. Well into the hours, I became aware of climbing a hill; the top had to be reached. The weight in me was dense, and I was barely able to move forward. The climb became steeper, and I went to my knees. The effort seemed to be taking a long time. I refused to relent and began to crawl. The look of my hands changed several times, and they were always manly hands. Only at the top did I realize the ascent was also a going back in time.

I stood at the top of the tallest mountain. The sky was perfectly blue, with so much sunshine. Warmth engulfed my whole being. I literally stood at the threshold of eternal life, the point of my resurrection. Everything was so clear to me back then, and still so clear to me today.

My body, like in a mirror, I was allowed to see it, my current one, so young and manly: 25 years old, I would say. The presentation was slim, muscular, but not overly muscular. All bodily imperfections were gone. I had a full head of light brown hair. I had reached **the Clarity**: the level where physical presentation is granted *unique perfection*. I was not a clone, not a robot, but instead a simple and unique "me," in a perfected body the Lord Almighty showed me He would reward me with later. (He will reward the reader in the same manner, after you repent and return to Him, even though there may first have to be time to serve out in JB purgatory.)

A week of afternoons has come and gone. Here I am again, on the Eau Galley Causeway. The feeling of freedom, the frequent breaks to look down at the river below and its surrounding landscapes, and the gazes into the clear blue sky above have helped my hand along. It is here, too, that I am best reminded of the incredible gift of salt and light the Lord God granted me 11 years ago.

There I was on a mountaintop, compelled to look to my right. Jesus and Mary stood 20 feet away. With blank facial expressions, they stared at me. Their position was at a higher place on the peak's ridge, and there was a gulf between us. They communicated without moving lips, asked that I not try to cross through **the veil** that separated us. Jesus and Mary thanked me and requested I go back. Silently, I agreed, then looked away, to look down, to ponder my return. Before departing, I turned to ask Jesus a question. After He answered, I began to jog down and soon entered hyper-speed through what seemed like a tunnel or a crazy type of elevator, before crashing into my sleeping body. I awoke to a beautiful new dawn, that spring morning in 2003.

While going up the spiritual mountain, I saw my hands change back to what they looked like during previous earth-terms. They were always that of a man, but a couple times they were not exactly beige. What an amazing reconnection to my soul's history! Because Jesus knew that I would be open to the enlightenment, He granted me the grace to receive it. Jesus and Mother Mary sent me back down here with the mission of helping others to see the real truth.

Earth-terms are preplanned in the spirit world; spirit-guides look for appropriate circumstances of entry for their designated subjects. Soul-persons must go through retributive justices and tough challenges partly due to previous earth-term mess-ups and partly for the purposes of correcting/strengthening the character and quality of the soul-person's sentient energy. The first time on earth, of course, is a God Blessed Birthment and not a "rebirthment." A more complete assessment will be done after body-death and time served in purgatory.

The early Christian Church talked of a soul's potential for multiple earth-terms; prior to the great divides in the Church, this truth was taught. Reader, did you know that? After Jesus' crucifixion, the first-generation of Christian teachers were the apostles and disciples who had walked with Him. These ones who Jesus taught—were they wrong? So why was the teaching of

God Blessed Rebirthment removed from Christian instruction and eventually forgotten about? The world back then was already weird enough. How much worse would the planet be today had this truth been allowed to remain in the mainstream? Jesus and the Father do not accept the term "reincarnation," and that's because it has been footballed around too much and now presents a diversion away from real truth.

Central to "the system of God Blessed Rebirthment" is God Himself. Hence, the word "God" must be included in the expression that refers to rebirthment. Pagans and their leader Satan don't like that. So, for the person who is open to the concept of God Blessed Rebirthment, when you are confronted with the in-your-face question "Hey, aren't you one of those who believes in reincarnation?" the best answer is, "No, I don't believe reincarnation, but I do believe in the fullness of God's infinite power to do whatever He decides, like allow a hundred year old woman to become pregnant and another woman to carry His Son in her womb by His Holy Will and not through sexual intercourse." Never fall into the traps that Satan and his servants set out before you. Always be on guard for them, his mainstream-media servants especially.

Not every soul-person is granted another earth-term. Some don't deserve another chance. Others have successfully graduated University of Earth, and they are now doctorates of the universe. The title "Doctor" is not used "up there." No earth-titles are allowed "up there," and that includes "President," "Senator," "Captain," "General," "Pope," "Father," "Pastor," "Dad," etc. The word "Father" can only be used for God, the word "Savior" for Jesus, the word "Mother" for Mary. The word "God" can be used for God the Father and Son Jesus. Besides our real spirit-names (explained later), the terms "friend," "brother," and "sister" are used between soul-persons. God the Father, His Son, and Mary can also be referred to as "Great Friend." As said before, the satanics use NS soul-persons' titles down there, but it's to belittle and humiliate.

[Spiritual note: Nothing takes place by happenstance in the upper spirit-world complex. On earth, the "human systems" are only *somewhat controlled* from above, in secret, invisible ways that do not significantly interfere with people's freedom to choose. If "up there" did constantly significantly interfere or apply complete control of things down here on our surface, we would be mere robots lacking free will, and the earth would not be in the moral toilet it is in right now. What free will does do is expose the good people, the bad people, and those caught in the gray in-between. When the earth's surface gets so bad, like it is now, God brings down His hard hand in order to erase the systems, so that new systems that are in His Will may evolve; in totality, it is called "purification." One just need read the Bible and the last 2,000 years of written history to see this truth. In the Foundation Testament, God the Father says He destroys cities and nations (and He often names them) so many times that it is literally impossible to keep track of unless a reader records them on a score sheet. God says to Isaiah, *"Behold, the LORD maketh the earth empty, and maketh it waste, and turneth it upside down, and scattereth abroad the inhabitants thereof. And it* [His judgment and punishment] *shall be with the people, so with the priest; as with the servant, so with his master; as with the maid; so with her mistress; as with the buyer, so with the seller* [and so on]. *The land shall be utterly emptied, and utterly spoiled: for the Lord hath spoken this word. The earth also is defiled under the inhabitants thereof; because they have transgressed the laws, changed the ordinance, broken the everlasting covenant. Therefore the curse devoured the earth, and they that dwell therein are desolate: therefore the inhabitants of the earth are burned, and few men* [and women] *are left." (24:1-3,5,6)* Not always does God put it in the mind of one nation's ruler to beat down the nation He wants beaten down. He tells His Prophet Amos of an earthquake two years before it is to happen: *And he* [God] *said, "Jerusalem and the habitations of the shepherds shall mourn, and the top of Carmel shall wither." (Amos 1-2)* Then there was ancient Egypt, all green and abundant with water and forests for thousands of years, prior to God passing judgment on the inhabitants' pagan ways, cursing them and their land, causing their beautiful area to turn into a vast arid desert that continues today.]

Each person is equally important to God; the salvation of ditch diggers, senators, salesmen, construction workers, and popes are of equal importance. The Lord detests how some persons down here can get so full of themselves. Jesus says of those who exalt themselves and those who do not: *"But many who are now first will be last, and many who are now last will be first." (Mark 10:31)* Today's professional athletes should keep that passage in mind, considering the radiant pride, love of money/bodily markings/fan worship, and lack of humility most show.

The other reason the enlightenment has been removed is because there bears little to no purpose in knowing it. This is the life we have right now! What are we going to make of it? Who cares about yester-centuries? What good comes from dwelling on the past? Fate is not a concept of God, for He wills today and tomorrow to be living, evolving, dynamic.

What possible good could come from knowing that the people around us were drunks, slobs, sport heroes, killers, kings, pastors, mill workers, or military privates/generals in previous stays here? Knowing such things would surely make us judgmental, even accusatory, and that's because humans tend to harp too much on the past. The information would certainly inhibit our abilities to properly, spontaneously interact with each other in the context of today's world. To seek prior-life information by way of regression hypnosis is a breach of the Divine rules. NOT ALLOWED. If it were allowed we would already know our details. Regression information might even be a total fabrication. The Foundation Testament shows how God will send a deceitful spirit to confuse (make fools out of) those who peeve Him.

"*I was a King Louis in a prior life.*"
"*You were? Which one?*"
"*I don't remember. And I didn't think to ask the hypnotist. But I do know this. He was king of England. I remember learning about him, or should I say myself, in high school history.*"
"*Was that before or after you dropped out?*"
"*Ah . . . I don't remember. Oh, ha-ha-ha, you're so funny.*"
"*Well, anyway, I was Marie Antoinette.*"
"*Who's she?*"
"*I don't know. I didn't think to ask the guy either.*"
"*Is it time for a doobie yet, or should we wait till noon?*"

At some point after the body dies off, the soul-person will become reconnected to his/her complete history from inception. Here presents another good reason why we should show a kind heart to all our neighbors because in a previous earth-term they might have been close to us. When we allow God into our minds and hearts, there eventually comes the realization that we are all brothers and sisters in the good spirit world. *Jesus asked, "Who is my mother and who are my brothers?" Then he looked at the people around him and said, "Here are my mother and my brothers. Anyone who* **obeys God** *is my brother or sister or mother." (Mark 3:33-35)*

Love of money and material items can blind our eyes to the Lord's presence. In Luke, Jesus says to a man stacked with possessions, *"You fool! Tonight you will die. Then who will get what you have stored up?" (12:15)* He then turns and says to the crowd, *"This is what happens to people who store up everything for themselves, but are poor in spirit of God." (12:20)*

Well now, how come God Blessed Rebirthment is not mentioned in the Bible? The answer is that even though the term itself is not used, its truth is revealed throughout the Bible. The Lord has removed readers' abilities to see it. In other words, Bible readers can go over a particular passage 50 times and it won't matter, for without a special grace from God, it'll be missed. God says to Isaiah, *"For the LORD hath poured out upon you* [humanity today] *the spirit of deep sleep, and hath closed your eyes: the prophets* [pastors] *and your rulers* [political leaders], *the seers* [advisers/media] *hath he covered. And the vision of all is become unto you as the words of a book that is sealed, which men* [and women] *deliver to one that is learned* [theologians], *saying, Read this, I pray thee: and he saith, I cannot; for it is sealed." (29:10-11)* At Jesus' time . . . *The apostles did not understand what Jesus was talking about.*

They could not understand, because the meaning of what he said was hidden from them. (Luke 18:34)

People back then knew about the soul's potential for multiple earth-terms. *The leaders in Jerusalem sent priests and temple helpers to ask John* [John the Baptist] *who he was. He told them plainly, "I am not the Messiah." Then when they asked him if he were Elijah, he said, "No, I am not!" (John 1:19-21)* Elijah lived eight centuries earlier. Obviously the priests and temple helpers knew that. John the Baptist denied that he was the revisiting soul of the great prophet, and this is where the rule is shown—the rule about earth people not being allowed to know about prior earth-terms. But what does Jesus say about John the Baptist?

The disciples asked Jesus, "Don't the teachers of the Law of Moses say that Elijah must come back before the Messiah does?" Jesus told them, "Elijah certainly will come and get everything ready. In fact, he has already come. But the people did not recognize him and treated him just as they wanted to. They will soon make the Son of Man suffer in the same way." Then the disciples understood that Jesus was talking to them about John the Baptist. (Matthew 17:10-13)

What else does Jesus say about it? *Now it happened that as he was praying alone, the disciples were with him; and he asked them, "Who do people say that I am?" And they answered, "John the Baptist, but others say Elijah; and others, one of the old prophets has risen." (Luke 9:18-19)* Jesus does not respond, "How can I be John the Baptist? He was alive till recently. And to be one of those ancient dead guys means some people around here believe in reincarnation. Let's go to Mount Sinai Hospital and see if they can be admitted for a psychiatric assessment." Instead, Jesus says, *"But who do you say that I am?" (Luke 9:20 & Matthew 16:13-15)* Peter answers, *"You are the Messiah, the Son of the living God." (Matthew 16:16)*

The disciples ask Jesus, *"Rabbi, who sinned, this man or his parents, that he was born blind?" (John 9:2)* One has to ask, "How can a man be born blind because of his sin? Is it possible to sin while in the mother's womb?" The fact that they ask Jesus the question means they believe a soul can sojourn on earth more than once. Jesus responds, *"It was not that the man sinned, or his parents, but that the works of God might be made manifest in him." (John 9:3)* Hence the term "God Blessed Rebirthment," which Jesus has given to His revealer's hand.

Jesus' answer shows how God's system melds justice with mercy, for the long-term good-growth of every soul. Together, God Blessed Rebirthment and purgatory constitute the majority share of God's infinitely genius system. We can call the latter "purgatory" or "place of the dead" or "limbo." Titles we humans apply are merely words and sometimes words can bring us to fussing with each other. God has a system and that is all we need to know; it is His, we are subject to it, and that is that, no matter how much we might want to disagree. The purpose of purgatory is to bring every soul properly back to God. Heaven cannot be achieved without God. Pagans don't like that.

Humanity is now inside the band of years known as End Time. God is allowing *some* release on His Divine Wisdom, so that more persons will come to accept His salt and light. But there is a catch. God Blessed Rebirthment cannot be taught to society but instead only "offered" to persons who are spiritually advanced in Godly schooling. Each person can accept or not accept the truth just like anybody else, but for the Godly persons who accept it, they will neither misuse the truth nor knead it down into pagan deceit, and they will be able to see how easy it would be for those godless tyrants to do exactly that, for they already do it with the greatest book ever, the Bible.

All four gospels have Jesus teaching love for neighbor. The Pharisees say to Jesus, *"Teacher, we know that you are honest. You teach the truth about what God wants people to do. And you treat everyone with the same respect, no matter who they are." (Matthew 12:16)* But that doesn't mean we should give out jewels to persons who aren't interested in or capable of receiving and handling them properly. *"Don't give to dogs what belongs to God. They will only turn and attack you. Don't throw pearls down in front of pigs. They will trample all over them." (Matthew 7:6)*

Chapter XLVI

JB Purgatory / Eternities / Paradise

JB purgatory has many levels of justice, correction, learning, rewiring. There is peace and to some degree happiness, but not bliss. Soul-persons review their good and not-so-good acts of demonstration from previous earth-terms. The JB levels are like as follows: obscure community college (low upper-level), state college (medium upper-level), and expensive private university (high upper-level). A soul must make it through each plane of instruction in order to merit entry into paradise and/or heaven. (Paradise is neither inside heaven nor part of purgatory.) The high upper-level deals with more subtle issues: e.g. mild displaced affections and lack of care for the physical aspects of God's earth; these can be as simple as why did the person not turn off lights not being used, throw litter on the ground, favor employment that destroyed the environment. The medium upper-level can be about how the soul-person frequently chose to be a thorn bush rather than a cedar tree or a lilac bush when interacting with people. An example is the person who was frequently late for work, causing the company and managers problems, money-loss, and hard feelings among co-workers, in turn sparking many of them to become like thorn bushes.

Heaven is the absolute highest spiritual place. Just prior to dying on the cross, Jesus told the repentant thief that He would see him in paradise before the end of the day. On the third day after His death, Jesus told Mary Magdalene not to hold on to Him because He had yet to ascend to the Father in heaven. God the Father is based in heaven. Jesus' words indicate that there is a separation between paradise and heaven. After delivering the guy to paradise, Jesus still had the Father's Will to do here on earth and down below, before His later ascension into heaven.

Yearly in the spirit world, Christmas is the most bountiful time for souls to gain heaven. Jesus *ascends them* as Christmas presents to the Father. Mary has been granted the grace to bring souls to Jesus on the same day, and that is because she has been given charge of a section of purgatory. During life, these soul-persons did not worship Mary but instead showed a strong devotion to her. Truth is that if these souls came to Jesus directly after body-death, without Mary interceding on their behalf and shielding them under her mantle, Jesus would rail at them before sending them to hell; many Catholics fall into this category, but only if they expressed a true devotion to Mother Mary. She and Jesus will eventually take these ones up to the Father.

One month later God sent the angel Gabriel to the town of Nazareth in Galilee with a message for a virgin named Mary. She was engaged to Joseph from the family of King David. The angel greeted Mary and said, "You are truly blessed! The Lord is with you." Mary was confused by the angel's words and wondered what they meant. Then the angel told Mary, "Don't be afraid! God is pleased with you, and you will have a son. His name will be Jesus. He will be great and will be called the Son of God Most High." (Luke 1:26-32) Thirty years later, Jesus attends a wedding. *Three days later Mary, the mother of Jesus, was at a wedding feast in the village of Cana in Galilee. Jesus and his disciples had also been invited and they were there. When the wine was all gone, Mary said to Jesus, "They don't have any more wine." Jesus replied, "Mother, my time hasn't yet come! You must not tell me what to do." Mary then said to the servants, "Do whatever Jesus tells you to do." (John 2:2-11)* Jesus does as His mother asks, makes wine from water. All Christians should consider Jesus' mother important. Revelation shows Mary having a high place in heaven. *Something important appeared in the sky. It was a woman whose clothes were the sun. The moon was under her feet, and a crown made of twelve stars was on her head. (Revelation 12:1)* No Christian has to go to Mary. But one certainly can, for it pleases her, and it pleases Jesus and God the Father. To say such is not blasphemy.

Paradises are wonderful places of love and friendship. They are invisible to our eyes and located in beautiful, remote areas. Genesis 3:23-24 refers to one. God expelled Adam and Eve from the Garden of Eden—a paradise on earth—because of their giving in to the serpent. Today still, by way of "a flaming sword," the Archangel Michael keeps Eden blocked from human eyes. There are many paradises. God owns the planet. Why wouldn't He use as much of it as possible? Does He have to explain His every detail to human beings?

Souls are rewarded stays in paradises and heaven. God determines the lengths of these "lifetimes." It might be a hundred years, considered short, like dying as a child. *"There shall be no more an infant of days, nor an old man that has not filled his days; for the child shall die a hundred years old;" (Isaiah 65:20)* (As far as the revealer knows, since the time of Isaiah there has never been a tot or a teenager that stayed a tot or a teenager for a hundred years. God is obviously referring to the time allotment He grants souls in paradise/ heaven.) Or a thousand years (not bad!). After a life in paradise is finished, a God Blessed Rebirthment must be done. Heaven's levels are based on what God determines as levels of perfection. The early levels require God Blessed Rebirthments, but only after a long period of time has been spent up there.

Earth's surface also has antipodeans to paradises; they are hardly-known-about stark zones remotely located; every continent has several. Generally speaking, only the locals know their exact locations and boundaries, and they make every effort to avoid entering them. The Bible talks of some. One is in the Book of Tobit (Catholic Holy Bible / Protestant Apocrypha). Archangel Raphael escorts the powerful killer-demon Asmodeus to the *remotest part of Egypt, and the angel bound him. (8:3)* The places are graveyard-portals for the "really bad" of the universe and are not to be walked on for any reason. God designates the following geographic area to be as such, when He says, *"For my sword shall be bathed in heaven: behold, it shall come down upon Idumea, and upon the people of my curse, to judgment. The sword of the LORD is filled with blood. . . . and a great slaughter in the land of Idumea. . . . And the streams thereof shall be turned to pitch and the dust thereof to brimstone, and land thereof shall become burning pitch. It shall not be quenched night nor day; the smoke thereof shall go up forever: from generation to generation it shall lie waste; none shall pass through it even forever and ever." (Isaiah 34:5,6,9,10)* God goes on to say that cormorants (daytime) and owls (at night) will hover over the land; the double-meaning is that the place will be guarded from the sky. Prison guards do not take well to human breaches and will sometimes release prisoner-entities onto them, in order to send a loud, clear message to the outside world. Prisoners crave to "inhale" the blood of life: as said before, the life-energy that lives in our blood, heart, and marrow. People enter these zones at their own peril. The terrible domains are kept separate and well away from hp-purgatory. "Family" is sometimes allowed inside for short visits. Another biblically talked-of antipodean is Gehenna.

There is a permanent gulf between the JB purgatory and the below-worlds. Soul-persons in the latter are considered NS and cannot cross over and up to the former without the benefit of a bridge. The bridges are the good soul-persons who have secretly crossed over from the good side. "Bridging" is one of the "good works" they do in order to gain merit and move up. The work can take place inside the netherworld or farther down, in the hp-cells, correctional rooms, and *wild zones* of sheol. The good workers interact with the poor souls in veiled ways, to help draw them to reflect/ repent/reject their rotten mannerisms.

Souls that have bridged from the bad to the good side are not allowed to enter community college right away; time and process are involved. They are at the lowest "saved" position and will prepare to become adept workers at helping the poor souls down there. It's not easy to go back down to the bad side. In order to appear as one of them, good workers have to get into the ways of fighting. They can "fall down" and end up back in the same crap they had previously escaped from. When that happens, they again have to find a bridge. It can take time; the below-worlds are vast.

Over time, souls grow resistant to temptations and cease falling down. They eventually gain enough merit to put away their shame/dishonor from a previous earth-term. In their minds, their good acts overwrite their bad ones, and they are allowed to move up the ladder, to a state college.

Every soul-person has a true name that stays with him/her forever; it is given at inception. We become reconnected to our eternal names and complete soul-history from inception once we make it into the high upper-level. Men and women stay as men and women and do not have God Blessed Rebirthments into the opposite gender or as animals. This is the type of nonsense Satan gets pagans to put out in order to pollute the real truth. (The soul's "inception" is not addressed in *ARR* but is in *MB*.)

Early in the Bible, God the Father makes direct reference to the rebirthment of a whole generation. God says to Abraham, *"As for yourself, you shall go to your fathers in peace; you shall be buried in a good old age. And they shall come back here in the fourth generation; for the iniquity of the Amorites is not yet complete." (Genesis 15:15-16)* His Word shows that He will send a chosen generation back into human body so that its members can teach and redirect the members of a troubled group, which He will also send back.

The prophet Isaiah says, *"Your dead shall live, their corpses shall rise. O dwellers in the dust, awake and sing for joy! For your dew is a radiant dew, and the earth shall give birth to those long dead." (Isaiah 26:19)* When God deems the souls down there have suffered for long enough, He does a General Judgment and raises death to life in a massive way, with a wave of His hand or a blow of a horn. Souls are granted a new eternity of opportunities at physical life on the surface. In the coming General Judgment, those who are still in JB purgatory will be assigned much better birth situations than those in hp-purgatory; many of the latter will be thrown into the lake of fire. The following is from the Book of Tobit: *Blessed is God who lives forever, and blessed is his kingdom. For he afflicts, and he shows mercy; he leads down to Hades, and he brings up again, and there is no one who can escape his hand. (13:2)*

Pastors courageous enough to speak about hell always assert that the place is eternal—*forever*. That would mean millions and billions of years. Wow! Thankfully, God doesn't work that way. "Forever" means an eternity, but it can also be more than one eternity. This is how our Lord works. Why not? The soul has to repent and agree to at least *try* to live the Christian rules.

"Eternities" are segments of God-time. It can be a thousand years, two thousand, or whatever God decides. Right after Jesus dies, He is briefly held in the Father's arms. God then sends His Son down into hell. For what? To rub salt in the wounds of the prisoner-souls? Here is what Peter says: *"Christ then preached to the spirits that were kept in prison. They had disobeyed God while Noah was building the boat, but God had been patient with them." (1 Peter 3:19-20)* Paul writes, *When it says, "He* [Jesus] *ascended," what does it mean but that he had also descended into the lower parts of the earth? He who descended is the same one who ascended far above all the heavens, so that he might fill all things. Therefore it is said, "When he ascended on high he made captivity itself captive; he gave gifts to his people." (Ephesians 4:8-9)* Jesus went down not to taunt but instead give the good news to the prisoners. By way of His Son, God the Father offered them a new eternity of opportunities for life on the surface. (Jesus made "captivity itself captive; he gave gifts to his people.") Most souls said, "Yes, Jesus, I want to give it a try."

There are more biblical references to souls from above being sent down here to be teachers. Prophet Jeremiah speaks of what God said to him: *"Now the word of the Lord came to me saying, 'Before I formed thee in the womb, I knew thee, and before you were born I consecrated you; I appointed you a prophet to the nations.'" (Jeremiah 1:5)* The prophet Isaiah reveals, *"The Lord called me before I was born." (Isaiah 49:1)* What does Jesus say about where He came from and why? *"I didn't come from heaven to do what I want! I came to do what the Father wants me to do. He sent me, and he wants to make certain that none of the ones he has given me will be lost." (John 6:38-39)* Jesus goes on to say that He was with the Father from before Abraham. *Jesus answered, "I tell you for certain that even before Abraham was, I was, and I am." (John 8:58)*

Back then, most of the people did not accept Jesus as Messiah. When the Pharisees, Sadducees, and teachers of the Law reject Jesus' miracles as proof, He scolds them and reveals that they came into the world from a lower level. *Jesus answered, "You are from below, but I am from above. You belong to this world, but I don't. That is why I said you will die with your sins unforgiven. If you don't have faith in me for who I am, you will die and your sins will not be forgiven." (John 8:23-24)* He even tells them their father is Satan. *"Your father is the devil, and you do exactly what he wants. He has always been a murderer and a liar." (John 8:44)*

Chapter XLVII

Thrust Units and Bond Souls

Bringing up exceptional situations is the non-believers' primary way to confound and counter those who are believers. "What about babies born with handicaps? How can a loving God do that?" Early Christian teachers are able to handle the question because the answer is in the Bible. Jesus says to His disciples, *"So if your hand causes you to sin, cut it off! You would be better off to go into life crippled than to have two hands and be thrown into the fires of hell that never go out. If your foot causes you to sin, chop it off. You would be better off to go into life lame than to have two feet and thrown into hell. If your eye causes you to sin, get rid of it. You would be better off to go into God's Kingdom with only one eye than to have two eyes and be thrown into hell." (Mark 9:42)* After the removal of God Blessed Rebirthment from Christian teaching, the meaning of the passage took on mystery. "We don't know what Jesus means. Only He knows. But please, *please*, do not cut off your hands or poke out your eyes."

Some persons carried out such atrocious acts of demonstration that even though they attended church later on, they will have to experience God Blessed Rebirthment(s) into mentally and/or physically debilitated units. An example might be as follows. An American soldier in WWI or II may have not shown mercy to surrendering enemy combatants. (Some soldiers may have raped/killed refugees.) The soldier survived the war and went on to lead a decent life. He went to church now and then and developed a feeling for Christ and a hope for eternal life. But he was lukewarm and never repented his cold-blooded act of demonstration. The soldier(s) he killed had a wife and children waiting back home. At the man's judgment, Jesus may, by way of secondary repentance, grant him escape from the lake of fire. But the man will later have to rebirth into a debilitated body. The body will be a **thrust unit** for the soul-person operating it.

There are other outcomes that demand the same path. Let's say a woman had a partial-birth abortion and later half-heartedly came to the Lord. Sometimes she attended church, but she never confessed to the pastor her selfish, debased, cold-blooded act of killing an innocent child and therefore never showed a proper act of demonstration of repentance. Jesus has let me know just how much physical pain and spiritual suffering these soul-children go through during a partial-birth abortion. The woman dies. In her judgment, Jesus doesn't mess around. She is shown the baby for a moment, and then she is either thrown into the lake of fire or offered secondary repentance. If the latter, a rigorous purgatory will be set for her; time in "the shores" and "the hall" will be included. Later, a short paradisiacal happiness may be allowed as encouragement to her spirit, prior to her God Blessed Rebirthment into a thrust unit.

No soul-person willingly goes to the lake of fire if a way of avoiding it is offered. Souls will beg for the Lord's mercy to be upon them and for the opportunity to have a future earth-term in a thrust unit. *They beg* to have their arms and hands removed, *they beg* to have their eyes poked out, *they beg* to get their brains damaged.

There are certain acts of demonstration that are sins against the Holy Spirit, and even if repented they cannot be forgiven "in totality," meaning they cannot be granted full remission, neither in the lifetime during which they happened nor in the next. Jesus reveals this truth right after the temple authorities accused Him of not having the Holy Spirit but instead a demon. What an insulting way to speak about God the Father's Son! It is not that the souls will be sent to hell, for the Lord, as the writer has already said and says again *for the reader's encouragement*, takes no joy in sending even one soul-person down there.

With the help of spirit guides, a soul-person will set positive plans with realistic goals to achieve during an ensuing God Blessed Rebirthment. A person who led a decent life but spoke in a way that insulted God's holiness will not have the sin completely remitted. Perhaps he/she will rebirth into a thrust unit that has autism, a stutter, another type of speech impediment, or a slower-than-normal brain. Maybe it will be something more subtle, like not very good eyesight.

Another sin against the Holy Spirit is to not forgive those who have sinned against us. We must keep in mind that we ourselves carried out poor acts of demonstration while alive. How can God's mercy and forgiveness be upon us when we refuse to forgive others? God is not a hypocrite. He recognizes souls who are, and He does not take well to being put to the test. This is shown in Jesus' parable (Matthew 18:21-35) about the official who was forgiven of his monetary debt but refuses to forgive someone else's. That person ends up back with his debts and worse. God will forgive every person who repents to Him, but only if the person has forgiven others. Jesus says, *"Whenever you stand up to pray, you must forgive what others have done to you. Then your Father in heaven will forgive your sins." (Mark 11:26)*

People who refuse to forgive others cannot enter that wonderful place above for the simple reason that *those others* might be up there or will be up there someday. People who refuse to forgive are, in effect, saying God should not forgive them. God certainly *will not* forgive them if they do not repent, but He *will* if they do. There are no hate, anger, deceit, and animosity in the upper realms of the spirit-world complex. Jesus says, *"If you forgive others for the wrongs they do to you, your Father in heaven will forgive you. But if you don't forgive others, your Father will not forgive your sins." "Don't condemn others, and God won't condemn you. God will be as hard on you as you are on others! He will treat you exactly as you treat them." (Matthew 6:14 & 7:1-2)* Jesus says in Luke's Gospel, *"I tell you, you will never get out* [of prison] *until you have paid the last penny." (15:59)* The statement is an oblique reference to purgatory.

A person may have been horribly mistreated. The one(s) who did the mistreating can be very hard to forgive. As mentioned earlier in Part IV, forgiveness is meant primarily for the forgiver and only secondarily for the forgiven. The forgiven person may break down in shame and apologize to the one who was mistreated. Maybe, maybe not. But a repentant former evildoer must still go through God's system of retributive justice and atonement during the stretch of life post-repentance and/or later in JB purgatory. The doer-of-terrible-acts does not simply get off. Repentance saved the person from the lake of fire and from long hauls in other hell levels. The soul-person may also have to come back in a thrust unit at a future time.

Timothy McVeigh is a good example to bring up for those who persist in refuting the existence of purgatory. In 1995, McVeigh carried out the senseless, brutal bombing of an Oklahoma City office building, killing 168 people, of which 19 were children under the age of six (680 other people were injured). Before he was executed in 2001, Christian pastors worked on McVeigh, to get him to repent. He refused. But had he done it, would he then go straight to paradise or heaven without having paid one cent of debt (except for his quick execution)? Would he blissfully reside up there with some of the soul-persons he had been happy to kill off, while their families and friends still suffer down here on earth from his heinous crime?

A human body that has spina bifida or cerebral palsy or brain disability is a difficult thrust unit for the soul-person housed inside of it. A life of constant challenge in a body like that can make the soul stronger than it was before: *a weightlifter gets stronger not by lifting feathers.*

Parents should try the best they can to teach and correct their brain-disabled children; these ones should not get a free ride away from being taught proper behavior and the understanding of boundaries; the teaching and correcting should be done within the measure of the child's ability to receive and comprehend. Some mentally handicapped children, perhaps even the majority, grow up to have calm spirits and become contributing adults to some degree. Others, as adults, can exhibit terrible, even atrocious behaviors. Besides being mentally disabled, some exhibit paranoid schizophrenia, and these ones can become very violent at times. The public is not much aware of the latter category. Today's behavior medications can be extremely effective and the difference between a mentally debilitated person having to be institutionalized or free to be out in public. I have witnessed this.

Some parents of high-behavior children do not like the idea of medicating them. Many believe the child will grow out of problem behaviors. My experience has never shown this outcome. In fact, after puberty sets in, behaviors can worsen to the point of frequent violent outbursts, including physical attacks against their own parents. Only later in life—in the 40s or 50s—may the behaviors begin to show signs of calming. My comment to parents who give their disabled children over to the State and insist that no medications be given them is this: "Then you take care of your child if you love him/her so much and think he/she is so easy. Oh, you don't like that idea." But most parents are fine with doctor-prescribed medications.

[Spiritual note: All persons of the Bible would be wise to keep in mind that God Himself stated man was created in His Image—*not as Him*, just in His Image. God is our Great Creator and Grand Shepherd through time and the universe; in other words, when we choose Him, He is our Forever Forward Shield. He shows, by way of Himself and later His Son Jesus, that He is the Infinitely Good Healer when He chooses to be. *What? Does He have to come down here and do everything for us? Poke out pointy little pebbles from our wounded knees and apply bandages?* He wants us to be in His Image, which means we have doctors, psychologists, nurses, emergency first responders, medical researchers, pharmaceutical makers, loving parents, pastors, etc. here on earth. God's Will is for us to be good-spirited helpers, because by being that way we become circuits of kindness for each other's souls. Love, trust, and faith in God are tremendous attributes to have, but it does not mean we should disassociate ourselves from humans who can help us in brotherly/sisterly ways. So it's okay to see medical doctors, psychiatrists, psychologists, and pastors; it's okay to take helpful medications when help is needed.]

Sometimes thrust units are allowed to birth for the purpose of bringing a parent or parents back into line. A child born blind because of sins of the parents is such a dim, unenlightened view of what sometimes is granted by God. A blind child may allow a parent to see the world with clearer vision. A child born with an obvious disability may help parents and siblings to recognize their own not-so-obvious disabilities. In the foreverness of the soul's journey through time and the universe, as it tries over and over to make its way back to freedom and into God's salt and light and oneness with **The Clarity**, earth-terms inside thrust units become retrospectively seen as tremendously helpful learning experiences, even though they were most certainly not considered to be that way while the earth-terms were in process.

A child does not have to be born with something big or obvious. Disabilities can be smaller things, like a three-year-old who needs thick glasses in order to see the world. A problem like this brings the potential to thrust the child's mind to heights it would otherwise never achieve. In a different way, the parents' eyes may become better focused, and their minds may also experience a type of thrust. Siblings, too, can join in. People who have done mission work with the disadvantaged and malnourished of Africa or Central America always say the experience changed them into the ways of better wisdom.

Though we are all brothers and sisters in the good spirit world, every soul-person has a small number of soul-persons for whom there is retained an extra-strong friendship. They are our **bond souls**. Bond souls are of the same primal pool (explained later). At initial entry into humanity, each soul-person experiences a "carved out" female counterpart; she is/becomes part of that **bond soul group**. As a pod, members travel together through time but do not all occupy human bodies at the same time. Mostly, the majority remains in spirit while one or a couple are carnate. To some degree, God allows the discarnate soul-persons to follow and observe us, even coach us, but not enough to interfere with our free will—rather just "draw" us into making good decisions.

As well, there are bad invisible spirits around us, and they too are allowed to influence us to some degree. Some of the bad souls may actually be our bond souls who are either stuck in the netherworld or have been temporarily let up from a below-world. These ones can have a drawing-down effect, ever tugging on our minds and hearts to do brainless or outright evil acts.

The revealer does not get big into the subject of unclean souls, evil spirits, demons, creature pools, and fallen angels in *American River Road (ARR)*, but I did so in the three previous efforts, particularly *MB*. That one recounts some of my interactions with the satanics and the one direct confrontation with Satan in 2000. Paul says, *"We are not fighting against humans. We are fighting against forces and authorities and against rulers of darkness and powers in the spiritual world. Finally, let the mighty strength of the Lord make you strong.*

Put on all the armor that God gives, so that you can defend yourself against the devil's tricks." (Ephesians 6:10-13) The Bible instructs the living not to seek conscious contact with "the invisible." The God-faithful are granted spiritual contact with God the Father and Son, *invisible,* during prayer, Bible reading, song, church attendance, and leading decent lives. *"Seek him* [God speaking of Himself] *that maketh the seven stars and Orion and turneth the shadow of death into the morning, and maketh the day darketh with night: that calleth for the waters of the sea, and poureth them out upon the face of the earth: the LORD is his name." (Amos 5:8)* Jesus and the Father may allow the JB souls to facilitate us in extra-special yet still imperceptible ways (graces), which in turn can be applied to their purgatorial merit sheets.

Sometimes a person takes a wrong path during earth-term. He/she ends up in a semi-private, psycho-type of swampy valley. Through a Guardian Angel, a bond soul may ask for God's permission to rebirth into a thrust unit as a way to help reel the lost person back in. It doesn't always work, but there is a decent chance it will.

After thrust units die, do the soul-persons go directly to paradise or heaven? Everyone wants to believe it. The religious often affirm it. The answer is, "We should not make that assertion." Ones that don't go to paradise or heaven may end up at a better position in their climb, but not all. God is judge. He knows the history of every soul-person. Some thrust units do even worse and end up doing a stretch in hell, before *possibly* being granted another difficult thrust unit.

Souls of dead babies do not necessarily go directly to heaven. Often they will go to "a place of waiting," where they will be cuddled and loved: *like* heaven. There will likely come eventual re-placements into physical life here. This may not happen until after the parents die, so that all of them may have a period of reuniting that will nurture healing of their sentient energies.

Woe to persons who plead for eugenics or so-called mercy killing. We need to help the disabled and downtrodden, for the benefits of their souls and the gaining of merit for ours. God loves and blesses their births into the world; otherwise, they would not be here.

Chapter XLVIII

Christian Faith Crossover

In late 1999, Jesus and God the Father asked me to be a revealer of spiritual truths and a deliverer of Divine messages; the truths and messages would help persons know how to achieve eternal life and not just go through life presuming on God's mercy; the reality of beneath-worlds and why so many soul-persons end up going down there would be revealed. Once I accepted the job, the following quote was given to me: *"Gird up your loins; stand up and tell the people everything I command you. Do not break down before them, or I will break you before them." (Jeremiah 1:17-19)* I carry God's order in my wallet and see it every time I open it.

The man's heart and brain required a period of intense training, the soul's resolve a regimen of hard testing. *MB* recounts the first seven years of those trials and tribulations. The Divine messages began in October 1999. The initial ones were from Archangel Michael; his last came on December 1. Jesus and God the Father began to give short messages in November and December. The years 2000 and 2001 brought the most messages from Jesus and the Father. Their communications got a little longer than at first, and the words were always very to the point. Some of the messages are below and a few more are at the back of the book.

October 11, 1999, message from Saint Michael: **"Your name is John. I know you well. You talk with me in church when you say the rosary. My name is Michael, and I speak every night with Ell** (the church-sister I was helping) **and Jesus. I love Ell and Christian** (Ell's grandson)**. Jesus gives me Ell and Christian to protect. Jesus saved her life and her special friend Joyce** (both in a car accident) **because Ell has come back to Jesus and the love Jesus had** lost. He stopped her from drinking for eight years. . . . Your best friend, Saint Michael"

November 21, 1999, message from Jesus: "Hello, John, it is Jesus talking to you. You have faith, love, and trust, but My Father is testing you right now to see if you have true faith, love, and trust, and whether or not you truly believe in My Father and Me. I love Ell. She and Christian are My children. I take Ell and she serves Me."

Later the same night, from God the Father: "I AM THE GOD OF ABRAHAM. I need both of you (Ell and me) to help My people come back to Me. Awake! Awake! My children, before it is too late. I am the Life and the End. I want My children to stop doing bad things and repent. Something can and will happen to the world."

March 8, 2000, message from Jesus: "Hello, John, it is Jesus talking to you. You know that you are Mine and I love you. I am happy you wrote My book *Threshold of the New Eternity*. John, you must pray hard for the world. Many, many people give their hearts to evil, and *some* people give their hearts to Me. Ell has given her heart to Me, and I love her very much. I know that she went to the casino. She feels bad about it, and I have forgiven her because she and Christian are Mine."

March 28, 2000, message from Jesus: "Hello, John. It is Jesus talking to you. How are you feeling today? Are you okay? I have a message for Ell and you. I gave you a mark on the forehead last Tuesday night at the healing mass. My Father, the Holy Spirit, and I were happy to see you both there. Ell, I will heal you and give you more love and patience. John, I have healed you from your anger, and now you have love and peace in your heart."

Later that same night—a message from God the Father for me to give out: "I am the God of Abraham talking to you. My people, I want you to ask Me for forgiveness, and to have faith and trust. Pray, My people, for peace on earth. You hate rather than love one another. I am upset that My people do not repent. There is too much thought about sex, and man-on-man, woman-on-woman are not right. I AM VERY ANGRY the government of Canada wants to pass a law legalizing same-sex marriage. This is against the Law of your Creator. I AM ANGRY ABOUT ABORTION, TOO. People who love Me should pray and pray for the world and go to church and receive the Body of My Son. OTHERS MUST REPENT NOW. I love you, My people—From God the Father, Holy Spirit, and Jesus."

The Divine messages are strict about repentance. The Catholic confessional is a well-known fact, and it is supposed to be entered fairly regularly, as a way to keep parishioners in constant reflection on personal conduct. Today, most Catholics don't bother with it much or even at all. In the above message, God the Father says OTHERS MUST REPENT. After the big-one primary repentance, all Christians need to stay in personal reflection (just like we do about our careers, families, eating habits, etc.), because no matter how hard we try not to, we mess up.

April 4, 2000, message from Jesus: "**My dear John, please give this message to My people. 'Wake up! Wake up! before it is too late. Repent, repent! Your sins live on sins: lying, corruption, drinking, gambling, murder, abortion, and sex, sex, and more sex. Do you, My people, really believe that these sins are hidden from Me and My Father? My dear people, you no longer have enough faith and trust. You do not love Me anymore. Come back to Me now. I am the Light. Repent, trust, love, and believe in Me, and you will be saved. BUT YOU MUST COME BACK. I love you, My people. Come back to Me—Jesus.'"**

July 24, 2000, message from Jesus for me to give out: "**My people, I am your Guardian and Good Shepherd. You must follow and respect Me, and you must believe and trust the people who take My place on earth. Some say that they take My place but do not teach My rules. They teach by their own sins. I will take care of these ones in due time, but most are with Me. It is time to pick up the Bible, for I will be coming to pick up many of you to take you to your true home—Paradise. No one should be left behind, but some will choose to stay. My people, do not choose to stay, for there is awareness of suffering in eternal death.**"

September 12, 2001, message from Jesus: "**I have a message for the world. What happened yesterday in New York is a warning. It is not finished yet. More is going to happen, and it will be much worse. Repent, My people, for it is time to turn away from the darkness and seek to enter My Light.**" (September 25, 2001, message from God the Father at back of book.)

Today's world has an almost infinite amount of evil deceptions and misinformation being presented as truth and choice. The highly enlightened Christian can be God's light in helping to change people back into the ways of goodness. But you need enough enlightenment to be able to do it. So, indirectly through you, reader, the book is meant for people whose blood turns cold as ice the instant they think of being in church. It is for the lukewarm, unfocused, wandering, and indifferent. It is for those who believe themselves to be insignificant, unworthy, unloved, unskilled, uneducated. For prisoners in obvious and not-so-obvious ways. For those who are caught in materialism and cannot seem to stop shopping in an attempt to suffocate their despair and inner loneliness. Shopping medicine never works, for despair and loneliness always return.

Jesus says that where there are two or three gathered in His name, there He is also. (Matthew 18:18-20) He didn't say "Where there are two or three Catholics" or "Where there are two or three Baptists or Pentecostals or Messianic." Every person is of equal importance to God. Going to Him is for each person to decide to do. He calls us back, yes, but He does not *make* anyone return. What joy could that possibly bring the Lord, to have to twist someone's arm?

Catholic churches are fine, but I am of the view that new Christians might find the institution intimidating to bordering on lunatic fringe. As well, joining the Catholic Church involves a lengthy process. I'm not trying to discourage anyone, just make aware. Every Catholic mass has a bloodless reenactment of Jesus' crucifixion and resurrection. Next, parishioners line up to receive the eucharistic bread and sometimes wine, which, they believe, have spiritually transformed (at the mass's moment known as "consecration") into the flesh and blood of Jesus. Jesus says, "Whoever does not eat my flesh cannot come to me. . . ." (John 6:53-56) The bread and wine now contain a tiny amount of heaven's life-energy: the Blood of Life. It is God the Father's infinite grace that humans, while alive here, have some extra access to heaven's life-energy by way of Jesus' flesh and blood and not from drinking the blood of dead people or animals and eating their raw hearts; the blood and bodies of the dead are meant to go into the ground, so that the spirits down there may have some.

Better suited for many people are the small community churches or the large evangelical centers. I am a fan of today's Southern Baptist and Pentecostal fortresses (Assemblies of God). Though a devoted Catholic, I as well consider myself a Southern Baptist. The SB church I have occasionally blogged into is located in South Carolina. I have a deep respect for the head pastor there. True evangelicals tend to be powerhouses on biblical teaching. I love that! The pastor is, like me, a dad, and he doesn't shy away from talking about the challenges of raising children in today's world, about politics, and about the rampant immorality scourging the soul of America and the world as a whole. Please understand that even though the Lord has graced the revealer in a unique way, I still seek the heartening help of good persons who can boldly speak the Word of God *in full truth*, something today's Catholic Church has run away from.

Having said that, there has to be added the element "caution" because not every church is equal when it comes to revealed truth—in particular, the truth about purgatory and praying for the dead. In Christianity, Catholicism hits the mark *dead* center. My message to non-Catholic Christians is this: "Don't be concerned about marking yourself 'too Catholic' just because you may decide to opt into accepting them." This is the only issue I have when listening to non-Catholic pastors. Sometimes they besmirch their Catholic brothers and sisters on these matters.

But today's Catholic Church and Christianity as a whole have entered what is called The Great Apostasy: the desertion of God's Word, Commandments, and Statutes in fullness, to be in favor of populist deceit. Only a remnant will remain true and righteous Christians at the end.

The majority of today's Catholic homilies are a single photocopied *one*—and a little on the strange side to boot. "We are all weak, and we are all sinners.... Just forgive everybody and don't judge.... God is love, He is only love. He does not judge anyone. No one judges us. We judge ourselves.... Love everyone and love everything. Just *lohhhve*, just *lohhhve*, just *lohhhve*. Do good works to show your *lohhhve*. It is a sin not to do good works.... Don't put down anyone and just accept all persons as they are, for by just being themselves they are perfect the way they are. Show them that you *lohhhve* and accept them just the way they are. All of us must be in unity because we are a world community. God is in control of everything here on earth. By thinking and being that way, you are like Jesus, for He is only *lohhhve* and does not judge anyone. But we are all human, we are all sinners, and we will never stop being sinners...." Prayers of the Faithful are another story: "Today, we pray to God that there be peace and unity among all families and peoples in the world. We also pray our political leaders show fairness to everyone and there be no discrimination against anyone for any reason. Finally, today, we pray that all people and world leaders recognize the sanctity of marriage." What the heck does that mean, *sanctity of marriage?* Isn't that why gays and lesbians want to get marriage licenses, because they believe in the sanctity of marriage? CATHOLIC CHURCH, WAKE UP! SMELL THE COFFEE! BE SPECIFIC ABOUT DO'S AND DON'TS! SPEAK OUT AGAINST *ALL* THE EVILS! STOP PUSHING CHRISTIANITY AWAY FROM GOD THE FATHER'S SOLID ROCK FOUNDATION, FOR IT CANNOT STAND ALONE! SUCCESSOR TO PETER, WHY ARE YOU DENYING JESUS? IN THE SPIRIT, YOU ARE CRIPPLING HIM! BELOVED JESUS IS ONCE AGAIN BEING CRUCIFIED BY THE PAGANS, HEATHENS, AND BETRAYERS AND ALL YOU CAN DO IS SMILE AND WAVE AND TRY TO BE MR. POPULAR! THE GUY CRUCIFIED NEXT TO JESUS SAID TO THE OTHER GUY, "DON'T YOU FEAR GOD?" CATHOLIC CHURCH, DON'T YOU FEAR GOD?

[Spiritual note: In Luke's Gospel (12:51-52), Jesus says to His disciples, *"Do you think I came to bring peace to earth? No indeed! I came to make people choose sides. A family of five will be divided, with two of them against the other three."* Matthew has Jesus saying: *"Don't think that I came to bring peace to the earth! I came to bring trouble, not peace. I came to turn sons against their fathers, daughters against their mothers, and daughters-in-law against their mothers-in-law. Your worst enemies will be in your own family. If you love your father and mother or even your sons and daughters more than me, you are not fit to be my disciple."* *(10:34-37)* To accept God *in full truth* means a person has the guaranteed hope of one day achieving eternal life, but it also means the person has to accept that she/he may be rejected and even belittled by those close by. So what! That's their problem! The born-again soul-person must be tenaciously selfish about her/his own personal salvation and only in that way can there be the confidence to kindly, respectfully reach out to help others and accept rejection gracefully.]

Love is not how many times the word "love" is said in 20 minutes. Love does turn a blind eye to evil lifestyles, hence validating a continuation in them. The bottom line is love is not about spouting out comfortable popular-isms. Populist preaching takes people away from God's commandments and statutes and ends up losing souls. Love is about loving someone enough to kindly tell her/him the truth about the narrow uphill path that leads to eternal life and about the other one—the wide and easy downhill highway that leads to the place God calls "death." Love is about educating listeners on repentance; love then hugs their souls and prays for them. Repenting is something evangelical pastors and Catholic priests tend to agree on, but most fall far too short on outlining the offences that shouldn't be done in the first place and require repenting if they have been.

Christian sermons should be like coffee; for the reader who prefers, let's say a good cup of English Breakfast or Orange Pekoe tea. Coffee or tea would not work without water—*obviously*. Adding water brings them to life for our taste buds to enjoy. When black, coffee is coffee, tea is tea. Many persons prefer to have milk/cream and/or sugar/honey added to their hot drinks. Even so, the coffee is still coffee, the tea still tea. But when the coffee/tea and water are removed, both cups are merely sweet milk. The coffee/tea is God's commandments and statutes as given in the Bible. Water gives them living spirit.

> *And it came to pass at the end of seven days, that the word of the Lord came unto me* [Prophet Ezekiel], *saying, "Son of man, I have made thee a watchman unto the house of Israel: therefore hear the word at my mouth and give them warning from me. When I say unto the wicked,*

Thou shalt surely die; and thou givest him not warning, nor speakest to warn the wicked from his wicked way, to save his life; the same wicked man shall die in his iniquity [evil ways]; *but his blood will I require at thine hand. Yet if thou warn the wicked, and he turn not from his wickedness, nor from his wicked way, he shall die in his iniquity; but thou hast delivered thy soul." (Ezekiel 3:16-19)*

Since Jesus' death, persons must repent to God through the Christ-venue in order to have their sins covered by Jesus' wounds and merit eternal life; otherwise, Satan will be there to accuse them. God will get very angry at soul-persons who belittled His Son and brushed off His wounds as meaningless. Woe to them! Eight centuries before Christ, God says to prophet Hosea, *"And they consider not in their hearts that I remember all their wickedness: now their own doings beset them about; they are before my face. They make the king* [most modern-day leaders] *glad with their wickedness, and their princes* [most leaders' underling politicians] *with their lies." (7:13)* Two centuries later, to prophet Ezekiel, *"Thus shall mine anger be accomplished, I will cause my fury to rest upon them, and I will be comforted: and they shall know that I the LORD have spoken it in my zeal, when I have accomplished my fury in them." (5:13)*

[Spiritual note: Jesus states that Jewish persons who do not accept Him as the Messiah must pass through Moses (John 5:45-47). Anyone who has read the first five books of the Bible knows that Moses does not mess around when challenged. He is very hard on those who rebel against God. He tries to shield them from God's wrath only if they repent. When Aaron and Miriam privately gossip against their brother Moses for marrying an Ethiopian woman, God becomes hot with wrath, but particularly so at the sister. (God obviously detests racist remarks.) Miriam instantly becomes leprous. Miriam and Aaron quickly admit to their a gross error. Moses begs the Lord to have mercy on them, and it works to a degree. *"Heal her now, Oh God, I beseech thee." And the Lord said unto Moses, "If her father had but spit in her face, should she not be ashamed seven days? Let her be shut out from the camp for seven days, and after that let her be received in again." (Numbers 12:13-14)* (Passage shows that God does not completely absolve the repentant until a reduced sentence in purgatory is served out. See?) But Moses does not die for humanity. In fact, fifteen hundred years after Moses' death, he and Elijah (the soul-persons of) are shown giving their blessings to Jesus when He is transfigured on the mountain. The three apostles Peter and brothers James and John witness it and hear God the Father speak from above, *"This is my own dear Son, and I am pleased with him. Listen to what he says!" (Matthew 17:5)* Denying Jesus the Christ is to call God a liar, another sin against the Holy Spirit.]

Today, no one seems to take the devil seriously. The fact that he is a very powerful fallen angel and an infinitely evil entity has been lost to the so-called modern world. Comedians joke about him like he is some kind of fable. Nowadays, almost all Protestant pastors and Catholic priests overlook him. As a result, there is no longer any teaching about the reality of hell and how to avoid going there.

Jokes about the devil are not funny to God, and they are not funny to Satan; it is an error joke about him. In the Catholic Church prior to the Vatican II conference, which took place in the front half of the 1960s, the conclusion of every Catholic service had attendees reciting the Saint Michael the Archangel Prayer: a special prayer requesting the archangel's help in warding off attacks from the invisible evil forces. Post-Vatican II, the practice ended, and soon parishioners began to hear some priests tell the occasional "little joke" about the fabled bad guy.

Pope John Paul II said the following in his book *Prayers and Devotions* (1984, pg 131): "A man who has a hardened heart and a degenerate conscience is a spiritually sick man, even though he may enjoy the fullness of his powers and physical capacities. Everything must be done to bring him back to a healthy soul." Populist preaching methods cannot do that.

Here is what the greatest evangelist would say to priests and pastors who refuse to speak out about the specific sins evildoers do: *"So with God and Christ as witnesses, I command you to preach God's message. Do it willingly, even if it isn't the popular thing to do." (2 Timothy 4:2)* Political correctness wasn't in the man. He saw the inclusion of hard truths as a requirement of the Christian faith. *"Do you think I am trying to please people? If I were doing that I would not be a servant of Christ." (Galatians 1:10)* The Holy Spirit is not weak, scared, fearful. The Holy Spirit does not back down from speaking Godly righteous truths *in their fullness*. The Holy Spirit is not populist. The Holy Spirit does not cover up or make excuses for evil acts of demonstration done by "the consecrated" and by doing so shield these evil perps from human justice. Human justice is God's justice, for we are made in His Image! But the Holy Spirit only coaches and does not make, because that would be interfering with God's rule about free will here on earth. Even priests, bishops, cardinals, popes, and Protestant pastors are not *made* to do anything by the Holy Spirit. The Holy Spirit does not ignore, cover up for, or transfer "the consecrated" evildoers, thus enabling them to continue their evil acts of demonstration against God and humanity, terribly sullying the integrity of Christianity. Only Satan's servants aid evil in this manner.

Sometimes church members are evil actors who bring discord and scandal into their parishes. Paul says, *"Warn troublemakers once or twice. Then don't have anything else to do with them. You know that their minds are twisted, and their own sins show how guilty they are." (Titus 3:10-11)* In other words, give them no duties and no authorities in the church. Kick them out when they persist in showing off their evil ways.

It is true that God is infinite love, mercy, and justice; the statement is not an oxymoron. For those who choose to be with Him, He is infinite love and mercy. For those who choose to negate Him, He is infinite justice. God Blessed Rebirthment and purgatory derive from God's infinite wisdom, and the two are part and parcel of God's infinite kindness and patience, which burst forth from His infinite wisdom—a wisdom that descends and crosses over into our physical realm in order to enter our human comprehension.

The impregnable salient defending the two conjoined concepts—God Blessed Rebirthment and purgatory—holds the cannons from which shoot the iron spheres of common sense. The spiritual cannonade is neither religious in nature nor secular, but of truth and crossover-wisdom. Truly, it is the Bible's real-life story about God's effort to raise up the collective human soul from its early dawn, its crude form, *its formlessness.*

Roughly eight billion people live on the earth right now. Let's say the average earthly lifespan is 70 years. Let's assume that the rate of population growth has been and will continue to be about the same for this century as it was in the last. That means in order to turn eight billion people in the next 70 years, an average of more than 110 million people must die every one of those years! This is a natural turn. In America this year, roughly four million people will die for all kinds of reasons, and this will be a natural turn.

Of the over one hundred million deaths that occurred in the world just last year, how many of them knew about God? How many repented before body-death? How many even knew about the concept of repentance? How many practiced a God-based religion and truly *tried* to live the Word of God *in its fullness*? Twenty percent? Ten percent? Probably far less than the latter figure, based on what I've observed in life. This part of the salient presents the strongest shooting position in defense of purgatory and God Blessed Rebirthment, since a primarily loving and merciful God wants to give souls ample opportunities to tune Him in prior to the end of the current eternity, *prior to the end of every eternity.*

[Spiritual note: Today, most Americans, including most of Christianity, are of the belief that persons who serve or have served in the military go straight to heaven when they die. This is the furthest thing from the truth, and it is certainly not in the Bible. I (my soul-person-self) have been taken by the Angel of God into the cell of an extremely famous dead military man of WWII (not the one who became President). I cannot say enough how much affection and respect I have for him; my parents' generation regarded him as the top-level architect (there were many excellent architects under him, of course) of America's victories in both war theaters. But he's in a form of prison cell down there and suffering in dark grayness, bearing the weight of the world on his shoulders, it seemed to me. Even in death, many soldiers continue to report to him; in fact, the Angel of God took me to a group of dead officers who surround and protect him, and they in turn took me down a passageway to his room. The Chief stayed sitting the whole time. To start, I saluted him, and he returned it. We talked briefly about how bad America's soul has become since the war ended. He agreed but was not accepting that the nation has to be brought down. Sadly, a very downtrodden man. As a result, I could not plead (be an intercessor) for him, and he stayed behind; all of his soldiers would have obediently followed him had he decided to come with me. In spirit, I am nothing more than a worker, and that's what he would have had to accept for himself: drop the grandiose earth-title and become a "worker." Tough go for some.

After reading the above passage, almost all pastors would think, "Jesus doesn't need that. He can just do whatever He wants whenever He wants." My response is, "Then why do you think He needs you as a pastor? And because you believe He does need you, you better be teaching His things and not your own ideas to His parishioners." But the bigger answer on this issue is that Jesus and God the Father want their "workers" to do it. This work allows workers to gain merit and move up. On top of that, is it proper for the Owner and His King to clean out the barns? Do not they have hired workers to do that, and that way the workers can earn a living and feed and protect their families?

To bridge over from the hp- to the JB purgatory, a soul-person must 1) have an intercessor (a "worker" who successfully bridges the soul-person), 2) repent and denounce his/her bad acts of demonstration (a very late secondary repentance), 3) willingly/gladly give up all earthly titles, 4) let go of pride and accept simple humility as the new strength/good quality of personal character, and 5) accept all of Jesus' work assignments (mostly given out by Angels of God and senior spirit-guides, but sometimes Queen Mary, King Jesus Himself, and even God the Father) to go back down and across to the bad side; part of fifth condition is the person, while in low-level JB purgatory (obscure community college) take on the title "worker" and keep his/her earth-term first name only.]

In heaven (as said in the previous chapter), "forever" is an eternity; that is how God and His angels and freedom souls speak. Again, "eternities" are segments of "God-time." Except for God's written Testaments, which lay out His Commandments and statutes as permanent fixtures that go forward, "before" is forgotten about and "after" is irrelevant because it has yet to begin. Only God the Father knows the "when." Because no one else knows, "after" does not exist. Get it? Jesus says, *"No one knows the day or hour. The angels in heaven don't know, and the Son himself doesn't know. Only the Father knows."* (Matthew 24:36)

In the Book of Isaiah, the Lord speaks of a coming new eternity: *"For behold, I create new heavens and a new earth: and the former shall not be remembered, nor come to mind." (65:17)* When Jesus died, the old eternity ended and the current one began. It is now in the process of ending. Judgment will come down on many soul-persons, carnate and discarnate. A tough transition will take humanity out of the current eternity and into the new one. **The transition** will include **the cataclysm** and **the confusion**, both of which will be for the purpose of awakening people from their immoralities. The confusion will be a prolonged valley of darkness that the soul of humanity must travel through in order to get to the valley's other side.

Hundreds of millions (billions!) of persons will be cast down, determined to have again and again failed God's Will and Word and His offer of repentance. *While God has overlooked the times of human ignorance, now he commands all people everywhere to repent, because he has fixed a day on which he will have judged in righteousness by a man whom he has appointed, and of this he has given assurance to all by raising him from the dead. (Acts 17: 30-31)*

Other soul-persons, less fortunate and born into circumstances devoid of God-based teaching, will have to go to gray holding areas below (hp-purgatory), where they will be kept waiting until a new opportunity on the surface is granted.

Jesus has given the revealer to the understanding that the word "day," in the phrase "day of judgment," does not translate directly into earth-time. It is God-time, meaning it could last years to decades. Persons who receive harsh judgments but are not dispatched to the lake of fire will have to endure multiple God Blessed Rebirthments into very difficult soul-learning circumstances; thrust units may be involved. For others it will be less harsh. Then there are the freedom souls God will send down from above: teachers, guides, positive entrepreneurial-types, positive influencers, and so forth. The upcoming, relatively peaceful eternity will last about a thousand years post the cataclysm and the transition to come.

Chapter XLIX

Secondary Repentance and Dead Presidents

In the early 1930s, Jesus began to dictate Divine messages to a young Polish woman. Faustina Kowalska, declared "Saint" in 2000 by Pope John Paul II, was a nun in her 20s when Jesus began to appear and speak to her. He expressed to the nun that humanity had arrived at a portal, beyond which lived eternal life in the Kingdom of God. The portal was His Heart, and from it flowed "unfathomable" love and mercy for souls who seek salvation. He explained that His love and mercy always override His justice for those who repent to Him. *My Heart overflows with great mercy for souls, and especially for poor sinners. If only they could understand that I am the best of Fathers to them and that it is for them that the Blood and Water flowed from My Heart as from a fount overflowing with mercy (diary note 367).*

Sister Faustina kept a diary of her daily life. Most of it was written after she became a nun, but it became particularly detailed once Jesus began to appear and speak to her. The detailed portion covers the 1930s to mid-1938, when she, due to terminal illness, became too weak to write. Sister died later that year, at the age of 33, the same age Jesus was crucified. Her final years involved intense sufferings. Even though she had been specially blessed, Jesus did not spare her from afflictions, but on the contrary gave them to her. *You are not living for yourself but for souls, and other souls will profit from your sufferings. Your prolonged suffering will give them the light and strength to accept my will. (67).* Another time, He said, *Do not be afraid of sufferings; I am with you. (151).* A little later, when she was in terrible pain: *My daughter, your sufferings will not last much longer (152). Do not weep; I am with you always (259). There is but one price at which souls are bought, and that is suffering united to my suffering on the cross. Pure love understands these words; carnal love will never understand them (324).*

With determined effort, her diary was made available outside Poland in 1979, but only in the Polish language for the Polish diaspora. It was not until 1987 that it came out book format in English: *Divine Mercy in My Soul, the Diary of Saint Maria Faustina Kowalska* (book available but not easy to find). In it, messages consistently tell of Jesus' mercy.

Sister often asked Jesus about the worst of sinners. *Let the greatest sinners place their trust in my mercy. They have the right before others to trust in the abyss of My mercy. My daughter, write about My mercy towards tormented souls. Souls that make an appeal to My mercy delight Me. To such souls I grant even more graces than they ask. I cannot punish even the greatest sinner if he makes an appeal to My compassion, but on the contrary, I **justify** him in My unfathomable and inscrutable mercy. He who refuses to pass through the door of My mercy must pass through the door of My justice (1146).*

When Sister Faustina asked Jesus how He can forgive the worst of sinners at the last second of their lives, He responded, *I have an eternity for punishing these, and so I am prolonging the time of mercy for the sake of sinners. But woe to them who do not recognize this time of My visitation (1160).*

[Spiritual note: Jesus used the word "justify," which means a *process* that will *eventually* grant entry into paradise or heaven. Justification may be difficult, depending on the amount of atonement and purification required. The important thing is the person repented, became enfolded into the heart of Jesus, and escaped the satanic correctional methods.]

Sister asked Jesus why the fallen angels were not granted the grace of repentance. He answered, *Because of their profound knowledge of God. No person on earth, even though a great saint, has such knowledge of God as an angel has (1332).*

[Spiritual note: Calling someone an angel is meant as a compliment or an encouragement, and though okay to do sparingly, it is figurative and not literal. After decades of hearing people talk like this, almost no one knows what an angel is other than just someone who does good deeds or has a pleasing personality. Angel spirits are of unique constitution. They are spirits sent to facilitate us. *Angels are merely spirits sent to serve people who are going to be saved. (Hebrews 1:14)* When we welcome strangers into our homes, we just might also be unwittingly welcoming an angel, meaning an invisible angel-spirit who has been ministering to the person. *Be sure to welcome strangers into your home. By doing this, some people have welcomed angels as guests, without even knowing it (Hebrews 13:2)* Jesus says, "Don't be cruel to any *of these little ones* [children]*! I promise you that their angels are always with my Father in heaven."* (Matthew 18:10, 14) *"When God raises people to life, they won't marry. They will be **like** angels in heaven."* (Matthew 22:30)]

Sister asked about sinners who are on their deathbeds and cannot speak or are in coma. Jesus answered that a faithful person praying nearby to the dying one can appeal to His mercy, and the prayers will count for that soul-person. He will instantly descend and save her/him from eternal death. But no one can be saved without repenting sins; to say otherwise would be the same as calling God the Father and Son liars.

With regard to the woman/man who is dying or has just died failing to repent, nearby in spirit (physically speaking, it can even be across the world) a faithful person can pray to Jesus' Divine Mercy. With it comes the guarantee that Jesus will grant her/him—now discarnate—a final opportunity to repent. The soul-person stands before the glorious, loving, merciful Christ. There is no vagueness and no cloudiness, only ultra-awareness. Naturally, standing with The Love in The Light, the soul-person wants to become part of it.

But remember that there is not full grace associated with secondary repentance. Also, the soul her-/himself will quickly come to the realization that there is a feeling of not being worthy enough to be around other soul-persons who had done better during life on earth. "I don't deserve this, Lord." And it is true. Jesus' grace is there to help out. Soon enough, off to JB purgatory the soul-person goes, where over time there will be many good works to carry out, enough to erase all feelings of unworthiness and overwrite the shame. Said before and reiterated here, suffering periods happen in JB purgatory, levels and lengths dependent on just how bad the sins Jesus' wounds had to cover over with the Father. The soul-person, though saved from the satanic correctional officers, may have done the most despicable acts during earth-term. Again, God the Father and Jesus are not pushovers! There has to be *some* answering! Reader, think about how Miriam repented and how Moses interceded for her. God removed her death sentence but still gave her a punishment of seven days exile.

On December 12, 1985, shortly after takeoff, Arrow Air Flight 1285 crashed and burned in Gander, Newfoundland, Canada. The charter jetliner was carrying 256 passengers, 248 of them American soldiers returning home after six months of peace-keeping deployment in the Middle East. The jet had landed at Gander in order to refuel. There were only a few seconds of notice, and all were instantly killed: ripped apart and incinerated.

Noontime November 22, 1963, found President Kennedy riding in a motorcade through Dealey Plaza in Dallas, Texas. A split-second was all it took for him to be assassinated, from piercing bullets that had entered his body, head, and brain. The President died without knowing what hit him. Basically, it was the shooter's way of shouting "Lights out, Kennedy!"

Almost a hundred years earlier, the same happened to another president. Like everyone in the world, presidents die. Most have time to reflect and repent, but do—DID—any of them? "Who needs to pray for dead presidents, anyway? They all go straight to heaven, don't they?" No, they absolutely do not! They have much to answer for. The revealer sometimes thinks to pray for them, and that is because in the Book of Ezekiel God the Father states that He will take into account none of the good done by a person who did not repent evil acts of demonstration. Furthermore, any person who had a grandiose position of power while on earth will have much more to review and deal with when before the Lord.

April 1968: At only 39 years old, Martin Luther King, Jr., was shot in the head while standing on the second-floor veranda of a motel in Memphis, Tennessee. He never regained consciousness and was pronounced dead an hour later. There was not even one second given for him to review the condition of his soul and repent his sins. In the 1980s, a board of experts determined that the doctor plagiarized part of his doctoral dissertation. Soon after his death, the public became aware that he was a secret womanizer while married. He carried on this lifestyle while at the same time being a Baptist pastor; he may have even had affairs with other men's wives. As to these facts being the truth, there seems to be no doubt. Of course, there are those who will always doubt and deny. Anyway, God knows the truth, and He does not judge based on human assumption and denial; He does not turn to a blind eye to not-repented evil.

September 11, 2001, saw the terrorist attacks on the twin towers in New York City. Two thousand seven hundred and fifty-two people died, most of them in a split-second. Two months later, on November 12, shortly after taking off from John F. Kennedy Airport, American Airlines Flight 587 nose-dived into the Queens, a borough of the same city. The passenger plane had 260 people on board. All instantly perished. Five persons on the ground were killed. That same day throughout America, individuals were killed in car accidents caused by drunk drivers.

None of the above persons had the time to properly reflect and repent. Were they heroes? Were any of them angels? They died tragically—yes, that's true. In the Bible, does not God say death sometimes comes as a thief in the night? The real truth is they were all victims before their time. But *that* was their time. Some, we must know, acted very heroically despite knowing they might die while trying to help others to live. Jesus says that there is no greater show of friendship than to give up one's life to save another (John 15:13).

Jesus also says, *"Out of your heart come evil thoughts, murder, unfaithfulness in marriage, vulgar deeds, stealing, telling lies, and insulting others. These are what make you unclean." (15:19-20) "You must obey God's commands better than the Pharisees and teachers of the Law obey them. If you don't, I promise you that you will never get into the kingdom of heaven." (Matthew 5:20)*

Again, none of the above persons had enough time to properly reflect and repent. Today's world knows that a particular assassinated president had done many *reprehensible acts of demonstration,* one of which was to literally rape a young woman while in the White House. He was known to have said that the American Bishops would need a redwood tree to knock down the doors of the White House if they ever wanted to get inside to see him.

Why does the revealer bring this stuff up? To hurt people's feelings? To dig up old bottles filled with pain? As Saint Paul might say in one of his letters, "I do it to shake people from their senseless thoughts and stupid ideas." Paul does not shy away from using the word "stupid"; in fact, he uses it often.

The bottom line is this: If you pray for your dead—family, friends, and other loved ones—you can help them out of their after-life situations (if they have not been relegated to the lake of fire for a specific, non-retractable period of time).

If you believe that there is no such thing as purgatory, that there is no good to come from praying for the dead, then you are saying that all the above soul-persons went to hell! There is just no other way to shape it for those who preach against the concepts. What exactly is so kind and merciful about a God Who does not have a system that delivers both justice and eventual salvation for the not-repentant persons who died suddenly, instantly? Secondary repentance, purgatory, and praying for the dead are extremely vital parts (graces) to the total make-up of God's infinite love, mercy, and *justice.*

The following example is extreme, and it is put forth so that the reader may receive the point in an even more obvious way. A child is abducted, molested, and slaughtered. The person who did it is never found. As the perp ages, he comes to regret what he did but never turns himself in and therefore never pays for the crime in any way while on earth. The child's family continues to suffer with the realization the perp will never be brought to justice. The man goes to a pastor and receives Christ. He does not reveal to the pastor just how evil an act of demonstration he had done, but instead only mentions that he did some bad things. Let's say he even tells a priest but still refuses to turn himself in, and that is because the man now has his own family and does not want to be shamed in their eyes. *He dies and goes straight to heaven?* Teaching like this takes not only the perp away from salvation, it also potentially takes others away, including victims' families and friends. Inside their hearts and minds, they might be brought to think, *What kind of God has no justice system for those who caused so much pain? On their deathbeds they get away with just saying I'm sorry to God and go straight to heaven?*

Sister Faustina asked Jesus about how He can tolerate so many sins and even the most horrendous of crimes and not punish them. As quoted earlier in the chapter: *I have an eternity for punishing these (1160). He who trusts in My mercy will not perish, for all his affairs are mine (723).* Hence, the reality of JB purgatory and God Blessed Rebirthments into thrust units.

So, do not praise the dead, do not presume positive or negative judgment on them, and do not build statues in their fleeting earthen images. Instead, do something constructive. Pray. If they are already in heaven, God will apply the prayer to the poor souls who never have anyone praying for them. No good-spirited prayer is wasted. Another option is to reserve a portion of prayer to the "Lord's unknown Will." God will apply it to whatever He wants, living or dead.

Prayer can be Bible reading, praising God in words and song, thoughtful reading from a prayer book, doing rosaries and other holy chaplets, and attending church. During prayer, say aloud your requests to Him. He already knows them, but we should never take His kindness, His attentiveness, *His bending down to us* for granted.

The first half of the twentieth century saw the Great Christian Revival sweeping across America. Millions of people repented and were baptized in the name of Christ. The "evangelical sweep-up" involved highly gifted pastors who worked in what seemed like superhuman capacities. For decades, these pastors traveled almost non-stop to carry out the miraculous works charged to them by God. Churches and community halls were jam-packed for sermons that lasted hours, even through the night. Waves of instantaneous healings beyond imagination took place. The pastors feared nothing, and they entered centers, one after another, where the devil was known to run the people's ways. The devil was always defeated. The book *God's Generals* (Roberts Liardon) details the magnificent works accomplished by such pastors as John G. Lake, Maria Wordworth-Etter, and Smith Wigglesworth. Most of these shiny lights went on to suffer many things before passing on.

Catholic Christians know nothing about the Revival, just as Evangelical Christians know nothing about the Divine Mercy. They happened in the same time period. Jesus says that in spirit we are all brothers and sisters when we belong to God. Paul says that we are all part of the body of Christ, when we accept Jesus as Lord.

Sister Faustina wrote down the following from Jesus: *I shall protect them* (the dying who pray to Him / the dying who cannot pray but are being prayed for by the living) *Myself at the hour of death, as My own glory. And even if the sins of the soul are as dark as night, when a sinner turns to My mercy he gives Me the greatest praise and is the glory of My passion. When a soul praises My goodness, Satan trembles before it and flees to the very bottom of hell (378).*

Truly faithful persons are Jesus' shiny lights on earth; they are shiny lights for their neighbors and the faithless members of their own families. When a faithful person has complete confidence in Jesus, it goes something like this: "Beloved Jesus, in You I know that I am saved. But, Lord, heaven won't be as wonderful as it could be if I know that my daughter/son (sister, father, etc.) won't make it up there. So I pray to You for her/him. Right now she/he is very far from you." Keep talking and praying to Jesus as if He is standing right there in front of you.

Even for parents who have already raised their children in a not-so-wonderful way and may even be out of their lives now—be cheered! Again first and foremost, you must be totally selfish about your own personal salvation. Always try to remain close to Jesus and the Father through the various religious avenues, and often pray about your concerns for your children.

Jesus may allow for circumstances to unfold that will bring a faithless person to recognize her/his dire state of soul condition and repent. Perhaps He will grant the soul-person an opportunity to do a secondary repentance and avoid eternal condemnation. Jesus does this for the sake of The Love—the love that binds Him to that faithful, prayerful shiny light. He certainly does not do it for of any merit due the person(s) being prayed for. Regarding the priest's story about the woman whose husband popped up from hell, the setting was in Italy. Tons of Italians pray for their dead; for anyone who knows Italy, this is a given. Jesus granted a tremendous grace for the porno-woman, so that she would have the opportunity to end her evil works and choose a life of good. Nothing she was doing at the time merited His favor. Someone in either the man or woman's family (probably both—it's Italy!) had been praying for one or both of these poor souls. Jesus and God the Father allowed for the visit to take place as an answer to the prayers. But the woman's free will was still there. She could have chosen to reject the grace.

Chapter L

Articles on Myths and Missing Links

Human Evolution: Myth or Missing Link? The evolution of the human body is irrelevant, but the body is not. A temporary vessel for the occupying energy-entity to use for implanting into itself sentient strength, intelligence, and good qualities—and then to magnify those qualities while at the same time shrink/eliminate those qualities that are not desirable—the body is utilized, then discarded.

The concept of "God" is a non sequitur for those who believe that we are nothing more than physical bodies evolved from ape. Failing repentance in life, soul-persons will not have this sin of false belief remitted. If a secondary repentance is granted, the soul-person will have to spend time in the "boogers and feces room" mentioned in prior reading.

The study of old bones is a unique form of entertainment that should never be seen as meaningful in ways that really count. Just interesting and entertaining, that's all.

Aliens: Myth or Missing Link? As to whether aliens exist or not, what difference does it make to the salvation of anyone's soul-person-self? None. A problem can happen when the subject of so-called aliens is taken too far. "Aliens" just might get the person into doing and saying things that will cause a falling off a cliff. So why even bother with the subject? Earth is lived on for specific reasons personal to the souls that have been allowed to take on human form.

The subject interests many, including me. The belief that there are aliens visiting us is not the real truth. To put it plainly, "aliens" don't exist. The cosmic term is "primal pools." The universe has many primal pools. Earth no longer has a primal pool of advanced intelligence—but the body, *the human body*, does belong to earth. It's not a contradiction, for, as said in a prior chapter, the unit has been brought forward. So what exactly does earth have?

The 1970s movie *Star Wars* has a planetary bar where beings from all over the galaxy go to relax, drink, discuss things, fight, and learn. Welcome to earth . . . *kind of.* In the movie, each primal pool shows a different physical presentation. The earth is the inside out of that bar. Here on earth, we all show a reasonably similar physical presentation.

All primal pools that have achieved **universal truth** know about the superiority of "the spirit" because that in and of itself is a universal truth. As said a few times already, an energy-entity, or "spirit-entity," is what the soul-person really is, and our physical bodies are—this, too, the revealer says again and again to stress the point—temporary vessels *used now and then* through endless time in order to teach, re-teach, correct, change, improve, implant, and magnify a spirit-entity's innate knowledge and strength/quality of exuding sentient energy.

All primal pools have members who have become ascended/re-ascended masters. Pools also have fallen members and lots of membership caught in the gray in-between. The fallen members are held prisoner inside the earth. The most classic of all primal-pool incidents is "Roswell," named after Roswell, New Mexico, near to where a spacecraft crashed, in 1947. The beings in the downed spacecraft had been invisibly involved in, by way of sentient energy projection (and even spirit-body overlap, as explained in *MB*), the development of atomic weapons; perhaps they were trying to block the development. If the latter, they failed. If the former, the craft was a renegade, for all primal pools agree that atomic/nuclear weapons are bad. But there has been and continues to be sharp disagreement as to what the primal pools can and should do about them. This is sole reason for the explosion in UFO sightings/visitations in the late 1940s and to this day continues. God cast judgment on the craft's crew, hurling them down to the ground. Once He makes that decision, it's too late for the objects of His wrath. Bible readers recognize lightning as one of God's weapons. Of the night the craft crashed, people in the area described the worst thunder and lightning they had ever witnessed.

The beings' bodies were either killed instantly or died later, and the occupying soul-entities were taken down into the earth by a unit of Satan's special forces. Satan knows what God expects him to do with those who get cast down.

Another job of the satanics is to make sure humanity remains hazy about UFOs and so-called aliens. Hence, Satan is given permission for hard apparitions of his special units from below. The "classic" Men in Black show up to warn, intimidate, and threaten persons who had a particularly strong UFO experience and even more so those involved in the recovery of materials from downed craft. Men in Black know things that they could not possibly know, and that is because beforehand they invisibly listened/observed.

The initial witness reports of UFO incidents are always the most accurate. After that, the military moves in to take control of "things." The military is *allowed* to record the information exactly as it had happened, and they are even *allowed* to haul away any and all foreign materials. BUT ONLY IF THEY AGREE TO COVER IT UP. (This agreement is not something that has been consciously made; human participants retain no conscious understanding as to why they get so angry and forceful against anything UFO.) Even so, using downed craft for earthly gain is not considered a blessed act by the heavenly court. All persons involved will eventually experience body-death, only to have much to answer for when before God. Governments are NOT ALLOWED to admit "aliens" exist, and humanity is definitely NOT ALLOWED to have open contact with primal pools. That is not what earth is for. God the Father created this place, and His rules are the only ones that should count. As for the general public—curiosity, intrigue, and mystery should and must stay as that. (More to come on the subject.)

As for the pastor or the parents of young children, when asked if aliens exist or not, the best answer is, "Whether or not there are other beings out there in God's universe is irrelevant to why each of us is here on earth. During life, always try to be most concerned about carrying on in God's laws, thanking and praising Him for the gift of life, and your attaining the ultimate goal of eternal life—the best thing to have in the whole universe and not a hoard of material items."

The Universal Ladder—First of Two Articles: The Universal Ladder is composed of "truth" and "knowledge." Though the two terms are similar, there is a difference. Whether intuitively seen and accepted or not, truth is a permanent fixture. The absolute truths of the universe are set by God and are not to be messed with by liberal politicians/judges on earth.

"Knowledge" is innate information that has been received "into" the living soul; an inanimate object cannot gain knowledge. Let me explain. In front of the television, a person can watch, let's say, baseball games; a person might even be able to watch an educational video on how wisdom teeth get extracted; the truths about the game and the toothy procedure can be learned in this manner. The television is a reasonably advanced scientific instrument, but it is inanimate. Intimate knowledge can only be obtained by actually getting involved in doing something, and a TV or video camera cannot do that. Do you see? That is why God made the earth for us, so that we may simultaneously gain knowledge and ascend (re-ascend) the ladder to higher and higher spiritual levels of God-tiered universal truths.

Truth and knowledge are like brother and sister. Together they climb the cosmic ladder, starting at a very low *vibration* in darkness, moving upward, emerging from darkness into grayness, into lighter grays, and finally into The

Light. It might take thousands of earth years for a soul-person to achieve (re-achieve) "light status." Some never make it.

The Missing Link: In outer space, well away from stars and planets, it would seem that there are no such things as "up" and "down." When in close proximity to the gravitational pull of a large object, such as a planet, then "up" and "down" move away from being vague concepts. Naturally, a line away from gravity is "up," the opposite "down." The planetary mass represents physical evidence to the larger reality of there existing stepped spiritual realms everywhere around us.

Jesus has shown His revealer that there are more universes than the one we see with our physical eyes. The universes are distinguished by their unique vibrations. The lowest vibration is sheer gravity, or anti-energy marked by pitch-blackness, and the highest is totally positive energy radiating brilliant white light.

Vibration contains tiered universes; our hard physical universe is one of them; most of the others are of a spiritual nature, though not all. The physical universe that the human body lives in is somewhat above the lowest vibration level, described before as dark dense gravity, yet close enough to be affected by it.

The word "vibration" is exactly that—*a word*. It is a human word that allows the mind to intuitively view larger truths. Vibration and not some million-year-old ape bone is the missing link to our past and our future.

The Universal Ladder—Second Article: As said, truth and knowledge are like brother and sister, and together they climb the cosmic ladder. Each higher-up step has its own truth and knowledge, which, together, hold mastery over the truth and knowledge of previous steps. In order to climb, one must have the desire to do so and at the same time be prepared to cut away from or at least modify former beliefs. Each ladder-step is a comfort level that contains personal beliefs and maxims "comfortable" to the person standing at that level. To climb a step is to break through a mental barrier. Beyond the barrier exists a new level of truth and knowledge that, once we get comfortable with, will allow us to feed our ever-hungry minds and hearts; like stomachs, minds and hearts get hungry. Each step up cuts away from a mental placenta so that a new one may attach.

As one moves up the universal ladder, there comes the realization that the previous step contained elements of untruth if not self-deceit that could not be perceived while positioned at that step. The bottom steps are placentas of bodily truth and knowledge: the belief that the physical is everything and that the spirit doesn't even exist. Pleasuring bodily desires/addictions is the focus in these persons' lives. Paul says in Galatians (5:19-21), *"Now the works of the flesh are plain: fornication, impurity, licentiousness, idolatry, sorcery, enmity, strife, jealousy, anger, selfishness, dissension, party spirit, envy, drunkenness, carousing and the like. . . . as I* [Paul] *have told you in times past, that they which do such things shall not inherit the kingdom of God."*

Persons in this category are extremely prone to falling into traps that will cause them to again and again carry out evil acts of demonstration against their own bodies and souls and against other people's bodies and souls. Often imbedded in their minds and hearts are negative/perverse beliefs about certain skin colors and ethnicities of human bodies. These persons could be termed racists and racism-accusers; both tend to be overly touchy/contentious about skin color. Persons who accuse others of being racist, whether the accusation is true or not, will have their own words/actions looked at very closely during judgment. Even things thought to have been said in private will be magnified as if through a loudspeaker. "Persons must never become the hate they hate. At least try not to." If persons are pure in their intentions and in their emitting soul-energy, they will do fine. "To accuse, you must be sure and pure, otherwise you will be accused." For example, had Lieutenant Chase been of a visible minority or a Caucasian of recent arrival from another area, surely every person in the world, except for those few in the know, would have said this was the reason no one was properly charged for his murder.

Not-repentant racists, false-/impure-accusers, race-baiters, and hypocrites are not allowed through heaven's gate—not right away. Each soul-person has to go through the Judge's complete assessment, and that is because other people's lives may have been negatively impacted. Not repented in life, every person answers for denigrating another's skin color. If secondary repentance is granted, the soul-person must sincerely repent, recant, and rebuke him-/ herself in order to be allowed into a purgatorial process of purification and atonement. A future God Blessed Rebirthment into the race that the person put down may be judged necessary. "Learn, soul-person! Learn! Why not? What else is there to do in endless time? Learn!"

An innocent baby's skin color is pure love and a gift from God. A baby's skin color, gender, and ethnicity are inert, in that they express neither action nor desire—they simply "are." At the end of an earth-term no person is judged on skin color, gender, or ethnicity. We are judged on the beliefs our minds and hearts held fast to at the time of our crossing over, we are judged on what good acts of demonstration we carried out during earth-term, and we are judged on the bad acts of demonstration we failed to recognize and repent and therefore still carry in us.

Men and women must be treated and paid the same for the same job done; obviously experience/longevity/competence/education should be considered, but in a gender-equal manner. Society must always treat/consider men and women as equals, with equal accesses/opportunities. Yet there must still exist a respectful separation in consideration to the differences in the two genders' physical makeup: e.g. separate men's and women's washrooms/locker rooms, separate men's and women's athletic competitions (mostly). In the latter example, compensations must be derived in a manner that is equal in consideration to the revenues created from viewer and market support, for double-standards, speaking out of two sides of the mouth, and hypocrisy are absolutely detested by the heavenly court. The court will harshly judge those who hollered "Hey, that's gender bias!" when the accusers were as bad or worse than the ones they accused. Jesus says, *"God will be as hard on you as you are on others. You can see speck in your friend's eye, but you don't notice the log in your own eye. How can you say, 'My friend, let me take the speck out of your eye,' when you don't see the log in your own eye?" (Matthew 7:2-4)*

With regard to equal access, the grand exception is the Catholic priesthood. It must remain male and celibate (no dating/marriage for priests). This is an immovable rule brought down by heaven and has nothing to do human rules and considerations. So, in other words, what business is it of anyone else? Persons who approach the institution or attempt to approach it with hostile intentions will die, and that includes those inside and outside the Church. In this paragraph, the revealer has employed the word "must." While here, we have free will, which means people can do whatever they want. I used "must" for the benefit of those who do not want face the wrath of God through Christ and have Satan take them down to the lake of fire.

At the upper end of the ladder lives the truth that the spirit is everything and the physical body a mere bio-vessel that is used for implanting/magnifying the strength/quality/attributes of a soul-entity's knowledge and projecting sentient energy. During earth-term, a person can implant/magnify his/her ability to love: to love God and thank Him for the gift of life; to love a parent and a child; to love a spouse and siblings; to feel love for a friend, a neighbor, nature, and a nation. The soul-person, while in the body, can learn to magnify many other desirable innate abilities: to be creative; to forgive and put behind; to commit and be loyal to; to respect, serve, and sacrifice; to be empathetic, gentle, and gentle when re-directing others; to be firm and when necessary forceful, but only just enough; to have sexual continence and control of one's temper; to live in fidelity to God's laws; to be more patient and compassionate. Galatians reads, "*. . . joy, peace, patience, kindness, goodness, long-suffering, gentleness, faith, modesty, self-control, chastity are with those who live in the spirit.*" These individuals dwell either very near The Light or in it. Hence, freedom souls are also called Children of The Light. *"While ye have light, believe in the light, that ye may be children of light." (John 12:36)*

Children of The Light are not only light bulbs for the people around them, they are also light bulbs for soul-persons of the netherworld and the lower-down regions that sometimes get "let up" so that they may hound us at certain times of the day and season (God's system). Their constant challenges to our innate goodness help to make us stronger and better-spirited, assuming we don't give in or we eventually stop giving in to their bad sentient projections.

The Fourth Dimension: Vibration is the real missing link. And there is more! The vibration vector—the fourth dimension in totality—is literally a passageway for one's coming aboard the higher reality of there existing many universes, all of which are simultaneous and overlapping; in other words, the fourth dimension is also a way of thinking that will allow the mind to perceive greater truth.

The fourth dimension is not viewable with our regular eyes because it exists above the three-dimensional prison cell in which our eyes are locked. But our minds are much, much larger than our eyes and therefore can visualize, if we choose, beyond the physical confines; the human brain and heart actually overlap into several vibrations.

The fourth dimension might be compared to a pad of paper: a stack of tightly tiered universes separated by—better, *connected by*—vibration. Again, the top sheet is brilliant white light, the bottom totally black. Ascending from the bottom, sheets graduate to lighter and lighter.

The change from one universe to the next, below or above, is not sharp; each level is affected by those closest to it, particularly the two that it is sandwiched between. Our physical surface of earth is closer to the bottom plane than the top. As a result, our plane gets moderately impacted by the ultra-dense gravity-plane located a few layers down.

Not all planes are physical. In fact, most are not. They are spiritual and metaphysical (thick spiritual). The sheet of paper just above the earth-sheet is high enough away from the bottom sheet so as not to be impacted by the suck of gravity. If an object can be raised in vibration, it will be loosed from its bond to gravity. Raising its vibration a little more will cause the physical unit to disappear from human eyesight; the unit still exists but is no longer in the grip of gravity and no longer seeable with our 3D-limited eyes. Raising the unit's vibration a little more will cause it to distort into a metaphysical state. From here, the unit can be lowered back down to its regular vibration, and it will look and be the same as it always was. Raising the unit too high in vibration will cause the physical structure to obliterate, leaving it only spiritual. From this level it is not possible to lower the unit back to a permanent physical presentation on our plane—but temporary, yes, as hard apparitions, needing of a power source.

[Spiritual note: The revealer has already talked of the hard apparitions of the "official" Men in Black. Satanic and powered from below, they are strange-looking, weird-acting, cold-souled males who have the scent of sulphur and the glow of black light about them.

Then there are the Godly apparitions from above. In the last couple hundred years, there have been many. The most famous is Mother Mary as our "Lady of Fatima," in Fatima, Portugal, where she appeared to three young peasant children in 1917. She came as a beautiful woman, simply yet elegantly robed, emitting from her sentient energy an ocean of love, gentleness, and kindness; she was surrounded with brilliant light, colorful flowers, and the smell of roses. *Messiah Bridge* heavily addresses why the mother of Jesus appeared there and in a few other places around the world, including Guadalupe, Mexico, at the bloody time in history outlined in a previous chapter.]

Things move faster and faster as one ascends vibration. If two persons were to stand next to each other while ascending, they would still look and move the same *to each other*, but they would be moving incredibly faster than they had been while residing at their normal plane of vibration. People back on earth would seem to be standing still or barely moving at all.

At each higher-up level of vibration, the earth's surface looks different, and so do the surfaces of our solar system's other planets; even the universe looks different. For example, from their perch on earth and at a particular higher-up level of vibration, Venus (and all the planets and stars of our galaxy) might look a little closer to earth. The surface they see would be solid and not made of overheated noxious gases. (The surfaces of the other planets would look different.) The planet would show a proper atmosphere and be very bright and happy-looking. Standing on Venus, the two would see earth as remarkably different than what they knew. Our planet would look a like a giant ball of water. God did that for us, His shepherded souls. It's biblical. *In the beginning God created the heaven and the earth. . . . And God said, Let there be a firmament in the midst of the waters, and let it divide the waters from the waters. And God made the firmament, and divided the waters which were under the firmament from the waters which were above the firmament: and it was so. And God called the firmament Heaven. . . . And God said, Let the waters under the heaven be gathered together unto one place, and let the dry land appear: and it was so. And God called the dry land Earth; and the gathering together of the waters called he Seas: and God saw that it was good. (Genesis 1:1,6-10)* Later on, at Noah's time, God flooded our surface by temporarily collapsing the vibration of the upper firmament. He is the Creator, and He can be a destroyer when He chooses to be. Says so Himself hundreds of times in the Foundation Testament.

Looking up on a cloudless day, we can see aqua-blue only, and this is a hint of our being underwater at a slightly higher-up vibration. At a slightly lower vibration than ours, the continents are exposed farther out into the oceans, showing solid land right to the edge of the shelves. Lower-vibration colonies are situated here and there along earth's continental shelves; they are "physical" and not spiritual. The Book of Revelation speaks of them.

A very dark surface exists on a low plane of vibration inside the earth; it is what we term as the "crust-mantle interface." The beings down there, at that vibration, consider it to be their surface. They see "only okay" the dark, hard land they walk on, and the sky above always shows as a solid sheet of dark gray cloud, which to us up here on the surface—at our higher-up vibration—is the solid crust, surface of which we walk on. The lava pools are lakes of orange flames; the biggest one is the official lake of fire; the hall of suffering is situated along a particular shoreline. I've spent time in the hall of suffering, and I've done some walking around and fighting down there on that surface: sheol. Some of my experiences are recounted in *MB*. It is a spiritual realm down there—again *sheol*. The Angel of God always takes soul-person-me at night, after my physical body has fallen asleep, because it is easier on the body-soul coalition. Spirit-entities feel almost as fully physical *to each other* as human bodies up here do; the heaviness of the pressing-down atmosphere (again, our crust but at a lower vibration) helps that.

Jesus revealed to "Seer Veronica of the Cross" as published in *Saint Michael's World Apostolate* that if human eyes could see the ships populating earth's upper stratosphere (highly advanced spaceships that can float and mostly reside at a higher vibration), people would think there was hardly any room for them to move around without bumping into each other.

Another way to look at vibration and the fourth dimension is to say the earth (or the universe) is a radio. When the dial gets turned, a different station is picked up. Even though our ears can only hear the one station, the others still exist. God is omniscient. He has ears and eyes that pick up every vibration. Anyway, He is the One Who set up the whole system a very long time ago, and He maintains control over it. *MB* contains much more enlightenment on vibration than this book does.

Jesus gave the following message in 2001: "**People are scared to come back to Me. They speak My Name badly, and there are many terrible sins in the world: corruption, gambling, excessive drinking, drug abuse, and the great holocaust of abortion. These are sins of not just an individual but, truly I tell you, these are sins of a culture and of a nation. You love your country that allows these sins against Me and My Father, but when you die will your country be there to protect you from the evils of darkness? COME BACK TO MY HEALING LIGHT AND MERCY NOW, WHILE YOU LIVE. Repent, repent and change your heart. Earth is a place to live, learn, grow, and walk in My laws. In human life, death is sure, but eternal life awaits your spirit. If you knew what happens in the fires of darkness of hell you would greatly desire to know Me and**

My Father again. My people, it is time to come back to My love. From Jesus the Savior, God the Father, and the Holy Spirit."

Continuing with primal pools: Shortly after a primal-pool incident, eyewitness reports may begin to change, not jibe anymore. Eyewitnesses may start to openly dispute with each other. Next, the military denies seeing anything or they say it was a meteor or whatever, *except what it really was.* Then come men in black from some secret part of the government, but these ones are real people and not the hard apparitions. The military is very smart. The high-ups figure "Why not? Let's give those nervous witnesses and UFOers what they want—some men in black suits and dark sunglasses." But, again, the reasons for their extreme efforts in this manner remain elusive to them. Anyway, after a while, the disagreements, the cover-up, the "explanation," the debunking, and the infusion of disinformation (those wild and weird claims as to what was seen and heard) transform the incident into a mess (Rendlesham Forest Incident an example). "Good job," I say. Generally speaking, persons of extremely strong faith in God will be the ones who are hard on those who are "into" UFOs. Even if they themselves were witness, it doesn't matter. What's the message? "God's Will." Persons who say they are Catholic, Baptist, or whatever but in reality are lax or fallen register the same as heathens and pagans. They are fair game for the parasitic lower primal pools. Those pools can be choosy. It's a silent form of intrusion that many in "UFO circles" believe with strong conviction was agreed to by a certain previous human leader. Almost every person in the world would say that it's ludicrous if not insanity to believe such an idea. Totally understandable.

The real answer lies in how nuclear detonations, including underground ones, impact not just our vibration level but also those just above and below. There are some primal pools that would in a flash destroy America and a few other nuclear countries if God's higher-up primal pools were not providing shield *in His Will*. God owns the earth and HE IS THE ONE WHO WILL DO THE DESTROYING; it will be done on His time and in His way and not on some pagan-Mayan timetable or by way of revenge-seeking parasitic primal pools. What God has allowed is for these primal pools to show bold acts of demonstration of their, His, and the universe's displeasure, to put it mildly, with nuclear weapons and power stations. These are not acts of aggression against countries or humanity, just against nuclear things because nuclear things can kill the planet.

Two things to consider on the matter. First, God's rule for this level of earth is that free will must be allowed to play out, so that each person's eternal destiny can be chosen by each person. Second, God does not contradict His Own rules. Part of the second is that the people of geopolitical nations are brought to reap the benefits of—or suffer the consequences from—the decisions of their leaders. The leaders and people as a whole are granted access to God's graces only if there is geopolitical repentance, which includes dumping any and all evil laws and taking on His rules; of course, individual repentance is there for each person's own salvation. Two biblical examples of this truth are with the people of the Kingdom of Nineveh and King David. Unlike them, America as a geopolitical entity has no interest in repenting and leaving Murky River's bottom, and that is why I believe God allowed a Presidential-Alien Pact to be made; it is still in place. "Allowed" doesn't mean He likes it. God allowed the beforehand meeting to take place, for it could not have happened without Him. He allowed the political leader to make a freewill decision without His sentient interference. (God shows in Exodus that when He wills to do so He places irreversible courses into a political leader's will, by His repeatedly "hardening the heart" of Pharaoh against Moses, each time after Pharaoh had already given in to Moses' demands.)

A particular parasitic primal pool insisted on being allowed to offer higher technologies to the most feared and righteous nuclear nation, so that the nation could lift its technology to a level such that it would never again see fit to use nuclear weaponry in wartime; by doing it, all other nations would conclude it foolhardy to challenge this nation, and the nation could be a sort of earthly police force. Terrorist groups present as a serious challenge to the belief. So do other nuclear nations fighting against other nuclear nations. That is why God and the higher-up primal pools *in His Will* know with certainty that zero nuclear weaponry is the best policy.

The parasitic primal pool wanted a give-back: basically a somewhat-restricted access to the nation's citizenry. On this matter, the revealer goes no further.

A footnote on Roswell. The day after the crash, the local newspaper reported the local military commander admitting to having the remains of a crashed "flying saucer." Many military personnel and civilians of repute have written and talked about what they saw and in some cases handled at the crash site and later on, at the local military base. Another day went by and a high-up military official arrived onto scene, to change the story to "it's a weather balloon." *Yes-yes, good job.* But the reason for this footnote is to show Roswell as the prime litmus test to expose UFO researchers/writers as credible or not. If they can't get Roswell right, then likely nothing else do they. Still, if I were to meet one of them, I would say, "Good job, friend. May I shake your hand?" (Another section to come on primal pools.)

What Exactly is Earth? As one climbs the cosmic ladder, there come step-up awakenings as to just how important the earth is. The arms of human love and satanic correctional services reach down into the valleys beneath earth and far out into the nighttime sky. We are not alone. We never have been. How could we be? We were created; we are shepherded. The human experience is a sojourn and we are the borrowers. Humanity—past, present, and future—is a vital part of a seemingly inextricable cosmic interface between good and evil. And there is a war going on. The good-draw emanating from the Beings of The Light are battling against the bad-suck coming from the beings of darkness, for the control, education, and allegiance of the massive amount of souls caught in the gray in-between. Jesus Christ is God the Father's Commander in Chief of the Forces of The Light. Jesus has revealed (through another of His seers, Vassula Ryden) that due to recent problems on earth, stability of the cosmos has been and continues to be threatened. The tension is not only about nuclear armaments but also about how so many soul-beings are falling into "prisoner classification." A few primal pools have the majority of their carnate members doing poorly, and this has brought fear/desperation to their local overlords who hover in the stratosphere. Some pools are doing okay, others pretty good.

Nevertheless, we must know that in the end, when God determines current time is over and a new time will begin, He is still in charge. He will judge through His Son Jesus Christ, and the good will go up and the bad will go down. Primal pools will be judged, some very harshly, and they will be forced down in vibration and lose their former positions, just like Lucifer and his angel-associates and the reptilians and the reptoids did.

Earth is obviously not even close to being at the center of the physical universe. In spirit, however, earth has been a very important center for a long time. Each soul-person enters earth-term with a pre-determined approximate-length of life, having goals and corrections to accomplish. As shown in Isaiah, length of life can sometimes be granted an extension. Because King Hezekiah begged and repented on his deathbed, God granted him another 15 years. Right after doing it, God reveals to Hezekiah—and to all future generations—His control of the planet's movement, spin, axis-tilt, and so forth. *"Behold, I will bring again the shadow of the degrees, which is gone down in the sun dial of Ahaz, ten degrees backward. So the sun returned ten degrees, by which degrees it was gone down." (Isaiah 38:8)* Five hundred years before Hezekiah, God even made the earth stand still for a day or so, to allow Joshua's army the necessary daylight to chase down and kill the fleeing armies of five Amorite kings (Joshua Chapter 10).

Earth is a grand field camp that has great views, fun outdoor activities, and delicious foods. For some, the place is temporary stopover prior to moving on to somewhere else in the universe. All sojourners are allowed to be here by God's permission. Beforehand, sojourners must agree to abide by His rules. Not so easy to do, considering Satan's influence. In a grander sense, earth is a place to learn to be peaceful. Sojourners can also learn to war successfully but in a peaceful manner, in their pursuits of godly righteousness. Earth is a proving ground. A soul is considered *not much* until it has graduated that tough, *very tough* school-earth.

Sometimes God assigns disputing primal pools to enter humanity so that they can war against each other within the confines of the planet, so that they may not be warring with each other *out there*. After the agreed-to timeframe ends, God is judge of outcome. The winner gets whatever it wanted in the dispute; the losing pool gets assigned down the ladder of power (it gets *de-powerized*). The grand-stage tussling on earth is mostly *not* about physical fights/wars, which usually spark from the side that is losing. Disputes get settled by way of sentient energy projections, to get members of the opposing pool(s) to do reprehensible acts, especially against the pool's own members. God's laws are "the rules" (much more on this matter in *MB*).

Finally, earth is a place where persons can merit their ship coming in, so to speak. A few graduate Earth Academy in such a fine way that they are rewarded a good position *on* a ship, literally, and perhaps even command of one. Sometimes a man—now joined by a woman-mate who brings him (and her) back to the feeling of "wholeness"—returns to an old command, having re-proved himself worthy of it. Good results might take few thousand years to achieve. Who in the universe is in a rush? We only have forever.

God created His earth on a multitude of pillars. He says so to the disenfranchised Job. *Then the Lord answered out of the whirlwind, and said, "Who is this that darkeneth counsel by words without knowledge? Gird up now thy loins like a man; for I will demand of thee, and answer thou me. Where wast thou when I laid the foundations of the earth? Declare, if thou hast understanding. . . . Can't thou bind the sweet influences of Pleiades, or loose the bands of Orion? Can't thou bring forth Mazzaroth in his season? Or canst thou guide Arcturus with his sons? Knowest thou the ordinances of heaven? Canst thou set the dominion thereof in the earth? Canst thou lift up thy voice to the clouds, that abundance of waters may cover thee? Canst thou send lightnings, that they may go, and say unto thee, here we are?" (Job 38:1-4, 31-35)* With such marvelous command of words, God again reveals Himself the Great Creator, Grand Shepherd, and Sovereign Leader of the universe. Even the Pleiadians and Arcturians bow down to Him; then they rush out to do what He told them to do. Even *they* recognize Him as their Forever Forward Shield through endless time and the endless universe. (Persons unfamiliar with UFO-olgy will not understand what the revealer said about Pleiadians and Arcturians.)

Some so-called theologians maintain that the Book of Job is an allegorical saga and Job a mere fictional character in it. The reason some say this is because they are stupid idiots who haven't read the Bible with any intensity. The Lord says to His prophet Ezekiel, *"Though these three men, Noah, Daniel, and Job were in it* [the world]*, they should deliver but their own souls by their righteousness, saith the Lord GOD. . . . Though these three men were in it, as I live, saith the Lord GOD, they shall deliver neither sons nor daughters; they only shall be delivered. . . ." (Ezekiel 14: 14 & 16)* After saying it twice, God goes on to say it twice more, which seems to imply that the three barely made it. But what is definite is God does not lie or speak from stupidity. Job lived, the story is real, and each person is responsible for his/her own salvation, no matter who the dad or mother is.

God does not judge us. We judge ourselves. Where exactly is that in the Bible? The reader might think, *I've never heard this. Is the writer making it up?* "No, I'm not." The falsehood infects "Catholic circles" and all of the fallen non-Catholic "chains." The God-does-not-judge-us-we-judge-ourselves "thing" is a contrived concept that has a nice liberal feel to it, and it travels between persons and groups that have never read the Bible, because if they had read it with any intensity, they would not dare speak in such a poor manner. Only in an indirect sense may there be some validity, in that our bad acts of demonstration during life and lack of recognizing and repenting them will end up being our judge. But it is still God the Father through His Son Who carries through on the process.

Jesus told him: "I came to judge the people of this world. I am here to give sight to the blind and to make blind everyone who can see." (John 9:39) "He [God the Father] *sent me. I did not come on my own." (John 8:42)* Paul says, *"After all, Christ will judge each of us for the good or the bad* [if we failed to repent the bad] *we do while living in these bodies." (2 Corinthians 4:10) "When Jesus Christ comes asking, he will be the judge of everyone,* **whether they are living or dead.***" (2 Timothy 4:1)* Jesus refers to Himself as judge: *"The Father doesn't judge anyone, but he has made his Son the judge of everyone." (John 5:22) "The Father has the power to give life, and he has given that same power to the Son. And he has given his Son the right to judge everyone, because he is the Son of Man." (John 5:26-27) "I cannot do anything on my own. The Father sent me, and he is the one who told me how to judge." (John 5:30) "You will know that I don't say anything on my own. I say only what the Father has taught me." (John 8:28)* How many times does Jesus need to say it? But later on, in the Gospel of John, He says, *"I am come a light into the world, that whoever believeth in me should not abide in darkness. And if any man hear my words and believe not, I judge him not: for I came not to judge the world, but to save the world. He that rejecteth me and receiveth not my words, hath one that judgeth him: the word that I have spoken, the same shall judge him on the last day." (John 12:46-48)* The first half of the passage seems to show Jesus contradicting His previous statements. The back half puts that idea to rest, when He says that the words He spoke will be the same as judge. Any time Jesus or God the Father seem to say something contradictory to other passages of direct Divine quotation, there truly has not been a contradiction. A proper interpretation must be made within the greater context of all passages of direct Divine quotation on any particular subject.

Doesn't God's judgment happen at the same time for all the living and dead? After we die, don't our souls just sleep in our graves? This is mostly myth. At the time of Jesus' visitation, the Pharisees and majority of Jewish people believed it. Today, members of the sect known as Jehovah Witness tout the same line, and it will be exactly that for them, as a punishment for their contradicting Jesus. Because these ones tend to lead good lives, Jesus punishes them because His Love binds Him to them. They don't sleep for more than a few years. In *MB*, I talk of being taken to the graves of a few JWs, to wake them up and intercede for them.

At news of His friend Lazarus' death, Jesus says to His disciples, *"Lazarus is dead! I am glad that I wasn't there, because now you will have a chance to put your faith in me. Let's go to him." (John 11:14-15)* Jesus gets there (Bethany) and sees Martha (Lazarus' sister) so very distraught. He says to her, *"Your brother will live again!"* Martha answers, *"I know that he will be raised to life on the last day* [Day of Judgment], *when all the dead are raised."* Jesus' comeback is *"I am the one who raises the dead to life! Everyone who has faith in me will live, even if they die. And anyone who lives because of faith in me will never really die. Do you believe this?"* She replies, *"Yes, Lord." (John 11:23-27)* Jesus raises Lazarus right then and there. JWs obviously don't believe in the fullness of power God the Father grants His Son.

After Jesus dies at Calvary, an earthquake comes. *At once the curtain in the temple was torn in two from top to bottom. The earth shook, and the rocks split apart. Graves opened, and many of God's people were raised to life. They left their graves, and after Jesus had risen to life* [three days later, on Easter], *they went into the holy city, where they were seen* [as apparitions] *by many people. (Matthew 27:51-53)* This is God the Father's act of demonstration of His offer to humanity through His Son. Later, Jesus ascends to the Father and takes those souls with Him.

In Revelation, Jesus states that He has the keys to the kingdoms of death. There, too, is the mention of Judgment Day. On that Last Day, soul-persons who have not made it out of JB purgatory and hp-purgatory will be subject to judgment as to their placements in and travels through the next eternity. Repeated from before, those from JB purgatory will get better birthing situations than those from hp-purgatory in the next eternity; many of the very evil ones in the latter will be condemned to the lake of fire. Jesus says in John 5:28-29, *"Don't be surprised! The time shall come when all the dead will hear the voice of the Son of Man and they will come out of their graves. Everyone who has done good things will rise to life, but everyone who has done evil things will rise and be condemned."*

All the apostles ran off and abandoned Jesus the night He was arrested. Every year on Good Friday and Easter this is what pastors preach.

The error gets my goat because it's a myth. All four gospels state that an apostle used a sword to strike one of the soldiers who had come to arrest Jesus. The soldier's ear was cut very badly: off or almost off. Jesus ordered Peter to put away the sword because what is to happen to the Son of Man must happen. Jesus then did another of His miracles, touching and healing the soldier's ear. The Gospels of Matthew and Mark claim that right after that, Jesus got arrested and all the apostles ran away. Luke's and John's gospels do not mention anyone running away. All four gospels say Peter followed Jesus and the soldiers at a close distance; later that night will come his infamous denial of Jesus. Only Gospel of John states that Apostle John, the writer of the gospel, also stayed near to Jesus, but for the other apostles not to see him must have meant he wasn't beside Peter. But they had run away, so how could they know? John's gospel goes on to say that the temple authorities recognized him a disciple of Jesus, and he was allowed to enter the court. He was given ample opportunity to deny the Lord, and he refused to. God did not interfere with John's free will. Satan tried (sentient energy projection) but could not get this apostle to back down. By not backing, John showed a fearless acceptance that he, too, might be accused and tortured, even killed. For the other apostles to regain God the Father's favor, after they had abandoned His Son—especially considering that they had seen His miracles and been given the same powers to heal people and stomp on snakes and demons—they would later have to do an *act of demonstration of fearless courage* by showing a preparedness to die for the flocks that they would bring to the Lord. Not only be prepared to be martyred but actually do it. (Each one came through.) This truth is shown later, after Jesus' resurrection, when the apostles were out in a fishing boat. A stranger standing on the shore shouted out to them to place their net on the other side of the boat. All except one thought, *Who the heck is he to tell us that?* Still, they did as the guy said and got a full net of fish. John said to Peter, "It's the Lord." Only John had the grace to recognize Jesus in a different form from what they knew. Peter's eyes were opened. He jumped out of the boat and swam to Jesus. After they ate and talked for a while, Peter asked Jesus if he (John) would have to die a martyr's death. Why would Peter single out John? The only answer can be that Jesus had revealed to him just how seriously disappointed God the Father was with the apostles who had abandoned Him. Basically, Peter's question inferred, "What about him—John? He didn't abandon you. Does he have to be killed or is he off the hook?" Jesus responded that it was none of Peter's business. The reason today's pastors use a single brushstroke that paints all the apostles the same color is because it blends in well with their populist preaching. Up until the late 1960s, the Catholic Church taught the real truth about the abandonment and sentence to martyrdom. That's how I first learned about it, from a teaching nun in Catechism class (formerly Catholic youths' version of Bible school). A huge problem in today's Christianity is most pastors and priests are not preaching and teaching God's Word *in its fullness*. Later, what will they say to Jesus? "Oops, sorry about that." "I did it my way, Lord, and not Yours."

The Baltimore Catholic Bible (1914) states Apostle John wrote his gospel 63 years after Jesus' resurrection; the other three gospels were already out there. The old man asked his students to do a general fast so that God would grant him the extra enlightenment warranting of a fourth gospel.

"You are saved by faith and faith alone." "You must show good works to be saved." Which instruction is true? The first is the correct statement: "You are saved by faith and faith alone." Two men were crucified alongside Jesus. One of the men railed at Jesus, the other acknowledged and repented his life of evil. Even though Jesus showed a hideous physical presentation, all bloodied and beaten to a pulp as he was, the second guy expressed a faith in Him; for him to do that took an incredible amount of belief and courage. The now-good guy said to the still-bad guy, *"Don't you fear God? Aren't you getting the same punishment as this man? We got what was coming to us, but he didn't do anything wrong." Then he said to Jesus, "Remember me when you come into your kingdom." Jesus replied, "I promise you that today you will be with me in paradise." (Luke 23:40-43)* But the repentant man showed no good works. How could he?

On his last day of earth-term, the repentant man was an incredible witness for the Lord. All there heard the criminal's humble contrition. Today, still, the broken, dying man remains the greatest example of the Lord's ocean of love and mercy for even the of worst sinners who repent.

In Chapter 18 of Luke, the Pharisee and tax collector go into the temple to pray. Back then, tax collectors for Caesar were considered traitors, and most of them were known to over-collect and pad their pockets. The Pharisee proudly prays whilst, Jesus says, *"The tax collector stood off at a distance and did not think himself good enough even to look up to heaven. He was so sorry for what he had done that he pounded his chest and prayed, 'God, have pity on me. I am such a sinner.' When the two men went home, it was the tax collector and not the Pharisee who was pleasing to God. If you put yourself above others, you will be put down. But if you humble yourselves, you will be honored." (9-14)*

After a person returns to the Lord, good works are fine to do. Some people don't have the time, money, opportunity. Others do. Some do not have the personality to turn on a dime and instantly become a bold do-gooder. Each person is unique, and each possesses certain types and levels of spiritual strengths. At minimum, a Christian should be kind-hearted, compassionate, friendly, obliging (hold that door open for the next person), and not a troublemaker.

Paul instructs Timothy: *"Timothy, you belong to God, so keep away from all these evil things. Try your best to please God and be like him. Be faithful, loving, dependable, and gentle." (1 Timothy 6:11) "Always do* [try to do] *the right thing. Be faithful, loving, and easy to get along with. Worship with people whose hearts are pure. Stay away from stupid and senseless arguments. These lead to trouble, and God's servants must not be troublemakers. They must be kind to everyone, and they must be good teachers and very patient." (2 Timothy 2:22-24) "Be humble when you correct people who oppose you. Maybe God will lead them to turn to him and learn the truth." (2 Timothy 2:25) "You must correct people and point out their sins. But cheer them up, and when you instruct them, always be patient." (2 Timothy 4:2)*

Apostle James puts the following in his general letter: *"My friends, what good is it to say you have faith, when you don't do anything to show that you really do have faith? Can that kind of faith save you? Faith that doesn't lead to good deeds is all alone and dead." (James 2:14,17)* Does this passage present as a biblical contradiction? God the Father and Jesus' direct words cannot be overridden. A discerner must refer to the Apostles' direct quotations of Jesus and/or God the Father, for they hold mastery. Only then can a proper interpretation of an apostle's passage be done, when a contradiction seems to have occurred.

At Bethany, *Mary* [Lazarus and Martha's sister] *took a very expensive bottle of perfume and poured it on Jesus' feet. She wiped them with her hair, and the sweet smell of the perfume filled the air.* The disciple Judas sees this and says, *"Why wasn't this perfume sold for three hundred silver coins and the money given to the poor?"* Jesus replies, *"Leave her alone! She has kept this for the day of my burial. You will always have the poor with you, but you won't always have me." (John 12: 3,5,7-8)* The Gospels also have Jesus instructing His disciples that when they do something for the poor, they also do it for Him. Then there's His parable about the Good Samaritan. Yes, of course we should want to— within our means and capabilities—carry out acts of demonstration that show our love of neighbor. But we must love God first and biggest, and only then will we end up not loving our neighbors' evil ways just to be friendly and agreeable.

Early in John's gospel, John says, *"But as many as received him* [Jesus], *to them he gave power to become the sons of God, even to them that believe unto his name." (1:12)* A serious problem happens when the passage is taken literally, in short, without further explanation—without proper reference to Jesus and the Father's direct words. Jesus says that for a person to be saved, he/she *must* repent and follow God's commandments, laws, and statutes better than the Pharisees and Sadducees do, and you can bet those two religious groups did not believe in gambling, same-sex marriage, abortion, pornography, tattoos, etc. Our so-called modern-day Protestant pastors and Catholic priests and hierarchy need to wake up, repent their apostasy, and start serving coffee!

In Galatians, Paul writes about the Law not being pleasing to God. He even says, *"If we can be acceptable to God by obeying the Law, it was useless for*

Christ to die." (2:21) Anyone who reads the Foundation Testament knows God's Laws are absolute, permanent, immovable. Considering Jesus and the Father's words hold mastery and none of the Apostles would ever be contradictory, what could Paul possibly be talking about? They are the human laws that were developed by religious leaders in order to control/subdue the people: e.g. how far one can go from home on the Sabbath, the maximum load the person can lift on that day, etc.

Jesus says, *"Don't suppose I came to do away with the Law and the Prophets. I did not come to do away with them but to give them their full meaning. Heaven and earth may disappear. But I promise you that not even a period or comma will ever disappear from the Law." (Matthew 5:17-16)* "The Law and Prophets" is a back-then way of referring to the Foundation Testament. Jesus didn't have much regard for laws instituted by rabbis. The Pharisees say to Jesus, *"Why are your disciples picking grain on the Sabbath? They are not supposed to do that!" (Matthew 12:2) "Is it right to heal people on the Sabbath?" (12:10)* Jesus shoots them down.

Religion is the cause of all wars. Wrong. Sin is the cause of all wars. The major sin that causes warring is bloated, warped nationalism, otherwise known as "national pride." Wars during the time spanning the Foundation Testament were almost unanimously *not* started because of religious differences. Instead, they were about one nation invading another in order to beat it into oblivion and gain its territory and material items. The Bible happens to be the primary informational source for many of the former-world battles. But The Book also has God saying that it is *sometimes* He Who brings nations into battle, when they've become too rife with riches, personal pride, immorality, abject greed, violence against neighbor, and hand-made statues.

The battles constituting The Crusades were the grand exception; those can mostly be attributed to religion. The last battle ended 600 years ago, in the early 1400s. Can we get past it?

A more fitting concept is that religion can be the cause of internal conflicts, in nations and in families. The good teams should never give in to the bad teams just to keep the peace. The Foundation Testament reveals that the Jewish nations of Judah and Israel sometimes battled against each other. The Bible shows why God considered Judah to be the good team most of the time. But sometimes not. As well, a whole host of other cities and nations *not*. The revealer asks the reader to take a timeout from *ARR* to read Jeremiah Chapter 25.

Then there's Northern Ireland, with its historical periods of Protestant-Catholic clashes. In the most recent disruption, which began in the 1970s, the so-called Catholic side carried assassins; in fact, they started the conflict by their marked killings. There is no way that God the Father and

Son considered that side good. But hatred blinds people. Read the Bible, I say. Paul instructs many times as follows: *"Always be glad because of the Lord! I will say it again: Be glad. Always be gentle with others."* (Philippians 4:4-5)

All those God-people are weird. Not quite. *Some* God-people are weird. These ones just need to read the Bible, repent, and start doing what God says. They also need to stop being in denial about global warming. "Look at the last forty years of satellite images of earth's icecaps! Stop choosing to be blind! Do what God wants! Take care of His earth!"

And who exactly are they that say God-people are weird? The godless heathens and pagans, of course, with their tattoos and earrings all over their bodies. Constant abuse of God's Holy Name, foul words, loud farts and burps, and hideous laughter dominate their noise-makings. They all love porn and violence of all kinds, and they smoke dope and teach their young brothers and sisters and children to do it. On weekends, they party their asses into the ground, drink their faces off, do drugs, and gamble their wallets away and somehow feel deprived if on a weekend they didn't get to do it. They belittle God-people and bellyache about what the government doesn't do for them. "And God-people are weird?" *"I often warned you that many people are living as enemies of the cross of Christ. And with tears in my eyes, I warn you again that they are headed for hell! They worship their stomachs and brag about all the disgusting things they do. All they can think about are things of this world."* (Philippians 3:17-19)

I pray to God for my ball team to win. Don't bother doing that. God deals with spheres the size of stars and planets. Why would He bother with a golf ball that is supposed to go into a ground hole? A basketball through a hoop? A football across a chalk line? Most sports were dreamed up by humans in the last couple hundred years so that participators and watchers could have some fun during time away from days of hard labor.

Free will and natural interactions of human bodies must be allowed to play out. Sports are neutral acts of demonstration that have the potential to deliver both positive and negative traits into souls. Players need to be careful about what they train into themselves, what they train themselves into, and what types of examples they are for others.

The Lord *may* answer prayers that are meant for body safety; but we have to be careful here because it is the person and not God who chooses for no truly "good" reason to be involved in activities that clearly and beforehand present dangerous to the physical body. Why would He protect the body of a professional football lineman? Especially one who paid money to have oodles of inked needles poked into his body and by doing so show as a poor example (in God's eyes) to the nation's youth? Prayers meant for the spirit are better received, for there is potential learning for the soul-person. Prayer may allow a person's spirit the grace to better handle losing or become a more humble winner. Prayer may spark the person TO REPENT! Again, the natural way of interaction cannot be interfered with for no good reason. A good reason is when God directly interferes in wars so that His side wins, as Moses' and Joshua's battles demonstrate.

There's no difference between Christians and Muslims. Both believe in the same God. These are fair statements that need addressing. Both faiths recognize, accept, and worship God the Father. Muslims mostly use "Allah" over "God" and do not use the term "the Father." Muslims accept Jesus as an important prophet and to some degree respect His Holy Name, depending on the type of Muslim. Non-Messianic Jews believe Jesus nothing. Christians (including Messianic Jews) recognize Jesus the Messiah; most believe Him to be the Son of God. Islam's holy book, Koran, states that anyone who calls Jesus "Son of God" is worthy of death. At Jesus' transfiguration on the mountain, God the Father Himself calls Jesus His Son. Is God worthy of death? Since His ascension, Jesus has sat at the Father's right hand in heaven. Apostle Peter says, *"Christ is now in heaven, where he sits at the right side of God. All angels, authorities, and powers are under his control." (1 Peter 3:22)*

Muslims and Christians believe that at the end of time Jesus will, with sword in hand, descend from heaven and defeat Satan from the hearts and minds of many people. The major gulf separating the two faiths is at the cross on Mount Calvary. Muslims believe that Jesus was not crucified but instead someone else was. Some geographic areas of Islam teach that it was Judas the betrayer who was crucified. This is a blatant falsehood and an atrocious thing to teach Islamic youth. Mother Mary did not recognize her own son? A betrayer died for our sins? A betrayer's wounds shield us from God the Father's wrath and His hard hand of justice? *"We know that God listens only to people who love and obey him. God doesn't listen to sinners." (John 9:31)*

Muslims say they accept the Foundation Testament and the four Gospels as being divinely inspired; the Koran references them several times. Islam believes God would not have allowed a prophet like Jesus to be killed. What exact Bible have they been reading? Prophets were almost always cruelly treated, and many were killed. In Acts, Stephen says to the Jewish authorities, *"You stubborn and hardheaded people! You are always fighting against the Holy Spirit, just as your ancestors did. Is there one prophet your ancestors didn't mistreat? They killed the prophets who told of the One Who Obeys God. And now you have turned against him* [Jesus] *and killed him." (Acts 7:52)* Stephen is then stoned to death.

Islam's great prophet Mohammed received his inspiration and Godly messages by way of Archangel Gabriel. After a time, Mohammed would have had to face Satan, as a test of his character and ability to discern. This is the "way of God," as shown in the Foundation Testament's Book of Job, when Satan goes before God to ask for an opportunity to test the Lord's good friend Job. Satan wants to see if Job can be brought to curse God. Job passes the test. An even greater indicator of God the Father allowing Satan his shots comes when Jesus is 40 days in the desert. Several times is Satan left to challenge and tempt God's Own Son.

Prior to His arrest, Jesus warns Peter that Satan went before God to ask for an opportunity to test the apostles. *"Simon* [Peter] *listen to me! Satan demanded the right to test each one of you, as a farmer does when he separates wheat from husks." (Luke 22:31)* Satan tested God's beloved King David, getting him to sin against God by doing a census (1 Chronicles Chapter 21).

Mohammed was tested by Satan. The Lord God allowed the devil his shots. There is just no other way to look at it. Again, Mohammed did not get free passage. If he had, then Satan would have bellyached up from below about the whole thing being rigged and unfair and on how the pathetic human never proved himself worthy to be a prophet. When it came to the subject of Jesus' crucifixion, Mohammed was unsuccessful in recognizing the first satanic concept offered him; he did not question the angel about it being contradictory to The Prophets and the Gospels. What does Jesus say when challenged on it? *Then Jesus explained clearly what he meant* [about His coming death]. *Peter took Jesus aside and told him to stop talking like that. But when Jesus turned and saw the disciples, he corrected Peter. He said to him, "Satan, get away from me! You are thinking like everyone else and not like God." (Mark 8:32-33)* There, Jesus says it. Can He be any clearer? Those who believe He would not be killed are thinking like Satan.

To believe/teach that it was a betrayer and thief (Judas was known to skim from the kitty) who died for our sins is, plain and simple, satanic. Mohammed failed the test, and as a result Satan was granted more room to rake and sift him. Next came the satanic offering about killing anyone who calls Jesus the Son of God. Archangel Gabriel said (Luke 1:35) to the inviolate Mary, "therefore also the holy thing born of thee shall be called Son of God." Is Gabriel, the very same archangel speaking to Mohammed, worthy of death? The falsehoods need to be acknowledged, repented, and removed from Islam. What are the chances of that ever happening? So you see, the gulf between the two faiths is permanent. And then to believe that to die while cold-bloodedly killing people will send the murderer straight to heaven, for the enjoyment of 72 virgins, which, by the way, is nowhere to be found in the Koran. Down there, the satanics mock, humiliate, and torture dead terrorists.

What about Mohammed? Just prior to being taken up into the sky, he gave out a beautiful prayer of forgiveness. But it was God Who lifted him up. Mohammed did not rise up on his own power. Even Jesus did not lift

Himself up; His Father did that. Seeing Mohammed float upward was a tremendous encouragement for his followers. But the man had yet to receive his personal life-review and final judgment. It is my belief that his repentance for later in life bowing down to worship three pagan female dieties and his last prayer were probably enough to get him reprieve from the lake of fire but not necessarily enough to get him out of a period of time in hell (including "the shores" and "the hall"). The writer also believes he was likely eventually placed in netherworld until the end of time, so that he could over and over again see just how badly his mistakes would mislead people and wreak havoc. I do not know for sure. God certainly does. All we need to do is read the Foundation and House Testaments to understand how He judges. That's what I did. And I have the Catholic teachings on purgatory and hell imbedded in my soul, though in the last five decades the Church has gone silent on the two afterlife places and now supplies zero to zilch teachings and warnings about them. (Please note that even though Mohammed made some huge mistakes, his name should not be disparaged, for God chose him a prophet. Most of the Koran is Holy Divinely-inspired revelation. Kind-hearted, peace-loving, God-loving, law-abiding Muslims are good people and not to be put down and insulted. God has granted them the grace to put aside Mohammed's significant errors.)

Still more on primal pools: Anything that shows reptile or reptile-like skin is considered low in the universe. Any ET that indicates reference to or reverence for anything reptile or reptile-like is considered low and might actually be a "re-pooled" energy-entity from a reptile primal pool. When Satan was cast down, those pools were punished along with him. Nudity is another bad one, but not totally. For the most part, "nudees" are considered "lowees." One particular primal pool—definitely not close to humanoid—has presentation that would be impossible to put clothes on. They are okay beings and not enemies, but they are extremely different-spirited and very sensitive about how they appear to others. The primal pool has a highly developed ability to project sentient energy, both positive and negative. They can appear as beautiful women or giant ugly monsters, depending on the situation. Their preference is to appear as they really are: 3-4 feet tall and dark brown; lots of thin, soft, hairy arms that extend to the ground; a head that looks somewhat like a large-brown-eyed giant lobster's, if the lobster were standing straight up. They prefer to be friendly and are quite humble. Too, they can show a short fuse and bite back real hard. But mostly the pool doesn't like to scare the daylights out of humans. The pool has some ascended masters who retain good self-control and are friendly. The ship I was allowed to see was like a giant, highly polished, smooth gold coin: 6-7 ft in height and 150-200 ft in diameter. Because of their appearance, God has a modicum of compassion for them. He allowed them to approach me, to request that I extract one of their discarnate members imprisoned in sheol. My free will was involved. In the past, the primal pool lost a war with the reptoids and retain fear of them. But God cast judgment on the reptoids when Satan was thrown down. The extraction was successful. The *why and how* can only be understood if one reads *MB*. They are somewhat beholden to me, and I, in turn, am forever hugely beholden Savior Jesus.

Most of the high-up primal pools are human-like and wear clothes (but not all the clothed pools are "nice"). Basically, this is how it goes: some primal pools are shorter, taller, more muscular, less muscular, on the hairy side, not so hairy, bigger skulled, smaller skulled, narrow skulled, wide skulled, lighter skinned, darker skinned, redder skinned, golden skinned. They follow God's rules and stay high up in vibration and mostly hidden from their members doing earth-term. *Right then the Spirit took control of me* [Revelation's John], *and right there in heaven I saw a throne and someone* [God the Father] *sitting on it. The one who was sitting there sparkled like precious stones of jasper and carnelian. A rainbow that looked like an emerald surrounded the throne. Twenty-four other thrones were in a circle around that throne. And on each of these thrones there was an elder* [leader of each of the 24 chosen primal pools] *dressed in white clothes and wearing a gold crown. Flashes of lightning and roars of thunder came out from the throne in the center of the circle. . . . At the same time the twenty-four elders knelt down before the one sitting on the throne. And as they worshipped the one who lives forever, they placed their crowns in front of the throne and said, "Our Lord and God, you are worthy to receive glory, honor, and power. You created all things, and by your decision they are and were created." (Revelation 4:2-5, 10-11)* Another important rule is that while on earth all beings are considered human. Later, after body-death, soul-persons do not have to return to their original primal-pool presentation, though they will forever retain memory of it. There may be a perfected earth-term presentation (a "re-pooled presentation") that the energy-entity prefers to show.

Messiah Bridge delves further into the subject of primal pools. *ARR* repeats almost nothing from that book, and what has been written above is almost entirely not in *MB*. Though *MB* came out seven years prior to this one, it is at a higher-up step on the universal ladder of enlightenment. The primal pools known as "short grays" and "tall grays" are revealed in it. The two are not horrible but they aren't exactly wonderful: they are silent parasitic. Their main objective—out of desperation—it to develop/incubate high-quality humanoid (and human-looking) physical bodies with brains (with the extra gland that can alter the physical body's level of vibration) that can adequately house their primal pools' discarnate souls. Only if a reader can accept what the revealer has presented in this offering should the earlier book be considered for reading. If you find the contents of this one "too wild and out there," forget the one from 2007. The terrible 4-5 feet tall primal pool known as "blood drinkers" (grotesque amphibian-like humanoids—naked, slimy) are in *MB*.

My vote is an emphatic NO to governments admitting to the existence of extraterrestrial beings and NO to open contact with any primal pool(s): review in 1,000 years. Humanity is just too selfish, too short-sighted, too fearful of body-death, too violent, too addicted, too depraved.

As with God Blessed Rebirthment, the truths about primal pools and earth's role in the cosmos should only be "offered" to individuals who are at a very high level of God-based spirituality. A person can be young, but not too young. The truly God-based will be able to see the revealing in the Light of God, and they will praise Him even more than they did before. On the other hand, heathens and pagans would use the information in an anti-God way and improve nothing about themselves. "See! All that God stuff is fiction! Aliens are the gods!"

The Catholic Church says Mary is Queen of the Universe. Come on, let's get serious. That's the biggest myth going. No, it's not. The revealer has already talked about Jesus' mother having her own wing of purgatory. It is a massive one, and she has been allowed it by God's grace. In *MB* I reveal Queen Mary as a mighty warrioress—when she decides to be that.

Most Catholics of predominantly Catholic nations show a strong devotion to Mary; they openly display her images and spend time praying the rosary in church and at home, for her help and intercession. But the problem is that many do not do what God says and end up helping evil win out in society. I explain by using the following example. The majority of Mexican and Filipino Catholics who emigrated to America vote for political candidates who are openly for s-s marriage and abortion at all stages of pregnancy. This is an extremely evil act of demonstration and failing repentance in life they are subject to God the Father and Son's full wrath and condemnation, no matter how many Our Fathers they prayed. The excuse that the person did not vote for the candidate for those reasons is not accepted. God's Will and Laws are not to be put aside because a candidate was handsome or spoke with gallantry or had pleasing-to-the-eye skin color/ethnicity/etc. Add to that, many of these persons retain unclean lips and eyes right into body-death, by their failing to have repented and ceased their loving to denigrate people behind their backs. This really bad habit is against the Fifth Commandment: *Thou shalt not kill.* Jesus says, *"You know that our ancestors were told, 'Do not murder' and 'A murderer must be brought to trial.' But I promise you that if you are angry with someone, you will have to stand trial. If you call someone a fool, you will be taken to court. And if you say that someone is worthless, you will be in danger of the fires of hell." (Matthew 5:21-22)* And then there's how they so enjoyed the taking in of sights of evil acts of demonstration on TV and in person.

Their anti-God ways were passed on to their children—God's little innocent children—as being fine.

God the Son cannot bring them anywhere near to God the Father. At these ones deaths, Jesus comes only because His Mother wants to be there, so that she can take the soul-persons with her and not let the satanics take them. He shows them His extreme anger and disappointment and tells them to go with His Mother right away and not be around Him for even one more second. Mary takes them to her wing of purgatory, consoles them only somewhat. On her plane *down there*, they continue to worship God *but now in full truth*. Confessions will be heard by priests that Mary also had to intercede for before Jesus' wrath. All will be required to go through very lengthy and rigorous purgatorial processes that will deliver sin-atonement and build merit. Mary will eventually be able to take them back to Jesus. Anyone who actually voted for s-s marriage in a referendum and **failed to repent and recant in life** is condemned; an abomination against God and heaven, it is an indelible mark of the beast left inside the soul-person after body-death; the final hope for the soul-person is for there to be someone in the world praying the Divine Mercy—and for Jesus to apply those prayers to that person and not someone else in the world; many, many people die at any given moment.

Catholicism has the following prayer: *Queen of the universe, Mediatrix of men to God, Refuge of all our hopes, have mercy on us.* Mary cannot forgive sins. All she can do is plead a better outcome for the ones who had a strong devotion to her motherly love. The prayer says it: *have mercy on us* [at our deaths please place us under your blue mantle of protection], *Queen of the Universe*, [by your being] *Refuge of all our hopes* [and our] *Mediatrix of men* [and women] *to God* [Who can be so fearsome a God when He sees the not-acknowledged and therefore not-repented evil we did during life].

Members of the 24 chosen primal pools incarnate in many countries on earth, but each has most of its members birthing into one or a few countries. If it were not for Mary, many primal pools would be producing poor results. Judgment would have most if not all of their members condemned to hell, and their pools would be judged very harshly: be lowered. The primal-pool leaders love and appreciate Mary to the nth degree. They bow and kiss her hand and thank her and do whatever she asks; in other words, they are "beholden" to her. So you see? She's Queen of the Universe. Woe to those who reduce/denigrate Mary and call themselves Christians!

Chapter LI

Fabulous Aching Heart Love

The Gospels have Jesus talking of "the good place above" in a vague manner. *"The kingdom of heaven is like what happens when someone finds treasure hidden in a field and buries it again. A person like that is happy and goes and sells everything in order to buy that field. The kingdom of Heaven is like what happens when a shop owner is looking for fine pearls. After finding a very valuable one, the owner goes and sells everything in order to buy that pearl." (Matthew 13:44-45) Jesus said, "What is God's kingdom like? What can I compare it with? It is like what happens when someone plants a mustard seed in a garden. The seed grows as big as a tree, and birds nest in its branches." Then Jesus said, "What can I compare God's kingdom with? It is like what happens when a woman mixes yeast into three batches of flour. Finally, the yeast rises." (Luke 13:18-20)* See what I mean? *Vague.*

In recent years, I have heard a few pastors assert that there is sex in heaven. Since no further explanation was provided, one can assume they meant sexual intercourse. This is an error. Something superior to sexual intercourse takes place up there, and to understand it requires that we, together, finally begin to climb the slope to the top of that mountain.

Heaven is about being in God's Kingdom with Him. Many cities are found throughout the Kingdom, the primary one being the *print* of the great faith-city Jerusalem ("print" explained in *MB*). Jesus Christ is the King, Who sits at the Right Hand of God the Father, Who occupies the Great Throne. If this is hard for some people down here to accept, it isn't up there. God's Will is living, absolute, unmovable. Doubt and ambivalence do not reside in heaven. Jesus told His disciples to believe, to have faith, to follow Him and have no doubt, and then and only then will they be open to the whole truth and have the guaranteed hope of gaining eternal life. Skeptics and debunkers don't make the cut. There are no such things as "balanced reporting" and agnosticism anywhere up there. So . . . please know that devil's advocates get no voice in the heavenly systems because they don't make it up there.

> Then with the help of the Spirit, he took me [Rev's John] *to the top of a very high mountain. There he showed me the holy city of Jerusalem coming down from God and heaven. I did not see a temple there. The Lord God All-Powerful and the Lamb were its temple. And the city did not need the sun or the moon. The glory of God was shining on it, and the Lamb was its light. (Revelation 21:10,22-23)*

There are overwhelming feelings of joy, bliss, and freedom in paradise and heaven. The perfected soul-body has firmness and outline, marvelous visual presentation, and it is not bound by weight, like the old human body was. Up there are indescribable light and positive energy that emit *into* us, and we are brought to feeling as one with them.

The euphoric feeling a youngster has on the first weekend of summer recess? Well, that feeling never leaves us while we are in heaven. There is complete rapture in the moment and at the same time an unending joy of looking forward. The Almighty Presences of God the Father and Jesus permeate the upper realms, and this takes residents to even further heights of happiness. Who on earth would not want to have the most loving, tender, and mighty of human fathers and big brothers? We have them in heaven. And we have a mother, in Mary. She is not only our mother; she is our parents' mother, our grandparents' mother, our great-grandparents' mother, right back to the time of Jesus' crucifixion. Before dying on the cross, Jesus says to Mary and Apostle John, the one who remained close by to Him during His trial and tortures, *"This man is now your son. She is now your mother." (John 19:26-27)*

In the former time, God the Father said He will send the Messiah to retrieve the lost children of Israel. As it would turn out, the Messiah also offers redemption to the rest of the world—that is, to the gentiles (the non-Jewish). God says to Moses that the people of Israel are a special lot unto Him. He also says, *"for all the earth is mine." (Exodus 19:5)* *"I [God] will also give thee [the Messiah] for a light to the Gentiles, that thou mayest be my salvation unto the end of the earth." (Isaiah 49:6)* *"Heaven is my throne, and earth is my footstool." (Isaiah 66:1 & Acts 7:49)*

What? Over 2,500 years ago God the Father promised to send the Messiah through the line of David and He has not come yet? If that were true, what exactly is God waiting for?

Forty years after the Messiah was murdered, God allowed Satan to mete out brutal punishment to His firstborn, the Jewish people. Many were slaughtered, the rest fled for their lives, Herod's temple in Jerusalem was demolished, and all the Jewish birth records were destroyed. So if the Messiah was not Jesus, how could it ever again be proven that a supposed-Messiah, born after the destruction, came through the house of David? This fact alone proves Jesus the Christ.

John's gospel reveals Caiaphas believed it better for one person than many to die for the sins of the nation. By saying it, Caiaphas demonstrated his belief that Jesus was the Messiah. ("Yeah-sure, he's probably the Messiah, seeing the stack of miracles he has done. But we don't need him around here anymore, reminding us about what we really should be doing.") Prior to His arrest, Jesus said that what is to happen to Him must happen, but it will be curtains for those who do it to Him. Since then, below the demolished temple there exists a dark spiritual prison; the souls of these particular dead of Israel are housed inside of it.

The Father is faithful to His Word. He is the most loving and merciful of fathers, but He does not tolerate His Word being stomped on by the rich and famous. Serves them right. Souls from even this purgatorial prison have been granted new earth-term opportunities to accept Jesus as Messiah. Two thousand years ago, Jesus informs the disbelieving Pharisees and teachers of the Law of Moses as follows: *"That's why you will be held guilty for the murder of every good person, beginning with the good man Abel. This also includes Barachiah's son Zechariah, the man you murdered between the temple and the altar. I can promise that you people living today will be punished for all these things!"* (Matthew 23:35-36) Seems Jesus is saying their current earth-terms are producing the same lousy results as their previous ones did.

For a person to prove his/her belief in Jesus as Messiah, a verbal proclamation followed by at least one successful *act of demonstration of sincerity* must take place on "the stage." There is just no other way to get off earth and regain freedom-soul status. Paul states,

> *"Do I mean that the people of Israel fell, never to get up again? Certainly not! Their failure made it possible for the gentiles to be saved, and this will make the people of Israel jealous. But if the rest of the world's people were helped so much by Israel's sin and loss, they will be helped even more by their return. When Israel rejected God, the rest of the people in the world were able to turn to him. So when God makes friends with Israel, it will be like bringing the dead back to life."* (Romans 11:11-12,15)

One day, Christian persecutor Saul of Tarsus is struck down while on the road to Damascus, a place where he intends to do more Christian-bashing. Jesus appears to him. *"Saul, Saul, why do you persecute me?" (Acts 9:4)* From then on, he takes the name Paul, and he will go on to become the greatest evangelist ever known. Coming out of the experience, Paul stays blind for several days, but his mind and heart forever remain before The Light and The Clarity of God. *"Things that are seen don't last forever, but things that are not seen are eternal. That's why we keep our minds on the things that cannot be seen." (2 Corinthians 4:18)* Though Paul does not use the term "The Clarity," he does refer to it in his own way. *"Now all we can see of God is like a cloudy picture in a mirror. Later we will see him face to face. We don't know everything, but then we will, just as God completely understands us." (1 Corinthians 13:12)*

Paul sometimes speaks in the veiled vernacular of God Blessed Rebirthment. Examples: *"For the creation waits with eager longing for the revealing of the children of God; for the creation was subjected to futility, not of its own will but by the will of the one who subjected it, in hope that the creation itself will be set free from its bondage to decay and will obtain the freedom of the glory of the children of God." (Romans 8:19-21)* *"Then, in the fullness of time God sent forth his Son born of woman, born under the new law, to deliver from the law* [rabbi laws] *those who were subjected to it, so that we might receive our status as adopted sons." (Galatians 4:4-5)* *"We know that the whole creation has been groaning in travail together until now." (Romans 8:22)* *"In the past, God forgave all this because people did not know what they were doing. But now he says everyone everywhere must turn to him." (Acts 17:30)*

King David's son Solomon was the great builder of Jerusalem. God's wisdom had settled on him like no other before, and his fame spread to the far reaches. One day a woman of stature visited him.

> And when the queen of Sheba heard of the fame of Solomon concerning the name of the Lord, she came to prove him with hard questions. And she came to Jerusalem with a very great train, with camels that bare spices, and very much gold, and precious stones: and when she was come to Solomon, she communed with him of all that was in her heart. And Solomon told her all her questions: there was not anything hid from the king, which he told her not. And when the queen of Sheba had seen all Solomon's wisdom, and the house he had built, and the meat of his table [and so on], there was no more spirit [resistance] in her. And she gave the king an hundred and twenty talents of gold, and of spices very great store, and precious stones: there came no more such abundance of spices as these which the queen of Sheba gave to King Solomon. And

King Solomon gave the queen of Sheba all her desire, whatsoever she asked, besides that [naughty, naughty] which Solomon gave her of his royal bounty. So she turned and went to her own country, she and her servants. (1 Kings 10:1-5,10,13)

The two received each other respectfully, kind-heartedly, as equals. But to share as they did, they had to rise to the level of "valuing" each other. Later in life, Solomon bitterly put down all that he owned and built, saying the buildings, fountains, courtyards, and jewels were nothing more than vanity.

In The Clarity, God shows that His hands do not offer us silver and gold or any precious stones, but instead something priceless: His universal heart and the inexhaustible treasures of love and wisdom contained inside it and from which our hearts were originally modeled.

[Spiritual note: Because of his worshipping young foreign women and offering sacrifices to their demon gods and goddesses, so that even as an old man he could keep gettin' some, Solomon fell out of God's grace. God allowed for the temple Solomon built to eventually be flattened, same as Herod's would be many centuries later. But because God favored Solomon's human dad, David, He did not allow Satan to split apart the Jewish kingdom until after Solomon died. *When Solomon was old, his wives turned away his heart after other gods; and his heart was not true to his Lord God, as was the heart of his father David. For Solomon followed Astarte the goddess of the Sidonians, and Milcom the abomination of the Ammonites. . . . Then Solomon built a high place for Chemosh the abomination of Moab, and for Molech the abomination of the Ammonites, on the mountain east of Jerusalem. . . . Therefore the Lord said to Solomon, "Since this has been your mind and you have not kept my covenant and my statutes that I have commanded you, I will surely tear the kingdom from you and give it to your servant. Yet for the sake of your father David I will not do it in your lifetime;" (1 Kings 11:4-5,7,11-12)*]

In heaven, a being is an intelligent, "super-corporeal" sentient energy-entity, dwelling up there with the Angels of God. To each other we feel just like physical bodies on earth do, and that is because every microscopic point within the body of soul-energy retains the exact knowledge of being in the human body and therefore retains the same abilities. When God grants a soul-person passage through the barrier-veil and into heaven, where the positively munificent energy, light, and living water are, the soul becomes magnified (powerized!). *"That's how it will be when our bodies are raised to life. These bodies will die, but the bodies that are raised will live forever. These ugly and weak bodies will become beautiful and strong. As surely as there are physical bodies, there are spiritual bodies. And our physical bodies will be changed* into spiritual bodies." (1 Corinthians 15:42-44) The evangelist says it again: "Brothers and sisters: When this perishable body puts on imperishability, and this mortal body puts on immortality, then the saying that is written will be fulfilled: 'Death has been swallowed up in victory.'" (1 Corinthians 15:54-55) And again: "Our Lord Jesus Christ has power over everything, and he will make these poor bodies of ours like his own glorious body." (Philippians 3:21)

Up there, men and women are especially respectful, kind-hearted, grounded in self-control, devoid of ego. Again, the soul-person lives as a sentient "super-corporeal" unit. To the eyes of others, each comes across as stunning: early to mid-20s, full head of hair, no blemishes. All bodily imperfections persons had to live with while on earth are gone. That big forehead? Gone! Rotund midsection and thundering thighs? Gone! Don't we know God knows how much persons detested those things? Did a person see him-/herself as too short or too tall? Up there everyone has the right height: not too tall, not too short. Nose big and bumpy? Acne? Hair too fine and a bit on the scraggly side? None of that stuff is allowed in heaven, unless someone actually wants it. No one does. God removes all imperfections from our visual presentations, and that way we may be so totally in love with the love of heaven and the infinite love of Him.

If a man and woman so choose and they are comfortable with each other in an extra-special way, they may agree to release their perimeters and merge for a while. In the "meld" takes place Fabulous Aching Heart Love, where two minds, two hearts, and that "other area below" overlap, to expose and explore each other's uniquely wonderful offerings, flavors if you will, and the resultant flame of passionate sharing—while *heavenly-powerized!*—is delirious magnificence that shows the old animal orgasm to have been nothing more than plain dry toast.

Up there, no one is selfish, possessive. No one but God has claim on souls, so there isn't marriage as we have it on earth. (There is something remotely similar, based partly on primal bond-souling and a heavenly "beholden system," both talked of in *MB*.) Here, we marry because the union has the potential to instill traits of goodness into our souls: the abilities to make and keep long-term commitment, retain loyalty and fidelity, and get spiritually stronger by overcoming obstacles together. Marriage is the best situation for birthing and raising children. A child wants and needs a devoted mother and father.

During the heavenly meld of man and woman, the two have a feeling of being whole again. In that wonderful state, they might even kiss each other's faces all over the place, smile, giggle, and inhale each other's uniquely perfected scents. It is a peak romantic rendezvous in the most intimate communion. A perfectly wonderful gift from God it is!

In God's most recent "stepped take-hold" of the original wild, ape-like species of earth, He assigned one of His shepherded beings into the re-formed male unit. *And the Lord God formed man of the dust of the ground, and breathed into his nostrils the breath of life; and the man became a living soul. And the Lord God planted a garden eastward in Eden; and there he put the man whom he had formed. (Genesis 2:7-8)* Adam was a next-step prototype and a far cry from the original unit. Way, way back, sex between the savages was crude and violent; there were no such things as love and romance.

God knew that the new male unit should not mix with the more primitive, previous-step female ones. That was another reason God relocated Adam to a secret location. And because God wanted the new man to have the company of an equally intelligent female rather than some lesser thing, He caused a sleep to come upon him. *And the Lord God caused a deep sleep to fall upon Adam, and he slept: and he took one of his ribs, and closed up the flesh instead thereof; And the rib, which the Lord God had taken from man, made he a woman, and he brought her unto man.* God's using the word "rib" was His simplified way of explaining to Moses—who, most believe, wrote down Genesis as God would have it—an infinitely complex, mystical process of Himself. At that moment, a portion of the male's soul was removed and placed into a feral female unit, and she became the prototype woman, Eve: intelligent, equal in stature but different in emotional and physical makeup. *And Adam said, This is now bone of my bones, and flesh of my flesh: she shall be called Woman, because she was taken out of Man. Therefore* [thence forward] *shall a man leave his father and his mother, and shall cleave unto his wife: and they shall be one flesh. (Genesis 2:23-24)*

Man-woman love created and blessed by the Great Creator God. A man and a woman, each longing, each searching to become reunited with that missing part of their wholeness, for the two are truly complementary natures yearning to come together to be as one. But they must find each other. And when they do, there is an intense desire to know more, to softly touch and kiss. Are they right for each other? Could they spend forever in loving harmony? Yes!

The Great Creator, Grand Shepherd, and Forever Forward Shield has given His shepherded souls a fantastic gift that is the envy of the entire cosmos: mystical romance. Wow! What a fantastic Father! And we generally make better parents than the savages did.

Chapter LII

Epilogue: How Men Cry

In the 1960s, Bolley's Famous Franks moved to a new location close to the Augusta-Hallowell line. It is still open. Gerard's Pizza also remains open. Pizzas from Woody's and Joe's are no more, as is Fairview Winery. Harriman & Black closed shortly after Cottles arrived.

Satellites Echo I and Echo II burned up at their reentries into the earth's atmosphere in 1967 and '68. Their missions to test radio signal deflections were deemed successful by an unnamed NASA sourse. On July 20, 1969, two astronauts of Apollo 11 crew landed on the moon. The Russians have yet to place a cosmonaut there.

The elegant Augusta House checked out its last travelers in the early 1970s. To make room for road expansion, the place was demolished in 1974. Out of the blue, Commonwealth Shoe and Leather Company closed in 1972. The area mourned terribly the loss of that one. At its peak, the place employed 400 people. The building still stands on the west side of Gardiner.

Marvelously hallmarking Wiscasset's shoreline for 66 years, the ghostly four-mast schooners *Hesper* and *Luther Little* were done in by a harsh storm in 1998.

Hallowell used to be the home of a real fine friend. She and I proved to each other that a man and woman can be close and not have the other stuff involved. She moved to Winthrop prior to 1976, but we had already grown apart, and she was with a man. On that lonely August evening at Freddies, I was not able to say goodbye to her, either. In the drive back to Gardiner, sadness engulfed my soul. The memory still haunts me. Another does as well—the smell of the river that night. The air was hot and sticky, the stench awful as ever. How could I not remember? I grew up with it. To this day, memories of those molecules remain imbedded inside my gray matter.

In high school, the writer had a second just-friend-woman from Hallowell. Because of her acute dyslexia, she asked that I not write to her because she would not be able to read it and did not want someone else to read it to her. Already in life, she had shown herself to be a very talented silversmith. Our friendship quickly dissipated after I left for Boston in 1972. Mike's high school sweetheart—they married in 1976—was another good friend. She and I were in many of the same classes in high school. For most of my life, the major problem for me was I liked women too much. Yet the man developed friendships with many women. Since late 1999, I have been celibate. I continue to have female just-friends. Some are close to my age and quite attractive. The man cannot deny what his eyes see, but I do not try to take things further. I guess the years of mental maturing have helped me in this area.

Persons who have had same-sex attraction since earliest remembrance are not going to become heterosexual just because they repent. Still, they can choose to repent their lives and current lifestyles and decide to take on the ways of "good friendships." Why not? Two men or two women who are in a carnal relationship can make the righteous decision to become like brothers or sisters, but there must never again be any kind of sexual interaction. Just be good friends. Why not? In addition, the person must immediately cease saying things like "I'm gay" or "I'm a gay bricklayer" or "I'm a gay priest" or "I'm a gay gold medalist" or "I'm a gay warehouse worker"; to continue in the repugnant manner would mean the person is still proclaiming/promoting his/her homosexuality; the manner is just one of the many booby traps Satan sets down as snares for humans; persons still caught in it at the time of body-death are NS. Heterosexuals never go around saying "I'm a straight basketball player," "I'm a heterosexual car salesman," "I'm a heterosexual Christian pastor," "I'm a straight gold medal winner."

With the decision to cease and repent comes the loss of the terrible fear of body-death and the gain of a guaranteed hope of achieving eternal life someday. *"We are people of flesh and blood. That is why Jesus became one of us. He died to destroy the devil, who had power over death. But he also died to rescue all of us who live each day in fear of dying."* (Hebrews 2:14-15)

[Final spiritual note: If Kandis and/or James were to come to me and say, "I'm gay," I would respond as follows. "I love you with all my heart and it is because of this love that I advise you to resist that lifestyle with all your might. If you do choose it, I will still love you the same, maybe even more, if that were possible, because I would so fear for the loss of being with you in the next life. But you must understand the truth that if you do not cease and repent while alive, you will be condemned to hell. It is a mortal sin for two men or two women to lie together as a man and women would. If I said anything less or gave you my blessing, it would mean I don't have a true love for you nor a true caring about your eternal salvation, and God would condemn me along with you. Honestly, dear daughter/son, I'm so totally selfish in my own quest for heaven. No one's getting in my way, not even you, my child who I love with all my heart but not as much as I love God the Father and Jesus. The love of God includes love of His Laws and Commandments. My hope is that you will choose right and not wrong, and I will pray for you to be strong against evil and that if you do choose evil, you will live long enough to cease and repent it before the thief in the night comes. If the Angel of Death does come and you are in a not-repentant state of mortal sin, God is very clear about your outcome. He says to the prophet Ezekiel, *'Behold, all souls are mine; as the soul of the father* and mother, *so also the soul of the son* and daughter *is mine: the soul that sinneth, it shall die,'* which means be condemned to hell. God says it more than once, that only the not-repentant sinner goes down there. So daughter/son, do care about your personal eternal salvation above all else while in this world."]

Decisions on a new life will have to be made. Apostle Peter says, *"You have already lived long enough like people who don't know God. You were immoral and followed your evil desires. You went around drinking and carrying on. In fact, you even worshipped disgusting idols. Now your former friends wonder why you stopped running around with them, and they curse you for it. But they will have to answer to God, who judges the living and the dead." (1 Peter 4:3-5)*

A sewage treatment plant serving the greater Gardiner area was completed in 1980, in South Gardiner. Treatment plants opened all along the Kennebec River during the 1970s and '80s. The river's odor soon disappeared, and in the mid-1980s, Atlantic bass, sturgeon, and salmon were once again swimming the natural waterway. A few more years passed before the river's fish were declared clean enough for human consumption. Sport fishing now abounds on the Kennebec, and yearly the industry brings in millions of tourist dollars.

In 1970, Phil Laithran accepted the job of assistant superintendent for the Kennebec Valley's central zone. The family moved to Augusta. Peter Laithran attended Cony High School and played a major part in the school's run for the state's Division 1 title. By a basket, the team finished second at the New England Tournament.

In the mid-'70s, the Bondys' tilted house was determined to be dangerously separating from its concrete foundation; it was officially condemned and demolished. A 7-Eleven store opened across the street from Christ Church in 1980. Gardiner Fruit shut down right after that.

Throughout the latter half of the twentieth century, a major goal of state conservationists was to secure governmental approval for the removal of the Edwards Dam. In 1997, the dam's license came up for renewal. The Federal Energy Regulatory Commission refused the dam company's request for more decades of fish-blockage. For the first time in United States history a dam was ordered removed for the purposes of returning a watershed to its early, more pristine ecology and economy. After it was taken out in 1999, migratory fish and American Eel were able to reach far up the Kennebec River and into many of its contributory rivers and streams.

In 2009, Amtrak re-instituted passenger-train service between Boston and Portland. The track was extended from Portland to Freeport and Brunswick in 2012. After landing in Brunswick, a suitcase-carrying traveler could then walk to the Maine Eastern Railroad Station and purchase a ticket to ride the scenic train to Rockland; that particular route had been put in place by the Morristown and Erie Railway (based in Pennsylvania) in 2003. On the way are stops in Bath and Wiscasset. To ride the MER's restored old coach and take in the spectacular views and unusual scents is considered by tourists and locals alike a real fine way to experience America. The route has received national recognition and tourist awards.

In 2002, Daniel had the idea to take the parents to Italy. Hard convincing had to done on dad to get him to go. The three hopped a plane to Rome. From there they drove to the American Cemetery and Memorial located just outside Anzio. Dad was 90, mother 84. While standing in front of a faded gravestone, dad broke down weeping as he slowly addressed his dead baby brother. "Henry, your brother Herve finally made it. This is my official goodbye to you. I guess I'll be joining you soon enough. You're still eighteen—go figure. Back then, none of us wanted to dwell on it, you getting killed and mother dropping dead. Hurt too much. Still does. Thanks for your sacrifice. I love you, and I have never forgotten you. Goodbye, Henry."

Two years passed and dad joined his brother. The night he died I could not make it to his bedside in New York City. That afternoon, Daniel held the phone to his ear so we could speak. The elderly man spoke in a small, frail voice that I barely recognized: "Charles, I'm so weak. This is it for me. My life, it's gone by like a flash. Goodbye, son. I love you." Because of being so choked up with tears, I could barely get out any words. "Thanks for being my father. I love you. Goodbye, Dad."

In the world from 1966 to 2016, five billion people died, give or take a few hundred million. This is a natural turn. Medical advances may matter on a personal level, but on a gross-number level they have almost no impact.

The Lawrence Welk Show ceased production in 1982. Mr. Welk passed away ten years later. A different one of his shows runs every Saturday night on the Spokane Public Broadcasting System. What comes around goes around, for I very much enjoy the show and try not to miss it.

․․․․․

2017

The after-work rush hour has begun, and the traffic is tightening. It's time for me to leave the causeway forever. The final few pages will be written on the soul-person's return to Calgary. The book will be available more than a year early. Close enough to 2016 to call it that, I figure.

The revealer retains no fear of the coming events, though a couple questions do linger. What will next year, 2017, bring? What will the years after that be like for humanity? The answers depend on the type of glasses a person wears. For me it will not be so much a *time* in history as a *place* for humanity: a launching pad to a planet of new hope, a land filled with milk and honey. Most people will see it differently, as a time of upheaval that brings terrible despair into the soul. There will be those who see it an opportunity to dance in the streets. As for these ones—militant activists, anarchists, looters—they will have proven themselves to be the worst of all peoples and thankfully their destinies to the lake of fire will be sealed off quickly.

God the Father and Jesus did not give the revealer 2017, but I have been given a definitive heads-up. The following message came in October 1999: "**I AM WHO I AM, the God of Abraham. I am very angry with My people. Repent before it is too late. When it is too late you go to hell! Come back to My love. Repent now before I destroy earth.**" God does not lie, and so I know with absolute certainty the earth *as we currently know it* will end sometime in the next few years. God the Father and Jesus have been training me all my life to be a witness to what is coming and a witness to why it has to happen. The Father and Jesus do not want me to go soft on the truth, to mince words, to be politically correct, to be soft-spine and populist, to serve honey and milk and call it coffee.

The cataclysm and *the confusion* must and will take place, for there is just no other way for humanity to get saved from the cesspool it is now drowning in. Humanity is in The Book of Revelation's time of "the dragon and two beasts" (Chapter 13). The dragon, Satan, has been allowed to give over much of his power to the two risen beasts. The first beast is constituted of an uncountable number of evil spirit-entities that have already been let up from under the sea. The second beast has already risen from the ground—"ground" meaning the beast is made up of living people (soul-persons housed in bodies made of the earth's elements) who have chosen to side with the spirit of evil. God has allowed this so that every person on the earth can be tested and once and for all prove allegiance. Will it be to Great God Above or to one or more of the false gods from below?

"I [Rev's John] saw a beast coming up from the sea ["sea" meaning in the spirit]. *This one had ten horns and seven heads, and a crown was on each of its ten horns.*

The ten horns are the categories of the not-repentant, let-up-from-below (to be around us so that they can challenge/tempt us) evil energy-entities as follows: 1) killers, the violent, paid brawlers, violence promoters, all members of Mafia/organized crime, 2) homosexuals, lesbians, pedophiles, rapists, 3) greedy money/gold/silver/diamond lovers/hoarders, 4) thieves, destroyers, looters, defacers (graffitists), forgers, insurance cheaters, liars who bring false lawsuits, anarchists, 5) porno women/men, those who openly present as sex symbols, nudists, prostitutes and those *of* prostitution, 6) blood drinkers, abortion doers/enablers, those into human experimentation/cloning 7) showoff daredevils, fire-eaters/-walkers, knife and needle lovers (including tattoo-ists/mutilators), 8) chronic gamblers, those of witchcraft, tarot card doers, diviners, mediums, devil-worshippers/-devotees (including those who do Satan's hand-signal), 9) anti-Semites, racists, false-accusers, skin-heads, Nazis/neo-Nazis, betrayers and haters of God's Word *in its fullness*, blasphemers, Bible/church/grave desecrators, atheists, God-haters, and 10) friends of illegal drugs and marijuana, traffickers, addicts, alcoholics.

"On each of the heads were names that were an insult to God. [The seven most notorious leaders—now very evil energy-entities (Nero the worst and the group's leader)—who openly hated/insulted God and worked to blot out His name from the earth.] *The beast that I saw had a body of a leopard, the feet of a bear, and the mouth of a lion. The dragon* [Satan] *handed over its own power and throne and great authority to this beast.* **Everyone on earth marveled at this beast** [Nero and his invisible, high-traveling demon-group that keeps supervision over the massive hoard of evil energy-entities all over the world], **and they worshipped the dragon** [Most of today's teenage and twenties Americans openly do the satanic hand-signal, which is a physical act of demonstration that expresses a devotion to Satan, and it is an appeal for his help and protection. It has even entered the Catholic Church, as a way for so-called religious persons, even some on the inside and at the highest of levels, to come across as being "cool," part of the "in" crowd.] *who had given its authority to the beast. The beast was allowed to brag and claim to be God, and for forty-two months it was allowed to rule* [the unbridled open display and promotion of all evils]. **The beast cursed God** [God's Commandments/laws/ordinances/statutes as outlined in the Foundation Testament], *and it cursed the name of God* [the successful removal of the names God and Jesus Christ from open display]. *It even cursed the place where God lives, as well as everyone who lives in heaven with God. It was allowed to fight against God's people and defeat*

them [evil's successful removal of God's human laws against immorality]. *I* [Rev's John] *saw another beast. This one came out of the ground* [again, ground meaning made of elements—meaning soul-persons in human bodies]. *It had two horns like a lamb, but spoke like a dragon.* ["Like a lamb but spoke like a dragon," meaning today's smooth-talking politicians, judges, actors/actresses/entertainers, persons of mainstream media, and so-called pastors and activists who speak out for or turn a blind eye to things that are against God's Will and Word.] *It worked for the beast whose fatal wound* [the invisible beast that had formerly concentrated itself inside the anti-God "Red Serpent" known as the Soviet Union, which had been brought, by the beast, to produce the world's most powerful intercontinental ballistic nuclear arsenal, known as "Satan Missiles," so that the world could be ended by way of nuclear holocaust—but the collapse of the Iron Curtain and Soviet Communism, as detailed in *MB*, brought the destruction and mothballing of the Satan Missiles] *had been healed* [meaning Satan's beast—his army of very evil spirit-entities: the high satanics—had successfully repositioned its end-the-world effort away from nuclear holocaust to moral holocaust outside of the Soviet Union]. *And it used all its authority to force the earth and its people to worship the beast* [that which openly promotes/markets rampant immorality (no more can a person get a job in Hollywood, the mainstream media, many so-called Christian denominations, the nation's ruling American Federal Democrat political party without first proclaiming approval of abortion and same-sex marriage and then agreeing to denounce those who are against the two items)]. *It worked mighty miracles* [the high satanics' End Time miracles constitute legalization of all things against God: abortion/partial-birth abortion, same-sex marriage, euthanasia, so-called mercy killing, open pornography, prostitution, open sexualized advertising of products and people, open abuse of God's Holy Name and removal of His Name and all Christian images, open sales & marketing of skin markings/cuttings, open gambling of all kinds promoted everywhere, open display of violence for entertainment, legalization of marijuana, open and proud displaying of the satanic hand signal, etc., all of which indicate the defeat of God's people] *and while the people watched, it* [Satan's servant-beast of high satanics] *even made fire* [evil sentient energy projections that set fire to the Word of God] *come down from the sky* [Paul mentions in his letters about the invisible evil forces in the air around us]." *(Revelation 13:1-4,5-7,11-13)*

When a person is truly with God, the exact year does not matter. The revealer *uses* 2017 as a wakeup call to help bring readers into the fold of believing, so that there can be enough time to reflect, repent, recant, and prepare for what is coming. If your heart and mind are right with God's Will and Word, you are a "green zone," for yourself and for those around you, including the wandering, confused netherworld souls, some of which may even be your bond souls. People will come to you for spiritual advice. Encourage others to be a green zone. A green-zone person must not be weak on expressing God's Word and Commandments/laws/statutes/ordinances *in full*. The strong coffee can be served with gentle kindness, firmness. Anyone who claims to be Christian and insists on serving sweetened milk is not a green zone and not a true Christian. In judgment, God will ask them why they did that. There is no "good" answer for such dereliction of Christian duty. Not one of these will be saved from spending a long haul below. Most importantly, a green-zone person must be tenaciously selfish about his/her own personal salvation.

An announcement—*The Knell*—will take place prior to the commencement of the cataclysmic period. It will be God's very public act of demonstration of His venting His rage, hate, and utter contempt for the *shame of failure associated with dereliction of righteous duty*.

God says to Prophet Jeremiah, "*I have forsaken my house, I have left mine heritage; I have given the dearly beloved of my soul to her enemies. Mine heritage unto me is like a lion in the forest; it crieth out against me: therefore I have hated it. Mine heritage unto me is like a speckled bird, the birds round about her are against her; come ye, assemble all the beasts of the field, cause them to come to devour. Many pastors have destroyed my vineyard, they have trodden my portion under foot, they have made my portion a desolate wilderness. They have made it desolate, and being desolate it mourneth unto me; the whole land is made desolate, because no man layeth it to heart. The spoilers are come upon all high places through the wilderness: for the sword of the LORD shall devour from one end of the land even to the other end of the land: no flesh shall have peace.*" (12:7-12)

Next will come Jesus' return to slay the anti-Christ—that which denigrated His Kingship. Then will come the cataclysm and the confusion. Worldwide exoduses similar to the Bible's Exodus will take place. Much, much culling will happen. God and all of heaven are right now on war footing; no one up there is in a good mood, they are in full armor, and their razor-sharp swords will soon be unsheathed, to slay all the evil forces currently in the world. "*I* [Rev's John] *looked and saw that heaven was open, and a white horse was there. Its rider was called Faithful and True, and he is always fair when he judges or goes to war. He had eyes like flames of fire, and he was wearing a lot of crowns. . . . The rider wore a robe that was covered with blood, and he was known as "The Word of God." He was followed by armies from heaven that rode on horses and were dressed in pure white linen. From his mouth a sharp sword went out to attack the nations. He will rule them with an iron rod and will show the fierce anger of God All-Powerful by trampling the grapes* [evil humans] *in the pit where wine is made. . . . The beast* [the diabolical leader(s) in the world] *and the false prophet* [the diabolical false-religious leader(s)] *were thrown into the lake of burning sulphur."* *(Revelation 19:11-13, 19)*

. . . . .

September 25, 2001, message from God the Father for me to give out: **"Pray and pray, My people. Change your life! I detest corruption, abortion, and lesbian and homosexual behavior. Your sins are very bad. I am happy when a country does not want to have war. It is not finished yet. I AM WHO I AM. Do you, My people, think that I do not see all? Open your eyes and open your hearts to Me. Repent, repent, NOW, while there is time. Do not wait, for you never know when I will come like a thief in the night. Your human life is a gift from Me. How will you face Me when you refuse to repent before I come? I am very wrathful now and My hand is straight up. I feel sad to know My people are going to hurt innocent people in the coming war. I love you, from Jesus and God the Father."**

August 14, 2003, message from Jesus for me to give out: **"If the Prime Minister of Canada does not change his stand on same-sex marriage, he will have consigned himself to hell. Will Canadian women be allowed to go topless in public?** (A short time after the message, a court in the province of Ontario approved women going topless in public.) **Canada, what are your leaders doing to your country? My people, the blackout in New York is a warning to turn away from the darkness in your souls and to come into My Light. If you do not change, much worse will take place. Jesus, your Savior."**

July 18, 2005, message from God the Father: **"John—the recent heat wave and forest fires in North America are a result of My wrath at the persistent immorality. You are a stiff-necked people. Canada has made a grave mistake, legalizing same-sex marriage. My Word cannot be changed and is not open for unrepentant sinners to debate. I AM WHO I AM. Every one of these lawmakers of evil will have to face Me. The world will get worse. The good people should know they will have to suffer with the bad, but a life in paradise awaits them. The unrepentant purveyors of their own vomit will be cast down. They will weep and gnash their teeth for their choosing to waste the gift of life and mislead souls. From God the Father, Son, and Holy Spirit."**

An overnight in 2006 found me in a room; it was after I had fallen asleep when the Angel of God removed soul-person-me from my physical body in order to bring me there. Other men were in the room, and all of us were in uniform. We stood, conversing about things. Soon, from above, a trumpet sounded and an angelic voice announced God the Father's arrival. Two men immediately vacated. I understood they were not allowed to be in His presence. Then, to our front, from beyond a white wall that was no longer there, a brilliant white light burst forth. We could see into the distance. God the Father, tall and wide, finely proportioned, with long glowing-white hair, wearing a long glowing-white robe, sporting massive sandals on His massive feet, walked toward us. He's a giant! A few steps were all it took for Him to make up what seemed a hundred yards. Thankfully, He was smiling. Under an arm He carried a scroll that contained plans. I was not allowed to consciously remember anything about the meeting.

In His visual presentation, God the Father expresses *universal majesty*. His face is remarkably macho-manly and friendly (when in a good mood), notably ruddy (reddish), and looks to be around 60 years old. He shows no wrinkles or any facial imperfections. His head and body are massive yet perfectly proportioned, and He is way oversized as compared to any human being, even the biggest and most muscular man. In a person's climb on the ladder—in one's "ascending the spirit world"—the soul desires to be become more and more *like* Him. This is another reason why primal pools want to sojourn earth: to attain a personal presentation that is uniquely pleasing to the eye and expresses an overall image that speaks to God's majesty.

A night in February 2013 had me waking in the presence of Archangel Michael, with God the Father speaking through His special agent. He stood about 15 feet away and was not in a good mood. "What makes you think you can call Me Father?" My mind answered, *Jesus*. At that, He grumbled something, came to me, touched my neck, and said, "Don't think this is the end of your suffering." I woke up with a neck feeling 75% better. For many years I've suffered with terrible upper back, neck, and shoulder pains from arthritis due to an early 1980s break in a neck vertebra. The real bad headaches started ten years ago. God was right. The relief didn't last.

The Divine encounter brought home the fact that God's wrath and justice are holy, not be viewed as a joyous occasion to look forward to. God says to His prophet Amos, *"Woe to you that desire the day of the Lord! To what end is it for you? The day of the Lord is darkness, and not light. As if a man did flee from a lion, and a bear met him; or went into a house and leaned his hand on the wall, and a serpent bit him."* (5:18-19)

I am truly blessed to have been born and raised in Gardiner, Maine: a small center not unlike most in the United States. On that mountain 13 years ago, a funny thought came to me. *Jesus, in all my times down there on earth, did I ever learn to sing?* I had always bemoaned my lack of melodic vocal cords. He looked at me funny and thought-projected back, *John, that is what I've been teaching you to do.*

Nancy Bondy and Ron Cates married in 1976. Early on, the couple developed a passion for backpacking through the mountains of New England. After 30 years of doing it, they wrote a book for other backpackers to use as an informative guide. I ordered a copy of *Mountains for Mortals: New England* (Ron & Nancy Chase, 2008) and very much enjoyed the read, vicariously backpacking my way through each of their sites, for I am no longer able to travel and definitely not able to backpack.

To this day, the Bible and *Treasure Island* remain near my bedside. The editor regrets never making it to Skowhegan.

Edwards Brothers Malloy
Thorofare, NJ USA
January 19, 2015